# The Complete works of Robert Browning

With Variant Readings & Annotations

Volume XI

EDITED BY

MICHAEL BRIGHT

OHIO UNIVERSITY PRESS
ATHENS, OHIO
BAYLOR UNIVERSITY
WACO, TEXAS
2008

THE COMPLETE WORKS OF ROBERT BROWNING

*Editorial Board*

ALLAN C. DOOLEY, General Editor

SUSAN CROWL

PARK HONAN, Founding Editor

ROMA A. KING, Founding Editor
General Editor, 1967–1985

JACK W. HERRING (1925–1999)
General Editor, 1985–1999

*Contributing Editors*

JOHN C. BERKEY

MICHAEL BRIGHT

ASHBY BLAND CROWDER

SUSAN E. DOOLEY

DAVID EWBANK

RITA S. PATTESON

Ohio University Press, Athens, Ohio 45701
© 2008 by Ohio University Press and Baylor University
Printed in the United States of America
All rights reserved

13 12 11 10 09 08     3 2 1

Ohio University Press books are printed on acid-free paper ∞™

Portrait of Robert Browning in 1875 by Rudolph Lehmann.
Courtesy of the Armstrong Browning Library.

Library of Congress Cataloging-in-Publication data
(Revised for vol. 11)

Browning, Robert, 1812–1889.
The complete works of Robert Browning, with variant readings & annotations.

Vol. 11 edited by Michael Bright.
Includes bibliographical references and indexes.
I. King, Roma A., 1914–     , ed.
II. Title.
PR4201.K5 1969  821'.8   68-18389
ISBN 978-0-8214-1839-0 (v. 11)

CONTENTS

I CONTENTS

This edition of the works of Robert Browning is intended to be complete. It will comprise at least seventeen volumes and will contain:

1. The entire contents of the first editions of Browning's works, arranged in their chronological order of publication. (The poems included in *Dramatic Lyrics, Dramatic Romances and Lyrics,* and *Men and Women,* for example, appear in the order of their first publication rather than in the order in which Browning rearranged them for later publication.)

2. All prefaces and dedications which Browning is known to have written for his own works and for those of Elizabeth Barrett Browning.

3. The two prose essays that Browning is known to have published: the review of a book on Tasso, generally referred to as the "Essay on Chatterton," and the preface for a collection of letters supposed to have been written by Percy Bysshe Shelley, generally referred to as the "Essay on Shelley."

4. The front matter and the table of contents of each of the collected editions (1849, 1863, 1865, 1868 [70, 75], 1888-1889) which Browning himself saw through the press.

5. Poems published during Browning's lifetime but not collected by him.

6. Poems not published during Browning's lifetime which have come to light since his death.

7. John Forster's *Thomas Wentworth, Earl of Strafford,* to which Browning contributed significantly, though the precise extent of his contribution has not been determined.

8. Variants appearing in primary and secondary materials as defined in Section II below.

9. Textual emendations.

10. Informational and explanatory notes for each work.

II PRIMARY AND SECONDARY MATERIALS

Aside from a handful of uncollected short works, all of Browning's works but *Asolando* (1889) went through two or more editions during his lifetime. Except for *Pauline* (1833), *Strafford* (1837), and *Sordello*

(1840), all the works published before 1849 were revised and corrected for the 1849 collection. *Strafford* and *Sordello* were revised and corrected for the collection of 1863, as were all the other works in that edition. Though no further poems were added in the collection of 1865, all the works were once again corrected and revised. The 1868 collection added a revised *Pauline* and *Dramatis Personae* (1864) to the other works, which were themselves again revised and corrected. A new edition of this collection in 1870 contained further revisions, and Browning corrected his text again for an 1875 reimpression. The printing of the last edition of the *Poetical Works* over which Browning exercised control began in 1888, and the first eight volumes are dated thus on their title-pages. Volumes 9 through 16 of this first impression are dated 1889, and we have designated them 1889a to distinguish them from the second impression of all 16 volumes, which was begun and completed in 1889. Some of the earlier volumes of the first impression sold out almost immediately, and in preparation for a second impression, Browning revised and corrected the first ten volumes before he left for Italy in late August,1889. The second impression, in which all sixteen volumes bear the date 1889 on their title-pages, consisted of a revised and corrected second impression of volumes 1-10, plus a second impression of volumes 11-16 altered by Browning in one instance. This impression we term 1889 (see section III below).

Existing manuscripts and editions are classified as either primary or secondary material. The primary materials include the following:

1. The manuscript of a work when such is known to exist.

2. Proof sheets, when known to exist, that contain authorial corrections and revisions.

3. The first and subsequent editions of a work that preserve evidence of Browning's intentions and were under his control.

4. The collected editions over which Browning exercised control:

1849—*Poems*. Two Volumes. London: Chapman and Hall.

1863—*The Poetical Works*. Three Volumes. London: Chapman and Hall.

1865—*The Poetical Works*. Three Volumes. London: Chapman and Hall.

1868—*The Poetical Works*. Six Volumes. London: Smith, Elder and Company.

1870—*The Poetical Works*. Six Volumes. London: Smith, Elder and Company. This resetting constituted a new edition, which was stereotyped and reimpressed several times; the 1875 impression contains revisions by Browning.

1888-1889—*The Poetical Works*. Sixteen Volumes. London: Smith,

Elder and Company. Exists in numerous stereotype impressions, of which two are primary material:

1888-1889a—The first impression, in which volumes 1-8 are dated 1888 and volumes 9-16 are dated 1889.

1889—The corrected second impression of volumes 1-10 and a second impression of volumes 11-16 altered by Browning only as stated in section III below; all dated 1889 on the title pages.

5. The corrections in Browning's hand in the Dykes Campbell copy of 1888-1889a, and the manuscript list of corrections to that impression in the Brown University Library (see section III below).

Other materials (including some in the poet's handwriting) that affected the text are secondary. Examples are: the copy of the first edition of *Pauline* which contains annotations by Browning and John Stuart Mill; the copies of the first edition of *Paracelsus* which contain corrections in Browning's hand; a very early manuscript of *A Blot in the 'Scutcheon* which Browning presented to William Macready, but not the one from which the first edition was printed; informal lists of corrections that Browning included in letters to friends, such as the corrections to *Men and Women* he sent to D. G. Rossetti; verbal and punctuational changes Browning essayed in presentation copies of his works or in his own copies, if not used by his printers; Elizabeth Barrett's suggestions for revisions in *A Soul's Tragedy* and certain poems in *Dramatic Romances and Lyrics;* and the edition of *Strafford* by Emily Hickey for which Browning made suggestions.

The text and variant readings of this edition derive from collation of primary materials as defined above. Secondary materials are occasionally discussed in the notes and sometimes play a part when emendation is required.

III  COPY-TEXT

The copy-text for this edition is Browning's final text: the first ten volumes of 1889 and the last six volumes of 1888-1889a, as described above. For this choice we offer the following explanation.

Manuscripts used as printer's copy for twenty of Browning's thirty-four book publications are known to exist; others may yet become available. These manuscripts, or, in their absence, the first editions of the works, might be considered as the most desirable copy-text. And this would be the case for an author who exercised little control over his text after the manuscript or first edition stage, or whose text clearly

became corrupted in a succession of editions. To preserve the inten-
tion of such an author, one would have to choose an early text and
emend it as evidence and judgment demanded.

With Browning, however, the situation is different, and our copy-
text choice results from that difference. Throughout his life Browning
continually revised his poetry. He did more than correct printer's er-
rors and clarify previously intended meanings; his texts themselves re-
mained fluid, subject to continuous alteration. As the manuscript
which he submitted to his publisher was no doubt already a product of
revision, so each subsequent edition under his control reflects the re-
sults of an ongoing process of creating, revising, and correcting. If we
were to choose the manuscript (where extant) or first edition as copy-
text, preserving Browning's intention would require extensive emen-
dation to capture the additions, revisions, and alterations which
Browning demonstrably made in later editions. By selecting Brown-
ing's final corrected text as our copy-text, emending it only to elimi-
nate errors and the consequences of changing house-styling, we pre-
sent his works in the form closest to that which he intended after years
of revision and polishing.

But this is true only if Browning in fact exercised extensive control
over the printing of his various editions. That he intended and at-
tempted to do so is apparent in his comments and his practice. In
1855, demanding accuracy from the printers, he pointed out to his
publisher Chapman, "I attach importance to the mere stops . . ." (De-
Vane and Knickerbocker, p. 83). There is evidence of his desire to con-
trol the details of his text as early as 1835, in the case of *Paracelsus*. The
*Paracelsus* manuscript, now in the Forster and Dyce collection in the
Victoria and Albert Museum Library, demonstrates a highly unconven-
tional system of punctuation. Of particular note is Browning's unre-
strained use of dashes, often in strings of two or three, instead of more
precise or orthodox punctuation marks. It appears that this was done
for its rhetorical effect. One sheet of Part 1 of the manuscript and all
but the first and last sheets of Part 3 have had punctuation revised in
pencil by someone other than Browning, perhaps J. Riggs, whose name
appears three times in the margins of Part 3. In addition to these revi-
sions, there are analogous punctuation revisions (in both pencil and
ink) which appear to be in Browning's hand, and a few verbal alter-
ations obviously in the poet's script.

A collation of the first edition (1835) with the manuscript reveals
that a major restyling of punctuation was carried out before *Paracelsus*
was published. However, the revisions incorporated into the first edi-
tion by no means slavishly follow the example set by the pencilled revi-

sions of Parts 1 and 3 of the manuscript. Apparently the surviving manuscript was not used as printer's copy for the first edition. Browning may have submitted a second manuscript, or he may have revised extensively in proof. The printers may have carried out the revisions to punctuation, with or without the poet's point by point involvement. With the present evidence, we cannot be conclusive about the extent of Browning's control over the first edition of *Paracelsus*. It can be stated, however, in the light of the incompleteness of the pencilled revisions and the frequent lack or correspondence between the pencilled revisions and the lines as printed in 1835, that Browning himself may have been responsible for the punctuation of the first edition of *Paracelsus*. Certainly he was responsible for the frequent instances in the first and subsequent editions where the punctuation defies conventional rules, as in the following examples:

> What though
> It be so?—if indeed the strong desire
> Eclipse the aim in me—if splendour break
> (Part I, ll. 329-331)

> I surely loved them—that last night, at least,
> When we . . . gone! gone! the better: I am saved
> (Part II, ll. 132-133)

> Of the body, even,)—what God is, what we are,
> (Part V, l. 642, 1849 reading)

The manuscripts of *Colombe's Birthday* (1844) and *Christmas-Eve and Easter-Day* (1850) were followed very carefully in the printing of the first editions. There are slight indications of minor house-styling, such as the spellings *colour* and *honour* for the manuscripts' *color* and *honor*. But the unorthodox punctuation, used to indicate elocutionary and rhetorical subtleties as well as syntactical relationships, is carried over almost unaltered from the manuscripts to the first editions. Similar evidence of Browning's painstaking attention to the smallest details in the printing of his poems can be seen in the manuscript and proof sheets of *The Ring and the Book* (1868-69). These materials reveal an interesting and significant pattern. It appears that Browning wrote swiftly, giving primary attention to wording and less to punctuation, being satisfied to use dashes to indicate almost any break in thought, syntax, or rhythm. Later, in the proof sheets for Books 1-6 of the poem and in the manuscript itself for Books 7-12, he changed the dashes to more specific and purposeful punctuation marks. The revised punctuation is what was printed, for the most part, in the first edition of *The Ring and the Book*; what further revisions there are conform to Browning's practice, though hardly to standard rules. Clearly Browning was in control of nearly every aspect of the published form of his works, even to the "mere stops."

Of still greater importance in our choice of copy-text is the substantial evidence that Browning took similar care with his collected editions. Though he characterized his changes for later editions as trivial and few in number, collations reveal thousands of revisions and corrections in each successive text. *Paracelsus,* for example, was extensively revised for the 1849 *Poems;* it was again reworked for the *Poetical Works* of 1863. *Sordello,* omitted in 1849, reappeared in 1863 with 181 new lines and short marginal glosses; Browning admitted only that it was "corrected *throughout*" (DeVane and Knickerbocker, p. 157). The poems of *Men and Women* (1855) were altered in numerous small but meaningful ways for both the 1863 and 1865 editions of the *Poetical Works* (see Allan C. Dooley, "The Textual Significance of Robert Browning's 1865 *Poetical Works*," *PBSA* 71 [1977], 212-18). Michael Hancher cites evidence of the poet's close supervision of the 1868 collected edition ("Browning and the *Poetical Works* of 1888-1889," *Browning Newsletter,* Spring, 1971, 25-27), and Michael Meredith has traced Browning's attentions to his text in the 1870 edition and an 1875 reimpression of it ("Learning's Crabbed Text," *SBHC* 13 [1985], 97-107); another perspective is offered in Allan C. Dooley's *Author and Printer in Victorian England* (1992), Ch. 4-5. Mrs. Orr, writing of the same period in Browning's life, reports his resentment of those who garbled his text by misplacing his stops (*Life,* pp. 357-58).

There is plentiful and irrefutable evidence that Browning controlled, in the same meticulous way, the text of his last collected edition, that which we term 1888-1889. Hancher has summarized the relevant information:

> The evidence is clear that Browning undertook the 1888-1889 edition of his *Poetical Works* intent on controlling even the smallest minutiae of the text. Though he at one time considered supplying biographical and explanatory notes to the poems, he finally decided against such a scheme, concluding, in his letter to Smith of 12 November 1887, "I am correcting them carefully, and *that* must suffice." On 13 January 1888, he wrote, regarding the six-volume edition of his collected works published in 1868 which was to serve as the printer's copy for the final edition: "I have thoroughly corrected the six volumes of the Works, and can let you have them at once." . . . Browning evidently kept a sharp eye on the production of all sixteen of the volumes, including those later volumes. . . . Browning returned proof for Volume 3 on 6 May 1888, commenting, "I have had, as usual, to congratulate myself on

the scrupulous accuracy of the Printers"; on 31 December he returned proofs of Volume 11, "corrected carefully"; and he returned "the corrected Proofs of Vol. XV" on 1 May 1889.

Throughout his long career, then, Browning continuously revised and corrected his works. Furthermore, his publishers took care to follow his directions exactly, accepting his changes and incorporating them into each successive edition. This is not to say that no one else had any effect whatsoever on Browning's text: Elizabeth Barrett made suggestions for revisions to *A Soul's Tragedy* and *Dramatic Romances and Lyrics.* Browning accepted some suggestions and rejected others, and those which he accepted we regard as his own. Mrs. Orr reports that Browning sent proof sheets to Joseph Milsand, a friend in France, for corrections (*Life,* p. 183), and that Browning accepted suggestions from friends and readers for the corrections of errors in his printed works. In some of the editions, there are slight evidences of minor house-styling in capitalization and the indication of quotations. But the evidence of Browning's own careful attention to revisions and corrections in both his manuscripts and proof sheets assures us that other persons played only a very minor role in the development of his text. We conclude that the vast majority of the alterations in the texts listed above as Primary Materials are Browning's own, and that only Browning's final corrected text, the result of years of careful work by the poet himself, reflects his full intentions.

The first impression of Browning's final collected edition (i.e., 1888-1889a) is not in and of itself the poet's final corrected text. By the spring of 1889 some of the early volumes of the first impression were already sold out, and by mid-August it was evident that a new one would be required. About this time James Dykes Campbell, Honorary Secretary of the London Browning Society, was informed by Browning that he was making further corrections to be incorporated into the new impression. According to Dykes Campbell, Browning had corrected the first ten volumes and offered to transcribe the corrections into Dykes Campbell's copy of 1888-1889a before leaving for Italy. The volumes altered in Browning's hand are now in the British Library and contain on the flyleaf of Volume I Dykes Campbell's note explaining precisely what happened. Of course, Dykes Campbell's copy was not the one used by the printer for the second impression. Nevertheless, these changes are indisputably Browning's and are those which, according to his own statement, he proposed to make in the new impression. This set of corrections carries, therefore, great authority.

Equally authoritative is a second set of corrections, also in Browning's hand, for part of 1888-1889a. In the poet's possession at the time of his death, this handwritten list was included in lot 179 of Sotheby, Wilkinson, and Hodge's auction of Browning materials in 1913; it is today located in the Brown University Library. The list contains corrections only to Volumes 4-10 of 1888-1889a. We know that Browning, on 26 July 1889, had completed and sent to Smith "the corrections for Vol. III in readiness for whenever you need them." By the latter part of August, according to Dykes Campbell, the poet had finished corrections for Volumes 1-10. Browning left for Italy on 29 August. The condition of the Brown University list does not indicate that it was ever used by the printer. Thus we surmise that the Brown list (completing the corrections through volume 10) may be the poet's copy of another list sent to his publisher. Whatever the case, the actual documents used by the printers—a set of marked volumes or handwritten lists—are not known to exist. A possible exception is a marked copy of *Red Cotton Night-Cap Country* (now in the Berg Collection of the New York Public Library) which seems to have been used by printers. Further materials used in preparing Browning's final edition may yet appear.

The matter is complicated further because neither set of corrections of 1888-1889a corresponds exactly to each other nor to the 1889 second impression. Each set contains corrections the other omits, and in a few cases the sets present alternative corrections of the same error. Our study of the Dykes Campbell copy of 1888-1889a reveals fifteen discrepancies between its corrections and the 1889 second impression. The Brown University list, which contains far fewer corrections, varies from the second impression in thirteen instances. Though neither of these sets of corrections was used by the printers, both are authoritative; we consider them legitimate textual variants, and record them as such. The lists are, of course, useful when emendation of the copy-text is required.

The value of the Dykes Campbell copy of 1888-1889a and the Brown University list is not that they render Browning's text perfect. The corrections to 1888-1889a must have existed in at least one other, still more authoritative form: the documents which Browning sent to his publisher. That this is so is indicated by the presence of required corrections in the second impression which neither the Dykes Campbell copy nor the Brown University list calls for. The significance of the existing sets of corrections is that they clearly indicate two important points: Browning's direct and active interest in the preparation of a corrected second impression of his final collected edition; and, given the high degree of correspondence between the two sets of corrections and the affected lines of the second impression, the concern of the printers to follow the poet's directives.

The second impression of 1888-1889 incorporated most of Browning's corrections to the first ten volumes of the first impression. There is no evidence whatever that any corrections beyond those which Browning sent to his publisher in the summer of 1889 were ever made. We choose, therefore, the 1889 corrected second impression of volumes 1-10 as copy-text for the works in those volumes. Corrections to the first impression were achieved by cutting the affected letters or punctuation out of the stereotype plates and pressing or soldering in the correct pieces of type. The corrected plates were then used for many copies, without changing the date on the title pages (except, of course, in volumes 17 [*Asolando*] and 18 [*New Poems*], added to the set by the publishers in 1894 and 1914 respectively). External evidence from publishers' catalogues and the advertisements bound into some volumes of 1889 indicate that copies of this impression were produced as late as 1913, although the dates on the title pages of volumes 1-16 remained 1889. Extensive plate deterioration is characteristic of the later copies, and use of the Hinman collator on early and late examples of 1889 reveals that the inserted corrections were somewhat fragile, some of them having decayed or disappeared entirely as the plates aged. (See Allan C. Dooley, "Browning's *Poetical Works* of 1888-1889," *SBHC* 7:1 [1978], 43-69.)

We do not use as copy-text volumes 11-16 of 1889, because there is no present evidence indicating that Browning exercised substantial control over this part of the second impression of 1888-1889. We do know that he made one correction, which he requested in a letter to Smith quoted by Hancher:

> I have just had pointed out to [me] that an error, I supposed corrected, still is to be found in the 13th Volume—(Aristophanes' Apology) page 143, line 9, where the word should be Opora—without an i. I should like it altered, if that may be possible.

This correction was indeed made in the second impression. Our collations of copies of volumes 11-16 of 1889a and 1889 show no other intentional changes. The later copies do show, however, extensive type batter, numerous scratches, and irregular inking. Therefore our copy-text for the works in the last six volumes of 1888-1889 is volumes 11-16 of 1888-1889a.

IV VARIANTS

In this edition we record, with a very few exceptions discussed below, all variants from the copy-text appearing in the manuscripts and in the editions under Browning's control. Our purpose in doing this is two-fold.

1. We enable the reader to reconstruct the text of a work as it stood at the various stages of its development.

2. We provide the materials necessary to an understanding of how Browning's growth and development as an artist are reflected in his successive revisions to his works.

As a consequence of this policy our variant listings inevitably contain some variants that were not created by Browning; printer's errors and readings that may result from house-styling will appear occasionally. But the evidence that Browning assumed responsibility for what was printed, and that he considered and used unorthodox punctuation as part of his meaning, is so persuasive that we must record even the smallest and oddest variants. The following examples, characteristic of Browning's revisions, illustrate the point:

> *Pauline,* l. 700:
>     1833: I am prepared—I have made life my own—
>     1868: I am prepared: I have made life my own.
> "Evelyn Hope," l. 41:
>     1855: I have lived, I shall say, so much since then,
>     1865: I have lived (I shall say) so much since then,
> "Bishop Blougram's Apology," l. 267:
>     1855: That's the first cabin-comfort I secure—
>     1865: That's the first-cabin comfort I secure:
> *The Ring and the Book,* Book 11 ("Guido"), l. 1064:
>     1869: What if you give up boys' and girls' fools'-play
>     1872: What if you give up boy and girl fools'-play
>     1889a: What if you give up boy-and-girl-fools' play

We have concluded that Browning himself is nearly always responsible for such changes. But even if he only accepted these changes (rather than originating them), their effect on syntax, rhythm, and meaning is so significant that they must be recorded in our variant listings.

The only variants we do not record are those which strongly appear to result from systematic house-styling. For example, Browning nowhere indicated that he wished to use typography to influence meaning, and our inference is that any changes in line-spacing, depth of paragraph indentation, and the like, were the responsibility of the printers of the various editions, not the poet himself. House-styling was also very probably the cause of certain variants in the apparatus of Browning's plays, including variants in stage directions which involve a change only in manner of statement, such as *Enter Hampden* instead of

*Hampden enters;* variants in the printing of stage directions, such as *Aside* instead of *aside,* or [*Aside.*] instead of [*Aside*], or [*Strafford.*] instead of [*Strafford*]; variants in character designations, such as *Lady Carlisle* instead of *Car* or *Carlisle.* Browning also accepted current convention for indicating quotations (see section V below ). Neither do we list changes in type face (except when used for emphasis), nor the presence or absence of a period at the end of the title of a work.

## V  ALTERATIONS TO THE COPY-TEXT

We have rearranged the sequence of works in the copy-text, so that they appear in the order of their first publication. This process involves the restoration to the original order of the poems included in *Dramatic Lyrics, Dramatic Romances and Lyrics,* and *Men and Women.* We realize, of course, that Browning himself was responsible for the rearrangement of these poems in the various collected editions; in his prefatory note for the 1888-1889 edition, however, he indicates that he desired a chronological presentation:

> The poems that follow are again, as before, printed in chronological order; but only so far as proves compatible with the prescribed size of each volume, which necessitates an occasional change in the distribution of its contents.

We would like both to indicate Browning's stated intentions about the placement of his poems and to present the poems in the order which suggests Browning's development as a poet. We have chosen, therefore, to present the poems in order of their first publication, with an indication in the notes as to their respective subsequent placement. We also include the tables of contents of the editions listed as Primary Materials above.

We have regularized or modernized the copy-text in the following minor ways:

1. We do not place a period at the end of the title of a work, though the copy-text does.

2. In some of Browning's editions, including the copy-text, the first word of each work is printed in capital letters. We have used the modern practice of capitalizing only the first letter.

3. The inconsistent use of both an ampersand and the word *and* has been regularized to the use of *and.*

4. We have eliminated the space between the two parts of a contraction; thus the copy-text's *it 's* is printed as *it's,* for example.

5. We uniformly place periods and commas within closing quotation marks.

6. We have employed throughout the modern practice of indicating quoted passages with quotation marks only at the beginning and end of the quotation. Throughout Browning's career, no matter which publisher or printer was handling his works, this matter was treated very inconsistently. In some of the poet's manuscripts and in most of his first editions, quotations are indicated by quotation marks only at the beginning and end. In the collected editions of 1863 and 1865, issued by Chapman and Hall, some quoted passages have quotation marks at the beginning of each line of the quotation, while others follow modern practice. In Smith, Elder's collected editions of 1868 and 1888-1889, quotation marks usually appear at the beginning of each line of a quotation. We have regularized and modernized what seems a matter of house-styling in both copy-text and variants.

The remaining way in which the copy-text is altered is by emendation. Our policy is to emend the copy-text to eliminate apparent errors of either Browning or his printers. It is evident that Browning did make errors and overlook mistakes, as shown by the following example from "One Word More," the last poem in *Men and Women*. Stanza sixteen of the copy-text opens with the following lines:

> What, there's nothing in the moon noteworthy?
> Nay: for if that moon could love a mortal,
> Use, to charm him (so to fit a fancy,
> All her magic ('tis the old sweet mythos)
> She . . .

Clearly the end punctuation in the third line is incorrect. A study of the various texts is illuminating. Following are the readings of the line in each of the editions for which Browning was responsible:

| MS: | fancy) | 1855: | fancy) | 1865: | fancy) | 1888: | fancy |
|-----|--------|-------|--------|-------|--------|-------|-------|
| P: | fancy) | 1863: | fancy) | 1868: | fancy) | 1889: | fancy, |

The omission of one parenthesis in 1888 was almost certainly a printer's error. Browning, in the Dykes Campbell copy corrections to 1888-1889a, missed or ignored the error. However, in the Brown University list of corrections, he indicated that *fancy* should be followed by a comma. This is the way the line appears in the corrected second impression of Volume 4, but the correction at best satisfies the demands of syntax only partially. Browning might have written the line:

> Use, to charm him, so to fit a fancy,

or, to maintain parallelism between the third and fourth lines:

> Use, to charm him (so to fit a fancy),

or he might simply have restored the earlier reading. Oversights of this nature demand emendation, and our choice would be to restore the punctuation of the manuscript through 1868. All of our emendations will be based, as far as possible, on the historical collation of the passage involved, the grammatical demands of the passage in context, and the poet's treatment of other similar passages. Fortunately, the multiple editions of most of the works provide the editor with ample textual evidence to make an informed and useful emendation.

All emendations to the copy-text are listed at the beginning of the Editorial Notes for each work. The variant listings for the copy-text also incorporate the emendations, which are preceded and followed there by the symbol indicating an editor's note.

## VI APPARATUS

1. *Variants.* In presenting the variants from the copy-text, we list at the bottom of each page readings from the known manuscripts, proof sheets of the editions when we have located them, and the first and subsequent editions.

A variant is generally preceded and followed by a pickup and a drop word (example a). No note terminates with a punctuation mark unless the punctuation mark comes at the end of the line; if a variant drops or adds a punctuation mark, the next word is added (example b). If the normal pickup word has appeared previously in the same line, the note begins with the word preceding it. If the normal drop word appears subsequently in the line, the next word is added (example c). If a capitalized pickup word occurs within the line, it is accompanied by the preceding word (example d). No pickup or drop words, however, are used for any variant consisting of an internal change, for example a hyphen in a compounded word, an apostrophe, a tense change or a spelling change (example e). A change in capitalization within a line of poetry will be preceded by a pickup word, for which, within an entry containing other variants, the < > is suitable (example f). No drop word is used when the variant comes at the end of a line (example g).

a.  [611]   *1840*:but that appeared   *1863*:but this appeared
b.  variant at end of line:          [109]   *1840*:intrigue:"   *1863*:intrigue.
    variant within line:          [82]   *1840*:forests like   *1863*:forests, like
c.  [132]   *1840*:too sleeps; but   *1863*:too sleeps: but          [77]   *1840*:that night
    by   *1863*:that, night by night,   *1888*:by night
d.  [295]   *1840*:at Padua to repulse the   *1863*:at Padua who repulsed the
e.  [284]   *1840*:are   *1863*:were
    [344]   *1840*:dying-day,   *1863*:dying day,
f.  capitalization change with no other variants:          [741]   *1840:*
    retaining Will,   *1863*:will,
    with other variants:          [843]   *1840*:Was < > Him back! Why   *1863*:Is
    < > back!" Why   *1865*:him
g.  [427]   *1840*:dregs:   *1863*:dregs.

Each recorded variant will be assumed to be incorporated in the next edition if there is no indication otherwise. This rule applies even in cases where the only change occurs in 1888-1889, although it means that the variant note duplicates the copy-text. A variant listing, then, traces the history of a line and brings it forward to the point where it matches the copy-text.

With regard to manuscript readings, our emphasis is on the textual development and sequence of revisions; visual details of the manuscripts are kept to a minimum. For economy of space, we use formulae such as §crossed out and replaced above by§, but these often cannot report fine details such as whether, when two words were crossed out, the accompanying punctuation was precisely cancelled also. Our MS entries provide enough information to reconstruct with reasonable accuracy B's initial and revised manuscript readings, but they cannot substitute for direct scrutiny of the documents themselves.

It should be noted that we omit drop words in manuscript entries where the final reading is identical to the printed editions—thus

MS:Silence, and all that ghastly §crossed out and replaced above by§ tinted pageant, base
Printed editions: Silence, and all that tinted pageant, base

is entered as

MS:that ghastly §crossed out and replaced above by§ tinted

in our variant listings.

An editor's note always refers to the single word or mark of punctuation immediately preceding or following the comment, unless otherwise specified.

In Browning's plays, all character designations which happen to occur in variant listings are standardized to the copy-text reading. In listing variants in the plays, we ignore character designations unless the designation comes within a numbered line. In such a case, the character designation is treated as any other word, and can be used as a pickup or drop word. When a character designation is used as a pickup word, however, the rule excluding capitalized pickup words (except at the beginning of a line) does not apply, and we do not revert to the next earliest uncapitalized pickup word.

2. *Line numbers.* Poetic lines are numbered in the traditional manner, taking one complete poetic line as one unit of counting. In prose passages the unit of counting is the type line of this edition.

3. *Table of signs in variant listings.* We have avoided all symbols and signs used by Browning himself. The following is a table of the signs used in the variant notes:

| | |
|---|---|
| § . . . § | Editor's note |
| < > | Words omitted |
| / | Line break |
| / / , / / / , . . . | Line break plus one or more lines without internal variants |

4 *Annotations.* In general principle, we have annotated proper names, phrases that function as proper names, and words or groups of words the full meaning of which requires factual, historical, or literary background. Thus we have attempted to hold interpretation to a minimum, although we realize that the act of selection itself is to some extent interpretive.

Notes, particularly on historical figures and events, tend to fullness and even to the tangential and unessential. As a result, some of the information provided may seem unnecessary to the scholar. On the other hand, it is not possible to assume that all who use this edition are fully equipped to assimilate unaided all of Browning's copious literary, historical, and mythological allusions. Thus we have directed our efforts toward a diverse audience.

TABLES

1. *Manuscripts.* We have located manuscripts for the following of Browning's works; the list is chronological.

*Paracelsus*
    Forster and Dyce Collection,
    Victoria and Albert Museum, London
*Colombe's Birthday*
    New York Public Library
*Christmas-Eve and Easter-Day*
    Forster and Dyce Collection,
    Victoria and Albert Museum, London
"Love Among the Ruins"
    Lowell Collection,
    Houghton Library, Harvard University
"The Twins"
    Pierpont Morgan Library, New York
"One Word More"
    Pierpont Morgan Library, New York
"James Lee's Wife," ll. 244-69
    Armstrong Browning Library, Baylor University
"May and Death"
    Armstrong Browning Library, Baylor University
"A Face"
    Armstrong Browning Library, Baylor University
*Dramatis Personae*
    Pierpont Morgan Library, New York
*The Ring and the Book*
    British Library, London
*Balaustion's Adventure*
    Balliol College Library, Oxford
*Prince Hohenstiel-Schwangau*
    Balliol College Library, Oxford
*Fifine at the Fair*
    Balliol College Library, Oxford
*Red Cotton Night-Cap Country*
    Balliol College Library, Oxford
*Aristophanes' Apology*
    Balliol College Library, Oxford
*The Inn Album*
    Balliol College Library, Oxford
*Of Pacchiarotto, and How He Worked in Distemper*
    Balliol College Library, Oxford
"Hervé Riel"
    Pierpont Morgan Library, New York

*The Agamemnon of Aeschylus*
    Balliol College Library, Oxford
*La Saisiaz and The Two Poets of Croisic*
    Balliol College Library, Oxford
*Dramatic Idylls*
    Balliol College Library, Oxford
*Dramatic Idylls, Second Series*
    Balliol College Library, Oxford
*Jocoseria*
    Balliol College Library, Oxford
*Ferishtah's Fancies*
    Balliol College Library, Oxford
*Parleyings With Certain People of Importance in Their Day*
    Balliol College Library, Oxford
*Asolando*
    Pierpont Morgan Library, New York

We have been unable to locate manuscripts for the following works, and request that persons with information about any of them communicate with us.

| | |
|---|---|
| *Pauline* | *The Return of the Druses* |
| *Strafford* | *A Blot in the 'Scutcheon* |
| *Sordello* | *Dramatic Romances and Lyrics* |
| *Pippa Passes* | *Luria* |
| *King Victor and King Charles* | *A Soul's Tragedy* |
| "Essay on Chatterton" | "Essay on Shelley" |
| *Dramatic Lyrics* | *Men and Women* |

2. *Editions referred to in Volume XI.* The following editions have been used in preparing the text and variants presented in this volume. The dates given below are used as symbols in the variant listings at the foot of each page. See the Editorial Notes for other texts collated or consulted.

1872    *Fifine at the Fair.*
        London: Smith, Elder and Company.

1875    *Red Cotton Night-Cap Country, or Turf and Towers.*
        London: Smith, Elder and Company.

1889a   *The Poetical Works.*
        Volumes 9-16. London: Smith, Elder and Company.

3. *Short titles and abbreviations.* The following short forms of reference have been used in the Editorial Notes:

| | |
|---|---|
| ABL | Armstrong Browning Library, Baylor University, Waco, TX |
| B | Browning |
| DeVane and Knickerbocker | *New Letters of Robert Browning,* ed. W. C. DeVane and K. L. Knickerbocker. New Haven, CT, 1950. |
| Domett | *The Diary of Alfred Domett 1872-1885,* ed. E. A. Horsman. Oxford, 1953. |
| EBB | Elizabeth Barrett Browning |
| Hood | *Letters of Robert Browning Collected by Thomas J. Wise,* ed. T. L. Hood. New Haven, CT, 1933. |
| Irvine and Honan | William Irvine and Park Honan. *The Book, the Ring, and the Poet.* New York, 1974. |
| McAleer, *DI* | *Dearest Isa: Robert Browning's Letters to Isabella Blagden,* ed. E. C. McAleer. Austin, TX, 1951. |
| *OED* | *The Oxford English Dictionary,* 2nd ed. Oxford, 1989. |
| Orr, *Hbk.* | Mrs. Sutherland Orr. *A Handbook to the Works of Robert Browning.* 6th ed. London, 1892. |
| Orr, *Life* | Mrs. Sutherland Orr. *Life and Letters of Robert Browning.* 2nd ed. London, 1891. |
| *Reconstruction* | *The Browning Collections, a Reconstruction, with Other Memorabilia,* comp. P. Kelley and B. A. Coley. Waco, TX; New York; Winfield, KS, and London, 1984. |

Citations and quotations from the Bible refer to the King James Version unless otherwise specified.

Citations and quotations from Shakespeare refer to T*he Riverside Shakespeare,* 2nd ed., ed. G. B. Evans, et al., Boston, 1997.

ACKNOWLEDGMENTS

For making available to us materials under their care, we thank the Armstrong Browning Library and its Browning Database at Baylor University; the Balliol College Library of Oxford University; the Henry E. Huntington Library; the Berg Collection, New York Public Library; the Humanities Research Center, University of Texas at Austin.

For assistance in preparing this volume, we particularly thank the following: John Krebs, Alan Tadiello, Marianne Tettlebaum, Andrew Wilson, Philip Kelley.

Extensive and invaluable research on *Red Cotton Night-Cap Country* was performed by Nathaniel Hart, who also composed a draft of the Editorial Notes. The present editors gratefully incorporated Prof. Hart's work into this edition.

Special recognition must be given to Susan E. Dooley, whose untimely death occurred as this volume was going to press. Susan worked tirelessly for over twenty years on this edition, often behind the scenes, organizing, researching, correcting, and inspiring. Her loss to the project, and to its General Editor, is immense.

# FIFINE AT THE FAIR

Edited by Michael Bright

# RED COTTON NIGHT-CAP COUNTRY

Annotations by Michael Bright
Text edited by Susan E. Dooley and Allan C. Dooley

# FIFINE AT THE FAIR

Edited by Michael Bright

# FIFINE AT THE FAIR

## DONE ELVIRE

Vous plaît-il, don Juan, nous éclaircir ces beaux mystères?

## DON JUAN

Madame, à vous dire la vérité . . .

## DONE ELVIRE

Ah! que vous savez mal vous défendre pour un homme de cour, et qui doit être accoutumé à ces sortes de choses! J'ai pitié de vous voir la confusion que vous avez. Que ne vous armez-vous le front d'une noble effronterie? Que ne me jurez-vous que vous êtes toujours dans les mêmes sentimens pour moi, que vous m'aimez toujours avec une ardeur sans égale, et que rien n'est capable de vous détacher de moi que la mort?

MOLIÈRE, Don Juan, acte i. sc. 3.

## DONNA ELVIRA

Don Juan, might you please to help one give a guess,
Hold up a candle, clear this fine mysteriousness?

## DON JUAN

Madam, if needs I must declare the truth,—in short . . .

## DONNA ELVIRA

Fie, for a man of mode, accustomed at the court
5  To such a style of thing, how awkwardly my lord
Attempts defence! You move compassion, that's the word—
Dumb-foundered and chap-fallen! Why don't you arm your brow
With noble impudence? Why don't you swear and vow
No sort of change is come to any sentiment
10  You ever had for me? Affection holds the bent,
You love me now as erst, with passion that makes pale
All ardour else: nor aught in nature can avail
To separate us two, save what, in stopping breath,
May peradventure stop devotion likewise—death!

*Epigraph 2*     12| MS:truth, in   *1872:*truth—in      15| MS:Falls to his fence!
*1872:*Attempts defence!      16| MS:chap fallen   *1872:*chap—fallen
23| MS:death?   *1872:*death!

*PROLOGUE*

AMPHIBIAN

I

The fancy I had to-day,
    Fancy which turned a fear!
I swam far out in the bay,
    Since waves laughed warm and clear.

II

I lay and looked at the sun,
    The noon-sun looked at me:
Between us two, no one
    Live creature, that I could see.

III

Yes! There came floating by
    Me, who lay floating too.
Such a strange butterfly!
    Creature as dear as new:

IV

Because the membraned wings
    So wonderful, so wide,
So sun-suffused, were things
    Like soul and nought beside.

V

A handbreadth over head!
    All of the sea my own,
It owned the sky instead;
    Both of us were alone.

---

*PROLOGUE: AMPHIBIAN*    [10]|  MS:too,  *1889a:*too.

## VI

I never shall join its flight,
For, nought buoys flesh in air.
If it touch the sea—good night!
Death sure and swift waits there.

## VII

Can the insect feel the better
For watching the uncouth play
Of limbs that slip the fetter,
Pretend as they were not clay?

## VIII

Undoubtedly I rejoice
That the air comports so well
With a creature which had the choice
Of the land once. Who can tell?

## IX

What if a certain soul
Which early slipped its sheath,
And has for its home the whole
Of heaven, thus look beneath,

## X

Thus watch one who, in the world,
Both lives and likes life's way,
Nor wishes the wings unfurled
That sleep in the worm, they say?

25

30

35

40

---

22| MS:For, what buoys <> air? *1872:*For, nought buoys <> air.    25| MS:Can it be all
the *1872:*Can the insect feel the    36| MS:beneath? *1872:*beneath,
37| MS:who in <> world *1872:*who, in <> world    40| MS:say *1872:*say?

### XI

But sometimes when the weather
   Is blue, and warm waves tempt
To free oneself of tether,
   And try a life exempt

### XII

45     From worldly noise and dust,
   In the sphere which overbrims
With passion and thought,—why, just
   Unable to fly, one swims!

### XIII

By passion and thought upborne,
50     One smiles to oneself— "They fare
Scarce better, they need not scorn
   Our sea, who live in the air!"

### XIV

Emancipate through passion
   And thought, with sea for sky,
55     We substitute, in a fashion,
   For heaven—poetry:

### XV

Which sea, to all intent,
   Gives flesh such noon-disport
As a finer element
60     Affords the spirit-sort.

---

43| MS:tether    *1872:*tether,      49| MS:upborne    *1872:*upborne,

### XVI

Whatever they are, we seem:
　　Imagine the thing they know;
All deeds they do, we dream;
　　Can heaven be else but so?

### XVII

65　　And meantime, yonder streak
　　Meets the horizon's verge;
That is the land, to seek
If we tire or dread the surge:

### XVIII

Land the solid and safe—
70　　To welcome again (confess!)
When, high and dry, we chafe
　　The body, and don the dress.

### XIX

Does she look, pity, wonder
　　At one who mimics flight,
75　Swims—heaven above, sea under,
　　Yet always earth in sight?

---

62| MS:know: *1872:*know; 63| MS:dream: *1872:*dream; 65| MS:meantime yonder *1872:*meantime, yonder 72| MS:body and *1872:*body, and

# FIFINE AT THE FAIR

*1872*

### I

O trip and skip, Elvire! Link arm in arm with me!
Like husband and like wife, together let us see
The tumbling-troop arrayed, the strollers on their stage,
Drawn up and under arms, and ready to engage.

### II

⁵     Now, who supposed the night would play us such a prank?
—That what was raw and brown, rough pole and shaven plank,
Mere bit of hoarding, half by trestle propped, half tub,
Would flaunt it forth as brisk as butterfly from grub?
This comes of sun and air, of Autumn afternoon,
¹⁰     And Pornic and Saint Gille, whose feast affords the boon—
This scaffold turned parterre, this flower-bed in full blow,
Bateleurs, baladines! We shall not miss the show!
They pace and promenade; they presently will dance:
What good were else i' the drum and fife? O pleasant land of France!

### III

¹⁵     Who saw them make their entry? At wink of eve, be sure!
They love to steal a march, nor lightly risk the lure.
They keep their treasure hid, nor stale (improvident)
Before the time is ripe, each wonder of their tent—
Yon six-legged sheep, to wit, and he who beats a gong,
²⁰     Lifts cap and waves salute, exhilarates the throng—
Their ape of many years and much adventure, grim

---

*FIFINE AT THE FAIR*     §MS in Balliol College Library. Ed. 1872, 1889a. See Editorial Notes§
*Title*  MS:Fifine §inserted to left of word or words illegibly crossed out§     ⁴|  MS:arms and
< > engage!   *1872:*arms, and < > engage.     ⁷|  MS:tressel §altered to§ trestle
⁹|  MS:air, of §inserted above§ Autumn and §deleted§     ¹⁰|  MS:Gille whose   *1872:*Gille,
whose     ¹³|  MS:They posture now §last two words crossed out and replaced above by one
word§ promenade and pace §transposed with *promenade*§     ¹⁴|  MS:pleant §altered to§
pleasant     ¹⁶|  MS:march nor   *1872:*march, nor     ¹⁷|  MS:nor §word illegibly crossed
out and replaced by§ stale     ¹⁹|  MS:sheep to-wit   *1872:*sheep, to wit

And grey with pitying fools who find a joke in him.
Or, best, the human beauty, Mimi, Toinette, Fifine,
Tricot fines down if fat, padding plumps up if lean,
25  Ere, shedding petticoat, modesty, and such toys,
They bounce forth, squalid girls transformed to gamesome boys.

### IV

No, no, thrice, Pornic, no! Perpend the authentic tale!
'Twas not for every Gawain to gaze upon the Grail!
But whoso went his rounds, when flew bat, flitted midge,
30  Might hear across the dusk,—where both roads join the bridge,
Hard by the little port,—creak a slow caravan,
A chimneyed house on wheels; so shyly-sheathed, began
To broaden out the bud which, bursting unaware,
Now takes away our breath, queen-tulip of the Fair!

### V

35  Yet morning promised much: for, pitched and slung and reared
On terrace 'neath the tower, 'twixt tree and tree appeared
An airy structure; how the pennon from its dome,
Frenetic to be free, makes one red stretch for home!
The home far and away, the distance where lives joy,
40  The cure, at once and ever, of world and world's annoy;
Since, what lolls full in front, a furlong from the booth,
But ocean-idleness, sky-blue and millpond-smooth?

### VI

Frenetic to be free! And, do you know, there beats
Something within my breast, as sensitive?—repeats
45  The fever of the flag? My heart makes just the same
Passionate stretch, fires up for lawlessness, lays claim
To share the life they lead: losels, who have and use

---

29| MS:rounds when  *1872:*rounds, when      32| MS:shyly-sheathed began
*1872:*shyly-sheathed, began      36| MS:neath  *1872:*'neath
38| MS:home,  *1872:*home!      44| MS:breast as  *1872:*breast, as
47| MS:lead, these §crossed out§ losels who §inserted above§  *1872:*lead: losels, who

The hour what way they will,—applaud them or abuse
Society, whereof myself am at the beck,
50 Whose call obey, and stoop to burden stiffest neck!

VII

Why is it that whene'er a faithful few combine
To cast allegiance off, play truant, nor repine,
Agree to bear the worst, forego the best in store
For us who, left behind, do duty as of yore,—
55 Why is it that, disgraced, they seem to relish life the more?
—Seem as they said "We know a secret passing praise
Or blame of such as you! Remain! we go our ways
With something you o'erlooked, forgot or chose to sweep
Clean out of door: our pearl picked from your rubbish-heap.
60 You care not for your loss, we calculate our gain.
All's right. Are you content? Why, so let things remain!
To the wood then, to the wild: free life, full liberty!"
And when they rendezvous beneath the inclement sky,
House by the hedge, reduced to brute-companionship,
65 —Misguided ones who gave society the slip,
And find too late how boon a parent they despised,
What ministration spurned, how sweet and civilized—
Then, left alone at last with self-sought wretchedness,
No interloper else!—why is it, can we guess?—
70 At somebody's expense, goes up so frank a laugh?

---

⁴⁹| MS:Society, of whom myself  *1872:*Society, whereof myself      ⁵⁰| MS:Whose call §two words inserted at beginning of line§ Obey §altered to§ obey the call, §last two words crossed out§ and §crossed out and then marked to restore§      ⁵¹| MS:§¶ called for§
⁵⁴| MS:For those §crossed out and replaced above by§ us who, stay §crossed out and replaced above by§ left      ⁵⁵| MS:§Line inserted between ll. 54 and 56 to create a triplet with the preceding two lines; ll. 53-55 are bracketed in the right margin§
⁵⁶| MS:secret well worth §last two words crossed out and replaced below by§ passing
⁵⁷| MS:you: remain! §altered to§ you! Remain!      ⁵⁹| MS:door, our <> from a §crossed out and replaced above by§ your rubbish-heap:  *1872:*door: our <> rubbish-heap.
⁶⁰| MS:for the §crossed out and replaced above by§ your <> calculate the §crossed out and replaced above by§ our gain:  *1872:*gain      ⁶¹| MS:right; are  *1872:*right. Are
⁶²| MS:wild, free  *1872:*wild: free      ⁶³| MS:when we §crossed out and replaced above by§ they      ⁶⁴|MS:Housed  *1872:*House      ⁶⁷|MS:spurned, how §crossed out and replaced above by§ so sweet  *1872:*spurned, how sweet      ⁶⁸|MS:Then,—left  *1872:*Then, left
⁶⁹| MS:it,—can  *1872:*it, can      ⁷⁰| MS:laugh,  *1872:*laugh?

As though they held the corn, and left us only chaff
From garners crammed and closed. And we indeed are clever
If we get grain as good, by thrashing straw for ever!

### VIII

  Still, truants as they are and purpose yet to be,
75 That nowise needs forbid they venture—as you see—
To cross confine, approach the once familiar roof
O' the kindly race their flight estranged: stand half aloof,
Sidle half up, press near, and proffer wares for sale
—In their phrase—make, in ours, white levy of black mail.
80 They, of the wild, require some touch of us the tame,
Since clothing, meat and drink, mean money all the same.

### IX

  If hunger, proverbs say, allures the wolf from wood,
Much more the bird must dare a dash at something good:
Must snatch up, bear away in beak, the trifle-treasure
85 To wood and wild, and then—O how enjoy at leisure!
Was never tree-built nest, you climbed and took, of bird
(Rare city-visitant, talked of, scarce seen or heard),
But, when you would dissect the structure, piece by piece,
You found, enwreathed amid the country-product—fleece
90 And feather, thistle-fluffs and bearded windlestraws—
Some shred of foreign silk, unravelling of gauze,
Bit, may be, of brocade, mid fur and blow-bell-down:

---

71| MS:corn and <> chaff, §comma crossed out§ *1872:*corn, and 72| MS:Their
§crossed out and replaced above by§ From <> closed, and <> indeed were §crossed out and
replaced above by§ are *1872:*closed. And 73| MS:grain to match §last two words crossed
out and replaced above by two words§ as good 74|MS:§¶ called for§ 76| MS:confines
§altered to§ confine 77| MS:race their <> estranged,—half stand aloof, *1872:*race,
their <> estranged: half *1889a:*race their <> estranged: stand half aloof, 78| MS:Half
sidle up *1889a:*Sidle half up 79| MS:phrase, but §crossed out and replaced above by
dash and word and comma§ —make, *1889a:*phrase—make, in 80| MS:They of <> wild
require *1872:*They, of <> wild, require 82| MS:And §crossed out and replaced above
by§ If 83| MS:good, *1872:*good: 86| MS:bird, *1889a:*bird 87| MS:Rare
<> heard, *1872:*(Rare <> heard) *1889a:*heard), 88| MS:you would §inserted above§
89| MS:country-product—fleece *1872:*country-product,—fleece *1889a:*country-product—
fleece 91| MS:unraveling *1889a:*unravelling 92| MS:Bit, of brocade, may be,
§transposed to§ Bit, may be, of brocade, <> and thistle-down: *1889a:*and blow-bell-down:

Filched plainly from mankind, dear tribute paid by town,
Which proved how oft the bird had plucked up heart of grace,
95   Swooped down at waif and stray, made furtively our place
Pay tax and toll, then borne the booty to enrich
Her paradise i' the waste; the how and why of which,
That is the secret, there the mystery that stings!

X

For, what they traffic in, consists of just the things
100   We,—proud ones who so scorn dwellers without the pale,
Bateleurs, baladines, white leviers of black mail,—
I say, they sell what we most pique us that we keep!
How comes it, all we hold so dear they count so cheap?

XI

What price should you impose, for instance, on repute,
105   Good fame, your own good fame and family's to boot?
Stay start of quick moustache, arrest the angry rise
Of eyebrow! All I asked is answered by surprise.
Now tell me: are you worth the cost of a cigar?
Go boldly, enter booth, disburse the coin at bar
110   Of doorway where presides the master of the troop,
And forthwith you survey his Graces in a group,
Live Picture, picturesque no doubt and close to life:
His sisters, right and left; the Grace in front, his wife.
Next, who is this performs the feat of the Trapeze?
115   Lo, she is launched, look—fie, the fairy!—how she flees
O'er all those heads thrust back,—mouths, eyes, one gape and stare,—
No scrap of skirt impedes free passage through the air,

---

93|  MS:tributes §altered to§ tribute      96|  MS:toll, and §crossed out and replaced above by§
then borne §altered to§ bore   *1872:*borne      97|  MS:waste—the  *1872:*waste; the
99|  MS:§¶ called for§ traffic with §crossed out and replaced above by§ in
100|  MS:proud ones §inserted above§ who despised §crossed out and replaced above by two
words§ so scorn      101|  MS:levy §altered to§ leviers      102|  MS:Or us §last two words
crossed out and replaced above by two words§ I say      104|  MS:§¶ called for§
107|  MS:surprize.  *1872:*surprise.      111|  MS:survey the §crossed out and replaced above
by§ his      113|  MS:left, the  *1872:*left;the      116|  MS:back,—mouths, §dash, word, and
comma inserted above§      117|  MS:Nor §altered to§ No

17

Till, plumb on the other side, she lights and laughs again,
That fairy-form, whereof each muscle, nay, each vein
120 The curious may inspect,—his daughter that he sells
Each rustic for five sous. Desiderate aught else
O' the vendor? As you leave his show, why, joke the man!
"You cheat: your six-legged sheep, I recollect, began
Both life and trade, last year, trimmed properly and clipt,
125 As the Twin-headed Babe, and Human Nondescript!"
What does he care? You paid his price, may pass your jest.
So values he repute, good fame, and all the rest!

XII

But try another tack; say: "I indulge caprice,
Who am Don and Duke, and Knight, beside, o' the Golden Fleece,
130 And, never mind how rich. Abandon this career!
Have hearth and home, nor let your womankind appear
Without as multiplied a coating as protects
An onion from the eye! Become, in all respects,
God-fearing householder, subsistent by brain-skill,
135 Hand-labour; win your bread whatever way you will,
So it be honestly,—and, while I have a purse,
Means shall not lack!"—His thanks will be the roundest curse
That ever rolled from lip.

XIII

Now, what is it?—returns
The question—heartens so this losel that he spurns
140 All we so prize? I want, put down in black and white,
What compensating joy, unknown and infinite,
Turns lawlessness to law, makes destitution—wealth,
Vice—virtue, and disease of soul and body—health?

---

119| MS:fairy-form whereof   *1872:*fairy-form, whereof       121| MS:sous: desiderate
*1872:*sous. Desiderate        125| MS:the Twin-headed Babe and    *1872:*the Twin-headed Babe,
and         128| MS:§¶ called for§ tack: say, "I < > caprice   *1872:*tack; say: "I < > caprice,
129| MS:and Duke and    *1872:*and Duke, and        130| MS:rich; abandon   *1872:*rich.
Abandon         133| MS:eye! Become in < > respects   *1872:*eye! Become, in < > respects,
138| MS:lip. §¶ called for§ So §crossed out and replaced above by§ Now

18

### XIV

Ah, the slow shake of head, the melancholy smile,
145   The sigh almost a sob! What's wrong, was right erewhile?
Why are we two at once such ocean-width apart?
Pale fingers press my arm, and sad eyes probe my heart.
Why is the wife in trouble?

### XV

This way, this way, Fifine!
Here's she, shall make my thoughts be surer what they mean!
150   First let me read the signs, pourtray you past mistake
The gipsy's foreign self, no swarth our sun could bake.
Yet where's a woolly trace degrades the wiry hair?
And note the Greek-nymph nose, and—oh, my Hebrew pair
Of eye and eye—o'earched by velvet of the mole—
155   That swim as in a sea, that dip and rise and roll,
Spilling the light around! While either ear is cut
Thin as a dusk-leaved rose carved from a cocoa-nut.
And then, her neck! now, grant you had the power to deck,
Just as your fancy pleased, the bistre-length of neck,
160   Could lay, to shine against its shade, a moonlike row
Of pearls, each round and white as bubble Cupids blow
Big out of mother's milk,—what pearl-moon would surpass
That string of mock-turquoise, those almandines of glass,
Where girlhood terminates? for with breasts'-birth commence
165   The boy, and page-costume, till pink and impudence
End admirably all: complete the creature trips
Our way now, brings sunshine upon her spangled hips,
As here she fronts us full, with pose half-frank, half-fierce!

---

147|   MS:and probing eyes §last two words crossed out and replaced above by three words§ sad
eyes probe      149|   MS:she shall    *1872:*she, shall      151|   MS:gypsey's <> bake;
*1872:*gypsy's <> bake.      152|   MS:trace degrades <> hair!    *1872:*trace, degrades <> hair?
*1889a:*trace degrades      154|   MS:eye o'earched <> mole,    *1872:*eye—o'earched <>
mole—      159|   MS:pleased, you §crossed out and replaced above by§ the
160|   MS:lay to <> moon-like    *1872:*lay, to    *1889a:*moonlike      161|   MS:pearl <> bubble,
Cupids    *1889a:*pearls <> bubble Cupids      163|   MS:turquoise, and §crossed out and
replaced above by§ those <> glass, §question mark erased and replaced by comma§
168|   MS:As now §crossed out and replaced above by§ here

### XVI

Words urged in vain, Elvire! You waste your quarte and tierce,
170 Lunge at a phantom here, try fence in fairy-land.
For me, I own defeat, ask but to understand
The acknowledged victory of whom I call my queen,
Sexless and bloodless sprite: though mischievous and mean,
Yet free and flower-like too, with loveliness for law,
175 And self-sustainment made morality.

### XVII

A flaw
Do you account i' the lily, of lands which travellers know,
That, just as golden gloom supersedes Northern snow
I' the chalice, so, about each pistil, spice is packed,—
Deliriously-drugged scent, in lieu of odour lacked,
180 With us, by bee and moth, their banquet to enhance
At morn and eve, when dew, the chilly sustenance,
Needs mixture of some chaste and temperate perfume?
I ask, is she in fault who guards such golden gloom,
Such dear and damning scent, by who cares what devices,
185 And takes the idle life of insects she entices
When, drowned to heart's desire, they satiate the inside
O' the lily, mark her wealth and manifest her pride?

### XVIII

But, wiser, we keep off, nor tempt the acrid juice;
Discreet we peer and praise, put rich things to right use.
190 No flavourous venomed bell,—the rose it is, I wot,
Only the rose, we pluck and place, unwronged a jot,

---

<sup>169|</sup> MS:carte    *1872:*quarte        <sup>173|</sup> MS:sprite, though    *1872:*sprite: though
<sup>175|</sup>MS:§¶ called for§        <sup>177|</sup> MS:That, whereas golden    *1872:*That, just as golden
<sup>178|</sup> MS:chalice, and about <> pistil spice <> packed    *1872:*chalice, so, about <> pistil, spice
<> packed,—        <sup>180|</sup> MS:moth their    *1872:*moth, their
<sup>181|</sup> MS:eve when    *1872:*eve, when        <sup>182|</sup> MS:perfume,—    *1872:*perfume?—
*1889a:*perfume?        <sup>183|</sup>MS:I say §crossed out and replaced above by§ ask
<sup>184|</sup> MS:by—who <> device    *1872:*by who <> devices,
<sup>185|</sup> MS:That takes <> insects, these entice    *1872:*And takes <> insects she entices
<sup>188|</sup> MS:§¶ called for§ But wiser we <> off nor <> juice    *1872:*But, wiser, we <> off,
nor <> juice;        <sup>189|</sup> MS:Discreet by §crossed out and replaced above by§ we

No worse for homage done by every devotee,
I' the proper loyal throne, on breast where rose should be.
Or if the simpler sweets we have to choose among,
195    Would taste between our teeth, and give its toy the tongue,—
O gorgeous poison-plague, on thee no hearts are set!
We gather daisy meek, or maiden violet:
I think it is Elvire we love, and not Fifine.

XIX

"How does she make my thoughts be sure of what they mean?"
200    Judge and be just! Suppose, an age and time long past
Renew for our behoof one pageant more, the last
O' the kind, sick Louis liked to see defile between
Him and the yawning grave, its passage served to screen.
With eye as grey as lead, with cheek as brown as bronze,
205    Here where we stand, shall sit and suffer Louis Onze:
The while from yonder tent parade forth, not—oh, no—
Bateleurs, baladines! but range themselves a-row
Those well-sung women-worthies whereof loud fame still finds
Some echo linger faint, less in our hearts than minds.

XX

210    See, Helen! pushed in front o' the world's worst night and storm,
By Lady Venus' hand on shoulder: the sweet form
Shrinkingly prominent, though mighty, like a moon
Outbreaking from a cloud, to put harsh things in tune,
And magically bring mankind to acquiesce

---

192| MS:For all the §last three words crossed out and replaced above by three words§ No worse
for 193| MS:be; *1872:*be 194| MS:sweets we *1872:*sweets, we *1889a:*sweets we
196| MS:O spicy §crossed out and replaced above by§ gorgeous poison-plague on
*1872:*poison-plague, on 197| MS:meek or *1872:*meek, or 198| MS:love and
*1872:*love, and 200| MS:just! Suppose an *1872:*just! Suppose, an
201| MS:Renewed *1872:*Renew 203| MS:grave its *1872:*grave, its
204-05| MS:§Two lines inserted between ll. 203 and 206§ 205| MS:stand, there sits and
suffers *1872:*stand, shall sit and suffer 206| MS:Suppose from < > paraded forth—oh
*1872:*The while from < > parade forth, not—oh 207| MS:ranged *1872:*range
210| MS:§¶ called for§ See, Helen,—pushed *1872:*See, Helen! pushed
211| MS:shoulder, the *1872:*shoulder: the 213| MS:from its §crossed out and replaced
above by§ a 214| MS:magically charm §crossed out and replaced above by§ bring

215 In its own ravage,—call no curse upon, but bless
(Beldame, a moment since) the outbreaking beauty, now,
That casts o'er all the blood a candour from her brow.
See, Cleopatra! bared, the entire and sinuous wealth
O' the shining shape; each orb of indolent ripe health,
220 Captured, just where it finds a fellow-orb as fine
I' the body: traced about by jewels which outline,
Fire-frame, and keep distinct, perfections—lest they melt
To soft smooth unity ere half their hold be felt:
Yet, o'er that white and wonder, a soul's predominance
225 I' the head so high and haught—except one thievish glance,
From back of oblong eye, intent to count the slain.
Hush,—O I know, Elvire! Be patient, more remain!
What say you to Saint . . . Pish! Whatever Saint you please,
Cold-pinnacled aloft o' the spire, prays calm the seas
230 From Pornic Church, and oft at midnight (peasants say)
Goes walking out to save from shipwreck: well she may!
For think how many a year has she been conversant
With nought but winds and rains, sharp courtesy and scant
O' the wintry snow that coats the pent-house of her shrine,
235 Covers each knee, climbs near, but spares the smile benign
Which seems to say "I looked for scarce so much from earth!"
She follows, one long thin pure finger in the girth
O' the girdle—whence the folds of garment, eye and eye,
Besprent with fleurs-de-lys, flow down and multiply
240 Around her feet,—and one, pressed hushingly to lip:
As if, while thus we made her march, some foundering ship
Might miss her from her post, nearer to God half-way

---

<sup>216</sup>| MS:—Beldame a <> since, the    *1872:* (Beldame, a <> since) the
<sup>218</sup>| MS:See, Cleopatra,—bared    *1872:* See, Cleopatra! bared
<sup>219</sup>| MS:indolent young health,    *1872:* indolent ripe health    <sup>221</sup>| MS:body, traced
*1872:* body: traced    <sup>222</sup>| MS:Fire-frame and hold §crossed out and replaced above by§ keep
<> perfections else would melt    *1872:* Fire-frame, and <> perfections—lest they melt
<sup>223</sup>| MS:hold were felt:    *1872:* hold be felt:    <sup>224</sup>| MS:Yet o'er    *1872:* Yet, o'er
<sup>225</sup>| MS:so haught and high—all §crossed out§ except <> glance    *1872:* so high and haught—
except <> glance,    <sup>226</sup>| MS:At back <> eye intent    *1872:* From back <> eye, intent
<sup>228</sup>| MS:to Saint . .   . Pish    *1872:* to Saint? . . Pish    *1889a:* to Saint . . . Pish
<sup>230</sup>| MS:midnight, peasants say,    *1872:* midnight (peasants say)
<sup>234</sup>| MS:penthouse    *1872:* pent-house    <sup>235</sup>| MS:near but    *1872:* near, but
<sup>238</sup>| MS:girdle, whence    *1872:* girdle—whence    <sup>240</sup>| MS:lip    *1872:* lip:

In heaven, and she inquired "Who that treads earth can pray?
I doubt if even she, the unashamed! though, sure,
245   She must have stripped herself only to clothe the poor."

### XXI

This time, enough's a feast, not one more form, Elvire!
Provided you allow that, bringing up the rear
O' the bevy I am loth to—by one bird—curtail,
First note may lead to last, an octave crown the scale,
250   And this feminity be followed—do not flout!—
By—who concludes the masque with curtsey, smile and pout,
Submissive-mutinous? No other than Fifine
Points toe, imposes haunch, and pleads with tambourine!

### XXII

"Well, what's the meaning here, what does the masque intend,
255   Which, unabridged, we saw file past us, with no end
Of fair ones, till Fifine came, closed the catalogue?"

### XXIII

Task fancy yet again! Suppose you cast this clog
Of flesh away (that weeps, upbraids, withstands my arm)
And pass to join your peers, paragon charm with charm,
260   As I shall show you may,—prove best of beauty there!
Yourself confront yourself! This, help me to declare
That yonder-you, who stand beside these, braving each
And blinking none, beat her who lured to Troy-town beach
The purple prows of Greece,—nay, beat Fifine; whose face,
265   Mark how I will inflame, when seigneur-like I place

---

243| MS:she thought "Who   *1889a:*she inquired "Who    246| MS:feast:not   *1872:*feast, not    248| MS:Of bevy   *1872:*O' the bevy    251| MS:By—who   *1872:*By who 252| MS:Submissive-mutinous: no   *1872:*Submissive-mutinous? No    253| MS:tambourine. *1872:*tambourine!    254| MS:intend   *1872:*intend,    256| MS:ones till   *1872:*ones, till    257| MS:§¶ called for§    260| MS:may,—the best < > there?   *1872:*may,—prove < > there!    262| MS:beside now, braving   *1872:*beside these, braving 264| MS:Greece—nay, §dash, word, and comma inserted above§ beat poor §crossed out§ Fifine, whose   *1872:*Fifine; whose    265| MS:inflame when   *1872:*inflame,

I' the tambourine, to spot the strained and piteous blank
Of pleading parchment, see, no less than a whole franc!

### XXIV

    Ah, do you mark the brown o' the cloud, made bright with fire
Through and through? as, old wiles succeeding to desire,
270    Quality (you and I) once more compassionate
A hapless infant, doomed (fie on such partial fate!)
To sink the inborn shame, waive privilege of sex,
And posture as you see, support the nods and becks
Of clowns that have their stare, nor always pay its price;
275    An infant born perchance as sensitive and nice
As any soul of you, proud dames, whom destiny
Keeps uncontaminate from stigma of the stye
She wallows in! You draw back skirts from filth like her
Who, possibly, braves scorn, if, scorned, she minister
280    To age, want, and disease of parents one or both;
Nay, peradventure, stoops to degradation, loth
That some just-budding sister, the dew yet on the rose,
Should have to share in turn the ignoble trade,—who knows?

### XXV

    Ay, who indeed! Myself know nothing, but dare guess
285    That off she trips in haste to hand the booty . . . yes,
'Twixt fold and fold of tent, there looms he, dim-discerned,
The ogre, lord of all those lavish limbs have earned!
—Brute-beast-face,—ravage, scar, scowl and malignancy,—
O' the Strong Man, whom (no doubt, her husband) by-and-by

---

266| MS:tambourine to   *1872:*tambourine, to    268|   MS:§¶ called for§ cloud made
*1872:*cloud, made    269| MS:through, as    *1872:*through? as    271|   MS:infant
doomed   *1872:*infant, doomed    274|   MS:stare nor < > price: §colon altered to
semicolon§   *1872:*stare, nor    275|   MS:That §crossed out and replaced above by§ An
276|   MS:dames! whom   *1872:*dames, whom    277|   MS:of that stye   *1872:*of the stye
278|   MS:in: you   *1872:*in! You    280|   MS:want and < > both;   *1872:*want, and
*1889a:*both,    281|   MS:Or §crossed out and replaced above by§ Nay    284|   MS:§ called
for§    286|   MS:tent there < > dim-discerned   *1872:*tent, there < > dim-discerned,
287|   MS:all those   *1872:*all, those   *1889a:*all those    289|   MS:the Strong Man whom—no
< > husband—by and by   *1872:*the Strong Man, whom (no < > husband) by   *1889a:*by-and-by

290     You shall behold do feats: lift up nor quail beneath
     A quintal in each hand, a cart-wheel 'twixt his teeth.
     Oh she prefers sheer strength to ineffective grace,
     Breeding and culture! seeks the essential in the case!
     To him has flown my franc; and welcome, if that squint
295     O' the diabolic eye so soften through absinthe,
     That, for once, tambourine, tunic and tricot 'scape
     Their customary curse "Not half the gain o' the ape!"
     Ay, they go in together!

## XXVI

                Yet still her phantom stays
     Opposite, where you stand: as steady 'neath our gaze—
300     The live Elvire's and mine—though fancy-stuff and mere
     Illusion; to be judged,—dream-figures,—without fear
     Or favour, those the false, by you and me the true.

## XXVII

     "What puts it in my head to make yourself judge you?"
     Well, it may be, the name of Helen brought to mind
305     A certain myth I mused in years long left behind:
     How she that fled from Greece with Paris whom she loved,
     And came to Troy, and there found shelter, and so proved
     Such cause of the world's woe,—how she, old stories call
     This creature, Helen's self, never saw Troy at all.
310     Jove had his fancy-fit, must needs take empty air,
     Fashion her likeness forth, and set the phantom there

---

290|   MS:feats, lift <> beneath    *1872:*feats: lift <> beneath,    *1889a:*beneath
291|   MS:cart wheel    *1872:*cart-wheel      292|   MS:Oh, she    *1889a:*Oh she
293|   MS:culture, seeks    *1872:*culture! seeks      294|   MS:franc: and    *1872:*franc; and
297|   MS:of   *1889a:*o'      298|   MS:together! §¶ called for§      299|   MS:stand as <>
gaze,—    *1889a:*stand: as <> gaze—      300|   MS:live Elvire's and mine,—though
*1872:*live Elvire's, and    *1889a:*live Elvire's and mine—though      301|   MS:Illusion, to
*1872:*Illusion; to      303|   MS:§¶ called for§      305|   MS:I liked §crossed out and replaced
above by§ knew §crossed out and replaced below by§ mused
307|   MS:And §crossed out and replaced above by§ That came <> Troy and there took §crossed
out and replaced above by§ found shelter and    *1872:*And came <> Troy, and <> shelter, and
308|   MS:woe,—how §inserted above§ she, that §crossed out§
310|   MS:air    *1872:*air,      311|   MS:forth and    *1872:*forth, and

I' the midst for sport, to try conclusions with the blind
And blundering race, the game create for Gods, mankind:
Experiment on these,—establish who would yearn
315    To give up life for her, who, other-minded, spurn
The best her eyes could smile,—make half the world sublime,
And half absurd, for just a phantom all the time!
Meanwhile true Helen's self sat, safe and far away,
By a great river-side, beneath a purer day,
320    With solitude around, tranquillity within;
Was able to lean forth, look, listen, through the din
And stir; could estimate the worthlessness or worth
Of Helen who inspired such passion to the earth,
A phantom all the time! That put it in my head,
325    To make yourself judge you—the phantom-wife instead
O' the tearful true Elvire!

XXVIII

I thank the smile at last

Which thins away the tear! Our sky was overcast,
And something fell; but day clears up: if there chanced rain,
The landscape glistens more. I have not vexed in vain
330    Elvire: because she knows, now she has stood the test,
How, this and this being good, herself may still be best
O' the beauty in review; because the flesh that claimed
Unduly my regard, she thought, the taste, she blamed
In me, for things extern, was all mistake, she finds,—
335    Or will find, when I prove that bodies show me minds,
That, through the outward sign, the inward grace allures,

---

313| MS:race, create as §crossed out and replaced above by§ mere game for Gods—mankind, *1872:*race, the game create for Gods, mankind:    314| MS:on men, establish    *1872:*on these,—establish    315| MS:other-minded; spurn    *1872:*other-minded, spurn
316| MS:sublime    *1872:*sublime,    317| MS:absurd, all for a    *1872:*absurd, for just a
320| MS:within:    *1872:*within;    322| MS:stir, could    *1872:*stir; could
323| MS:Of Helen that inspired    *1872:*Of Helen who inspired    326| MS:true Elvire! §¶ called for§    327| MS:sky seemed §crossed out and replaced above by§ was
332| MS:review: because    *1872:*review; because    333| MS:taste she    *1872:*taste, she
334| MS:me for < > externe < > finds;    *1872:*me, for < > finds,—    *1889a:*extern
335| MS:Nor can I better prove    *1872:*Or will find, when I prove
336| MS:sign the    *1872:*sign, the

And sparks from heaven transpierce earth's coarsest covertures,—
All by demonstrating the value of Fifine!

## XXIX

   Partake my confidence! No creature's made so mean
340   But that, some way, it boasts, could we investigate,
Its supreme worth: fulfils, by ordinance of fate,
Its momentary task, gets glory all its own,
Tastes triumph in the world, pre-eminent, alone.
Where is the single grain of sand, mid millions heaped
345   Confusedly on the beach, but, did we know, has leaped
Or will leap, would we wait, i' the century, some once,
To the very throne of things?—earth's brightest for the nonce,
When sunshine shall impinge on just that grain's facette
Which fronts him fullest, first, returns his ray with jet
350   Of promptest praise, thanks God best in creation's name!
As firm is my belief, quick sense perceives the same
Self-vindicating flash illustrate every man
And woman of our mass, and prove, throughout the plan,
No detail but, in place allotted it, was prime
355   And perfect.

## XXX

   Witness her, kept waiting all this time!
What happy angle makes Fifine reverberate
Sunshine, least sand-grain, she, of shadiest social state?
No adamantine shield, polished like Helen there,
Fit to absorb the sun, regorge him till the glare,
360   Dazing the universe, draw Troy-ward those blind beaks
Of equal-sided ships rowed by the well-greaved Greeks!

---

337| MS:covertures,   *1872:*covertures,—   338| MS:Than by <> Fifine.   *1872:*All by <>
Fifine!   339| MS:§¶ called for§ confidence: §colon altered to exclamation point§ no
§altered to§ No   341| MS:worth, fulfils   *1872:*worth: fulfils   344| MS:sand, from
§crossed out and replaced above by§ mid   346| MS:leap, did §crossed out and replaced
above by§ would   348| MS:When sunrise shall   *1872:*When sunshine shall
350| MS:praise, and §crossed out§ thanks God §inserted above§   353| MS:of the mass
*1872:*of our mass   355| MS:perfect. §¶ called for§ <> her kept   *1872:*her, kept
357| MS:Most shine, least   *1872:*Sunshine, least   358| MS:shield polished   *1872:*shield,
polished   361| MS:Greeks:   *1872:*Greeks!

No Asian mirror, like yon Ptolemaic witch
Able to fix sun fast and tame sun down, enrich,
Not burn the world with beams thus flatteringly rolled
365    About her, head to foot, turned slavish snakes of gold!
And oh, no tinted pane of oriel sanctity,
Does our Fifine afford, such as permits supply
Of lustrous heaven, revealed, far more than mundane sight
Could master, to thy cell, pure Saint! where, else too bright,
370    So suits thy sense the orb, that, what outside was noon,
Pales, through thy lozenged blue, to meek benefic moon!
What then? does that prevent each dunghill, we may pass
Daily, from boasting too its bit of looking-glass,
Its sherd which, sun-smit, shines, shoots arrowy fire  beyond
375    That satin-muffled mope, your sulky diamond?


                    XXXI

And now, the mingled ray she shoots, I decompose.
Her antecedents, take for execrable! Gloze
No whit on your premiss: let be, there was no worst
Of degradation spared Fifine: ordained from first
380    To last, in body and soul, for one life-long debauch,
The Pariah of the North, the European Nautch!
This, far from seek to hide, she puts in evidence
Calmly, displays the brand, bids pry without offence
Your finger on the place. You comment "Fancy us

---

<sup>362</sup>| MS:mirror like    *1872:*mirror, like        <sup>363</sup>|MS:fix him fast <> tame him down
*1872:*fix sun fast <> tame sun down        <sup>364</sup>|    MS:beams that flatteringly    *1872:*beams thus
flatteringly    <sup>365</sup>|    MS:And §crossed out and replaced above by§ Soft §crossed out§ kissed
§crossed out and replaced above by§ About <> gold.    *1872:*gold!
<sup>366</sup>|    MS:oh no painted §altered to§ tinted <> sanctity    *1872:*oh, no <> sanctity,
<sup>367</sup>|    MS:Well §crossed out and replaced above by§ Does        <sup>368</sup>|    MS:revealed beyond what
§last two words crossed out and replaced above by three words§ far more than    *1872:*revealed,
far        <sup>370</sup>|    MS:suits the orb thy sense §last four words transposed to§ thy sense the orb <>
outside made §crossed out and replaced above by§ was        <sup>371</sup>|    MS:blue, to §crossed out and
replaced above by§ a meek    *1872:*blue, to meek        <sup>372</sup>|    MS:then, does    *1872:*then? does
<sup>375</sup>|    MS:That velvet §crossed out and replaced above by§ satin        <sup>376</sup>|    MS:§¶ called for§
This is §last two words crossed out and replaced by one word§ Behold the <> decompose;
*1872:*And now, the <> decompose.        <sup>377</sup>|    MS:antecedents take    *1872:*antecedents, take
<sup>379</sup>|    MS:spared Fifine, ordained    *1872:*spared Fifine: ordained
<sup>384</sup>|    MS:Our finger <> place, bears comment    *1872:*Your finger <> place. You comment

385 So operated on, maltreated, mangled thus!
Such torture in our case, had we survived an hour?
Some other sort of flesh and blood must be, with power
Appropriate to the vile, unsensitive, tough-thonged,
In lieu of our fine nerve! Be sure, she was not wronged
390 Too much: you must not think she winced at prick as we!"
Come, come, that's what you say, or would, were thoughts but free.


XXXII

Well then, thus much confessed, what wonder if there steal
Unchallenged to my heart the force of one appeal
She makes, and justice stamp the sole claim she asserts?
395 So absolutely good is truth, truth never hurts
The teller, whose worst crime gets somehow grace, avowed.
To me, that silent pose and prayer proclaimed aloud
"Know all of me outside, the rest be emptiness
For such as you! I call attention to my dress,
400 Coiffure, outlandish features, lithe memorable limbs,
Piquant entreaty, all that eye-glance over-skims.
Does this give pleasure? Then, repay the pleasure, put
Its price i' the tambourine! Do you seek further? Tut!
I'm just my instrument,—sound hollow: mere smooth skin
405 Stretched o'er gilt framework, I: rub-dub, nought else within—

---

389| MS:of our §over *the*§        391| MS:would, if §crossed out and replaced above by§ were
thoughts were §crossed out and replaced above by§ but        392| MS:§¶ called for§
393| MS:to our §crossed out and replaced above by§ my < > of that §crossed out and replaced
above by§ one        394| MS:She does make—justice    *1872:*She makes, and justice
396| MS:gets one §crossed out and replaced above by§ somehow grace, if §crossed out§ avowed;
*1872:*avowed.        397| MS:And when that    *1872:*To me, that        398| MS:See §crossed out
and replaced above by§ Know        400| MS:features, memorable limbs    *1872:*features, and
memorable limbs,    *1889a:*features, lithe memorable        401| MS:And §crossed out§ piquant
§altered to§ Piquant gesture §crossed out and replaced above by§ pleading §crossed out and
replaced by word and comma§ entreaty, all that §crossed out and replaced above by§ your eye-
glance    *1872:*all that eye-glance        402| MS:this much satisfy? §crossed out and replaced
above by§ pleasure? Then, §word and comma inserted above§        403| MS:§illegible
erasure§ the tambourine my §crossed out and replaced above by§ Its price! §last four words
transposed to§ Its price the tambourine! Would §crossed out and replaced above by§ Do
*1872:*price i' the        404| MS:mere stretched §crossed out and replaced above by§ smooth
405| MS:And §crossed out and replaced above by two words§ Stretched o'er painted §crossed
out and replaced above by§ gilt < > within!—    *1872:*within—

Always, for such as you!—if I have use elsewhere,—
If certain bells, now mute, can jingle, need you care?
Be it enough, there's truth i' the pleading, which comports
With no word spoken out in cottages or courts,
410 Since all I plead is 'Pay for just the sight you see,
And give no credit to another charm in me!'
Do I say, like your Love? 'To praise my face is well,
But, who would know my worth, must search my heart to tell!'
Do I say, like your Wife? 'Had I passed in review
415 The produce of the globe, my man of men were—you!'
Do I say, like your Helen? 'Yield yourself up, obey
Implicitly, nor pause to question, to survey
Even the worshipful! prostrate you at my shrine!
Shall you dare controvert what the world counts divine?
420 Array your private taste, own liking of the sense,
Own longing of the soul, against the impudence
Of history, the blare and bullying of verse?
As if man ever yet saw reason to disburse
The amount of what sense liked, soul longed for,—given, devised
425 As love, forsooth,—until the price was recognized
As moderate enough by divers fellow-men!
Then, with his warrant safe that these would love too, then,
Sure that particular gain implies a public loss,
And that no smile he buys but proves a slash across
430 The face, a stab into the side of somebody—

---

406| MS:you: for other §last two words crossed out and replaced above by three words§ if I have
1872:you!—if        407| MS:mute, should §crossed out and replaced above by§ can
408| MS:Be it §last two words inserted above at beginning of line§ <> there's so much §last two
words crossed out§ <> the question, it §last two words crossed out and replaced above by two
words§ pleading, which        410-11| MS:§two lines inserted above l. 412§
410| MS:When all <> is 'Pay    1872:Since all <> is 'Pay        411| MS:me!"    1872:me!'
412| MS:love, "To    1872:Love? 'To        413| MS:tell!"    1872:tell!'        414| MS:wife,
"Had    1872:Wife? 'Had        415| you!"    1872:you!'        416| MS:your Helen, "Yield
1872:your Helen? 'Yield        418| MS:worshipful-prostrate you first §inserted above§
at shrine §crossed out and replaced by§ shrine!        419| MS:divine,    1872:divine?
420| MS:Set up §last two words crossed out and replaced above by§ Array        427| MS:safe
these fain would <> then    1872:safe that these would <> then,        428| MS:Assured
§replaced above by two words§ Sure that <> implies the public    1872:implies a public
429| MS:And that no kiss §last three words crossed out and replaced above by three words§ not a
smile <> a cut §crossed out and replaced above by§ slash    1872:And that no smile
430| MS:a punch §crossed out and replaced above by§ stab <> somebody,    1872:somebody—

Sure that, along with love's main-purchase, he will buy
Up the whole stock of earth's uncharitableness,
Envy and hatred,—then, decides he to profess
His estimate of one, by love discerned, though dim
435 To all the world beside: since what's the world to him?'
Do I say, like your Queen of Egypt? 'Who foregoes
My cup of witchcraft—fault be on the fool! He knows
Nothing of how I pack my wine-press, turn its winch
Three-times-three, all the time to song and dance, nor flinch
440 From charming on and on, till at the last I squeeze
Out the exhaustive drop that leaves behind mere lees
And dregs, vapidity, thought essence heretofore!
Sup of my sorcery, old pleasures please no more!
Be great, be good, love, learn, have potency of hand
445 Or heart or head,—what boots? You die, nor understand
What bliss might be in life: you ate the grapes, but  knew
Never the taste of wine, such vintage as I brew!'
Do I say, like your Saint? 'An exquisitest touch
Bides in the birth of things: no after-time can much
450 Enhance that fine, that faint, fugitive first of all!
What colour paints the cup o' the May-rose, like the small
Suspicion of a blush which doubtfully begins?
What sound outwarbles brook, while, at the source, it wins

---

431| MS:with her, the §crossed out and replaced above by word and hyphen§ main-purchase
*1872:*with love's main-purchase        432| MS:Up §inserted in left margin§ The §altered to§
the        433| MS:hatred,—then decide    *1872:*hatred,—then, decides
434| MS:one—love had discerned though    *1872:*one, love <> discerned, though
*1889a:*one, by love discerned        435| MS:beside, since <> him?"    *1872:*beside: since
*1889a:*him?'        436| MS:of Egypt "Who    *1872:*of Egypt? 'Who
441| MS:Out §inserted in left margin§ The §altered to§ the        442| MS:dregs, in §crossed
out§ <> thought pleasure §crossed out and replaced above by§ essence
443| MS:sorcery, pleasure would §crossed out and then restored§ please    *1872:*sorcery, old
pleasures please        445| MS:die nor    *1872:*die, nor        446| MS:What thing might be to
live: you <> grapes but    *1872:*What bliss might be in life: you <> grapes, but
447| MS:brew!"    *1872:*brew!'        448| MS:your Saint, "The §crossed out and replaced above
by§ An    *1872:*your Saint? 'An        451| MS:o' the white §crossed out and replaced above by§
snow rose like    *1872:*o' the    May-rose, like        452| MS:a red §crossed out and replaced
above by§ blush        453| MS:sound reveals the §last two words crossed out and replaced
above by three words§ so soft as §last three words crossed out and replaced above by§
out-warbles brook so soft as §last four words crossed out and replaced above by three words§
while at the source it    *1872:*brook, while, at <> source, it    *1889a:*outwarbles

That moss and stone dispart, allow its bubblings breathe?
455 What taste excels the fruit, just where sharp flavours sheathe
Their sting, and let encroach the honey that allays?
And so with soul and sense; when sanctity betrays
First fear lest earth below seem real as heaven above,
And holy worship, late, change soon to sinful love—
460 Where is the plenitude of passion which endures
Comparison with that, I ask of amateurs?'
Do I say, like Elvire" . . .

### XXXIII

(Your husband holds you fast
Will have you listen, learn your character at last!)
"Do I say?—like her mixed unrest and discontent,
465 Reproachfulness and scorn, with that submission blent
So strangely, in the face, by sad smiles and gay tears,—
Quiescence which attacks, rebellion which endears,—
Say? 'As you loved me once, could you but love me now!
Years probably have graved their passage on my brow,
470 Lips turn more rarely red, eyes sparkle less than erst;
Such tribute body pays to time; but, unamerced,
The soul retains, nay, boasts old treasure multiplied.
Though dew-prime flee,—mature at noonday, love defied

---

454| MS:That §inserted in left margin§ <> stone to §crossed out§ unlock, and let §last two
words crossed out and replaced above by§ allow    *1872:*stone dispart, allow
455| MS:fruit's just    *1872:*fruit, just          458| MS:First that the earth <> seems    *1872:*First
fear lest earth <> seem          459| MS:And what was worship late turns now to nearly love—
*1872:*And holy worship, late, change soon to sinful love—          460| MS:passion that endures
*1872:*passion which endures          461| MS:that, I §crossed out, replaced above by illegibly
crossed out word, and then restored§ <> amateurs?"    *1872:*amateurs?'          462| MS:like
Elvire . .  . §¶ called for§ (Your    *1872:*like Elvire". . .§¶§ (Your          464| MS:Do <> say,—
like <> mixed Unrest and Discontent,    *1872:*"Do <> say?—like <> unrest <> discontent,
465| MS:and Scorn with that Submission    *1872:*scorn, with <> submission
466| MS:strangely in <> face by <> tears,    *1872:*strangely, in <> face, by <> tears,—
467| MS:Quiescence that attacks, rebellion that endears,—    *1872:*Quiescence which attacks,
rebellion which endears,—          468| MS:Say "As    *1872:*Say? 'As
470| MS:Lips redden, I suppose, eyes    *1872:*Lips turn more rarely red, eyes
471| MS:time: but    *1872:*time; but          472| MS:nay boasts    *1872:*nay, boasts
473| MS:Well might the dew-prime flee since noon §inserted above§ day's affection §crossed out
and replaced above by two words§ truth defied §first word crossed out and replaced above by§
love    *1872:*Though dew-prime flee,—mature at noonday, love

Chance, the wind, change, the rain: love, strenuous all the more

475 For storm, struck deeper root and choicer fruitage bore,

Despite the rocking world; yet truth struck root in vain:

While tenderness bears fruit, you praise, not taste again.

Why? They are yours, which once were hardly yours, might go

To grace another's ground: and then—the hopes we know,

480 The fears we keep in mind!—when, ours to arbitrate,

Your part was to bow neck, bid fall decree of fate.

Then, O the knotty point—white-night's work to revolve—

What meant that smile, that sigh? Not Solon's self could solve!

Then, O the deep surmise what one word might express,

485 And if what seemed her "No" may not have meant her "Yes!"

Then, such annoy, for cause—calm welcome, such acquist

Of rapture if, refused her arm, hand touched her wrist!

Now, what's a smile to you? Poor candle that lights up

The decent household gloom which sends you out to sup.

490 A tear? worse! warns that health requires you keep aloof

From nuptial chamber, since rain penetrates the roof!

Soul, body got and gained, inalienably safe

Your own, become despised; more worth has any waif

Or stray from neighbour's pale: pouch that,—'tis pleasure, pride,

495 Novelty, property, and larceny beside!

Preposterous thought! to find no value fixed in things,

To covet all you see, hear, dream of, till fate brings

---

474| MS:rain; and strenuous   *1872:*rain: love, strenuous        476| MS:world: but truth <>
vain,   *1872:*world; yet truth   *1889a:*vain:        477| MS:And tenderness <> you eye §crossed
out and replaced above by word and comma§ praise,        478| MS:yours which   *1872:*yours,
which        479| MS:ground and   *1872:*ground: and        481| MS:neck, when §crossed out
and replaced above by§ bid <> fate!   *1872:*fate.        482| MS:point—a §crossed out and
replaced above by word and hyphen§ white-        483| MS:sigh—not   *1872:*sigh? Not
484| MS:Then, ah the <> express   *1872:*Then, O the <> express,        485| MS:If what was
§altered to§ resounded   "No" <> have echoed "Yes!"   *1872:*And if what sounded "No"
*1889a:*what seemed her "No" <> have meant her "Yes!"        486| MS:annoy could cause cold
welcome   *1872:*annoy, for cause—calm welcome        487| MS:rapture—hand, refused the
arm, yet touched the wrist!   *1872:*rapture, that, refused <> arm, hand touched
*1889a:*rapture if refused her arm <> touched her wrist!        489| MS:gloom when §crossed
out and replaced above by§ ere you go out <> sup!   *1872:*gloom which sends you out <> sup.
490| MS:warning,—health   *1872:*warns that health        491| MS:chamber since
*1872:*chamber, since        492| MS:For all is got <> safe   *1872:*safe,   *1889a:*Soul, body got
<> safe        493| MS:own, and, so, despised   *1889a:*own, become despised

About that, what you want, you gain; then follows change.
Give you the sun to keep, forthwith must fancy range:
500 A goodly lamp, no doubt,—yet might you catch her hair
And capture, as she frisks, the fen-fire dancing there!
What do I say? at least a meteor's half in heaven;
Provided filth but shine, my husband hankers even
After putridity that's phosphorescent, cribs
505 The rustic's tallow-rush, makes spoil of urchins' squibs,
In short prefers to me—chaste, temperate, serene—
What sputters green and blue, this fizgig called Fifine!' "

### XXXIV

So all your sex mistake! Strange that so plain a fact
Should raise such dire debate! Few families were racked
510 By torture self-supplied, did Nature grant but this—
That women comprehend mental analysis!

### XXXV

Elvire, do you recall when, years ago, our home
The intimation reached, a certain pride of Rome,
Authenticated piece, in the third, last and best
515 Manner,—whatever fools and connoisseurs contest,—
No particle disturbed by rude restorer's touch,
The palaced picture-pearl, so long eluding clutch
Of creditor, at last, the Rafael might—could we
But come to terms—change lord, pass from the Prince to me?

---

498| MS:that what <> then comes a change.   *1872:*that, what   *1889a:*then follows change.
500| MS:might I catch his hair   *1872:*might you catch her hair   501| MS:as he frisks, the §crossed out and replaced above by§ brave Jack-o'-lantern there!"   *1872:*as she frisks, the fen-fire dancing there!   502| MS:least the meteor drops §crossed out and replaced above by§ fell from heaven;   *1872:*least a meteor's half in heaven;   503| MS:Provided that §crossed out§ filth §over illegible word§ but §inserted above§ <> hankers §over illegible erasure§
505| MS:His   *1872:*The   507| MS:called Fifine!"   *1872:*called Fifine!' "
509| MS:debate in families,—unracked   *1872:*debate! Few families were racked
510| MS:self-supplied, would Nature   *1872:*self-supplied, did Nature   512| MS:§¶ called for§ recal <> ago, at §crossed out and replaced above by§ our   *1889a:*recall
513| MS:First §crossed out and replaced above by§ The <> reached,—a   *1872:*reached, a
515| MS:Manner, whatever <> contest,   *1872:*Manner,—whatever <> contest,—
516| MS:particle displaced by the restorer's   *1872:*particle disturbed by rude restorer's

<sup>520</sup> I think you recollect my fever of a year:
How the Prince would, and how he would not; now,—too dear
That promise was, he made his grandsire so long since;
Rather to boast "I own a Rafael" than "am Prince!"
And now, the fancy soothed—if really sell he must
<sup>525</sup> His birthright for a mess of pottage—such a thrust
I' the vitals of the Prince were mollified by balm,
Could he prevail upon his stomach to bear qualm,
And bequeath Liberty (because a purchaser
Was ready with the sum—a trifle!) yes, transfer
<sup>530</sup> His heart at all events to that land where, at least,
Free institutions reign! And so, its price increased
Five-fold (Americans are such importunates!),
Soon must his Rafael start for the United States.
O alternating bursts of hope now, then despair!
<sup>535</sup> At last, the bargain's struck, I'm all but beggared, there
The Rafael faces me, in fine, no dream at all,
My housemate, evermore to glorify my wall.
A week must pass, before heart-palpitations sink,
In gloating o'er my gain, so late I edged the brink
<sup>540</sup> Of doom; a fortnight more, I spent in Paradise:
"Was outline e'er so true, could colouring entice
So calm, did harmony and quiet so avail?
How right, how resolute, the action tells the tale!"

---

<sup>520|</sup> MS:year— *1872:*year: <sup>521|</sup> MS:how Prince §crossed out and replaced above by§ he
<> not: now *1872:*not; now <sup>522|</sup> MS:promise which he *1872:*promise was, he
<sup>523|</sup> MS:am Prince"! *1872:*am Prince!" <sup>528|</sup> MS:Bequeath to Liberty—because
*1872:*And bequeath Liberty (because <sup>529|</sup> MS:sum—he minded to transfer *1872:*sum—
a trifle!) yes, transfer <sup>530|</sup> MS:to some land where at least *1872:*to that land where, at
least, <sup>533|</sup> MS:must §inserted above§ Rafael may be §last two words crossed out and
replaced above by two words§ start for resigned §altered to *Resigned* and the first five words
transposed to§ Resigned must Raphael start for to §crossed out§ *1872:*Soon must his Raphael
start <sup>534|</sup> MS:bursts, first hope and then *1872:*bursts of hope; *1889a:*hope now, then
<sup>535|</sup> MS:last the *1872:*last, the <sup>536|</sup> MS:me in *1872:*me, in <sup>537|</sup> MS:evermore
the glory of my *1872:*evermore to glorify my <sup>538|</sup> MS:week I pass, before the §crossed
out and replaced above by§ such palpitations sink, *1872:*before heart-palpitations sink,
*1889a:*week must pass <sup>539|</sup> MS:so lately on the *1889a:*so late I edged the
<sup>540|</sup> MS:Of loss; a <> more I <> in Paradise *1872:*more, I <> in Paradise: *1889a:*Of doom;
a <sup>541|</sup> MS:true, did colouring *1872:*true, could colouring
<sup>542|</sup> MS:So calmly, quietude and harmony avail? *1872:*So calm did harmony and quiet so
avail? <sup>543|</sup> MS:How, right and resolute, the *1872:*How right, how resolute, the

A month, I bid my friends congratulate their best:
⁵⁴⁵ "You happy Don!" (to me): "The blockhead!" (to the rest):
"No doubt he thinks his daub original, poor dupe!"
Then I resume my life: one chamber must not coop
Man's life in, though it boast a marvel like my prize.
Next year, I saunter past with unaverted eyes,
⁵⁵⁰ Nay, loll and turn my back: perchance to overlook
With relish, leaf by leaf, Doré's last picture-book.

XXXVI

Imagine that a voice reproached me from its frame:
"Here do I hang, and may! Your Rafael, just the same,
'Tis only you that change: no ecstasies of yore!
⁵⁵⁵ No purposed suicide distracts you any more!"
Prompt would my answer meet such frivolous attack:
"You misappropriate sensations. What men lack,
And labour to obtain, is hoped and feared about
After a fashion; what they once obtain, makes doubt,
⁵⁶⁰ Expectancy's old fret and fume, henceforward void.
But do they think to hold such havings unalloyed
By novel hopes and fears, of fashion just as new,
To correspond i' the scale? Nowise, I promise you!
Mine you are, therefore mine will be, as fit to cheer
⁵⁶⁵ My soul and glad my sense to-day as this-day-year.
So, any sketch or scrap, pochade, caricature,

---

⁵⁴⁴| MS:month I   *1872*:month, I      ⁵⁴⁵| MS:happy man!" (to   *1872*:happy Don!" to
⁵⁴⁸| MS:My life <> prize:   *1872*:prize.   *1889a*:Man's life      ⁵⁴⁹| MS:And now §last two
words crossed out and replaced above by two words and comma§ This year,
*1889a*:Next year      ⁵⁵⁰| MS:Nay, sit §crossed out and replaced above by§ loll <> back,
perchance   *1872*:back: perchance      ⁵⁵²| MS:§¶ called for§ Suppose, Elvire, a <> from the
§crossed out and replaced above by§ its   *1872*:Imagine that a      ⁵⁵³| MS:hang and may!
Your Rafael just   *1872*:hang, and may! Your Rafael, just      ⁵⁵⁶| MS:answer turn such
*1889a*:answer meet such      ⁵⁵⁷| MS:sensations; what I lack   *1872*:sensations. What <> lack,
*1889a*:sensations. What men lack,      ⁵⁵⁸| MS:obtain, I §crossed out and replaced above by§
is      ⁵⁵⁹| MS:fashion: what I do §crossed out and replaced above by§ once
*1872*:fashion; what   *1889a*:what they once      ⁵⁶⁰| MS:Expectancy, old <> and titillation,
void;   *1872*:and fume, henceforward void.   *1889a*:Expectancy's old      ⁵⁶¹| MS:do I think
*1889a*:do they think      ⁵⁶²| MS:hope <> fear   *1889a*:hopes <> fears
⁵⁶⁵| MS:this-day-year:   *1872*:this-day-year.      ⁵⁶⁸| MS:sieze and then forever throw aside,
*1872*:seize <> aside   *1889a*:seize, enjoy, then tire of, throw aside,

36

Made in a moment, meant a moment to endure,
I snap at, seize, enjoy, then tire of, throw aside,
Find you in your old place. But if a servant cried
570    'Fire in the gallery!'—methinks, were I engaged
In Doré, elbow-deep, picture-books million-paged
To the four winds would pack, sped by the heartiest curse
Was ever launched from lip, to strew the universe.
Would not I brave the best o' the burning, bear away
575    Either my perfect piece in safety, or else stay
And share its fate, be made its martyr nor repine?
Inextricably wed, such ashes mixed with mine!"

### XXXVII

For which I get the eye, the hand, the heart, the whole
O' the wondrous wife again!

### XXXVIII

But no, play out your *rôle*
580    I' the pageant! 'Tis not fit your phantom leave the stage:
I want you, there, to make you, here, confess you wage
Successful warfare, pique those proud ones, and advance
Claim to . . . equality? nay, but predominance
In *physique* o'er them all, where Helen heads the scene
585    Closed by its tiniest of tail-tips, pert Fifine.

---

569| MS:And find <> your place   *1889a:*Find <> your old place   570| MS:"Fire <> gallery!"—Methinks   *1872:*'Fire <> gallery!'—methinks   571| MS:elbow-deep, portfolio million-paged,   *1872:*portfolios million-paged   *1889a:*elbow-deep, picture-books million-paged   572| MS:winds should they pack   *1872:*winds would pack   573| MS:universe; *1889a:*universe.   574| MS:While I would brave the worst §crossed out and replaced above by§ best   *1889a:*Would not I brave   575| MS:Either the §crossed out and replaced above by§ my   576| MS:fate: §comma crossed out and replaced by colon§ if made a martyr, why repine?   *1889a:*fate, be made its martyr nor repine   578| MS:which I have §crossed out and replaced above by§ get   579| MS:again! §¶ called for§ <> rôle   *1872:rôle* 581| MS:make yourself §last five letters crossed out and replaced above by comma, word, and comma§ , here,   582| MS:warfare, with §crossed out and replaced above by§ pique <> ones, may advance   *1872:*ones, and advance   583| MS:Claim—to equality? Nay   *1872:*Claim to . . . equality? nay   584| MS:physique <> all, from §crossed out and replaced above by§ where Helen that §crossed out§ heads the §inserted above§ scene,   *1872:*scene *1889a:physique* 585| MS:Down to its <> pert Fifine:   *1872:*Closed by its <> pert Fifine.

How ravishingly pure you stand in pale constraint!
My new-created shape, without or touch or taint,
Inviolate of life and worldliness and sin—
Fettered, I hold my flower, her own cup's weight would win
590 From off the tall slight stalk a-top of which she turns
And trembles, makes appeal to one who roughly earns
Her thanks instead of blame, (did lily only know),
By thus constraining length of lily, letting snow
Of cup-crown, that's her face, look from its guardian stake,
595 Superb on all that crawls beneath, and mutely make
Defiance, with the mouth's white movement of disdain,
To all that stoops, retires and hovers round again!
How windingly the limbs delay to lead up, reach
Where, crowned, the head waits calm: as if reluctant, each,
600 That eye should traverse quick such lengths of loveliness,
From feet, which just are found embedded in the dress
Deep swathed about with folds and flowings virginal,
Up to the pleated breasts, rebellious 'neath their pall,
As if the vesture's snow were moulding sleep not death,

---

<sup>586</sup>|  MS:So ravishingly <> constraint,  *1872:*How ravishingly <> constraint!
<sup>587</sup>|  MS:The new-created  *1872:*My new-created  <sup>589</sup>|  MS:Emprisoned like a § last three
words crossed out and replaced above by word, comma, and word§ Fettered, my lily-flower,
§hyphen, word, and comma inserted above§ which else rough winds would  *1872:*Fettered, I
hold my flower, her own cup's weight would  <sup>590</sup>|  MS:off the tender §last two words
crossed out and replaced above by three words§ yon tall slight <> which there turns  *1872:*off
the tall <> which she turns  <sup>591</sup>|  MS:to who proves friendly, earns  *1872:*to one who
roughly earns  <sup>592</sup>|  MS:Her §crossed out and replaced above by§ Your gratitude,—by
right and §crossed out§ did she §crossed out and replaced above by§ lily <> know,—
*1872:*Her thanks instead of blame, (did <> know),  <sup>593</sup>|  MS:By nailing fast §last three
words crossed out and replaced above by two words§ Enlacing thus the length of limbs to let
that §altered to§ the snow  *1872:*By thus constraining length of lily, letting snow
<sup>594</sup>|  MS:O' the cup-crown, called her §last two words crossed out and replaced above by two
words§ that's your face  *1872:*Of cup-crown, that's her face  <sup>595</sup>|  MS:In safety on what
crawls below, and  *1872:*Superb on all that crawls beneath, and  <sup>596</sup>|  MS:Defiance with
that white §crossed out§ mouth's mild §crossed out and replaced above by§ white <> disdain
*1872:*Defiance, with the mouth's <> disdain,  <sup>597</sup>|  MS:On §crossed out and replaced
above by§ To  <sup>598</sup>|  MS:So windingly  *1872:*How windingly  <sup>599</sup>|  MS:Where quite
the <> calm: as if §last two words inserted above§ reluctant, all and §last two words crossed out§
*1872:*Where, crowned, the  <sup>600</sup>|  MS:loveliness  *1872:*loveliness,  <sup>601</sup>|  MS:feet that
§crossed out and replaced above by§ which just begin §crossed out and replaced above by two
words§ are found  *1872:*feet, which  <sup>603</sup>|  MS:the pleated §inserted above§ breasts that
beat §last two words crossed out§ rebellious 'neath the pall  *1872:*breasts, rebellious <> their
pall,  <sup>604</sup>|  MS:O' the vesture, as its snow <> death  *1872:*As if the vesture's snow <> death,

605 Must melt and so release; whereat, from the fine sheath,
The flower-cup-crown starts free, the face is unconcealed,
And what shall now divert me, once the sweet face revealed,
From all I loved so long, so lingeringly left?

### XXXIX

Because indeed your face fits into just the cleft
610 O' the heart of me, Elvire, makes right and whole once more
All that was half itself without you! As before,
My truant finds its place! Doubtlessly sea-shells yearn,
If plundered by sad chance: would pray their pearls return,
Let negligently slip away into the wave!
615 Never may eyes desist, those eyes so grey and grave,
From their slow sure supply of the effluent soul within!
And, would you humour me? I dare to ask, unpin
The web of that brown hair! O'erwash o' the sudden, but
As promptly, too, disclose, on either side, the jut
620 Of alabaster brow! So part rich rillets dyed
Deep by the woodland leaf, when down they pour, each side
O' the rock-top, pushed by Spring!

---

605| MS:And must release the life: whereat from <> sheath    *1872:*Must melt and must release; whereat, from <> sheath,    606| MS:The flower's cup-crown <> face looks forth revealed §last three words crossed out and replaced above by two words and comma§ is unconcealed, *1872:*The flower-cup-crown    607| MS:And how shall eye revert, once    *1872:*And what shall now divert, once    *1889a:*divert me, once    608| MS:To all it loved    *1872:*From all I loved    609| MS:§¶ called for§ into shall §crossed out§    610| MS:me, Elvire, and §crossed out§ makes complete §crossed out and replaced above by three words§ right and whole    612| MS:My pearl is §last two words crossed out and replaced above by§ truant's in its place: be sure the §crossed out and replaced above by§ e'en sea-shells yearn—    *1872:*truant <> place! Because e'en <> yearn,    *1889a:*truant finds its! Doubtlessly    613| MS:Plundered by any chance—to §crossed out and replaced above by§ would have their pearl    *1872:*chance: would *1889a:*If plundered by sad chance: would pray <> pearls    615| MS:Oh §crossed out§ never §altered to§ Never may they §inserted above§ desist    *1889a:*may eyes desist    617| MS:me,—in tragic phrase, unpin    *1872:*me? I dare to ask, unpin    618| MS:hair, o'erwash    *1872:*hair! O'erwash    619| MS:promptly part again, on <> side their jut    *1872:*promptly, too, disclose, on <> side, the jut    620| MS:brow, as do those rillets    *1872:*brow! So part, those    *1889a:*part rich rillets    621| MS:Deep with the *1872:*Deep by the    622| MS:by Spring . . . §¶ called for§ "And    *1872:*by Spring! §¶§ "And

### XL

"And where i' the world is all
This wonder, you detail so trippingly, espied?
My mirror would reflect a tall, thin, pale, deep-eyed
<sub></sub>625 Personage, pretty once, it may be, doubtless still
Loving,—a certain grace yet lingers, if you will,—
But all this wonder, where?"

### XLI

Why, where but in the sense
And soul of me, Art's judge? Art is my evidence
That something was, is, might be; but no more thing itself,
<sub></sub>630 Than flame is fuel. Once the verse-book laid on shelf,
The picture turned to wall, the music fled from ear,—
Each beauty, born of each, grows clearer and more clear,
Mine henceforth, ever mine!

### XLII

But if I would re-trace
Effect, in Art, to cause,—corroborate, erase
<sub></sub>635 What's right or wrong i' the lines, test fancy in my brain

---

<sub>623|</sub>  MS:wonder, you §crossed out and replaced above by§ I detail    *1872:*wonder, you detail
<sub>624|</sub>  MS:The §crossed out and replaced above by§ My §crossed out and replaced above by§ Your
mirror    *1889a:*My mirror        <sub>625|</sub>  MS:be, that is §last two words crossed out and replaced
above by§ doubtless still    *1872:*still,    *1889a:*still        <sub>626|</sub>  MS:if you §crossed out and
replaced above by§ I will,—    *1889a:*if you will,—        <sub>627|</sub>  MS:where?" §¶ called for§
<sub>628|</sub>  MS:me, the judge of Art? I boast my §last three words crossed out and replaced above
by§art-evidence    *1872:*Art-evidence,    *1889a:*me, Art's judge? Art is my evidence
<sub>629|</sub>  MS:That §inserted in left margin§ Thing §altered to§ thing was, or §crossed out and
replaced above by word and comma§ is, thing §crossed out§ <> be, but §inserted above§ <>
more the §crossed out§ <> itself    *1872:*be; but <> itself,    *1889a:*That something was
<sub>630|</sub>  MS:is ember §crossed out and replaced above by word and period§ fuel.   Once §inserted
above illegibly crossed out word § <> verse-book laid §inserted above illegibly crossed out
word§ on the §inserted above and then crossed out§        <sub>631|</sub>  MS:picture §next word illegibly
crossed out§ out of heart §crossed out and replaced above by§ sight, the music's §altered to§
music gone §crossed out and replaced above by§ fled    *1872:*picture turned to wall, the
<sub>632|</sub>  MS:But what was §last three words crossed out and replaced above by two words§ Each
beauty born <> each grows    *1872:*beauty, born <> each, grows
<sub>633|</sub>  MS:mine! §¶ called for§ Suppose I    *1872:*mine! §¶§ But if I
<sub>634|</sub>  MS:Effect to cause, some day,—corroborate    *1872:*Effect, in Art, to cause,—corroborate
<sub>635|</sub>  MS:lines, o' the §last two words crossed out and replaced above by§ test

By fact which gave it birth? I re-peruse in vain
The verse, I fail to find that vision of delight
I' the Bazzi's lost-profile, eye-edge so exquisite.
And, music: what? that burst of pillared cloud by day
640 And pillared fire by night, was product, must we say,
Of modulating just, by enharmonic change,—
The augmented sixth resolved,—from out the straighter range
Of D sharp minor,—leap of disimprisoned thrall,—
Into thy light and life, D major natural?

### XLIII

645 Elvire, will you partake in what I shall impart?
I seem to understand the way heart chooses heart
By help of the outside form,—a reason for our wild
Diversity in choice,—why each grows reconciled
To what is absent, what superfluous in the mask
650 Of flesh that's meant to yield—did nature ply her task
As artist should,—precise the features of the soul,
Which, if in any case they found expression, whole
I' the traits, would give a type, undoubtedly display
A novel, true, distinct perfection in its way.
655 Never shall I believe any two souls were made
Similar; granting, then, each soul of every grade
Was meant to be itself, prove in itself complete
And, in completion, good,—nay, best o' the kind,—as meet
Needs must it be that show on the outside correspond

---

636| MS:By the §crossed out§    637| MS:verse: I    *1872*:verse, I    638| MS:the Razzi's
lost-profile nose nearly out of sight §last five words crossed out and replaced above by dash,
three words, and period§ —eye-edge so exquisite.    *1872*:profile, eye-edge    *1889a*:the Bazzi's
lost-profile    642| MS:resolved,—into §crossed out and replaced above by two words§ from
out    643| MS:minor, to D major's liberty §last three words crossed out and replaced above
by dash, four words, comma, and dash§ —leap of disimprisoned thrall,—    644| MS:natural!
*1872*:natural?    648| MS:in taste,—why    *1872*:in choice,—why    649| MS:mask
*1872*:mask:    *1889a*:mask    650| MS:Material which would yield    *1872*:Material meant to
yield    *1889a*:Of flesh that's meant    651| MS:soul:    *1872*:soul;    *1889a*:soul
655| MS:Since how §last two words crossed out and replaced above by§ Never <> believe any
§inserted above§ <> were ever §crossed out§    656| MS:Similar: granting    *1872*:Similar;
granting    657| MS:itself, and in    *1889a*:itself, prove in    658| MS:And §crossed out
and replaced above by§ So <> good,—so §crossed out and replaced above by§ nay    *1872*:And

660 With inward substance,—flesh, the dress which soul has donned,
Exactly reproduce,—were only justice done
Inside and outside too—types perfect everyone.
How happens it that here we meet a mystery
Insoluble to man, a plaguy puzzle? Why
665 Each soul is either made imperfect, and deserves
As rude a face to match; or else a bungler swerves,
And nature, on a soul worth rendering aright,
Works ill, or proves perverse, or, in her own despite,
—Here too much, there too little,—bids each face, more or less,
670 Retire from beauty, make approach to ugliness?
And yet succeeds the same: since, what is wanting to success,
If somehow every face, no matter how deform,
Evidence, to some one of hearts on earth, that, warm
Beneath the veriest ash, there hides a spark of soul
675 Which, quickened by love's breath, may yet pervade the whole
O' the grey, and, free again, be fire?—of worth the same,
Howe'er produced, for, great or little, flame is flame.
A mystery, whereof solution is to seek.

XLIV

I find it in the fact that each soul, just as weak
680 Its own way as its fellow,—departure from design
As flagrant in the flesh,—goes striving to combine
With what shall right the wrong, the under or above
The standard: supplement unloveliness by love.

---

660| MS:flesh, that §altered to§ the      661| MS:reproduce perfect,—were justice
*1872:*reproduce,—were only justice      662| MS:types all and everyone,—   *1872:*types
perfect everyone.      663| MS:But in as much as § last five words crossed out and replaced
above by four words§ Why   §crossed out and replaced by§ How happens it that
664| MS:man, the plaguy puzzle? §question mark over illegibly erased punctuation§ why
§altered to§ Why   *1872:*man, a plaguy      665| MS:Either is each soul made   *1889a:*Each
soul is either made      666| MS:Only a <> match,—or   *1872:*As rude a <> match; or
667| MS:nature, with a   *1872:*nature, on a      669| MS:little,—makes each face more <> less
*1872:*face, more <> less,   *1889a:*little,—bids each      670| MS:beauty and approach
*1872:*beauty, and   *1889a:*beauty, make approach      671| MS:same, since what but §last two
words inserted above§ this is life's success   *1872:*same: since, what is wanting to success,
672| MS:That somehow   *1872:*If somehow      676| MS:fire, of <> same   *1872:*fire?—of
<> same,      677| MS:produced, since, great   *1872:*produced, for, great
683| MS:standard, supplement <> Love:   *1872:*standard: supplement <> love.

—Ask Plato else! And this corroborates the sage,
685   That Art,—which I may style the love of loving, rage
Of knowing, seeing, feeling the absolute truth of things
For truth's sake, whole and sole, not any good, truth brings
The knower, seer, feeler, beside,—instinctive Art
Must fumble for the whole, once fixing on a part
690   However poor, surpass the fragment, and aspire
To reconstruct thereby the ultimate entire.
Art, working with a will, discards the superflux,
Contributes to defect, toils on till,—*fiat lux,*—
There's the restored, the prime, the individual type!

### XLV

695   Look, for example now! This piece of broken pipe
(Some shipman's solace erst) shall act as crayon; and
What tablet better serves my purpose than the sand?
—Smooth slab whereon I draw, no matter with what skill,
A face, and yet another, and yet another still.
700   There lie my three prime types of beauty!

### XLVI

                        Laugh your best!
"Exaggeration and absurdity?" Confessed!
Yet, what may that face mean, no matter for its nose,
A yard long, or its chin, a foot short?

### XLVII

                      "You suppose,
Horror?" Exactly! What's the odds if, more or less
705   By yard or foot, the features do manage to express
Such meaning in the main? Were I of Gérôme's force,
Nor feeble as you see, quick should my crayon course
O'er outline, curb, excite, till,—so completion speeds

---

685|  MS:That Art—which   *1872:*That Art,—which    686|  MS:things,
*1872:*things    687|  MS:good truth   *1872:*good, truth
690|  MS:fragment and   *1872:*fragement, and    708|  MS:till,—see how brow recedes,
§last four words replaced above by three words§ so completion speeds

With Gérôme well at work,—observe how brow recedes,
710  Head shudders back on spine, as if one haled the hair,
Would have the full-face front what pin-point eye's sharp stare
Announces; mouth agape to drink the flowing fate,
While chin protrudes to meet the burst o' the wave: elate
Almost, spurred on to brave necessity, expend
715  All life left, in one flash, as fire does at its end.
Retrenchment and addition effect a masterpiece,
Not change i' the motive: here diminish, there increase—
And who wants Horror, has it.

### XLVIII

Who wants some other show
Of soul, may seek elsewhere—this second of the row?
720  What does it give for germ, monadic mere intent
Of mind in face, faint first of meanings ever meant?
Why, possibly, a grin, that, strengthened, grows a laugh;
That, softened, leaves a smile; that, tempered, bids you quaff
At such a magic cup as English Reynolds once
725  Compounded: for the witch pulls out of you response
Like Garrick's to Thalia, however due may be
Your homage claimed by that stiff-stoled Melpomene!

### XLIX

And just this one face more! Pardon the bold pretence!
May there not lurk some hint, struggle toward evidence
730  In that compressed mouth, those strained nostrils, steadfast eyes
Of utter passion, absolute self-sacrifice,

---

711| MS:have the §inserted above§ <> front fate, which §last two words crossed out and
replaced above by§ what     712| MS:Announces, mouth   *1872:*Announces; mouth
713| MS:to break §crossed out and replaced above by§ meet          714| MS:to meet § crossed
out and replaced above by§ brave     716| MS:effect the §crossed out and replaced above by§
a     719| MS:sould may   *1872:*soul, may     721| MS:face, what §crossed out and
replaced above by§ faint     722| MS:laugh   *1872:*laugh;     723| MS:softened, gr §two
letters crossed out§ <> smile, that   *1872:*smile; that     724| MS:such another §crossed out
and replaced above by two words§  a magic     725| MS:Compounded: how his §last two
words crossed out and replaced above by two words§ for the <> out of §inserted above§
731| MS:passion, whole and sole §last three words crossed out and replaced above by§ absolute

Which,—could I but subdue the wild grotesque, refine
That bulge of brow, make blunt that nose's aquiline,
And let, although compressed, a point of pulp appear
735    I' the mouth,—would give at last the portrait of Elvire?

L

Well, and if so succeed hand-practice on awry
Preposterous art-mistake, shall soul-proficiency,
Despair,—when exercised on nature, which at worst
Always implies success, however crossed and curst
740    By failure,—such as art would emulate in vain?
Shall any soul despair of setting free again
Trait after trait, until the type as wholly start
Forth, visible to sense, as that minutest part,
(Whate'er the chance) which first arresting eye, warned soul
745    That, under wrong enough and ravage, lay the whole
O' the loveliness it "loved"—I take the accepted phrase?

LI

So I account for tastes: each chooses, none gainsays
The fancy of his fellow, a paradise for him,
A hell for all beside. You can but crown the brim
750    O' the cup; if it be full, what matters less or more?
Let each, i' the world, amend his love, as I, o' the shore
My sketch, and the result as undisputed be!
Their handiwork to them, and my Elvire to me:

---

733| MS:brow, and §crossed out and replaced above by§ make    735| MS:Elvire!
*1872:*Elvire?    736| MS:§¶ called for§    739| MS:success,—however  *1889a:*success,
however    742| MS:type entirely start  *1872:*type as wholly start    743| MS:sense as
*1872:*sense, as    744| MS:Whate'er < > chance, which  *1872:* (Whate'er < > chance) which
746| MS:"loved"—I find §crossed out and replaced above by§ take    747| MS:§¶ called for§
749| MS:beside: fill each cup to §last four words crossed out and replaced above by four words§
you can but crown  *1872:*beside. You    750-52| What matters less or more?
As undisputed be— §this line expanded to three lines by insertions§ O' the cup; if it be full,
what matters less or more? / Let each i' the world amend his love, as I, o' the shore, /
My sketch, and the result as undisputed be—  *1872:*each, i' < > world, amend < > be!
*1889a:*shore.    753| MS:Their loves to all the world as this §last seven words
crossed out and replaced below by five words§ handiwork to them, and

—Result more beautiful than beauty's self, when lo,
755 What was my Rafael turns my Michelagnolo!

LII

For, we two boast, beside our pearl, a diamond.
I' the palace-gallery, the corridor beyond,
Upheaves itself a marble, a magnitude man-shaped
As snow might be. One hand,—the Master's,—smoothed and scraped
760 That mass, he hammered on and hewed at, till he hurled
Life out of death, and left a challenge: for the world,
Death still,—since who shall dare, close to the image, say
If this be purposed Art, or mere mimetic play
Of Nature?—wont to deal with crag or cloud, as stuff
765 To fashion novel forms, like forms we know, enough
For recognition, but enough unlike the same,
To leave no hope ourselves may profit by her game;
Death therefore to the world. Step back a pace or two!
And then, who dares dispute the gradual birth its due
770 Of breathing life, or breathless immortality,
Where out she stands, and yet stops short, half bold, half shy,

---

754| MS:Of power §last two words crossed out and replaced in left margin by§ Result <> self,
for §crossed out and replaced above by§ when   *1872:*—Result
756| MS:§¶ called for§ Our palace boasts <> diamond:   *1872:*For, we two boast <> diamond.
757| MS:Go from the gallery: i' §inserted above§ the   *1872:*I' the palace-gallery, the
758| MS:Shows §illegibly crossed out word§ marble bulk, mere §last five words crossed out and
replaced above by five words§ Upheaves itself a marble, a magnitude of snow §last two words
crossed out and replaced above by§ half §crossed out and replaced above by word and hyphen§
man-shaped          759| MS:As snow might be; one §last five words inserted above illegibly
crossed out words§ hand,—a §crossed out and replaced above by§ the   *1872:*be.   One
760| MS:mass he hammered on and hewed at, §last six words and comma inserted above§ <>
he §next three words illegibly crossed out§   *1872:*mass, he          761| MS:left this §crossed out
and replaced above by§ a          762| MS:still: for §crossed out and replaced above by§ since <>
the creature §crossed out and replaced above by§ image   *1872:*still,—since          763|
MS:purposed Art or   *1872:*purposed Art, or          764| MS:Of Nature, wont   *1872:*Of Nature?
wont          766| MS:same   *1872:*same,          767| MS: For any §last two words crossed out and
replaced above by§ To let no §last three words crossed out and replaced below by three words§
To leave no          768| MS:world: step §crossed out and replaced above by illegibly crossed out
word, then replaced above by word, exclamation mark, and dash§ Nay!—back
*1872:*world. Step back          769| MS:dares deny §crossed out and replaced above by§ dispute
the sudden §crossed out and replaced above by§ gradual          770| MS:Of breathing life
§words inserted above last three words and then illegibly crossed out§
771| MS:When §over illegible word§ out there stands, *1872:*Where out she stands,

Hesitates on the threshold of things, since partly blent
With stuff she needs must quit, her native element
I' the mind o' the Master,—what's the creature, dear-divine
775 Yet earthly-awful too, so manly-feminine,
Pretends this white advance? What startling brain-escape
Of Michelagnolo takes elemental shape?
I think he meant the daughter of the old man o' the sea,
Emerging from her wave, goddess Eidotheé—
780 She who, in elvish sport, spite with benevolence
Mixed Mab-wise up, must needs instruct the Hero whence
Salvation dawns o'er that mad misery of his isle.
Yes, she imparts to him, by what a pranksome wile
He may surprise her sire, asleep beneath a rock,
785 When he has told their tale, amid his web-foot flock
Of sea-beasts, "fine fat seals with bitter breath!" laughs she
At whom she likes to save, no less: Eidotheé,
Whom you shall never face evolved, in earth, in air,
In wave; but, manifest i' the soul's domain, why, there
790 She ravishingly moves to meet you, all through aid
O' the soul! Bid shine what should, dismiss into the shade
What should not be,—and there triumphs the paramount

---

773| MS:stuff it needs <> quit, its §crossed out, replaced above by illegibly crossed out word, and then restored§ native   *1872*:stuff she needs <> quit, her native     774-77| MS:§these four lines inserted from back of previous leaf§       774| MS:the master, what the §altered to§the Master. What the   *1872*:the Master,—what's the       778| MS:think it is §last two words crossed out and replaced above by two words§ he meant <> man of   *1872*:man o'
779| MS:goddess Eidotheé— §first two letters of last word inserted above illegibly crossed out words§       780-87| MS:§these eight lines inserted from back of previous leaf§
782| MS:Escape may §last two words crossed out and replaced above by§ Salvation dawn §altered to§ dawns <> isle:   *1872*:isle.
783| MS:him by   *1872*:him, by       785| MS:tale amidst §altered to§ amid
786| MS:Of sea-sheep, §second half of last word and comma crossed out and replaced above by word and comma§ beasts, fine <> breath! laughs   *1872*:sea-beasts, "fine <> breath!" laughs
787| MS:she means §crossed out and replaced above by§ likes <> save, G §letter crossed out§
788| MS:Whom §over illegible word§ you §inserted above§
789| MSS:domain, there, §last word and comma crossed out and replaced above by word and comma§ why,       790| MS:you, paramount §crossed out and replaced above by illegibly crossed out word or words§ all through aid §last three words inserted to the right§
791-93| MS:§these three lines inserted from back of previous leaf to replace line crossed out§ Emprize o' the master! §colon altered to exclamation mark§ would §altered to§ Would you know how the world makes §followed by illegibly crossed out word§
791| MS:soul! §comma altered to exclamation mark§ bid §altered to§ Bid

Emprise o' the Master! But, attempt to make account
Of what the sense, without soul's help, perceives? I bought
795   That work—(despite plain proof, whose hand it was had wrought
I' the rough: I think we trace the tool of triple tooth,
Here, there and everywhere)—bought dearly that uncouth
Unwieldy bulk, for just ten dollars—"Bulk, would fetch—
Converted into lime—some five pauls!" grinned a wretch,
800   Who, bound on business, paused to hear the bargaining,
And would have pitied me "but for the fun o' the thing!"

LIII

Shall such a wretch be—you? Must—while I show Elvire
Shaming all other forms, seen as I see her here
I' the soul,—this other-you perversely look outside,
805   And ask me, "Where i' the world is charm to be descried
I' the tall thin personage, with paled eye, pensive face,
Any amount of love, and some remains of grace?"
See yourself in my soul!

LIV

And what a world for each
Must somehow be i' the soul,—accept that mode of speech,—

793| MS:the master §altered to§ Master      794| MS:sense perceives without the soul
§transposed to§ sense, without the soul, perceives      *1889a:*sense, without soul's help, perceives
795| MS:despite the §crossed out and replaced above by§ plain proof whose      *1872:*proof,
whose      796| MS:rough,—I < > we see §crossed out and replaced above by§ trace < > tool,
the §crossed out and replaced above by§ of triple-toothed,      *1872:*rough: I < > triple-tooth,
*1889a:*tool of      798| MS:bulk for < > dollars—"which would      *1872:*bulk, for < > dollars—
"Bulk, would      799| MS:§first words illegibly crossed out and replaced above by illegibly
crossed out words§ converted §altered to§ Converted < > lime—some five pauls" §last three
words and quotation mark inserted below§ remarked §crossed out and replaced above by§ this
§crossed out and replaced above by§ grinned      800| MS:Who, bound §next word illegibly
crossed out§ on business, paused to §last five words inserted above§ heard §altered to§ hear
802| MS:§¶ called for§ you? who §crossed out and replaced above by word and dash§ Must—
803| MS:Shaming §inserted above illegibly crossed out word§      804| MS:perversely look
§inserted above illegibly crossed out word§      805| MS:And §inserted above two illegibly
crossed out words§ ask me, " §word, comma, and quotation mark inserted above§ where < > is
all the §last two words crossed out and replaced above by§ any §crossed out§ charm to be §last
two words inserted above§      *1889a:*me, "Where      806| MS:personage, with §inserted
above§ < > eye, and §crossed out§ pensive §inserted above illegibly crossed out word§
808| MS:soul! §¶ called for§      809| MS:in      *1872:*i'

810     Whether an aura gird the soul, wherein it seems
       To float and move, a belt of all the glints and gleams
       It struck from out that world, its weaklier fellows found
       So dead and cold; or whether these not so much surround,
       As pass into the soul itself, add worth to worth,
815     As wine enriches blood, and straightway send it forth,
       Conquering and to conquer, through all eternity,
       That's battle without end.

LV

                  I search but cannot see
       What purpose serves the soul that strives, or world it tries
       Conclusions with, unless the fruit of victories
820     Stay, one and all, stored up and guaranteed its own
       For ever, by some mode whereby shall be made known
       The gain of every life. Death reads the title clear—
       What each soul for itself conquered from out things here:
       Since, in the seeing soul, all worth lies, I assert,—
825     And nought i' the world, which, save for soul that sees, inert
       Was, is, and would be ever,—stuff for transmuting,—null
       And void until man's breath evoke the beautiful—
       But, touched aright, prompt yields each particle its tongue
       Of elemental flame,—no matter whence flame sprung
830     From gums and spice, or else from straw and rottenness,

---

813|  MS:cold: or   *1872:*cold; or     815|  MS:wine makes §crossed out§ rich §altered to§ enriches the §crossed out§ blood, the better §last two words crossed out and replaced above by two words§ and straightway < > forth.  *1872:*forth,     816|  MS:eternity  *1872:*eternity,   817|  MS:That's §over illegible erasure§ < > end! §¶ called for§ I   *1872:*end. §¶§ I   818|  MS:strives, this §crossed out and replaced above by§ or     820|  MS:Stay, one and all, §last four words and two commas inserted above three illegibly crossed out words§   821|  MS:Forever  *1872:*For ever     822|  MS:§line inserted above l. 823§ life; death  *1872:*life. Death     824|  MS:the seeeing §inserted above§ soul that sees §last two words crossed out§ < > worth lies, §word and comma inserted above inserted above illegibly crossed out word§     825|  MS:world which  *1872:*world, which     826|  MS:for transmuting, §word and comma inserted above illegibly crossed out word§ —full §altered to§ null   827|  MS:And void §last two words inserted to left§ Til §altered to§ until man's breath §last two words inserted above illegibly crossed out word§ evokes §inserted above§  *1872:*evoke   828|  MS:aright, yields prompt, §transposed to§ prompt yields, each  *1872:*yields each   829|  MS:flame, no < > whence it sprung—  *1872:*flame,—no < > whence flame sprung   830|  MS:spice, true wood, or  §last three words crossed out and replaced above by three words§ or else from rottenness and straw §last three words transposed to§ straw and rottenness

So long as soul has power to make them burn, express
What lights and warms henceforth, leaves only ash behind,
Howe'er the chance: if soul be privileged to find
Food so soon that, by first snatch of eye, suck of breath,
835    It can absorb pure life: or, rather, meeting death
I' the shape of ugliness, by fortunate recoil
So put on its resource, it find therein a foil
For a new birth of life, the challenged soul's response
To ugliness and death,—creation for the nonce.

LVI

840    I gather heart through just such conquests of the soul,
Through evocation out of that which, on the whole,
Was rough, ungainly, partial accomplishment, at best,
And—what, at worst, save failure to spit at and detest?—
—Through transference of all, achieved in visible things,
845    To where, secured from wrong, rest soul's imaginings—
Through ardour to bring help just where completion halts,
Do justice to the purpose, ignore the slips and faults—

---

*1872:*rottenness,    832|    MS:henceforth, and §inserted above illegibly crossed out word§ it
but §inserted above§ ash behind    *1872:*henceforth, leaves only ash behind,
833|    MS:In either case §last three words crossed out and replaced above by three words§
Howe'er the chance,—if soul was §crossed out and replaced above by§ be    *1872:*chance: if
834|    MS:Food so soon §last three words inserted above illegibly crossed out words§ that at < >
eye suck    *1872:*that, at < > eye, suck        835|    MS:It had but to §last three words crossed out
and replaced above by§ may absorb < > or, rather, §word and comma inserted above§
*1872:*It shall absorb        836|    MS:I' the shape of §last three words inserted above illegibly
crossed out words§ ugliness, §next two words illegibly crossed out§
837|    MS:§first word illegibly erased§ put < > resource, that
§crossed out and then restored§ shape becomes §inserted above illegibly crossed out word§ the
foil    *1872:*So put < > resource, it finds therein a foil        838|    MS:If a sudden §crossed out
and replaced above by§ new < > life, creation for the nonce §last four words crossed out and
replaced above by three words§ challenged soul's response    *1872:*For a < > life, the
840|    MS:§¶ called for§ I cannot think but that these §crossed out and replaced above by§ such
*1872:*I gather heart through just such        841|    MS:These §crossed out and replaced above
by§ Such evocations §altered to§ evocation    *1872:*Through evocation
843|    MS:worst, except    §crossed out and replaced above by two words§ save failure
844|    MS:This §crossed out and replaced above by dash and word§ —Such transference < > all
achieved    *1872:*—Through transference < > all, achieved        845|    MS:To live, §last word
and comma crossed out and replaced above by word and comma§ rest, secure from wrong, mid
mere imaginings—    *1889a:*To where, secured from, wrong, rest soul's imaginings—
846|    MS:This §crossed out and replaced above by§ Such    *1872:*Through

And, last, through waging with deformity a fight
Which wrings thence, at the end, precise its opposite.
850 I praise the loyalty o' the scholar,—stung by taunt
Of fools "Does this evince thy Master men so vaunt?
Did he then perpetrate the plain abortion here?"
Who cries "His work am I! full fraught by him, I clear
His fame from each result of accident and time,
855 Myself restore his work to its fresh morning-prime,
Not daring touch the mass of marble, fools deride,
But putting my idea in plaster by its side,
His, since mine; I, he made, vindicate who made me!"

LVII

For, you must know, I too achieved Eidotheé,
860 In silence and by night—dared justify the lines
Plain to my soul, although, to sense, that triple-tine's
Achievement halt half-way, break down, or leave a blank.
If she stood forth at last, the Master was to thank!
Yet may there not have smiled approval in his eyes—
865 That one at least was left who, born to recognize
Perfection in the piece imperfect, worked, that night,
In silence, such his faith, until the apposite

---

848| MS:And, last as best §last two words crossed out and replaced above by two words§ not least, with stark deformity this §crossed out and replaced above by§ such fight   *1872:*last, not   *1889a:*last, through waging with deformity a fight        849| MS:Which §crossed out and replaced above by§ As wrings thence, at at <> opposite—   *1872:*Which wrings thence, at <> opposite.        850| MS:As if §crossed out and replaced above by§ though the   *1872:*I praise the        851| MS:Of the §crossed out§ <> thy Master they §crossed out and then restored§ so   *1889a:*thy Master men so        852| MS:here?—"   *1872:*here?"—   *1889a:*here?"
853| MS:Cried "His best work am I—full-fraught   *1872:*Who cries "His work am I! full fraught        854| MS:time:   *1872:*time,        855| MS:Thus I restore the §crossed out and replaced above by§ his <> morning-prime   *1872:*And thus, restore <> morning-prime:   *1889a:*Myself restore <> morning-prime,        856| MS:the lines §crossed out and replaced above by§ mass of his, you §last two words crossed out and replaced above by word and comma§ marble, fools §crossed out and then restored§        857| MS:idea on §altered to§ in canvas §crossed out and replaced above by§ plaster by their §crossed out and replaced above by§ its        858| MS:mine; whom §crossed out and replaced above by word and comma§ I, <> made, to §crossed out§
859-71| MS:§these lines inserted from back of previous leaf§        865| MS:That §inserted to left§ one scholar still §last two words crossed out and replaced above by two words§ at least        867| MS:the exquisite §crossed out and replaced above by§ apposite

51

Design was out of him, truth palpable once more?
And then,—for at one blow, its fragments strewed the floor,—
870    Recalled the same to live within his soul as heretofore.

### LVIII

And, even as I hold and have Eidotheé,
I say, I cannot think that gain,—which would not be
Except a special soul had gained it,—that such gain
Can ever be estranged, do aught but appertain
875    Immortally, by right firm, indefeasible,
To who performed the feat, through God's grace and man's will!
Gain, never shared by those who practised with earth's stuff,
And spoiled whate'er they touched, leaving its roughness rough,
Its blankness bare, and, when the ugliness opposed,
880    Either struck work or laughed "He doted or he dozed!"

### LIX

While, oh, how all the more will love become intense
Hereafter, when "to love" means yearning to dispense,
Each soul, its own amount of gain through its own mode
Of practising with life, upon some soul which owed
885    Its treasure, all diverse and yet in worth the same,
To new work and changed way! Things furnish you rose-flame,

---

868|   MS:more— *1872:*more; *1889a:*more?      871|   MS:§¶ called for§ And, just as I return
by right Eidotheé,   *1872:*And, even as I hold and have Eidotheé,      872|   MS:I say, §last two
words and comma inserted above§ < > think but that these §last three words crossed out and
replaced above by§ such gains   *1872:*think that gains   *1889a:*gain      873|   MS:Save for the
special soul that gains them,—and such §last two words crossed out and replaced above by§
human gain   *1872:*Except a special soul had gained them,—that such gain   *1889a:*gained it,—
that      874|   MS:Is alienated ever, does aught   *1872:*Can ever be estranged, do aught
875|   MS:Immortally, and §crossed out§ < > right firm, §word and comma inserted above§
876|   MS:To the §crossed out§ soul which did the feat through   *1872:*To who performed the
feat, through      877|   MS:Not to be shared < > with the §crossed out and replaced above by§
earth's   *1872:*Gain never shared      878|   MS:whatever   *1872:*whate'er
880|   MS:Either shut eye §last two words crossed out and replaced above by two words§ struck
work < > or He   *1872:*or he      881|   MS:§¶ called for§      883|   MS:gain by §crossed out
and replaced above by§ through      886|   MS:Through §crossed out and replaced above by§
To change in §crossed out and replaced above by§ i' the work and way! Things feed for §last two
words crossed out and replaced above by§ furnish   *1872:*To new work and changed way

Which burn up red, green, blue, nay, yellow more than needs,
For me, I nowise doubt; why doubt a time succeeds
When each one may impart, and each receive, both share
890   The chemic secret, learn,—where I lit force, why there
You drew forth lambent pity,—where I found only food
For self-indulgence, you still blew a spark at brood
I' the greyest ember, stopped not till self-sacrifice imbued
Heaven's face with flame? What joy, when each may supplement
895   The other, changing each as changed, till, wholly blent,
Our old things shall be new, and, what we both ignite,
Fuse, lose the varicolor in achromatic white!
Exemplifying law, apparent even now
In the eternal progress,—love's law, which I avow
900   And thus would formulate: each soul lives, longs and works
For itself, by itself,—because a lodestar lurks,
An other than itself,—in whatsoe'er the niche
Of mistiest heaven it hide, whoe'er the Glumdalclich
May grasp the Gulliver: or it, or he, or she—

---

887| MS:up red and §last two words crossed out and replaced above by two words and two commas§ red, green, blue, and §replaced above by word and comma§ nay,
888| MS:nowise doubt: why   *1872:*nowise doubt; why       889| MS:When each is to §last two words crossed out and replaced above by two words§ one may impart and  *1872:*impart, and
890| MS:learn, where   *1872:*learn,—where       891| MS:pity, where   *1872:*pity,—where
893| MS:ember till now §last two words crossed out§ stopped not §inserted above§ < > self-sacrifice   *1872:*ember, stopped < > self-sacrifice imbued       894| MS:Aspired to heaven? §colon altered to question mark§ What joy when each shall §crossed out and replaced above by§ may   *1872:*Heaven's face with flame? What joy, when      895| MS:each as   *1872:*each, as   *1889a:*each as      896| MS:All §crossed out and replaced above by§ The old < > and, what §comma and word inserted§ we henceforth §crossed out and replaced above by§ both  *1872:*Our old      897| MS:And §crossed out and replaced above by word and comma§ Fuse, < > in unprismatic §crossed out and replaced above by§ achromatic
898| MS:Exemplifying §inserted above illegibly crossed out word§ law clear to me §last three words crossed out and replaced above by§ apparent   *1872:*law, apparent
899| MS:progress,—the §inserted above§ law which §inserted above§ I believe §crossed out and replaced above by§ accept §crossed out and replaced above by illegibly crossed out word§  *1872:*progress,—love's law, which I avow      900| MS:And thus would §last two words inserted above§ formulate: this fashion §last two words crossed out§ < > soul exists §crossed out and replaced above by two words and comma§ live, longs      901| MS:by itself, because  *1872:*by itself,—because      902| MS:itself, in   *1872:*itself,—      903| MS:heaven may cover §crossed out and replaced above by§ hide   *1872:*heaven it hide
904| MS:Attract its gaze, divine, human, or both, may §last eight words crossed out and replaced above by seven words§ May grasp the §next word illegibly crossed out§ of §crossed out§ Gulliver, or it, or be §altered to§ he   *1872:*the Gulliver:or

905    *Theosutos e broteios eper kekramene,—*
     (For fun's sake, where the phrase has fastened, leave it fixed!
     So soft it says,—"God, man, or both together mixed"!)
     This, guessed at through the flesh, by parts which prove the whole,
     This constitutes the soul discernible by soul
910    —Elvire, by me!

LX

        "And then"—(Pray you, permit remain
     This hand upon my arm!—your cheek dried, if you deign,
     Choosing my shoulder)—"then"—(Stand up for, boldly state
     The objection in its length and breadth!) "you abdicate,
     With boast yet on your lip, soul's empire, and accept
915    The rule of sense; the Man, from monarch's throne has stept—
     Leapt, rather, at one bound, to base, and there lies, Brute.
     You talk of soul,—how soul, in search of soul to suit,
     Must needs review the sex, the army, rank and file
     Of womankind, report no face nor form so vile
920    But that a certain worth, by certain signs, may thence
     Evolve itself and stand confessed—to soul—by sense.
     Sense? Oh, the loyal bee endeavours for the hive!
     Disinterested hunts the flower-field through, alive

---

905| MS:Theosutos e broteios eper kekramene,— §last five words, comma, and dash inserted above cancelled Greek words θεόσυτος, ἢ βρότειος, ἤπερ κεκραμένη§   *1872:Theosutos e broteios eper kekramene,—*   906| MS:§line inserted above and illegibly crossed out§ (For fun's §inserted above illegibly crossed out word§   907| MS:So soft it says §last four words inserted above illegibly crossed out words§ ,—God <> mixed)—   *1872:*mixed!)   *1889a:*says,—"God <> mixed"!)   908| MS:Transparent through <> flesh (thus I resume §parenthesis and last three words crossed out and replaced above by four words§ by parts which prove <> whole) §parenthesis crossed out§   *1872:*This, guessed at through <> flesh, by <> whole, 909| MS:Which constitutes   *1872:*This constitutes   910| MS:then"—Ay, "then," Elvire! §last three words and exclamation mark crossed out§   911| MS:arm, your cheek dry §altered to§ dried   *1872:*arm!—your   912| MS:"then!"—(stand §altered to§ Stand *1889a:*"then"—(Stand   913| MS:breadth!) "You   *1889a:*breadth!) "you 914| MS:on my §crossed out and replaced above by§ your 915| MS:man §altered to§ Man from   *1872:*Man, from   916| MS:base and <> brute. §altered to§ Brute.   *1872:*base, and   917| MS:You §over illegible erasure§ <> how soul in *1872:*how soul, in   919| MS:womankind, report §over illegible erasure§ 921| MS:sense:   *1872:*sense.   922| MS:Sense? I believe §last two words crossed out and replaced above by word and comma§ Oh, the loyal §inserted above§ <> the best §crossed out§ hive—   *1872:*hive!   923| MS:alive—   *1872:*alive

Not one mean moment, no,—suppose on flower he light,
<sup>925</sup> To his peculiar drop, petal-dew perquisite,
Matter-of-course snatched snack: unless he taste, how try?
This, light on tongue-tip laid, allows him pack his thigh,
Transport all he counts prize, provision for the comb,
Food for the future day,—a banquet, but at home!
<sup>930</sup> Soul? Ere you reach Fifine's, some flesh may be to pass!
That bombéd brow, that eye, a kindling chrysopras,
Beneath its stiff black lash, inquisitive how speeds
Each functionary limb, how play of foot succeeds,
And how you let escape or duly sympathize
<sup>935</sup> With gastroknemian grace,—true, your soul tastes and tries,
And trifles time with these, but, fear not, will arrive
At essence in the core, bring honey home to hive,
Brain-stock and heart-stuff both—to strike objectors dumb—
Since only soul affords the soul fit pabulum!
<sup>940</sup> Be frank for charity! Who is it you deceive—
Yourself or me or God, with all this make-believe?"

### LXI

And frank I will respond as you interrogate.
Ah, Music, wouldst thou help! Words struggle with the weight
So feebly of the False, thick element between

---

924| MS:Never one §last two words crossed out and replaced above by three words§ Not one
mean moment, he §crossed out and replaced above by§ no      925| MS:peculiar gain, §last
word and comma crossed out and replaced above by word and comma§ drop,
926| MS:snatched §inserted above illegibly crossed out word§ meal §crossed out and replaced
above by§ snack (unless <> try?)   *1872:*snack: unless <> try?      927| MS:Which, laid
§crossed out and replaced above by§ light on tongue— §word and hyphen inserted above§ tip
of tongue— §last two words and comma crossed out and replaced above by word and comma§
laid, <> him load §crossed out and replaced above by§ pack   *1872:*This, light
928| MS:With §crossed out and replaced above by§ Transport <> counts true §crossed out§
931| MS:eye's §altered to§ eye      932| MS:Inquisitive, beneath <> lash, how   *1872:*Beneath
<> lash, inquisitive how      934| MS:And how you §last two words inserted above illegibly
crossed out words§      935| MS:The gastro-knemian grace,—these §crossed out and replaced
above by word and comma§ true, our §altered to§ your   *1872:*With gastr-knemian
*1889a:*gastroknemian      936| MS:May §crossed out and replaced above by§ And trifle
§altered to§ trifles time, perchance, but   *1872:*time with these, but      937| MS:core, bring
§over illegible word§ honey thence to   *1872:*honey home to      938| MS:both—to §over
illegible erasure§ pabulum.   *1872:*pabulum!      939| MS:pabulum.   *1872:*pabulum!      940| MS:charity,—who
*1872:*charity! Who      944| MS:the False, the §altered to§ thick

55

945     Our soul, the True, and Truth! which, but that intervene
       False shows of things, were reached as easily by thought
       Reducible to word, as now by yearnings wrought
       Up with thy fine free force, oh Music, that canst thrid,
       Electrically win a passage through the lid
950     Of earthly sepulchre, our words may push against,
       Hardly transpierce as thou! Not dissipate, thou deign'st,
       So much as tricksily elude what words attempt
       To heave away, i' the mass, and let the soul, exempt
       From all that vapoury obstruction, view, instead
955     Of glimmer underneath, a glory overhead.
       Not feebly, like our phrase, against the barrier go
       In suspirative swell the authentic notes I know,
       By help whereof, I would our souls were found without
       The pale, above the dense and dim which breeds the doubt!
960     But Music, dumb for you, withdraws her help from me;
       And, since to weary words recourse again must be,
       At least permit they rest their burthen here and there,
       Music-like: cover space! My answer,—need you care
       If it exceed the bounds, reply to questioning
965     You never meant should plague? Once fairly on the wing,
       Let me flap far and wide!

---

945|   MS:Truth which   *1872:*Truth! which      948|   MS:fine free   *1872:*fine, free
*1889a:*fine free     950|   MS:Of the §crossed out§ <> sepulchre, which §inserted above§
words vainly §crossed out and replaced above by§ may   *1872:*sepulchre, our words
951|   MS:Never §crossed out and replaced above by§ Hardly <> dissipate thou   *1872:*dissipate,
thou     953|   MS:away i' <> mass and   *1872:*away, i' <> mass, and     955|   MS:Of the
§crossed out§ <> underneath, the glory   *1872:*underneath, a glory     956|   MS:Not thus
but otherwise against   *1872:*Not feebly, like our phrase, against     957|   MS:swell the
§inserted above§     958|   MS:whereof, somehow the §last two words crossed out and replaced
above by three words§ I would our soul §altered to§ souls is §crossed out and replaced above by§
were     960|   MS:Since §crossed out and replaced above by§ But music <> you, refuses
§crossed out and replaced above by two words§ withdraws her help to §crossed out and replaced
above by§ from   *1872:*But Music     961|   MS:And since §inserted above§ to the §crossed
out§   *1872:*And, since     962|   MS:they range at pleasure §last two words inserted above§
here <> there   *1872:*they rest their burthen here <> there,     963|   MS:Music-like,—cover
space! §colon altered to exclamation mark§ my §altered to§ My   *1872:*Music-like: cover
965|   MS:That §crossed out and replaced above by§ You <> meant to §crossed out and replaced
above by§ should     966|   MS:me fly far <> wide! §¶ called for§   *1872:*me flap far

LXII

For this is just the time,
The place, the mood in you and me, when all things chime.
Clash forth life's common chord, whence, list how there ascend
Harmonics far and faint, till our perception end,—
970   Reverberated notes whence we construct the scale
Embracing what we know and feel and are! How fail
To find or, better, lose your question, in this quick
Reply which nature yields, ample and catholic?
For, arm in arm, we two have reached, nay, passed, you see,
975   The village-precinct; sun sets mild on Sainte Marie—
We only catch the spire, and yet I seem to know
What's hid i' the turn o' the hill: how all the graves must glow
Soberly, as each warms its little iron cross,
Flourished about with gold, and graced (if private loss
980   Be fresh) with stiff rope-wreath of yellow crisp bead-blooms
Which tempt down birds to pay their supper, mid the tombs,
With prattle good as song, amuse the dead awhile,
If couched they hear beneath the matted camomile!

---

968| MS:whence list *1872:*whence, list          972| MS:or else forget §last two words crossed out
and replaced above by dash, word, dash, and two words§ —best—o'er look your question for the
nonce, §last three words and comma crossed out and replaced above by three words§ in this
quick *1872:*or, better, lose your          973| MS:Answer §inserted above, then crossed out and
replaced by§ Reply <> nature meets the soul in §last four words crossed out and replaced above
by word, comma, and two words§ yields, complete and catholic? §question mark inserted and
next words illegibly crossed out§ *1872:*yields, ample          974| MS:two, have *1872:*two have
975| MS:village-precinct: sun sets slow §crossed out and replaced above by§ soft on
*1872:*village-precinct; sun sets mild on          977| MS:hill; how *1872:*hill: how
978| MS:each lifts §crossed out and replaced above by§ warms          979| gold and,—if the
private *1872:*gold, and graced (if private          980| MS:Be recent, §word and comma crossed
out and replaced above by word and comma§ fresh, its stiff §inserted above§ <> of beaded
§crossed out§ yellow crisp bead- §last two words and hyphen inserted above§ *1872:*fresh) with
stiff <> yellow, crisp          981| MS:To §crossed out and replaced above by§ Which <> birds
which sing at §last three words crossed out and replaced above by three words§ to pay their
982| MS:With not unlike §last two words crossed out and replaced above by two words§ prattle
good <> awhile *1872:*awhile,          983| MS:If couched §inserted above§ they can hear §last
two words crossed out and replaced above by two words§ give up §last two words crossed out and
*hear* restored§ <> matted §illegibly crossed out words inserted above§

## LXIII

Bid them good-bye before last friend has sung and supped!
985  Because we pick our path and need our eyes,—abrupt
Descent enough,—but here's the beach, and there's the bay,
And, opposite, the streak of Île Noirmoutier.
Thither the waters tend; they freshen as they haste,
At feel o' the night-wind, though, by cliff and cliff embraced,
990  This breadth of blue retains its self-possession still;
As you and I intend to do, who take our fill
Of sights and sounds—soft sound, the countless hum and skip
Of insects we disturb, and that good fellowship
Of rabbits our foot-fall sends huddling, each to hide
995  He best knows how and where; and what whirred past, wings wide?
That was an owl, their young may justlier apprehend!
Though you refuse to speak, your beating heart, my friend,
I feel against my arm,—though your bent head forbids
A look into your eyes, yet, on my cheek, their lids
1000 That ope and shut, soft send a silken thrill the same.
Well, out of all and each these nothings, comes—what came
Often enough before, the something that would aim
Once more at the old mark: the impulse to at last
Succeed where hitherto was failure in the past,
1005 And yet again essay the adventure. Clearlier sings
No bird to its couched corpse "Into the truth of things—
Out of their falseness rise, and reach thou, and remain!"

---

<sup>984</sup>| MS:§¶ called for§ last bird §crossed out and replaced above by§ friend
<sup>985</sup>| MS:our way §crossed out and replaced above by§ path       <sup>987</sup>| MS:of Isle Noirmontier,
*1872:*of Isle Noirmontier.   *1889a:*of Île Noirmontier.       <sup>988</sup>| MS:Whither the <> tend,
that freshen   *1872:*Thither the <> tend; they freshen       <sup>990</sup>| MS:breadth of blue §last two
words inserted above§ <> its blue and §last two words crossed out§ <> still,   *1872:*still;
<sup>992</sup>| MS:Of the §crossed out§ <> sounds—that §crossed out and replaced above by§ soft sound,
that §crossed out and replaced above by§ the countless hum and §last two words inserted above§
<sup>993</sup>| MS:Of the §crossed out§       <sup>994</sup>| MS:Of the §crossed out§ rabbits, our <> huddling
each   *1872:*huddling, each   *1889a:*rabbits our       <sup>995</sup>| MS:knows how and §last two words
inserted above§ where: <> past you, §last word crossed out§ wings so §crossed out§
<sup>996</sup>| MS:apprehend:   *1872:*apprehend!       <sup>997</sup>| MS:And, though you do not speak
*1872:*Though you refuse to speak       <sup>999</sup>| MS:I look <> yet on <> cheek their
*1872:*A look <> yet, on <> cheek, their       <sup>1000</sup>| MS:shut and send <> same,—
*1872:*shut, soft send <> same.       <sup>1003</sup>| MS:mark, the   *1872:*mark: the
<sup>1005</sup>| MS:To yet <> adventure: softlier sings   *1872:*And yet <> adventure. Clearlier sings
<sup>1006</sup>| MS:No §inserted to left§ Bird §altered to§ bird like §crossed out§ to the §crossed out and
replaced above by§ its <> corpse, "Into   *1889a:*corpse "Into       <sup>1007</sup>| MS:rise and <> thou

## LXIV

"That rise into the true out of the false—explain?"
May an example serve? In yonder bay I bathed,
1010 This sunny morning: swam my best, then hung, half swathed
With chill, and half with warmth, i' the channel's midmost deep:
You know how one—not treads, but stands in water? Keep
Body and limbs below, hold head back, uplift chin,
And, for the rest, leave care! If brow, eyes, mouth, should win
1015 Their freedom,—excellent! If they must brook the surge,
No matter though they sink, let but the nose emerge.
So, all of me in brine lay soaking: did I care
One jot? I kept alive by man's due breath of air
I' the nostrils, high and dry. At times, o'er these would run
1020 The ripple, even wash the wavelet,—morning's sun
Tempted advance, no doubt: and always flash of froth,
Fish-outbreak, bubbling by, would find me nothing loth
To rise and look around; then all was overswept
With dark and death at once. But trust the old adept!
1025 Back went again the head, a merest motion made,
Fin-fashion, either hand, and nostril soon conveyed
Assurance light and life were still in reach as erst:
Always the last and,—wait and watch,—sometimes the first.

---

and    *1872:*rise, and <> thou, and        1008|    MS:§¶ called for§        1009|    MS:Will §crossed
out and replaced above by§ May <> bay, I    *1889a:*bay I        1010|    MS:morning, swam <>
hung, soft §crossed out and replaced above by§ half    *1872:*morning: swam        1011|    MS:With chill, half §last two words inserted above§ warmth about, in §altered to§ i'
*1872:*chill, and half with warmth, i'        1013|    MS:hold resolv §incomplete word crossed out
and replaced above by§ head        1014|    MS:care! §colon altered to exclamation mark§ if
§altered to§ If brow, and §crossed out§ eyes, mouth §inserted above§ should    *1872:*mouth,
should        1015|    MS:freedom, well! §word and exclamation mark crossed out and replaced
above by word and exclamation mark§ excellent! If they §last two words inserted above illegibly
crossed out words§    *1872:*freedom,—excellent        1016|    MS:And §crossed out and replaced
above by§ No <> sink, provided §crossed out and replaced above by three words§ let but the
1017|    MS:So all    *1872:*So, all        1019|    MS:dry. Even o'er    *1872:*dry. At times, o'er
1020|    MS:ripple, wash at times the wavelet,—for the sun    *1872:*ripple, even wash the
*1889a:*wavelet,—morning's sun        1021|    MS:doubt, and    *1872:*doubt: and
1022|    MS:And fish of §last three words crossed out and replaced above by hyphenated word and
comma§ Fish-outbreak,        1024|    MS:once; but—trust <> adept!—    *1872:*once. But <>
adept!        1025|    MS:made    *1872:*made,        1027|    MS:The news that life and light §last
three words transposed to§ light and life    *1889a:*Assurance light        1028|    MS:last and,—wait
and watch §dash and last three words inserted above illegibly crossed out words§

Try to ascend breast-high? wave arms wide free of tether?
1030 Be in the air and leave the water altogether?
Under went all again, till I resigned myself
To only breathe the air, that's footed by an elf,
And only swim the water, that's native to a fish.
But there is no denying that, ere I curbed my wish,
1035 And schooled my restive arms, salt entered mouth and eyes
Often enough—sun, sky, and air so tantalize!
Still, the adept swims, this accorded, that denied;
Can always breathe, sometimes see and be satisfied!

LXV

I liken to this play o' the body,—fruitless strife
1040 To slip the sea and hold the heaven,—my spirit's life
'Twixt false, whence it would break, and true, where it would bide.
I move in, yet resist, am upborne every side
By what I beat against, an element too gross
To live in, did not soul duly obtain her dose
1045 Of life-breath, and inhale from truth's pure plenitude
Above her, snatch and gain enough to just illude
With hope that some brave bound may baffle evermore
The obstructing medium, make who swam henceforward soar:
—Gain scarcely snatched when, foiled by the very effort, sowse,
1050 Underneath ducks the soul, her truthward yearnings dowse

---

<sup>1029</sup>| MS:breast-high, wave <> tether,    *1872:*breast-high? wave <> tether?
<sup>1030</sup>| MS:altogether!   *1872:*altogether?     <sup>1031</sup>| MS:Under goes all <> resign   *1872:*Under went all <> resigned     <sup>1032</sup>| MS:To only §inserted above§     <sup>1033</sup>| MS:To only bathe in §last two words crossed out and replaced above by two words§ swim the   *1872:*And only <sup>1034</sup>| MS:denying, sun and sky tantalize §last four words crossed out and replaced above by six words and comma§ that ere I curbed my wish,   *1872:*denying that, ere     <sup>1035</sup>| MS:salt was in mouth   *1872:*salt entered mouth     <sup>1036</sup>| MS:enough—so much §last two words crossed out§ sky and air so §last three words inserted above§   *1872:*sky, and     <sup>1037</sup>| MS:adept knows §crossed out and replaced above by§swims <> denied,   *1872:*denied;     <sup>1038</sup>| MS:Bids §crossed out and replaced above by§ Can     <sup>1039</sup>| MS:§¶ called for§ body, fruitless *1889a:*body,—fruitless     <sup>1040</sup>| MS:heaven, my §over illegible word§   *1889a:*heaven,—     <sup>1044</sup>| MS:not life §crossed out and replaced above by§ soul     <sup>1048</sup>| MS:make no longer swim but §last four words crossed out and replaced above by illegibly crossed out words, and then replaced by two words, comma, and word§ who swam, henceforward   *1872:*swam henceforward     <sup>1049</sup>| But not so much but, §last five words and comma crossed out and replaced above by dash, four words, and comma§ —Gain scarcely snatched when,

Deeper in falsehood! ay, but fitted less and less
To bear in nose and mouth old briny bitterness
Proved alien more and more: since each experience proves
Air—the essential good, not sea, wherein who moves
1055 Must thence, in the act, escape, apart from will or wish.
Move a mere hand to take waterweed, jelly-fish,
Upward you tend! And yet our business with the sea
Is not with air, but just o' the water, watery:
We must endure the false, no particle of which
1060 Do we acquaint us with, but up we mount a pitch
Above it, find our head reach truth, while hands explore
The false below: so much while here we bathe,—no more!

### LXVI

Now, there is one prime point (hear and be edified!)
One truth more true for me than any truth beside—
1065 To-wit, that I am I, who have the power to swim,
The skill to understand the law whereby each limb
May bear to keep immersed, since, in return, made sure
That its mere movement lifts head clean through coverture.
By practice with the false, I reach the true? Why, thence
1070 It follows, that the more I gain self-confidence,
Get proof I know the trick, can float, sink, rise, at will,
The better I submit to what I have the skill
To conquer in my turn, even now, and by and by
Leave wholly for the land, and there laugh, shake me dry
1075 To last drop, saturate with noonday—no need more
Of wet and fret, plagued once: on Pornic's placid shore,
Abundant air to breathe, sufficient sun to feel!

---

1051| MS:falsehood? ay—but   *1872:*falsehood! ay, but        1052| MS:bitterness—
*1872:*bitterness        1055| MS:wish:   *1872:*wish.        1057| MS:tend; and   *1872:*tend! And
1061| MS:head in truth while feet §crossed out and replaced above by§ hands   *1872:*head reach
truth, while        1063| MS:§¶ called for§        1065| MS:swim   *1872:*swim,
1070| MS:follows that <> I §over illegible erasure§   *1872:*follows, that
1073| MS:turn even <> and, by   *1872:*turn, even <> and by
1074| MS:land and   *1872:*land, and        1075| MS:with sunshine, no
*1872:*with noonday—no        1076| MS:O' the wet <> once, for Pornic's on the shore—
*1872:*Of wet <> once: on Pornic's placid shore,        1077| MS:Plenty §over illegible erasure§
of air <> breathe, plenty of sun   *1872:*Abundant air <> breathe, sufficient sun

Meantime I buoy myself: no whit my senses reel
When over me there breaks a billow; nor, elate
1080  Too much by some brief taste, I quaff intemperate
The air, o'ertop breast-high the wave-environment.
Full well I know the thing I grasp, as if intent
To hold,—my wandering wave,—will not be grasped at all:
The solid-seeming grasped, the handful great or small
1085  Must go to nothing, glide through fingers fast enough;
But none the less, to treat liquidity as stuff—
Though failure—certainly succeeds beyond its aim,
Sends head above, past thing that hands miss, all the same.

### LXVII

So with this wash o' the world, wherein life-long we drift;
1090  We push and paddle through the foam by making shift
To breathe above at whiles when, after deepest duck
Down underneath the show, we put forth hand and pluck
At what seems somehow like reality—a soul.
I catch at this and that, to capture and control,
1095  Presume I hold a prize, discover that my pains
Are run to nought: my hands are baulked, my head regains
The surface where I breathe and look about, a space.
The soul that helped me mount? Swallowed up in the race
O' the tide, come who knows whence, gone gaily who knows where!
1100  I thought the prize was mine; I flattered myself there.
It did its duty, though: I felt it, it felt me,
Or, where I look about and breathe, I should not be.
The main point is—the false fluidity was bound .

1081|  MS:air, breast-high o'ertop §last two words transposed to§ o'ertop breast-high
1082|  MS:know the <> grasp at, §last word crossed out§ as if §inserted above§  *1872:*know, the
*1889a:*know the      1085|  MS:enough  *1872:*enough;      1086|  MS:stuff,  *1872:*stuff—
1087|  MS:failure, certainly <> aim,  *1872:*failure—certainly <> aim      1088|  MS:above, far
past the thing hands miss  *1872:*miss, the  *1889a:*above, past thing that hands miss, all the
1089|  MS:§¶ called for§ world wherein  *1872:*world, wherein      1090|  MS:the froth §crossed
out and replaced above by§ foam      1097|  MS:surface by a bound § last three words crossed
out and replaced above by three words§ where I breathe <> about a space:  *1872:*about, a
space.      1099|  MS:come God knows <> gaily God knows  *1872:*come who knows <> gaily
who knows      1100|  MS:there:  *1872:*there.      1101|  MS:me:  *1872:*me;  *1889a:*me,
1102|  MS:Otherwise §crossed out and replaced above by word, comma, and word§ Or, where

Acknowledge that it frothed o'er substance, nowise found
1105 Fluid, but firm and true. Man, outcast, "howls,"—at rods?
If "sent in playful spray a-shivering to his gods!"
Childishest childe, man makes thereby no bad exchange.
Stay with the flat-fish, thou! We like the upper range
Where the "gods" live, perchance the dæmons also dwell:
1110 Where operates a Power, which every throb and swell
Of human heart invites that human soul approach,
"Sent" near and nearer still, however "spray" encroach
On "shivering" flesh below, to altitudes, which gained,
Evil proves good, wrong right, obscurity explained,
1115 And "howling" childishness. Whose howl have we to thank,
If all the dogs 'gan bark and puppies whine, till sank
Each yelper's tail 'twixt legs? for Huntsman Commonsense
Came to the rescue, bade prompt thwack of thong dispense
Quiet i' the kennel; taught that ocean might be blue,
1120 And rolling and much more, and yet the soul have, too,
Its touch of God's own flame, which He may so expand
"Who measurèd the waters i' the hollow of His hand"
That ocean's self shall dry, turn dew-drop in respect
Of all-triumphant fire, matter with intellect
1125 Once fairly matched; bade him who egged on hounds to bay,

---

1104| MS:To recognize it <> substance nowise    *1872:*Acknowledge that it <> substance,
nowise        1105| MS:Fluid but <> true: the §crossed out and replaced above by word and
comma§ Man, outcast, Man §crossed out and replaced above by word in quotation marks§
"howls",—what odds,—    *1872:*Fluid, but <> true|  Man <> "howls,"—at rods?—
1106| MS:Is §crossed out and replaced above by§ Sea §crossed out and replaced to left by§ If <>
Gods?"  *1872:*gods!"        1107| MS:Child §altered to§ Childishest by thy leave, §last three
words and comma crossed out and replaced above by word and comma§ childe,
1109| MS:Where the "Gods" <> perchance the Daemons <> dwell,    *1872:*"gods" <> daemons
*1889a:*dwell:        1110| MS:a Power which    *1872:*a Power, which        1111| MS:O'the
human    *1872:*Of human        1112| MS:"Sends"    *1872:*"Sent"        1113| MS:below, that
§crossed out and replaced above by§ to altitude    *1872:*altitudes        1115| MS:"howling,"
childishness §over illegible erasure§ :whose    *1872:*"howling" childishness. Whose
1116| MS:puppies yelp §crossed out and replaced above by§ whine        1117| MS:twixt legs
when Huntsman    *1872:*'twixt legs? for Huntsman        1118| MS:rescue, caused prompt
*1889a:*rescue, bade prompt        1119-25| MS:§seven lines inserted from slip pasted to right
margin§        1121| MS:flame which    *1872:*flame, which        1122| MS:measured
*1872:*measuréd  *1889a:*measurèd        1123| MS:dry, a §crossed out and replaced above by§
turn        1124| MS:O' the all-triumphant fire, match but §last two words crossed out and
replaced above by§ matter    *1872:*Of all-triumphant fire

Go curse, i' the poultry yard, his kind: "there let him lay"
The swan's one addled egg: which yet shall put to use,
Rub breast-bone warm against, so many a sterile goose!

LXVIII

No, I want sky not sea, prefer the larks to shrimps,
1130 And never dive so deep but that I get a glimpse
O' the blue above, a breath of the air around. Elvire,
I seize—by catching at the melted beryl here,
The tawny hair that just has trickled off,—Fifine!
Did not we two trip forth to just enjoy the scene,
1135 The tumbling-troop arrayed, the strollers on their stage,
Drawn up and under arms, and ready to engage—
Dabble, and there an end, with foam and froth o'er face,
Till suddenly Fifine suggested change of place?
Now we taste æther, scorn the wave, and interchange apace
1140 No ordinary thoughts, but such as evidence
The cultivated mind in both. On what pretence
Are you and I to sneer at who lent help to hand,
And gave the lucky lift?

---

<sup>1126</sup>|   MS:Go practice §crossed out and replaced above by two words§ curse mankind §altered
to§ his kind in the poultry-yard "there   *1872:*Go curse, i' the poultry yard, his kind: "there
<sup>1127</sup>|   MS:The swan's one §last two words inserted above§ < > egg, which yet may §crossed out
and replaced above by illegibly crossed out word, perhaps *will*, and then replaced above by§
shall < > to cackling §crossed out§   *1872:*egg: which          <sup>1128</sup>|   MS:against, some §crossed out
and replaced above by three words§ full §crossed out and replaced above by§ so many a
<sup>1129</sup>|   MS:§¶ called for§ sea, and get a §last three words crossed out and replaced above by§
prefer          <sup>1131</sup>|   MS:around—Elvire—   *1872:*around. Elvire,          <sup>1132</sup>|   MS:I seize, §two
words and comma inserted to left§ By §altered to§ by < > that bit of §last two words crossed out§
*1872:*seize—by          <sup>1133</sup>|   MS:tawny wavelet just   *1872:*tawny hair that just
<sup>1135</sup>|   MS:stage   *1872:*stage,          <sup>1136</sup>|   MS:arms and   *1872:*arms, and
<sup>1137</sup>|   MS:Dabble, §word and comma inserted above§ And   *1872:*and
<sup>1138</sup>|   MS:Till suddenly Fifine suggested change of place, §line crossed out and then restored§
*1872:*place?          <sup>1139</sup>|   MS:Till §crossed out and replaced to left by§ When we < > aether
straight, you see, §last two words and comma inserted above§ and   *1872:*Now we < > aether,
scorn the wave, and          <sup>1141</sup>|   MS:both! §colon altered to exclamation point§ on §altered to§
On   *1889a:*both. On          <sup>1143</sup>|   MS:the lucky §inserted above§ lift? §¶ called for§

64

LXIX

Still sour? I understand!
One ugly circumstance discredits my fair plan—
1145   That Woman does the work: I waive the help of Man.
"Why should experiment be tried with only waves,
When solid spars float round? Still some Thalassia saves
Too pertinaciously, as though no Triton, bluff
As e'er blew brine from conch, were free to help enough!
1150   Surely, to recognize a man, his mates serve best!
Why is there not the same or greater interest
In the strong spouse as in the pretty partner, pray,
Were recognition just your object, as you say,
Amid this element o' the false?"

LXX

We come to terms.
1155   I need to be proved true; and nothing so confirms
One's faith in the prime point that one's alive, not dead,
In all Descents to Hell whereof I ever read,
As when a phantom there, male enemy or friend,
Or merely stranger-shade, is struck, is forced suspend

---

1144|   MS:One ugly §inserted above§ circumstance that casts §last two words crossed out§ discredit §altered to§ discredits on the §last two words crossed out and replaced above by two words§ my fair       1145|   MS:That §inserted to left§ <> does all §crossed out§ <> work: you §crossed out and replaced above by§ I want no help from Man.   *1872:*work: I waive the help of Man.       1146|   MS:"Why must §crossed out and replaced above by§ should
1147|   MS:round? §dash altered to question mark§ the §altered to§ The white §last two words crossed out and replaced above by two words§ Still some       1148|   Too §crossed out and then restored§ <> as if §crossed out and replaced above by§ though no §crossed out and then restored§ Tritons §altered to§ Triton       1149|   MS:blew brine from §last two words inserted above§ conch, abound §crossed out and replaced above by§ were <> to proffer §crossed out§
1152|   MSS:the Strong Spouse §crossed out, replaced above by illegibly crossed out word, and then restored§ <> in Fifine §crossed out§ the pretty §inserted above§ <> pray,   *1872:*strong spouse <> pray?   *1889a:*pray,       1154|   MS:false?" §¶ called for§ We <> terms:   *1872:*false." §¶§ We <> terms.   *1889a:*false?" §¶§ We       1155|   MS:You §crossed out and replaced above by§ We need   *1872:*I need       1156|   MS:in the §altered from another word by illegibly crossing out last letter or letters§ <> point, of life as §last three words crossed out and replaced above by two words§ that one's alive not   *1872:*alive, not       1158|   MS:there, old §inserted above§ enemy   *1872:*there, male enemy       1159|   MS:Or merely §inserted above§ stranger-ghost §hyphen and second half of word crossed out and replaced above by hyphen and word§ -shade just §crossed out and replaced above by§ is   *1872:*stranger-shade, is

<sup>1160</sup>   His passage: "You that breathe, along with us the ghosts?"
Here, why must it be still a woman that accosts?

### LXXI

Because, one woman's worth, in that respect, such hairy hosts
Of the other sex and sort! Men? Say you have the power
To make them yours, rule men, throughout life's little hour,
<sup>1165</sup>   According to the phrase; what follows? Men, you make,
By ruling them, your own: each man for his own sake
Accepts you as his guide, avails him of what worth
He apprehends in you to sublimate his earth
With fire: content, if so you convoy him through night,
<sup>1170</sup>   That you shall play the sun, and he, the satellite,
Pilfer your light and heat and virtue, starry pelf,
While, caught up by your course, he turns upon himself.
Women rush into you, and there remain absorbed.
Beside, 'tis only men completely formed, full-orbed,
<sup>1175</sup>   Are fit to follow track, keep pace, illustrate so
The leader: any sort of woman may bestow
Her atom on the star, or clod she counts for such,—
Each little making less bigger by just that much.

---

<sup>1161|</sup>   MS:§this line inserted above following line§ accosts?"   *1872:*accosts?
<sup>1162|</sup>   MS:§¶ called for§ Ah, but §last two words crossed out and replaced to left by§ Because one
woman's worth in < > respect such hairy §inserted below§   *1872:*Because, one < > worth, in
< > respect, such   <sup>1163|</sup>   MS:sort! of creature §last two words crossed out and replaced
above by three words§ Men? Say you   <sup>1164|</sup>   MS:yours, be §crossed out§ ruled §altered
to§ rule men, §last word and comma inserted above§   <sup>1165|</sup>   MS:As §crossed out and
replaced above by two words§ According to < > phrase: is, well, §last two words and two commas
crossed out§ what then §crossed out and replaced above by§ follows   *1872:*phrase; what
<sup>1166|</sup>   MS:own—which each for   *1872:*own: each man for   <sup>1168|</sup>   MS:apprehends in
§inserted above illegibly crossed out word§   <sup>1170|</sup>   MS:sun and he the satellite—
*1872:*sun, and he, the satellite,   <sup>1171|</sup>   MS:Procure so much §last two words crossed out and
replaced above by§ him light, and   *1872:*Pilfer your light and
<sup>1172|</sup>   MS:And §crossed out and replaced above by§ While < > up in your course, keep §crossed
out and replaced above by§ he turning §altered to§ turns on §altered to§ upon itself. §altered
to§ himself.   *1872:*up by your   <sup>1173|</sup>   MS:you and   *1872:*you, and
<sup>1174|</sup>   MS:completely-formed   *1872:*completely formed   <sup>1176|</sup>   MS:any clod that pleases
§last three words crossed out and replaced above by three words§ sort of woman
<sup>1177|</sup>   MS:or mass §crossed out and replaced above by§ clod she §over illegible erasure§
<sup>1178|</sup>   MS:Each §inserted to left§ Little §altered to§ little §next word illegibly crossed out§
making you §crossed out and replaced above by§ less < > much:   *1872:*much.

Women grow you, while men depend on you at best.
1180 And what dependence! Bring and put him to the test,
Your specimen disciple, a handbreadth separate
From you, he almost seemed to touch before! Abate
Complacency you will, I judge, at what's divulged!
Some flabbiness you fixed, some vacancy outbulged,
1185 Some—much—nay, all, perhaps, the outward man's your work:
But, inside man?—find him, wherever he may lurk,
And where's a touch of you in his true self?

### LXXII

I wish
Some wind would waft this way a glassy bubble-fish
O' the kind the sea inflates, and show you, once detached
1190 From wave . . . or no, the event is better told than watched:
Still may the thing float free, globose and opaline
All over, save where just the amethysts combine
To blue their best, rim-round the sea-flower with a tinge
Earth's violet never knew! Well, 'neath that gem-tipped fringe,
1195 A head lurks—of a kind—that acts as stomach too;
Then comes the emptiness which out the water blew
So big and belly-like, but, dry of water drained,
Withers away nine-tenths. Ah, but a tenth remained!
That was the creature's self: no more akin to sea,

---

1181| MS:disciple, held but §last two words crossed out§ one handbreadth of §crossed out§
*1872:*disciple, a handbreadth        1182| MS:you he   *1872:*you, he        1183| MS:divulged:
*1872:*divulged!        1185| MS:Some,—much <> all perhaps of §crossed out§   *1872:*Some—
much <> all, perhaps        1186| MS:But, the §crossed out§ <> man,—find that, wherever it
may   *1872:*man?—find him, wherever he may        1187| MS:in the man's §crossed out§ <>
self? §¶ called for§        1188| MS:You wave §last two words crossed out and replaced above by
two words§ Some wind <> way one of those jelly- §last four words and hyphen crossed out and
replaced above by three words and hyphen§ a glassy bubble-        1189| MS:That sort §last two
words crossed out and replaced above by three words§ O' the kind        1190| MS:watched,
*1872:*watched:        1191| MS:float free §over illegible erasure§        1194| MS:knew: well
*1872:*knew! Well        1195| MS:too,   *1872:*too;        1197| MS:belly-like, which, thence the
§last three words crossed out and replaced above by three words§ but, dry of
1198| MS:nine-tenths: suppose a <> remained,   *1872:*nine-tenths. Ah, but a <> remained!
1199| MS:self, no <> sea.   *1872:*self: no <> sea,

1200   Poor rudimental head and stomach, you agree,
      Than sea's akin to sun who yonder dips his edge.

LXXIII

    But take the rill which ends a race o'er yonder ledge
    O' the fissured cliff, to find its fate in smoke below!
    Disengage that, and ask—what news of life, you know
1205   It led, that long lone way, through pasture, plain and waste?
    All's gone to give the sea! no touch of earth, no taste
    Of air, reserved to tell how rushes used to bring
    The butterfly and bee, and fisher-bird that's king
    O' the purple kind, about the snow-soft silver-sweet
1210   Infant of mist and dew; only these atoms fleet,
    Embittered evermore, to make the sea one drop
    More big thereby—if thought keep count where sense must stop.

LXXIV

    The full-blown ingrate, mere recipient of the brine,
    That takes all and gives nought, is Man; the feminine
1215   Rillet that, taking all and giving nought in turn,

---

1200|  MS:rudimental head, §word and comma inserted above§ rag-stomach though it be
*1872:*head and stomach, you agree,     1201|  MS:Than sea to yonder §last two words crossed
out and replaced above by three words§ has part in sun now dipping his red edge:   *1872:*Than
sea's akin to who dips yonder his <> edge.   *1889a:*to sun who yonder dips his edge.
1202|  MS:§¶ called for§ But take the §last two words crossed out, replaced above by illegibly
crossed out word, and then restored§ rillet, run to waste §last three words crossed out and
replaced above by three words§ ends its race   *1872:*rillet, ends a race   *1889a:*the rill, which
ends     1203|  MS:cliff and §crossed out and replaced above by§ to finds §altered to§ find its
way §crossed out and replaced above by§ fate <> below—   *1872:*cliff, <> to below!
1204|  MS:of the §crossed out§ life, we know   *1872:*life, you know     1205|  MS:Was §crossed
out and replaced above by§ It led, all §crossed out§ <> long lone §inserted above§
1206|  MS:All <> sea! §colon altered to exclamation point§ no §altered to§ No   *1872:*All's <>
sea! no     1208|  MS:butterfly, and <> and fishing-bird §altered to§ fisher-bird
*1872:*butterfly and     1209|  MS:about the soft and silver-sweet   *1872:*about the snow-soft,
silver-sweet   *1889a:*snow-soft silver-sweet     1210|  MS:Child §crossed out and replaced above
by§ Infant of the §crossed out§ <> dew; whereof §crossed out and replaced above by§ only the
§altered to§ these     1212|  MS:thereby—since §crossed out and replaced above by§ if <>
keeps §altered to§ keep <> senses §altered to§ sense must §inserted above§
1213-18|  MS:§Six lines inserted from back of previous leaf§     1213|  MS:§¶ called for§
1214|  MS:is Man: the *1872:*so Man; the     1215|  MS:Rillet that §over comma§ taking all and
giving nought   *1872:*that, giving all and taking nought   *1889a:*that, taking all and giving nought

Goes headlong to her death i' the sea, without concern
For the old inland life, snow-soft and silver-clear,
That's woman—typified from Fifine to Elvire.

LXXV

Then, how diverse the modes prescribed to who would deal
<sup></sup>1220  With either kind of creature! 'Tis Man, you seek to seal
Your very own? Resolve, for first step, to discard
Nine-tenths of what you are! To make, you must be marred,—
To raise your race, must stoop,—to teach them aught, must learn
Ignorance, meet half-way what most you hope to spurn
1225  I' the sequel. Change yourself, dissimulate the thought
And vulgarize the word, and see the deed be brought
To look like nothing done with any such intent
As teach men—though perchance it teach, by accident!
So may you master men: assured that if you show
1230  One point of mastery, departure from the low
And level,—head or heart-revolt at long disguise,
Immurement, stifling soul in mediocrities,—
If inadvertently a gesture, much more, word
Reveal the hunter no companion for the herd,
1235  His chance of capture's gone. Success means, they may snuff,
Examine, and report,—a brother, sure enough,

---

1216| MS:in <> sea without   *1872*:i' <> sea, without      1217| MS:life, so soft and sweet and
clear,   *1872*:life, snow-soft and silver-clear,      1218| MS:woman, typified   *1872*:woman—
typified      1219| MS:And §crossed out§ then, §altered to§ Then, how §inserted above§ the
diverse §last two words transposed to§ diverse the      1220| MS:creature! Your own you
*1872*:creature! 'Tis Man, you      1221| MS:The man-sort? Be §crossed out and replaced
above by word and comma§ Why, Resolved §altered to§ resolve   *1872*:Your very own? Resolve
1222| MS:are: to   *1872*:are! To      1225| MS:sequel, don disguise, §last two words and
comma crossed out and replaced above by dash, two words, and comma§ —change yourself,
*1872*:sequel. Change      1227| MS:nothing done §inserted above§      1228| MS:it may, by
*1872*:it teach, by      1229| MS:So does §crossed out and replaced above by§ may man
§altered to§ you <> if he §crossed out and replaced above by§ you      1230| MSS:mastery,
plan §crossed out and replaced above by§ departure      1232| MS:In mediocrity §last two
words crossed out and replaced above by§ Immurement stifling   *1872*:Immurement, stifling
1233| MS:He §crossed out and replaced above by§ If inadvertently—by §dash and word crossed
out and replaced above by§ a      1235| MS:chance o' the capture's <> gone: success
*1872*:chance of capture's <> gone. Success      1236| MS:Examine and report,
a brother sure enough   *1872*:Examine, and report,—a brother, sure enough,

Disports him in brute-guise; for skin is truly skin,
Horns, hoofs are hoofs and horns, and all, outside and in,
Is veritable beast, whom fellow-beasts resigned
1240 May follow, made a prize in honest pride, behind
One of themselves and not creation's upstart lord!
Well, there's your prize i' the pound—much joy may it afford
My Indian! Make survey and tell me,—was it worth
You acted part so well, went all-fours upon earth
1245 The live-long day, brayed, belled, and all to bring to pass
That stags should deign eat hay when winter stints them grass?

LXXVI

So much for men, and how disguise may make them mind
Their master. But you have to deal with womankind?
Abandon stratagem for strategy! Cast quite
1250 The vile disguise away, try truth clean-opposite
Such creep-and-crawl, stand forth all man and, might it chance,
Somewhat of angel too!—whate'er inheritance,
Actual on earth, in heaven prospective, be your boast,
Lay claim to! Your best self revealed at uttermost,—
1255 That's the wise way o' the strong! And e'en should falsehood tempt
The weaker sort to swerve,—at least the lie's exempt
From slur, that's loathlier still, of aiming to debase

---

<sup>1237</sup>| MS:brute-guise; §colon altered to semicolon§ <> is very §crossed out and replaced above
by§ truly      <sup>1238</sup>| MS:Horns, hoofs, are      *1872:*Horns, hoofs are      <sup>1239</sup>| MS:The
§crossed out and replaced above by§ Is      <sup>1240</sup>| MS:To follow to the snare in      *1872:*May
follow, made a prize in      <sup>1241</sup>| MS:lord.      *1872:*lord!      <sup>1242</sup>| MS:afford,      *1872:*afford
<sup>1244</sup>| MS:went belly-wise on earth      *1872:*went all-fours upon on earth      *1889a:*upon earth
<sup>1246</sup>| MS:should feed on §last two words crossed out and replaced above by two words§ learn eat
<> winter kills the §last two words crossed out and replaced above by two words§ stints them
*1872:*should deign eat      <sup>1247</sup>| MS:§¶ called for§ men and how a man §last two words
crossed out and replaced above by§ disguised §altered to§ disguise may §crossed out and
replaced above by illegibly crossed out word, then restored§      *1872:*men, and
<sup>1248</sup>| MS:master: but put case he §crossed out and replaced above by§ you deals §altered to§
deal <> womankind,      *1872:*master. But you have to deal <> womankind?
<sup>1249</sup>| MS:strategy! §colon altered to exclamation point§ take §altered to§ Take quite
*1872:*strategy! Cast quite      <sup>1251</sup>| MS:The §crossed out and replaced to left by§ Such
<sup>1252</sup>| MS:Some §altered to§ Somewhat of §crossed out§ the god besides,— §last two words,
comma, and dash crossed out and replaced above by two words, exclamation point, and dash§
angel too!—      *1872:*Somewhat of angel      <sup>1256</sup>| MS:sort of these §last two words crossed out
and replaced above by two words§ to swerve      <sup>1257</sup>| MS:From something of §last two words
crossed out and replaced above by two words and comma§ slur, that's

Rather than elevate its object. Mimic grace,
Not make deformity your mask! Be sick by stealth,
1260 Nor traffic with disease—malingering in health!
No more of: "Countrymen, I boast me one like you—
My lot, the common strength, the common weakness too!
I think the thoughts you think; and if I have the knack
Of fitting thoughts to words, you peradventure lack,
1265 Envy me not the chance, yourselves more fortunate!
Many the loaded ship self-sunk through treasure-freight,
Many the pregnant brain brought never child to birth,
Many the great heart broke beneath its girdle-girth!
Be mine the privilege to supplement defect,
1270 Give dumbness voice, and let the labouring intellect
Find utterance in word, or possibly in deed!
What though I seem to go before? 'tis you that lead!
I follow what I see so plain—the general mind
Projected pillar-wise, flame kindled by the kind,
1275 Which dwarfs the unit—me—to insignificance!
Halt you, I stop forthwith,—proceed, I too advance!"

LXXVII

Ay, that's the way to take with men you wish to lead,
Instruct and benefit. Small prospect you succeed
With women so! Be all that's great and good and wise,
1280 August, sublime—swell out your frog the right ox-size—

---

<sup>1258</sup>| MS:object, mimics §altered to§ mimic   *1872:*object. Mimic     <sup>1259</sup>| MS:your §over
illegible word§ mask,—be §over illegible word§   *1872:*mask! Be      <sup>1260</sup>| MS:Nor ape
disease for gain—malingering   *1872:*Nor traffic with disease—malingering
<sup>1261</sup>| MS:one as you—   *1872:*one like you—      <sup>1262</sup>| MS:My §inserted above illegibly
crossed out word§ be §crossed out and replaced above by§ lot the <> too—
*1872:*lot, the <> too!      <sup>1263</sup>| MS:think your §crossed out and replaced above by§ the <>
you think, §word inserted above illegibly crossed out word§ and   *1872:*you think; and
<sup>1264</sup>| MS:words you   *1872:*words, you      <sup>1265</sup>| MS:not §crossed out
and then restored§ <> yourselves, the fortunate!   *1872:*yourselves more fortunate!
<sup>1266</sup>| MS:thro'   *1872:*through      <sup>1267</sup>| MSS:brain too heavy proves §inserted above§ for a
§crossed out§ birth   *1872:*brain brings never child to birth,   *1889a:*brain brought never
<sup>1268</sup>| MS:the pent §inserted above§ heart pent all §last two words crossed out and replaced
above by§ bursts beneath   *1872:*the great heart   *1889a:*heart broke beneath
<sup>1272</sup>| MS:though I seem to §last two words inserted above§ <> before?
§colon altered to question mark§ <> lead—   *1872:*lead!      <sup>1277</sup>| MS:§¶ called for§
<sup>1278</sup>| MS:benefit: no prospect   *1872:*benefit. Small prospect

71

He's buoyed like a balloon, to soar, not burst, you'll see!
The more you prove yourself, less fear the prize will flee
The captor. Here you start after no pompous stag
Who condescends be snared, with toss of horn, and brag
1285   Of bray, and ramp of hoof; you have not to subdue
The foe through letting him imagine he snares you!
'Tis rather with . . .

### LXXVIII

Ah, thanks! quick—where the dipping disk
Shows red against the rise and fall o' the fin! there frisk
In shoal the—porpoises? Dolphins, they shall and must
1290   Cut through the freshening clear—dolphins, my instance just!
'Tis fable, therefore truth: who has to do with these,
Needs never practise trick of going hands and knees
As beasts require. Art fain the fish to captivate?
Gather thy greatness round, Arion! Stand in state,
1295   As when the banqueting thrilled conscious—like a rose
Throughout its hundred leaves at that approach it knows
Of music in the bird—while Corinth grew one breast
A-throb for song and thee; nay, Periander pressed
The Methymnæan hand, and felt a king indeed, and guessed
1300   How Phœbus' self might give that great mouth of the gods

---

1281|   MS:He §altered to§ He's turns to §last two words crossed out and replaced above by two words§ buoyed like <> ballon and §crossed out and replaced above by§ to soars, §altered to§soar, not bursts §altered to§ burst   *1872:*ballon, to     1282|   MS:you prove §inserted above illegibly crossed out word§ —yourself—less   *1872:*prove yourself, less
1283|   MS:captor: here the case is with no   *1872:*captor. Here you start after no
1284|   MS:Proceeding to be <> horn and   *1872:*Who condescends be <> horn, and
1285|   MS:hoof—you §over illegible word§   *1872:*hoof; you     1286|   MS:he beats you!
*1872:*he snares you!     1287|   MS:§¶ called for§ quick—there, the   *1872:*quick—where the
1288|   MS:of   *1872:*o'     1289|   MS:porpoises? §colon altered to question mark§
1291|   MS:And §crossed out and replaced above by§ 'Tis fable therefore truth: §illegible punctuation mark altered to colon§ <> these   *1872:*fable, therefore <> these,
1292|   MS:practice   *1872:*practise     1293|   MS:require, §colon altered to comma§ Art §over illegible word§   *1872:*require. Art     1295|   MS:conscious as §crossed out and replaced above by§ like   *1872:*conscious—like     1297|   MS:bird, and §crossed out and replaced above by§ while   *1872:*bird—while     1298|   MS:Wide-open to thy song while §last five words crossed out and replaced above by eight words and two commas§ A-throb on fire §last two words crossed out§ for song and thee, nay,   *1872:*thee; nay     1300|   MS:How Phoebus self might give §last five words inserted above illegibly crossed out words§   *1872:*How Phoebus'

Such a magnificence of song! The pillar nods,
Rocks roof, and trembles door, gigantic, post and jamb,
As harp and voice rend air—the shattering dithyramb!
So stand thou, and assume the robe that tingles yet
1305   With triumph; strike the harp, whose every golden fret
Still smoulders with the flame, was late at fingers' end—
So, standing on the bench o' the ship, let voice expend
Thy soul, sing, unalloyed by meaner mode, thine own,
The Orthian lay; then leap from music's lofty throne,
1310   Into the lowest surge, make fearlessly thy launch!
Whatever storm may threat, some dolphin will be staunch!
Whatever roughness rage, some exquisite sea-thing
Will surely rise to save, will bear—palpitating—
One proud humility of love beneath its load—
1315   Stem tide, part wave, till both roll on, thy jewell'd road
Of triumph, and the grim o' the gulph grow wonder-white
I' the phosphorescent wake; and still the exquisite
Sea-thing stems on, saves still, palpitatingly thus,

---

1301|   MS:By §crossed out and replaced above by§ Such a §inserted above illegibly crossed out
word§ <> of praise §crossed out and replaced above by§ song      1302|   MS:The §crossed
out§ roof §altered to§ Roof rocks and the gate's §last two words crossed out and replaced above
by three words and two commas§ giant door, see, a-tremble §altered to§ trembles, post
*1872:*Rocks roof, and trembles door, gigantic, post      1303|   MS:At §altered to§ A harp <>
voice rush forth §last two words crossed out and replaced above by two words and dash§ rend
air—   *1872:*As harp      1304|   MS:thou and   *1872:*thou, and      1305|   MS:triumph, strike
<> harp, with §altered to§ whose   *1872:*triumph; strike      1306|   MS:flame was <> finger's
*1872:*flame, was   *1889a:*fingers'      1307|   MS:voice intone §crossed out and replaced above
by§ expend      1308|   MS:All §crossed out and replaced above by three words and comma§
Thy soul, sing unalloyed by aught of §last two words crossed out§   *1872:*sing, unalloyed
1309|   MS:The Orthrian §altered to§ Orthian, lay, then leap from music's lofty throne, §last four
words inserted above§   *1872:*Orthian lay; then      1310|   MS:Into the lowest surge §last four
words inserted between ll. 1309 and 1310§ make fearlessly thy launch! §last four words and
exclamation point inserted from second half of l. 1309§   *1872:*surge, make
1311|   threat, the §crossed out and replaced above by§ some dolphins §altered to§ dolphin
1313|   MS:Will surely §inserted above§ <> palpitating— §dash crossed out§   *1872:*palpitating—
1314|   MS:With §crossed out and replaced above by§ The proud   *1872:*One proud
1315|   MS:The while, until the wave §last five words and comma crossed out and replaced above
by six words and comma§ Stem tide, part wave till both smooths §altered to§ smooth thee §over
illegible word§ one jewelled   *1872:*wave, till both roll on, thy jewell'd      1316|   MS:triumph,
and §crossed out and then restored§ the dark §crossed out and replaced above by§ grim <> the
depth §crossed out and replaced above by§ gulph foams §inserted above illegibly crossed out
word§ wonder-white   *1872:*gulph grow wonder-white      1318|   MS:Sea-thing §inserted above
illegibly crossed out word§ saves §crossed out and replaced above by§ stems on, and on, §last
two words and comma crossed out and replaced above by two words and comma§ saves still,

Lands safe at length its load of love at Tænarus,
1320    True woman-creature!

### LXXIX

Man? Ah, would you prove what power
Marks man,—what fruit his tree may yield, beyond the sour
And stinted crab, he calls love-apple, which remains
After you toil and moil your utmost,—all, love gains
By lavishing manure?—try quite the other plan!
1325    And, to obtain the strong true product of a man,
.   Set him to hate a little! Leave cherishing his root,
And rather prune his branch, nip off the pettiest shoot
Superfluous on his bough! I promise, you shall learn
By what grace came the goat, of all beasts else, to earn
1330    Such favour with the god o' the grape: 'twas only he
Who, browsing on its tops, first stung fertility
Into the stock's heart, stayed much growth of tendril-twine,
Some faintish flower, perhaps, but gained the indignant wine,
Wrath of the red press! Catch the puniest of the kind—
1335    Man-animalcule, starved body, stunted mind,
And, as you nip the blotch 'twixt thumb and finger-nail,

---

1319|  MS:Landing §altered to§ Lands safe §inserted above§ at last §crossed out and replaced above by§ length       1320|  MS:The §crossed out and replaced above by§ True woman-creature! §¶ called for§ <> prove the §crossed out and replaced above by§ what
1321|  MS:Of §crossed out and replaced above by§ Marks <> fruit his tree §last two words inserted above§ <> beyond that §crossed out and replaced above by§ the
1323|  MS:utmost,—what love    1872:utmost,—all love       1324|  MS:manure? §comma altered to question mark§ <> plan—    1872:plan!       1325|  MS:§this line inserted above l. 1326§ And to <> man    1872:And, to <> man,       1326|  MS:little, leave    1872:little! Leave
1327|  MS:And trust to pruning-hook §last three words crossed out and replaced above by four words§ rather prune his branch       1328|  MS:bough: I    1872:bough! I
1329|  MS:How it was that §last four words crossed out and replaced above by four words§ By what grace came <> beasts, came §comma and last word crossed out and replaced above by word and comma§ else,       1330|  MS:favor <> the god §altered to§ God <> was only §inserted above§    1872:the god    1889a:favour       1331|  MS:By §crossed out and replaced above by word and comma§ Who, <> its shoots §crossed out and replaced above by word and comma§ tops,       1332|  MS:the vine §crossed out§ <> tendril-twine    1872:tendril-twine,
1333|  MS:And §crossed out and replaced above by§ Some <> flowers, perhaps, §last word and comma inserted above§ <> the red §crossed out§       1334|  MS:the red §inserted above§
1335|  MS:Man-animalcule, starved §inserted above illegibly crossed out word§ body, §comma over illegible letter§       1336|  MS:you hold §crossed out and replaced above by§ nip the mite §crossed out and replaced above by§ blotch twixt    1872:'twixt

Admire how heaven above and earth below avail
No jot to soothe the mite, sore at God's prime offence
In making mites at all,—coax from its impotence
1340 One virile drop of thought, or word, or deed, by strain
To propagate for once—which nature rendered vain,
Who lets first failure stay, yet cares not to record
Mistake that seems to cast opprobrium on the Lord!
Such were the gain from love's best pains! But let the elf
1345 Be touched with hate, because some real man bears himself
Manlike in body and soul, and, since he lives, must thwart
And furify and set a-fizz this counterpart
O' the pismire that's surprised to effervescence, if,
By chance, black bottle come in contact with chalk cliff,
1350 Acid with alkali! Then thrice the bulk, out blows
Our insect, does its kind, and cuckoo-spits some rose!

---

1337| MS:how God §crossed out and replaced above by§ heaven <> and man §crossed out and replaced above by§ earth        1338| MS:to make §crossed out and replaced above by§ soothe the thing, §last word and comma crossed out and replaced above by word and comma§ mite, forgive §crossed out and replaced above by two words§ sore at God's §crossed out replaced above by three words§ all that the §last three words crossed out and *God's* restored§
1339| MS:In making §last two words crossed out and replaced above by three words§ That God should mites   *1872:*In making mites        1340| MS:§first word illegibly crossed out, replaced above by illegibly crossed out word(s), and then replaced to left by§ One virile drop of §last two words inserted above§ thought or §inserted above§ word or §inserted above§ deed by strain §inserted above§   *1872:*thought, or word, or deed,        1341-43| §three lines inserted from right§        1341| MS:vain   *1872:*vain,        1342| MS:Who §over illegible word§ lets her failure   *1872:*lets first failure        1343| MS:Mistake that §over illegible word§ <> the Lord:   *1872:*the Lord!        1344| MS:Therefore no good in love's best pains! §last seven words and exclamation point inserted above l. 1345§ But let the elf §last four words inserted from l. 1340, originally the last part of that line§   *1872:*Such were the gain from love's        1345| MS:Be pricked with hate, see just one §last two words crossed out and replaced above by two words§ because some <> man bear §altered to§ bears   *1872:*Be touched with        1346| MS:Aright §crossed out and replaced above by§ Manlike in flesh and soul, who §crossed out and replaced above by§ and <> must cross §crossed out and replaced above by§ thwart   *1872:*in body and        1347| MS:And §inserted above illegibly crossed out word§ furify, §comma crossed out and replaced above by§ and set all §crossed out§        1348| MS:surprized <> effervescence if   *1872:*surprised <> effervescence, if,        1349| MS:It find its §crossed out, replaced above by illegibly crossed out word, and then restored§ bottle §inserted above illegibly crossed out word§ brought §crossed out and replaced above by§ come <> with chalk §crossed out, replaced above by illegibly crossed out word, and then restored§ cliff—   *1872:*By chance, black bottle <> cliff,        1350| MS:alkali—till, §word and comma crossed out and replaced above by word and dash§ then—thrice <> bulk, there grows §last two words crossed out§   *1872:*alkali! Then thrice        1351| MS:And §crossed out and replaced above by§ The §crossed out and replaced to left by§ Our insect, for what end? to §three words, question mark, and word crossed out and replaced

75

## LXXX

No—'tis ungainly work, the ruling men, at best!
The graceful instinct's right: 'tis women stand confessed
Auxiliary, the gain that never goes away,
1355 Takes nothing and gives all: Elvire, Fifine, 'tis they
Convince,—if little, much, no matter!—one degree
The more, at least, convince unreasonable me
That I am, anyhow, a truth, though all else seem
And be not; if I dream, at least I know I dream.
1360 The falsity, beside, is fleeting: I can stand
Still, and let truth come back,—your steadying touch of hand
Assists me to remain self-centred, fixed amid
All on the move. Believe in me, at once you bid
Myself believe that, since one soul has disengaged
1365 Mine from the shows of things, so much is fact: I waged
No foolish warfare, then, with shades, myself a shade,
Here in the world—may hope my pains will be repaid!
How false things are, I judge: how changeable, I learn
When, where and how it is I shall see truth return,
1370 That I expect to know, because Fifine knows me!—
How much more, if Elvire!

---

above by§ three words, comma, and word§ does its kind, and          1352| MS:§¶ called for§
1354|  MS:The §crossed out§ auxiliary §altered to§ Auxiliary, one §altered to§ the
1355|  MS:all— §dash crossed out and replaced above by colon§ Elvire, Fifine are they     *1872*:all:
Elvire, Fifine, 'tis they          1356|  MS:Convince you §crossed out§          1359|  MS:dream.
§comma altered to period§          1360|  MS:fleeting,— §comma and dash crossed out and
replaced above by colon§          1361|  MS:let things §crossed out and replaced above by§ truth
come round §crossed out and replaced above by§ back,—the §crossed out and replaced above
by§ your          1362|  MS:Assists so much §last two words crossed out and replaced above by two
words§ me to          1363|  MS:Things §crossed out and replaced above by§ All <> move: believe
<> me, at once §last two words inserted above§     *1872*:move. Believe          1364|  MS:that since
your §crossed out and replaced above by§ one     *1872*:that, since          1367|  MS:§line inserted
above l. 1368§ world, may <> repaid.     *1872*:world—may <> repaid!          1368|  MS:judge,
how <> learn,     *1872*:judge: how <> learn:     *1889a*:learn          1369|  MS:When, where
§inserted above§ <> how once more §last two words crossed out and replaced above by two
words and comma§ it is,          1370|  MS:That I shall hope §last two words crossed out and
replaced above by§ expect <> because Elvire §crossed out and replaced above by§ Fifine
1371|  MS:How §inserted to left§ Much <> if Elvire! §¶ called for§ why not must §last two words
crossed out§ not only She?"     *1872*:much <> not, only she?     *1872*:much <> not, only she?

## LXXXI

"And why not, only she?
Since there can be for each, one Best, no more, such Best,
For body and mind of him, abolishes the rest
O' the simply Good and Better. You please select Elvire
<sup>1375</sup> To give you this belief in truth, dispel the fear
Yourself are, after all, as false as what surrounds;
And why not be content? When we two watched the rounds
The boatman made, 'twixt shoal and sandbank, yesterday,
As, at dead slack of tide, he chose to push his way,
<sup>1380</sup> With oar and pole, across the creek, and reach the isle
After a world of pains—my word provoked your smile,
Yet none the less deserved reply: ''Twere wiser wait
The turn o' the tide, and find conveyance for his freight—
How easily—within the ship to purpose moored,'
<sup>1385</sup> Managed by sails, not oars! But no,—the man 's allured
By liking for the new and hard in his exploit!
First come shall serve! He makes,—courageous and adroit,—
The merest willow-leaf of boat do duty, bear
His merchandise across: once over, needs he care
<sup>1390</sup> If folk arrive by ship, six hours hence, fresh and gay?'
No: he scorns commonplace, affects the unusual way;
And good Elvire is moored, with not a breath to flap
The yards of her, no lift of ripple to o'erlap

---

<sup>1372</sup>| MS:there must §crossed out and replaced above by§ can be one <> more, for man §crossed out and replaced above by§ each, such   *1872:*be for each, one <> more, such   <sup>1374</sup>| MS:and Better: you   *1872:*and Better. You   <sup>1376</sup>| MS:surrounds:   *1872:*surrounds;   <sup>1381</sup>| MS:smile   *1872:*smile,   <sup>1382</sup>| MS:Yet still awaits §last two words crossed out and replaced above by four words§ none the less deserved reply: the m §last word and letter crossed out and replaced above by single quotation mark, apostrophe, and two words§ ''T were   <sup>1383</sup>| MS:and take §crossed out and replaced above by§ find <> freight   *1872:*freight—   <sup>1384</sup>| MS:'So easily—since, see—the skiff to   *1872:*'How easily—within the ship to   <sup>1385</sup>| MS:oars! §colon altered to exclamation point§ but §altered to§ But   <sup>1386</sup>| MS:exploit:   *1872:*exploit!   <sup>1387</sup>| MS:serve: he   *1872:*serve! He   <sup>1389</sup>| MS:merchandize   *1872:*merchandise   <sup>1390</sup>| MS:If you and I §last two words crossed out§ arrive by ship, §last two words and comma inserted above§ <> hence fresh   *1872:*If folk arrive <> hence, fresh   <sup>1391</sup>| MS:No: §word and colon inserted to left§ He §altered to§ he scorns the §crossed out§ <> way,   *1872:*way;   <sup>1392</sup>| MS:The §crossed out and replaced to left by§ And   <sup>1393</sup>| MS:In §crossed out§ the §altered to§ The sail §crossed out and replaced above by§ yards <> no wash §crossed out and replaced above by§ lift of wave §crossed out and replaced above by§ ripple to overlap §altered to§ o'erlap

Keel, much less, prow. What care? since here's a cockle-shell,
1395 Fifine, that's taut and crank, and carries just as well
Such seamanship as yours!"

LXXXII

Alack, our life is lent,
From first to last, the whole, for this experiment
Of proving what I say—that we ourselves are true!
I would there were one voyage, and then no more to do
1400 But tread the firmland, tempt the uncertain sea no more.
I would we might dispense with change of shore for shore
To evidence our skill, demonstrate—in no dream
It was, we tided o'er the trouble of the stream.
I would the steady voyage, and not the fitful trip,—
1405 Elvire, and not Fifine,—might test our seamanship.
But why expend one's breath to tell you, change of boat
Means change of tactics too? Come see the same afloat
To-morrow, all the change, new stowage fore and aft
O' the cargo; then, to cross requires new sailor-craft!
1410 To-day, one step from stern to bow keeps boat in trim:
To-morrow, some big stone,—or woe to boat and him!—
Must ballast both. That man stands for Mind, paramount
Throughout the adventure: ay, howe'er you make account,

---

1394| MS:prow: what care, since   *1872:*prow. What care? since   1395| MS:Fifine to wit §last two words crossed out§ that's taut and §last two words inserted above§ crank and   *1872:*Fifine, that's <> crank, and   1396| MS:Such §crossed out, replaced above by two illegibly crossed out words, and then restored§ sea-manship as §crossed out, replaced above by illegibly crossed out word, and then restored§ yours!" §¶ called for§   *1872:*seamanship   1400| MS:more: *1872:*more.   1401| MS:with further flitting o'er §last three words crossed out and replaced above by five words and comma§ change of shore for shore,   *1872:*for shore   1403| MS:was we <> stream! §colon altered to exclamation point§   *1872:*was, we <> stream.   1404| MS:voyage and   *1872:*voyage, and   1405| MS:Elvire and <> seamanship! *1872:*Elvire, and <> seamanship.   1407| MS:too? §colon altered to question mark§ when §crossed out and replaced above by§ Come <> a-float   *1872:*afloat   1408| MS:change, one fresh§last two words crossed out and replaced above by two words§ some shift from §inserted above illegibly crossed out word§ fore to §over illegible word§ aft   *1872:*change, new stowage fore and aft   1409| MS:cargo; §colon altered to semicolon§ and the case §last three words crossed out and replaced above by word, comma, and two words§ then, to cross <> sailorcraft!   *1872:*sailor-craft!   1410| MS:from bench to <> keep §next letter crossed out§   *1872:*from stern to <> keeps   1412| MS:man shall be the §crossed out§ mind §altered to§ Mind   *1872:*man stands for Mind   1413| MS:adventure—ay   *1872:*adventure: ay

'Tis mind that navigates,—skips over, twists between
<sup>1415</sup> The bales i' the boat,—now gives importance to the mean,
And now abates the pride of life, accepts all fact,
Discards all fiction,—steers Fifine, and cries, i' the act,
"Thou art so bad, and yet so delicate a brown!
Wouldst tell no end of lies : I talk to smile or frown!
<sup>1420</sup> Wouldst rob me: do men blame a squirrel, lithe and sly,
For pilfering the nut she adds to hoard? Nor I."
Elvire is true, as truth, honesty's self, alack!
The worse! too safe the ship, the transport there and back
Too certain! one may loll and lounge and leave the helm,
<sup>1425</sup> Let wind and tide do work: no fear that waves o'erwhelm
The steady-going bark, as sure to feel her way
Blindfold across, reach land, next year as yesterday!
How can I but suspect, the true feat were to slip
Down side, transfer myself to cockle-shell from ship,
<sup>1430</sup> And try if, trusting to sea-tracklessness, I class
With those around whose breast grew oak and triple brass:
Who dreaded no degree of death, but, with dry eyes,

---

<sup>1415</sup>| MS:boat, now §over illegible word§   *1872:*boat,—now   <sup>1416</sup>| MS:And §over illegible word§ < > accepts the §crossed out§   <sup>1417</sup>| MS:fiction—steers < > in < > act,— *1872:*fiction,—steers < > act,   *1889a:*i'   <sup>1419</sup>| MS:lies: I trust they §last two words crossed out and replaced above by two words§ talk to   <sup>1420</sup>| MS:me,—do you §crossed out and replaced above by§ men < > squirrel lithe < > sly   *1872:*me: do < > squirrel, lithe < > sly,   <sup>1421</sup>| MS:nut she < > I.   *1872:*nut, she   *1889a:*nut she §emended to§ hoard? Nor I." §see Editorial Notes§   <sup>1422</sup>| MS:You would not lies nor robs, are goodness' §last eight words crossed out and replaced above by seven words§ Elvire is §next word illegibly crossed out§ true as truth, honesty's self—Alack!   *1872:*true, as < > self, alack!   <sup>1423</sup>| MS:The ship's §crossed out and replaced above by word and exclamation point§ worse! < > safe §two illegibly crossed out words inserted above§ the ship, §two words and comma inserted above§   <sup>1424</sup>| MS:certain! §colon altered to exclamation point§   <sup>1426</sup>| MS:bark, that's §crossed out and replaced above by word and comma§ as, sure to feel §over illegible word§   *1872:*as sure   <sup>1427</sup>| MS:Blindfold < > land, to-day §crossed out and replaced above by two words§ next year < > yesterday.   *1872:*Blind-fold < > yesterday! *1889a:*Blindfold   <sup>1428</sup>| MS:can one §crossed out and replaced above by§ I < > suspect 'twere the real feat to   *1872:*suspect, the true feat were to   <sup>1430</sup>| MS:if, trusting to §last two words inserted above, followed by three illegibly crossed out words§ sea-truculence, §word and comma inserted above and then written out again in right margin§ I *1872:*to sea-tracklessness, I   <sup>1431</sup>| MS:With those §last two words inserted below§ around whose breast grew §inserted below illegibly crossed out word§ oak and triple brass §last eight words originally part of l. 1430§   <sup>1432</sup>| MS:Who, dreaded §next letter crossed out§ < > death, as §crossed out and replaced above by word and comma§ but,   *1872:*Who dreaded

79

Surveyed the turgid main and its monstrosities—
And rendered futile so, the prudent Power's decree
<sup>1435</sup> Of separate earth and disassociating sea;
Since, how is it observed, if impious vessels leap
Across, and tempt a thing they should not touch—the deep?
(See Horace to the boat, wherein, for Athens bound,
When Virgil must embark—Jove keep him safe and sound!—
<sup>1440</sup> The poet bade his friend start on the watery road,
Much re-assured by this so comfortable ode.)

## LXXXIII

Then, never grudge my poor Fifine her compliment!
The rakish craft could slip her moorings in the tent,
And, hoisting every stitch of spangled canvas, steer
<sup>1445</sup> Through divers rocks and shoals,—in fine, deposit here
Your Virgil of a spouse, in Attica: yea, thrid
The mob of men, select the special virtue hid
In him, forsooth, and say—or rather, smile so sweet,

---

<sup>1433|</sup>  MS:They saw §last two words crossed out and replaced above by§ Surveyed <> main with §crossed out and replaced above by§ and        <sup>1434|</sup>  MS:And proved that all in vain §last five words crossed out and replaced above by four words§ rendered futile so, a prudent *1872:*so, the prudent        <sup>1435|</sup>  MS:falling§crossed out and replaced above by two words§ Which cut from earth the disassociating §inserted above illegibly crossed out word or words§ sea,    *1872:*Of separate earth and disassociating sea;        <sup>1436|</sup>  MS:If §crossed out and replaced to left by§ Since, just the same as ever, these impious    *1872:*Since, how is it observed, if impious       <sup>1437|</sup>  MS:and cheat a <> they dare not <> deep.    *1872:*and tempt a <> they should not <> deep?       <sup>1438|</sup>  MS:(See §inserted above illegibly crossed out word§ <> the ship §crossed out and replaced above by§ boat        <sup>1439|</sup>  MS:When §inserted to left of illegibly crossed out word§        <sup>1441|</sup>  MS:By §crossed out and replaced above by§ With §crossed out and replaced above by§ Much reassurance §altered to§ re-assured of this §last two words crossed out and replaced above by three words§ by dint of comfortable    *1872:*by this so comfortable
<sup>1442|</sup>  MS:§¶ called for§ And shall you §last three words crossed out and replaced above by word, comma, and word§ Then, never        <sup>1443|</sup>  MS:Whose gypsey gear, trim §next word illegibly crossed out§ she's besprent §last seven words crossed out and replaced above by eleven words and comma, the first word being illegibly crossed out§ The rakish craft §inserted above illegibly crossed out word§ which §crossed out and replaced above by§ could slipped §altered to§ slip her moorings in the tent,        <sup>1444|</sup>  MS:Turban at top, tricot at underneath, could §next word illegible§ thrid §last nine words crossed out and replaced above by eight words§ And hoisting every stitch of spangled sail §crossed out and replaced to right by§ canvas, steer    *1872:*And, hoisting       <sup>1445|</sup>  MS:§line inserted above l. 1447§ Straight up to me §last four words crossed out§        <sup>1446|</sup>  MS:§line inserted to right§        <sup>1447|</sup>  MS:And §crossed out and replaced

"Of all the multitude, you—I prefer to cheat!
1450　Are you for Athens bound? I can perform the trip,
Shove little pinnace off, while yon superior ship,
The Elvire, refits in port!" So, off we push from beach
Of Pornic town, and lo, ere eye can wink, we reach
The Long Walls, and I prove that Athens is no dream,
1455　For there the temples rise! they are, they nowise seem!
Earth is not all one lie, this truth attests me true!
Thanks therefore to Fifine! Elvire, I'm back with you!
Share in the memories! Embark I trust we shall
Together some fine day, and so, for good and all,
1460　Bid Pornic Town adieu,—then, just the strait to cross,
And we reach harbour, safe, in Iostephanos!

LXXXIV

How quickly night comes! Lo, already 'tis the land
Turns sea-like; overcrept by grey, the plains expand,
Assume significance; while ocean dwindles, shrinks

---

above by§ The 　　　　1448| MS:or rather, §word and comma inserted above§ <> so §next word
illegibly crossed out§ sweet 　*1872:*sweet, 　　　1451| MS:My §crossed out and replaced above
by§ Shove <> pinnace gay with streamer, §last three words and comma crossed out and
replaced above by word and comma§ off, <> yon superior §inserted above
1452| MS:The Elvire, §last two words and comma inserted to left§ Refits §altered to§ refits <>
port! §colon altered to exclamation point§ <> we put from 　*1872:*we push from
1454| MS:The long §altered to§ Long walls §altered to§ Walls, and I prove §over illegible word§
<> dream 　*1872:*dream, 　　　1455| MS:temples tower, §word and comma crossed out and
replaced above by word and colon§ rise: they <> seem, 　*1872:*rise! they <> seem!
1456| MS:attests it §crossed out and replaced above by§ me true, 　*1872:*true!
1457| MS:Your help, §last two words and comma crossed out and replaced to left by two words§
Thanks for §crossed out and replaced above by two words§ therefore to <> you! §colon altered
to exclamation point§ 　　　1458| MS:memories! §colon altered to exclamation point§ we
meditate return §last three words crossed out and replaced above by§ embark 　*1872:*memories!
Embark 　　　1459| MS:and then §crossed out and replaced above by§ so <> all, §next word
illegibly crossed out§ cross §crossed out§ 　　　1460| MS:Abide i' the city, safe in §last six words
crossed out and replaced above by five words§ Gain nor lease, were Athene §last five words
crossed out§ Bid Pornic Town, adieu,—then, just the strait to cross, 　*1872:*Bid Pornic Town
adieu 　　　1461| MS:§line inserted above l. 1462§ safe in 　*1872:*safe, in
1462| MS:§¶ called for§ quick §altered to§ quickly <> comes! Turn round §last two words
crossed out and replaced above by word and comma§ Lo, 　　　1463| MS:sea-like: overcrept
*1872:*sea-like; overcrept 　　　1464| MS:Grow great and mean no more, §last six words and
comma crossed out and replaced above by two words and comma§ Assume significance, while
the sea §last two words crossed out and replaced above by§ ocean 　*1872:*significance; while

1465 Into a pettier bound: its plash and plaint, methinks,
Six steps away, how both retire, as if their part
Were played, another force were free to prove her art,
Protagonist in turn! Are you unterrified?
All false, all fleeting too! And nowhere things abide,
1470 And everywhere we strain that things should stay,—the one
Truth, that ourselves are true!

LXXXV

A word, and I have done.
Is it not just our hate of falsehood, fleetingness,
And the mere part, things play, that constitutes express
The inmost charm of this Fifine and all her tribe?
1475 Actors! We also act, but only they inscribe
Their style and title so, and preface, only they,
Performance with "A lie is all we do or say."
Wherein but there can be the attraction, Falsehood's bribe,
That wins so surely o'er to Fifine and her tribe
1480 The liking, nay the love of who hate Falsehood most,
Except that these alone of mankind make their boast
"Frankly, we simulate!" To feign, means—to have grace

---

1465| MS:bound, its noise §crossed out and replaced above by§ plash and fret, §word and
comma crossed out and replaced above by word and comma§ plaint, methinks; §colon altered
to semicolon§  *1872:*bound: its <> methinks,      1466| MS:away, and §crossed out and
replaced above by§ how <> retire! as  *1872:*retire, as      1468| MS:In turn protagonist: §last
three words transposed and altered to§ Protagonist in turn: are  *1872:*turn! Are
1469| MS:no where <> abide  *1872:*nowhere <> abide,      1471| MS:true! §colon altered to
exclamation point, and ¶ called for§ <> word and  *1872:*word, and
1472| MS:just through §crossed out and replaced above by§ our      1473| MS:the mere
§inserted above§ part all §crossed out§ <> play, that §crossed out, replaced above by *which*, and
then restored§  *1872:*part, things      1475| MS:They also play their part, §last five words and
comma crossed out and replaced above by word, semicolon, three words, comma, and four
words§ Actors; we also act, but only they inscribe  *1872:*Actors! We      1476| MS:Their style
and title so: §last five words and colon inserted above l. 1477§ but preface  *1872:*so, and preface
1478| MS:Wherein but here can be §last four words crossed out and replaced above by three
words§ do you detect§ last three words crossed out and the original four words restored§ but
here can be <> bribe  *1872:*but there, can <> bribe,  *1889a:*there can
1479| MS:o'er just those §last two words crossed out and replaced above by five words§ to Fifine
and her tribe      1480| MS:§line inserted above l. 1481§ who hate §crossed out and then
restored§ Falsehood §inserted above illegibly crossed out word§
1481| MS:But in the §last three words crossed out and replaced above by two words§ Except that
these §over illegible word§      1482| MS:simulate! §colon altered to exclamation point§

And so get gratitude! This ruler of the race,
Crowned, sceptred, stoled to suit,—'tis not that you detect
1485 The cobbler in the king, but that he makes effect
By seeming the reverse of what you know to be
The man, the mind, whole form, fashion and quality.
Mistake his false for true, one minute,—there's an end
Of the admiration! Truth, we grieve at or rejoice:
1490 'Tis only falsehood, plain in gesture, look and voice,
That brings the praise desired, since profit comes thereby.
The histrionic truth is in the natural lie.
Because the man who wept the tears was, all the time,
Happy enough; because the other man, a-grime
1495 With guilt, was, at the least, as white as I and you;
Because the timid type of bashful maidhood, who
Starts at her own pure shade, already numbers seven
Born babes and, in a month, will turn their odd to even;
Because the saucy prince would prove, could you unfurl
1500 Some yards of wrap, a meek and meritorious girl—
Precisely as you see success attained by each
O' the mimes, do you approve, not foolishly impeach
The falsehood!

LXXXVI

That's the first o' the truths found: all things, slow
Or quick i' the passage, come at last to that, you know!
1505 Each has a false outside, whereby a truth is forced

---

<sup>1483</sup>| MS:And to §crossed out and replaced above by§ so <> gratitude! §colon altered to
exclamation point§ this §altered to§ This        <sup>1487</sup>| MS:mind, the whole §inserted above§ <>
fashion, and §crossed out§ quality.   *1872:*mind, whole <> fashion, and quality.   *1889a:*fashion and
<sup>1489</sup>| MS:admiration! §colon altered to exclamation point§ truth's §altered to§ Truth to
§crossed out and replaced above by§ we   *1872:*Truth, we        <sup>1490</sup>| MS:'Tis §inserted to left§
Only <> gesture, look §inserted above§   *1872:*only        <sup>1491</sup>| MS:praise—desired since
*1872:*praise desired, since        <sup>1492</sup>| MS:You must §last two words crossed out and replaced
above by two words§ The histrionic        <sup>1494</sup>| MS:enough: because   *1872:*enough; because
<sup>1495</sup>| MS:white as you §crossed out and replaced above by§ I <> you:   *1872:*you;
<sup>1498</sup>| MS:even:   *1872:*even;        <sup>1499</sup>| MS:Because yo §incomplete word crossed out and
replaced above by§ the        <sup>1502</sup>| MS:the mimes §over illegible word§
<sup>1503</sup>| MS:falsehood! §colon altered to exclamation point, and ¶ called for§ that's §altered to§
That's        <sup>1504</sup>| MS:come to §crossed out and replaced above by§ that §crossed out§

To issue from within: truth, falsehood, are divorced
By the excepted eye, at the rare season, for
The happy moment. Life means—learning to abhor
The false, and love the true, truth treasured snatch by snatch,
1510   Waifs counted at their worth. And when with strays they match
I' the parti-coloured world,—when, under foul, shines fair,
And truth, displayed i' the point, flashes forth everywhere
I' the circle, manifest to soul, though hid from sense,
And no obstruction more affects this confidence,—
1515   When faith is ripe for sight,—why, reasonably, then
Comes the great clearing-up. Wait threescore years and ten!

### LXXXVII

Therefore I prize stage-play, the honest cheating; thence
The impulse pricked, when fife and drum bade Fair commence,
To bid you trip and skip, link arm in arm with me,
1520   Like husband and like wife, and so together see
The tumbling-troop arrayed, the strollers on their stage
Drawn up and under arms, and ready to engage.
And if I started thence upon abstruser themes . . .
Well, 'twas a dream, pricked too!

### LXXXVIII

A poet never dreams:
1525   We prose-folk always do: we miss the proper duct
For thoughts on things unseen, which stagnate and obstruct
The system, therefore; mind, sound in a body sane,
Keeps thoughts apart from facts, and to one flowing vein
Confines its sense of that which is not, but might be,
1530   And leaves the rest alone. What ghosts do poets see?

---

1506|   MS:within: two qualities divorced   *1872*:within: truth, falsehood, are divorced
1509|   MS:false and   *1872*:false, and     1510|   MS:worth: and   *1872*:worth. And
1511|   MS:particolored   *1872*:parti-colored     1513|   MS:soul though   *1872*:soul, though
1517|   MS:§¶ called for§ cheating: thence   *1872*:cheating; thence     1520|   MS:wife and
*1872*:wife, and     1522|   MS:arms and   *1872*:arms, and     1524|   MS:too! §¶ called for§
1525|   MS:always,—minds that miss   *1872*:always do: we miss
1527|   MS:therefore: mind sound <> sane   *1872*:therefore; mind, sound <> sane,
1529| MS:be, §colon erased and replaced by comma§

What dæmons fear? what man or thing misapprehend?
Unchoked, the channel's flush, the fancy's free to spend
Its special self aright in manner, time and place.
Never believe that who create the busy race
<sup></sup>O' the brain, bring poetry to birth, such act performed,
Feel trouble them, the same, such residue as warmed
My prosy blood, this morn,—intrusive fancies, meant
For outbreak and escape by quite another vent!
Whence follows that, asleep, my dreamings oft exceed
The bound. But you shall hear.

LXXXIX

I smoked. The webs o' the weed,
With many a break i' the mesh, were floating to re-form
Cupola-wise above: chased thither by soft warm
Inflow of air without; since I—of mind to muse, to clench
The gain of soul and body, got by their noon-day drench
In sun and sea,—had flung both frames o' the window wide,
To soak my body still and let soul soar beside.

1535, 1540, 1545 (margin line numbers)

---

1531| MS:fear, what   *1872:*fear? what        1533| MS:in manner §over illegible erasure§
1534| MS:that one creator of the race   *1872:*that who create the busy race
1535| MS:brain, who used §altered to§ uses his §crossed out§ might in the act, that §crossed out§
and replaced above by§ such   *1872:*brain, bring poetry to birth, such
1536| MS:Felt §altered to§ Feels trouble, all the same, such §over illegible word§ residue that
§crossed out and replaced above by§ as   *1872:*Feel trouble them, the
1537| MS:His §crossed out and replaced above by two words§ My prosy blood, at work or play
§last four words crossed out and replaced above by two words, comma, and dash§ this morn,—
intrusive stuff, was §last two words crossed out and replaced above by word and comma§ fancy,
*1872:*fancies        1539| MS:that I dream, asleep §last three words transposed to§ that, asleep I
dream,—awake indeed,—   *1872:*asleep, my dreamings oft exceed        1540| MS:As chanced,
this very day. §last three words and period crossed out and replaced above by dash, four words,
and period§ —but you shall hear. §¶ called for§ The smokey- §word and hyphen inserted
above§ webs of the fine §crossed out§ weed,   *1872:*The bound. But <> hear. I smoked. The
webs o' the weed,        1542| MS:Cupola-wise §inserted above§ Above §altered to§ above:
§colon inserted§ me, §word and comma crossed out§ chased on high §last two words crossed
out and replaced above by§ thither by the in-flow §last two words crossed out§ soft, and §crossed
out§        1543| MS:In-flow §inserted to left§ Of the §crossed out§ air from outside §last two
words crossed out and replaced above by§ without, since, I was §crossed out and replaced above
by dash§ —of <> to muse, to §last two words inserted above§   *1872:*Inflow of <> without;
since   *1889a:*since I        1544| MS:body got   *1872:*body, got
1545| MS:Of §crossed out and replaced to left by§ In <> sea, so §crossed out and replaced
above by dash and word§ —I   *1889a:*sea,—had flung        1546| MS:To §over illegible
erasure§ soaked §altered to§ soak my body §inserted above§ still, and   *1889a:*still and

In came the country sounds and sights and smells—that fine
Sharp needle in the nose from our fermenting wine!
In came a dragon-fly with whir and stir, then out,
1550　　Off and away: in came,—kept coming, rather,—pout
Succeeding smile, and take-away still close on give,—
One loose long creeper-branch, tremblingly sensitive
To risks which blooms and leaves,—each leaf tongue-broad, each bloom
Mid-finger-deep,—must run by prying in the room
1555　　Of one who loves and grasps and spoils and speculates.
All so far plain enough to sight and sense: but, weights,
Measures and numbers,—ah, could one apply such test
To other visitants that came at no request
Of who kept open house,—to fancies manifold
1560　　From this four-cornered world, the memories new and old,
The antenatal prime experience—what know I?—
The initiatory love preparing us to die—
Such were a crowd to count, a sight to see, a prize
To turn to profit, were but fleshly ears and eyes
1565　　Able to cope with those o' the spirit!

XC

Therefore,—since
Thought hankers after speech, while no speech may evince
Feeling like music,—mine, o'erburthened with each gift
From every visitant, at last resolved to shift

---

[1548]　MS:nose is §crossed out§ from our §inserted above§　　　[1549]　MS:whir of §crossed out
and replaced above by§ enough §crossed out and replaced above by two words§ and stir
[1550]　MS:coming, going §crossed out and replaced above by§ rather
[1552]　MS:creeper's branch §last two words altered to§ creeperbranch　　*1872:*creeper-branch
[1553]　MS:Of all its §last three words crossed out and replaced above by two words and comma§
To what §crossed out§ danger, blooms　　*1872:*To risk, which blooms　　*1889a:*risks which
[1554]　MS:must brave by　　*1872:*must run by　　　　[1555]　MS:speculates:—　　*1872:*speculates.
[1556]　MS:Each and §last two words crossed out§ all §altered to§ All, so far, §comma, two words,
and comma inserted above§ plain enough §crossed out and then restored§ < > but,—weights,
*1872:*but, weights,　　*1889a:*All so far plain　　　　[1557]　MS:apply the test
*1872:*apply such test　　　　[1565]　MS:spirit! §colon altered to exclamation point, and ¶ called
for§ Therefore,— §dash inserted§　　　　[1566]　MS:Thought always craves for §last three words
crossed out and replaced above by two words§ hankers after speech, and §crossed out and
replaced above by§ while < > speech will §crossed out and replaced above by§ may

Its burthen to the back of some musician dead
1570 And gone, who feeling once what I feel now, instead
Of words, sought sounds, and saved for ever, in the same,
Truth that escapes prose,—nay, puts poetry to shame.
I read the note, I strike the key, I bid *record*
The instrument—thanks greet the veritable word!
1575 And not in vain I urge: "O dead and gone away,
Assist who struggles yet, thy strength become my stay,
Thy record serve as well to register—I felt
And knew thus much of truth! With me, must knowledge melt
Into surmise and doubt and disbelief, unless
1580 Thy music reassure—I gave no idle guess,
But gained a certitude I yet may hardly keep!
What care? since round is piled a monumental heap
Of music that conserves the assurance, thou as well
Wast certain of the same! thou, master of the spell,
1585 Mad'st moonbeams marble, didst *record* what other men
Feel only to forget!" Who was it helped me, then?
What master's work first came responsive to my call,
Found my eye, fixed my choice?

---

1569| MS:Nay §crossed out and replaced above by§ Its      1570| MS:once what §inserted
above illegibly erased word§ <> feel, found instead    *1872:*feel now, instead
1571| MS:words, the §crossed out and replaced above by§ fit sounds    *1872:*words, sought
sounds      1572| MS:What clean §last two words crossed out and replaced above by two
words§ Truth that <> shame:    *1872:*shame.      1573| MS:One reads <> note, one strikes
<> key, one bids    *1872:*key, one    *1889a:*I read <> note, I strike <> key, I bid
1575| MS:One cries, and not in vain §last six words transposed and altered to§ And not in vain
One cries, O    *1872:*one cries: "O    *1889a:*vain I urge: "O      1576| MS:become his §crossed
out and replaced above by§ my      1577| MS:register I §inserted above illegibly crossed out
word§    *1872:*register—I      1578| MS:truth! With him §crossed out and replaced above by§
me, must §over illegible word§      1580| MS:reassure he §crossed out and replaced above by§
I    *1872:*reassure—I      1581| MS:certitude,—himself §altered to§ myself may
*1872:*certitude, myself    *1889a:*certitude, I yet may      1582| MS:care? while round
*1872:*care? since round      1583| MS:conserves experience—thou    *1872:*conserves the
assurance, thou      1584| MS:same, and, master    *1872:*same! thou, master
1585| MS:Made <> marble, left on record that all men    *1872:*Mad'st <> marble, didst *record*
what other men      1586| MS:Who §over illegible word§ live and die so feel some once, and,
now and then,    *1872:*Feel only to forget! Who was it helped me, then?    *1889a:*forget!"
1587| MS:Some . . who is it to be? on which work first let fall    *1872:*What master's work first
came responsive to my call,      1588| MS:My finger, and §last two words crossed out and
replaced above by three words§ eye and fix <> choice? §¶ called for§ Why, Schumann's
Carnival!    *1872:*Found my eye, fixed <> Why, Schumann's "Carnival!"

XCI

Why, Schumann's "Carnival!"
My choice chimed in, you see, exactly with the sounds
<sup>1590</sup> And sights of yestereve when, going on my rounds,
Where both roads join the bridge, I heard across the dusk
Creak a slow caravan, and saw arrive the husk
O' the spice-nut, which peeled off this morning, and displayed,
'Twixt tree and tree, a tent whence the red pennon made
<sup>1595</sup> Its vivid reach for home and ocean-idleness—
And where, my heart surmised, at that same moment,—yes,—
Tugging her *tricot* on,—yet tenderly, lest stitch
Announce the crack of doom, reveal disaster which
Our Pornic's modest stock of merceries in vain
<sup>1600</sup> Were ransacked to retrieve,—there, cautiously a-strain,
(My heart surmised) must crouch in that tent's corner, curved
Like Spring-month's russet moon, some girl by fate reserved
To give me once again the electric snap and spark
Which prove, when finger finds out finger in the dark
<sup>1605</sup> O' the world, there's fire and life and truth there, link but hands
And pass the secret on. Lo, link by link, expands
The circle, lengthens out the chain, till one embrace
Of high with low is found uniting the whole race,
Not simply you and me and our Fifine, but all
<sup>1610</sup> The world: the Fair expands into the Carnival,
And Carnival again to . . . ah, but that's my dream!

---

<sup>1589|</sup>  MS:—Choice chiming  *1889a:*My choice chimed  <sup>1590|</sup>  MS:rounds  *1872:*rounds,
<sup>1592|</sup>  MS:caravan and  *1872:*caravan, and  <sup>1593|</sup>  MS:morning and  *1872:*morning, and
<sup>1594|</sup>  MS:and tree a  *1872:*and tree, a  <sup>1595|</sup>  MS:Its vivid §inserted above§
<sup>1597|</sup>  MS:tricot <> yet tender lest some stitch  *1872:*yet tenderly, lest stitch  *1889a: tricot*
<sup>1599|</sup>  MS:All §crossed out and replaced above by§ Our Pornic's modest stock of § last three
words inserted above§ merceries, in  *1872:*merceries in  <sup>1600|</sup>  MS:to repair §altered to§
retrieve  <sup>1601|</sup>  MS:My <> surmised, must  *1872:* (My <> surmised) must
<sup>1602|</sup>  MS:Like April's §crossed out and replaced above by§ Spring-month's
<sup>1604|</sup>  MS:prove when  *1872:*prove, when  <sup>1605|</sup>  MS:there, chain §crossed out and
replaced above by two words§ link but  <sup>1606|</sup>  MS:on!—till, link  *1872:*on! till
*1889a:*on. Lo, link  <sup>1607|</sup>  MS:chain, till §crossed out and replaced above by§ and one
*1889a:*chain, till one  <sup>1609|</sup>  MS:all the §erased§  <sup>1610|</sup>  MS:world—the <> the
Carnival  *1889a:*world: the <> the Carnival,  <sup>1611|</sup>  MS:to—ah  *1872:*to . . . ah

## XCII

I somehow played the piece: remarked on each old theme
I' the new dress; saw how food o' the soul, the stuff that's made
To furnish man with thought and feeling, is purveyed
<sup>1615</sup> Substantially the same from age to age, with change
Of the outside only for successive feasters. Range
The banquet-room o' the world, from the dim farthest head
O' the table, to its foot, for you and me bespread,
This merry morn, we find sufficient fare, I trow.
<sup>1620</sup> But, novel? Scrape away the sauce; and taste, below,
The verity o' the viand,—you shall perceive there went
To board-head just the dish which other condiment
Makes palatable now: guests came, sat down, fell-to,
Rose up, wiped mouth, went way,—lived, died,—and never knew
<sup>1625</sup> That generations yet should, seeking sustenance,
Still find the selfsame fare, with somewhat to enhance
Its flavour, in the kind of cooking. As with hates
And loves and fears and hopes, so with what emulates
The same, expresses hates, loves, fears and hopes in Art:
<sup>1630</sup> The forms, the themes—no one without its counterpart
Ages ago; no one but, mumbled the due time
I' the mouth of the eater, needs be cooked again in rhyme,
Dished up anew in paint, sauce-smothered fresh in sound,

---

<sup>1612|</sup>　MS:§¶ called for§　　　<sup>1613|</sup>　MS:dress: how the food　　*1872:*dress; saw how food
<sup>1614|</sup>　MS:To yield §crossed out and replaced above by§ furnish　　　<sup>1616|</sup>　MS:for the feasters:
range　　*1872:*for successive feasters. Range　　　<sup>1617|</sup>　MS:from the dim §last two words
inserted above§　　　<sup>1618|</sup>　MS:foot for < > bespread　　*1872:*foot, for < > bespread,
<sup>1619|</sup>　MS:To-day §crossed out and replaced above by§ This merry morning with sufficient < >
trow:　　*1872:*merry morn, we find sufficient < > trow.　　　<sup>1620|</sup>　MS:novel? Put aside §last
two words crossed out and replaced above by two words§ Scrape away < > sauce and prick
§crossed out and replaced above by§ taste below　　*1872:*sauce; and taste, below,
<sup>1621|</sup>　MS:viand,—and you shall find there　　*1872:*viand,—you shall perceive there
<sup>1622|</sup>　MS:board-head the same §crossed out and replaced above by§ one dish
*1872:*board-head just the dish　　　<sup>1624|</sup>　MS:up, wiped mouth, §last two words and comma
inserted above§ and went their §inserted above and then crossed out§ away §altered to§ way,—
lived, died,— §dash, two words, comma, and dash inserted above§ < > knew,　　*1872:*mouth,
went < > knew　　　<sup>1625|</sup>　MS:How many a generation should still seek sustenance　　*1872:*That
generations yet should, seeking sustenance,　　　<sup>1626|</sup>　MS:And find < > with something
§altered to§ somewhat　　*1872:*Still find　　　<sup>1627|</sup>　MS:flavour in　　*1872:*flavour, in
<sup>1629|</sup>　MS:in Art,—　　*1872:*in Art:　　　<sup>1631|</sup>　MS:ago, no　　*1872:*ago; no
<sup>1633|</sup>　MS:Fashioned afresh §last two words crossed out and replaced above by three words§
Dished up anew < > paint, dress §crossed out and replaced above by§ sauce

To suit the wisdom-tooth, just cut, of the age, that's found
1635 With gums obtuse to gust and smack which relished so
The meat o' the meal folk made some fifty years ago.
But don't suppose the new was able to efface
The old without a struggle, a pang! The commonplace
Still clung about his heart, long after all the rest
1640 O' the natural man, at eye and ear, was caught, confessed
The charm of change, although wry lip and wrinkled nose
Owned ancient virtue more conducive to repose
Than modern nothings roused to somethings by some shred
Of pungency, perchance garlic in amber's stead.
1645 And so on, till one day, another age, by due
Rotation, pries, sniffs, smacks, discovers old is new,
And sauce, our sires pronounced insipid, proves again
Sole piquant, may resume its titillating reign—
With music, most of all the arts, since change is there
1650 The law, and not the lapse: the precious means the rare,
And not the absolute in all good save surprise.
So I remarked upon our Schumann's victories

---

1634| MS:the infant §crossed out and replaced above by§ altered §crossed out§ taste §crossed
out and replaced above by three words§ wisdom-tooth just cut of the infant §inserted above and
then crossed out and replaced above by§ bestial §crossed out§ *1872:*wisdom-tooth, just cut, of
1635| MS:smack that §crossed out and replaced above by§ which       1636| MS:meat which
made §last two words crossed out and replaced above by§ o' <> meal was made §last two words
inserted above§ *1872:*meal folks made       1637| MS:Yet §altered to§ But
1638| MS:pang: the   *1872:*pang! The       1639| MS:about the heart   *1872:*about his heart
1640| MS:man was caught at eye and ear, confessed   *1872:*man, at eye and ear, was caught,
confessed       1641| MS:After §crossed out and replaced above by dash and two words§ —Safe
through the first essay, wry <> nose,—   *1872:*The charm of change, although wry <> nose
1642| MS:The ancient virtue too §crossed out and replaced above by§ more   *1872:*Owned
ancient       1643| MS:modern trash turned right §crossed out and replaced above by§ rich
and rousing by   *1872:*modern nothing roused to something by   *1889a:*nothings
1644| MS:Of pungent stuff, what §inserted above§ though but §crossed out§ garlic <> stead?
§exclamation point altered to question mark§   *1872:*Of pungency, perchance   *1889a:*stead.
1646| MS:Rotation, stumbles back and finds our §last five words crossed out and replaced above
by word, comma, word, comma, and two words§ pries, sniffs, and pries §last two words crossed
out and replaced above by§ tastes, pronounces §crossed out and replaced to right by§ discovers
old things §crossed out and replaced above by§ is new,   *1872:*sniffs, smacks, discovers <> new.
*1889a:*new,       1648| MS:The §crossed out and replaced above by§ Sole piquant, and resumes
<> reign   *1872:*reign—   *1872:*piquant, may resume       1649| MS:With §over illegible word
1650| MS:lapse; the <> rare   *1872:*lapse: the <> rare,       1651| MS:the perfect gift §last two
words crossed out and replaced above by two words§ absolute in <> surprize.   *1872:*surprise.

Over the commonplace, how faded phrase grew fine,
And palled perfection—piqued, upstartled by that brine,
1655   His pickle—bit the mouth and burnt the tongue aright,
Beyond the merely good no longer exquisite:
Then took things as I found, and thanked without demur
The pretty piece—played through that movement, you prefer,
Where dance and shuffle past,—he scolding while she pouts,
1660   She canting while he calms, —in those eternal bouts
Of age, the dog—with youth, the cat—by rose-festoon
Tied teasingly enough—Columbine, Pantaloon:
She, toe-tips and *staccato,*—*legato* shakes his poll
And shambles in pursuit, the senior. *Fi la folle!*
1665   Lie to him! get his gold and pay its price! begin
Your trade betimes, nor wait till you've wed Harlequin
And need, at the week's end, to play the duteous wife,
And swear you still love slaps and leapings more than life!
Pretty! I say.

---

1654|   MS:perfection, steeped and §last two words crossed out and replaced above by word, dash, word and hyphen§ stung—up-startled   *1872:*perfection, piqued, up-startled
*1889a:*perfection—piqued, upstartled     1655|   MS:pickle, burnt the mouth and bit §last five words transposed to§ pickle, bit the mouth and burnt the <> aright   *1872:*aright,
*1889a:*pickle—bit     1656|   MS:the merely §crossed out and then restored§ beautiful §crossed out and replaced above by§ good not §crossed out and replaced above by two words§ no longer exquisite,—   *1872:*exquisite:     1657|   MS:Then frankly §crossed out and replaced above by§ took bade §crossed out and replaced above by illegibly crossed out word§ him lead, and marched §two words, comma, and two words crossed out and replaced above by four words, comma, and two words§ things as I found, and thanked     1658|   MS:piece—got past §last two words crossed out and replaced above by two words§ played through
1659|   MS:past, he   *1872:*past,—he     1660|   MS:calms, in   *1872:*calms,—in
1661|   MS:dog, with <> cat, whom ros §word and partial word crossed out and replaced above by two words§ by rose-festoon   *1872:*dog—with <> cat—by
1662|   MS:Ties up to §last two words crossed out§ teazing §altered to§ teazingly for ever—
Columbine, Panataloon,   *1872:*Tied   *1889a:*teasingly enough—Columbine, Pantaloon:
1664|   MS:pursuit the senior. §colon altered to period§   *fi,* §altered to§ *Fi, la   1872:*pursuit, the senior. *Fi la*     1665|   MS:him, get <> price, begin   *1872:*him! get <> price! begin
1666|   MS:betimes nor   *1872:*betimes, nor     1667|   MS:A single §inserted above§ week, §last three words and comma crossed out§ before §altered to§ Before at the week's end §last four words inserted above§ you play <> wife   *1872:*And need, at <> end, to play <> wife,
1668|   MS:And tell him that t §last three words and partial word crossed out and replaced above by two words§ swear you <> love his §crossed out and replaced above by two words§ slaps and leaping   *1872:*leapings     1669|   MS:Pretty! §semicolon altered to exclamation point§ I say. §colon altered to period, and ¶ called for§ and §altered to§ And

91

## XCIII

And so I somehow-nohow played
1670 The whole o' the pretty piece; and then . . . whatever weighed
My eyes down, furled the films about my wits? suppose,
The morning-bath,—the sweet monotony of those
Three keys, flat, flat and flat, never a sharp at all,—
Or else the brain's fatigue, forced even here to fall
1675 Into the same old track, and recognize the shift
From old to new, and back to old again, and,—swift
Or slow, no matter,—still the certainty of change,
Conviction we shall find the false, where'er we range,
In art no less than nature: or what if wrist were numb,
1680 And over-tense the muscle, abductor of the thumb,
Taxed by those tenths' and twelfths' unconscionable stretch?
Howe'er it came to pass, I soon was far to fetch—
Gone off in company with Music!

## XCIV

Whither bound
Except for Venice? She it was, by instinct found
1685 Carnival-country proper, who far below the perch
Where I was pinnacled, showed, opposite, Mark's Church,
And, underneath, Mark's Square, with those two lines of street,

---

1670| MS:piece: and then . . whatever  *1872:*piece; and  *1889a:*then . . . whatever
1671| MS:down, wound §crossed out and replaced above by§ furled <> wits,—suppose,
*1872:*wits? suppose,  1673| MS:and flat,— §dash erased§ and not §last two words crossed
out and replaced above by§ never  1675| MS:track and <> the change §crossed out and
replaced above by§ shift  *1872:*track, and  1676| MS:new and then §crossed out and
replaced above by§ back <> again, and, swift  *1872:*new, and  *1889a:*again, and,—swift
1677| MS:matter, still  *1889a:*matter,—still  1678| MS:false where'er  *1872:*false, where'er
1679| MS:In Art <> nature,—or  *1889a:*In art <> nature: or
1680| MS:And over-stretched §altered to§ over-tasked the abductor muscle, §last two words
transposed to§ the muscle, abductor  *1872:*And over-tense  1681| MS:Taxed §over
illegible erasure§ <> stretch,—  *1872:*stretch?  1682| MS:fetch,  *1872:*fetch,—
*1889a:*fetch—  1683| MS:with Schuman §crossed out and replaced above by word and
punctuation§ music §altered to§ Music. §comma altered to period§ whither § altered to§
Whither  1684| MS:instinct crowned §crossed out and replaced above by word and
comma§ found,  *1889a:*found  1685| MS:who underneath my §last two words crossed out
and replaced above by three words§ far below the  1686| MS:opposite, her §crossed out
and replaced above by§ Mark's church, §altered to§ Church,  1687| MS:underneath, her
§altered to§ his square  *1872:*underneath, Mark's square  *1889a:*Square

*Procuratié*-sides, each leading to my feet—
Since from above I gazed, however I got there.

## XCV

1690    And what I gazed upon was a prodigious Fair,
Concourse immense of men and women, crowned or casqued,
Turbaned or tiar'd, wreathed, plumed, hatted or wigged, but
    masked—
Always masked,—only, how? No face-shape, beast or bird,
Nay, fish and reptile even, but someone had preferred,
1695   From out its frontispiece, feathered or scaled or curled,
To make the vizard whence himself should view the world,
And where the world believed himself was manifest.
Yet when you came to look, mixed up among the rest
More funnily by far, were masks to imitate
1700   Humanity's mishap: the wrinkled brow, bald pate
And rheumy eyes of Age, peak'd chin and parchment chap,
Were signs of day-work done, and wage-time near,—mishap
Merely; but, Age reduced to simple greed and guile,
Worn apathetic else as some smooth slab, erewhile

---

1688| MS:That constitute the §last three words crossed out and replaced above by word and hyphen§ *Pocuratié*-sides, each §over illegible erasure§    1689| MS:Since §inserted above§ I gazing §altered to§ gazed from above, however < > there. §dash crossed out and replaced by period§   *1889a:*Since from above I gazed, however   1690| MS:§¶ called for§ fair, *1889a:*Fair,   1691| MS:Or flock at least §last four words crossed out and replaced above by two words§ Concourse immense < > crowned and §crossed out and replaced above by§ or casqued  *1872:*casqued,   1692| MS:Turbaned and §crossed out and replaced above by§ or tiar'd, plumed, wreathed, §last two words transposed to§ wreathed, plumed, hatted §inserted above§ < > but always §crossed out§   1693| MS:Only, §word and comma crossed out and replaced above by§ Always masked,—only, §dash, word, and comma inserted above§ how? No face- §last word and hyphen inserted above§   1694| MS:preferred  *1872:*preferred,   1695| MS:§line inserted above l. 1696§   1697| MS:world should find §last two words crossed out and replaced above by§ believed   1698| MS:But §crossed out and replaced above by§ Yet   1700| MS:Humanity's mishaps §crossed out and replaced above by§ disgraced §crossed out and the original word restored§ mishaps; §comma crossed out and replaced by semicolon§ the §inserted above§  *1872:*mishap: the   1701| MS:of Age, peaked §altered to§ peak'd   1702| MS:of work-day §altered to§ day-work done and rest at hand §last three words crossed out and replaced above by two words§ wage-time near  *1872:*done, and   1703| MS:to simple §inserted above§ greediness §altered to§ greed   1704| MS:And §crossed out and replaced above by§ Worn < > as some §inserted above§ smooth worn §crossed out§ slab erewhile  *1872:*slab, erewhile

<sup>1705</sup> A clear-cut man-at-arms i' the pavement, till foot's tread
Effaced the sculpture, left the stone you saw instead,—
Was not that terrible beyond the mere uncouth?
Well, and perhaps the next revolting you was Youth,
Stark ignorance and crude conceit, half smirk, half stare
<sup>1710</sup> On that frank fool-face, gay beneath its head of hair
Which covers nothing.

XCVI

These, you are to understand,
Were the mere hard and sharp distinctions. On each hand,
I soon became aware, flocked the infinitude
Of passions, loves and hates, man pampers till his mood
<sup>1715</sup> Becomes himself, the whole sole face we name him by,
Nor want denotement else, if age or youth supply
The rest of him: old, young,—classed creature: in the main
A love, a hate, a hope, a fear, each soul a-strain
Some one way through the flesh—the face, an evidence
<sup>1720</sup> O' the soul at work inside; and, all the more intense,
So much the more grotesque.

XCVII

"Why should each soul be tasked
Some one way, by one love or else one hate?" I asked.

---

<sup>1705|</sup> MS:A marble §crossed out and replaced above by§ clear-cut man of mark §last two words crossed out and replaced above by two hyphens and two words§ -at-arms <> till foot's §over illegible erasure§ <sup>1706|</sup> MS:left that §altered to§ the <> you see §altered to§ saw <sup>1707|</sup> MS:§line inserted above l. 1708§ <sup>1711|</sup> MS:nothing. §colon altered to period, and ¶ called for§ these §altered to§ These <sup>1712|</sup> MS:distinctions: on *1872:*distinctions. On <sup>1714|</sup> MS:till the §crossed out and replaced above by§ his <sup>1715|</sup> MS:face we recognize, §last two words and comma crossed out and replaced above by four words and comma§ we name him by, <sup>1716|</sup> MS:youth supplies §altered to§ supply <sup>1717|</sup> MS:The §over illegible erasure§ <> him: old, young,— §last two words, commas, and dash inserted above§ <> creature: §either comma or semicolon altered to colon§ <sup>1718|</sup> MS:fear, §comma over illegibly erased word§ <sup>1719|</sup> MS:flesh, the face, the §over illegible word§ evidence §last four words and commas inserted above§ *1872:*flesh—the *1889a:*face, an evidence <sup>1720|</sup> MS:Of the thing at work inside: §last six words and colon inserted above§ and *1872:*O' the soul at <> inside; and <sup>1721|</sup> MS:So much §inserted above§ The §altered to§ the <> grotesque. §comma and dash crossed out and replaced by period, and ¶ called for§ "why §altered to§ "Why

When it occurred to me, from all these sights beneath
There rose not any sound: a crowd, yet dumb as death!

XCVIII

1725     Soon I knew why. (Propose a riddle, and 'tis solved
Forthwith—in dream!) They spoke; but,—since on me devolved
To see, and understand by sight,—the vulgar speech
Might be dispensed with. "He who cannot see, must reach
As best he may the truth of men by help of words
1730 They please to speak, must fare at will of who affords
The banquet,"—so I thought. "Who sees not; hears and so
Gets to believe; myself it is that, seeing, know,
And, knowing, can dispense with voice and vanity
Of speech. What hinders then, that, drawing closer, I
1735 Put privilege to use, see and know better still
These *simulacra*, taste the profit of my skill,
Down in the midst?"

XCIX

    And plumb I pitched into the square—
A groundling like the rest. What think you happened there?
Precise the contrary of what one would expect!
1740 For,—whereas so much more monstrosities deflect
From nature and the type, as you the more approach
Their precinct,—here, I found brutality encroach
Less on the human, lie the lightlier as I looked
The nearlier on these faces that seemed but now so crook'd

---

1723| MS:me, §colon altered to comma§ from §first letter of word over illegible letter§
1725| §¶ called for§ But I know §altered to§ knew why. §exclamation point altered to period§
*1889a:*Soon I     1726| MS:dream!) §exclamation point and parenthesis over illegible
erasure§ <> spoke: §semicolon altered to colon§ but     *1872:*spoke; but
1728| MS:with; he     *1872:*with. "He     1731| MS:banquet: such an one sees not, but hears,
and     *1872:*banquet,"—so I thought. "Who sees not, hears and     1732| MS:believe: myself
*1872:*believe; myself     1734| MS:Beside §crossed out and replaced above by two words§ Of
speech: what     *1872:*speech. What     1737| MS:midst?" §¶ called for§ <> into the Square—
*1872:*square—     1738| MS:A §illegibly crossed out word inserted above§
1739| MS:Precise §inserted to left§ The §altered to§ the <> expect! §colon altered to
exclamation point§     1741| MS:type, the more that §inserted above and then crossed out§
you §altered to§ yourself approach     *1889a:*type, as you the more approach
1744| MS:The nearer on each face that     *1872:*on these faces     *1889a:*The nearlier

<sup></sup>1745 And clawed away from God's prime purpose. They diverged
A little from the type, but somehow rather urged
To pity than disgust: the prominent, before,
Now dwindled into mere distinctness, nothing more.
Still, at first sight, stood forth undoubtedly the fact
1750 Some deviation was: in no one case there lacked
The certain sign and mark,—say hint, say, trick of lip
Or twist of nose,—that proved a fault in workmanship,
Change in the prime design, some hesitancy here
And there, which checked the man and let the beast appear;
1755 But that was all.

C

All: yet enough to bid each tongue
Lie in abeyance still. They talked, themselves among,
Of themselves, to themselves; I saw the mouths at play,
The gesture that enforced, the eye that strove to say
The same thing as the voice, and seldom gained its point
1760 —That this was so, I saw; but all seemed out of joint
I' the vocal medium 'twixt the world and me. I gained
Knowledge by notice, not by giving ear,—attained
To truth by what men seemed, not said: to me one glance

---

1745| MS:purpose; just §crossed out and replaced above by§ these diverged   *1872:*purpose.
They diverged       1746| MS:the true man §last two words crossed out and replaced above by§
animal §crossed out§ type, but somehow §inserted above§       1747| MS:than abhorrence
§crossed out and replaced above by four words and three punctuation marks§ disgust: the
prominent, before,       1748| MS:Was §crossed out and replaced above by§ Now dwindling
§altered to§ dwindled to §altered to§ into mere distinctness §last four letters over illegible
erasure§       1750| MS:That deviation   *1872:*Some deviation       1751| MS:The little
§crossed out and replaced above by§ certain <> mark, nay hint, nay, trick   *1872:*mark, say
hint, say, trick   *1889a:*mark,—say       1752| MS:nose, that   *1889a:*nose,—that
1754| MS:appear   *1872:*appear;       1755| MS:was all, §¶ called for§ and §crossed out and
replaced above by word and colon§ All: yet <> tongue §over illegible erasure§   *1872:*was all.
All; yet   *1889a:*was all. All: yet       1756| MS:still: they   *1872:*still. They
1757| MS:themselves: §semicolon altered to colon§ I   *1872:*themselves; I       1759| MS:point—
§dash crossed out§       1760| MS:saw, but   *1872:*saw; but       1761| MS:me. §comma
altered to period§ I took §crossed out§       1762| MS:ear,— §semicolon altered to comma and
dash§ attained §inserted above§       1763| MS:§line inserted above l. 1764§ me, one §inserted
above§ look §inserted above, then crossed out and replaced to right by§ glance   *1872:*me one

Was worth whole histories of noisy utterance,

1765 —At least, to me in dream.

CI

And presently I found

That, just as ugliness had withered, so unwound
Itself, and perished off, repugnance to what wrong
Might linger yet i' the make of man. My will was strong
I' the matter; I could pick and choose, project my weight:
1770 (Remember how we saw the boatman trim his freight!)
Determine to observe, or manage to escape,
Or make divergency assume another shape
By shift of point of sight in me the observer: thus
Corrected, added to, subtracted from,—discuss
1775 Each variant quality, and brute-beast touch was turned
Into mankind's safeguard! Force, guile, were arms which earned
My praise, not blame at all: for we must learn to live,
Case-hardened at all points, not bare and sensitive,
But plated for defence, nay, furnished for attack,
1780 With spikes at the due place, that neither front nor back
May suffer in that squeeze with nature, we find—life.
Are we not here to learn the good of peace through strife,
Of love through hate, and reach knowledge by ignorance?
Why, those are helps thereto, which late we eyed askance,
1785 And nicknamed unaware! just so, a sword we call
Superfluous, and cry out against, at festival:

---

1764| MS:worth to me §last two words crossed out§    1765| MS:—To me at least, §last four
words and comma transposed and altered to§ —At least, to me <> dream. §¶ called for§
1768| MS:man: my    *1872:*man. My    1769| MS:matter, I <> weight    *1872:*matter; I
*1889a:*weight:    1775| MS:The §crossed out and replaced above by§ Each <> quality, the
§crossed out and replaced above by§ and    1776| MS:safeguard; force    *1872:*safeguard!
Force    1777| MS:all: for    *1872:*all! for    *1889a:*all: for    1778| MS:not weakly §crossed
out and replaced above by two words§ bare and    1779| MS:defence, and §crossed out and
replaced above by word and comma§ nay, <> attack    *1872:*attack,    1780| MS:With points
§crossed out and replaced above by§ spikes    1781| MS:find— §dash inserted§
1783| MS:hate, attain §crossed out and replaced above by two words§ and reach
1784| MS:thereto, at §crossed out§ which late §inserted above§ we look §crossed out and
replaced above by§ eyed    1785| MS:unaware! §colon altered to exclamation point§ just
§altered to§ Just    1786| MS:Superfluous and    *1872:*Superfluous, and

97

Wear it in time of war, its clink and clatter grate
O' the ear to purpose then!

CII

I found, one must abate
One's scorn of the soul's casing, distinct from the soul's self—
1790   Which is the centre-drop: whereas the pride in pelf,
The lust to seem the thing it cannot be, the greed
For praise, and all the rest seen outside,—these indeed
Are the hard polished cold crystal environment
Of those strange orbs unearthed i' the Druid temple, meant
1795   For divination (so the learned please to think)
Wherein you may admire one dew-drop roll and wink,
All unaffected by—quite alien to—what sealed
And saved it long ago: though how it got congealed
I shall not give a guess, nor how, by power occult,
1800   The solid surface-shield was outcome and result
Of simple dew at work to save itself amid
The unwatery force around; protected thus, dew slid
Safe through all opposites, impatient to absorb

---

<sup>1788</sup>|   MS:Somehow §crossed out and replaced above by three words§ O' the ear <> then. §¶
called for§ I found one   *1872:*then! §¶§ I found, one        <sup>1789</sup>|   MS:soul's arms §crossed out
and replaced above by§ case, distinct   *1872:*soul's casing, distinct        <sup>1790</sup>|   MS:centre-
drop,—whereas the thirst for §last two words crossed out and replaced above by two words§
pride in   *1872:*centre-drop; whereas   *1889a:*centre-drop: whereas        <sup>1791</sup>|   MS:it is
§crossed out and replaced above by§ can not   *1872:*cannot        <sup>1794</sup>|   MS:Of that §altered to§
those        <sup>1795</sup>|   MS:divination—so <> learned lean to think—   *1872:*divination (so <> think)
*1889a:*learned please to        <sup>1796</sup>|   MS:one live §crossed out and replaced above by word and
hyphen§ dew-drop flit §crossed out and replaced above by§ roll        <sup>1798</sup>|   MS:ago: §comma
and dash altered to colon§        <sup>1799</sup>|   MS:I know not—that §crossed out and replaced above
by§ how it serves its purpose—that, I perceive §last eleven-word line crossed out and replaced
above by eleven-word line§ I shall not give a guess—nor how, by power occult,   *1872:*guess, nor
<sup>1800</sup>|   MS:surface-shield, the dew, by power §last four words and two commas crossed out and
replaced above by two words, comma, and two words§ in question, was result   *1872:*surface-
shield was outcome and result        <sup>1802</sup>|   MS:around; and §crossed out§ thus protected, §last
two words transposed to§ protected thus, thrid §crossed out and replaced to right by two words§
dew slid        <sup>1803</sup>|   MS:The maze of §last three words crossed out and replaced above by three
words§ Safe through all opposites impatient   *1889a:*opposites, impatient

98

Its spot of life, and last for ever in the orb
1805   We, now, from hand to hand pass with impunity.

CIII

And the delight wherewith I watch this crowd must be
Akin to that which crowns the chemist when he winds
Thread up and up, till clue be fairly clutched,—unbinds
The composite, ties fast the simple to its mate,
1810   And, tracing each effect back to its cause, elate,
Constructs in fancy, from the fewest primitives,
The complex and complete, all diverse life, that lives
Not only in beast, bird, fish, reptile, insect, but
The very plants and earths and ores. Just so I glut
1815   My hunger both to be and know the thing I am,
By contrast with the thing I am not; so, through sham
And outside, I arrive at inmost real, probe
And prove how the nude form obtained the chequered robe.

CIV

—Experience, I am glad to master soon or late,
1820   Here, there and everywhere i' the world, without debate!

---

1804| MS:life, which §crossed out and replaced above by§ and lasts  *1889a:*last
1805| MS:We, pass §crossed out and replaced above by word and comma§ now, <> to hand pass
§over illegible erasure§    1806| MS:§¶ called for§    1808| MS:be fairly §inserted above§
1810| MS:§line inserted above l. 1811§ And tracing <> elate  *1872:*And, tracing <> elate,
1812| MS:The complex §inserted above§ ultimate, all  *1872:*complex and complete, all
1813| MS:in man §crossed out§ <> bird, fish, §word and comma inserted above§ reptile, §word
crossed out, replaced above by *and*, and then restored§ insect,—but  *1872:*insect, but
1814| MS:The very §inserted above§ plants, and earths, and ores. §colon altered to period§ just
§altered to§ Just  *1872:*plants and earths and    1815| MS:hunger both <> be, and
*1872:*hunger, both <> be and  *1889a:*hunger both
1816| MS:contrast of §crossed out and replaced above by§ with <> thing: I <> not: as,
§word over illegible erasure§ through  *1872:*thing I <> not; so, through
1818| MS:prove how §inserted above§ <> form wears §crossed out and replaced above by two
words§ came by the variegated §crossed out and replaced below by§ motley §crossed out and
replaced above by§ chequered robe,—  *1872:*form obtained the <> robe.
1819-20| MS:§two lines inserted at top of page§    1820| MS:debate:  *1872:*debate!

Only, in Venice why? What reason for Mark's Square
Rather than Timbuctoo?

CV

And I became aware,
Scarcely the word escaped my lips, that swift ensued
In silence and by stealth, and yet with certitude,
1825   A formidable change of the amphitheatre
Which held the Carnival; although the human stir
Continued just the same amid that shift of scene.

CVI

For as on edifice of cloud i' the grey and green
Of evening,—built about some glory of the west,
1830   To barricade the sun's departure, —manifest,
He plays, pre-eminently gold, gilds vapour, crag and crest
Which bend in rapt suspense above the act and deed
They cluster round and keep their very own, nor heed
The world at watch; while we, breathlessly at the base
1835   O' the castellated bulk, note momently the mace
Of night fall here, fall there, bring change with every blow,
Alike to sharpened shaft and broadened portico

---

1822|  MS:than Timbuctoo? §¶ called for§ <> aware  *1872:*aware,
1823|  MS:Even as the <> that there ensued  *1872:*Scarcely the <> that swift ensued
1826|  MS:That held <> Carnival, whereof the noiseless §crossed out and replaced above by§
human  *1872:*Which held <> Carnival; although   1827|  MS:Continued all §crossed out
and replaced above by§ just <> same for all §inserted above§ that <> scene:  *1872:*same amid
that <> scene.    1828|  MS:§¶ called for§ as the §crossed out and replaced above by§ some
edifice  *1872:*as on edifice    1829|  MS:glory in §altered to§ of    1830|  MS:Which
§crossed out and replaced above by§ To    1831|  MS:He plays, §last two words and comma
inserted to left§ Pre-eminently §altered to§ pre-eminently gold, to all those §last three words
crossed out and replaced above by two words and comma§ on vapour, crags §altered to§ crag
and crests §altered to§ crest  *1872:*gold, gilds vapour    1832|  MS:Held §crossed out and
replaced above by§ Bent in sublime suspense about §altered to§ above  *1872:*Which bend in
rapt suspense    1833|  MS:own; §semicolon blotted out§ nor  *1872:*own, nor
1834|  MS:watch without: which, breathless at  *1872:*watch; while we, breathlessly at
1836|  MS:Of leaden §crossed out§ night <> there, find nought resist its stress §last five words
crossed out and replaced above by five words§ bring change with every blow  *1872:*blow,
1837|  MS:But bow from §last three words crossed out and replaced above by two words§ Alike to
<> shaft, to §crossed out§ and caverned breath below  *1872:*shaft and broadened portico

I' the structure: heights and depths, beneath the leaden stress,
Crumble and melt and mix together, coälesce
1840   Re-form, but sadder still, subdued yet more and more
By every fresh defeat, till wearied eyes need pore
No longer on the dull impoverished decadence
Of all that pomp of pile in towering evidence
So lately: —

CVII

Even thus nor otherwise, meseemed
1845   That if I fixed my gaze awhile on what I dreamed
Was Venice' Square, Mark's Church, the scheme was straight
     unschemed,
A subtle something had its way within the heart
Of each and every house I watched, with counterpart
Of tremor through the front and outward face, until
1850   Mutation was at end; impassive and stock-still
Stood now the ancient house, grown—new, is scarce the phrase,
Since older, in a sense,—altered to . . . what i' the ways,

---

1838| MS:Of bastions; §last two words and semicolon crossed out and replaced above by two words and colon§ The structure: cloud and cloud, beneath   *1872:*I' the structure: heights and depths, beneath   1839| MS:mix partly, or co-alesce,   *1872:*mix together, coalesce,   *1889a:*coälesce   1840| MS:sadder still, §last word and comma inserted above§ subdued and never §last two words crossed out and replaced above by two words§ yet more
1841| MS:every fresh §over illegible word§ defeat, until §altered to§ til eyes wearied §last two words transposed to§ wearied eyes need §inserted above§   *1872:*till
1842| MS:the mean grey colourless §last three words crossed out and replaced above by two words§ dull impoverished   1843| MS:From §crossed out and replaced above by§ Of < > that towering §inserted above illegibly crossed out word§ pomp < > in evidence *1872:*that pomp < > in towering evidence   1844| MS:lately: §¶ called for§ even §altered to§ Even   *1872:*lately:—   1846| MS:Was Venice' §crossed out, replaced above by "Mark's", and then restored§ Square, Mark's Church, §last two words and comma inserted beneath illegibly crossed out words§ < > was all §crossed out and replaced above by§ straight
1847| MS:something worked §crossed out and replaced above by three words§ had its way < > the stony §crossed out§   1849| MS:Of tremor §last two letters over illegible erasure§
1850| MS:Mutatin grew §crossed out and replaced above by§ was complete, the ancient house, stock-still,   *1872:*was at end; impassive and stock-still   1851| MS:Stood for inspection now, grown—new, I dare not say, §last four words and comma crossed out and replaced above by four words and comma§ is scarce the phrase,   *1872:*Stood now the ancient house, grown
1852| MS:sense, altered to—, every-day, §last word crossed out and replaced above by three words§ go your ways,   *1872:*sense,—altered to . . . what i' the ways,

Ourselves are wont to see, coërced by city, town
Or village, anywhere i' the world, pace up or down
1855　Europe! In all the maze, no single tenement
I saw, but I could claim acquaintance with.

### CVIII

There went
Conviction to my soul, that what I took of late
For Venice was the world; its Carnival—the state
Of mankind, masquerade in life-long permanence
1860　For all time, and no one particular feast-day. Whence
'Twas easy to infer what meant my late disgust
At the brute-pageant, each grotesque of greed and lust
And idle hate, and love as impotent for good—
When from my pride of place I passed the interlude
1865　In critical review; and what, the wonder that ensued
When, from such pinnacled pre-eminence, I found
Somehow the proper goal for wisdom was the ground
And not the sky,—so, slid sagaciously betimes

---

1853| MS:What §crossed out, replaced above by *And*, and then restored§ one §crossed out and replaced above by§ you submits §altered to§ submit to bear, coërced    *1872:*Ourselves are wont to see, coërced    1854| MS:village anywhere < > world, this modern time §last three words crossed out and replaced above by four words§ go §crossed out and replaced above by§ pace up or down    *1872:*village, anywhere    1855| MS:Europe, this §altered to§ maze,—no    *1872:*Europe! In all the maze, no
1856| MS:But < > claim §over illegible erasure§ once more acquaintance with! §colon altered to exclamation point, and ¶ called for§ there §altered to§ There    *1872:*I say, but < > claim acquaintance    1860| MS:time—and < > particular gaudy- §word and hyphen crossed out and replaced above by word and hyphen§ feast-day; whence    *1872:*time, and < > feast-day. Whence    1861| MS:to conclude §crossed out and replaced above by§ infer that §crossed out and then restored§ my late §inserted above and then crossed out§ sublime disgust    *1872:*infer what meant my late disgust    1862| MS:At that brute-pageant    *1872:*At the brute-pageant    1863| MS:And foolish §crossed out and replaced above by§ idle
1864| MS:When §first letter altered from A§ from my pinnacle §crossed out and replaced above by three words§ pride of place < > the interlude §inserted above illegibly crossed out word§
1865| MS:review: and then, the sudden change of mood §last four words crossed out and replaced above by three words§ wonder that ensued    *1872:*review; and what, the
1866| MS:When from < > pre-eminence I    *1872:*When, from < > pre-eminence, I
1867| MS:proper place §crossed out and replaced above by§ goal    1868| MS:sky,—so §over illegible erasure§ wisely §inserted above§ slipped as down a silver-smooth §last four words crossed out and replaced above by§ betimes    *1872:*so, slid sagaciously betimes

Down heaven's baluster-rope, to reach the mob of mimes
1870 And mummers; whereby came discovery there was just
Enough and not too much of hate, love, greed and lust,
Could one discerningly but hold the balance, shift
The weight from scale to scale, do justice to the drift
Of nature, and explain the glories by the shames
1875 Mixed up in man, one stuff miscalled by different names
According to what stage i' the process turned his rough,
Even as I gazed, to smooth—only get close enough!
—What was all this except the lesson of a life?

CIX

And—consequent upon the learning how from strife
1880 Grew peace—from evil, good—came knowledge that, to get
Acquaintance with the way o' the world, we must nor fret
Nor fume, on altitudes of self-sufficiency,
But bid a frank farewell to what—we think—should be,
And, with as good a grace, welcome what is—we find.

CX

1885 *Is*—for the hour, observe! Since something to my mind

---

1869| MS:Down heaven's §inserted to left§ Baluster-rope §altered to§ baluster-rope, of heaven §last two words crossed out§ and reached the mob §over illegible erasure§ uncouth §crossed out and replaced to right by two words§ of mimes    *1872:*baluster-rope, to reach
1870| MS:Of mimes, and §last three words and comma crossed out and replaced above by two words and comma§ And mummers, made at once discovery    *1872:*mummers; whereby came discovery    1872| MS:If one discerningly adjusted §next word illegibly crossed out§ scale §last three words crossed out and replaced above by four words and comma§ could hold the balance,    *1872:*Could one discerningly but hold    1873| MS:weights    *1872:*weight
1876| MS:process whereby §crossed out and replaced above by two words§ turns the rough    *1872:*turned his rough    *1889a:*rough,    1877| MS:From smooth, §last two words and comma crossed out§ even §altered to§ Even as you gaze, to smooth— §last two words and dash inserted above§    *1872:*as I gazed    1878| MS:Why—what was this *1872:*—What was all this    1879| MS:§¶ called for§ the learning §crossed out, replaced above by *knowledge*, and then restored§ that §crossed out and replaced above by§ how
1880| MS:Comes peace <> good—the learning §crossed out and replaced above by§ knowledge *1872:*Grew peace <> good—came knowledge    1881| MS:Such knowledge of §last three words crossed out and replaced above by two words§ Acquaintance with
1882| MS:fume, idle §crossed out and replaced above by two words§ on altitudes
1885| MS:§¶ called for§ hour, at least! §colon altered to exclamation point§ for §crossed out and replaced above by§ since §altered to§ Since    *1872:*hour, observe! Since

Suggested soon the fancy, nay, certitude that change,
Never suspending touch, continued to derange
What architecture, we, walled up within the cirque
O' the world, consider fixed as fate, not fairy-work.
1890 For those were temples, sure, which tremblingly grew blank
From bright, then broke afresh in triumph,—ah, but sank
As soon, for liquid change through artery and vein
O' the very marble wound its way! And first a stain
Would startle and offend amid the glory; next,
1895 Spot swift succeeded spot, but found me less perplexed
By portents; then as 'twere a sleepiness soft stole
Over the stately fane, and shadow sucked the whole
*Façade* into itself, made uniformly earth
What was a piece of heaven; till, lo, a second birth,
1900 And the veil broke away because of something new
Inside, that pushed to gain an outlet, paused in view
At last, and proved a growth of stone or brick or wood
Which, alien to the aim o' the Builder, somehow stood
The test, could satisfy, if not the early race
1905 For whom he built, at least our present populace,
Who must not bear the blame for what, blamed, proves mishap
Of the Artist: his work gone, another fills the gap,
Serves the prime purpose so. Undoubtedly there spreads

---

1886| MS:Suggests the <> nay, the certitude <> change   *1872:*Suggested soon the <> nay,
certitude <> change,        1887| MS:suspends its touch, §word over illegible erasure§
continues   *1872:*suspending touch, continued        1888| MS:What §first letter of word over
illegible letter§        1889| MS:fixed and sure §last two words crossed out and replaced above by
two words§ as fate        1892| MS:change, through   *1872:*change through
1893| MS:marble made §crossed out and replaced above by§ wound <> way: and
*1872:*way! And        1894| MS:Would fright you and <> glory, next
*1872:*Would startle and <> glory; next,        1895| MS:Out came a second §last four words
crossed out and replaced above by three words§ Spot swift succeeded spot, which §crossed out
and replaced above by§ and found you less   *1872:*spot, but found me less
1896| MS:portents; §semicolon over illegible erasure§ <> sleepiness that stole   *1872:*sleepiness
soft stole        1897| MS:fane, a §altered to§ and        1898| MS:Façade   *1889a:Façade*
1903| MS:aim of §altered to§ o' the artist, calmly §last two words and comma crossed out and
replaced above by two words and comma§ builder, somehow   *1872:*the Builder
1904| MS:test, could §first two letters of last word over illegible letters§
1905| MS:our present §inserted above§ populace   *1872:*populace,        1906| MS:not suffer for
the §last three words crossed out and replaced above by seven words and two commas§ bear the
blame for what proves, blamed, mishap   *1872:*what, blamed, proves mishap

104

Building around, above, which makes men lift their heads
1910 To look at, or look through, or look—for aught I care—
Over: if only up, it is, not down, they stare,
"Commercing with the skies," and not the pavement in the Square.

CXI

But are they only temples that subdivide, collapse,
And tower again, transformed? Academies, perhaps!
1915 Domes where dwells Learning, seats of Science, bower and hall
Which house Philosophy—do these, too, rise and fall,
Based though foundations be on steadfast mother-earth,
With no chimeric claim to supermundane birth,
No boast that, dropped from cloud, they did not grow from ground?
1920 Why, these fare worst of all! these vanish and are found
Nowhere, by who tasks eye some twice within his term
Of threescore years and ten, for tidings what each germ
Has burgeoned out into, whereof the promise stunned
His ear with such acclaim,—praise-payment to refund
1925 The praisers, never doubt, some twice before they die
Whose days are long i' the land.

CXII

Alack, Philosophy!
Despite the chop and change, diminished or increased,

---

1908| MS:Serves §over illegible erasure§ <> so, undoubtedly    *1872:*so. Undoubtedly
1910| MS:To §over illegible erasure§ <> at, or look §last two words inserted above§ through, or
look, for <> care,    *1872:*through, or look—for <> care—    1911| MS:Over, so long as
§inserted above§ up <> is not down, §last two words and comma inserted above§ they send
their §last two words crossed out§    *1872:*Over: if only up,    1913| MS:§¶ called for§ that
swell, sink §last two words crossed out§    1914| MS:And §crossed out and then restored§
stand apart or else collapse §last five words crossed out and replaced above by three words,
question mark, word, and comma§ tower again transformed? Academies, perhaps,
*1872:*again, transformed <> perhaps!    1918| MS:claims §altered to§ claim
1919| MS:boast, §comma erased§ <> cloud, and §crossed out and replaced above by§ they
1920| MS:all, these    *1872:*all! these    1921| MS:eye, some    *1872:*eye some
1922| MS:three-score <> what the germ    *1872:*what each germ    *1889a:*threescore
1923| MS:the advent §crossed out and replaced above by§ promise    1924| MS:praise-
payment men §crossed out and replaced above by§ to    1925| MS:Honestly ( §parenthesis
over comma§ never fear! §exclamation point over comma§ ) §parenthesis inserted§ some <>
before he die    *1872:*The praisers, never doubt, some <> before they die
1926| MS:land. §¶ called for§    1927| MS:Despite §over illegible erasure§

Patched-up and plastered-o'er, Religion stands at least
I' the temple-type. But thou? Here gape I, all agog
1930 These thirty years, to learn how tadpole turns to frog;
And thrice at least have gazed with mild astonishment,
As, skyward up and up, some fire-new fabric sent
Its challenge to mankind that, clustered underneath
To hear the word, they straight believe, ay, in the teeth
1935 O' the Past, clap hands and hail triumphant Truth's outbreak—
Tadpole-frog-theory propounded past mistake!
In vain! A something ails the edifice, it bends,
It bows, it buries . . . Haste! cry "Heads below" to friends—
But have no fear they find, when smother shall subside,
1940 Some substitution perk with unabated pride
I' the predecessor's place!

CXIII

No,—the one voice which failed
Never, the preachment's coign of vantage nothing ailed,—
That had the luck to lodge i' the house not made with hands!
And all it preached was this: "Truth builds upon the sands,
1945 Though stationed on a rock: and so her work decays,
And so she builds afresh, with like result. Nought stays
But just the fact that Truth not only is, but fain

---

<sup>1928|</sup> MS:plastered-o'er, Religion §first two letters of last word over illegible erasure§
<sup>1929|</sup> MS:temple-type. §comma altered to period§ but §altered to§ But <> agog,   *1872:*agog
<sup>1930|</sup> MS:frog   *1872:*frog;   <sup>1931|</sup> MS:astonishment   *1872:*astonishment,
<sup>1932|</sup> MS:As skyward §inserted above§ <> and up, its spires §last two words crossed out and
replaced above by two words and hyphen§ some fire-   *1872:*As, skyward   <sup>1933|</sup> MS:to the
world close- §last four words and hyphen crossed out and replaced above by two words and
comma§ mankind that, clustering §altered to§ clustered beneath §altered to§ underneath
*1872:*underneath—   *1889a:*underneath   <sup>1934|</sup> MS:They §over illegible word§ hear <>
word and strait believe   *1889a:*To hear <> word, they straight believe   <sup>1935|</sup> MS:the Past,
clap hands §last two words over illegible words§ <> truth's   *1872:*Truth's
<sup>1937|</sup> MS:vain! A §over illegible erasure§ something §first two letters over illegible erasure§
<sup>1938|</sup> MS:it topples o'er: cry <> below!" to   *1872:*it buries . . . Haste! cry <> below" to
<sup>1939|</sup> MS:But never §crossed out and replaced above by two words§ have no   <sup>1941|</sup> MS:place!
§¶ called for§   <sup>1943|</sup> MS:That came, because it lodged <> hands   *1872:*That had the luck
to lodge <> hands!   <sup>1944|</sup> MS:preached was §over illegible erasure§ this: Truth §inserted
above illegibly crossed out word§ <> sands   *1872:*this: "Truth <> sands,   <sup>1945|</sup> MS:rock,
and   *1872:*rock: and   <sup>1946|</sup> MS:with §over illegible erasure§ <> result—nought
§over illegible erasure§   *1872:*result. Nought   <sup>1947|</sup> MS:truth   *1872:*Truth

106

Would have men know she needs must be, by each so plain
Attempt to visibly inhabit where they dwell."
1950 Her works are work, while she is she; that work does well
Which lasts mankind their life-time through, and lets believe
One generation more, that, though sand run through sieve,
Yet earth now reached is rock, and what we moderns find
Erected here is Truth, who, 'stablished to her mind
1955 I' the fulness of the days, will never change in show
More than in substance erst: men thought they knew; we know!

### CXIV

Do you, my generation? Well, let the blocks prove mist
I' the main enclosure,—church and college, if they list,
Be something for a time, and everything anon,
1960 And anything awhile, as fit is off or on,
Till they grow nothing, soon to re-appear no less
As something,—shape re-shaped, till out of shapelessness
Come shape again as sure! no doubt, or round or square
Or polygon its front, sonic building will be there,
1965 Do duty in that nook o' the wall o' the world where once
The Architect saw fit precisely to ensconce
College or church, and bid such bulwark guard the line
O' the barrier round about, humanity's confine.

---

1948| MS:have them §crossed out and replaced above by§ men <> by these so   1872:by each so
1949| MS:Attempts <> where they §crossed out and then restored§ dwell:   1872:Attempt <>
dwell."   1950| MS:They are her §last three words crossed out and replaced above by three
words§ Her works are work, not §crossed out and replaced above by§ while she herself: §last
word and colon crossed out and replaced above by two words and colon§ is she: that   1872:she;
that   1951| MS:lasts mankind §inserted above§   1952| MS:that though §inserted
above§ sand has §crossed out§ run through §last three letters of last word inserted above§
1872:that, though   1953| MS:All §crossed out and replaced§ Yet earth and all §last two
words crossed out§ henceforth is   1872:earth now reached is   1954| MS:Established
§crossed out and replaced above by§ Erected there is   1872:Erected here is
1955| MS:knew: we   1872:knew; we   1957| MS:§¶ called for§ generation? Why, let
1872:generation? Well, let   1963| MS:Comes again shape as sure, because, be §crossed out
and replaced above by§ or   1872:Come shape again as sure! no doubt, or
1965| MS:that space §crossed out and replaced above by§ nook
1967| MS:church and   1872:church, and   1968| MS:confine:   1872:confine.

CXV

Leave watching change at work i' the greater scale, on these
1970    The main supports, and turn to their interstices
Filled up by fabrics too, less costly and less rare,
Yet of importance, yet essential to the Fair
They help to circumscribe, instruct and regulate!
See, where each booth-front boasts, in letters small or great,
1975    Its specialty, proclaims its privilege to stop
A breach, beside the best!

CXVI

Here History keeps shop,
Tells how past deeds were done, so and not otherwise:
"Man! hold truth evermore! forget the early lies!"
There sits Morality, demure behind her stall,
1980    Dealing out life and death: "This is the thing to call
Right, and this other, wrong; thus think, thus do, thus say,
Thus joy, thus suffer!—not to-day as yesterday—
Yesterday's doctrine dead, this only shall endure!
Obey its voice and live!"—enjoins the dame demure.
1985    While Art gives flag to breeze, bids drum beat, trumpet blow,
Inviting eye and ear to yonder raree-show.

---

1969| MS:§no ¶§ watching restlessness §crossed out and replaced above by three words§ change at work <> scale, §exclamation point altered to comma§ On §altered to§ on    *1872:*§¶§
1970| MS:The prime supports    *1872:*The main supports       1973| MS:regulate! §colon altered to exclamation point§       1976| MS:best! §¶ called for§       1977| MS:Tells how §over illegible word§ things really §last two words crossed out and replaced above by two words§ past deeds were done, §word and comma inserted above§ <> otherwise;    *1872:*otherwise:
1978| MS:Truth, now and §last two words crossed out and replaced above by two words§ hold truth evermore,—forget the early §over illegible erasure§ lies!    *1872:*"Man! hold <> evermore! forget <> lies!"       1979| MS:sits Morality, demure §inserted above§
1980| MS:death: "this §altered to§ "This       1981| MS:wrong,—thus think §over illegible word§    *1872:*wrong; thus       1982| MS:suffer—not    *1872:*suffer!—not
1983| MS:That doctrine was mistake! §dash altered to exclamation point§ this §altered to§ This <> endure! §colon altered to exclamation point§    *1872:*Yesterday's doctrine dead, this
1984| MS:Obey my voice    *1872:*Obey its voice       1985| MS:flag the while §last two words crossed out and replaced above by two words, comma, dash, and word§ to breeze,—bids drums §altered to§ drum beat, and §inserted above and then crossed out§ trumpets §altered to§ trumpet    *1872:*breeze, bids       1986| MS:to yonder §altered from illegible word§

Up goes the canvas, hauled to height of pole. I think,
We know the way—long lost, late learned—to paint! A wink
Of eye, and lo, the pose! the statue on its plinth!
1990 How could we moderns miss the heart o' the labyrinth
Perversely all these years, permit the Greek seclude
His secret till to-day? And here's another feud
Now happily composed: inspect this quartett-score!
Got long past melody, no word has Music more
1995 To say to mortal man! But is the bard to be
Behindhand? Here's his book, and now perhaps you see
At length what poetry can do!

### CXVII

Why, that's stability
Itself, that change on change we sorrowfully saw
Creep o'er the prouder piles! We acquiesced in law
2000 When the fine gold grew dim i' the temple, when the brass
Which pillared that so brave abode where Knowledge was,
Bowed and resigned the trust; but, bear all this caprice,
Harlequinade where swift to birth succeeds decease
Of hue at every turn o' the tinsel-flag which flames

---

1987|  MS:the canvas §first letter over illegible erasure§ <> of scaff §partial word crossed out and replaced above by word and colon§ pole: I   *1872:*pole.  I       1988|  MS:way—long lost, late learned— §dash, last four words, and dash inserted above§       1989|  MS:pose! §exclamation point inserted§ o' §crossed out§       1991|  MS:years, and let §last two words crossed out and replaced above by§ permit       1993|  MS:this music-score!   *1872:*this quartett-score!
1994|  MS:You have the §last three words crossed out and replaced above by two words§ Receive her ultimate, no word shall §crossed out and replaced above by§ has music   *1872:*Got long past melody, no <> Music       1995|  MS:To offer §crossed out and replaced above by three words§ say to mortal man! §¶ called for and then crossed out§       1997|  MS:At length, §last two words and comma inserted above§ What <> do! §¶ called for§   *1872:*what
1998|  MS:Itself, that §illegibly altered and then restored§       1999|  MS:piles! §colon altered to exclamation point§ we §altered to§ We       2000|  MS:grows dim of §crossed out and replaced above by§ i' <> temple, and §crossed out and replaced above by§ when   *1872:*grew
2001|  MS:where knowledge §altered to§ Knowledge was   *1872:*was,
2002|  Bows <> resigns their §altered to§ the <> but, all §crossed out and replaced above by two words§ bear all this mere §crossed out§ caprice—   *1872:*Bowed <> resigned <> caprice,
2003|  MS:Harlequinade of Art, §last two words crossed out§ where, swift, to §last two words and two commas inserted above§   *1872:*Harlequinade where swift to
2004|  MS:tinsel which proclaims §last two words crossed out and replaced above by hyphen and three words§ -flag which flames

2005 While Art holds booth in Fair? Such glories chased by shames
Like these, distract beyond the solemn and august
Procedure to decay, evanishment in dust,
Of those marmoreal domes,—above vicissitude,
We used to hope!

CXVIII

"So, all is change, in fine," pursued
2010 The preachment to a pause. When—"All is permanence!"
Returned a voice. Within? without? No matter whence
The explanation came: for, understand, I ought
To simply say—"I saw," each thing I say "I thought."
Since ever as, unrolled, the strange scene-picture grew
2015 Before me, sight flashed first, though mental comment too
Would follow in a trice, come hobblingly to halt.

CXIX

So, what did I see next but,—much as when the vault
I' the west,—wherein we watch the vapoury manifold
Transfiguration,—tired turns blaze to black,—behold,
2020 Peak reconciled to base, dark ending feud with bright,
The multiform subsides, becomes the definite.

---

2005| MS:Where §inserted to left§ Art holds her §crossed out§ <> in the §crossed out§ fair, §altered to§ Fair? those §crossed out and replaced above by§ Such    *1872:*While Art
2006| MS:Distract, distress beyond    *1872:*Like these, distract beyond        2007| MS:Procedure §first five letters inserted above illegibly crossed out letters§ <> dust §punctuation illegibly crossed out§    *1872:*dust,        2009| MS:hope! §¶ called for§ <> fine" pursued    *1872:*fine," pursued        2010| MS:preachment to a pause. §last three words and period inserted above§ When—"Nay, §quotation mark, word, and comma crossed out§        2011| MS:voice—within? §comma altered to question mark§ without? I say not §last three words crossed out and replaced above by two words§ No matter    *1872:*voice. Within        2013| MS:say—I saw, each thing I say—I thought:    *1872:*thing I say I thought.    *1889a:*say—"I saw," each thing I say "I thought."        2015| MS:sight flashed first §last two words inserted above illegibly crossed out word§        2017| MS:§¶ called for§        2018| MS:vapoury manifold    *1872:*vapoury, manifold    *1889a:*vapoury manifold        2019| MS:Transfiguration, bids §crossed out and replaced above by dash§ —tired would turn to rest,—behold    *1889a:*tired turns blaze to black,—behold,        2020| MS:Cloud §crossed out and replaced above by§ Peak <> to cloud §crossed out and replaced above by§ base, dark grows at peace §last three words crossed out and replaced above by three words§ ends its feud    *1872:*dark ending feud        2021| MS:subsides, into §crossed out and replaced above by two words§ is found <> definite;    *1872:*definite.    *1889a:*subsides, becomes the

Contrasting life and strife, where battle they i' the blank
Severity of peace in death, for which we thank
One wind that comes to quell the concourse, drive at last
2025 Things to a shape which suits the close of things, and cast
Palpably o'er vexed earth heaven's mantle of repose?

CXX

Just so, in Venice' Square, that things were at the close
Was signalled to my sense; for I perceived arrest
O' the change all round about. As if some impulse pressed
2030 Each gently into each, what was distinctness, late,
Grew vague, and, line from line no longer separate,
No matter what its style, edifice . . . shall I say,
Died into edifice? I find no simpler way
Of saying how, without or dash or shock or trace
2035 Of violence, I found unity in the place
Of temple, tower,—nay, hall and house and hut,—one blank
Severity of peace in death; to which they sank
Resigned enough, till . . . ah, conjecture, I beseech,
What special blank did they agree to, all and each?
2040 What common shape was that wherein they mutely merged
Likes and dislikes of form, so plain before?

CXXI

I urged
Your step this way, prolonged our path of enterprise

---

<sup>2022|</sup> MS:Contrasting life §altered to§ lifes and strife §altered to§ strifes <> they in §altered to§
i'   *1889a:*life <> strife        <sup>2023|</sup> MS:Severe §altered to§ Severity of death and peace, for
*1889a:*of peace in death, for        <sup>2024|</sup> MS:One final §crossed out§ cloud that §over illegible
erasure§ <> concourse, falls at   *1872:*fall   *1889a:*One wind that <> concourse, drive at
<sup>2025|</sup> MS:Into the §crossed out and replaced above by§ a shape befits the   *1889a:*Things to a
shape which suits the        <sup>2026|</sup> o'er the §crossed out and replaced above by§ vexed <>
repose? §colon altered to question mark§        <sup>2027|</sup> MS:§¶ called for§        <sup>2028|</sup> MS:sense;
when §crossed out and replaced above by§ for        <sup>2033|</sup> MS:edifice,—till §crossed out§ I find
no §inserted above§   *1872:*edifice? I        <sup>2036|</sup> MS:tower, and hall   *1872:*tower,—nay, hall
<sup>2037|</sup> MS:of death and peace: they soft §last two words crossed out and replaced above by two
words§ to which   *1872:*peace; to   *1889a:*of peace in death; to
<sup>2039|</sup> MS:What severe blankness they agreed   *1872:*What special blank did they agree
<sup>2040|</sup> MS:shape it was wherein   *1872:*shape was that wherein
<sup>2041|</sup> MS:form, so plain §last two words inserted above§ before? §¶ called for§

To where we stand at last, in order that your eyes
Might see the very thing, and save my tongue describe
2045 The Druid monument which fronts you. Could I bribe
Nature to come in aid, illustrate what I mean,
What wants there she should lend to solemnize the scene?

CXXII

How does it strike you, this construction gaunt and grey—
Sole object, these piled stones, that gleam unground-away
2050 By twilight's hungry jaw, which champs fine all beside
I' the solitary waste we grope through? Oh, no guide
Need we to grope our way and reach the monstrous door
Of granite! Take my word, the deeper you explore
That caverned passage, filled with fancies to the brim,
2055 The less will you approve the adventure! such a grim
Bar-sinister soon blocks abrupt your path, and ends
All with a cold dread shape,—shape whereon Learning spends
Labour, and leaves the text obscurer for the gloss,
While Ignorance reads right—recoiling from that Cross!
2060 Whence came the mass and mass, strange quality of stone
Unquarried anywhere i' the region round? Unknown!
Just as unknown, how such enormity could be
Conveyed by land, or else transported over sea,

---

<sup>2043</sup>| MS:at length §crossed out and replaced above by§ last    <sup>2045</sup>| MS:you: could
*1872:*you. Could    <sup>2047</sup>| MS:she could lend to help the special §last three words crossed out
and replaced above by§ solemnize scene?    *1872:*she would lend <> solemnize the scene?
<sup>2048</sup>| MS:§¶ called for§ grey?    *1889a:*grey—    <sup>2049</sup>| MS:unground away
*1889a:*unground-away    <sup>2050</sup>| MS:By the §crossed out§ <> jaw which champs black
§crossed out and replaced above by§ fine    *1872:*jaw, which    <sup>2051</sup>| MS:solitary field
§crossed out and replaced above by§ waste <> grope across §crossed out and replaced above by
three words§ through thus far; §last two words crossed out§ oh, §word and comma inserted
above§    *1872:*through. Oh    *1889a:*through? Oh    <sup>2052</sup>| MS:However, need we now to
reach the double §crossed out and replaced above by§ monstrous    *1889a:*Need we to grope our
way and reach    <sup>2054</sup>| MS:with blackness §crossed out and replaced above by§ fancies
<sup>2055</sup>| MS:adventure: such    *1872:*adventure! such    <sup>2056</sup>| MS:Bar-sinister that §crossed out
and replaced above by§ soon    <sup>2057</sup>| MS:shape, that §crossed out§ —shape which §crossed
out and replaced above by§ whereon <> spends,    *1872:*spends
<sup>2058</sup>| MS:Ne §partial word crossed out§ labour §altered to§ Labour,
§next word illegibly crossed out§ still §crossed out and replaced above by two words§ and leaves
the §crossed out and then restored§    <sup>2062</sup>| MS:as how this and that enormity
*1872:*as unknown, how such enormity    <sup>2063</sup>| MS:land or <> sea    *1872:*land, or <> sea,

And laid in order, so, precisely each on each,
2065 As you and I would build a grotto where the beach
Sheds shell—to last an hour: this building lasts from age
To age the same. But why?

CXXIII

Ask Learning! I engage
You get a prosy wherefore, shall help you to advance
In knowledge just as much as helps you Ignorance
2070 Surmising, in the mouth of peasant-lad or lass,
"I heard my father say he understood it was
A building, people built as soon as earth was made
Almost, because they might forget (they were afraid)
Earth did not make itself, but came of Somebody.
2075 They laboured that their work might last, and show thereby
He stays, while we and earth, and all things come and go.
Come whence? Go whither? That, when come and gone, we know
Perhaps, but not while earth and all things need our best
Attention: we must wait and die to know the rest.
2080 Ask, if that's true, what use in setting up the pile?
To make one fear and hope: remind us, all the while
We come and go, outside there's Somebody that stays;
A circumstance which ought to make us mind our ways,
Because,—whatever end we answer by this life,—
2085 Next time, best chance must be for who, with toil and strife,

---

2064| MS:order, last, precisely <> on each   *1872*:order, so, precisely   *1889a:*on each,
2067| MS:same: but why? §¶ called for§ Ask Learning,—I   *1872:*same. But why? §¶§ Ask
Learning! I      2068|   MS:a why and §last two words crossed out and replaced above by two
words§ prosy of §crossed out§ <> you make §crossed out and replaced above by§ to
2069| MS:In knowing §altered to§ knowledge      2070|   MS:Surmising,—in <> lass,—
*1872:*Surmising, in <> lass,      2072|   MS:A place which §last two words crossed out and
replaced above by word and comma§ building, people built §over illegible erasure§
2074|   MS:Earth but §inserted above§ came of somebody; and §crossed out§ did not make itself,
§last eight words transposed to§ did not make itself, but came of somebody;   *1889a:*Somebody.
2076|   MS:and what's about us §last three words crossed out and replaced above by four words§
earth and all things <> go:   *1872:*earth, and <> go.      2080|   MS:Ask §inserted to left§ if
§over illegible erasure§ that's be all, §last two words and comma crossed out and replaced above
by word and comma§ true,   *1872:*Ask, if      2081|   MS:hope, remind   *1872:*hope: remind
2082|   MS:go, that §crossed out§ <> somebody <> stays   *1872:*Somebody <> stays;
2083|   MS:which tends §crossed out and replaced above by§ ought

113

Manages now to live most like what he was meant
Become: since who succeeds so far, 'tis evident,
Stands foremost on the file; who fails, has less to hope
From new promotion. That's the rule—with even a rope
2090 Of mushrooms, like this rope I dangle! those that grew
Greatest and roundest, all in life they had to do,
Gain a reward, a grace they never dreamed, I think;
Since, outside white as milk and inside black as ink,
They go to the Great House to make a dainty dish
2095 For Don and Donna; while this basket-load, I wish
Well off my arm, it breaks,—no starveling of the heap
But had his share of dew, his proper length of sleep
I' the sunshine: yet, of all, the outcome is—this queer
Cribbed quantity of dwarfs which burthen basket here
2100 Till I reach home; 'tis there that, having run their rigs,
They end their earthly race, are flung as food for pigs.
Any more use I see? Well, you must know, there lies
Something, the Curé says, that points to mysteries
Above our grasp: a huge stone pillar, once upright,
2105 Now laid at length, half-lost—discreetly shunning sight
I' the bush and briar, because of stories in the air—
Hints what it signified, and why was stationed there,
Once on a time. In vain the Curé tasked his lungs—
Showed, in a preachment, how, at bottom of the rungs
2110 O' the ladder, Jacob saw, where heavenly angels stept
Up and down, lay a stone which served him, while he slept,

---

2086| MS:Managed §altered to§ Manages now §inserted above§      2088| MS:file, who
*1872:*file; who      2089| MS:promotion: that's   *1872:*promotion. That's
2090| MS:mushrooms like <> dangle: those   *1872:*mushrooms, like <> dangle! those
2092| MS:think,   *1872:*think;      2095| MS:and Donna: while   *1872:*and Donna; while
2096| MS:arm it   *1872:*arm, it      2097| MS:his fill §crossed out and replaced above by§ share
<> dew, his proper §inserted above§ length of lazy §crossed out§      2098| MS:sunshine,—
yet  *1872:*sunshine: yet      2100| MS:home: 'tis   *1872:*home; 'tis      2101| MS:They end
§over illegible erasure§ on peace and §last three words crossed out and replaced above by three
words§ their earthly race      2104| MS:grasp, a   *1872:*grasp: a      2106| MS:briar: because
*1872:*briar, because      2107| MS:Of §crossed out and replaced above by§ Hints
2109| MS:a sermon §crossed out and replaced above by word and comma§ preachment,
2110| MS:ladder, Jacob saw, §last two words and comma inserted above§ whereon §altered to§
where heavenly §inserted below illegibly crossed out word§      2111| MS:down, served
§crossed out and replaced above by illegibly crossed out word, then replaced below by§ lay <>
stone for pillow §last two words crossed out and replaced above by three words and comma§

114

For pillow; when he woke, he set the same upright
As pillar, and a-top poured oil: things requisite
To instruct posterity, there mounts from floor to roof,
2115 A staircase, earth to heaven; and also put in proof,
When we have scaled the sky, we well may let alone
What raised us from the ground, and,—paying to the stone
Proper respect, of course,—take staff and go our way,
Leaving the Pagan night for Christian break of day.
2120 'For,' preached he, 'what they dreamed, these Pagans wide-awake
We Christians may behold. How strange, then, were mistake
Did anybody style the stone,—because of drop
Remaining there from oil which Jacob poured a-top, —
Itself the Gate of Heaven, itself the end, and not
2125 The means thereto!' Thus preached the Curé, and no jot
The more persuaded people but that, what once a thing
Meant and had right to mean, it still must mean. So cling
Folk somehow to the prime authoritative speech,
And so distrust report, it seems as they could reach
2130 Far better the arch-word, whereon their fate depends,
Through rude charactery, than all the grace it lends,
That lettering of your scribes! who flourish pen apace

---

which served him, 2112| MS:pillow: when *1872:*pillow; when 2114| posterity—
there *1872:*posterity, there 2115| MS:proof— *1872:*proof, 2116| MS:have
witnessed heaven §last two words crossed out and replaced above by three words and comma§
scaled the sky, 2117| MS:ground, to §crossed out and replaced above by word, comma,
and dash§ and,—paying §inserted above illegible erasure§ 2119| MS:for Christian
§inserted above§ 2120| MS:'For,' said §crossed out and replaced above by§ preached
2121| MS:behold; how *1872:*behold. How 2123| MS:there of §crossed out and replaced
above by§ from 2124| MS:'Itself §quotation mark and word inserted to left§ The §altered
to§ the 2125| MS:'These §altered to§ 'The <> thereto!' Thus §over illegible word§
2126| MS:more, persuaded *1872:*more persuaded 2127| MS:and had §over illegible
word§ <> must mean. §dash altered to period§ so §altered to§ So 2128| MS:Folks §over
illegible erasure§ *1872:*Folk 2130| MS:Far §inserted to left§ Better the one §last three
words crossed out, replaced above by illegibly crossed out words, and then restored§ word on
which their §over illegible word§ *1872:*better the arch-word, whereon their
2131| MS:Through the §crossed out§ <> charactery than all §crossed out and replaced above
by§ through the grace which lends *1872:*charactery, than all the grace it lends,
2132| MS:lettering these §crossed out and replaced above by§ your scribes §altered to§ scribe
who flourish §altered to§ flourished pen, indeed, §word crossed out and replaced above by§
apace, *1872:*lettering of <> scribes! who flourish pen apace

115

And ornament the text, they say—we say, efface.

Hence, when the earth began its life afresh in May,

2135  And fruit-trees bloomed, and waves would wanton, and the bay

Ruffle its wealth of weed, and stranger-birds arrive,

And beasts take each a mate,—folk, too, found sensitive,

Surmised the old grey stone upright there, through such tracts

Of solitariness and silence, kept the facts

2140  Entrusted it, could deal out doctrine, did it please:

No fresh and frothy draught, but liquor on the lees,

Strong, savage and sincere: first bleedings from a vine

Whereof the product now do Curés so refine

To insipidity, that, when heart sinks, we strive

2145  And strike from the old stone the old restorative.

'Which is?'—why, go and ask our grandames how they used

To dance around it, till the Curé disabused

Their ignorance, and bade the parish in a band

---

2133| MS:Abundantly, and leave §word, comma, and two words crossed out and replaced above by six words, comma, and two words§ Apace and render so and ornament, they say §last eight words, except *ornament*, crossed out§ the text less plain to read §last four words crossed out and replaced below by dash, two words, comma, three words, and period§ —we say, fine strokes efface.   *1872:*And ornament < > text, they say—we say, efface.      2134| MS:§first word illegibly crossed out and replaced to left by word and comma§ Hence,      2135| MS:And the bough §last two words crossed out and replaced above by§ fruit-trees      2136| MS:Slow all §last two words crossed out and replaced above by§ Ruffle      2137| MS:each his §crossed out and replaced above by§ a mate, folk, §word and comma over illegible erasure§ too were sensitive   *1872:*mate,—folk, too, found sensitive,      2138| MS:And knew §crossed out and replaced above by§ guessed < > stone, upright there, heard and knew §last three words crossed out and replaced above by three words§ through such §next word illegibly crossed out and replaced above by§ tracts   *1872:*Surmised the < > stone upright      2139| MS:silence, kept §over illegible word§      2140| MS:it, can §altered to§ could < > doctrine, if §crossed out and replaced above by§ did < > please,   *1872:*please:      2141| MS:Not fine and frothed, perhaps, §last four words and two commas crossed out and replaced above by three words and comma§ frothy-light to drink, but   *1872:*No fresh and frothy draught, but
2142| MS:Strong, homely §crossed out and replaced above by§savage < > sincere, first bleedings of that §last two words crossed out and replaced above by two words§ from a   *1872:*sincere: first
2143| MS:Whereof the product so do Curés now §last seven words inserted above illegibly crossed out words§ refine   *1872:*product now do Curés so refine
2144| MS:that, when §over illegible word§ < > sinks, must §crossed out and replaced above by§ we      2145| MS:Strike out §last two words inserted above illegibly crossed out words§ from §crossed out and replaced above by§ of the < > restorative;   *1872:*And strike from out the < > restorative.   *1889a:*from the      2146| MS:Which §first letter altered from illegible letter§ is?— §word, question mark, and dash over illegible erasure§ why   *1872:*'Which is?'—why
2148| MS:Their §last two letters over illegible letters§ < > the parish §over illegible word§

Lay flat the obtrusive thing that cumbered so the land!
2150  And there, accordingly, in bush and briar it—'bides
Its time to rise again!' (so somebody derides,
That's pert from Paris) 'since, yon spire, you keep erect
Yonder, and pray beneath, is nothing, I suspect,
But just the symbol's self, expressed in slate for rock,
2155  Art's smooth for Nature's rough, new chip from the old block!'
There, sir, my say is said! Thanks, and Saint Gille increase
The wealth bestowed so well!"—wherewith he pockets piece,
Doffs cap, and takes the road. I leave in Learning's clutch
More money for his book, but scarcely gain as much.

### CXXIV

2160     To this it was, this same primæval monument,
That, in my dream, I saw building with building blent
Fall: each on each they fast and founderingly went
Confusion-ward; but thence again subsided fast,
Became the mound you see. Magnificently massed
2165  Indeed, those mammoth-stones, piled by the Protoplast
Temple-wise in my dream! beyond compare with fanes
Which, solid-looking late, had left no least remains
I' the bald and blank, now sole usurper of the plains
Of heaven, diversified and beautiful before.

---

2149| MS:flat the §over illegible erasure§ ugly §first letter ove illegible erasure§ <> cumbered
thus §over illegible word§ the land! §colon altered to exclamation point§    *1872:*the obtrusive
thing <> cumbered so the          2151| MS:again!' So §inserted above illegibly crossed out
word§    *1872:*again!' (so          2152| MS:That's pert §over illegible word§ from Paris, 'since yon
<> you have erect    *1872:*from Paris) 'since, yon <> you keep erect
2153| MS:Yonder,' pursues the joke 'is    *1872:*Yonder, and pray beneath, is
2154| MS:'More or less than the same, expressed    *1872:*'But just the symbol's self, expressed
2155| MS:'Art's smooth §last two words inserted above illegibly crossed out word§ for Nature's
§first letter of last word over illegible letter§ <> chip for the    *1872:*chip from the
2156| MS:There, Sir <> said! Thanks, Sir, §word and comma crossed out and replaced above
by§ and    *1872:*sir          2157| MS:wealth that's used so    *1872:*wealth bestowed so
2158| MS:Doffs §first letter over illegible letter§ <> and takes the §last two words crossed out,
replaced above by illegibly erased words, and then restored§ road. §word and period inserted
above and over illegible word§          2159| MS:but do not learn §last three words crossed out
and replaced above by two words§ scarcely gain          2160| MS:§¶ called for§
2162| MS:Fall; each    *1872:*Fall: each          2164| MS:see: magnificently
*1872:*see. Magnificently          2166| MS:dream, beyond    *1872:*dream! beyond
2168| MS:blank about, usurper    *1872:*blank, now sole usurper
2169| MS:heaven diversified <> before;    *1872:*heaven, diversified <> before.

2170     And yet simplicity appeared to speak no more
Nor less to me than spoke the compound. At the core,
One and no other word, as in the crust of late,
Whispered, which, audible through the transition-state,
Was no loud utterance in even the ultimate
2175     Disposure. For as some imperial chord subsists,
Steadily underlies the accidental mists
Of music springing thence, that run their mazy race
Around, and sink, absorbed, back to the triad base,—
So, out of that one word, each variant rose and fell
2180     And left the same "All's change, but permanence as well."
—Grave note whence—list aloft!—harmonics sound, that mean:
"Truth inside, and outside, truth also; and between
Each, falsehood that is change, as truth is permanence.
The individual soul works through the shows of sense,
2185     (Which, ever proving false, still promise to be true)
Up to an outer soul as individual too;
And, through the fleeting, lives to die into the fixed,
And reach at length 'God, man, or both together mixed,'
Transparent through the flesh, by parts which prove a whole,
2190     By hints which make the soul discernible by soul—
Let only soul look up, not down, not hate but love,
As truth successively takes shape, one grade above
Its last presentment, tempts as it were truth indeed
Revealed this time; so tempts, till we attain to read

---

2171|   MS:compound; at <> core   *1872:*compound. At <> core,      2172|   MS:word than in
*1872:*word, as in      2173|   MS:Which, whispered, but distinct through <> transition state,
*1872:*Whispered, which, audible through <> transition-state,      2174|   MS:in this the
*1872:*in even the      2175|   MS:Disposure; much as   *1872:*Disposure. For as
2177|   MS:music that spring thence and run   *1872:*music springing thence, that run
2178|   MS:sink absorbed, §last word and comma inserted above§ <> to that triad of the §last two
words crossed out§ base,   *1872:*sink, absorbed <> to the triad base,—
2179|   MS:word, the variants   *1872:*word, each variant      2181|   MS:note enough, whence soft
harmonics sound, which mean:   *1872:*note whence—list aloft!—harmonics sound, that mean:
2183|   MS:change as   *1872:*change, as      2186|   MS:too   *1872:*too;      2187|   MS:And
through <> fleeting lives <> fixed   *1872:*And, through <> fleeting, lives <> fixed,
2188|   MS:mixed'   *1872:*mixed,'      2189|   MS:flesh by <> whole   *1872:*flesh, by <> whole,
2190|   MS:And constitute the <> by soul   *1872:*By hints which make the <> by soul—
2191|   MS:If §first letter over illegible letter§ soul <> down, nor hate but, rather, love
*1872:*Let only soul <> down, not hate but love,      2192|   MS:shape one   *1872:*shape, one
2194|   MS:time; so §over illegible erasure§ tempts till   *1872:*tempts, till

2195 The signs aright, and learn, by failure, truth is forced
To manifest itself through falsehood; whence divorced
By the excepted eye, at the rare season, for
The happy moment, truth instructs us to abhor
The false, and prize the true, obtainable thereby.
2200 Then do we understand the value of a lie;
Its purpose served, its truth once safe deposited,
Each lie, superfluous now, leaves, in the singer's stead,
The indubitable song; the historic personage
Put by, leaves prominent the impulse of his age;
2205 Truth sets aside speech, act, time, place, indeed, but brings
Nakedly forward now the principle of things
Highest and least."

CXXV

Wherewith change ends. What change to dread
When, disengaged at last from every veil, instead
Of type remains the truth? once—falsehood: but anon
2210 *Theosuton e broteion eper kekramenon,*
Something as true as soul is true, though veils between
Prove false and fleet away. As I mean, did he mean,

---

2195| MS:aright and  *1872:*aright, and         2198| MS:moment, you an §last two words, or
word and partial word, crossed out and replaced above by two words§ life means learning to
*1872:*moment, truth instructs us to         2199| MS:thereby:  *1872:*thereby.
2200| MS:Since, so we <> lie  *1872:*Then do we <> lie;         2201| MS:Whose purpose served,
§word inserted above illegibly crossed out word§ and §crossed out and replaced above by§ once
safe its truth deposited  *1872:*Its purpose served, its truth once safe deposited,
2202| MS:The lie <> stead  *1872:*Each lie <> stead,         2203| MS:The imperishable
§crossed out and replaced above by§ indubitable lay; the  *1872:*indubitable song; the
2204| MS:Puts by, makes prominent  *1872:*Put by, leaves prominent         2205| MS:Aside sets
speech and act and time and place, and brings  *1872:*Truth sets aside speech, act, time, place,
indeed, but brings         2206| MS:things."  *1872:*things         2207| MS:§¶ called for§
Wherewith <> ends, no doubt; what <> change can be §last two words crossed out and
replaced above by two words§ to dread  *1872:*Highest and least." §¶§ Wherewith <> ends.
What  *1889a:*ends. What change         2208| MS:When §over illegible word§ disengaged
*1872:*When, disengaged         2209| MS:type we see the truth? Now—falsehood, but
*1872:*type remains the truth? Once—falsehood: but  *1889a:*truth? once
2211| MS:is true, and all between  *1872:*is true, though veils between
2212| MS:Is §inserted to left§ False §altered to§ false and to§crossed out§ fleets away.  I wonder,
did  *1872:*Are false <> fleet away.  As I mean, did  *1889a:*Prove false

The poet whose bird-phrase sits, singing in my ear
A mystery not unlike? What through the dark and drear
2215　Brought comfort to the Titan? Emerging from the lymph,
"God, man, or mixture" proved only to be a nymph:
"From whom the clink on clink of metal" (money, judged
Abundant in my purse) "struck" (bumped at, till it budged)
"The modesty, her soul's habitual resident"
2220　(Where late the sisterhood were lively in their tent)
"As out of wingèd car" (that caravan on wheels)
"Impulsively she rushed, no slippers to her heels,"
And "Fear not, friends we flock!" soft smiled the sea-Fifine—
Primitive of the veils (if he meant what I mean)
2225　The poet's Titan learned to lift, ere "Three-formed Fate,
*Moirai Trimorphoi*" stood unmasked the Ultimate.

CXXVI

Enough o' the dream! You see how poetry turns prose.
Announcing wonder-work, I dwindle at the close
Down to mere commonplace old facts which everybody knows.
2230　So dreaming disappoints! The fresh and strange at first,
Soon wears to trite and tame, nor warrants the outburst
Of heart with which we hail those heights, at very brink
Of heaven, whereto one least of lifts would lead, we think,
But wherefrom quick decline conducts our step, we find,
2235　To homely earth, old facts familiar left behind.

---

2213| MS:whose soft §crossed out and replaced above by word and hyphen§ bird-phrase keeps §crossed out and replaced above by§ sits singing <> ear, *1872:*sits, singing <> ear
2214| MS:A §inserted above illegibly crossed out word§ mystery like this? What §next two words illegibly crossed out and replaced above by three illegible words§ made appear §crossed out and replaced above by§ clear *1872:*mystery not unlike? What through the dark and drear
2215| MS:This comfort *1872:*Brought comfort　　　2216| MS:only an ocean §last two words crossed out and replaced above by two words§ a certain nymph! *1872:*only to be a nymph:
2218| MS:at till *1872:*at, till　　　2220| MS:the sistered §altered to§ sisterhood
2221| MS:winged *1872:*wingèd　　　2222| MS:heels" *1872:*heels,"
2224| MS:First §crossed out and replaced above by§ Primitive <> the many §crossed out§
2229| MS:commonplace which *1889a:*commonplace old facts which　　　2230| MS:But
dreaming disappoints. The *1889a:*So dreaming disappoints! The　　　2231| MS:wear <> warrant
*1889a:*wears <> warrants　　　2232| MS:heights at *1872:*heights, at　　　2233| MS:think:
*1872:*think; *1889a:*think,　　　2234| MS:Wherefrom, one quick *1872:*But wherefrom quick
2235| MS:earth and fact *1872:*earth, and *1889a:*earth, old facts

Did not this monument, for instance, long ago
Say all it had to say, show all it had to show,
Nor promise to do duty more in dream?

### CXXVII

Awaking so,
What if we, homeward-bound, all peace and some fatigue,
2240  Trudge, soberly complete our tramp of near a league,
Last little mile which makes the circuit just, Elvire?
We end where we began: that consequence is clear.
All peace and some fatigue, wherever we were nursed
To life, we bosom us on death, find last is first
2245  And thenceforth final too.

### CXXVIII

"Why final? Why the more
Worth credence now than when such truth proved false before?"
Because a novel point impresses now: each lie
Redounded to the praise of man, was victory
Man's nature had both right to get, and might to gain,
2250  And by no means implied submission to the reign
Of other quite as real a nature, that saw fit
To have its way with man, not man his way with it.
This time, acknowledgment and acquiescence quell
Their contrary in man; promotion proves as well
2255  Defeat: and Truth, unlike the False with Truth's outside,
Neither plumes up his will, nor puffs him out with pride.
I fancy, there must lurk some cogency i' the claim,
Man, such abatement made, submits to, all the same.
Soul finds no triumph, here, to register like Sense
2260  With whom 'tis ask and have,—the want, the evidence
That the thing wanted, soon or late, will be supplied.

---

<sup>2247</sup>|   MS:impresses here: §last word and colon crossed out and replaced above by word and colon§ now:     <sup>2249</sup>|   MS:get and   *1872:*get, and     <sup>2251</sup>|   MS:nature that
<sup>1872</sup>*:*nature, that     <sup>2254</sup>|   MS:man: promotion   *1872:*man; promotion
<sup>2257</sup>|   MS:claim   *1872:*claim,     <sup>2259</sup>|   MS:no victory §crossed out and replaced above by two words and two commas§ triumph, here,     <sup>2261</sup>|   MS:supplied   *1872:*supplied.

This indeed plumes up will; this, sure, puffs out with pride,
When, reading records right, man's instincts still attest
Promotion comes to Sense because Sense likes it best;
2265    For bodies sprouted legs, through a desire to run:
While hands, when fain to filch, got fingers one by one,
And nature, that's ourself, accommodative brings
To bear that, tired of legs which walk, we now bud wings
Since of a mind to fly. Such savour in the nose
2270    Of Sense, would stimulate Soul sweetly, I suppose,
Soul with its proper itch of instinct, prompting clear
To recognize soul's self Soul's only master here
Alike from first to last. But, if time's pressure, light's
Or rather, dark's approach, wrest thoroughly the rights
2275    Of rule away, and bid the soul submissive bear
Another soul than it play master everywhere
In great and small,—this time, I fancy, none disputes
There's something in the fact that such conclusion suits
Nowise the pride of man, nor yet chimes in with attributes
2280    Conspicuous in the lord of nature. He receives
And not demands—not first likes faith and then believes.

CXXIX

And as with the last essence so with its first faint type.
Inconstancy means raw, 'tis faith alone means ripe
I' the soul which runs its round: no matter how it range
2285    From Helen to Fifine, Elvire bids back the change
To permanence. Here, too, love ends where love began.
Such ending looks like law, because the natural man
Inclines the other way, feels lordlier free than bound.
Poor pabulum for pride when the first love is found

---

2262|   MS:will, this   *1872:*will; this      2270|   MS:stimulate Soul sweetly, §last word and comma inserted above illegibly crossed out word§      2271|   MS:That owns its < > instinct, prompting §altered to§ prompts us §inserted above§ clear   *1872:*Soul with its < > prompting clear
2272|   MS:self soul's   *1889a:*self Soul's      2273|   MS:From first to last alike §last five words transposed and altered to§ Alike from first to last. Whence, if   *1872:*But, if
2274|   MS:approach wrest   *1872:*approach, wrest      2275|   MS:away and   *1872:*away, and
2279|   MS:nor chimes with   *1872:*nor yet chimes in with
2280|   MS:nature. He §over illegible erasure§      2286|   MS:permanence. §comma altered to period§ here §altered to§ Here      2288|   MS:bound:   *1872:*bound.

2290 Last also! and, so far from realizing gain,
Each step aside just proves divergency in vain.
The wanderer brings home no profit from his quest
Beyond the sad surmise that keeping house were best
Could life begin anew. His problem posed aright
2295 Was—"From the given point evolve the infinite!"
· Not—"Spend thyself in space, endeavouring to joint
Together, and so make infinite, point and point:
Fix into one Elvire a Fair-ful of Fifines!"
Fifine, the foam-flake, she: Elvire, the sea's self, means
2300 Capacity at need to shower how many such!
And yet we left her calm profundity, to clutch
Foam-flutter, bell on bell, that, bursting at a touch,
Blistered us for our pains. But wise, we want no more
O' the fickle element. Enough of foam and roar!
2305 Land-locked, we live and die henceforth: for here's the villa-door.

CXXX

How pallidly you pause o' the threshold! Hardly night,
Which drapes you, ought to make real flesh and blood so white!
Touch me, and so appear alive to all intents!
Will the saint vanish from the sinner that repents?
2310 Suppose you are a ghost! A memory, a hope,
A fear, a conscience! Quick! Give back the hand I grope
I' the dusk for!

CXXXI

That is well. Our double horoscope
I cast, while you concur. Discard that simile

---

2290| MS:also; and *1872:*also! and          2291| MS:aside was §crossed out and replaced above by§ proves just divergency *1872:*aside just proves divergency          2294| MS:anew: his *1872:*anew. His          2295| MS:Was—"from §altered to§ "From <> infinite!" §colon altered to exclamation point§          2296| MS:Not—"spend §altered to§ "Spend
2302| MS:The §crossed out and replaced above by word and hyphen§ Foam-flutter, of §crossed out§ bell of §altered to§ on          2303| MS:pains. §¶§ But *1872:*pains. §no ¶§ But
2304| MS:element: enough <> roar *1872:*element. Enough <> roar!
2305| MS:the villa §inserted above§ door *1872:*villa-door          2306| MS:§no ¶§ *1872:*§¶§
2308| MS:me and *1872:*me, and          2309| MS:§line inserted above l. 2310§
2310| MS:ghost. A *1872:*ghost! A

O' the fickle element! Elvire is land not sea—
2315 The solid land, the safe. All these word-bubbles came
O' the sea, and bite like salt. The unlucky bath's to blame.
This hand of yours on heart of mine, no more the bay
I beat, nor bask beneath the blue! In Pornic, say,
The Mayor shall catalogue me duly domiciled,
2320 Contributable, good-companion of the guild
And mystery of marriage. I stickle for the town,
And not this tower apart; because, though, half-way down,
Its mullions wink o'erwebbed with bloomy greenness, yet
Who mounts to staircase top may tempt the parapet,
2325 And sudden there's the sea! No memories to arouse,
No fancies to delude! Our honest civic house
Of the earth be earthy too!—or graced perchance with shell
Made prize of long ago, picked haply where the swell
Menaced a little once—or seaweed-branch that yet
2330 Dampens and softens, notes a freak of wind, a fret
Of wave: though, why on earth should sea-change mend or mar
The calm contemplative householders that we are?
So shall the seasons fleet, while our two selves abide:
E'en past astonishment how sunrise and springtide

---

<sup>2314</sup>| MS:element! §colon altered to exclamation point§ <> is earth §crossed out and replaced
above by§ land       <sup>2316</sup>| MS:and taste of brine. §last four words and period crossed out and
replaced above by three words and period§ bite like salt.       <sup>2318</sup>| MS:beat nor *1872:*beat,
nor       <sup>2323</sup>| MS:The windows are close §last four words crossed out and replaced above by
four words and hyphen§ Its mullions wink o'er- <> with creeping §crossed out and replaced
above by§ bloomy       <sup>2324</sup>| MS:Who climbs §crossed out and replaced above by§ mounts to
very §crossed out and replaced above by§ staircase top, may §inserted above illegibly crossed out
word§ out on §last two words crossed out and replaced above by two words§ tempt the
*1889a:*top may       <sup>2325</sup>| MS:And sudden, §last word and comma inserted above§ <> sea! We
want §last two words crossed out§ no §altered to§ No
<sup>2326</sup>| MS:fancies, to       *1889a:*fancies to       <sup>2327</sup>| MS:earth, be       §inserted above§ earthy
too!—or §word, exclamation point, dash, and word inserted above§ <> with some stray §last
two words crossed out§       *1872:*earth be       <sup>2329</sup>| MS:seaweed branch       *1872:*seaweed-branch
<sup>2330</sup>| MS:Softens and so §last three words crossed out and replaced above by three words and
comma§ Dampens and softens, denotes §altered to§ notes a shaft §crossed out and replaced
above by§ freak       <sup>2331</sup>| MS:though what §crossed out and replaced above by§
why <> earth should §over illegible erasure§ sea-change matter now §last two words
crossed out and replaced above by three words§ mend or mar       *1872:*though, why
<sup>2332</sup>| MS:contemplative— §dash crossed out§       <sup>2333</sup>| MS:seasons pass §crossed out and
replaced above by§ fleet the while ourselves abide       *1872:*fleet, while our two selves abide:
<sup>2334</sup>| MS:Long §crossed out and replaced above by§ E'en

<sup>2335</sup> Could tempt one forth to swim; the more if time appoints
That swimming grow a task for one's rheumatic joints.
Such honest civic house, behold, I constitute
Our villa! Be but flesh and blood, and smile to boot!
Enter for good and all! then fate bolt fast the door,
<sup>2340</sup> Shut you and me inside, never to wander more!

CXXXII

Only,—you do not use to apprehend attack!
No doubt, the way I march, one idle arm, thrown slack
Behind me, leaves the open hand defenceless at the back,
Should an impertinent on tiptoe steal, and stuff
<sup>2345</sup> —Whatever can it be? A letter sure enough,
Pushed betwixt palm and glove! That largess of a franc?
Perhaps inconsciously,—to better help the blank
O' the nest, her tambourine, and, laying egg, persuade
A family to follow, the nest-egg that I laid
<sup>2350</sup> May have contained,—but just to foil suspicious folk,—
Between two silver whites a yellow double yolk!
Oh, threaten no farewell! five minutes shall suffice
To clear the matter up. I go, and in a trice
Return; five minutes past, expect me! If in vain—
<sup>2355</sup> Why, slip from flesh and blood, and play the ghost again!

---

<sup>2335</sup>| MS:Could ever §crossed out§ tempt one forth §last two words inserted above§ <> swim:
the more that time  *1872:*swim; the more if time     <sup>2336</sup>| MS:Swimming grows difficult to
one's  *1872:*That swimming grow a task for one's     <sup>2337-38</sup>| MS:§two lines inserted above l.
2339§     <sup>2338</sup>| MS:villa—be  *1872:*villa! Be     <sup>2339</sup>| MS:all, and fate  *1872:*all! then fate
<sup>2341</sup>| MS:§line inserted above l. 2342§     <sup>2342</sup>| MS:All the same, one must still §last six words
and comma inserted above and then crossed out§ No doubt, that §altered to§ the <> I walk
§crossed out and replaced above by§ march <> arm thrown  *1872:*arm, thrown
<sup>2343</sup>| MS:the open §inserted above§ hand     <sup>2345</sup>| MS:enough  *1872:*enough,
<sup>2346</sup>| MS:betwixt hand §crossed out and replaced above by§ palm <> glove! That §next word
inserted above and then illegibly erased§     <sup>2348</sup>| MS:nest, the tambourine, and laying egg,
persuade §last four words inserted above§     <sup>2349</sup>| MS:A family to follow,
§last four words and comma inserted below§     <sup>2350</sup>| MS:contained,—perchance
§crossed out and replaced above by two words§ but just     <sup>2352</sup>| MS:Oh, this is §last two
words crossed out and replaced above by two words§ speak no farewell! §colon altered to
exclamation point§ <> minutes so suffice  *1872:*Oh, threaten no <> minutes shall suffice
<sup>2353</sup>| MS:go—and  *1872:*go, and     <sup>2355</sup>| MS:Slip  *1872:*Why, slip §following last line of
poem§ L. D. I. E. / Begun Dec 6. 71. Finished May 11. '72.

## EPILOGUE

THE HOUSEHOLDER

I

Savage I was sitting in my house, late, lone:
  Dreary, weary with the long day's work:
Head of me, heart of me, stupid as a stone:
  Tongue-tied now, now blaspheming like a Turk;
5 When, in a moment, just a knock, call, cry,
  Half a pang and all a rapture, there again were we!—
"What, and is it really you again?" quoth I:
"I again, what else did you expect?" quoth She.

II    ˙

"Never mind, hie away from this old house—
10   Every crumbling brick embrowned with sin and shame!
Quick, in its corners ere certain shapes arouse!
  Let them—every devil of the night—lay claim,
Make and mend, or rap and rend, for me! Good-bye!
  God be their guard from disturbance at their glee,
15 Till, crash, comes down the carcass in a, heap!" quoth I:
"Nay, but there's a decency required!" quoth She.

III

"Ah, but if you knew how time has dragged, days, nights!
  All the neighbour-talk with man and maid—such men!
All the fuss and trouble of street-sounds, window-sights:
20   All the worry of flapping door and echoing roof; and then,

---

EPILOGUE: THE HOUSEHOLDER        6| MS:we!    1872:we!—
9| MS:house!    1872:house—        10| MS:shame.    1872:shame!
12| MS:night lay    1872:night—lay        13| MS:mend or    1872:mend, or
14| MS:glee    1872:glee,        16| MS:"Nay    1889a:'Nay §emended to§ "Nay §see Editorial
Notes§        17| MS:nights:    1872:nights!        18| MS:with worthy men—such    1872:with
man and maid—such        19| MS:the fussy trouble of window-sounds and sights,    1872:the
fuss and trouble of street-sounds, window-sights:        20| MS:roof: and    1872:roof; and

All the fancies . . . Who were they had leave, dared try
    Darker arts that almost struck despair in me?
If you knew but how I dwelt down here!" quoth I:
    "And was I so better off up there?" quoth She.

IV

25    "Help and get it over! *Re-united to his wife*
    (How draw up the paper lets the parish-people know?)
*Lies M., or N., departed from this life,*
    *Day the this or that, month and year the so and so.*
What i' the way of final flourish? Prose, verse? Try!
30    *Affliction sore long time he bore*, or, what is it to be?
*Till God did please to grant him ease.* Do end!" quoth I:
    "I end with—Love is all and Death is nought!" quoth She.

---

27|   MS:*or N, departed*   *1872:or N., departed*      30|   MS:*sore long* <> *bore*, say, §last word crossed out and replaced above by§ or,   *1872:sore, long*   *1889a:sore long*
31|   MS:quoth I.   *1872:*quoth I:      32|   MS:§following last line of poem§ L. D. I. E.   RB.

RED COTTON NIGHT-CAP COUNTRY


Annotations by Michael Bright
Text edited by Susan E. Dooley and Allan C. Dooley

RED COTTON NIGHT-CAP COUNTRY, OR TURF AND TOWERS

TO

MISS THACKERAY

MS:§no dedication§  *CP3:*To Miss Thackeray

# RED COTTON NIGHT-CAP COUNTRY, OR TURF AND TOWERS

1873


I

  And so, here happily we meet, fair friend!
Again once more, as if the years rolled back
And this our meeting-place were just that Rome
Out in the champaign, say, o'er-rioted
<sup>5</sup> By verdure, ravage, and gay winds that war
Against strong sunshine settled to his sleep;
Or on the Paris Boulevard, might it prove,
You and I came together saunteringly,
Bound for some shop-front in the Place Vendôme—
<sup>10</sup> Gold-smithy and Golconda mine, that makes
"The Firm-Miranda" blazed about the world—
Or, what if it were London, where my toe
Trespassed upon your flounce? "Small blame," you smile,
Seeing the Staircase Party in the Square
<sup>15</sup> Was Small and Early, and you broke no rib.

---

*RED COTTON NIGHT-CAP COUNTRY, OR TURF AND TOWERS*     §MS in Balliol College
Library, Oxford. Ed. P1873 (P2, P2a, P3, P3a, P4), 1873, C1873, 1889a. See Editorial Notes and
Table of Editions§

*Title*| MS: Red <> Night Cap Country. / or, Turf and Towers. §last four words crossed out and
then restored§   *P2:*Night-Cap Country: / or Turf   *P3:*Country / or   *1889a:*Country, / or
<sup>2</sup>| MS:back, *1873:*back     <sup>5</sup>| MS:ravage, all §crossed out and replaced above by§ and the
futile §inserted above§ winds that blow §last two words crossed out and replaced above by§
which §crossed out§ war   *P2:*and gay winds that war     <sup>6</sup>| MS:And the §last two words
crossed out and replaced above by§ Against <> to its §crossed out and replaced above by§ his
sleep:   *P2:*sleep;     <sup>7</sup>| MS:Or Paris on the Boulevard <> it be, §crossed out and replaced
above by§ prove,   *P2:*Or on the Paris Boulevard     <sup>8</sup>| MS:§line added between present ll. 7
and 9§ to-gether   *P2:*together     <sup>9</sup>| MS:the Street of Peace—   *CP2:*the *Street of Peace—*
*CP3:*the Street of Peace—   *CP4:*the Place Vendôme—     <sup>11</sup>| MS:Mellerio, Brothers, blazed
<> world:— §dash crossed out§   *P2:*"Mellerio, Brothers" blazed <> world—
*CP2:*"*Mellerio, Brothers*"   *P3:*"Mellerio, Brothers"   *CP3:*"Flammario, Brothers"   *P4:*"Mellerio,
Brothers"   *CP4:* "The Firm-Miranda" blazed     <sup>12</sup>| MS:were London, and my
*P2:*were London, where my     <sup>13</sup>| MS:your skirt? "Small   *P2:*your flounce? "Small
<sup>14</sup>| MS:the Stair-case   *1889a:*the Staircase     <sup>15</sup>| MS:and Early, and I crushed §last two
words crossed out and replaced above by two words§ you broke

Even as we met where we have met so oft,
Now meet we on this unpretending beach
Below the little village: little, ay!
But pleasant, may my gratitude subjoin?
20  Meek, hitherto un-Murrayed bathing-place,
Best loved of sea-coast-nook-ful Normandy!
That, just behind you, is mine own hired house:
With right of pathway through the field in front,
No prejudice to all its growth unsheaved
25  Of emerald luzern bursting into blue.
Be sure I keep the path that hugs the wall,
Of mornings, as I pad from door to gate!
Yon yellow—what if not wild-mustard flower?—
Of that, my naked sole makes lawful prize,
30  Bruising the acrid aromatics out,
Till, what they preface, good salt savours sting
From, first, the sifted sands, then sands in slab,
Smooth save for pipy wreath-work of the worm:
(Granite and mussel-shell are ground alike
35  To glittering paste,—the live worm troubles yet.)
Then, dry and moist, the varech limit-line,
Burnt cinder-black, with brown uncrumpled swathe
Of berried softness, sea-swoln thrice its size;
And, lo, the wave protrudes a lip at last,
40  And flecks my foot with froth, nor tempts in vain.

Such is Saint-Rambert, wilder very much

---

¹⁹| MS:And pleasant  *P2:*But pleasant      ²¹|  *P4:*lovved  *CP4:*loved <> Normandy!
§crossed out and then restored§      ²²|  MS:house,  *P2:*house:
²³|  MS:of path- §word and hyphen inserted above§ way  *1889a:*pathway
²⁵|  MS:blue:. §colon crossed out§      ²⁷|  MS:mornings as I trip from <> gate.
*P2:*mornings, as I pad from <> gate!      ²⁸|  MS:The §crossed out and replaced above by§
Yon      ²⁹|  MS:naked foot makes  *P2:*naked sole makes
³¹|  MS:preface, the salt savours come §crossed out§ sting  *P2:*preface, good salt
³²|  MS:With §crossed out and replaced above by§ From      ³³|  MS:pipy wreathings §last four
letters crossed out and replaced above by§ -work      ³⁴|  MS:muscle-shell  *1889a:*mussel-shell
³⁶|  MS:limit-line  *P2:*limit line,      ³⁷|  MS:Mixed §crossed out and replaced above by§
Burnt      ³⁸|  MS:thrice the §crossed out and replaced above by§ its
⁴⁰|  MS:And tips the §last two words crossed out and replaced above by two words§ flecks my
⁴¹|  MS:is Saint Aubin  *CP2:*is Saint-Aubin  *CP4:*is Saint-Rambert

Than Joyeux, that famed Joyous-Gard of yours,
Some five miles farther down; much homelier too—
Right for me,—right for you the fine and fair!
45   Only, I could endure a transfer—wrought
By angels famed still, through our countryside,
For weights they fetched and carried in old time
When nothing like the need was—transfer, just
Of Joyeux church, exchanged for yonder prig,
50   Our brand-new stone cream-coloured masterpiece.

Well—and you know, and not since this one year,
The quiet seaside country? So do I:
Who like it, in a manner, just because
Nothing is prominently likeable
55   To vulgar eye without a soul behind,
Which, breaking surface, brings before the ball
Of sight, a beauty buried everywhere.
If we have souls, know how to see and use,
One place performs, like any other place,
60   The proper service every place on earth
Was framed to furnish man with: serves alike
To give him note that, through the place he sees,
A place is signified he never saw,
But, if he lack not soul, may learn to know.

---

⁴²|   MS:Than Lion, that famed Lionesse of   *P2a:*§in another hand than B's, *Joyeux* and *Joyous-Gard* are written above *Lion* and *Lionesse*§   *CP4:*Than Joyeux, that famed Joyous-Gard of
⁴³|   MS:down:, §comma crossed out§ and §crossed out and replaced above by§ much
*P2:*down; much        ⁴⁴|   MS:me, right < > fair!— §dash crossed out§   *P2:*me,—right
⁴⁵|   MS:endure the §crossed out and replaced above by§ a        ⁴⁶|   MS:angels famous,
through   *P2:*angels famed still, through        ⁴⁷|   MS:Who used to §last three words crossed
out and replaced above by three words§ For weights they fetch §altered to§ fetched and carry
§altered to§ carried        ⁴⁸|   MS:transfer, well, §crossed out and replaced above by§ just
⁴⁹|   MS:Of Lion Church   *P2a:*Of Lion church §in another hand than B's, *Joyeux* is written
above *Lion*§   *CP4:*Of Joyeux church        ⁵⁰|   MS:The §crossed out and replaced above by§
Our        ⁵¹|   MS:Well, and   *P2:*Well—and        ⁵²|   MS:This §altered to§ The
⁵³|   MS:And §crossed out and restored; replaced above by§ Who §crossed out§   *C1873:*Who
⁵⁵|   MS:eyes §altered to§ eye        ⁵⁷|   MS:Of sight, §last two words and comma inserted
above§ The §altered to§ the beauty that lies §last two words crossed out§ buried   *P2:*sight, a
beauty        ⁶¹|   MS:with, §comma crossed out and replaced above by colon§
⁶³|   MS:Is signified, a place §marked for transposition to§ a place Is signified, he
*P2:*A place is signified he        ⁶⁴|   MS:he have the §last two words crossed out and replaced
above by two words§ lack not < > learn of so §last two words crossed out§ to

65    Earth's ugliest walled and ceiled imprisonment
      May suffer, through its single rent in roof,
      Admittance of a cataract of light
      Beyond attainment through earth's palace-panes
      Pinholed athwart their windowed filagree
70    By twinklings sobered from the sun outside.
      Doubtless the High Street of our village here
      Imposes hardly as Rome's Corso could:
      And our projected race for sailing-boats
      Next Sunday, when we celebrate our Saint,
75    Falls very short of that attractiveness,
      That artistry in festive spectacle,
      Paris ensures you when she welcomes back
      (When shall it be?), the Assembly from Versailles;
      While the best fashion and intelligence
80    Collected at the counter of our Mayor
      (Dry goods he deals in, grocery beside)
      What time the post-bag brings the news from Vire,—
      I fear me much, it scarce would hold its own,
      That circle, that assorted sense and wit,
85    With Five o'clock Tea in a house we know.


      Still, 'tis the check that gives the leap its lift.
      The nullity of cultivated souls,
      Even advantaged by their news from Vire,
      Only conduces to enforce the truth

---

65| MS:Our §crossed out and replaced above by§ Earth's ugliest cieling §crossed out and replaced above by§ walled and cieled *P2:*ceiled    66| MS:rent of §crossed out and replaced above by§ in    68| MS:attainment by the §crossed out and replaced above by§ earth's palace panes *P2:*attainment through earth's palace-panes    69| MS:Pinholed throughout their <> fillagree  *P2:*Pinholed athwart their<> filagree    71| MS:here, *P2:*here    72| MS:as the Corso could—  *P2:*as Rome's Corso could:    73| MS:And that §crossed out and replaced above by§ our    74| MS:our Saint—  *P2:*our Saint,    75| MS:Falls somehow §crossed out and replaced above by§ very    78| MS:from Versailles:— §dash crossed out§  *P2:*from Versailles;    81-82| MS:§lines reversed; marked for transposition§    82| MS:from Caen,—  *CP4:*from Vire,—    85| MS:five §altered to§ Five    85-86| MS:§no ¶§  *P2:*§¶§    86| MS:lift,. §period crossed out§    87| MS:cultivated man §crossed out§ souls,    88| MS:Even with §crossed out§ ad §inserted above§ vantaged of §crossed out and replaced above by§ the news from Caen,  *P2:*by their news  *CP4:*from Vire,    89| MS:to present §crossed out and replaced above by§ enforce the fact §crossed out§ truth

90    That, thirty paces off, this natural blue
      Broods o'er a bag of secrets, all unbroached,
      Beneath the bosom of the placid deep,
      Since first the Post Director sealed them safe;
      And formidable I perceive this fact—
95    Little Saint-Rambert touches the great sea.
      From London, Paris, Rome, where men are men,
      Not mice, and mice not Mayors presumably,
      Thought scarce may leap so fast, alight so far.

      But this is a pretence, you understand,
100   Disparagement in play, to parry thrust
      Of possible objector: nullity
      And ugliness, the taunt be his, not mine
      Nor yours,—I think we know the world too well!
      Did you walk hither, jog it by the plain,
105   Or jaunt it by the highway, braving bruise
      From springless and uncushioned vehicle?
      Much, was there not, in place and people both,
      To lend an eye to? and what eye like yours—
      The learned eye is still the loving one!
110   Our land: its quietude, productiveness,
      Its length and breadth of grain-crop, meadow-ground,
      Its orchards in the pasture, farms a-field

---

⁹⁰| MS:off, the savage sea §last two words crossed out and replaced above by two words§ natural
blue    *P2:*off, this natural        ⁹¹| MS:unbroached    *P2:*unbroached,        ⁹²| · MS:§line
inserted between present ll. 91 and 93§ Beneath §added in margin§ Within §crossed out§ the
<> of the natural §crossed out and replaced above by§ placid green,    *P2:*placid deep,
⁹⁵| MS:Little Saint Aubin touches <> sea;. §semicolon crossed out§    *CP2:*Little Saint-Aubin
*CP4:*Little Saint-Rambert touches        ⁹⁷| MS:§line added between present ll. 96 and 98§ and
mice not minded like our §last three words crossed out§ Mayors, presumably    *P2:*not Mayors
presumably,        ⁹⁸| MS:Perhaps §crossed out§ we §altered to§ We might not leap
*P2:*Thought scarce may leap        ⁹⁸⁻⁹⁹| MS:§¶ called for§    *P2:*§no¶§    *1889a:*§no ¶; emended
to restore ¶; §see Editorial Notes§        ¹⁰¹| MS:objector—nullity    *P2:*objector: nullity
¹⁰²| MS:taunt is his <> mine,    *P2:*taunt be his <> mine        ¹⁰³| MS:Not yours <> the
head §crossed out and replaced above by§ world    *P2:*Nor yours        ¹⁰⁴| MS:the fields
§crossed out and replaced above by§ plain        ¹⁰⁸| MS:and an §altered to§ what
¹¹⁰| MS:The land, its    *P2:*Our land; its    *C1873:*land: its        ¹¹¹| MS:The length    *P2:*Its
length        ¹¹²| MS:The orchards <> farms §*s* crossed out and restored§    *P2:*Its orchards

And hamlets on the road-edge, nought you missed
Of one and all the sweet rusticities!
115 From stalwart strider by the waggon-side,
Brightening the acre with his purple blouse,
To those dark-featured comely women-folk,
Healthy and tall, at work, and work indeed,
On every cottage door-step, plying brisk
120 Bobbins that bob you ladies out such lace!
Oh, you observed! and how that nimble play
Of finger formed the sole exception, bobbed
The one disturbance to the peace of things,
Where nobody esteems it worth his while,
125 If time upon the clock-face goes asleep,
To give the rusted hands a helpful push.
Nobody lifts an energetic thumb
And index to remove some dead and gone
Notice which, posted on the barn, repeats
130 For truth what two years' passage made a lie.
Still is for sale, next June, that same château
With all its immobilities,—were sold
Duly next June behind the last but last;
And, woe's me, still placards the Emperor
135 His confidence in war he means to wage,
God aiding and the rural populace.
No: rain and wind must rub the rags away
And let the lazy land untroubled snore.

Ah, in good truth? and did the drowsihead

---

¹¹³| MS:hamlets §*s* crossed out and restored§ on the roads-edge §altered to§ road-edge, much
you    *P2:*road-edge, nought you          ¹¹⁷| MS:To the dark-featured    *P2:*To those dark-
featured         ¹²⁰| MS:The §crossed out§ bobbins §altered to§ Bobbins <> you §inserted
above§         ¹²⁵| MS:When time <> clock-face go §crossed out§ falls §crossed out and
replaced above by§ seems §crossed out§ goes §inserted above§ asleep,    *P2:*If time
¹²⁶| MS:push:. §colon crossed out§          ¹²⁹| MS:Notice that, pasted on
*P2:*Notice which, posted on          ¹³⁰| MS:passage makes the lie;. §semicolon crossed out§
*P2:*passage made the          ¹³¹| MS:chateau    *P2:*château
¹³⁴| MS:still proclaims §crossed out and replaced above by§ placards
¹³⁵| MS:war about to be,    *P2:*war he means to wage,          ¹³⁷| MS:No, rain    *P2:*No: rain
¹³⁸⁻³⁹| MS:§¶ called for§    *1889a:*§¶no ¶; emended to restore § ¶; §see Editorial Notes§
¹³⁹| MS:the sleepyhead §altered to§ sleepihead §altered to§ drowsihead

140    So suit, so soothe the learned loving eye,
       That you were minded to confer a crown,
       (Does not the poppy boast such?) —call the land
       By one slow hither-thither stretching, fast
       Subsiding-into-slumber sort of name,
145    Symbolic of the place and people too,
       *"White Cotton Night-cap Country?"* Excellent!
       For they do, all, dear women young and old,
       Upon the heads of them bear notably
       This badge of soul and body in repose;
150    Nor its fine thimble fits the acorn-top,
       Keeps woolly ward above that oval brown,
       Its placid feature, more than muffler makes
       A safeguard, circumvents intelligence
       In—what shall evermore be named and famed,
155    If happy nomenclature aught avail,
       *"White Cotton Night-cap Country."*


                            Do I hear—
       Oh, better, very best of all the news—
       You mean to catch and cage the winged word,
       And make it breed and multiply at home
160    Till Norman idlesse stock our England too?
       Normandy shown minute yet magnified

---

[140]|   MS:So suit and §last two words inserted above§ soothe <> eye of you §last two words
crossed out§   *P2*:suit, so soothe <> eye,        [142]|   MS:such?— §altered to§ such?) call
*C1873:*such?) —call        [143]|   MS:stretching, §word illegibly crossed out§ swift §crossed out
and replaced above by§ fast        [144]|   MS:name   *P2*:name,        [146]|   MS: *"White Cotton Night
Cap*   *P2*: *"White Cotton Night-cap*        [147]|   MS:For §inserted above§ And they <> women old
and young, §last three words marked for transposition to§ young and old,   *P2*:For they
[149]|   MS:repose—   *P2*:repose;        [150]|   MS:Nor §added in margin§ Its §altered to§ its fine
§inserted above§ thimble does not cup §crossed out and replaced above by§ cover §last three
words crossed out and replaced above by§ fits the §crossed out and restored§ acorn-close, up
§last two words crossed out and replaced above by§ more §crossed out§ top,
[151]|   MS:Whitening §crossed out and replaced above by four words§ Keeps wooll §crossed out§
woolly ward <> that §altered to§ the oval brown, its face, phyz, §last three words crossed out§
*P2*:above that oval        [152]|   MS:Than §crossed out and replaced above by§ More §crossed out§
Its        [153]|   MS:safeguard circumvent   *P2*:safeguard, circumvents        [154]|   MS:In what <>
be loved by me §last three words crossed out and replaced above by two words§ named, and
*P2*:In—what <> named and        [156]|   MS: *"White Cotton Night Cap*   *P2*: *"White Cotton Night-cap*
[160]|   MS:Till Norman pleasantness stock England   *P2*:Till Norman idlesse stock our England
[161]|   MS:Normandy shown §inserted above§ minuted §altered to§ minute

In one of those small books, the truly great,
We never know enough, yet know so well?
How I foresee the cursive diamond-dints,—
<sup>165</sup> Composite pen that plays the pencil too,—
As, touch the page and up the glamour goes,
And filmily o'er grain-crop, meadow-ground,
O'er orchard in the pasture, farm a-field
And hamlet on the road-edge, floats and forms
<sup>170</sup> And falls, at lazy last of all, the Cap
That crowns the country! we, awake outside,
Farther than ever from the imminence
Of what cool comfort, what close coverture
Your magic, deftly weaving, shall surround
<sup>175</sup> The unconscious captives with. Be theirs to drowse
Trammeled, and ours to watch the trammel-trick!
Ours be it, as we con the book of books,
To wonder how is winking possible!

All hail, "White Cotton Night-cap Country," then!
<sup>180</sup> And yet, as on the beach you promise book,—
On beach, mere razor-edge 'twixt earth and sea,
I stand at such a distance from the world
That 'tis the whole world which obtains regard,
Rather than any part, though part presumed
<sup>185</sup> A perfect little province in itself,
When wayfare made acquaintance first therewith.

---

<sup>168</sup>| MS:The §crossed out and replaced above by§ O'er orchards §altered to§ orchard
<sup>171</sup>| MS:country! only §crossed out§ we, awake §inserted above§ <sup>173</sup>| MS:Of that §altered
to§ what < > comfort, that §altered to§ what <sup>174</sup>| MS:weaving, webs §crossed out and
replaced above by§ shall around §altered to§ surround <sup>175</sup>| MS:inconscious captives with:
§inserted above§ deep be §last two words crossed out and replaced above by§ while theirs
*P2:*unconscious captives with. Be theirs <sup>176</sup>| MS:Trammeled; §altered to§ Trammeled,
while we who §last three words crossed out and replaced above by three words§ be ours to < >
trammel-trick, *P2:*Trammeled, and ours < > trammel-trick! <sup>178</sup>| MS:possible
*P2:*possible! <sup>179</sup>| MS:hail < > Night Cap *P2:*hail < > Night-cap
<sup>180</sup>| MS:you tell me this,— *P2:*you promise book,— <sup>181</sup>| MS:This beach, this razor-edge
*P2:*On beach, mere razor-edge <sup>182</sup>| MS:One stands *P2:*I stand <sup>183</sup>| MS:whole for
which one has an eye §last two words crossed out and replaced above by§ regard, *P2:*whole
world which obtains regard, <sup>184</sup>| MS:part, though part §last two words crossed out and
replaced above by two words§ at first §crossed out; original reading restored§

So standing, therefore, on this edge of things,
What if the backward glance I gave, return
Loaded with other spoils of vagrancy
190  Than I despatched it for, till I propose
The question—puzzled by the sudden store
Officious fancy plumps beneath my nose—
"Which sort of Night-cap have you glorified?"

You would be gracious to my ignorance:
195  "What other Night-cap than the normal one?—
Old honest guardian of man's head and hair
In its elastic yet continuous, soft,
No less persisting, circumambient gripe,—
Night's notice, life is respited from day!
200  Its form and fashion vary, suiting so
Each seasonable want of youth and age.
In infancy, the rosy naked ball
Of brain, and that faint golden fluff it bears,
Are smothered from disaster,—nurses know
205  By what foam-fabric; but when youth succeeds,
The sterling value of the article
Discards adornment, cap is cap henceforth
Unfeathered by the futile row on row.
Manhood strains hard a sturdy stocking-stuff
210  O'er well-deserving head and ears: the cone
Is tassel-tipt, commendably takes pride,

---

<sup>187</sup>| MS:So, standing  *P2:*So standing      <sup>188</sup>| MS:returns §altered to§ return
<sup>190</sup>| MS:for, and §crossed out and replaced above by§ till      <sup>193</sup>| MS:of Night-Cap §altered
to§ Night Cap will you §crossed out and replaced above by§ be §crossed out; original reading
restored; *will* crossed out and replaced above by§ have you glorified?" *P2:*of Night-cap
*1889a:*glorified?' §emended to§ glorified?" §see Editorial Notes§      <sup>194</sup>| MS:to
impertinence: *P2:*to my ignorance:      <sup>195</sup>| MS:night cap §altered to§ Night Cap
*P2:*other Night-cap      <sup>198</sup>| MS:gripe, *P2:*gripe,—      <sup>199</sup>| MS:Night's summons that
the Day desist from din §last seven words crossed out and replaced above by six words§ notice,
life is respited from Day! *P2:*day!      <sup>201</sup>| MS:The §crossed out and replaced above by§
Each <> wants §altered to§ want      <sup>204</sup>| MS:nurses name  *P2:*nurses know
<sup>205</sup>| MS:The §crossed out and replaced above by two words§ By what foamy-fabric §altered to§
foam-fabric: but  *P2:*foam-fabric; but      <sup>209</sup>| MS:strains on the sturdy  *P2:*strains hard a
sturdy      <sup>211</sup>| MS:tassel-tipt, a commendable pride,  *P2:*tassel-tipt, commendably takes pride,

Announcing workday done and wages pouched,
And liberty obtained to sleep, nay, snore.
Unwise, he peradventure shall essay
215   The sweets of independency for once—
Waive its advantage on his wedding-night:
Fool, only to resume it, night the next,
And never part companionship again.
Since, with advancing years, night's solace soon
220   Intrudes upon the daybreak dubious life,
Persuades it to appear the thing it is,
Half-sleep; and so, encroaching more and more,
It lingers long past the abstemious meal
Of morning, and, as prompt to serve, precedes
225   The supper-summons, gruel grown a feast.
Finally, when the last sleep finds the eye
So tired it cannot even shut itself,
Does not a kind domestic hand unite
Friend to friend, lid from lid to part no more,
230   Consigned alike to that receptacle
So bleak without, so warm and white within?

"Night-caps, night's comfort of the human race:
Their usage may be growing obsolete,
Still, in the main, the institution stays.
235   And though yourself may possibly have lived,
And probably will die, undignified—

---

²¹²|  MS:workday-done   *P2:*workday done     ²¹⁴|  MS:peradventure may essay
*P2:*peradventure shall essay     ²¹⁷|  MS:Fool, he §crossed out and replaced above by two
words§ only to resumes §altered to§ resume it, night §inserted above§
²¹⁸|  MS:And §added in margin§ Never to §crossed out§ part   *P2:*never
²¹⁹|  MS:Nay, §crossed out and replaced above by§ Since, <> nights'   *P2:*night's
²²⁰|  MS:the daylight §second syllable crossed out and replaced above by§ break <> life,
*1889a:*life §emended to§ life, §see Editorial Notes§     ²²⁸|  MS:kind domestic's hands §last
two words altered to§ domestic hand     ²²⁹|  MS:to friend, meeting now §last two words
crossed out and replaced above by three words§ lid meets lid §*meets* crossed out and replaced
below by§ with   *P2:*lid from lid     ²³¹|  MS:without, where all is §last three words crossed
out and replaced above by three words§ so warm and     ²³²|  MS: §line added between
present ll. 231 and 233§ Night caps, night  *P2:*Night-caps   *C1873:*"Night-caps, night's
²³⁴|  MS:stays;  *P2:*stays.     ²³⁵|  MS:may probably §crossed out and replaced above by§
possibly     ²³⁶|  MS:And pos §crossed out§ probably

The Never-night-capped—more experienced folk
Laugh you back answer—What should Night-cap be
Save Night-cap pure and simple? Sorts of such?
240 Take cotton for the medium, cast an eye
This side to comfort, lambswool or the like,
That side to frilly cambric costliness,
And all between proves Night-cap proper." Add
"Fiddle!" and I confess the argument.

245 Only, your ignoramus here again
Proceeds as tardily to recognize
Distinctions: ask him what a fiddle means,
And "Just a fiddle" seems the apt reply.
Yet, is not there, while we two pace the beach,
250 This blessed moment, at your Kensington,
A special Fiddle-Show and rare array
Of all the sorts were ever set to cheek,
'Stablished on clavicle, sawn bow-hand-wise,
Or touched lute-fashion and forefinger-plucked?
255 I doubt not there be duly catalogued
Achievements all and some of Italy,
Guarnerius, Straduarius,—old and new,
Augustly rude, refined to finicking,
This mammoth with his belly full of blare,
260 That mouse of music—inch-long silvery wheeze.
And here a specimen has effloresced

---

237| MS:The Never-night capped   *1873:*The Never-night-capped       238|   MS:Will laugh in
answer What <> night-cap §altered to§ Night-Cap   *P2:*Laugh you back answer—What <>
Night-cap       239|   MS:But night cap §last two words altered to§ Night Cap   *P2:*Save Night-
cap       243|   MS:And thats §crossed out§ all between is night cap§last two words altered to§
Night Cap   *P2:*between proves Night-cap       244|   MS:and I succumb to §last two words
crossed out and replaced above by two words§ confess the       245|   MS:ignoramus even so
§last two crossed out§ here       246|   MS:Would there again be §last three words crossed out
and replaced above by§ would §crossed out§ yet as   *P2:*Proceeds as <> recognise
*1889a:*recognize       248|   MS:seems his apt   *P2:*seems the apt       251|   MS:special Fiddle-
show §altered to§ Fiddle-Show       253|   MS:On shoulder, §crossed out and replaced above
by§ clavicle, sawn by §crossed out§ bow-hand-wise,       254|   MS:lute-fashion by §crossed out
and replaced above by§ and fore-finger's-plucked? §altered to§ fore-finger-plucked?
*1889a:*forefinger-plucked?       256|   MS:The achievements   *P2:*Achievements
259|   MS:bellyful   *P2:*belly full       260|   MS:The mouse   *P2:*That mouse

Into the scroll-head, there subsides supreme,
And with the tail-piece satisfies mankind.
Why should I speak of woods, grains, stains and streaks,
265    The topaz varnish or the ruby gum?
We preferably pause where tickets teach
"Over this sample would Corelli croon,
Grieving, by minors, like the cushat-dove,
Most dulcet Giga, dreamiest Saraband."
270    "From this did Paganini comb the fierce
Electric sparks, or to tenuity
Pull forth the inmost wailing of the wire—
No cat-gut could swoon out so much of soul!"

Three hundred violin-varieties
275    Exposed to public view! And dare I doubt
Some future enterprise shall give the world
Quite as remarkable a Night-cap-show?
Methinks, we, arm-in-arm, that festal day,
Pace the long range of relics shrined aright,
280    Framed, glazed, each cushioned curiosity,
And so begin to smile and to inspect:
"Pope's sickly head-sustainment, damped with dews
Wrung from the all-unfair fight: such a frame—
Though doctor and the devil helped their best—
285    Fought such a world that, waiving doctor's help,

---

262| MS:supreme   *P2*:supreme,     264| MS:woods, and §inserted above and crossed out§ grains §inserted above§ stains, polish play §last two words crossed out and replaced above by two words§ and streaks,     267| MS:sample did §crossed out and replaced above by§ would < > croon §over perhaps *crow*§   *P2*:croon,     268| MS:§line added between present ll. 267 and 269§ minors like   *P2*:minors, like     269| MS:The §crossed out and replaced above by§ Most gentlest §altered to§ gentle Giga, softest §altered to§ sleepiest Saraband.   *P2*:sleepiest Saraband."   *CP2*:Most dulcet Giga, dreamiest Saraband."     270| MS:the fiery §altered to§ fierce §crossed out§ fierce     273| MS:cat-gut ever held such captive §last four words crossed out and replaced above by five words§ could enclose §crossed out and replaced above by§ outswoon so much of §inserted above§   *P2*:could swoon out so     276| MS:That §crossed out and replaced above by§ Some     277| MS:a night cap-Show? §altered to§ a Night Cap-Show?   *P2*:a Night-cap-show?     278| MS:arm in arm   *P2*:arm-in-arm     280| MS:each object on its velvet ground, §last five words crossed out and replaced above by two words§ cushioned curiosity,     283| MS:fight—such   *C1873*:fight: such     284| MS:devil did their   *P2*:devil helped their     285| MS:With such < > that, waved §altered to§ waving the §crossed out§ doctor off,   *P2*:Fought such < > that, waiving doctor's help,

Had the mean devil at its service too!
Voltaire's imperial velvet! Hogarth eyed
The thumb-nail record of some alley-phyz,
Then chucklingly clapped yonder cosiness
290   On pate, and painted with true flesh and blood!
Poor hectic Cowper's soothing sarsnet-stripe!"
And so we profit by the catalogue,
Somehow our smile subsiding more and more,
Till we decline into . . . but no! shut eyes
295   And hurry past the shame uncoffined here,
The hangman's toilet! If we needs must trench,
For science' sake which craves completeness still,
On the sad confine, not the district's self,
The object that shall close review may be . . .

300   Well, it is French, and here are we in France:
It is historic, and we live to learn,
And try to learn by reading story-books.
It is an incident of 'Ninety-two,
And, twelve months since, the Commune had the sway.
305   Therefore resolve that, after all the Whites
Presented you, a solitary Red
Shall pain us both, a minute and no more!
Do not you see poor Louis pushed to front
Of palace-window, in persuasion's name,
310   A spectacle above the howling mob
Who tasted, as it were, with tiger-smack,

---

286|   MS:at command to book. §last three words crossed out and replaced above by three words§ their service too.   *P2:*at its service too!      288|   MS:His §crossed out and replaced above by§ The thumb-nail <> some alley-face §altered to§ alley-phyz,   *P2:*alley-phiz,   *1889a:*alley-phyz, 291|   MS:Poor feverish §crossed out and replaced above by§ hectic 293|   MS:Somehow the smile   *P2:*Somehow our smile      294|   MS:into . . . but   *P2:*into . . but   *1889a:*into . . . but      295|   MS:uncoffined thus,   *P2:*uncoffined here, 296|   MS:toilet! No, §crossed out§ If      299-300|   MS:§no ¶§   *P2:*§¶§ 300|   MS:in France—   *P2:*in France:      302|   MS:story-books, §altered to§ story-books. 303|   MS:of 'ninety-two,   *P2:*of 'Ninety-two,      307|   MS:pain the eye §last two words crossed out and replaced above by two words§ us both a   *CP4:*both, a      309|   MS:Of palace §inserted above§ window in   *P2:*palace-window, in      311|   MS:tasted as   *P2:*tasted, as

The outstart, the first spirit of blood on brow,
The Phrygian symbol, the new crown of thorns,
The Cap of Freedom? See the feeble mirth
315  At odds with that half-purpose to be strong
And merely patient under misery!
And note the ejaculation, ground so hard
Between his teeth, that only God could hear,
As the lean pale proud insignificance
320  With the sharp-featured liver-worried stare
Out of the two grey points that did him stead
And passed their eagle-owner to the front
Better than his mob-elbowed undersize,—
The Corsican lieutenant commented
325  "Had I but one good regiment of my own,
How soon should volleys to the due amount
Lay stiff upon the street-flags this *canaille!*
As for the droll there, he that plays the king
And screws out smile with a Red night-cap on,
330  He's done for! Somebody must take his place."
White Cotton Night-cap Country: excellent!
Why not Red Cotton Night-cap Country too?


"Why not say swans are black and blackbirds white,
Because the instances exist?" you ask.

---

³¹²| MS:The apparition of §last two words crossed out and replaced above by two words§
outstart, the first stain of §last two words inserted above; *stain* crossed out and replaced by *spirit*§
³¹³| MS:That hideous §last two words crossed out and replaced above by one word§ The
Phrygian symbolled §altered to§ symbol, mockery §crossed out and replaced above by three
words§ that §altered to§ the new Crown of    *P2:*crown        ³¹⁵| MS:half purpose
*P2:*half-purpose        ³¹⁷| MS:And hear §crossed out and replaced above by§ see the    *P2:*And
note the        ³¹⁸| MS:teeth that only §inserted above§    *P2:*teeth, that        ³¹⁹| MS:lean
little insignificance    *P2:*lean pale proud insignificance        ³²⁰| MS:liver-worried face
§crossed out§ stare        ³²¹| MS:grey eyes §crossed out and replaced above by§ points
³²²| MS:§line added between present ll. 321 and 323§ And got their owner passage to    *P2:*And
passed their eagle-owner to        ³²³| MS:than that mob-elbowed    *P2:*than his mob-elbowed
³²⁴| MS:lieutenant—commenting    *P2:*lieutenant commented        ³²⁶| MS:vollies
*1889a:*volleys        ³²⁷| MS:Lay flat §crossed out and replaced above by§ stiff <> canaille!
*1889a: canaille!*        ³²⁹| MS:a Red Night-Cap    *P2:*a Red night-cap        ³³⁰| MS:for!
somebody <> his turn §crossed out and replaced above by§ place."    *1889a:*for! Somebody
³³¹| MS§line added between present ll. 330 and 332§ White Cotton Night Cap    *P2:*White
Cotton Night-cap        ³³²| MS:not Red Cotton Night Cap    *P2:* not Red Cotton Night-cap
³³³| MS:white    *P2:*white,        ³³⁴| MS:exist, §altered to§ exist?" you ask? §altered to§ ask.

<sup>335</sup> "Enough that white, not red, predominates,
Is normal, typical, in cleric phrase
*Quod semel, semper, et ubique.*" Here,
Applying such a name to such a land,
Especially you find inopportune,
<sup>340</sup> Impertinent, my scruple whether white
Or red describes the local colour best.
"Let be" (you say), "the universe at large
Supplied us with exceptions to the rule,
So manifold, they bore no passing-by,—
<sup>345</sup> Little Saint-Rambert has conserved at least
The pure tradition: white from head to heel,
Where is a hint of the ungracious hue?
See, we have traversed with hop, step and jump,
From heel to head, the main-street in a trice,
<sup>350</sup> Measured the garment (help my metaphor!)
Not merely criticized the cap, forsooth;
And were you pricked by that collecting-itch,
That pruriency for writing o'er your reds
'Rare, rarer, rarest, not rare but unique,'—
<sup>355</sup> The shelf, Saint-Rambert, of your cabinet,
Unlabelled,—virginal, no Rahab-thread
For blushing token of the spy's success,—

---

<sup>335|</sup> MS:white not red predominates *P2:* white, not red, predominates  <sup>338|</sup> MS:§line
added between present ll. 337 and 339§ to such a place, §crossed out and replaced above by§
land §crossed out§ spot, §inserted below§ ˈ *CP2:*to such a land,  <sup>340|</sup> MS:Impertinent, the
scruple *P2:*Impertinent, my scruple  <sup>342|</sup> MS:be," (you say) §last two words and
parentheses inserted above§ "the  *1889a:*be" (you say), the  <sup>343|</sup> MS:Supplies you
§crossed out and replaced above by§ us  *P2:*Supplied  <sup>344|</sup> MS:they bear no passing-by:
*P2:*passing-by,—  *CP2a:*bear §*ea* crossed out; no correction made§  *CP2:*bore
<sup>345|</sup> MS:Little Saint-Aubin *P2:*Little Saint Aubin  *CP2:*Little Saint-Aubin  *CP4:*Little Saint-
Rambert  <sup>348|</sup> MS:jump *P2:*jump,  <sup>350|</sup> MS:help with §crossed out and replaced
above by§ my  <sup>351|</sup> MS:criticized *P2:*criticised  *1889a:*criticized  <sup>353|</sup> MS:reds—
*CP2:*reds  <sup>354|</sup> MS:but—unique!' *P2:*but unique,'—  <sup>355|</sup> MS:shelf Saint Aubin of
*P2:*shelf, Saint Aubin, of  *CP2:*shelf, Saint-Aubin  *CP4:*shelf, Saint-Rambert, of
<sup>356|</sup> MS:Would shame you,— §last three words crossed out and replaced above by one word and
comma§ Unlabelled, virginal, show §crossed out§ no Rahab's-thread §altered to§ Rahab-thread
*P2:*Unlabelled,—virginal  <sup>357|</sup> MS:To testify the §last three words crossed out and
replaced above by three words§ As blushing token  *P2:*For blushing

Would taunt with vacancy, I undertake!
What, yonder is your best apology,
360   Pretence at most approach to naughtiness,
Impingement of the ruddy on the blank?
This is the criminal Saint-Rambertese
Who smuggled in tobacco, half-a-pound!
The Octroi found it out and fined the wretch.
365   This other is the culprit who despatched
A hare, he thought a hedgehog (clods obstruct),
Unfurnished with Permission for the Chase!
As to the womankind—renounce from those
The hope of getting a companion-tinge,
370   First faint touch promising romantic fault!"

Enough: there stands Red Cotton Night-cap shelf—
A cavern's ostentatious vacancy—
My contribution to the show; while yours—
Whites heap your row of pegs from every hedge
375   Outside, and house inside Saint-Rambert here—
We soon have come to end of. See, the church
With its white steeple gives your challenge point,
Perks as it were the night-cap of the town,

---

358|   MS:Would line about §last two words crossed out and replaced above by one word§
decorate its pain §last three words crossed out and replaced below by three words§ taunt with
vacancy, I prophesy §crossed out and replaced above by§ undertake!
360|   MS:Pretence of an approach   *P2:*Pretence at some approach   *CP2:*at most approach
362|   MS:This is §altered and transposed to§ Is this §original reading restored§ the criminal
Saint Aubinese   *CP2:*criminal Saint-Aubinese   *CP4:*criminal Saint-Rambertese
363|   MS:That §crossed out and replaced above by§ Who <> half a pound;   *P2:*half-a-pound!
365|   MS:dispatched   *1889a:*despatched        366|   MS:hedgehog, (in the §last two words
crossed out§ clods were close §last two words crossed out and replaced above by§ obstruct)
*1889a:*hedgehod (clods obstruct),        367|   MS:the Chase.   *P2:*the Chase!
368|   MS:from them   *P2:*from those        371|   MS:Enough, there <> Night Cap Case—
*P2:*Enough: there <> Night-cap shelf—        372|   MS:vacancy,   *P2:*vacancy—
373|   MS:show: while   *P2:*show; while        374|   MS:You fill §last two words crossed out and
replaced above by two words§ White, heaps your   *P2:*White heaped your   *CP2:*White, heaps
your   *1889a:*Whites heap your        375|   MS:Outside and inside Saint Aubin   *P2:*Outside,
and   *CP2:*inside Saint-Aubin   *CP4:*inside Saint-Rambert        376|   MS:of: see the   *P2:*of.
See, the        378|   MS:were the Night Cap <> Town,   *P2:*were the night-cap <> town,

Starchedly warrants all beneath is matched
380    By all above, one snowy innocence!

You put me on my mettle. British maid
And British man, suppose we have it out
Here in the fields, decide the question so?
Then, British fashion, shake hands hard again,
385    Go home together, friends the more confirmed
That one of us—assuredly myself—
Looks puffy about eye, and pink at nose?
Which "pink" reminds me that the arduousness
We both acknowledge in the enterprise,
390    Claims, counts upon a large and liberal
Acceptance of as good as victory
In whatsoever just escapes defeat.
You must be generous, strain point, and call
Victory, any the least flush of pink
395    Made prize of, labelled scarlet for the nonce—
Faintest pretension to be wrong and red
And picturesque, that varies by a splotch
The righteous flat of insipidity.

Quick to the quest, then—forward, the firm foot!
400    Onward, the quarry-overtaking eye!
For, what is this, by way of march-tune, makes
The musicalest buzzing at my ear

---

379|   MS:A §crossed out§ Starchedly assurance §crossed out and replaced above by§ warrants
380|   MS:innocence." §quotation marks crossed out§   *P2:*innocence!
381|   MS:mettle,—British   *P2:*mettle. British     382|   *P2:*we fight it   *CP2:*we have it
383|   MS:so,   *P2:*so?     386|   MS:of them §crossed out and replaced above by§ us
389|   MS:Y §crossed out§ We < > in the §last two words crossed out and replaced above by two
words illegibly crossed out; original reading restored§     391|   MS:of as seeming like defeat
§last three words crossed out and replaced above by three words§ good as victory
392|   MS:§line added between present ll. 391 and 393§ defeat:   *P2:*defeat.
393|   MS:Escaped: §crossed out§ you < > strain point §inserted above§ and   *P2:*You < > point,
and     395|   MS:I capture and call sanguine §last five words crossed out and replaced above
by five words§ Made prize of, labelled scarlet     396|   MS:The §crossed out§ faintest §altered
to§ Faintest of §crossed out§ pretensions §altered to§ pretension     397|   MS:picturesque
and vary   *P2:*picturesque, that varies     399|   MS:forward the best §crossed out and replaced
above by§ firm foot,   *CP2:*forward, the firm foot!     400|   MS:Onward the   *CP2:*Onward,
the     401|   MS:For what   *1889a:*For, what     402|   MS:ear?   *P2:*ear

By reassurance of that promise old
*Though sins are scarlet they shall be as wool?*
405　Whence—what fantastic hope do I deduce?
I am no Liebig: when the dyer dyes
A texture, can the red dye prime the white?
And if we washed well, wrung the texture hard,
Would we arrive, here, there and everywhere,
410　At a fierce ground beneath the surface meek?

I take the first chance, rub to threads what rag
Shall flutter snowily in sight. For see!
Already these few yards upon the rise,
Our back to brave Saint-Rambert, how we reach
415　The open, at a dozen steps or strides!
Turn round and look about, a breathing-while!
There lie, outspread at equidistance, thorpes
And villages and towns along the coast,
Distinguishable, each and all alike,
420　By white persistent Night-cap, spire on spire.
Take the left: yonder town is—what say you
If I say "Londres"? Ay, the mother-mouse
(Reversing fable, as truth can and will)
Which gave our mountain of a London birth!
425　This is the Conqueror's country, bear in mind,

---

⁴⁰³| MS:The reassurance *P2:*By reassurance 　　⁴⁰⁴| MS:*wool. P2:wool?*
⁴⁰⁷| MS:texture, does §crossed out and replaced above by§ can 　　⁴⁰⁸| MS:if one §crossed
out and replaced above by§ we 　　⁴⁰⁹| MS:Would one §crossed out and replaced above by§
we 　　⁴¹⁰| MS:At the §crossed out and replaced above by§ a < > beneath that surface
*P2:*beneath the surface 　　⁴¹⁴| MS:back turned §crossed out§ to brave §inserted above§
Saint Aubin, how *CP2:*brave Saint-Aubin how *CP4:*brave Saint-Rambert, how
⁴¹⁷| MS:lie out-spread at equidistance, see, *P2:*equidistance thorpes *CP2:*lie, out-spread at
equidistance, thorpes *1889a:*outspread 　　⁴¹⁸| MS:Take the left §last three words crossed
out and replaced above by two words§ The villages or towns < > coast; *P2:*And villages and
towns < > coast, 　　⁴¹⁹| MS:distinguishable each, and *P2:* distinguishable, each and
⁴²⁰| MS:By that persistent night cap §last two words altered to§ Night Cap of a spire
*P2:*By white persistent Night-cap, spire on spire. 　　⁴²¹| MS:left,—that §crossed out and
replaced above by two words§ yonder town is . . what now do §last two words crossed out§ you
say §last two words transposed§ *P2:*left: yonder < > is—what 　　⁴²²| MS:say "Douvres"? Ay
*CP4:*say "Londres"? Ay 　　⁴²⁴| MS:a Dover birth. *P2:*birth: *CP2:*birth! *CP4:*a London
birth! 　　⁴²⁵| *CP4:*the Conqueror's §last two words crossed out and restored§

And Londres-district blooms with London-pride.
Turn round: La Roche, to right, where oysters thrive:
Monlieu—the lighthouse is a telegraph;
This, full in front, Saint-Rambert; then succeeds
430    Villeneuve, and Pons the Young with Pons the Old,
And—ere faith points to Joyeux, out of sight,
A little nearer—oh, La Ravissante!

There now is something like a Night-cap spire,
Donned by no ordinary Notre-Dame!
435    For, one of the three safety-guards of France,.
You front now, lady! Nothing intercepts
The privilege, by crow-flight, two miles far.
She and her sisters Lourdes and La Salette
Are at this moment hailed the cynosure
440    Of poor dear France, such waves have buffeted
Since she eschewed infallibility
And chose to steer by the vague compass-box.
This same midsummer month, a week ago,
Was not the memorable day observed
445    For reinstatement of the misused Three
In old supremacy for evermore?
Did not the faithful flock in pilgrimage
By railway, diligence and steamer—nay

---

<sup>426|</sup>   MS:And Dover-district <> London-pride.) §parenthesis crossed out§   *CP4:*And Londre-
district     <sup>427|</sup>   MS:Next comes Courseulle—where coarsish oysters   *P2:*Turn round:
Courseulle, to right, where oysters   *CP4:*round: La Roche, to     <sup>428|</sup>   MS:Bernièrs—the
light-house   *P2:*lighthouse   *CP4:*Monlieu—the     <sup>429|</sup>   MS:front, Saint Aubin; now
§crossed out and replaced above by§ then   *CP2:*front, Saint-Aubin   *CP4:*front, Saint-Rambert;
then     <sup>430|</sup>   MS:Langrune, and Luc the Young, and Luc the Old,   *P2:*Langrune <> Young
with Luc   *CP4:*Villeneuve, and Pons the <> with Pons the     <sup>431|</sup>   MS:ere we get to Lion
last in sight,   *P2:*ere faith gets to Lion, out of sight,   *CP2:*faith points to   *CP4:*to Jòyeux, out
<sup>432|</sup>   MS:little inland §crossed out and replaced above by§ nearer,—Oh, La Délibrande!
*P2:*nearer—oh   *CP4:*oh, La Ravissante!     <sup>433|</sup>   MS:a night cap §last two words altered to§
Night Cap   *P2:*a Night-cap     <sup>434|</sup>   MS:That extraordinary Notre-Dame!   *P2:*Donned by no
ordinary Notre-Dame!   *1889a:*ordinary Notre-Dame §emended to§ Notre-Dame! §see Editorial
Notes§     <sup>435|</sup>   MS:'Tis one <> three miracles of France   *P2:*For, one <> France,
*CP3:*three safety-guards of     <sup>437|</sup>   MS:crow-flight, four miles   *P2:*crow-flight, two miles
<sup>438|</sup>   MS:That, with the sisters   *P2:*She and her sisters     <sup>439|</sup>   MS:Is at   *P2:*Are at
<sup>440|</sup>   MS:buffeted,   *P2:*buffeted     <sup>442|</sup>   MS:the mad compass-box.   *P2:*the vague compass-box.
<sup>445|</sup>   MS:re-instatement   *P2:*reinstatement     <sup>448|</sup>   MS:diligence, and   *P2:* diligence and

On foot with staff and scrip, to see the sights
450   Assured them? And I say best sight was here:
And nothing justified the rival Two
In their pretension to equality;
Our folk laid out their ticket-money best,
And wiseliest, if they walked, wore shoe away;
455   Not who went farther only to fare worse.
For, what was seen at Lourdes and La Salette
Except a couple of the common cures
Such as all three can boast of, any day?
While here it was, here and by no means there,
460   That the Pope's self sent two great real gold crowns
As thick with jewelry as thick could stick,
His present to the Virgin and her Babe—
Provided for—who knows not?—by that fund,
Count Alessandro Sforza's legacy,
465   Which goes to crown some Virgin every year.
But this year, poor Pope was in prison-house,
And money had to go for something else;
And therefore, though their present seemed the Pope's,
The faithful of our province raised the sum
470   Preached and prayed out of—nowise purse alone.
Gentle and simple paid in kind, not cash,
The most part: the great lady gave her brooch,
The peasant-girl her hair-pin; 'twas the rough

---

450| MS:sight by much   *P2:*sight was here:          451| MS:Was here, and nowise at §last three
words crossed out and replaced above by two words§ nor gratified §altered to§ justified <> Two,
*P2:*And nothing justified <> Two          452| MS:§line added between present ll. 451 and 453§
pretention   *P2:*pretension          453| MS:And those laid   *P2:*Our folk laid
455| MS:Than §crossed out and replaced above by§ Not          456| MS:For what   *P2:*For, what
457| MS:But just a   *P2:*Except a          460| MS:That §inserted above§ The §altered to§ the
Pope's himself §altered to§ self          461| MS:thick can stick,   *P2:*thick could stick,
463| MS:fund   *P2:*fund,          465| MS:year;   *P2:*year.          466| MS:Though §crossed out
and replaced above by§ But <> year, being in the prison-house,   *P2:*year, Pope was in
*1889a:*year, poor Pope was in prison-house,          467| MS:The money <> else,   *P2:*And
money <> else;          468| MS:though the present was §crossed out and replaced above by§
seemed   *P2:*though their present          469| MS:The people §crossed out and replaced above
by§ faithful <> province paid its price §last three words crossed out and replaced above by two
words§ furnished cash—   *P2:*province raised the sum—   *CP2:*sum
470| MS:alone;   *P2:*alone.          472| MS:her ring, §crossed out and replaced above by§
brooch,          473| MS:peasant-girl, her   *1889a:*peasant-girl her

Bluff farmer mainly who,—admonished well
475 By wife to care lest his new colewort-crop
Stray sorrowfully sparse like last year's seed,—
Lugged from reluctant pouch the fifty-franc,
And had the Curé's hope that rain would cease.
And so, the sum in evidence at length,
480 Next step was to obtain the donative
By the spontaneous bounty of the Pope—
No easy matter, since his Holiness
Had turned a deaf ear, long and long ago,
To much entreaty on our Bishop's part,
485 Commendably we boast. "But no," quoth he,
"Image and image needs must take their turn:
Here stand a dozen as importunate."
Well, we were patient; but the cup ran o'er
When—who was it pressed in and took the prize
490 But our own offset, set far off indeed
To grow by help of our especial name,
She of the Ravissante—in Martinique!
"What?" cried our patience at the boiling-point,
"The daughter crowned, the mother's head goes bare?
495 Bishop of Raimbaux!"—that's our diocese—
"Thou hast a summons to repair to Rome,
Be efficacious at the Council there:
Now is the time or never! Right our wrong!
Hie thee away, thou valued Morillon,

---

475| MS:his next §inserted above; crossed out and replaced by§ new colewort crop
*P2:*colewort-crop       476| MS:Come §crossed out and replaced above by§ Stray sorrowfully
up §crossed out and replaced above by§ sparse       477| MS:Lugged out of leathern §last
three words crossed out and replaced above by two words§ from reluctant
481| MS:of the Pope   *CP2:*of the Pope:   *P3:*of the Pope—       482| MS:—No   *P2:*No
483| MS:ear long <> ago   *P2:*ear, long <> ago,       484| MS:part   *P2:*part,
485| MS:They §crossed out and replaced above by§ We commendably boast; "But   *P2:*boast.
"But   *CP3:*Commendably we boast   *P4:*We commendably boast   *CP4:*Commendably we boast
486| MS:must want §crossed out and replaced above by§ take <> turn;   *P2:*turn:
487| MS:Here are §crossed out and replaced above by§ stand
488| MS:patient: but   *P2:*patient; but       492| MS:the Delivrande—in   *P2:*the Délivrande—
in   *CP4:*the Ravissante—in       493| MS:our passion §crossed out and replaced above by§
patience <> boiling point,   *CP2:*boiling-point,       495| MS:of Bayeux"—that's
*CP2:*of Bayeux!"—that's   *CP4:*of Raimbaux!"—that's       498| MS:wrong!" §quotation mark
crossed out§   *P2:*wrong   *CP2:*wrong!       499| MS:thou priceless §crossed out
and replaced above by§ valued Hugonin,   *CP2:*valued Morillon,

500 And have the promise, thou who hast the vote!"
So said, so done, so followed in due course
(To cut the story short) this festival,
This famous Twenty-second, seven days since.


Oh, but you heard at Joyeux! Pilgrimage,
505 Concourse, procession with, to head the host,
Cardinal Mirecourt, quenching lesser lights:
The leafy street-length through, decked end to end
With August-strippage, and adorned with flags
That would have waved right well but that it rained
510 Just this picked day, by some perversity.
And so were placed, on Mother and on Babe,
The pair of crowns: the Mother's, you must see!
Miranda, the great Paris goldsmith, made
The marvel,—he's a neighbour: that's his park
515 Before you, tree-topped wall we walk toward.
His shop it was turned out the masterpiece,
Probably at his own expenditure;
Anyhow, his was the munificence
Contributed the central and supreme
520 Splendour that crowns the crown itself, The Stone.
Not even Paris, ransacked, could supply
That gem: he had to forage in New-York,
This jeweller, and country-gentleman,
And most undoubted devotee beside!
525 Worthily wived, too: since his wife it was

---

503| MS:famous twenty-second  *P2*:famous Twenty-second   504| MS:at Lion! Pilgrimage,
*CP4*:at Joyeux! Pilgrimage,   506| MS:Cardinal Bonnechose, quenching <> lights,
*P2*:lights:  *CP4*:Cardinal Mirecourt, quenching   507| MS:The leafy §inserted above§
508| MS:With August strippage  *P2*:With August-strippage   510| MS:Just that one August
§last three words crossed out and replaced above by two words§ this picked   511| MS:on
Babe  *P2*:on Babe,   512| MS:the Mother's, in a word, §last three words crossed out and
replaced above by three words§ you must see:  *P2*:see!   513| MS:Mellerio, the <> Paris
§inserted above§ goldsmith's §altered to§ goldsmith, master-piece— §crossed out and replaced
above by§ artistic §crossed out§ made §inserted above§  *CP3*:Flammario, the  *P4*:Mellerio, the
*CP4*:Miranda, the   514| MS:neighbour, that's his house §crossed out and replaced above
by§ park  *P2*:neighbour: that's   516| MS:was, turned  *1889a*:was turned
517| MS:expenditure—  *P2*:expenditure;   520| MS:Splendor <> Stone—  *P2*:itself, The
Stone.  *1889a*:Splendour   522| MS:in Madrid,  *CP4*:in New-York,
524| MS:beside.  *P2*:beside!   525| MS:too—since <> was,  *P2*:too: since <> was

Bestowed "with friendly hand"—befitting phrase!
The lace which trims the coronation-robe—
Stiff wear—a mint of wealth on the brocade.

Do go and see what I saw yesterday!
530    And, for that matter, see in fancy still,
Since . . .

There now! Even for unthankful me,
Who stuck to my devotions at high-tide
That festal morning, never had a mind
To trudge the little league and join the crowd—
535    Even for me is miracle vouchsafed!
How pointless proves the sneer at miracles!
As if, contrariwise to all we want
And reasonably look to find, they graced
Merely those graced-before, grace helps no whit,
540    Unless, made whole, they need physician still.
I—sceptical in every inch of me—
Did I deserve that, from the liquid name
"Miranda,"—faceted as lovelily
As his own gift, the gem,—a shaft should shine,
545    Bear me along, another Abaris,
Nor let me light till, lo, the Red is reached,
And yonder lies in luminosity!

---

528-29|    MS:§¶ called for§    *1889a:*§no ¶; emended to restore ¶. See Editorial Notes§
531|    MS:Since . . §¶§ There now! even for the, §crossed out§ unthankful man §crossed out§ me
*P2:*now! Even <> me,    *1889a:*Since . . . §¶§ There            532|    MS:to his §crossed out and
replaced above by§ my            533|    MS:had the grace §crossed out and replaced above by§ mind
*P2:*had a mind            534|    MS:the little §crossed out and restored§ half-league, §inserted above§
way and §last two words crossed out§ join    *P2:*the little league and join
536|    MS:miracles—: §dash crossed out§    *P2:*miracles!            538|    MS:grace    *P2:*graced
539|    MS:Merely the graced-before    *P2:*Merely those graced-before
540|    MS:Unless the whole need the physician most §crossed out and replaced above by§ now
§crossed out§ still.    *P2:*Unless, made whole, they need physician
542|    MS:that from that liquid    *P2:*that, from the liquid
543|    MS:"Mellerio," facetted    *P2:* "Mellerio,"—faceted    *CP4:*"Miranda,"—faceted
544|    MS:gem, a <> should go §crossed out§ shine    *P2:*gem,—a
546|    MS:till—lo    *P2:*till, lo            547|    MS:And §inserted above§ Yonder it §crossed out§ lies

Look, lady! where I bade you glance but now!
Next habitation, though two miles away,—
550    No tenement for man or beast between,—
That, park and domicile, is country-seat
Of this same good Miranda! I accept
The augury. Or there, or nowhere else,
Will I establish that a Night-cap gleams
555    Of visionary Red, not White for once!
"Heaven" saith the sage "is with us, here inside
Each man:" "Hell also," simpleness subjoins,
By White and Red describing human flesh.

And yet as we continue, quicken pace,
560    Approach the object which determines me
Victorious or defeated, more forlorn
My chance seems,—that is certainty at least.
Halt midway, reconnoitre! Either side
The path we traverse (turn and see) stretch fields
565    Without a hedge: one level, scallop-striped
With bands of beet and turnip and luzern,
Limited only by each colour's end,

---

*P2:*yonder    548|   MS:lady! Nay, §crossed out and replaced above by§ where < > you note,
but now,    *CP2:*you glance, but now!    *1889a:*glance but    549|   MS:That, though < > away,
next house of all, §last three words crossed out and replaced above by one word§ *habitat,*
*P2: habitat,—*    *CP2:*Next habitation, though < > away,—    550|   MS:for fo §crossed out and
replaced above by§ man < > between,    *P2:*between,—    551|   MS:Is, park and domicile, the
country-seat    *CP2:*That, park and domicile, is country-seat    552|   MS:good Mellerio! I
*CP3:*good Flammario! I    *P4:*good Mellerio! I    *CP4:*good Miranda! I    553|   MS:augury: or
*P2:*augury. Or    554|   MS:a night-cap §altered to§ Night-Cap stands    *P2:*a Night-cap
*CP2:*a Night-cap gleams    556|   MS:Heaven, saith the sage, is    *P2:*"Heaven," saith the sage,
"is    *CP2* "Heaven" saith the sage "is    557|   MS:A §crossed out and replaced above by§ Each
man: "Hell also," simple I subjoin §last three words altered to§ simpleness subjoins,    *P2:*man:"
"Hell    558|   MS:Red and White, §transposed to§ White and Red, properly describing flesh.
*P2:*By White and Red describing human flesh.    559|   MS:continue, walk, with §last two
words crossed out§ quickened §altered to§ quicken    560|   MS:And near the object that
determined you §crossed out§ me    *P2:*object which determines    *CP4:*Approach the
562|   MS:certainty itself. §crossed out§ at least!    *CP2:*least.    *P3:*least,    *CP3:*least.
563|   MS:midway, and §crossed out§ reconnoitre: either    *P2:*reconnoitre! Either
564|   MS:traverse—turn and see—are §crossed out and replaced above by§ stretch
*CP2:*traverse (turn and see!) stretch    *P3:*see) stretch    565|   MS:hedge—one
*P2:*hedge: one    566|   MS:beets §altered to§ beet and turnips §altered to§ turnip, and
*P2:*turnip and    567|   MS:by the colour's    *P2:*by each colour's

Shelves down,—we stand upon an eminence,—
To where the earth-shell scallops out the sea,
570    A sweep of semicircle; and at edge—
Just as the milk-white incrustations stud
At intervals some shell-extremity,
So do the little growths attract us here,
Towns with each name I told you: say, they touch
575    The sea, and the sea them, and all is said,
So sleeps and sets to slumber that broad blue!
The people are as peaceful as the place.
This, that I call "the path" is road, highway;
But has there passed us by a market-cart,
580    Man, woman, child, or dog to wag a tail?
True, I saw weeders stooping in a field;
But—formidably white the Cap's extent!

Round again! Come, appearance promises!
The boundary, the park-wall, ancient brick,
585    Upholds a second wall of tree-heads high
Which overlean its top, a solid green.
That surely ought to shut in mysteries!
A jeweller—no unsuggestive craft!
Trade that admits of much romance, indeed.
590    For, whom but goldsmiths used old monarchs pledge
Regalia to, or seek a ransom from,
Or pray to furnish dowry, at a pinch,

---

568|   *CP2:*down (we <> eminence)   *P3:*down,—we <> eminence,—       569|   MS:To what
§altered to§ where the earth- §inserted above§ shell     570|   MS:semicircle: and §inserted
above§   *P2:*semicircle; and     571|   MS:milkwhite   *P2:*milk-white     572|   MS:intervals
the shell-extremity,   *P2:*intervals, some shell-extremity,     573|   MS:attract the eye, §last two
crossed out§ us here,     574|   MS:you: and §crossed out and replaced above by§ say, they
575|   MS:said—   *CP2:*said,     576|   MS:blue.   *P2:*blue!     578|   MS:This, I call "path" is
road, is main highway;   *P2:*This, that I call "the path" is road, highway;
579|   MS:But—has   *P2:*But has     581|   MS:weeders busy §crossed out and replaced above
by§ stooping <> field:   *P2:*field;     582|   MS:the cap's §altered to§ Cap's projects! §crossed
out and replaced above by§ extent!     583|   MS:again! come §altered to§ Come
585|   MS:Holding, a <> wall, the §comma and last word crossed out and replaced above by§ of
*P2:*Upholds a     586|   MS:That §crossed out and replaced above by§ Which <> green,
*P2:*green.     587|   MS:mysteries.   *P2:*mysteries!     588|   MS:A Jeweller   *P2:*jeweller
590|   MS:Who but their goldsmiths do the §crossed out and replaced above by§ old
*P2:*For, whom but goldsmiths used old     592|   MS:Or get to   *P2:*Or pray to

According to authentic story-books?
Why, such have revolutionized this land
595  With diamond-necklace-dealing! not to speak
Of families turned upside-down, because
The gay wives went and pawned clandestinely
Jewels, and figured, till found out, with paste,
Or else redeemed them—how, is horrible!
600  Then there are those enormous criminals
That love their ware and cannot lose their love,
And murder you to get your purchase back.
Others go courting after such a stone,
Make it their mistress, marry for their wife,
605  And find out, some day, it was false the while,
As ever wife or mistress, man too fond
Has named his Pilgrim, Hermit, Ace of Hearts.

Beside—what style of edifice begins
To grow in sight at last and top the scene?
610  That grey roof, with the range of *lucarnes*, four
I count, and that erection in the midst—
Clock-house, or chapel-spire, or what, above?
Conventual, that, beyond manorial, sure!
And reason good; for Clairvaux, such its name,
615  Was built of old to be a Priory,
Dependence on that Abbey-for-the-Males

---

593| MS:storybooks?  *P2*:story-books?      594| MS:Why, they have  *P2*:Why, such have
595| MS:diamond-necklace-dealing—not  *P2*:diamond-necklace-dealing! not
597| MS:the gay §inserted above§ wives go and pawn  *P2*:wives went and pawned
598| MS:Jewels and plate, replaced §last two words crossed out and replaced above by four words§ figure, till found out, with paste: and sham. §last two words crossed out§  *P2*:Jewels, and figured, <> paste,      599| MS:redeem <> horrible.  *P2*:redeemed <> horrible!
603| MS:Yes, they go  *P2*:Others go      604| MS:marry like their wife  *P2*:marry for their wife,      605| MS:And then find out, §inserted above§ one day, all §crossed out§ the while was false §last four words transposed to§ was false the while  *P2*:And find out, some day, it was <> while,      607| MS:To §crossed out and replaced above by§ Would name his  *P2*:Has named his      608| MS:Besides §altered to§ Beside      610| MS:of mansardes §crossed out and replaced above by§ lucarnes, four  *C1873: lucarnes*      611| MS:count, with that *P2*:count, and that      612| MS:what—above?  *P2*:what, above?      613| MS:Conventual that  *P2*:Conventual, that      614| MS:for Tailleville, such  *CP3*:for Mailleville, such  *P4*:for Tailleville, such  *CP4*:for Clairvaux, such      616| MS:Dependance  *P2*:Dependence

Our Conqueror founded in world-famous Caen,
And where his body sought the sepulture
It was not to retain: you know the tale.
620 Such Priory was Clairvaux, prosperous
Hundreds of years; but nothing lasts below,
And when the Red Cap pushed the Crown aside,
The Priory became, like all its peers,
A National Domain: which, bought and sold
625 And resold, needs must change, with ownership,
Both outside show and inside use; at length
The messuage, three-and-twenty years ago,
Became the purchase of rewarded worth
Impersonate in Father—I must stoop
630 To French phrase for precision's sake, I fear—
Father Miranda, goldsmith of renown:
By birth a Madrilene, by domicile
And sojourning accepted French at last.
His energy it was which, trade transferred
635 To Paris, throve as with a golden thumb,
Established in the Place Vendôme. He bought
Not building only, but belongings far
And wide, at Gonthier there, Monlieu, Villeneuve,
A plentiful estate: which, twelve years since,

---

617| MS:The §crossed out and replaced above by§ Our <> founded, in    P2:founded in
*CP4:*Our Conqueror §crossed out and restored§ founded <> Caen §crossed out and restored§
618| MS:sepulture,    *1889a:*sepulture          620| MS:And §crossed out and replaced above by§
Such <> was Tailleville, prosperous    *CP3a:*was Mailleville, prosperous    *P4:*was Tailleville,
prosperous    *CP4:*was Clairvaux, prosperous          623| MS:This Priory became like <> peers
*P2:*The Priory became, like <> peers,          624| MS:A National Domain: was bought
*P2:*A National Domain: which, bought          625| MS:Resold, and, §last two words altered and
transposed to§ And, Resold, chopped and changed, with    *P2:*And resold, needs must change,
with          626| MS:Its outside <> use, until    *P2:*Both outside <> use; at length
627| MS:The place, just three and twenty    *P2:*The messuage, three-and-twenty
631| MS:Father Mellerio, goldsmith of renown,    *P2:*renown:    *CP3a:*Father Flammario,
goldsmith    *P4:*Father Mellerio, goldsmith    *CP4:*Father Miranda, goldsmith
632| MS:birth, a Turinese, by    *CP4:*birth, a Madrilene, by    *1889a:*birth a
633| MS:sojourning, accepted    *1889a:*sojourning accepted          634| MS:was that, transferred
trade §last two words transposed to§ trade transferred    *P2:*was which, trade
635| MS:thrived    *P2:*throve          636| MS:the Street of Peace. He
*CP4:*the Place Vendôme. He          638| MS:at Bernières, Beny, and Langrune,
*P2:*at Bény there, Bernières, Langrune,    *CP4:*at Gonthier there, Monlieu, Villeneuve,

640   Passed, at the good man's natural demise,
To Son and Heir Miranda—Clairvaux here,
The Paris shop, the mansion—not to say
Palatial residence on Quai Rousseau,
With money, moveables, a mine of wealth—
645   And young Léonce Miranda got it all.


Ah, but—whose might the transformation be?
Were you prepared for this, now? As we talked,
We walked, we entered the half-privacy,
The partly-guarded precinct: passed beside
650   The little paled-off islet, trees and turf,
Then found us in the main ash-avenue
Under the blessing of its branchage-roof.
Till, on emergence, what affronts our gaze ?
Priory—Conqueror—Abbey-for-the-Males—
655   Hey, presto, pass, who conjured all away?
Look through the railwork of the gate: a park
—Yes, but *à l'Anglaise*, as they compliment!
Grass like green velvet, gravel-walks like gold,
Bosses of shrubs, embosomings of flowers,
660   Lead you—through sprinkled trees of tiny breed
Disporting, within reach of coverture,
By some habitual acquiescent oak
Or elm, that thinks, and lets the youngsters laugh—
Lead, lift at last your soul that walks the air,

---

641| MS:and Heir Mellerio,—Tailleville here,　*P2:*and Heir Mellerio—Tailleville　*CP3a:*and Heir Flammario—Mailleville here,　*P4:*and Heir Mellerio—Tailleville　*CP4:*and Heir Miranda—Clairvaux here,　　642| MS:shop, with §over *a*§ Mansion <> say,　*P2:*shop, the mansion <> say　643| MS:residence— §dash crossed out§ on Quai Voltaire,　*CP4:*on Quai Rousseau,　　644| MS:And money, §inserted above§ <> wealth,—　*P2:*With money, <> wealth—　　645| MS:young Antoine Mellerio got　*CP3a:*young Antoine Flammario got　*P4:*young Antoine Mellerio got　*CP4:*young Alphonse §crossed out and replaced above by§ Léonce Miranda got　　649| MS:precinct, passed　*P2:*precinct: passed　652| MS:branchage-roof:　*P2:*branchage-roof.　　654| MS:Priory,—Conqueror,—Abbey-for-the-Males—　*P2:*Priory—Conqueror—Abbey-for-the-Males—　*P4:*Priory—Conqueror §last word crossed out and restored§　　660| MS:Wind you,—through <> tree　*P2:*Wind you—through <> trees　*1889a:*Lead you　　663| MS:youngster laugh,　*P2:*youngsters laugh—　664| MS:Waft you at last, your　*P2:*Wind, waft at last your　*1889a:*Lead, lift at

665 Up to the house-front, or its back perhaps—
Whether façade or no, one coquetry
Of coloured brick and carved stone! Stucco? Well,
The daintiness is cheery, that I know,
And all the sportive floral framework fits
670 The lightsome purpose of the architect.
Those *lucarnes* which I called conventual, late,
Those are the outlets in the *mansarde*-roof;
And, underneath, what long light elegance
Of windows here suggests how brave inside
675 Lurk eyeballed gems they play the eyelids to!
Festive arrangements look through such, be sure!
And now the tower a-top, I took for clock's
Or bell's abode, turns out a quaint device,
Pillared and temple-treated Belvedere—
680 Pavilion safe within its railed-about
Sublimity of area—whence what stretch
Of sea and land, throughout the seasons' change,
Must greet the solitary! Or suppose
—If what the husband likes, the wife likes too—
685 The happy pair of students cloistered high,
Alone in April kiss when Spring arrives!
Or no, he mounts there by himself to meet
Winds, welcome wafts of sea-smell, first white bird

---

665|  MS:the House-front  *P2:*the house-front   667|  MS:carved-stone! §exclamation mark
over question mark§ stucco §altered to§ Stucco  *P2:*carved stone   668|  MS:The panneling
§crossed out and replaced above by§ daintiness   669|  MS:all that §altered to§ the
670|  MS:The pleasant purpose  *P2:*The lightsome purpose   671|  MS:lucarnes that I
*P2:*lucarnes which I  *C1873:* lucarnes   672|  MS:mansard-roof:  *P2:*mansard-roof;
*C1873: mansarde*-roof;   673|  MS:underneath, the §crossed out and replaced above by§ what
674|  MS:windows, that suggest how brave the §crossed out and replaced above by§ a ball
*P2:*windows here suggests how brave inside   675|  MS:Of sight inside they <> the eyelid to!
*P2:*Lurk eyeballed gems they <> the eyelids to!   677|  MS:And see, the
*P2:*And now the   678|  MS:a daintiness §crossed out§ quaint
679|  MS:temple- §above illegible word§ treated Belvidere—  *P2:*temple-treated Belvedere—
681|  *P3:*stretch,  *1889a:*stretch   682|  MS:seasons change,  *P2:*seasons, change,
*CP2:*seasons' change,  *P3:*seasons change,  *CP3:*seasons' change,
683|  MS:solitary!—or suppose  *P2:*solitary! Or suppose,  *1889a:*suppose
685|  MS:The §crossed out and replaced above by§ Some happy<> cloistered there §crossed out
and replaced above by§ high:  *P2:*The happy <> high,   686|  MS:Fancy, in April when the
Spring  *P2:*Alone in  *1889a:*in April kiss when Spring   688|  MS:The §crossed out§
Winds, welcome, §inserted above§ wafts  *P2:*welcome wafts §see Editorial Notes§

That flaps thus far to taste the land again,
690  And all the promise of the youthful year;
Then he descends, unbosoms straight his store
Of blessings in the bud, and both embrace,
Husband and wife, since earth is Paradise,
And man at peace with God. You see it all?

695  Let us complete our survey, go right round
The place: for here, it may be, we surprise
The Priory,—these solid walls, big barns,
Grey orchard-grounds, huge four-square stores for stock,
Betoken where the Church was busy once.
700  Soon must we come upon the Chapel's self.
No doubt next turn will treat us to . . . Aha,
Again our expectation proves at fault!
Still the bright graceful modern—not to say
Modish adornment, meets us: *Parc Anglais,*
705  Tree-sprinkle, shrub-embossment as before.
See, the sun splits on yonder bauble world
Of silvered glass concentring, every side,
All the adjacent wonder, made minute
And touched grotesque by ball-convexity!
710  Just so, a sense that something is amiss,
Something is out of sorts in the display,
Affects us, past denial, everywhere.
The right erection for the Fields, the Wood,
(Fields—but *Elysées,* wood—but *de Boulogne*)

---

690| MS:year:— §dash crossed out§ *P2:*year;      691| MS:descends, unbosoming §altered to§ unbosoms straight §inserted above§      694| MS:with God. I §erased and replaced above by§ You      696| MS:place then,—here *P2:*place: for here      698| MS:And garden-grounds §*And* and *garden* crossed out and replaced above by two words§ Old orchard §*Old* crossed out and replaced by§ Grey      699| MS:Betoken where §crossed out and replaced above by§ that the <> once— *P2:*Betoken where the <> once.      700| MS:And here we *P2:*Soon must we      701| MS:to . . . Aha, *P2:*to . . Aha, *1889a:*to . . . Aha,      703| MS:This, the <> say, *P2:*Still the <> say      705| MS:shrub embossment as before—. §dash crossed out§ *P2:*shrub-embossment      706| MS:sun plays §crossed out and replaced above by§ splits      707| MS:Of looking §crossed out and replaced above by§ silvered glass, that §crossed out§ concentring *P2:*glass concentring      709| MS:by its §crossed out and replaced above by§ ball-convexity!      710| MS:so, much §crossed out and replaced above by§ a      714| MS:but Elysées—wood *P2:*but Elysées, wood

715    Is peradventure wrong for wood and fields
       When Vire, not Paris, plays the Capital.

       So may a good man have deficient taste;
       Since Son and Heir Miranda, he it was
       Who, six years now elapsed, achieved the work
720    And truly made a wilderness to smile.
       Here did their domesticity reside,
       A happy husband and as happy wife,
       Till . . . how can I in conscience longer keep
       My little secret that the man is dead
725    I, for artistic purpose, talk about
       As if he lived still? No, these two years now,
       Has he been dead. You ought to sympathize,
       Not mock the sturdy effort to redeem
       My pledge, and wring you out some tragedy
730    From even such a perfect commonplace!
       Suppose I boast the death of such desert
       My tragic bit of Red? Who contravenes
       Assertion that a tragedy exists
       In any stoppage of benevolence,
735    Utility, devotion above all?
       Benevolent? There never was his like:
       For poverty, he had an open hand
       . . . Or stop—I use the wrong expression here—

---

715| MS:Is peradventure §inserted above§          716| MS:When Caen, not   *CP4:*When Vire,
not          718| MS:and Heir Mellerio, he   *CP3a:*and Heir Flammario, he   *P4:*and Heir
Mellerio, he   *CP4:*and Heir Miranda, he          719| MS:That, six   *P2:*Who, six
720| MS:And truly §inserted above§ made a wilderness to smile. indeed. §crossed out§
722| MS:The §crossed out and replaced above by§ A happy          723| MS:Till . . how
*1889a:*Till . . . how          724| MS:secret, that   *P2:*secret that          725| MS:I, §over W̷e̷§ for
<> purpose, talked §altered to§ talk          727| MS:sympathise—   *C1873:*sympathise,
*1889a:*sympathize,          728| MS:At all my §last three words crossed out and replaced above by
three words§ Not mock the studry strivings §crossed out and replaced above by§ effort
729| MS:pledge and <> tragedy,   *P2:*pledge, and <> tragedy          730| MS:common-place.
*P2:*common-place!   *1889a:*commonplace!          731| MS:Suppose I make §crossed out and
replaced above by§ boast <> such a man §last two words crossed out§ desert
733| MS:That §crossed out and replaced above by§ Assertion that the §crossed out and replaced
above by§ such element exists   *P2:*that a tragedy exists          734| MS:In such a §last two words
crossed out and replaced above by one word§ any          736| MS:Benevolent? Why never
*P2:*Benevolent? There never          738| MS: . . Or   *1889a:* . . . Or

An open purse, then, ever at appeal;
740  So that the unreflecting rather taxed
Profusion than penuriousness in alms.
One, in his day and generation, deemed
Of use to the community? I trust
Clairvaux thus renovated, regalized,
745  Paris expounded thus to Normandy,
Answers that question. Was the man devout?
After a life—one mere munificence
To Church and all things churchly, men or mice,—
Dying, his last bequeathment gave land, goods,
750  Cash, every stick and stiver, to the Church,
And notably to that church yonder, that
Beloved of his soul, La Ravissante—
Wherefrom, the latest of his gifts, the Stone
Gratefully bore me as on arrow-flash
755  To Clairvaux, as I told you.

                              "Ay, to find
Your Red desiderated article,
Where every scratch and scrape provokes my White
To all the more superb a prominence!
Why, 'tis the story served up fresh again—
760  How it befell the restive prophet old
Who came and tried to curse, but blessed the land.
Come, your last chance! he disinherited
Children: he made his widow mourn too much

---

739| MS:at demand §crossed out and replaced above by§ appeal—   *P2:*appeal;
744| MS:Tailleville thus renovate and regalized,   *P2:*regalised,   *CP3a:*Mailleville thus
*P4:*Tailleville thus   *CP4:*Clairvaux thus   *1889a:*thus renovated, regalized,
745| MS:This §crossed out§ Paris   *CP4:*to Normandy §crossed out and restored§
746| MS:question. Does "devout" conclude?   *P2:*question. Was the man devout?
749| MS:bequeathment was, land   *P2:*bequeathment gave, land   *1889a:*gave land
750| MS:stiver to   *P2:*stiver,   751| MS:that Church   *P2:*church
752| MS:soul, La Delivrande—   *P2:*soul, La Délivrande—   *CP4:*soul, La Ravissante—
753| MS:gifts, that Stone   *CP2:*gifts, the Stone   754| MS:me on an arrow-flash
*P2:*me as on arrow-flash   755| MS:To Tailleville, as   *CP4:*To Clairvaux, as
756| MS:The Red   *P2:*Your Red   757| MS:provokes the White   *P2:*provokes my White
760| MS:restive Prophet   *P2:*prophet   761| MS:curse but   *1889a:*curse, but
763| MS:Children, he <> mourn indeed §crossed out§ too   *P2:*Children: he

By this endowment of the other Bride—
765  Nor understood that gold and jewelry
Adorn her in a figure, not a fact.
You make that White, I want, so very white,
'Tis I say now—some trace of Red should be
Somewhere in this Miranda-sanctitude!"

770  Not here, at all events, sweet mocking friend!
For he was childless; and what heirs he had
Were an uncertain sort of Cousinry
Scarce claiming kindred so as to withhold
The donor's purpose though fantastical:
775  Heirs, for that matter, wanting no increase
Of wealth, since rich already as himself;
Heirs that had taken trouble off his hands,
Bought that productive goldsmith-business he,
With abnegation wise as rare, renounced
780  Precisely at a time of life when youth,
Nigh on departure, bids mid-age discard
Life's other loves and likings in a pack,
To keep, in lucre, comfort worth them all.
This Cousinry are they who boast the shop

---

765| MS:Nor §over *Not*§ understanding §altered to§ understood that §inserted above§ jewelry
and gold §last three words transposed to§ gold and jewelry     767| MS:§line added between
present ll. 766 and 768§ make the White I want so   *P2:*want, so   *1889a:*make that White, I
769| MS:Somewhere, in this Mellerio sanctitude!"   *P2:*Somewhere in   *CP2:*this Mellerio-
sanctitude!"   *CP3a:*this Flammario-sanctitude   *P4:*this Mellerio-sanctitude!"
*CP4:*this Miranda-sanctitude!"     771| MS:childless—and   *P2:*childless; and
772| MS:uncertain kind §crossed out and replaced above by§ sort of cousinry   *P2:*of Cousinry
773| MS:Not §crossed out and replaced above by§ Scarce <> withold   *P2:*withhold
774| MS:The man's mind that his wish should have its way— §last nine words crossed out and
replaced above by four words§ donor's purpose though fantastical:
775| MS:Nay §crossed out and replaced above by§ Heirs     776| MS:Of riches, §crossed out
and replaced above by two words§ wealth, since <> himself—   *P2:*himself;
777| MS:Seeing they took the §crossed out and replaced above by§ a trouble
*P2:*Heirs that had taken trouble     778| MS:goldsmith-business, he,   *1889a:*goldsmith-
business he,     780| MS:at the time   *P2:*at a time     781| MS:About §crossed out and
replaced above by two words§ Nigh on     782| MS:All §crossed out and replaced above by§
Life's     783| MS:And keep   *P2:*To keep     784| MS:cousinry   *P2:*This Cousinry

785   Of "Firm-Miranda, London and New-York."
    Cousins are an unconscionable kind;   ·
    But these—pretension surely on their part
    To share inheritance were too absurd!

    "Remains then, he dealt wrongly by his wife,
790   Despoiled her somehow by such testament?"
    Farther than ever from the mark, fair friend!
    The man's love for his wife exceeded bounds
    Rather than failed the limit. 'Twas to live
    Hers and hers only, to abolish earth
795   Outside—since Paris holds the pick of earth—
    He turned his back, shut eyes, stopped ears to all
    · Delicious Paris tempts her children with,
    And fled away to this far solitude—
    She peopling solitude sufficiently!
800   She, partner in each heavenward flight sublime,
    Was, with each condescension to the ground,
    Duly associate also: hand in hand,
    . . . Or side by side, I say by preference—
    On every good work sidelingly they went.
805   Hers was the instigation—none but she
    Willed that, if death should summon first her lord,
    Though she, sad relict, must drag residue
    Of days encumbered by this load of wealth—
    (Submitted to with something of a grace

---

785| MS:"Mellerio, Brothers—Meller, people say."   *CP3a:*"Flammario, Brothers—Flammar, people   *P4:*"Mellerio, Brothers—Meller, people   *CP4:*Of "The §quotation mark and last word crossed out§ "Firm Miranda, (London and New Y§remainder of correction concealed in binding§   *1873:*Of "Firm-Miranda, London and New-York."   786| MS:kind—   *P2:*kind;
788| MS:absurd.   *P2:*absurd!   789| MS:Remains   *P2:*"Remains
790| MS:testament?   *P2:*testament?"   793| MS:limit: 'twas   *P2:*limit. 'Twas
794| MS:only, and abolish   *P2:*only, to abolish   795| MS:of it— §crossed out and replaced above by§ earth—   796| MS:all,   *CP3:*all   799| MS:peopled   *1889a:*peopling
800| MS:in his heaven-ward flights   *P2:*in each heavenward flight
801| MS:condescention   *P2:*condescension   802| MS:in hand—   *P2:*in hand,
803| MS:Or   *P2:* . . Or   *1889a:* . . . Or   804| MS:In every < > sidlingly   *P2:*On every
*C1873:*sidelingly   807| MS:His relict should but drag her residue   *P2:*Though she, sad relict, must drag residue   809| MS:Submitted   *CP2:*(Submitted

810  So long as her surviving vigilance
     Might worthily administer, convert
     Wealth to God's glory and the good of man,
     Give, as in life, so now in death, effect
     To cherished purpose)—yet she begged and prayed
815  That, when no longer she could supervise
     The House, it should become a Hospital:
     For the support whereof, lands, goods and cash
     Alike will go, in happy guardianship,
     To yonder church, La Ravissante: who debt
820  To God and man undoubtedly will pay.


     "Not of the world, your heroine!"


                              Do you know
     I saw her yesterday—set eyes upon
     The veritable personage, no dream?
     I in the morning strolled this way, as oft,
825  And stood at entry of the avenue.
     When, out from that first garden-gate, we gazed
     Upon and through, a small procession swept—
     Madame Miranda with attendants five.
     First, of herself: she wore a soft and white
830  Engaging dress, with velvet stripes and squares
     Severely black, yet scarce discouraging:

---

810|  MS:as the survivor's vigilance   *P2:*as she surviving vigilance   *CP2:*as her surviving
812|  MS:man,—   *CP2:*man,   813|  MS:And §crossed out and replaced above by§ Give
814|  MS:purpose: therefore, was it planned   *P2:*purpose:—yet, she begged and prayed
*CP2:*purpose)—yet she   815|  MS:That, she no §inserted above§ longer left to supervise,
*P2:*That, when no longer she could supervise,   *CP2:*supervise   816|  MS:The House
should thenceforth be a Hospital   *P2:*The House it should become a Hospital:
*CP2:*The House, it   817|  MS:Whereof to the support §last four words altered and
transposed to§ To the support whereof   *P2:*For the   818|  MS:Alike should go <>
guardianship   *P2:*Alike will go <> guardianship,   819|  MS:By yonder Church, La
Delivrande, who   *P2:*To yonder church, La Délivrande: who   *CP4:*church, La Ravissante: who
820|  MS:and Man   *P2:*man   821|  MS:Not <> world, this lady! §¶§   *P2:*"Not <> world,
your heroine!" §¶§   825|  *P2:*avenue;   *CP2:*avenue.   826|  MS:When out
*P2:*When, out   827|  MS:swept   *P2:*swept—   828|  MS:Madame Mellerio with
*CP3a:*Madame Flammario with   *P4:*Madame Mellerio with   *CP4:*Madame Miranda with

Fresh Paris-manufacture! (Vire's would do?
I doubt it, but confess my ignorance.)
Her figure? somewhat small and darlinglike.
835    Her face? well, singularly colourless,
For first thing: which scarce suits a blonde, you know.
Pretty you would not call her: though perhaps
Attaining to the ends of prettiness
And somewhat more, suppose enough of soul.
840    Then she is forty full: you cannot judge
What beauty was her portion at eighteen,
The age she married at. So, colourless
I stick to, and if featureless I add,
Your notion grows completer: for, although
845    I noticed that her nose was aquiline,
The whole effect amounts with me to—blank!
I never saw what I could less describe.
The eyes, for instance, unforgettable
Which ought to be, are out of mind as sight.

850    Yet is there not conceivably a face,
A set of wax-like features, blank at first,
Which, as you bendingly grow warm above,
Begins to take impressment from your breath?
Which, as your will itself were plastic here
855    Nor needed exercise of handicraft,
From formless moulds itself to correspond

---

832| MS:Fresh Paris-manufacture: Caen would    *P2:*Fresh Paris-manufacture; (Caen's would
*CP2:*Fresh Paris-manufacture! (Caen's    *CP4:*Fresh Paris-manufacture! (Vire's would
833| MS:ignorance.  *P2:*ignorance.)    834| MS:figure—somewhat < > darlinglike,
*CP2:*figure? somwhat  *1889a:*darlinglike.    835| MS:face—well < > colourless
*P2:*colourless,  *CP2:*face? well, singularly colour-free,  *CP3:*singularly colourless,
836| MS:thing, which  *P2:*thing: which    837| MS:you could not < > her—though
*P2:*you would not < > her: though    838| MS:prettiness,  *CP2:*prettiness
840| MS:full—you  *CP2:*full: you    841| MS:beauty who §crossed out§ was
842| MS:at: so  *P2:*at. So    843| MS:to—though §crossed out and replaced above by§ and if
"featureless" might §crossed out§ I  *CP2:*to, and  *CP3:*if featureless I    844| MS:completer,
for  *P2:*completer: for    846| MS:blank:  *P2:*blank!    849| MS:That ought
*CP2:*Which ought    849-50| MS:§no ¶§  *P2:*§¶§    850| MS:not conceivably §inserted
above§    851| MS:Some set  *P2:*A set    853| MS:Begin  *P2:*Begins
854| MS:And, as < > will were only plastic  *P2:*Which, as < > will itself were plastic
856| MS:The formless, fixed, begins to  *P2:*formless moulds itself to  *CP2:*From formless

With all you think and feel and are—in fine
Grows a new revelation of yourself,
Who know now for the first time what you want?
860　Here has been something that could wait awhile,
Learn your requirement, nor take shape before,
But, by adopting it, make palpable
Your right to an importance of your own,
Companions somehow were so slow to see!
865　—Far delicater solace to conceit
Than should some absolute and final face,
Fit representative of soul inside,
Summon you to surrender—in no way
Your breath's impressment, nor, in stranger's guise,
870　Yourself—or why of force to challenge you?
Why should your soul's reflection rule your soul?
("You" means not you, nor me, nor anyone
Framed, for a reason I shall keep suppressed,
To rather want a master than a slave:
875　The slavish still aspires to dominate!)
So, all I say is, that the face, to me
One blur of blank, might flash significance
To who had seen his soul reflected there
By that symmetric silvery phantom-like
880　Figure, with other five processional.
The first, a black-dressed matron—maybe, maid—
Mature, and dragonish of aspect,—marched;

---

859| MS:want.　*CP2:*want?　860| MS:awhile—　*CP2:*awhile,　861| MS:before—
*P2:*before,　862| MS:And by < > it make　*P2:*But by　*CP2:*But, by < > it, make
866| MS:Than when the absolute　*P2:*Than should some absolute
868| MS:Summons < > surrender—by no means　*P2:*Summon < > surrender—in no way
869| MS:§line added betweeen ll. 868 and 870§ impressment,—in a stranger's
*P2:*impressment, nor, in stranger's　870-72| MS:you? / ("You"—is §crossed out and
replaced above by§ means < > you, nor I, nor　*P2:*you? / Why should your soul's reflexion rule
your soul? / ("You" means < > you, nor me, nor　*1889a:*reflection　873| MS:Made
§crossed out and replaced above by§ Framed, for what reason　*P2:*for a reason
874| MS:slave—　*P2:*slave:　877| MS:might have significance　*P2:*might flash significance
878| MS:who saw grow §last two words crossed out and replaced above by two words§ had seen
his own §crossed out and replaced above by§ soul < > there,　*P2:*there
879| MS:By §added in margin§ that §over perhaps§ The white §crossed out§ symmetric silent
phantom-like　*P2:*symmetric silvery phantom-like　880| MS:Figure with < > professional.—
§dash crossed out§　*P2:*Figure, with　881| MS:may be, maid　*1889a:*maybe, maid—

Then four came tripping in a joyous flock,
Two giant goats and two prodigious sheep
885    Pure as the arctic fox that suits the snow
Tripped, trotted, turned the march to merriment,
But ambled at their mistress' heel—for why?
A rod of guidance marked the *Châtelaine*,
And ever and anon would sceptre wave,
890    And silky subject leave meandering.
Nay, one great naked sheep-face stopped to ask
Who was the stranger, snuffed inquisitive
My hand that made acquaintance with its nose,
Examined why the hand—of man at least—
895    Patted so lightly, warmly, so like life!
Are they such silly natures after all?
And thus accompanied, the paled-off space,
Isleted shrubs and verdure, gained the group;
Till, as I gave a furtive glance, and saw
900    Her back-hair was a block of solid gold,
The gate shut out my harmless question—Hair
So young and yellow, crowning sanctity,
And claiming solitude . . . can hair be false ?


"Shut in the hair and with it your last hope
905    Yellow might on inspection pass for Red!—
Red, Red, where is the tinge of promised Red
In this old tale of town and country life,
This rise and progress of a family?
First comes the bustling man of enterprise,
910    The fortune-founding father, rightly rough,

---

883| MS:flock—  *CP2*:flock,          884| MS:sheep,  *CP2*:sheep
885|  MS:the Arctic <> snow,  *P2*:arctic  *1889a*:snow          888|  MS:the Chatellaine, §altered
to§ the Chatelaine,  *CP2*:the Châtelaine,  *C1873*:the *Châtelaine*,          890|  MS:silky creature
leave  *P2*:silky subject leave          893|  MS:The hand  *P2*:My hand          895|  MS:warmly, so
§inserted above§ like the §crossed out§ life;  *P2*:life!          898|  MS:group; §semicolon deleted
and restored§          899|  MS:And as  *P2*:Till, as          901|  MS:out impertinent regard. §last
two words crossed out and replaced above by four words§ my harmless §inserted above§
question—"hair  *CP2*:question "Hair  *CP3*:question—Hair
903|  MS:solitude . . can it §crossed out and replaced above by§ hair be false?"  *CP3*:false?
*1889a*:solitude . . . can          907|  MS:life,? §question mark crossed out§

As who must grub and grab, play pioneer.
Then, with a light and airy step, succeeds
The son, surveys the fabric of his sire
And enters home, unsmirched from top to toe.
915   Polish and education qualify
Their fortunate possessor to confine
His occupancy to the first-floor suite
Rather than keep exploring needlessly
Where dwelt his sire content with cellarage:
920   Industry bustles underneath, no doubt,
And supervisors should not sit too close.
Next, rooms built, there's the furniture to buy,
And what adornment like a worthy wife?
In comes she like some foreign cabinet,
925   Purchased indeed, but purifying quick
What space receives it from all traffic-taint.
She tells of other habits, palace-life;
Royalty may have pried into those depths
Of sandal-wooded drawer, and set a-creak
930   That pygmy portal pranked with lazuli.
More fit by far the ignoble we replace
By objects suited to such visitant
Than that we desecrate her dignity

---

911| MS:must play §last two words crossed out and replaced above by two words§ grub and grab and §crossed out and replaced above by§ play pioneer   P2:pioneer.
912| MS:succeeds   *1889a:*succee §emended to§ succeeds §see Editorial Notes§
913| MS:sire,   *1889a:*sire      914| MS:from head §crossed out and replaced above by§ top to heel §crossed out and replaced above by§ toe.      918| MS:than explorations §altered to§ exploration, needless now,   P2:than keep exploring needlessly      919| MS:cellerage.
*P2:*cellerage;      920| MS:Industry goes on §last two words crossed out and replaced above by§ bustles <> doubt,   P2:doubt;   *1889a:*doubt;      921| MS:The supervisor should not go §crossed out and replaced above by§ sit too close,   P2:close.   *1889a:*And supervisors
922| MS:And §crossed out and replaced above by§ Next, walls built   P2:Next, rooms built
924| MS:some precious cabinet,   P2:some foreign cabinet,      925-26| MS:quick / <> receives her, from its traffic-taint.   P2:but, from its traffic-taint, / <> her, purifying quick. *CP2:*but purifying quick / <> her, from its traffic-taint.   P3:quick,   CP3:quick   *1889a:* quick / <> receives it from all traffic-taint.      928| MS:Princes §crossed out and replaced above by§ Royalty      929| MS:drawer, have §crossed out and replaced above by§ or set   P2:drawer, and set      931| MS:far, the ignoble be §crossed out and replaced above by§ were replaced *1889a:*far the ignoble we replace      932| MS:visitant,   *1889a:*visitant
933| MS:that the dignity be desecrate   *1889a:*that we desecrate her dignity

By neighbourhood of vulgar table, chair,
935 Which haply helped old age to smoke and doze.
The end is, an exchange of city-stir
And too intrusive burgess-fellowship,
For rural isolated elegance,
Careless simplicity, how preferable!
940 There one may fairly throw behind one's back
The used-up worn-out Past, we want away,
And make a fresh beginning of stale life.
'In just the place'—does anyone object?—
'Where aboriginal gentility
945 Will scout the upstart, twit him with each trick
Of townish trade-mark that stamps word and deed,
And most of all resent that here town-dross
He daubs with money-colour to deceive!'
Rashly objected! Is there not the Church
950 To intercede and bring benefic truce
At outset? She it is shall equalize
The labourers i' the vineyard, last as first.
Pay court to her, she stops impertinence.
'Duke, once your sires crusaded it, we know:
955 Our friend the newcomer observes, no less,
Your chapel, rich with their emblazonry,
Wants roofing—might he but supply the means!

---

935| MS:helped the father §last two words crossed out and replaced above by three words§ old
age to            936| MS:of city noise §crossed out and replaced above by§ stir    *1889a:*city-stir
937| MS:And that intrusive    *P2:*And too intrusive            938| MS:elegance—    *CP2:*elegance,
*P3:*elegance    *CP3:*elegance,            941| MS:past    *1889a:*worn-out Past
942| MS:of our life.    *P2:*of stale life.            942-44| MS:life. /  'Where all the resident §last
three words crossed out and replaced above by two words§ aboriginal gentility
*P2:*life. /  'In just the place'—does anyone object?—            945| MS:'Will <> with the §crossed
out and replaced above by§ each    *P2:*Will            946| MS:'Of town, trade-mark <> stamps each
word    *P2:*Of    *1889a:*Of townish trade-mark <> stamps word            947| MS: 'And <> here
the dirt    *P2:*And    *1889a:*here town-dross            948| MS:'Is daubed    *P2:*Is    *1889a:*He daubs
951| MS:equalize    *P2:*equalise    *1889a:*equalize            952-54| MS:in the <> first. /  'Duke, once
§inserted above§    *P2:*first. /  Pay court to her, she stops impertinence. /  'Duke    *1889a:*i'
955| MS:'Our <> newcomer confides, to me, §last two words crossed out§ no
*P2:*Our <> newcomer observes, no            956| MS:'Your chapel covered with their coat of arms
§last three words crossed out and replaced above by one word§ blazonry,
*P2:*Your chapel, rich with their emblazonry,            957| MS:'Wants    *P2:*Wants

Marquise, you gave the honour of your name,
Titular patronage, abundant will
960   To what should be an Orphan Institute:
Gave everything but funds, in brief; and these,
Our friend, the lady newly resident,
Proposes to contribute, by your leave!'
Brothers and sisters lie they in thy lap,
965   Thou none-excluding, all-collecting Church!
Sure, one has half a foot i' the hierarchy
Of birth, when 'Nay, my dear,' laughs out the Duke,
'I'm the crown's cushion-carrier, but the crown—
Who gave its central glory, I or you?'
970   When Marquise jokes 'My quest, forsooth? Each doit
I scrape together goes for Peter-pence
To purvey bread and water in his bonds
For Peter's self imprisoned—Lord, how long?
Yours, yours alone the bounty, dear my dame,
975   You plumped the purse which, poured into the plate,
Made the Archbishop open brows so broad!
And if you really mean to give that length
Of lovely lace to edge the robe!' . . . Ah, friends,
Gem better serves so than by calling crowd
980   Round shop-front to admire the million's-worth!

---

958|   MS:'Marquise,—you <> honor   P2:Marquise, you <> honour     959|   MS:'Titular
patronage, and much good will,   P2:Titular patronage, abundant will,   CP2:will
960|   MS:'To <> Institute,   P2:To <> Institute:     961|   MS:'Everything but the funds, in
short §crossed out and replaced above by§ brief: and these   P2:Gave everything but funds <>
these,   CP2:brief; and     962|   MS:'Our   P2:Our     963|   MS:'Proposes <> leave!
P2:Proposes <> leave!'     965|   MS:none-excluding all-collecting   1889a:none-excluding,
all-collecting     966|   MS:O, one   P2:Sure, one     967|   MS:when "Nay, my dear,"
§altered to§ when 'Nay, my dear,' laughs <> Duke   P2:the Duke,     968|   MS:'I shall
§crossed out and replaced above by§ may be cushion-carrier   1889a:'I'm the crown's cushion-
carrier     969|   MS: 'Y §crossed out§ Who gave the §crossed out and restored§ centre-glory,
you or I §last three words transposed to§ I or you?'   P2:Who gave its central glory, I
970|   MS:The Marquise jokes "My §altered to§ 'My   P2:When Marquise
971|   MS:to-gether   P2:together     975|   MS:That plumped the purse, which
P2:You plumped   CP2:purse which     976|   MS:open eyes §crossed out and replaced above
by§ brows     978|   MS:robe!" §altered to§ robe!'—Good lack, §last two words crossed out§ Ah
me—   P2:me!   CP2:robe!' . . Ah, friends,   1889a:robe!' . . . Ah
979|   MS:Stone §crossed out and replaced above by§ Gem <> so, than to §crossed out and
replaced above by§ by calling §over perhaps *call a*§   1889a:so than
980|   MS:Round window to <> million's-worth;   P2:Round shop-front to <> million's worth!

175

Lace gets more homage than from *lorgnette*-stare,
And comment coarse to match, (should one display
One's robe a trifle o'er the *baignoire*-edge)
'Well may she line her slippers with the like,
985    If minded so! their shop it was produced
That wonderful *parure*, the other day,
Whereof the Baron said it beggared him.'
And so the paired Mirandas built their house,
Enjoyed their fortune, sighed for family,
990    Found friends would serve their purpose quite as well,
And come, at need, from Paris—anyhow,
With evident alacrity, from Vire—
Endeavour at the chase, at least succeed
In smoking, eating, drinking, laughing, and
995    Preferring country, oh so much to town!
Thus lived the husband; though his wife would sigh
In confidence, when Countesses were kind,
'Cut off from Paris and society!'
White, White, I once more round you in the ears!
1000    Though you have marked it, in a corner, yours

---

981| MS:Lace lacks no §last two words crossed out and replaced above by two words§ gets more homage than §inserted above§ from the §crossed out§ lorgnette-stare, *C1873: lorgnette*-stare, 982-83| MS:§lines inserted between present ll. 981 and 984§ 982| MS:match, should *P2*:match, (should 983| MS:baignoire-edge, *P2*:baignoire-edge,) *C1873: baignoire*-edge,) 984| MS:"Well §altered to§ 'Well 985| MS:so; their <> was, produced *CP3*:so! their *1889a*:was produced 987| MS:said, it *1889a*:said it 988| MS:paired Mellerios built *CP3a*:paired Flammarios built *P4*:paired Mellerios built *CP4*:paired Mirandas built 989| MS:their Tainville, sighed *P2*:their Tailleville, sighed *CP2*:their fortune, sighed 990| MS:purpose quite as §last two words inserted above§ much, the same, §last two words crossed out§ *CP2*:as well, *P4*:as much, *1873*:as well, 991| MS:come at call—from Paris, at a pinch, §last three words crossed out§ anyhow, *P2*:call, from Paris,—anyhow, *CP2*:come, at need, from Paris—anyhow, 992| MS:From Caen, with evident alacrity,— *CP2*:From Caen,—with <> alacrity, *P3*:With evident alacrity, from Caen— *CP4*:from Vire— 993| MS:chase and quite §last two words crossed out and replaced above by dash and two words§ —at least *P2*:chase, at 994| MS:laughing there. *P2*:there, *CP2*:laughing, and 996| MS:At least, §last two words crossed out and replaced above by two words§ So lived the husband—for §crossed out and replaced above by§ though *P2*:Thus lived the husband; though 998| MS:society!" §altered to§ society!' 999| MS:Red—Red, §last two words crossed out and replaced above by two words§ White, White, 1000| MS:Well, §crossed out and replaced above by§ Though <> it in a corner yours *P2*:it, in a corner, yours

Henceforth,—Red-lettered 'Failure' very plain,
I shall acknowledge, on the snowy hem
Of ordinary Night-cap! Come, enough!
We have gone round its cotton vastitude,
1005   Or half-round, for the end's consistent still,
A *cul-de-sac* with stoppage at the sea.
Here we return upon our steps. One look
May bid good morning—properly good night—
To civic bliss, Miranda and his mate!
1010   Are we to rise and go?"

No, sit and stay!
Now comes my moment, with the thrilling throw
Of curtain from each side a shrouded case.
Don't the rings shriek an ominous "Ha! ha!
*So* you take Human Nature upon trust?"
1015   List but with like trust to an incident
Which speedily shall make quite Red enough
Burn out of yonder spotless napery!

Sit on the little mound here, whence you seize
The whole of the gay front sun-satisfied,
1020   One laugh of colour and embellishment!

---

1001| MS:Henceforth,—red-lettered an initial plain §last three words crossed out and replaced above by two words§ failure very plain, §*plain* restored§   P2:red-lettered Failure
CP2:red-lettered 'Failure'   *1889a:*Henceforth,—Red-lettered        1002-3| MS:shall remember
< > the virgin snow / Of what proves, just as I expected, pure §entire line crossed out§ / And pure and §last two words inserted above§ simple specimen of §last two words crossed out§ night-cap! §altered to§ Night-Cap! Come   P2:snow, / The pure < > Night-cap! Come
CP2:shall acknowledge < > the snowy hem / Of ordinary Night-cap! Come   P3:acknowedge
CP4:acknowledge        1006| MS:*cul-de-sac,* this §crossed out and replaced above by§ and stoppage   P2:*cul-de-sac* with stoppage        1008| MS:May §over illegible word§
1009| MS:To bourgeois bliss, Mellerio and his mate.   P2:To civic bliss, < > mate!
CP3a:bliss, Flammario and   P4:bliss, Mellerio and   CP4:bliss, Miranda and
1010| MS:§¶§ No, to §crossed out§ sit        1011| MS:moment, and §crossed out and replaced above by§ with   1013| MS:ominous "Ha Ha—   P2:ominous "Ha! ha!        1015| MS:but a little to   P2:but with like trust to        1016| MS:Or two §last two words crossed out§ that §altered to§ That speedily shall §last two words inserted above§   P2:Which speedily
1017-18| MS:§¶ called for§   *1889a:*§no ¶; emended to restore ¶; see Editorial Notes§
1018| MS:the little §inserted above§        1020| MS:embellishment.   P2:embellishment!

Because it was there,—past those laurustines,
On that smooth gravel-sweep 'twixt flowers and sward,—
There tragic death befell; and not one grace
Outspread before you but is registered
1025 In that sinistrous coil these last two years
Were occupied in winding smooth again.

"True?" Well, at least it was concluded so,
Sworn to be truth, allowed by Law as such
(With my concurrence, if it matter here)
1030 A month ago: at Vire they tried the case.

---

[1021]| MS:past the laurustines, *P2:*past those laurustines, [1022]| MS:On the smooth gravel sweep *P2:*On that smooth gravel-sweep [1023]| MS:That tragic < > befell, and *P2:*There tragic < > befell; and [1024]| MS:before you §inserted above§ [1025]| MS:coil, these *1889a:*coil these [1026]| MS:Were taken §crossed out and replaced above by§ occupied in winding out §crossed out and replaced above by§ smooth [1026-27]| MS:§no ¶§ *P2:*§¶§ [1028]| MS:such, *1889a:*such [1029]| MS:With < > if that matter here *P2:*(With < > if it matter here) [1030]| MS:ago: they tried the case at Caen. §rule; note in B's hand "Leave half-sheet" *CP4:*ago: at Vire they tried the case.

II

Monsieur Léonce Miranda, then, . . . but stay!
Permit me a preliminary word,
And, after, all shall go so straight to end!

Have you, the travelled lady, found yourself
⁵   Inside a ruin, fane or bath or cirque,
Renowned in story, dear through youthful dream?
If not,—imagination serves as well.
Try fancy-land, go back a thousand years,
Or forward, half the number, and confront
¹⁰  Some work of art gnawn hollow by Time's tooth,—
Hellenic temple, Roman theatre,
Gothic cathedral, Gallic Tuileries,
But ruined, one and whichsoe'er you like.
Obstructions choke what still remains intact,
¹⁵  Yet proffer change that's picturesque in turn;
Since little life begins where great life ends,
And vegetation soon amalgamates,
Smooths novel shape from out the shapeless old,
Till broken column, battered cornice block
²⁰  The centre with a bulk half weeds and flowers,
Half relics you devoutly recognize.

---

¹|  MS:Monsieur Antoine Mellerio, then,—but first §crossed out§ no:  *P2*:but stay!
*CP2*:then, . . but  *CP3a*:Monsieur Antoine Flammario, then  *P4*:Monsieur Antoine Mellerio,
then  *CP4*:Monsieur Alphonse §crossed out and replaced above by§ Léonce Miranda, then
*1889a*:then, . . . but      ³⁻⁴|  MS:§no ¶§  *P2*:§¶§      ⁵|  MS:ruin, temple, theatre cir §last
three words crossed out§ fane, or bath, or  *P2*:fane or bath or      ⁹|  MS:and you note §last
two words crossed out§ confront      ¹⁰|  MS:§line added between present ll. 9 and 11§ art
deposed by circumstance, §last three words crossed out and replaced below by five words§
gnawn hollow by time's tooth—  *P2*:by Time's tooth,—      ¹¹|  MS:Athenian §crossed out
and replaced above by§ Hellenic      ¹³|  MS:But ruined, §crossed out and replaced above
by§ ravage, §crossed out, restoring *ruined*,§ <> whichso'er  *P2*:whichsoe'er
¹⁴|  MS:Obstructions §last letter crossed out and restored§ choaks §altered to§ choak
*P2*:choke      ¹⁵|  MS:Yet want not §last two words crossed out and replaced above by§ furnish
picturesqueness in their turn;  *P2*:Yet proffer change that's picturesque in turn;
¹⁸|  MS:Makes a new §last three words crossed out and replaced above by two words§ Smooths
novel shape from §inserted above§ out of §crossed out§ the  *P2*:Smoothes  *CP2*:Smooths
¹⁹|  MS:And §crossed out and replaced above by§ Till broken pillar §crossed out and replaced
above by§ column <> cornice, build §crossed out§ block  *CP2*:cornice block
²⁰|  MS:centre, §comma crossed out§      ²¹|  *P2*:recognise.  *1889a*:recognize.

Devoutly recognizing,—hark, a voice
Not to be disregarded! "Man worked here
Once on a time; here needs again to work;
25    Ruins obstruct, which man must remedy."
Would you demur "Let Time fulfil his task,
And, till the scythe-sweep find no obstacle,
Let man be patient"?

                    The reply were prompt:
"Glisteningly beneath the May-night moon,
30    Herbage and floral coverture bedeck
Yon splintered mass amidst the solitude:
Wolves occupy the background, or some snake
Glides by at distance; picturesque enough!
Therefore, preserve it? Nay, pour daylight in,—
35    The mound proves swarming with humanity.
There never was a thorough solitude,
Now you look nearer: mortal busy life
First of all brought the crumblings down on pate,
Which trip man's foot still, plague his passage much,

---

²²| *P2*:recognising    *1889a*:recognizing        ²³| MS:disregarded!—"Man   *CP2*:disregarded!
"Man          ²⁴| MS:time; he §crossed out and replaced above by§ here needs again §inserted
above§ to work once more; §last two words crossed out§        ²⁵| MS:This is §last two words
crossed out and replaced above by§ Ruins obstruction §altered to§ obstruct, you §crossed out§
which man §last two words inserted above§ must remedy!" *P2*:remedy."         ²⁶| MS:How
§crossed out§ would §altered to§ Would you say? §crossed out and replaced above by§ demur
"Let time §altered to§ Time   *P2*:demur—"Let   *CP2*:demur "Let        ²⁸| MS:Let all be as it
is §last five words crossed out and replaced above by three words§ man be patient?" §¶§ The
§inserted above§ Reply   *P2*:reply        ³⁰| MS:floral tenderness §crossed out and replaced
above by§ coverture bedeck §over perhaps *beseem*§        ³¹| MS:The splintered mass that
makes the   *P2*:You splintered   *CP2*:Yon splintered mass amidst the        ³²| MS:Wolves in
§crossed out and replaced above by§ occupy the background, may be, §last two words crossed
out§ or        ³³| MS:Conceived §crossed out and replaced above by two words§ Glides off
§crossed out§ by §inserted above§ at distance: picturesque   *1889a*:distance; picturesque
³⁴| MS:Therefore, §added in margin§ Preserve §altered to§ preserve it? But I §last two words
crossed out and replaced above by§ Nay, pour broad §crossed out§ daylight
³⁵| MS:mound is §crossed out and replaced above by§ proves <> humanity:   *CP2*:humanity.
³⁶| MS:a proper §inserted above§ solitude, at all, §last two words crossed out§   *CP2*:a thorough
solitude,        ³⁸| MS:all, brought   *P2*:all brought        ³⁹| MS:trip man's §inserted above§
foot still, and §crossed out§ plague mans §crossed out and replaced above by§ his

40 And prove—what seems to you so picturesque
To him is . . . but experiment yourself
On how conducive to a happy home
Will be the circumstance your bed for base
Boasts tessellated pavement,—equally
45 Affected by the scorpion for his nest,—
While what o'erroofs bed is an architrave,
Marble, and not unlikely to crush man
To mummy, should its venerable prop,
Some fig-tree-stump, play traitor underneath.
50 Be wise! Decide! For conservation's sake,
Clear the arena forthwith! lest the tread
Of too-much-tried impatience trample out
Solid and unsubstantial to one blank
Mud-mixture, picturesque to nobody,—
55 And, task done, quarrel with the parts intact
Whence came the filtered fine dust, whence the crash
Bides but its time to follow. Quick conclude
Removal, time effects so tardily,
Of what is plain obstruction; rubbish cleared,

---

40] MS:Seeing that what to you is picturesque *P2:*And prove that    *CP2:*prove—what seems to you so picturesque, *P3:*picturesque    41] MS:is . . well, experiment *CP2:*is . . but experiment *1889a:*is . . . but    43] MS:May §crossed out and replaced above by§ Would be the fact of your §last three words crossed out and replaced above by two words§ circumstance that bed is based *P2:*circumstance, your bed for base *CP2:*Will be *1889a:*circumstance your    44] MS:On tesselated *P2:*Boasts tesselated    46] MS:o'erroofs you is *P2:*o'erroofs bed is    47] MS:True §crossed out§ marble §altered to§ Marble, and not §last two words inserted above§ never §crossed out and replaced above by§ little §crossed out§ likely §altered to§ unlikely    48] MS:mummy, while §crossed out and replaced above by§ though its *P2:*mummy, should its    49] MS:The §crossed out and replaced above by§ Some fig-tree-stump, does duty staunch beneath. *P2:*The fig-tree-stump, play traitor underneath. *CP2:*Some fig-tree-stump    50] MS:Be wise—decide, for §last four words altered to§ Be wise! Decide! For *P2:*Be wise!—Decide! For *CP2:*Be wise! Decide! For    51] MS:forthwith, lest *CP2:*forthwith! lest    52] MS:Of ignorant §crossed out and replaced above by§ too-much-tried    55] MS:And §crossed out and replaced above by§ Nay, that done <> intact— *P2:*And, that <> intact *CP2:*And, task done    56] MS:Thence §altered to§ Whence came <> dust, thence §altered to§ whence    57] MS:Bided §altered to§ Bides but §inserted above§ its <> follow. best §altered to§ Best conclude *CP2:*follow. Quick, §comma crossed out§ conclude    58] MS:The §crossed out and replaced above by§ Removal, we were §crossed out and replaced above by§ began so *P2:*Removal, time effects so    59] MS:§added in margin§ Of p §crossed out§ is <> obstruction: for the rest, *P2:*Of what is *CP2:*obstruction; rubbish cleared *CP3:*cleared,

60    Let partial-ruin stand while ruin may,
      And serve world's use, since use is manifold.
      Repair wreck, stanchion wall to heart's content,
      But never think of renovation pure
      And simple, which involves creation too.
65    Transform and welcome! Yon tall tower may help
      (Though built to be a belfry and nought else)
      Some Father Secchi to tick Venus off
      In transit: never bring there bell again,
      To damage him aloft, brain us below,
70    When new vibrations bury both in brick!"

      Monsieur Léonce Miranda, furnishing
      The application at his cost, poor soul!
      Was instanced how,—because the world lay strewn
      With ravage of opinions in his path,
75    And neither he, nor any friendly wit,
      Knew and could teach him which was firm, which frail,
      In his adventure to walk straight through life
      The partial-ruin,—in such enterprise,
      He straggled into rubbish, struggled on,

---

80   And stumbled out again observably.
     "Yon buttress still can back me up," he judged:
     And at a touch down came both he and it.
     "A certain statue, I was warned against,
     Now, by good fortune, lies well under foot,
85   And cannot tempt to folly any more:"
     So, lifting eye, aloft since safety lay,
     What did he light on? the Idalian shape,
     The undeposed, erectly Victrix still!
     "These steps ascend the labyrinthine stair
90   Whence, darkling and on all-fours, out I stand
     Exalt and safe, and bid low earth adieu—
     For so instructs 'Advice to who would climb:' "
     And all at once the climbing landed him
     —Where, is my story.

                    Take its moral first.
95   Do you advise a climber? Have respect
     To the poor head, with more or less of brains
     To spill, should breakage follow your advice!
     Head-break to him will be heart-break to you
     For having preached "Disturb no ruins here!

---

80| MS:stumbled §altered to§ stumbles  *P2:*stumbled        81| MS:"That buttress <> up,"
quoth §crossed out§ he  *P2:*"You buttress  *CP2:*"Yon buttress        83| MS:Up from the
wreck §last four words crossed out and replaced above by five words§ "A certain statue, I was
84| MS:That §crossed out and replaced above by§ Now <> underfoot," §quotation mark
crossed out§  *P2:*under foot,        85| MS:§line added between present ll. 84 and 86§ folly"
§quotation mark crossed out§ more"—quoth he:  *P2:*folly any more:'  *CP2:*more:"
*P3:*more:'  *1873:*more:"        86| MS:eye, in air where §crossed out and replaced below by§
since  *P2:*eye, aloft since        87| MS:What comes he on but the <> shape  *P2:*shape,
*CP3:*What did he light on? The §altered to§ the        88| MS:All §crossed out and replaced
above by§ The        89| MS:stair,  *P2:*stair        90| MS:out we §crossed out and replaced
above by§ I        91| MS:Sublime §crossed out and replaced above by§ Exalt and
92| MS:so I read 'Advice <> climb.' "  *P2:*so instructs 'Advice <> climb:' "
93| MS:all at once §last two words inserted above§  *CP2:*landed him §*ed* and *him* crossed out
and restored§        94| MS:Where, §over perhaps *There*§ is <> story: §altered to§ story. §¶§
take §altered to§ Take the moral  *P2:*§¶§ Take its moral        95| MS:advise the climber
*P2:*advise a climber        96| MS:head of him, §last two words crossed out§ with
97| MS:Of brains §last two words crossed out§ to §altered to§ To spill, if breakage <> advice,
*P2:*To spill, should breakage <> advice.  *CP2:*advice!        98| MS:you,  *CP2:*you
99| MS:So, never say "Disturb  *P2:*For having preached "Disturb

<sup>100</sup>  Are not they crumbling of their own accord?
Meantime, let poets, painters keep a prize!
Beside, a sage pedestrian picks his way."
A sage pedestrian—such as you and I!
What if there trip, in merry carelessness,
<sup>105</sup>  And come to grief, a weak and foolish child?
Be cautious how you counsel climbing, then!

Are you adventurous and climb yourself?
Plant the foot warily, accept a staff,
Stamp only where you probe the standing-point,
<sup>110</sup>  Move forward, well assured that move you may:
Where you mistrust advance, stop short, there stick!
This makes advancing slow and difficult?
Hear what comes of the endeavour of brisk youth
To foot it fast and easy! Keep this same
<sup>115</sup>  Notion of outside mound and inside mash,
Towers yet intact round turfy rottenness,
Symbolic partial-ravage,—keep in mind!
Here fortune placed his feet who first of all

---

<sup>101</sup>|  MS:And §crossed out and replaced above by§ Then, meantime, let the painter keep the §crossed out and replaced above by§ a    *P2:*Meantime, let poets, painters keep
<sup>102</sup>|  MS:a strong wise man will §last four words crossed out and replaced above by two words§ sage pedestrian pick §altered to§ picks his eye §crossed out§ way."      <sup>103</sup>|  MS:§line added between present ll. 102 and 104§ you yourself! §crossed out§ and      <sup>104</sup>|  MS:What if §last two words added in margin§ Suppose §crossed out§ there trips §altered to§ trip
<sup>105-7</sup>|  MS:And comes §altered to§ come <> a yound §crossed out and replaced above by§ weak <> child? / §no ¶§ Are    *P2:*child? / Be cautious how you counsel climbing, then! /§¶§ Are
<sup>108</sup>|  MS:Use your §last two words crossed out and replaced above by two words§ Plant the
<sup>109</sup>|  MS:Stamp §over perhaps *Stand*§      <sup>110</sup>|  MS:Move forward, §inserted above§ with man's best §last three words crossed out and replaced above by§ well assurance §altered to§ assured that §inserted above§ move he §crossed out and replaced above by§ you may,    *P2:*may:
<sup>111</sup>|  MS:short and stick!    *C1873:*short, there stick!      <sup>113</sup>|  MS:what came of endeavour in a §last two words crossed out and replaced above by two words§ of brisk man    *P2:*brisk youth    *C1873:*came of the endeavour    *1889a:*comes      <sup>114</sup>|  MS: easy,—keep §altered to§ easy! keep    *P2:*easy! Keep      <sup>115</sup>|  MS:      <sup>115-16</sup>|  MS:§two lines added between present ll. 114 and 117§ outside shell and <> / <> intact and turfy    *P2:*outside mound and    *CP2:*intact round turfy      <sup>117</sup>|  MS:Symbolic partial §inserted below§ ravage in your mind,; §comma crossed out§ the which §last two words crossed out§    *P2:*ravage, in <> mind!    *CP2:*partial-ravage,—keep in mind!      <sup>118</sup>|  MS:I strew such round the feet which §over *where*§ first    *CP2:*There fortune placed his feet who first §over illegible correction§    *CP3:*Here fortune

184

Found no incumbrance, till head found . . . But hear!

<sup>120</sup> This son and heir then of the jeweller,
Monsieur Léonce Miranda, at his birth,
Mixed the Castilian passionate blind blood
With answerable gush, his mother's gift,
Of spirit, French and critical and cold.
<sup>125</sup> Such mixture makes a battle in the brain,
Ending as faith or doubt gets uppermost;
Then will has way a moment, but no more:
So nicely-balanced are the adverse strengths,
That victory entails reverse next time.
<sup>130</sup> The tactics of the two are different
And equalize the odds: for blood comes first,
Surrounding life with undisputed faith.
But presently, a new antagonist,
By scarce-suspected passage in the dark,
<sup>135</sup> Steals spirit, fingers at each crevice found
Athwart faith's stronghold, fronts the astonished man:

---

<sup>119|</sup> MS:I §crossed out§ found §altered to§ Found the §crossed out and replaced above by§ no
incumbrance, and they §last two words crossed out and replaced above by two words§ till head
found . . But  *1889a:*head found . . . But    <sup>121|</sup> MS:§line added between lines 120 and
122§ Monsieur Antoine Mellerio at   *CP3a:*Monsieur Antoine Flammario at   *P4:*Monsieur
Antoine Mellerio at   *CP4:*Monsieur Alphonse §crossed out and replaced above by§ Léonce
Miranda    <sup>122|</sup> MS:the Italian passionate   *CP4:*the Castilian passionate
<sup>124|</sup> MS:spirit French and cold and critical §last three words transposed to§ critical and cold.
*P2:*spirit, French    <sup>126|</sup> MS:as this §crossed out and replaced above by§ faith or that
§crossed out and replaced above by§ doubt is uppermost;   *P2:*doubt gets uppermost;
<sup>127|</sup> MS:And §crossed out and replaced above by§ Then <> moment, and §crossed out and
replaced above by§ but no more,   *1889a:*more:    <sup>128|</sup> MS:For §crossed out and replaced
above by§ So    <sup>129|</sup> MS:And victory obtains §crossed out and replaced above by§ entails
*C1873:*That victory    <sup>131|</sup> *P2:*first.  *CP2:*first,    <sup>132|</sup> MS:Begins the life <>
undisputed sway §crossed out and replaced above by§ faith;  *P2:*faith.  *CP2:*Surrounding life
<sup>133|</sup> MS:Afterward gets §crossed out and replaced above by§ grow to be antagonist   *CP2:*But
presently, a new antagonist,    <sup>134|</sup> MS:Those scarce-suspected dealings in the dark
*CP2:*Grow §crossed out and replaced above by§ By scarce-suspected passage in the dark,
<sup>135|</sup> MS:When spirit fingers   *P2:*When spirit, fingering at   *CP2:*Steals §crossed out and restored;
replaced above by§ Your §crossed out§ spirit, §comma crossed out and restored§ fingers at
<sup>136|</sup> MS:Athwart the bulwark, §crossed out and restored; replaced above by perhaps *massy*§
§crossed out§ fronts <> man,   *CP2:*Athwart faith's stronghold, fronts <> man—   *P3:*man:

"Such pains to keep me far, yet here stand I,
Your doubt inside the faith-defence of you!"

With faith it was friends bulwarked him about
140   From infancy to boyhood; so, by youth,
He stood impenetrably circuited,
Heaven-high and low as hell: what lacked he thus,
Guarded against aggression, storm or sap?
What foe would dare approach? Historic Doubt?
145   Ay, were there some half-knowledge to attack!
Batter doubt's best, sheer ignorance will beat.
Acumen metaphysic?—drills its way
Through what, I wonder! A thick feather-bed
Of thoughtlessness, no operating tool—
150   Framed to transpierce the flint-stone—fumbles at,
With chance of finding an impediment!
This Ravissante, now: when he saw the church
For the first time, and to his dying-day,
His firm belief was that the name fell fit
155   From the Delivering Virgin, niched and known;
As if there wanted records to attest
The appellation was a pleasantry,
A pious rendering of Rare Vissante,

---

137| MS:"All this to <> me out §crossed out and replaced above by§ far   *P2:*"Such pains to
138-39| MS:§no ¶§   *P2:*§¶§   139| MS:was they bulwarked   *CP2:*was friends bulwarked
141| MS:It was §crossed out and replaced above by§ stood the impenetrable circuit, high
*CP2:*Faith stood   *1889a:*He stood impenetrably circuited,   142| MS:As heaven, and <>
he there,? §question mark crossed out§   *P2:*heaven and   *1889a:*Heaven-high and <> he thus,
143| MS:Guarded §inserted above§ Against aggression <> sap,   *P2:*against   *CP2:*sap?
144| MS:Whatever the approach? Historic   *CP2:*What foe would dare approach? Historic
145| MS:there §letters illegibly crossed out§ some <> attack—   *P2:*attack!
146| MS:Batter you best, here's §crossed out and replaced above by§ sheer <> beat!   *P2:*beat.
*CP2:*Batter doubt's best   147| MS:metaphysic—drilling §altered to§ drills its §inserted
above§   *CP2:*metaphysic?—drills   148| MS:tool,—   *P2:*tool—   150| MS:to transfix
the flint-stone,—fumbles   *P2:*to transpierce the flint-stone—fumbles   151| MS:of piercing
an   *P2:*of finding an   152| MS:This Delivrande, now   *P2:*This Délivrande, now
*CP4:*This Ravissante, now   153| MS:time, as to his dying day,   *P2:*time, and to his dying-
day,   155| MS:From the §over *her*,§ <> niched there first;   *P2:*first.
*CP2:*niched and known.   *P3:*known   *CP3:*known;   156| MS:The first instructed §last
three words crossed out and replaced above by four words§ As if there wanted
158| MS:of Dell Yvrande   *P2:* of Dell Yvrande,   *CP4:*of Rare Vissante,

The proper name which erst our province bore.
160   He would have told you that Saint Aldabert
Founded the church, (Heaven early favoured France,)
About the second century from Christ;
Though the true man was Bishop of Raimbaux,
Eleventh in succession, Eldobert,
165   Who flourished after some six hundred years.
He it was brought the image "from afar,"
(Made out of stone the place produces still)
"Infantine Art divinely artless," (Art
In the decrepitude of Decadence,)
170   And set it up a-working miracles
Until the Northmen's fury laid it low,
Not long, however: an egregious sheep,
Zealous with scratching hoof and routing horn,
Unearthed the image in good Mailleville's time,
175   Count of the country. "If the tale be false,
Why stands it carved above the portal plain?"
Monsieur Léonce Miranda used to ask.
To Londres went the prize in solemn pomp,
But, liking old abode and loathing new,
180   Was borne—this time, by angels—back again.

---

[159]  MS:erst the §crossed out and replaced above by§ our     [160]  MS:that Saint Regnobert
*CP4:*that Saint Aldabert     [161]  MS:church, (Heaven early §inserted above§ favoured
France,) so soon, §last two words and comma crossed out§     [162]  MS:About the end of §last
three words crossed out§ the first §crossed out and replaced above by§ second
[163]  MS:Though §inserted above§ The <> was the §crossed out§ Bishop of Bayeux,
*P2:*Though the    *CP4:*of Raimbaux,     [164]  MS:succession, Ragnebert,   *CP4:*succession,
Eldobert,     [165]  MS:florished <> years;   *P2:*flourished   *CP2:*years.
[168]  MS:artless" (Art   *CP2:*artless," (Art     [169]  MS:of Decadence)    *1889a:*of Decadence,)
[170]  MS:miracles,   *CP2:*miracles     [171]  MS:From when the <> it flat,   *CP2:*Until the <>
it low,     [172]  MS:Till that day when §last four words crossed out and replaced above by four
words§ Until the pains of an   *P2:*Until that day when an   *CP2:*—Not long, however: an
*P3:*Not     [173]  MS:scratching foot §crossed out and replaced above by§ hoof
[174]  MS:good Beaudoin's time,   *CP4:*good Mailleville's time,
[175]  MS:country: "If   *P2:*country. "If     [177]  MS:Monsieur Antoine Mellerio used to think
§crossed out§ ask.   *CP3a:*Monsieur Antoine Flammario used   *P4:*Monsieur Antoine Mellerio
used   *CP4:*Monsieur Alphonse §crossed out and replaced above by§ Léonce Miranda used
[178]  MS:To Dover went   *CP2:*To Douvres went   *CP4:*To Londres went
[179]  MS:But liked the old abode, so from the new   *P2:*liked its old <> so, from
*CP2:*But liking the old abode and loathing new,     [180]  MS:again   *P2:*again.

And, reinaugurated, miracle
Succeeded miracle, a lengthy list,
Until indeed the culmination came—
Archbishop Chaumont prayed a prayer and vowed
185    A vow—gained prayer and paid vow properly—
For the conversion of Prince Vertgalant.
These facts, sucked in along with mother's-milk,
Monsieur Léonce Miranda would dispute
As soon as that his hands were flesh and bone,
190    Milk-nourished two-and-twenty years before.

So fortified by blind Castilian blood,
What say you to the chances of French cold
Critical spirit, should Voltaire besiege
"Alp, Apennine, and fortified redoubt"?
195    Ay, would such spirit please to play faith's game
Faith's way, attack where faith defends so well!
But then it shifts, tries other strategy.
Coldness grows warmth, the critical becomes
Unquestioning acceptance. "Share and share

---

181|  MS:And, thus began §crossed out§ inaugurated, did §crossed out§ miracles   *P2:*miracle
*CP2:*And, once §crossed out§ reinaugurated, miracle     182|  MS:Succeeded to §crossed out§
miracles and lengthened list   *P2:*miracle   *CP2:*miracle, a lengthy list,     183|  MS:indeed a
culmination   *CP2:*indeed the culmination     184|  MS:Archbishop Quelen prayed
*CP4:*Archbishop Chaumont prayed     186|  MS:of Prince Talleyrand.   *CP4:*of Prince
Vertgalant.     187|  MS:Which §crossed out and replaced above by§ These
188|   MS:Monsieur Antoine Mellerio would   *P2:*Monsieur Antoine Mellerio   *CP3a:*Monsieur
Antoine Flammario would   *P4:*Monsieur Antoine Mellerio would   *CP4:*Monsieur Alphonse
§crossed out and replaced above by§ Léonce Miranda would     189|  MS:and blood,
*P2:*and bone,     190-91|  MS:§no¶§   *P2:*§¶§   *1889a:*§no ¶§; emended to restore ¶; see
Editorial Notes§     191|  MS:§line added between present ll. 190 and 192§   by blood, blind,
passionate,   *P2:*by blind Italian blood,   *CP2:*Thus fortified   *P3:*So fortified   *CP4:*blind
Castilian blood,     192|  MS:of that cold   *P2:*of French cold     195|  MS:Ay, but §crossed
out and replaced above by§ would the spirit will not §last two words crossed out and replaced
above by two words§ please to play our §crossed out and replaced above by§ faith's   *P2:*would
such spirit     196|  MS:Our §crossed out and replaced above by§ Faith's <> where we
§crossed out and replaced above by§ faith <> well!—   *P2:*well!     197|  MS:then it §crossed
out and replaced above by§ doubt shifts <> strategy,   *P2:*strategy.   *CP2:*then it shifts
199|  MS:acceptance, shares and shares   *CP2:*acceptance: "Share and share   *P3:*acceptance. "Share

200    Alike in facts, to truth add other truth!
      Why with old truth needs new truth disagree?"

      Thus doubt was found invading faith, this time,
      By help of not the spirit but the flesh:
      Fat Rabelais chuckled, where faith lay in wait
205    For lean Voltaire's grimace—French, either foe.
      Accordingly, while round about our friend
      Ran faith without a break which learned eye
      Could find at two-and-twenty years of age,
      The twenty-two-years-old frank footstep soon
210    Assured itself there spread a standing-space
      Flowery and comfortable, nowise rock
      Nor pebble-pavement roughed for champion's tread
      Who scorns discomfort, pacing at his post.
      Tall, long-limbed, shoulder right and shoulder left,
215    And 'twixt *acromia* such a latitude,
      Black heaps of hair on head, and blacker bush
      O'er-rioting chin, cheek and throat and chest,—
      His brown meridional temperament
      Told him—or rather pricked into his sense
220    Plainer than language—"Pleasant station here!
      Youth, strength, and lustihood can sleep on turf

---

200-4|  MS:Alike of §crossed out and replaced above by§ in facts, this truth, the other too: / §no
¶§ And,—doubt still found <> faith,— this time, / Fat   *P2:*too. / §¶§ And doubt was found
<> faith, this time, / By help not of the spirit, but the flesh: / Fat   *CP2:*in facts,— §altered to
*truths* and restored§ to truth, add other truth / §no  ¶§ Why with the old truth needs new truth
disagree §punctuation hidden in binding§ / §¶§ Thus doubt <> / By help of not the spirit but
<> / Fat   *P3:*other truth! / <> disagree?" ///      205|  MS:grimace—French, both the
§last two words crossed out and replaced above by§ either    206|  MS:friend §over illegible word§
207|  MS:break his §crossed out and replaced above by§ which
209|  MS:frank foot of him §last two words crossed out and replaced above by two words§ step
here   *P2:*frank footstep soon    212|  MS:The proper §last two words crossed out and
replaced above by two words§ Nor pebble-pavement meet §inserted above§ for a §crossed out§
champion's   *P2:*pebble-pavement roughed for    213|  MS:That §crossed out and replaced
above by§ Who, safe in court, paces sentinel §crossed out§ at   *P2:*Who scorns discomfort, paces
at   *CP2:*pacing    214|  MS:long-limbed, shoulder this §crossed out and replaced above by§
right <> left   *P2:*left,    217|  MS:O'errioting <> throat as well,— §last two crossed out and
replaced above by§ and chest,   *P2:*O'er-rioting <> chest,—    218|  MS:This brown
*CP2:*His brown    220|  MS:language "Pleasant   *P2:*language—"Pleasant

Yet pace the stony platform afterward:
First signal of a foe and up they start!
Saint Eldobert, at all such vanity,
225    Nay—sinfulness, had shaken head austere.
Had he? But did Prince Vertgalant? And yet,
After how long a slumber, of what sort,
Was it, he stretched octogenary joints
And, nigh on Day-of-Judgment trumpet-blast,
230    Jumped up and manned wall, brisk as any bee?"

Nor Rabelais nor Voltaire, but Sganarelle,
You comprehend, was pushing through the chink!
That stager in the saint's correct costume,
Who ever has his speech in readiness
235    For thickhead juvenility at fault:
"Go pace yon platform and play sentinel!
You won't? The worse! but still a worse might hap.
Stay then, provided that you keep in sight
The battlement, one bold leap lands you by!
240    Resolve not desperately 'Wall or turf,
Choose this, choose that, but no alternative!'
No! Earth left once were left for good and all:

---

222| MS:And pace <> afterward— *P2:*Yet pace <> afterward:       223| MS:up I §crossed
out and replaced above by§ you start!" *P2:*up they start!       224| MS:Saint Regnobert, at
*CP4:*Saint Eldobert, at       226| MS:did Prince Talleyrand? And *P2:*he! But *CP4:*did Prince
Vertgalant? And    *1889a:*he? But       228| MS:Did §crossed out and replaced above by§ Was it
the octogenary stretched his joints    *P2:*it he stretched octogenary joints    *CP2:*Was it, he
229| MS:And, just at §last two words crossed out and replaced above by two words§ nigh on Day-
of-Judgment trumpet-call §last word crossed out and replaced above by§ blast,
230| MS:bee? *P2:*Bee?"       230-31| MS:§no ¶§ *P2:*§¶§       231| MS:Nor Rabelias, nor
*CP2:*Nor Rabelais nor       234| MS:his rede §crossed out and replaced above by§ speech
235| MS:thick-head    *1889a:*thickhead       236| MS:pace the platform *CP2:*pace yon
platform       237| MS:hap: *P2:*hap.       238| MS:Compose yourself, and keep in sight, the
same,    *CP2:*Stay §over illegible word§ then—provided that you keep in sight §altered to§ view
§crossed out; *sight* restored§ the same, §last two words crossed out§ *P3:*then, provided
239| MS:That battlement    *CP2:*The battlement, §altered to§ battlement,— §dash crossed out§
one <> by! §altered to§ there! §crossed out; *by!* restored§       240| MS:Never be desperate,
cry §over *say*§ —'Wall or turf— *P2:*Never cry desperately— 'Wall or turf, *CP2:*Resolve not
desperately 'Wall       241| *P2:*that, there's no *CP2:*that, but no
242| MS:§line added between present ll. 241 and 243§ But: 'Earth <> once is *P2:*But—'Earth
<> once were    *CP2:*No! Earth    *P3:*No! 'Earth    *CP4:*No! Earth

'With Heaven you may accommodate yourself.' "

Saint Eldobert—I much approve his mode;
245  With sinner Vertgalant I sympathize;
But histrionic Sganarelle, who prompts
While pulling back, refuses yet concedes,—
Whether he preach in chair, or print in book,
Or whisper due sustainment to weak flesh,
250  Counting his sham beads threaded on a lie—
Surely, one should bid pack that mountebank!
Surely, he must have momentary fits
Of self-sufficient stage-forgetfulness,
Escapings of the actor-lassitude
255  When he allows the grace to show the grin,
Which ought to let even thickheads recognize
(Through all the busy and benefic part,—
Bridge-building, or rock-riving, or good clean
Transport of church and congregation both
260  From this to that place with no harm at all,)
The Devil, that old stager, at his trick
Of general utility, who leads
Downward, perhaps, but fiddles all the way!

---

243|  MS:With Heaven one may accommodate oneself.' "  *CP2*:With Heaven you may accommodate yourself." *P3*:yourself.' "  *CP3*:'With  244|  MS:Saint Regnobert—I <> mode: *CP2*:mode;  *CP4*:Saint Eldobert—I  245|  MS:With Sinner Talleyrand I sympathize: *P2*:sinner  *CP2*:sympathize;  *CP4*:sinner Vertgalant I  247|  MS:In pulling <> refuses and concedes,  *P2*:While pulling <> refuses yet concedes,—  250-52|  MS:lie!— / Surely, there must be momentary  *P2*:lie!— / Surely, one should bid pack the mountebank! / Surely, there *CP2*: / <> pack that mountebank! / Surely, he must have momentary  *P3*:lie— //  255|  *CP2*:When he §crossed out and restored§  256|  MS:And §crossed out and replaced above by two words§ Should let even you, dear thickhead, recognize  *P2*:Which ought to let even thickheads recognize—  *CP2*:recognize  *CP4*:Which §missing *W*inserted§  257|  MS:Through <> part—  *P2*:part,—  *CP2*: (Through  258|  MS:rock-riving, or that clean  *P2*:rock-riving, or good clean  260|  MS:all,—  *CP2*:all,—) §dash crossed out and restored§  *P3*:all,)  261|  MS:The old persisting Devil at  *P2*:The Devil, that old stager, at  263|  MS:Astray §crossed out and replaced above by§ Hell-ward, perhaps <> the while. §crossed out and replaced above by§ way.  *P2*:Down-ward, perhaps  *CP2*:way!  *1889a*:Downward

Therefore, no sooner does our candidate
265 For saintship spotlessly emerge soul-cleansed
From First Communion to mount guard at post,
Paris-proof, top to toe, than up there starts
The Spirit of the Boulevard—you know Who—
With jocund "So, a structure fixed as fate,
270 Faith's tower joins on to tower, no ring more round,
Full fifty years at distance, too, from youth!
Once reach that precinct and there fight your best,
As looking back you wonder what has come
Of daisy-dappled turf you danced across!
275 Few flowers that played with youth shall pester age,
However age esteem the courtesy;
And Eldobert was something past his prime,
Stocked Caen with churches ere he tried hand here.
Saint-Sauveur, Notre-Dame, Saint-Pierre, Saint-Jean
280 Attest his handiwork commenced betimes.
He probably would preach that turf is mud.
Suppose it mud, through mud one picks a way,

---

264| MS:In fine §last two words crossed out and replaced above by§ Therefore <> did    *P2:*does
268| MS:who—    *P2:*know Who—          269| MS:jocund "So the bastion's §crossed out and
replaced above by§ structure <> fate    *P2:*jocund, "So, the structure's fixed    *CP2:*jocund "So a
structure fixed <> fate,    *P3:*jocund, "So    *CP3:*jocund "So          270| MS:And tower joins
hand §crossed out and replaced above by§ on to    *CP2:*Faith's tower          271| MS:But §over
*Full*§ fifty <> distance, too §crossed out and replaced above by§ full, from    *P2:*Full fifty <>
distance, too, from          272| MS:reach their precinct and, I promise you,    *P2:*reach that
precinct    *CP2:*and there fight your best,          273| MS:Look back and you shall wonder
*CP2:*As, looking back, you wonder          274| MS:Of all the daisied turf    *P2:*Of daisy-dappled
turf          275| MS:Little that <> age—    *CP2:*Few flowers that played with §last two words
crossed out, replaced by *tempted*, and then restored§ youth shall pester §crossed out, replaced by
*old*, and then restored§ age—    *P3:*age,          276| MS:courtesy.    *CP2:*courtesy;
277| MS:Saint §crossed out and replaced above by§ Our Regnobert, good man, was well in years,
§last six words crossed out and replaced above by five words§ was something past his prime
*P2:*prime,    *CP2:*And Regnobert    *CP4:*And Eldobert was          278| MS:he church-build
§crossed out and replaced above by two words§ tried hand, here,    *CP2:*here.    *CP4:*Stocked
Caen §crossed out and restored§          279| *P2:*Saint-Sauveur, <> Saint-Jean,    *CP2:* Saint-
Sauveur, <> Saint-Jean    *P3:* Saint-Sauveur, <> Saint-Jean,    *CP3:* Saint-Sauveur, <> Saint-Jean
280| MS:handiwork began betimes:    *P2:*handiwork commenced betimes:    *CP2:*Attest, his <>
betimes.    *1889a:*Attest his          281| MS:would cry §crossed out and replaced above by§
preach    *CP2:*would preach that §last two words crossed out, replaced by *tell you*, and then
restored§ turf <> mud. §period altered to colon and then restored§
282| *CP2:*way, §comma altered to exclamation mark and then restored§

And when, clay-clogged, the struggler steps to stone,
He uncakes shoe, arrives in manlier guise
285   Than carried pick-a-back by Eldobert
Big-baby-fashion, lest his leathers leak!
All that parade about Prince Vertgalant
Amounts to—your Castilian helps enough—
*Inveni ovem quæ perierat:*
290   But ask the pretty votive statue-thing
What the lost sheep's meantime amusements were
Till the Archbishop found him! That stays blank:
They washed the fleece well and forgot the rest.
Make haste, since time flies, to determine, though!"

295   Thus opportunely took up parable,—
Admonishing Miranda just emerged
Pure from The Ravissante and Paris-proof,—
Saint Sganarelle: then slipped aside, changed mask,
And made re-entry as a gentleman
300   Born of the Boulevard, with another speech
I spare you.

So, the year or two revolved,

---

283|  MS:the traveller §crossed out and replaced above by§ struggler     284|  MS:in manly §altered to§ manlier style §crossed out§ guise     285|  MS:Not §crossed out and replaced above by§ Than <> by Regnobert  *CP4*:by Eldobert     286|  MS:Like a §last two words crossed out§ big §altered to§ Big-baby-fashion, §last word inserted above§ lest <> leathers spo §crossed out§ leak.  *CP2*:leak!     287|  MS:All thats §altered to§ that recorded of Prince Talleyrand  *P2*:that parade about Prince  *CP4*:about Prince Vertgalant     288|  MS:Amounts <> your Italian helps  *CP4*:your Castilian helps     289|  *P2*: perierat. *1889a: perierat:*     290|  MS:We §added in margin§ Quoth Quelen in §last three words crossed out and replaced below by one word§ read the §over *his*§ pretty votive statue- §inserted above§ thing—  *P2*:But ask the  *CP2*:statue-thing     291|  MS:amusements §*s* added§ was §crossed out§ were     292|  MS:him, wisely §crossed out and replaced above by two words§ that stays  *P2*:him! That     294|  MS:haste, though, to determine, since time flies," §last seven words transposed to§ haste, since time flies, to determine, though!"     295|  MS:To §crossed out and replaced above by§ Thus  *P2*:parable,  *CP2*:parable,—     296|  MS:Admonished our Mellerio thus §crossed out and replaced above by§ just  *CP2*:Admonishing Mellerio *CP4*:Admonishing Miranda just     297|  MS:White §crossed out and replaced above by§ Pure <> The §over *La*§ Delivrande  *P2*:from The Délivrande  *CP4*:from The Ravissante     299|  MS:gentleman,  *CP2*:gentleman     300|  MS:Spirit o' the <> speech,  *P2*:Born of the *1889a*:speech     301|  MS:§¶§ So the <> revolved  *P2*:§¶§ So, the <> revolved,

And ever the young man was dutiful
To altar and to hearth: had confidence
In the whole Ravissantish history.
305 Voltaire? Who ought to know so much of him,—
Old sciolist, whom only boys think sage,—
As one whose father's house upon the Quai
Neighboured the very house where that Voltaire
Died mad and raving, not without a burst
310 Of squibs and crackers too significant?
Father and mother hailed their best of sons,
Type of obedience, domesticity,
Never such an example inside doors!
Outside, as well not keep too close a watch;
315 Youth must be left to some discretion there.
And what discretion proved, I find deposed
At Vire, confirmed by his own words: to wit,
How, with the sprightliness of twenty-five,
Five—and not twenty, for he gave their names
320 With laudable precision—were the few
Appointed by him unto mistress-ship;
While, meritoriously the whole long week
A votary of commerce only, week
Ended, "at shut of shop on Saturday,
325 Do I, as is my wont, get drunk," he writes
In airy record to a confidant.

---

302| MS:man was faithful found §last three words crossed out and replaced above by two words§
was dutiful       303| MS:had faith—as first, §last three words crossed out§ confidence
304| MS:In The §over *La*§ Delivrande, the whole history.    *P2:*In the whole Délivrandish history.
*CP4:*whole Ravissantish history.       306| MS:§line added between present ll. 305 and 307§
The mocking §crossed out§ sciolist, the mimic §last two words crossed out and replaced above
by four words§ whom only fools think    *P2:*Old sciolist <> only boys think
310| MS:crackers, too    *1889a:*crackers too       316| MS:And §added in margin§ What
§altered to§ what that §crossed out§ discretion       317| MS:At Caen, confirmed
*CP4:*At Vire, confirmed       318| MS:That §crossed out and replaced above by§ How <>
spriteliness    *1889a:*sprightliness       319| MS:twenty—nay, he    *P2:*twenty—for he
*CP2:*Five— §dash altered to parenthesis and then restored§ and <> twenty, for
320| *CP2:*precision—were §dash altered to parenthesis and then restored§
321| MS:mistress ship;    *P2:*mistress-ship;       323| MS:commerce, only    *P2:*commerce only
324| MS:Ended, at    *P2:*Ended, "at       325| MS:"Do I    *P2:*Do, I

"Bragging and lies!" replied the apologist:
"And do I lose by that?" laughed Somebody
At the Court-edge a-tiptoe, mid the crowd,
330  In his own clothes, a-listening to men's Law.

Thus while, prospectively a combatant,
The volunteer bent brows, clenched jaws, and fierce
Whistled the march-tune "Warrior to the wall!"
Something like flowery laughters round his feet
335  Tangled him of a sudden with "Sleep first!"
And fairly flat upon the turf sprawled he
And let strange creatures make his mouth their home.

Anyhow, 'tis the nature of the soul
To seek a show of durability,
340  Nor, changing, plainly be the slave of change.
Outside the turf, the towers: but, round the turf,
A tent may rise, a temporary shroud,
Mock-faith to suit a mimic dwelling-place:
Tent which, while screening jollity inside
345  From the external circuit—evermore
A menace to who lags when he should march—

---

<sup>327</sup>| MS:"He §crossed out§ bragged §altered to§ Bragging and lied §altered to§ lies!" said
§crossed out and replaced above by§ replied        <sup>328</sup>| MS:"And §crossed out, restored, and
then replaced above by§ What §crossed out§ do I lose thereby §crossed out and replaced above
by two words§ by that?"—laughed Somebody,  *P2:*that?" laughed  *1889a:*laughed Somebody
<sup>329</sup>| MS:§line added between present ll. 328 and 330§ the Court-edge, a-tiptoe mid
*P2:*the Court-edge a-tiptoe, mid        <sup>330</sup>| MS:to the §crossed out and replaced above by§
men's Law.  *P2:*law.  *CP2:*men's Law.        <sup>330-31</sup>| MS:§no ¶§  *P2:*§¶§
<sup>331-37</sup>| MS:§on verso; marked for insertion between present ll. 330 and 338§
<sup>333</sup>| MS:march tune, "Warrior  *P2:*march-tune "Warrior        <sup>335</sup>| MS:Were, of a sudden,
found §crossed out§ at him with  *P2:*Tangled him of a sudden, with  *CP3:*sudden with
<sup>336</sup>| MS:turf lay he  *P2:*turf sprawled he        <sup>337-38</sup>| MS:§¶§  *1889a:*§no ¶; emended to
restore ¶; see Editorial Notes§        <sup>338</sup>| MS:Anyhow §crossed out and replaced above by§
Certainly §crossed out; original reading restored§        <sup>342</sup>| MS:temporary wall §crossed out§
shroud,        <sup>343</sup>| MS:Of §crossed out and replaced above by§ Mock faith adapted to the
pleasure-ground; §last four words crossed out and replaced above by six words§ to suit a mimic
dwelling place,  *P2:*Mock-faith < > dwelling-place:  *CP2:*Mock faith  *P3:*Mock-faith
<sup>344</sup>| MS:Which while it screen the jollity  *P2:*Tent which, while screening jollity
<sup>345</sup>| MS:circuit menacing  *P2:*circuit evermore  *CP2:*circuit—evermore  *P3:*circuit-evermore
*CP3:*circuit—evermore        <sup>346</sup>| MS:At distance who must rise and march one day—
*P2:*A menace to who lags when he should march—

Yet stands a-tremble, ready to collapse
At touch of foot: turf is acknowledged grass,
And grass, though pillowy, held contemptible
350   Compared with solid rock, the rampired ridge.
To truth a pretty homage thus we pay
By testifying—what we dally with,
Falsehood, (which, never fear we take for truth!)
We may enjoy, but then—how we despise!

355   Accordingly, on weighty business bound,
Monsieur Léonce Miranda stooped to play,
But, with experience, soon reduced the game
To principles, and thenceforth played by rule:
Rule, dignifying sport as sport, proclaimed
360   No less that sport was sport and nothing more.
He understood the worth of womankind,—
To furnish man—provisionally—sport:
Sport transitive—such earth's amusements are:
But, seeing that amusements pall by use,
365   Variety therein is requisite.

---

347| MS:Yet §added in margin§ Stands on the §crossed out§ tremble, ready
*P2:*stands a-tremble, ready      348| MS:At kick of foot; reminded that §last two words crossed out§ turf is §crossed out and replaced above by two words§ is acknowledged   *P2:*At touch of
*CP2:*foot: turf      349| MS:though pleasant, §illegible word crossed out and replaced above by§ held   *P2:*though pillowy, held      350| MS:with solid §crossed out and replaced above by two words§ stand for §crossed out; original reading restored§ rock by which we swear;.
§semicolon crossed out§   *P2:*rock, the rampired ridge.      351| MS:To truth, §last two words and comma added in margin§ What §crossed out and replaced above by§ a <> homage do §crossed out and replaced above by§ thus we pay, to truth §last two words crossed out§
*CP2:*pay   *C1873:*truth a      352| MS:testifying—Thus, §crossed out and replaced above by§ what <> with,—   *CP2:*with,      353| MS:Falsehood,—never <> for thee §crossed out§ truth!   *P2:*Falsehood,—which, never   *CP2:*Falsehood, (which <> truth!)      354| MS:We §word illegibly crossed out§ may      355| MS:§line added between present ll. 354 and 356§
356| MS: Monsieur Antoine Mellorio stooped   *P2:*Monsieur Antoine Mellerio
*CP3a:*Monsieur Antoine Flammario stooped   *P4:*Monsieur Antoine Mellerio stooped
*CP4:*Monsieur Alphonse §crossed out and replaced above by§ Léonce Miranda stooped
358| MS:and played thenceforth §last two words transposed to§ thenceforth played
359| MS:Which, dignifying   *P2:*Rule, dignifying      363| MS:transitive—such, §last word and comma crossed out and replaced above by§ since earth's   *P2:*transitive—such earth's
364| MS:Here most of all does §last five words crossed out and replaced above by four words§ But, seeing that such pleasures pall   *P2:*that amusements pall
365| MS:Variety is therefore §last two words crossed out and replaced above by§ therein is

And since the serious work of life were wronged
Should we bestow importance on our play,
It follows, in such womankind-pursuit,
Cheating is lawful chase. We have to spend
370   An hour—they want a lifetime thrown away:
We seek to tickle sense—they ask for soul,
As if soul had no higher ends to serve!
A stag-hunt gives the royal creature law:
Bat-fowling is all fair with birds at roost,
375   The lantern and the clapnet suit the hedge.
Which must explain why, bent on Boulevard game,
Monsieur Léonce Miranda decently
Was prudent in his pleasure—passed himself
Off on the fragile fair about his path
380   As the gay devil rich in mere good looks,
Youth, hope—what matter though the purse be void?
"If I were only young Miranda, now,
Instead of a poor clerkly drudge at desk
All day, poor artist vainly bruising brush
385   On palette, poor musician scraping gut
With horsehair teased that no harmonics come!

---

366| MS:And since §last two words inserted above§ The §altered to§ the <> wronged indeed §crossed out§       368| MS:Accordingly, §crossed out and replaced above by§ Therefore, in all such §last two words inserted above§   P2:It follows, in such       369| MS:chase: we have an hour §last two words crossed out§ to   P2:chase. We       370| MS:To spend §last two words crossed out and replaced above by two words§ An hour, they   P2:hour—they
371| MS:to soothe our §last two words crossed out and replaced above by§ tickle
373| MS:law, §altered to§ law:       375| MS:clapnet fits the hedge;   P2:clapnet suits the CP2:hedge.       376| MS:§line added between present ll. 375 and 377§   CP3:Which must §last two words crossed out and replaced by two words So I; original reading restored§
377| MS:Monsieur Antoine Mellerio decently   CP3a:Monsieur Antoine Flammario decently P4:Monsieur Antoine Mellerio decently       CP4:Monsieur Alphonse §crossed out and replaced above by§ Léonce Miranda decently       380| MS:the poor §crossed out and replaced above by§ gay <> in his §crossed out and replaced above by§ mere
381| MS:matter if the   P2:matter though the       382| MS:"If we were only §inserted above§ young Mellerio now,   P2:"If I were   CP2:young Mellerio, now,   CP3a:young Flammario, now, P4:young Mellerio, now,   CP4:young Miranda, now,       383| MS:of the §crossed out and replaced above by§ a poor clerk §altered to§ clerkly condemned to §last two words crossed out and replaced above by two words§ drudge at       384| MS:artist drudge at §last two words crossed out and replaced above by two words§ vainly bruising       385| MS:And §crossed out and replaced above by§ On       386| MS:teazed <> come!—   P2:come!   1889a:teased

Then would I love with liberality,
Then would I pay!—who now shall be repaid,
Repaid alike for present pain and past,
390    If Mademoiselle permit the contre-danse,
Sing 'Gay in garret youth at twenty lives,'
And afterward accept a lemonade!"

Such sweet facilities of intercourse
Afford the Winter-Garden and Mabille!
395    "Oh, I unite"—runs on the confidence,
Poor fellow, that was read in open Court,
—"Amusement with discretion: never fear
My *escapades* cost more than market-price!
No durably-attached Miranda-dupe,
400    Sucked dry of substance by two clinging lips,
Promising marriage, and performing it!
Trust me, I know the world, and know myself,
And know where duty takes me—in good time!"

Thus fortified and realistic, then,
405    At all points thus against illusion armed,
He wisely did New Year inaugurate
By playing truant to the favoured five:

---

387-88| MS:§lines added between present ll. 386 and 389§ would he love <> / <> would he pay <> no must be   *P2:*would I love <> / <> would I pay   *CP2:*/<> now shall be
389| MS:Repaid for all, pains past §crossed out and replaced below by§ present and pains to be §last two words crossed out and replaced below by§ past,   *P2:*pain <> pain   *CP2:*Repaid alike for present pain and past,     390| MS:Should Mademoiselle   *P2:*If Mademoiselle
391| MS:§line added between present ll. 390 and 392§ Sing "Gay <> lives,"   *P2:*Sing 'Gay <> lives,'     392| MS:limonade   *P2:*lemonade     394| MS:the Winter-Garden, or Mabille. *P2:*the Winter-Garden and Mabille.   *CP2:*and Mabille!     395| MS:confidence *P2:*confidence,     396| MS:§line added between present ll. 395 and 397§
398| MS:escapades   *C1873: escapades*     399| MS:A durably-attached Mellerio-dupe *CP2:*Now durably-attached   *CP3a:*durably-attached Flammario-dupe,   *P4:*durably-attached Mellerio-dupe,   *CP4:*durably-attached Miranda-dupe,     401| MS:it,   *P2:*it?   *CP2:*it!
403| MS:know my §crossed out and replaced above by§ where duty waits §crossed out and replaced above by§ takes     404| MS:fortified already grown was §last three words crossed out and replaced above by two words and comma§ and realistic, then,
405| MS:Thus at all points against §last five words transposed to§ At all points thus against
406| *CP2:*did New-Year   *CP3:*did New Year     407| MS:five   *P2:*five:

And sat installed at "The Varieties,"—
Playhouse appropriately named,—to note
410 (Prying amid the turf that's flowery there)
What primrose, firstling of the year, might push
The snows aside to deck his button-hole—
Unnoticed by that outline sad, severe,
(Though fifty good long years removed from youth)
415 That tower and tower,—our image, bear in mind!


No sooner was he seated than, behold,
Out burst a polyanthus! He was 'ware
Of a young woman niched in neighbourhood;
And ere one moment flitted, fast was he
420 Found captive to the beauty evermore,
For life, for death, for heaven, for hell, her own.
Philosophy, bewail thy fate! Adieu,
Youth realistic and illusion-proof!
Monsieur Léonce Miranda,—hero late
425 Who "understood the worth of womankind,"
"Who found therein—provisionally—sport,"—
Felt, in the flitting of a moment, fool

---

408-9| MS:And, §crossed out and replaced above by word illegibly crossed out; original reading
restored§ all alone at "the §altered to§ "The <> / Appropriate playhouse,—sate installed to see
P2:And all <> / <> sat    CP2:Sitting installed at <> / Playhouse appropriately named,—to
§crossed out and replaced above by§ took §crossed out; original reading restored§
P3:And sat installed        410| MS:§line added between present ll. 409 and 411§ turf, we talked
about)    CP2:turf, that's frequent §crossed out and replaced above by§ flowery there)
P3:turf that's flowery the)    CP3:flowery there)    P4:flowery the)    CP4:flowery there)
411|    CP2:What §crossed out and replaced above by§ If §crossed out; original reading restored§
414|    MS:And §crossed out and replaced above by§ But fifty <> youth,    CP2:Though fifty
CP3: (Though <> youth)        415|    MS:Of tower    CP3:That tower
417|    MS:polyanthus. he §altered to§ He    P2:polyanthus! He
418|    MS:neighbourhood,    P2: neighbourhood:    CP2: neighbourhood;
419|    MS:moment's flitting §last two words altered to§ moment flitted        420|    MS:Found
bondslave to    1889a:Found captive to        421|    MS:§line added between present ll. 420 and
422§        424|    MS:§line added in top margin§ Monsieur Antoine Mellerio,—hero
CP3a:Monsieur Antoine Flammario,—hero    P4:Monsieur Antoine Mellerio,—hero
CP4:Monsieur Alphonse §crossed out and replaced above by§ Léonce Miranda,—hero
425|    MS:womankind—    P2:womankind,"        426|    MS:To furnish man provisionally sport,"—
P2: "Who found therein—provisionally—sport,"—        427|    MS:moment, Fool    P2:fool

Was he, and folly all that seemed so wise,
And the best proof of wisdom's birth would be
430  That he made all endeavour, body, soul,
By any means, at any sacrifice
Of labour, wealth, repute, and (—well, the time
For choosing between heaven on earth, and heaven
In heaven, was not at hand immediately—)
435  Made all endeavour, without loss incurred
Of one least minute, to obtain her love.
"Sport transitive?" "Variety required?"
"In loving were a lifetime thrown away?"
How singularly may young men mistake!
440  The fault must be repaired with energy.


Monsieur Léonce Miranda ate her up
With eye-devouring; when the unconscious fair
Passed from the close-packed hall, he pressed behind;
She mounted vehicle, he did the same,
445  Coach stopped, and cab fast followed, at one door—
Good house in unexceptionable street.
Out stepped the lady,—never think, alone!
A mother was not wanting to the maid,
Or, may be, wife, or widow, might one say?
450  Out stepped and properly down flung himself
Monsieur Léonce Miranda at her feet—
And never left them after, so to speak,
For twenty years, till his last hour of life,

---

428| MS:all he thought §last two words crossed out and replaced above by three words§ that
seemed so— §dash and two illegible words crossed out§ wise,        430| MS:body, and §crossed
out§ soul,        432| MS:repute and  *P2:*repute, and        433| MS:earth and  *P2:*earth, and
434| MS:heaven was  *CP2:*heaven, was        437| MS:transitive"? "Variety we lack §last two
words crossed out and replaced above by§ required?"  *P2:*transitive?" "Variety
438| MS:"In love §altered to§ loving <> a whole §crossed out§ life-time  *P2:*lifetime
441| MS:Monsieur Antoine Mellerio ate  *CP3a:*Monsieur Antoine Flammario ate
*P4:*Monsieur Antoine Mellerio ate  *CP4:*Monsieur Alphonse §crossed out and replaced above
by§ Léonce Miran[da] §hidden in binding§ ate        442| MS:eye-devouring, when
§last two words altered to§ eye-devouring. When  *P2:*eye-devouring; when
443| MS:the close-packed §inserted above§        445| MS:fast-following  *P2:*fast following
*CP2:*followed        446| MS:street—  *P2:*street.        451| MS:Monsieur Antoine Mellerio at
*CP4:*Monsieur Alphonse §crossed out and replaced above by§ Léonce Miranda at
453| MS:twenty-years, to his <> life  *P2:*twenty years <> life,  *CP2:*years, till his

When he released them, as precipitate.
455    Love proffered and accepted then and there!
Such potency in word and look has truth.

Truth I say, truth I mean: this love was true,
And the rest happened by due consequence.
By which we are to learn that there exists
460    A falsish false, for truth's inside the same,
And truth that's only half true, falsish truth.
The better for both parties! folk may taunt
That half your rock-built wall is rubble-heap:
Answer them, half their flowery turf is stones!
465    Our friend had hitherto been decking coat
If not with stones, with weeds that stones befit,
With dandelions—"primrose-buds," smirked he;
This proved a polyanthus on his breast,
Prize-lawful or prize-lawless, flower the same.
470    So with his other instance of mistake:
Was Christianity the Ravissante?

And what a flower of flowers he chanced on now!
To primrose, polyanthus I prefer
As illustration, from the fancy-fact
475    That out of simple came the composite
By culture: that the florist bedded thick

---

457| MS:Truth I mean §crossed out and replaced above by§ say,      460-62| MS:§one line
expanded to three lines; l. 460 first read§ A falsish false, and a true true: folks may taunt §fourth
through seventh word crossed out and replaced above by four words§ truth's inside the same, §l.
461 added above§ §five words added below to create l. 462§ The better for both parties! folks
may taunt    *1889a*:folk      463| MS:half the §crossed out and replaced below by§ your
464| MS:is weeds §crossed out and replaced above by§ stones!      466| MS:§line added
between present ll. 465 and 467§      467| MS:he:   *CP2*:he;      468| MS:This was §crossed
out and replaced above by§ proved      470| MS:§line added between present ll. 469 and 471§
471| MS:Was Christianity the §over *La*§ Delivrande?   *P2*:the Délivrande?   *CP4*:the Ravissante?
472| MS:flowers was chanced on here §crossed out and replaced above by§ now!   *CP3*:flowers
he chanced      474| MS:As style and title §last three words crossed out and replaced above
by§ illustration from   *P2*:illustration, from      475| MS:That from the plain was nursed §last
three words crossed out and replaced above by two words§ simple came   *P2*:That out of simple
476| MS:By hor §crossed out and replaced above by§ culture, that the florist took manure §last
two words crossed out and replaced above by two words§ bedded thick   *P2*:culture: that

His primrose-root in ruddle, bullock's blood,
Ochre and devils'-dung, for aught I know,
Until the pale and pure grew fiery-fine,
480 Ruby and topaz, rightly named anew.
This lady was no product of the plain;
Social manure had raised a rarity.
Clara de Millefleurs (note the happy name)
Blazed in the full-blown glory of her Spring.
485 Peerlessly perfect, form and face: for both—
"Imagine what, at seventeen, may have proved
Miss Pages, the actress: Pages herself, my dear!"
Noble she was, the name denotes: and rich?
"The apartment in this Coliseum Street,
490 Furnished, my dear, with such an elegance,
Testifies wealth, my dear, sufficiently!
What quality, what style and title, eh?
Well now, waive nonsense, you and I are boys
No longer: somewhere must a screw be slack!
495 Don't fancy, Duchesses descend at door
From carriage-step to stranger prostrate stretched,
And bid him take heart, and deliver mind,
March in and make himself at ease forthwith,—
However broad his chest and black his beard,
500 And comely his belongings,—all through love
Protested in a world of ways save one
Hinting at marriage!"—marriage which yet means

---

477| MS:The §crossed out and replaced above by§ His      482-83| MS:§¶§   P2:§no ¶§
483| MS:Anna de Beaupré—note <> name—   CP2: Anna de Beaupré (note <> name!)
P3:name).   P4:name)   CP2:Clara de Millefleurs (note      484| MS:Was in   P2:Blazed in
486| MS:"Imagine what   P2:"Imagine, what      487| MS:Miss §inserted above§
488| MS:was—the <> rich—   CP2:was, the <> rich?      489| MS:in the Street Miromesnil
§last two words transposed to§ Miromesnil Street,   CP3:in this Miromesnil   CP4:this Coliseum
Street,      491| MS:Testifies that §crossed out and replaced above by§ wealth <> sufficiently."
§quotation mark crossed out§   P2:sufficiently!      493| MS:now, no §crossed out and
replaced above by§ waive      494| MS:longer—somewhere <> be loose §crossed out§ slack!
P2:longer: somewhere      495| MS:Don't tell me §last two words crossed out and replaced
above by§ fancy      497| MS:heart and   CP2:heart, and      499| MS:However black
§crossed out and replaced above by§ broad his chest, and   P2:chest and      500| MS:And
manly §altered to§ comely      501| MS:one—   CP3:one      502| MS:at marriage—
marriage, which   P2:at marriage"—marriage which   CP2:at marriage!"—marriage

Only the obvious method, easiest help
To satisfaction of love's first demand,
505    That love endure eternally: "my dear,
Somewhere or other must a screw be slack!"

Truth is the proper policy: from truth—
Whate'er the force wherewith you fling your speech—
Be sure that speech will lift you, by rebound,
510    Somewhere above the lowness of a lie!
Monsieur Léonce Miranda heard too true
A tale—perhaps I may subjoin, too trite!
As the meek martyr takes her statued stand
Above our pity, claims our worship just
515    Because of what she puts in evidence,
Signal of suffering, badge of torture borne
In days gone by, shame then but glory now,
Barb, in the breast, turned aureole for the front!
So, half timidity, composure half,
520    Clara de Millefleurs told her martyrdom.

Of poor though noble parentage, deprived
Too early of a father's guardianship,
What wonder if the prodigality
Of nature in the girl, whose mental gifts

---

504|  MS:demand—  *P2:*demand,    505|  MS:eternally,—my dear,!" §exclamation mark
crossed out§  *P2:*eternally,—"my dear,  *CP2:*eternally: "My §altered to§ "my
506|  MS:§line added between present ll. 505 and 507§
508|  MS:speech,— §comma crossed out§  *P2:*speech,—
510|  MS:above a portion with the low!  *CP2:*above the lowness of a lie  *P3:*of lie!
*CP3:*of a lie!  *P4:*of lie!  *CP4:*of a lie!    511-12|  MS:Monsieur Antoine Mellerio heard a tale
/ Too true,—I fear I may  *P2:*/ Too true,—perhaps I may  *CP3:*heard too true / A tale,—
perhaps  *P4:*heard a tale / Too true,—perhaps  *CP4:*Monsieur Alphonse §crossed out and
replaced above by§ Léonce Miranda heard too true / A tale,—perhaps  *1873:*/ <> tale—
perhaps    512-13|  MS:§¶§  *1873:*§no ¶§    514|  MS:pity, nay, our worship—why,
*P2:*pity, claims our  *CP2:*worship just    515|  MS:If not for what  *CP2:*Because of what
516|  MS:The §crossed out§ signal §altered to§ Signal    518-20|  MS:Barb in <> front? / §¶§
Anna de Beaupré told  *P2:*front? / So, half timidity, composure half, / §no ¶§ Anna <>
martrydom.  *CP2:*front!— / So <> / <> martyrdom.  *P3:*front! / So  *CP4:*Clara de
Millefleurs told  *1889a:*Barb, in    520-21|  MS:§no ¶§  *P2:*§¶§    521|  MS:Of parents,
poor though noble, born, deprived  *P2:*Of poor though noble parentage, deprived
524|  MS:girl whose mental gift  *P2:*girl, whose mental gifts

525 Matched her external dowry, form and face—
If these suggested a too prompt resource
To the resourceless mother? "Try the Stage
And so escape starvation! Prejudice
Defames Mimetic Art: be yours to prove
530 That gold and dross may meet and never mix,
Purity plunge in pitch yet soil no plume!"

All was prepared in London—(you conceive
The natural shrinking from publicity
In Paris, where the name excites remark)
535 London was ready for the grand *début*;
When some perverse ill-fortune, incident
To art mimetic, some malicious thrust
Of Jealousy who sidles 'twixt the scenes
Or pops up sudden from the prompter's hole,—
540 Somehow the brilliant bubble burst in suds.
Want followed: in a foreign land, the pair!
O hurry over the catastrophe—
Mother too sorely tempted, daughter tried
Scarcely so much as circumvented, say!
545 Caged unsuspecting artless innocence!

Monsieur Léonce Miranda tell the rest!—
The rather that he told it in a style
To puzzle Court Guide students, much more me.

---

525| MS:Matched that external   *P2:*Matched her external        527| MS:mother: "try §altered
to§ "Try   *P2:*mother? "Try the stage   *CP4:*the Stage        529| MS:Defames the §crossed out§
Art Mimetic §last two words transposed to§ Mimetic Art. Be hers §crossed out and replaced
above by§ yours   *P2:*Defames Mimetic Art: be        531| MS:And purity touch filth §crossed
out and replaced above by§ pitch <> no hand!"   *P2:*Purity plunge in pitch   *CP2:*no plume!"
534| MS:remark)—   *P2:*remark)        535| MS:*debût*;   *P2:*debût;   *C1873:debût*;   *1889a:début*;
536| MS:When, some   *CP2:*When some        537| MS:To Art Mimetic   *P2:*To art mimetic
538| MS:Of jealousy <> scenes,   *P2:*jealousy, who <> scenes   *CP2:*jealousy who
*CP3:*Of Jealousy        539| MS:hole,   *P2:*hole,—        544| MS:say,   *CP2:*say!
545| MS:That §crossed out and replaced above by§ Caged        546| MS:Monsieur Antoine
Mellerio tell   *P2:*Monsieur Antonio Mellerio   *CP2:*Monsieur Antoine Mellerio
*CP3a:*Monsieur Antoine Flammario tell   *P4:*Monsieur Antoine Mellerio tell
*CP4:*Monsieur Alphonse §crossed out and replaced above by§ Léonce Miranda tell
548| MS:puzzle Red-Book §crossed out and replaced above by two words§ Court Guide

"Brief, she became the favourite of Lord N.,
550  An aged but illustrious Duke, thereby
Breaking the heart of his competitor
The Prince of O. Behold her palaced straight
In splendour, clothed in diamonds"(phrase how fit!),
"Giving tone to the City by the Thames!
555  Lord N., the aged but illustrious Duke,
Was even on the point of wedding her,
Giving his name to her" (why not to us ?)
"But that her better angel interposed.
She fled from such a fate to Paris back,
560  A fortnight since: conceive Lord N.'s despair!
Duke as he is, there's no invading France.
He must restrict pursuit to postal plague
Of writing letters daily, duly read
As darlingly she hands them to myself,
565  The privileged supplanter, who therewith
Light a cigar and see abundant blue"—
(Either of heaven or else Havanna-smoke.)
"Think! she, who helped herself to diamonds late,
In passion of disinterestedness
570  Now—will accept no tribute of my love
Beyond a paltry ring, three Louis'-worth!
Little she knows I have the rummaging
Of old Papa's shop in the Place Vendôme!"
So wrote entrancedly to confidant

---

549|  MS:the favoured of Lord N,  *P2:*of Lord N.,  *CP2:*the favourite of
553|  MS:splendor <> diamonds,"—(tis the §last two words crossed out§ phrase <> fit!)
*P2:*diamonds," (phrase  *1889a:*splendour <> fit!),  554|  MS:the City by §crossed out and
replaced above by§ on §crossed out; *by* restored§  555|  MS:Lord N, the  *P2:*Lord N., the
556|  MS:her—  *1889a:*her,  557|  MS:Bestowing §crossed out and replaced above by two
words§ Giving his name on §crossed out and replaced above by§ to her" (if not on §crossed out
and replaced above by§ to us)  *P2:*her" (why not to us?)  558|  MS:But  *P2:*"But
560|  MS:conceive Lord N's  *P2:*conceive Lord N.'s  561|  MS:he was  *P2:*he is
562|  MS:He but restricted his pursuit to plague  *P2:*He must restrict pursuit to just a plague
*CP2a:*§*postal* inserted above§  *CP2:*to postal a plague  *P3:*to postal plague
563|  MS:Of daily letter-writing, duly  *P2:*Of writing letters daily, duly  566|  MS:Lights
§altered to§ Light <> and sees §altered to§ see  567|  MS:or else §inserted above§
568|  MS:"Why, §crossed out and replaced above by§ "Dear! she  *P2:*"Think! she
573|  MS:the Street of Peace!"  *CP4:*the Place Vendôme!"  573-74|  MS:§¶ called for§
*P2:*§no ¶§  574|  MS:confidant,  *1889a:*confidant

<sup>575</sup>  Monsieur Léonce Miranda. Surely now,
If Heaven, that sees all, understands no less,
It finds temptation pardonable here,
It mitigates the promised punishment,
It recognizes that to tarry just
<sup>580</sup>  An April hour amid such dainty turf
Means no rebellion against task imposed
Of journey to the distant wall one day?
Monsieur Léonce Miranda puts the case!
Love, he is purposed to renounce, abjure;
<sup>585</sup>  But meanwhile, is the case a common one?
Is it the vulgar sin, none hates as he ?


Which question, put directly to "his dear"
(His brother—I will tell you in a trice)
Was doubtless meant, by due meandering,
<sup>590</sup>  To reach, to fall not unobserved before
The auditory cavern 'neath the cope
Of Her, the placable, the Ravissante.
But here's the drawback, that the image smiles,
Smiles on, smiles ever, says to supplicant
<sup>595</sup>  "Ay, ay, ay"—like some kindly weathercock
Which, stuck fast at Set Fair, Favonian Breeze,

---

<sup>575|</sup>  MS:Monsieur Antoine Mellerio. Surely  *CP3a:*Monsieur Antoine Flammario. Surely
*P4:*Monsieur Antoine Mellerio. Surely  *CP4:*Monsieur Alphonse §crossed out and replaced
above by§ Léonce Miranda. Surely  <sup>579|</sup>  MS:that, to  *CP2:*that to  <sup>580|</sup>  MS:amid the
§crossed out§ such <> turf,  *CP2:*turf  <sup>581|</sup>  MS:rebellion to the §last two words crossed
out and replaced above by§ against  <sup>582|</sup>  MS:day.  *P2:*day!  *1889a:*day?
<sup>583|</sup>  MS:§line added between present ll. 582 and 584§ Monsieur Antoine Mellerio—mark the
*P2:*Monsieur Antoine Mellerio puts the  *CP3a:*Monsieur Antoine Flammario puts
*P4:*Monsieur Antoine Mellerio puts  *CP4:*Monsieur Alphonse §crossed out and replaced above
by§ Léonce Miranda puts  <sup>584|</sup>  MS:Love he §over perhaps we§ are §crossed out and
replaced above by§ is <> abjure—  *CP2:*Love, he <> abjure;
<sup>585|</sup>  MS:is it quite §last two words crossed out and replaced above by two words§ the case a
common case §crossed out and replaced above by§ one,  *CP2:*one?
<sup>586-87|</sup>  MS:§¶§  *1889a:*§no ¶; emended to restore ¶; see Editorial Notes§
<sup>588|</sup>  MS:§line added between present ll. 587 and 589§  <sup>590|</sup>  MS:reach—to  *CP2:*reach, to
<sup>592|</sup>  MS:the amenable at Delivrande.  *P2:*at Délivrande.  *CP2:*the placable at  *CP4:*placable,
the Ravissante.  <sup>594|</sup>  MS:supplicant,  *CP4:*supplicant  <sup>595|</sup>  MS:"Yes, yes, yes §last
three words crossed out and replaced above by three words§ Ay, Ay, Ay  *P2:*"Ay, ay, ay
<sup>596|</sup>  MS:That, §inserted above§ Stuck <> Fair, and §crossed out§ Favonian  *P2:*Which, stuck

Still warrants you from rain, though Auster's lead
Bring down the sky above your cloakless mirth.
Had he proposed this question to, nor "dear"
600 Nor Ravissante, but prompt to the Police,
The Commissary of his Quarter, now—
There had been shaggy eyebrows elevate
With twinkling apprehension in each orb
Beneath, and when the sudden shut of mouth
605 Relaxed,—lip pressing lip, lest out should plump
The pride of knowledge in too frank a flow,—
Then, fact on fact forthcoming, dose were dealt
Of truth remedial in sufficiency
To save a chicken threatened with the pip,
610 Head-staggers and a tumble from its perch.

Alack, it was the lady's self that made
The revelation, after certain days
—Nor so unwisely! As the haschisch-man
Prepares a novice to receive his drug,
615 Adroitly hides the soil with sudden spread
Of carpet ere he seats his customer:
Then shows him how to smoke himself about
With Paradise; and only when, at puff
Of pipe, the Houri dances round the brain
620 Of dreamer, does he judge no need is now
For circumspection and punctiliousness;
He may resume the serviceable scrap

---

597| MS:That §crossed out and replaced above by§ Still < > rain with Auster's   *P2:*rain though
Auster's   *CP2:*rain, though        598| MS:Loading the §over illegible word§ sky < > your
cloaklessness. §altered to§ cloakless mirth.   *P2:*Bring down the        600| MS:Nor Delivrande
*P2:*Nor Délivrande   *CP4:*Nor Ravissante        603| MS:each ball §crossed out§ orb
604| MS:shut relaxed §crossed out and replaced above by two words§ of mouth
605| MS:Of mouth §last two words crossed out and replaced above by§ Relaxed,—lip over lip
*CP4:*Relaxed,—lip pressing lip        608| MS:remedial, in   *1889a:*remedial in
610| MS:Head-staggers, and   *CP2:*Head-staggers and        612| MS:days: §colon crossed out§
613| MS:haschisch-man   *P2:*haschisch-man        614| MS:receive the §crossed out and replaced
above by§ his        616| MS:customer,   *P2:*customer:        618| MS:With Paradise: and
*P2:*With Paradise; and        620| MS:is more §crossed out§ now
621| MS:punctiliousness,   *P2:*punctiliousness;        622| MS:And §crossed out and replaced
above by§ So plucks §crossed out and replaced by§ pulls away §crossed out and replaced
above by two words§ may resume   *CP2:*He may   *P3:*Hc   *CP3:*He   *P4:*Hc   *CP4:*He

That made the votary unaware of muck.
Just thus the lady, when her brewage—love—
625 Was well a-fume about the novice-brain,
Saw she might boldly pluck from underneath
Her lover the preliminary lie.

Clara de Millefleurs, of the noble race,
Was Lucie Steiner, child to Dominique
630 And Magdalen Commercy; born at Sierck,
About the bottom of the Social Couch.
The father having come and gone again,
The mother and the daughter found their way
To Paris, and professed mode-merchandize,
635 Were milliners, we English roughlier say;
And soon a fellow-lodger in the house,
Monsieur Ulysse Muhlhausen, young and smart,
Tailor by trade, perceived his housemate's youth,
Smartness, and beauty over and above.
640 Courtship was brief, and marriage followed quick,
And quicklier—impecuniosity.
The young pair quitted Paris to reside
At London: which repaid the compliment
But scurvily, since not a whit the more
645 Trade prospered by the Thames than by the Seine.
Failing all other, as a last resource,

---

623| MS:muck:  *CP2:*muck.    624-27| MS:§four lines added in margin and marked for
insertion between present ll. 623 and 628§    626| *P2:*pluck, from   *1889a:*pluck from
627| *P2:*lover, the   *1889a:*lover the    628| MS:Anna de Beaupré, of   *CP4:*Clara de
Millefleurs, of    629| MS:Was Sophy Trayer, child to Dominic   *P2:*to Dominique
*CP3a:*Was Lucie Mayer, child to Ferdinand   *P4:*to Dominique   *CP4:*Was Lucie Steiner, child
630| MS:And Magdalen Lalory; both §crossed out and replaced above by§ born at Metz
*P2:*at Metz,   *CP3a:*And Caroline Aman[ ]; born §letters hidden in binding§   *P4:*And
Magdalen Lalory; born   *CP4:*And Magdalen Commercy; born at Sierc[k], §last letter hidden in
binding§    637| MS:Monsieur Achille Debacker, young and brisk,   *P2:*and smart,
*CP3a:*Monsieur Ulysse Durlach, young   *P4:*Monsieur Ubysse Debacker young   *CP4:*Monsieur
Achille §crossed out§ Ulysse Muhlhausen young   *1889a:*Monsieur Ulysse Muhlhausen, young
638| MS:house-mate's   *1889a:*housemate's    639| MS:Briskness, and <> above;
*P2:*Smartness, and   *CP2:*above.    641| MS:And quicker—impecuniosity.   *CP2:*And
quicklier—impecuniosity.    643| MS:At London—which   *P2:*At London: which

"He would have trafficked in his wife,"—she said.
If for that cause they quarrelled, 'twas, I fear,
Rather from reclamation of her rights
650 To wifely independence, than as wronged
Otherwise by the course of life proposed:
Since, on escape to Paris back again
From horror and the husband,—ill-exchanged
For safe maternal home recovered thus,—
655 I find her domiciled and dominant
In that apartment, Coliseum Street,
Where all the splendid magic met and mazed
Monsieur Léonce Miranda's venturous eye.
Only, the same was furnished at the cost
660 Of someone notable in days long since,
Carlino Centofanti: he it was
Found entertaining unawares—if not
An angel, yet a youth in search of one.
Why this revealment after reticence?
665 Wherefore, beginning "Millefleurs," end at all
Steiner, Muhlhausen, and the ugly rest?
Because the unsocial purse-comptrolling wight,
Carlino Centofanti,—made aware
By misadventure that his bounty, crumbs
670 From table, comforted a visitant,—
Took churlish leave, and left, too, debts to pay.

---

647| MS:said.  *P2:*said.  648| MS:quarreled  *P2:*quarrelled  651| MS:proposed,
*P2:*proposed:  652| MS:again,  *1889a:*again  654| MS:For the maternal  *P2:*For safe
maternal  656| MS:apartment, Rue §crossed out§ Miromesnil Street,  *CP4:*apartment,
Coliseum Street. §crossed out and restored§  658| MS:Monsieur Antoine Mellerio's
venturous eye:  *P2:*eye.  *CP3a:*Monsieur Antoine Flammario's venturous  *P4:*Monsieur
Antoine Mellerio's venturous  *CP4:*Monsieur Alphonse §crossed out and replaced above by§
Léonce Mirand[a's]  §last letters hidden in binding§ venturous  660| MS:days gone by
§last two words crossed out and replaced above by two words§ long since,
661| MS:Miranda di Mongino: he it was,  *CP4:*Carlo Centofanti: he  *1889a:*was
663-64| MS:§¶§  *1889a:*§no ¶§  665| MS:beginning "Beaupre," end  *CP4:*beginning
"Millefleur," end  666| MS:Trayer, Debacker, and  *CP3a:*Mayer, Durlach, and  *P4:*Trayer,
Debacker, and  *CP4:*Steiner, Muhlhausen, and  667| MS:purse-comptrolling prince
§crossed out§ wight,  668| MS:Miranda di Mongino, made  *CP4:*Carlino Centofanti, made
*C1873:*Carlo Centofanti,—made  669| MS:bounty—crumbs  *C1873:*bounty, crumbs
670| MS:table—comforted a visitant,  *C1873:*table, comforted a visitant,—  671| MS:leave
and  *P2:*leave, and  675| MS:therefore had §crossed out and replaced above by§ might

Loaded with debts, the lady needs must bring
Her soul to bear assistance from a friend
Beside that paltry ring, three Louis'-worth;
675 And therefore might the little circumstance
That Monsieur Léonce had the rummaging
Of old Papa's shop in the Place Vendôme
Pass, perhaps, not so unobservably.

Frail shadow of a woman in the flesh,
680 These very eyes of mine saw yesterday,
Would I re-tell this story of your woes,
Would I have heart to do you detriment
By pinning all this shame and sorrow plain
To that poor *chignon*,—staying with me still,
685 Though form and face have well-nigh faded now,—
But that men read it, rough in brutal print,
As two years since some functionary's voice
Rattled all this—and more by very much—
Into the ear of vulgar Court and crowd?
690 Whence, by reverberation, rumblings grew
To what had proved a week-long roar in France,
Had not the dreadful cannonry drowned all.
Was, now, the answer of your advocate
More than just this? "The shame fell long ago,
695 The sorrow keeps increasing: God forbid
We judge man by the faults of youth in age!"

---

676| MS:That Monsieur Antoine had    *CP4:*That Monsieur Alphonse §crossed out and replaced
above by§ Léonce had        677| MS:the Street of Peace,    *CP4:*the Place Vendome    *1873:*the
Place Vendôme,    *1889a:*the Place Vendôme        679| MS:Dear §crossed out and replaced
above by§ Frail <> of the §crossed out and replaced above by§ a        680| MS:saw yestermorn
§altered to§ yesterday,        681| MS:§line added between present ll. 680 and 682§
684| MS:chignon    *C1873: chignon*        685| MS:well nigh    *1889a:*well-nigh
686| MS:that men §inserted above§        689| MS:of Caen?—Caen's Court and crowd,—
*P2:*of Caen—Caen's    *CP2:*of Caen, Caen's <> crowd,    *CP4:*of vulgar Court
690| MS:Whence by reverberation, rumbling grew    *P2:*rumblings    *CP2:*Whence, by
692| MS:But that §last two words crossed out and replaced above by§ Only, the    *P2:*Did not the
<> drown all.    *CP2:*Had not <> drowned        694| MSthis—"The    *CP2a:*this?—"The
*CP2:*this? "The:        696-98| MS:The §crossed out and replaced above by§ We <> man, by <>
youth, is age!" / That youth of yours be like <> avenue    *P2:*age!" / Permit me the expression
of a hope / Your youth proceeded like <> avenue,    *1889a:*man by <> youth in <> / /

210

Permit me the expression of a hope
Your youth proceeded like your avenue,
Stepping by bush, and tree, and taller tree,
700  Until, columnar, at the house they end.
So might your creeping youth columnar rise
And reach, by year and year, symmetrical,
To where all shade stops short, shade's service done.
Bushes on either side, and boughs above,
705  Darken, deform the path else sun would streak;
And, cornered half-way somewhere, I suspect
Stagnation and a horse-pond: hurry past!
For here's the house, the happy half-and-half
Existence—such as stands for happiness
710  True and entire, howe'er the squeamish talk!
Twenty years long, you may have loved this man;
He must have loved you; that's a pleasant life,
Whatever was your right to lead the same.
The white domestic pigeon pairs secure,
715  Nay, does mere duty by bestowing egg
In authorized compartment, warm and safe,
Boarding about, and gilded spire above,
Hoisted on pole, to dogs' and cats' despair!
But I have spied a veriest trap of twigs
720  On tree-top, every straw a thievery,
Where the wild dove—despite the fowler's snare,

---

⁶⁹⁹|  MS:by bush, and §last two words inserted above§ tree, and taller §inserted above§ tree;
until the house §last three words crossed out§  *P2:*taller tree,        ⁷⁰⁰|  MS:§line added
between present ll. 699 and 702§        ⁷⁰¹|  MS:§added in margin§ So may what crept in youth,
columnar rise  *CP2:*So might your creeping youth  *1889a:*youth columnar        ⁷⁰²|  MS:And
§added in margin§ Is §crossed out§ reach, §over *Reaching*, over perhaps *reached*§ by <> and
year, maturity §crossed out§ symmetrical,  *P2:*reach by  *CP2:*reach, by        ⁷⁰³|  MS:§line
added between present ll. 702 and 704§ all treks stop short, their service  *P2:*all shade stops
short, shade's service        ⁷⁰⁴|  MS:The §crossed out§ bushes §altered to§ Bushes <> side, the
§crossed out and replaced below by§ and        ⁷⁰⁵|  MS:streak—  *P2:*path, else  *CP2:*streak;
*1889a:*path else        ⁷⁰⁶|  MS:halfway  *1889a:*half-way        ⁷⁰⁷|  MS:horse-pond,—hurry
past,  *P2:*past!  *CP2:*horse-pond: hurry        ⁷⁰⁸|  MS:And §crossed out and replaced above
by§ For <> half and half  *P2:*half-and-half        ⁷¹⁰|  MS:Whole §crossed out and replaced
above by§ True        ⁷¹²|  MS:a happy life,  *1889a:*a pleasant life,        ⁷¹³|  MS:was the
§crossed out and replaced above by§ your        ⁷¹⁷|  MS:about and  *CP2:*about, and
⁷¹⁸|  MS:pole to <> despair;  *P2:*pole, to <> despair!        ⁷²¹|  MS:dove,—despite the
fowler's gin §crossed out and replaced above by§ snare,  *P2:*dove—despite

The sportsman's shot, the urchin's stone,—crooned gay,
And solely gave her heart to what she hatched,
Nor minded a malignant world below.

725 *I* throw first stone forsooth? 'Tis mere assault
Of playful sugarplum against your cheek,
Which, if it makes cheek tingle, wipes off rouge!
*You,* my worst woman? Ah, that touches pride,
Puts on his mettle the exhibitor

730 Of Night-caps, if you taunt him "This, no doubt,—
Now we have got to Female-garniture,—
Crowns your collection, Reddest of the row!"
O unimaginative ignorance
Of what dye's depth keeps best apart from worst

735 In womankind!—how heaven's own pure may seem
To blush aurorally beside such blanched
Divineness as the women-wreaths named White:
While hell, eruptive and fuliginous,
Sickens to very pallor as I point

740 Her place to a Red clout called woman too!
Hail, heads that ever had such glory once
Touch you a moment, like God's cloven tongues
Of fire! your lambent aureoles lost may leave
You marked yet, dear beyond true diadems:

745 And hold, each foot, nor spurn, to man's disgrace,

---

<sup>722</sup>| MS:urchin's aim,—crooned   *P2:*urchin's stone,—crooned      <sup>725</sup>| MS:forsooth? A
§crossed out and replaced above by§ 'Tis      <sup>728</sup>| MS:You   *P2: You*
<sup>730</sup>| MS:Of Night-caps §altered to§ Of Night-Caps, to be §last two words crossed out and
replaced above by two words§ if you taunted §altered to§ taunt him §inserted above§
*P2:*Of Night-caps      <sup>733</sup>| MS:ignorance!   *P2:*ignorance      <sup>734</sup>| MS:What depth of dye
keeps   *CP2:*Of what dye's depth keeps      <sup>735</sup>| MS:womankind,—how Heaven's
*P2:*womankind! how   *P3:*how heaven's      <sup>736</sup>| MS:To take auroral tint beside
*CP2:*To blush aurorally beside      <sup>737</sup>| MS:the woman I name White:
*P2:*the women-wreaths named White:      <sup>738</sup>| MS:While Hell   *P3:*While hell
<sup>740</sup>| MS:place there to my §crossed out and replaced above by§ a Red called Woman
*P2:*place   <> Red clout called Woman   *P3:*woman      <sup>741</sup>| MS:Hail, head of mine, that
had the glory once   *P2:*Hail, heads that ever had such glory      <sup>742</sup>| MS:Touch thee a <>
tongue   *P2:*Touch you a <> tongues      <sup>743</sup>| MS:fire, thy lambent aureole lost, that leaves
*P2:*fire, your lambent aureoles <> leave   *1889a:*fire! your <> lost may leave
<sup>744</sup>| MS:A mark yet <> beyond all diadems!   *P2:*You marked yet   *1889a:*beyond true diadems:
<sup>745</sup>| MS:withhold, my foot <> to thy disgrace,   *P2:*hold, each foot <> to man's disgrace,

What other twist of fetid rag may fall!
Let slink into the sewer the cupping-cloth!

Lucie, much solaced, I re-finger you,
The medium article; if ruddy-marked
With iron-mould, your cambric,—clean at least
From poison-speck of rot and purulence.
Lucie Muhlhausen said—"Such thing am I:
Love me, or love me not!" Miranda said
"I do love, more than ever, most for this."
The revelation of the very truth
Proved the concluding necessary shake
Which bids the tardy mixture crystallize
Or else stay ever liquid: shoot up shaft,
Durably diamond, or evaporate—
Sluggish solution through a minute's slip.
Monsieur Léonce Miranda took his soul
In both his hands, as if it were a vase,
To see what came of the convulsion there,
And found, amid subsidence, love new-born
So sparklingly resplendent, old was new.
"Whatever be my lady's present, past,

---

$^{746}$|　MS:That other <> fetid §inserted above§ rag, that §crossed out and replaced above by§
which fell!　*P2:*What other <> rag may fall!　　　$^{747}$|　MS:Let slip §altered to§ slink
$^{748}$|　MS:Sophy, with §crossed out§ much <> you　*P2:*Sophie <> you,　*CP3a:*Lucie, much
*P4:*Sophie, muc*h*　*CP4:*Lucie, much　　　$^{750}$|　MS:iron-mould, thy §crossed out and replaced
above by§ your　　　$^{751}$|　MS:of blood §crossed out and replaced above by§ rot and purulence!
*1889a:*purulence.　　　$^{752-54}$|　MS:§lines added between present ll. 751 and 755§
$^{752}$|　MS:Sophy Debacker said　*P2:*Sophie　*CP3a:*Lucie Durlach said　*P4:*Sophy Debacker said
*CP4:*Lucie Muhlhausen said　　　$^{753}$|　MS:not!" Mellerio said　*P2:*said,　*P3:*said
*CP3a:*not!" Flammario said　*P4:*not!" Mellerio said　*CP4:*not!" Miranda said
$^{755}$|　MS:This §altered to§ The <> truth,　*1889a:*truth　　　$^{757}$|　MS:That bids <> crystalize
*C1873:*crystallize　*1889a:*Which bids　　　$^{758}$|　MS:Or else §inserted above§ stay forever
§altered to§ ever　　　$^{760}$|　MS:solution that lets §last two words crossed out and replaced
above by two words§ through a　　　$^{761}$|　MS:Monsieur Antoine Mellorio took　*P2:*Mellerio
*CP3a:*§first five letters of *Mellerio* crossed out§　*CP4:*Monsieur Alphonse §crossed out and
replaced above by§ Léonce Miranda took　　　$^{764}$|　MS:found, love born §last two words
crossed out and replaced above by§ sparkle §crossed out§ amid §altered to§ mid the §crossed
out§ subsidence, <> new-born—　*P2:*found, amid subsidence　*CP2:*new-born
$^{765}$|　MS:§line added in margin between present ll. 764 and 766§　　　$^{766}$|　MS:be this woman's
§last two words crossed out and replaced above by two words§ my lady's <> past　*P2:*past,

Or future, this is certain of my soul,
I love her: in despite of all I know,
Defiance of the much I have to fear,
770    I venture happiness on what I hope,
And love her from this day for evermore:
No prejudice to old profound respect
For certain Powers! I trust they bear in mind
A most peculiar case, and straighten out
775    What's crooked there, before we close accounts.
Renounce the world for them—some day I will:
Meantime, to me let her become the world!"


Thus mutely might our friend soliloquize
Over the tradesmen's bills, his Clara's gift—
780    In the apartment, Coliseum Street,
Carlino Centofanti's legacy,
Provided rent and taxes were discharged—
In face of Steiner now, De Millefleurs once,
The tailor's wife and runaway confessed.


785    On such a lady if election light,
(According to a social prejudice)

---

768| MS:her: in    *CP2:*her! in    *1889a:*her: in        769| MS:the rest §crossed out and replaced
above by§ much        770| MS:But §crossed out and replaced above by§ I venturing §altered
to§ venture my soul §last two words crossed out and replaced above by§ happiness
771| MS:I §altered to§ And < > forevermore—    *P2:*for evermore!    *1889a:*evermore:
772| MS:to my §crossed out and replaced above by§ old        773| MS:certain Powers—I trust
will take §crossed out and replaced above by§ bear    *P2:*trust they bear    *CP2:*certain Powers! I
774| MS:My §crossed out and replaced above by§ A < > straigten    *P2:*straighten
775| MS:crooked now §crossed out and replaced above by§ there        778| MS:So mutely
*P2:*Thus, mutely    *1889a:*Thus mutely        779| MS:his Sophy's gift—    *P2:*his Anna's gift—
*CP4:*his Clara's gift—        780| MS:apartment, Street Miromesnil §last two words transposed
to§ Miromesnil Street    *P2:*apartment, Miromesnil Street,    *CP4:*apartment, Coliseum Street,
781| MS:Miranda di Mongino's legacy—    *P2:*legacy.    *CP4:*Carlino Centofanti's legacy,
782| MS:discharged.    *P2:*discharged—        783| MS:of Trayer now, de Beaupré once,
*CP3a:*of Mayer now, de    *P4:*of Trayer now, de    *CP4:*of Steiner now, De Millefleurs once,
784| MS:Confessed §altered to§ confessed §moved to end of line§ the §altered to§ The tailor's
784-85| MS:§no ¶§    *P2:*§¶§        785| MS:Now, on such lady if election falls §altered to§ fall,
*P2:*On such a lady if election light,        786| MS:§line added in margin and marked for
insertion between present ll. 785 and 787§

If henceforth "all the world" she constitute
For any lover,—needs must he renounce
Our world in ordinary, walked about
790 By couples loving as its laws prescribe,—
Renunciation sometimes difficult.
But, in this instance, time and place and thing
Combined to simplify experiment,
And make Miranda, in the current phrase,
795 Master the situation passably.

For first facility, his brother died—
Who was, I should have told you, confidant,
Adviser, referee and substitute,
All from a distance: but I knew how soon
800 This younger brother, lost in Portugal,
Had to depart and leave our friend at large.
Cut off abruptly from companionship
With brother-soul of bulk about as big,
(Obvious recipient—by intelligence
805 And sympathy, poor little pair of souls—
Of much affection and some foolishness)
Monsieur Léonce Miranda, meant to lean
By nature, needs must shift the leaning-place

---

787| MS:If §over perhaps *To*§ henceforth §inserted above§ constitutes §crossed out§ his
§crossed out and replaced above by§ she §crossed out§ "all        788| MS:lover, needs
*P2*:lover,—needs        789| MS:Our §added in margin§ The §crossed out§ world
790| MS:as its laws §last two words inserted above; *its* crossed out and replaced by *our*§
*1889a*:as its laws        791| MS:§line added between present ll. 790 and 792§ *P2*:difficult
enough. *CP3*:difficult.        792| MS:But §added in margin§ And, §crossed out§ in
794| MS:make Mellerio, in    *CP3a*:make Flammario, in    *P4*:make Mellerio, in    *CP4*:make
Miranda, in        795| MS:situation: notice, now! §last two words crossed out and replaced
above by§ passably.        795-96| MS:§no ¶§ *P2*:§¶§        796| MS:For §added in margin§
First §altered to§ first of all, did §last three words crossed out and replaced above by§ facility, his
brother come to §last two words crossed out§ died. *CP2*:died—        797| MS:I < > you who
was confidant,    *CP2*:Who was, I < > you, confidant,        799| MS:distance—but
*P2*:distance: but        800| MS:§line added between present ll. 799 and 801§ in Italy,
*CP4*:in Portugal,        801| MS:He §crossed out§ had §altered to§ Had
804| MS:recipient,—by    *CP2*:recipient—by        805| MS:§line added between present ll. 804
and 806§        806| MS:foolishness)—    *CP2*:foolishness)        807| MS:Monsieur Antoine
Mellerio, meant    *CP3a*:Monsieur Antoine Flammario, meant    *P4*:Monsieur Antoine Mellerio,
meant    *CP4*:Monsieur Léonce Miranda, meant        808| MS:nature, had his only §last three
words crossed out and replaced above by four words§ needs must shift the

To his love's bosom from his brother's neck,
810   Or fall flat unrelieved of freight sublime.

Next died the lord of the Aladdin's cave,
Master o' the mint and keeper of the keys
Of chests chokeful with gold and silver changed
By Art to forms where wealth forgot itself,
815   And caskets where reposed each pullet-egg
Of diamond, slipping flame from fifty slants.
In short, the father of the family
Took his departure also from our scene,
Leaving a fat succession to his heir
820   Monsieur Léonce Miranda,—"fortunate
If ever man was, in a father's death,"
(So commented the world,—not he, too kind,
Could that be, rather than scarce kind enough)
Indisputably fortunate so far,
825   That little of incumbrance in his path,
Which money kicks aside, would lie there long.

And finally, a rough but wholesome shock,
An accident which comes to kill or cure,
A jerk which mends a dislocated joint!

---

810| MS:of sympathy. §crossed out and replaced above by two words§ freight sublime.
810-11| MS:§no ¶§ P2:§¶§      812| MS:the Mint P2:mint      813-14| MS:§lines added in margin and marked for insertion between present ll. 812 and 815§      813| MS:chests, choakful of §crossed out and replaced above by§ with P2:chests choakful 1889a:chokeful
815| MS:To §crossed out and replaced above by§ And <> reposed some §crossed out and replaced above by§ each pigeon-egg §pigeon crossed out and replaced above by§ pullet
816| MS:diamond, fire a-slip §last two words crossed out and replaced above by two words§ slipping flame <> slants— CP2:slants.      818| MS:from this §crossed out and replaced above by§ our      819| MS:heir— CP2:heir      820| MS:Monsieur Antoine Mellerio,— "fortunate CP3a:Monsieur Antoine Flammario,—"fortunate P4:Monsieur Antoine Mellerio,—"fortunate CP4:Monsieur Alphonse §crossed out and replaced above by§ Léonce Miranda,—"fortunate      822| MS:world, not he: too CP2:world,—not he, too
823| MS:If §crossed out§ that could §last two words transposed and altered to§ Could that <> than not §crossed out and replaced above by§ scarce      824| MS:Indisputably §inserted above§ Fortunate §altered to§ fortunate      825| MS:his way §crossed out§ path,
826| MS:money could remove §last two words crossed out and replaced above by two words§ kicks aside, would      826-27| MS:§no ¶§ P2:§¶§      827| MS:finally a P2:finally, a
829| MS:Like §crossed out and replaced above by§ A <> joint, P2:joint!

830   Such happy chance, at cost of twinge, no doubt,
      Into the socket back again put truth,
      And stopped the limb from longer dragging lie.
      For love suggested "Better shamble on,
      And bear your lameness with what grace you may!"
835   And but for this rude wholesome accident,
      Continuance of disguise and subterfuge,
      Retention of first falsehood as to name
      And nature in the lady, might have proved
      Too necessary for abandonment.
840   Monsieur Léonce Miranda probably
      Had else been loath to cast the mask aside,
      So politic, so self-preservative,
      Therefore so pardonable—though so wrong!
      For see the bugbear ill the background! Breathe
845   But ugly name, and wind is sure to waft
      The husband news of the wife's whereabout:
      From where he lies perdue in London town,
      Forth steps the needy tailor on the stage,
      Deity-like from dusk machine of fog,

---

831|   MS:Put truth, §last two words and comma moved to end of line§ into §altered to§ Into
*P2:*put          832|   MS:And saved §crossed out and replaced above by§ stopped the limb which
else had dragged, perhaps. §last five words crossed out and replaced above by four words§ from
longer dragging lie,   *CP2:*lie.          833|   MS:Had love suggested—"Better   *CP2:*For love
suggested "Better          835|   MS:§line added between present ll. 834 and 836§ But for < > rude
though wholesome   *1873:*And but < > rude wholesome          836|   MS:Which means,— §last
two words crossed out§ necessity §crossed out and replaced above by§ continuance   §altered
to§ Continuance of the §inserted above and crossed out§ disguise and §last two words inserted
above§          837|   MS:In keeping up that old disguise of §last seven words crossed out and
replaced above by six words§ Retention of first falsehood as to          838|   MS:lady, long had
plagued   §last three words crossed out and replaced above by three words§ might have proved
839|   MS:§line added between present ll. 838 and 840§ abandonment:   *CP2:*abandonment.
840|   MS:Monsieur Antoine Mellerio probably   *CP3a:*Monsieur Antoine Flammario probably
*P4:*Monsieur Antoine Mellerio probably   *CP4:*Monsieur Léonce Miranda probably
841|   MS:§line added between present ll. 840 and 842§          842|   MS:So §added in margin§ As
§crossed out§ politic, necessitous—   §crossed out and replaced above by three words§ so and
§crossed out§ self-perservative,          843|   MS:And §crossed out§ therefore §altered to§
Therefore so §last two words inserted above§          846|   MS:whereabout—   *P2:*whereabout!
*CP2:*whereabout:          846-49|   MS:whereabout— / Forth steps the needy tailor on the stage, /
From where he lies perdue in London town, / God §crossed out and replaced above by§ Deity-
like from far §crossed out and replaced above by§ dusk machine of London §crossed out§ fog,
*P2:*whereabout! / / /   *CP2:*whereabout: / §ll. 847 and 848 transposed§

217

850 And claims his consort, or his consort's worth
In rubies which her price is far above.
Hard to propitiate, harder to oppose,—
Who but the man's self came to banish fear,
A pleasant apparition, such as shocks
855 A moment, tells a tale, then goes for good!

Monsieur Ulysse Muhlhausen proved no less
Nor more than "Gustave," lodging opposite
Monsieur Léonce Miranda's diamond-cave
And ruby-mine, and lacking little thence
860 Save that its gnome would keep the captive safe,
Never return his Clara to his arms.
For why? He was become the man in vogue,
The indispensable to who went clothed
Nor cared encounter Paris-fashion's blame,—
865 Such miracle could London absence work.
Rolling in riches—so translate "the vogue"—
Rather his object was to keep off claw
Should griffin scent the gold, should wife lay claim
To lawful portion at a future day,
870 Than tempt his partner from her private spoils.
Best forage each for each, nor coupled hunt!

---

852| MS:oppose   *P2:*oppose,—         853| MS:What §altered to§ Who          854| MS:as frights
§crossed out§ shocks          855| MS:tells good news, §last two words crossed out and replaced
above by two words§ a tale, and goes again §crossed out§ for   *P2:*tale, then goes
855-56| MS:§no ¶§   *P2:*§¶§          856| MS:Monsieur Achille Debacker proved   *CP3a:*Monsieur
Ulysse Durlach proved   *P4:*Monsieur Achille Debacker proved   *CP4:*Monsieur Ulysse
Muhlhausen proved          857| MS:than "Alfred," lodging   *CP3a:*than "Gustave," lodging
*P4:*than "Alfred," lodging   *CP4:*than "Gustave," lodging          858| MS:§line added between
present ll. 857 and 859§ Monsieur Antoine Mellerio's diamond-cave   *CP3a:*Monsieur Antoine
Flammario's diamond-cave   *P4:*Monsieur Antoine Mellerio's diamond-cave   *CP4:*Monsieur
Alphonse §crossed out and replaced above by§ Léonce Miranda's diamond-cave
859| MS:And §over *The*§          860| MS:But §crossed out and replaced above by§ Save <>
would hold §crossed out and replaced above by§ keep          861| MS:§line added between
present ll. 860 and 862§ his Anna to   *CP2:*his Clara to          864| MS:In Paris and §crossed out
and replaced above by§ nor encountered fashion's blame,—   *CP2:*Nor would §crossed out and
replaced above by§ cared encounter Paris fashion's   *1889a:*encounter Paris-fashion's
866|   *CP2:*riches—so <> vogue"— §dashes altered to parentheses and restored§
868|   MS:Of griffin from the   *CP2:*Should griffin scent the          870|   MS:spoils:   *CP2:*spoils.
871|   MS:§line added between present ll. 870 and 872§ hunt.   *P2:*hunt!

Pursuantly, one morning,—knock at door
With knuckle, dry authoritative cough,
And easy stamp of foot, broke startlingly
875   On household slumber, Coliseum Street:
"Admittance in the name of Law!" In marched
The Commissary and subordinate.
One glance sufficed them. "A marital pair:
We certify, and bid good morning, sir!
880   Madame, a thousand pardons!" Whereupon
Monsieur Ulysse Muhlhausen, otherwise
Called "Gustave" for conveniency of trade,
Deposing in due form complaint of wrong,
Made his demand of remedy—divorce
885   From bed, board, share of name, and part in goods.
Monsieur Léonce Miranda owned his fault,
Protested his pure ignorance, from first
To last, of rights infringed in "Gustave's" case:
Submitted him to judgment. Law decreed
890   "Body and goods be henceforth separate!"
And thereupon each party took its way
This right, this left, rejoicing, to abide
Estranged yet amicable, opposites

---

872| MS:Accordingly, one   *CP2:*Pursuantly, one      875| MS:The §crossed out and replaced above by two words§ On household slumbering §altered to§ slumbers §altered to§ slumber, Street Miromesnil   §last two words transposed to§ Miromesnil Street:   *CP4:*slumber, Coliseum Street:     876| MS:law!" In   *CP2:*of Law!" In      877| MS:subordinates §altered to§ subordinate:   *CP2:*subordinate.     878| MS:them §inserted§      879| MS:We §over *I*§ certify, <> Sir—   *P2:*sir—   *CP2:*sir!     880| MS:Madam   *P2:*Madame
881| MS:Monsieur Achille Debacker, known by name §last three words crossed out§ otherwise *CP3a:*Monsieur Ulysse Durlach, otherwise   *P4:*Monsieur Achille Debacker otherwise *CP4:*Monsieur Ulysse Muhlhausen otherwise   *1889a:*Monsieur Ulysse Muhlhausen, otherwise
882| MS:Of §crossed out and replaced above by§ Called "Alfred,' for   *P2:*Called "Alfred," for *CP2:*Called "Alfred" for   *CP3a:*Called "Gustave" for   *P4:*Called "Alfred" for   *CP4:*Called "Gustave" for      884| MS:And §crossed out§ makes §altered to§ Made his §inserted above§
886| MS:Monsieur Antoine Mellerio owned   *CP4:*Monsieur Alphonse §crossed out and replaced above by§ Léonce Miranda owned     887| MS:Protested (with truth) §last two words crossed out§ his pure §inserted above§     888| MS:in "Alfred's" case: *CP4:*in "Gustave's" case:     889| MS:Submits §altered to§ Submitted him §inserted below§ to judgment. Judgment §crossed out and replaced above by§ Law straight §crossed out and replaced above by§ quick §crossed out§ decrees §altered to§ decreed *CP2:*§revisions attempted and crossed out§     891| MS:party takes §crossed out and replaced above by§ took its way   *CP2:*way,     892| MS:abide—   *CP2:*abide

219

In life as in respective dwelling-place.
895 Still does one read on his establishment
Huge-lettered "Gustave,"—gold out-glittering
"Miranda, goldsmith," just across the street"—
"A first-rate hand at riding-habits"—say
The instructed—"special cut of chamber-robes."

900 Thus by a rude in seeming—rightlier judged
Beneficent surprise, publicity
Stopped further fear and trembling, and what tale
Cowardice thinks a covert: one bold splash
Into the mid-shame, and the shiver ends,
905 Though cramp and drowning may begin perhaps.

To cite just one more point which crowned success:
Madame, Miranda's mother, most of all
An obstacle to his projected life
In licence, as a daughter of the Church,
910 Duteous, exemplary, severe by right—
Moreover one most thoroughly beloved
Without a rival till the other sort
Possessed her son,—first storm of anger spent,
She seemed, though grumblingly and grudgingly,
915 To let be what needs must be, acquiesce.

---

896| MS:Huge-lettered "Alfred," gold   *CP2:*Huge-lettered "Alfred,"—gold   *CP3a:*Huge-lettered "Gustave,"—gold   *P4:*Huge-lettered "Alfred,"—gold   *CP4:*Huge-lettered "Gustave,"—gold
897| MS:"Mellerio, goldsmith < > the way §crossed out and replaced above by§ street: *CP2:*street—   *CP3a:*"Flammario, goldsmith   *P4:*"Mellerio, goldsmith   *CP4:*"Miranda, goldsmith        898| MS:A < > riding-habits—say   *CP2:*riding-habits—say §dash altered to parenthesis and restored§   *CP4:*"A < > riding-habits"—say        899| MS:instructed—"specialty of Amazones."   *CP2:*instructed—"specialty §dash altered to parenthsis and restored§ *CP4:*instructed—"special cut of chamber-robes."        900| MS:Thus §over perhaps *So*§ by < > seeming—rightly judged,   *CP2:*seeming—rightlier judged        902| MS:Stopped need of §last two words crossed out and replaced above by§ further < > what his §crossed out§ tale
906| MS:cite another §crossed out and replaced above by three words§ just one more
907| MS:Madame Mellorio, Mother   *P2:*Madame Mellerio, mother   *CP2:*Madame, Mellerio's mother   P3a:Madame, Flammario's mother   *P4:*Madame, Mellerio's mother *CP4:*Madame, Miranda's mother        908| MS:to the projected   *CP2:*to his projected
914| MS:Seemed, grumblingly and grudgingly no doubt,   *C1873:*She seemed, though grumblingly and grudgingly,        915| MS:To acquiesce, nor strive with what must be. *CP4:*To acquiesce, let be what needs must be.   *C1873:*To let < > be, acquiesce.

"With Heaven—accommodation possible!"
Saint Sganarelle had preached with such effect,
She saw now mitigating circumstance.
"The erring one was most unfortunate,
920  No question: but worse Magdalens repent.
Were Clara free, did only Law allow,
What fitter choice in marriage could have made
Léonce or anybody?" 'Tis alleged
And evidenced, I find, by advocate
925  "Never did she consider such a tie
As baleful, springe to snap whate'er the cost."
And when the couple were in safety once
At Clairvaux, motherly, considerate,
She shrank not from advice. "Since safe you be,
930  Safely abide! for winter, I know well,
Is troublesome in a cold country-house.
I recommend the south room, that we styled,
Your sire and I, the winter-chamber."

                                          Chance
Or purpose,—who can read the mystery?—
935  Combined, I say, to bid "Entrench yourself,

---

⁹¹⁶⁻¹⁸| MS: "With Heaven,— accommodation possible!" / §line added between present ll. 916
and 918§ Could not the tempted §altered to§ Tempter leave this ear alone? / She saw much
mitigating circumstance:  *P2:* ("With Heaven—accommodation < > / < > alone?) / She < >
circumstance.  *CP2:* "With < > / Saint Sganarelle had preached with such effect, / She now saw
mitigating  *P3:* / Saint Sgandrette had < > / She saw now  *CP3:* / Saint Sganarelle had < > /
⁹¹⁹| MS:The *CP2:* "The       ⁹²⁰| MS:question—but far worse than she repent.  *P2:* question:
but  *CP2:* but worse Magdalens repent.  *P3:* worse Magdalen's  *CP3:* worse Magdalens
⁹²¹| MS:Had she been free < > only law  *P2:* Were Anna free  *CP2:* only Law
*CP4:* Were Clara free       ⁹²³| MS:Antoine or anybody? "Never"—('tis  *P2:* anybody?— 'Tis
*CP2:* anybody?" 'Tis  *CP4:* Léonce or       ⁹²⁴| MS:advocate)  *P2:* advocate,  *CP2:* advocate
⁹²⁶| MS:As shameful, to be snapt whate'er the cost:"  *P2:* cost."  *CP2:* As baleful, springe to
snap whate'er  *P3:* As baleful, springe       ⁹²⁷| MS:in fast retreat §last two words crossed out
and replaced above by two words§ safety once       ⁹²⁸| MS:At Taneville, motherly  *P2:* At
Tailleville, motherly  *CP2:* At Clairvaux, motherly       ⁹²⁹| MS:shrunk < > advice, "since
§altered to§ Since  *P2:* advice. "Since  *CP4:* shrank       ⁹³⁰| MS:abide!—and winter  *P2:* and
Winter  *CP2:* abide! for Winter  *C1873:* winter       ⁹³¹| MS:country-house;  *P2:* country-
house.       ⁹³²| MS:the South  *P2:* south       ⁹³³| MS:and I, The Winter-Chamber." §¶§
Chance,  *P2:* and I, the  *CP2:* the Winter-chamber." §¶§ Chance  *C1873:* winter-chamber
⁹³⁵| MS:Combined, in short §last two words crossed out and replaced above by two words§ I say

Monsieur Léonce Miranda, on this turf,
About this flower, so firmly that, as tent
Rises on every side around you both,
The question shall become,—Which arrogates
940   Stability, this tent or those far towers?
May not the temporary structure suit
The stable circuit, co-exist in peace?—
Always until the proper time, no fear!
'Lay flat your tent!' is easier said than done."

945   So, with the best of auspices, betook
Themselves Léonce Miranda and his bride—
Provisionary—to their Clairvaux house,
Never to leave it—till the proper time.

I told you what was Clairvaux-Priory
950   Ere the improper time: an old demesne
With memories,—relic half, and ruin whole,—
The very place, then, to repair the wits
Worn out with Paris-traffic, when its lord,
Miranda's father, took his month of ease
955   Purchased by industry. What contrast here!
Repose, and solitude, and healthy ways.
That ticking at the back of head, he took

---

936|   MS:Monsieur Antoine Mellerio, on   *CP4:*Monsieur Alphonse §crossed out and replaced
above by§ Léonce Miranda, on        938|   MS:Rises around you both on every side,   *P2:*Rises
on every side around you both,          940|   MS:Stability, the tent or towers afar—   *P2:*afar?
*C1873:*Stability, this tent or those far towers?          942|   MS:The circuit-wall, and co-exist
*P2:*The stable circuit, co-exist          944|   MS:Meantime, 'Lay flat!' is   *P2:* 'Lay flat your tent'! is
*CP2:*tent!' is          945|   MS:auspices betook   *P2:*auspices, betook          946|   MS:Monsieur
§crossed out and replaced above by§ Themselves Antoine Mellorio and his Bride
*P2:*Themselves Antoine Mellerio and his bride—   *CP4:*Themselves Alphonse §crossed out and
replaced above by§ Léonce Miranda and          947|   MS:Provisionary, to their Tailleville house
*P2:*Provisionary—to   *CP4:*their Clairvaux house,          949|   MS:was Tailleville-Priory
*CP4:*was Clairvaux-Priory          950|   MS:In the   *P2:*Ere the          951|   MS:relic, half, and ruin,
whole,—   *1889a:*relic half, and ruin whole,—          953|   MS:with Paris-traffic when the
§crossed out and replaced above by§ its lord   *P2:*with Paris-traffic, when its lord,
954|   MS:Mellerio-father took   *CP2:*Mellerio's father took   *CP4:*Miranda's father
*1889a:*father, took          955|   MS:industry. What solider §crossed out§ contrast here—
*CP2:*here!          956|   MS:Repose, tranquil §crossed out and replaced above by two words§ and
solitude, and healthy feel!   *P2:*healthy ways!   *1889a:*ways.

For motion of an inmate, stopped at once,
Proved nothing but the pavement's rattle left
960 Behind at Paris: here was holiday.
Welcome the quaint succeeding to the spruce,
The large and lumbersome and—might he breathe
In whisper to his own ear—dignified
And gentry-fashioned old-style haunts of sleep!
965 Palatial gloomy chambers for parade,
And passage-lengths of lost significance,
Never constructed as receptacle,
At his odd hours, for him their actual lord
By dint of diamond-dealing, goldsmithry.
970 Therefore Miranda's father chopped and changed
Nor roof-tile nor yet floor-brick, undismayed
By rains a-top or rats at bottom there.
Such contrast is so piquant for a month!
But now arrived quite other occupants
975 Whose cry was "Permanency,—life and death
Here, here, not elsewhere, change is all we dread!"
Their dwelling-place must be adapted, then,
To inmates, no mere truants from the town,

---

958| MS:motions    CP2:motion          959| MS:Proved themselves but <> rattle, left
*P2:*Proved itself but    *CP2:*Proved nothing but <> rattle left          960| MS:Behind our
§crossed out and replaced above by§ his holiday—his §over perhaps *a*§ month of pride!
*CP2:*Behind at Paris: here was holiday!    *P3:*holiday—    *CP3:*holiday!    *1889a:*holiday.
961| MS:Pleasant the    *P2:*Welcome the          962| MS:lumbersome and . . may §altered to§
might one §crossed out and replaced above by§ he    *P2:*lumbersome and—might
963| MS:to one's §crossed out and replaced above by§ his <> ear? . . dignified
*P2:*ear—dignified          964| MS:sleep,    *CP2:*sleep!— §dash crossed out§
966| MS:significance,—    *CP2:*significance,          967| MS:receptacle    *CP2:*receptacle,
968| MS:hours of who is §last three words crossed out and replaced above by three words§ for
him the actual    *P2:*him their actual    *CP2:*hours, for          970| MS:Therefore Mellerio-father
chopped    *P2:*Therefore Mellerio father    *CP2:*Therefore Mellerio's father    *CP4:*Therefore
Miranda's father          971| MS:floor-brick,—uncompelled §altered to§ till compelled
*P2:*floor-brick, undismayed          972-74| MS:By rain a-top, or <> there. / But now we have §last
two words crossed out and replaced above by§ arrived    *P2:*a-top or <> there. / Such contrasts
are so piquant for a month! / But    *CP2:*By rains <> / Such contrast is so <> /
975| MS:cry was §over *is*§          976| MS:Be §added in margin§ Here §altered to§ here, and
§crossed out§ not elsewhere, with no dread of §last four words crossed out§ change
*P2:*Here, here, not          977| MS:This dwelling-place accordingly §crossed out and replaced
above by two words§ must be <> then    *P2:*Their dwelling-place <> then,
978| MS:town,— §dash crossed out§

No temporary sojourners, forsooth,
980　At Clairvaux: change it into Paradise!

Fair friend,—who listen and let talk, alas!—
You would, in even such a state of things,
Pronounce,—or am I wrong?—for bidding stay
The old-world inconvenience, fresh as found.
985　All folk of individuality
Prefer to be reminded now and then,
Though at the cost of vulgar cosiness,
That the shell-outside only harbours man
The vital and progressive, meant to build,
990　When build he may, with quite a difference,
Some time, in that far land we dream about,
Where every man is his own architect.
But then the couple here in question, each
At one in project for a happy life,
995　Were by no acceptation of the word
So individual that they must aspire
To architecture all-appropriate
And, therefore, in this world impossible:
They needed house to suit the circumstance,

---

979| MS:§line added between present ll. 978 and 980§ forsooth   *P2:*forsooth,
980| MS:At §added in margin§ This §crossed out§ Tailleville: they intend for §last three words crossed out and replaced below by four words§ change it then to Paradise!   *P2:*it into Paradise! *CP2:*At Clairvaux: change   981| MS:Fair §over *Dear*§ Friend <> listen while I §last two words crossed out and replaced below by two words§ and let <> alas,—   *P2:*Fair friend <> alas!—   983| MS:wrong?,—for letting §crossed out and replaced above by§ bidding *P2:*wrong?—for   985| MS:folks   *1889a:*folk   986| MS:reminded, now *1889a:*reminded now   988| MS:only houses you §crossed out§ man   *P2:*only harbours man   989| MS:build   *P2:*build,   990| MS:When you do, §last two words crossed out and replaced above by three words§ build he may, with   991| MS:Having §crossed out and replaced above by two words§ Some day §crossed out and replaced above by§ Time, <> far clime §crossed out and replaced above by§ land <> about, §crossed out and restored§ may be §last two words crossed out§   993| MS:couple now in   *CP2:*couple here in   994| *CP2:*At one §last two words crossed out§ Agreed §crossed out; original reading restored§   995| MS:Were §word illegibly crossed out§ by   997| MS:architecture thus §crossed out and replaced above by§ all-appropriate   998-99| MS:§lines added between present ll. 997 and 1000§ And §added in margin§ Therefore in this world §last three words inserted above§ impossible: / they §altered to§ They <> the neighbourhood §crossed out and replaced above by§ circumstance,   *P2:*And therefore   *CP2:*And, therefore, in

<sup></sup>1000 Proprietors, not tenants for a term.
Despite a certain marking, here and there,
Of fleecy black or white distinguishment,
These vulgar sheep wore the flock's uniform.
*They* love the country, *they* renounce the town?
1005 They gave a kick, as our Italians say,
To Paris ere it turned and kicked themselves!
Acquaintances might prove too hard to seek,
Or the reverse of hard to find, perchance,
Since Monsieur Gustave's apparition there.
1010 And let me call remark upon the list
Of notabilities invoked, in Court
At Vire, to witness, by their phrases culled
From correspondence, what was the esteem
Of those we pay respect to, for "the pair
1015 Whereof they knew the inner life," 'tis said.
Three, and three only, answered the appeal.
First, Monsieur Vaillant, music-publisher,
"Begs Madame will accept civilities."
Next, Alexandre Dumas,—sire, not son,—
1020 "Sends compliments to Madame and to you."

---

<sup>1000|</sup> MS:Exact the size of §last four words crossed out and replaced above by two words§
Proprietors, not <sup>1001|</sup> MS:here or §crossed out and replaced above by§ and   *P2:*marking
here   *CP2:*marking, here <sup>1003-5|</sup> MS:Two, or one §last three words crossed out and
replaced above by§ These <> of what a §last three words crossed out and replaced above by two
words§ wore the <> uniform. / They gave <> as the Italians   *P2:*uniform. / They love the
country, they renounce the town? / They gave   *CP2:*uniform. / *They* <> country, *they* <> /
*P3:* // <> as our Italians <sup>1006|</sup> MS:it turned and   §last two words inserted above§
kicked, §comma crossed out§ perchance, §crossed out§ themselves;   *P2:*themselves!
<sup>1007|</sup> MS:might be §crossed out and replaced above by§ prove <> seek   *P2:*seek,
<sup>1009|</sup> MS:Since Monsieur Alfred's apparition   *CP4:*Since Monsieur Gustave's apparition
<sup>1012|</sup> MS:At Caen, to   *CP4:*At Vire, to <sup>1014|</sup> MS:we hold in honor §last three words
crossed out and replaced above by three words§ pay respect to, for the   *CP2:*we pay respect to,
§last four words crossed out and restored; replaced by two words§ held estimable, §last two
words crossed out§   *P3:*for "the <sup>1015|</sup> MS:the domesticity. §crossed out and replaced
above by four words§ inner life, 'tis said.   *CP2:*"Whereof <> life," 'tis   *P3:*Whereof
<sup>1016|</sup> MS:Three and, three   *CP2:*Three, and three   *P3:*Three and three, only, answered
*CP3:*Three, and three only, answered <sup>1017|</sup> MS:First, Monsieur Meriel, Music-publisher,
*P2:*First, Monsieur Mériel, music-publisher,   *CP4:*First, Monsieur Vaillant, music-publisher,
<sup>1018|</sup> MS:Next §crossed out§ "Begs <sup>1019|</sup> MS:Next, Alexander   *P2:*Next Alexandre
<sup>1020|</sup> MS:My §crossed out§ "Sends <> you,"   *P2:*you."

And last—but now prepare for England's voice!
I will not mar nor make—here's word for word—
"A rich proprietor of Paris, he
To whom belonged that beauteous *Bagatelle*
1025     Close to the wood of Boulogne, Hertford hight,
Assures of homages and compliments
Affectionate"—not now Miranda but
"Madame Muhlhausen." (Was this friend, the Duke
Redoubtable in rivalry before ?)
1030     Such was the evidence when evidence
Was wanted, then if ever, to the worth
Whereat acquaintances in Paris prized
Monsieur Léonce Miranda's household charm.
No wonder, then, his impulse was to live,
1035     In Norman solitude, the Paris life:
Surround himself with Art transported thence,
And nature like those famed Elysian Fields:
Then, warm up the right colour out of both,
By Boulevard friendships tempted to come taste
1040     How Paris lived again in little there.

Monsieur Léonce Miranda practised Art.
Do let a man for once live as man likes!

---

1021|   MS:last—and §crossed out and replaced above by§ but here prepare <> voice—
*P2*:but now prepare <> voice!     1022|   MS:will nor mar   *P2*:will not mar
1026|   MS:Assures his §crossed out§ of     1027|   MS:Affectionate—not now Mellerio but
*P2*:Affectionate"—not   *CP4*:now Miranda but     1028|   MS:Madame Debacker." (Was this
lord, the   *P2*:"Madame   *P3*:this friend, the   *CP4*:"Madame Muhlhausen." (Was
1033|   MS:Monsieur Antoine Mellerio's household   *CP4*:Monsieur Alphonse §crossed out and
replaced above by§ Léonce Miranda's household     1033-34|   MS:§¶§   *P2*:§no ¶§
1034|   MS:Accordingly, his <> live   *P2*:impulse, was   *CP2*:No wonder, then, his impulse was to
live,     1035|   MS:The Paris life: in Norman solitude, §last six words altered and transposed
to§ In Norman solitude, the Paris life:   *CP4*:In Norman §crossed out and restored§
1036|   MS:with art, transported   *P2*:with Art, transported   *CP4*:with Art transported
1037|   MS:nature modish as §last two words crossed out and replaced above by two words§
fashioned like the Elysian   *CP2*:And Nature like those famed Elysian   *CP2(3a)*:nature
*P3*:nature like theose   *CP3*:those     1038|   MS:And §crossed out and replaced above by§
Then, warm     1039|   MS:come see   *P2*:come taste     1040-42|   MS:there. / §no ¶§ Do
*P2*:there. / §¶§ Monsieur Antoine Mellerio practised Art. / Do   *CP4*:§¶§ Monsieur Alphonse
§crossed out and replaced above by§ Léonce Miranda practised

Politics? Spend your life, to spare the world's:
Improve each unit by some particle
<sup>1045</sup> Of joy the more, deteriorate the orb
Entire, your own: poor profit, dismal loss!
Write books, paint pictures, or make music—since
Your nature leans to such life-exercise!
Ay, but such exercise begins too soon,
<sup>1050</sup> Concludes too late, demands life whole and sole,
Artistry being battle with the age
It lives in! Half life,—silence, while you learn
What has been done; the other half,—attempt
At speech, amid world's wail of wonderment—
<sup>1055</sup> "Here's something done was never done before!"
To be the very breath that moves the age
Means not to have breath drive you bubble-like
Before it—but yourself to blow: that's strain;
Strain's worry through the life-time, till there's peace;
<sup>1060</sup> We know where peace expects the artist-soul.

---

<sup>1043-47</sup>| MS:§See Editorial Notes for an explanation of B's revisions to these lines§   MS:Politics?
Spend your §inserted above; crossed out and replaced above by§ his own §inserted above§ life,
so to save / The world of lives, each unit's particle / Of joy that's life, and lose the orb entire, /
Your §crossed out and replaced above by§ His own aforesaid!   Artistry, perhaps? / Write
*P2:/// <> aforesaid! Artist then: but how? / Write   CP2:Politics? Spend your own full life, to
<> / <> each scanty particle / Of joy you give, so much subtracted from / The orb entire, your
own.   Be Artist then! / Write   CP2(3a): <> your life to save the world: / Improve each unit by
some particle / Of joy the more, deteriorate the orb / Entire, your own: poor profit, dismal loss!
/ Write   P3:Politics? Spend yonr §sic§ life, to spare the world's: // <> own poor prnfit, §sic§
<> / Write   CP3:your // <> own: poor profit, <> / Write        <sup>1048</sup>|   MS:Yo §crossed out§
His nature leaned to such an exercise?   CP2:Your nature leans to such life-exercise!
P3:life—exercise!   CP3:life-exercise!        <sup>1050</sup>|   MS:demands him §crossed out and replaced
above by§ life <> sole.   P2:sole,   1889a:sole §emended to§ sole, §see Editorial Notes§
<sup>1051</sup>|   MS:Such life will be one battle   P2:Artistry being battle with the age
<sup>1052</sup>|   MS:in: half-life <> while he learns   P2:in Half life <> while you learn   CP2:in! Half
<sup>1054</sup>|   MS:world's cry of   CP2:world's wail of        <sup>1055</sup>|   MS:That is to do, §last four words
crossed out and replaced above by three words§ Here's something done, was <> before!
CP2:"Here's <> before!"   1889a:done was        <sup>1056</sup>|   MS:be the spirit,—breath <> age,
P2:be the very breath   1889a:age        <sup>1057</sup>|   MS:not, to have it §crossed out and replaced
above by§ breath drive man bubble-like   P2:drive you bubble-like   1889a:not to
<sup>1058</sup>|   MS:but himself §inserted above§ to <> strain,   P2:but yourself to   CP2:strain;
P3:strain"   CP4:strain;        <sup>1059</sup>|   MS:And tempest §last two words crossed out and replaced
above by two words§ Strain's— §dash crossed out§ worry <> life-time—till   P2:life-time, till

227

Monsieur Léonce Miranda knew as much.
Therefore in Art he nowise cared to be
Creative; but creation, that had birth
In storminess long years before was born
1065    Monsieur Léonce Miranda,—Art, enjoyed
Like fleshly objects of the chace that tempt
In cookery, not in capture—these might feast
The dilettante, furnish tavern-fare
Open to all with purses open too.
1070    To sit free and take tribute *seigneur*-like—
Now, not too lavish of acknowledgment,
Now, self-indulgently profuse of pay,
Always Art's *seigneur*, not Art's serving-man
Whate'er the style and title and degree,—
1075    That is the quiet life and easy death
Monsieur Léonce Miranda would approve
Wholly—provided (back I go again
To the first simile) that while glasses clink,
And viands steam, and banqueting laughs high,

---

<sup>1060-62</sup>|  MS:You §crossed out and replaced above by§ We < > where it §crossed out and replaced
above by§ peace expects §crossed out and replaced above by§ allays §crossed out and replaced
above by§ expects the stormy soul. / §no ¶; l. 1062 added between present ll. 1060 and 1063§
Therefore in art he nowise thought to    *P2:*the artist-soul. / §¶§ Monsieur Antoine Mellerio
knew as much. / Therefore < > nowise cared to    *CP2:* // < > in Art    *CP4:*Monsieur Alphonse
§crossed out and replaced above by§ Léonce Miranda knew < > /    *1889a:* / §no ¶; emended to
restore ¶; see Editorial Notes§        <sup>1063</sup>|   MS:Creative: but    *CP2:*Creative; but
<sup>1064</sup>|   MS:storminess so §crossed out§ long years §inserted above§        <sup>1065</sup>|   MS:Monsieur
Antoine Mellerio,—art    *P2:* Monsieur Antoine Mellerio,—Art    *CP4:*Monsieur Alphonse
§crossed out and replaced above by§ Léonce Miranda,—Art        <sup>1066</sup>|   MS:the chase that
please    *P2:*the chace that tempt        <sup>1067</sup>|   MS:not capture—these §over *there*§ he §crossed
out and replaced above by§ might feasts, §altered to§ feast    *CP2:*not capture,—these
*P2:*not capture—these    *C1873:*not in capture        <sup>1068</sup>|   MS:dilettante, on the §last two words
crossed out and replaced above by§ furnish        <sup>1069</sup>|   MS:all whose purse is open too—
*P2:*too.    *CP2:*all with purses open        <sup>1070</sup>|   MS:There sits §altered to§ sit < > and takes
§altered to§ take < > seigneur-like—    *P2:*To sit    *C1873: seigneur*-like—
<sup>1071</sup>|   MS:acknowledgement,    *P2:*acknowledgment,        <sup>1072</sup>|   MS:Now self-indulgently
*P2:*Now, self-indulgently        <sup>1073</sup>|   MS:Always the §crossed out and replaced above by§ art's
seigneur, not the §crossed out and replaced above by§ art's serving man,    *P2:*Always Art's < >
not Art's    *CP2:*serving-man,    *C1873: seigneur    1889a:*serving man        <sup>1074</sup>|   MS:degree!
*P2:*degree,—        <sup>1076</sup>|   MS:Monsieur Antoine Mellerio would approve,    *P2:*approve
*CP4:*Monsieur Alphonse §crossed out and replaced above by§ Léonce Miranda would
<sup>1078</sup>|   MS:simile) that §inserted above§ while the §crossed out§ glasses        <sup>1079</sup>|   MS:and
banqueting's §altered to§ banqueting at §crossed out§ is high    *P2:*banqueting laughs high,

1080 All that's outside the temporary tent,
The dim grim outline of the circuit-wall,
Forgets to menace "Soon or late will drop
Pavilion, soon or late you needs must march,
And laggards will be sorry they were slack!
1085 Always—unless excuse sound plausible!"

Monsieur Léonce Miranda knew as much:
Whence his determination just to paint
So creditably as might help the eye
To comprehend how painter's eye grew dim
1090 Ere it produced L'Ingegno's piece of work—
So to become musician that his ear
Should judge, by its own tickling and turmoil,
Who made the Solemn Mass might well die deaf—
So cultivate a literary knack
1095 That, by experience how it wiles the time,
He might imagine how a poet, rapt
In rhyming wholly, grew so poor at last
By carelessness about his banker's-book,
That the Sieur Boileau (to provoke our smile)
1100 Began abruptly,—when he paid devoir

---

1081| MS:circuit-wall   *P2*:circuit-wall,          1082| MS:menace: §altered to§ menace—"Soon
*P2*:menace,—"Soon   *CP2*:menace "Soon          1083| MS:Pavilion, and the §crossed out and
replaced above by§ your onward march must beat,   *CP2*:Pavilion, soon or late you needs must
march,          1084| MS:laggards may §crossed out and replaced above by§ will < > were late—
§crossed out and replaced above by§ slack!"   *P2*:slack!          1085| MS:excuse be §crossed out
and replaced above by§ sound plausible!   *P2*:plausible!"          1085-86| MS:§¶§   *1889a*:§no ¶;
emended to restore ¶; see Editorial Notes§          1086| MS:§line added between present ll. 1085
and 1087§ Monsieur Antoine Mellerio knew   *P2*:knew all that:   *CP2*:knew as much:
*CP4*:Monsieur Alphonse §crossed out and replaced above by§ Léonce Miranda knew
1087| MS:Whence the §crossed out and replaced below by§ his determination so to
*CP2*:determination just to          1088| MS:Just §crossed out§ as §altered to§ As much as,
§inserted above§ and no more than helps the eye   *CP2*:So creditably as might help
1089| MS:comprehend the §crossed out and replaced above by§ a painter's   *CP2*:comprehend
how painter's          1090|. MS:Ere he produced L'Ingenio's piece   *P2*:Ere it produced
L'Ingeno's   *CP2*:produced L'Ingegno's          1092| MS:judge by < > turmoil   *P2*:judge, by < >
turmoil,          1095| MS:by it §crossed out§ experience          1096 MS:One may imagine
*P2*:He might may imagine   *CP2*:He might imagine how §crossed out and replaced above by two
words§ some old §last two words crossed out; original reading restored§
1097| MS:wholly, got §over perhaps *gets*§ so   *P2*:wholly, grew so          1098| MS:banker's book,
*P2*:banker's-book,          1100| MS:Begins §altered to§ Began < > he pays §altered to§ paid

To Louis Quatorze as he dined in state,—
"Sire, send a drop of broth to Pierre Corneille
Now dying and in want of sustenance!"
—I say, these half-hour playings at life's toil,
1105    Diversified by billiards, riding, sport—
With now and then a visitor—Dumas,
Hertford—to check no aspiration's flight—
While Clara, like a diamond in the dark,
Should extract shining from what else were shade,
1110    And multiply chance rays a million-fold,—
How could he doubt that all offence outside,—
Wrong to the towers, which, pillowed on the turf,
He thus shut eyes to,—were as good as gone?

So, down went Clairvaux-Priory to dust,
1115    And up there rose, in lieu, yon structure gay
Above the Norman ghosts: and where the stretch
Of barren country girdled house about,
Behold the Park, the English preference!
Thus made undoubtedly a desert smile
1120    Monsieur Léonce Miranda.

Ay, but she?
One should not so merge soul in soul, you think?

---

[1101]  MS:he dines §altered to§ dined     [1102]  MS:to Pierre Corneille,   *CP2:* to Pierre Corneille     [1107]  MS:Hertford—who §crossed out and replaced above by§ to checks our §crossed out and replaced above by§ no <> flight? §altered to§ flight—   *P2:*to check no *CP2:*§dashes replaced with parentheses and restored§     [1108]  MS:With Anna, like *CP2:*While Anna, like   *CP4:*While Clara, like     [1109]  MS:To extract shining where wont §last two words crossed out and replaced above by three words§ from what else   *CP2:*Should extract     [1110]  MS:multipy   *P2:*multiply     [1111]  MS:outside, *CP2:*outside,—     [1112]  MS:§line added between present ll. 1111 and 1113§ to the Towers which <> the Turf, *P2:*to the towers, which <> turf,     [1113]  MS:to, were *CP2:*to,—were     [1114]  MS:went Tailleville Priory *P2:*went Tailleville-Priory *CP4:*went Clairvaux-Priory     [1115]  MS:And in its place uprose §last four words crossed out and replaced above by five words§ up there rose, in lieu, yon     [1116]  *P2:*and when the *CP2:*and where the *CP4:*Above the Norman §crossed out and restored§     [1118]  MS:preference, *P2:*preference!     [1119]  MS:Making §crossed out and replaced above by two words§ So made the desert smile undoubtedly §last four words transposed to§ undoubtedly the desert smile, *CP2:*Thus made undoubtedly a desert *1889a:*smile     [1120]  MS: Monsieur Antoine Mellerio. §¶§ <> She? *P2:*she? *CP4:*Monsieur Alphonse §crossed out and replaced above by§ Léonce Miranda. §¶§

And I think: only, let us wait, nor want
Two things at once—her turn will come in time.
A cork-float danced upon the tide, we saw,
1125 This morning, blinding-bright with briny dews:
There was no disengaging soaked from sound,
Earth-product from the sister-element.
But when we turn, the tide will turn, I think,
And bare on beach will lie exposed the buoy:
1130 A very proper time to try, with foot
And even finger, which was buoying wave,
Which merely buoyant substance,—power to lift,
And power to be sent skyward passively.
Meanwhile, no separation of the pair!

---

1125| MS:dews— *P2*:dews: 1127| MS:sister-element; *P2*:sister-element.
1128| MS:will turn, as well §last two words crossed out§ I 1129| MS:And bare §inserted
above§ on the §crossed out§ beach will lie §over perhaps *be*§ exposed the buoy.
*P2*:buoy: 1130| MS:And then will be the §last five words crossed out and replaced above by
three words§ A very proper < > try with *CP2*:try, with 1131| MS:which of it §last two
words inserted above and crossed out§ was frothy §inserted above and crossed out§ dancing
§inserted above§ wave, *P2*:was buoying wave, 1132| MS:Which merely §inserted above§
buoyant substance,—which was §last two words crossed out§ power
1133| MS:Or §added in margin§ Which §crossed out§ power to be raised §crossed out and
replaced above by§ sent < > passively: *P2*:passively. *CP2*:And power
1134| MS:Meanwhile, inseparable let §last two words crossed out and replaced above by two
words§ no separation §double rule; B notes in margin *Leave half sheet*§

231

III

And so slipt pleasantly away five years
Of Paradisiac dream; till, as there flit
Premonitory symptoms, pricks of pain,
Because the dreamer has to start awake
⁵ And find disease dwelt active all the while
In head or stomach through his night-long sleep,—
So happened here disturbance to content.

Monsieur Léonce Miranda's last of cares,
Ere he composed himself, had been to make
¹⁰ Provision that, while sleeping safe he lay,
Somebody else should, dragon-like, let fall
Never a lid, coiled round the apple-stem,
But watch the precious fruitage. Somebody
Kept shop, in short, played Paris-substitute.
¹⁵ Himself, shrewd, well-trained, early-exercised,
Could take in, at an eye-glance, luck or loss—
Know commerce throve, though lazily uplift
On elbow merely: leave his bed, forsooth?
Such active service was the substitute's.

---

²| MS:dream; but §crossed out and replaced above by§ till, as      ³| MS:symptoms—pricks
of pain— *CP2:*symptoms, pricks of pain,      ⁵| MS:disease was §crossed out and replaced
above by§ dwelt      ⁶| MS:stomach though §altered to§ through his §crossed out and
restored§ nightlong §inserted above§ sleep, §crossed out and restored§ he dozed away,— §last
three words crossed out§  *P2:*night-long sleep,—      ⁷| MS:happened this §crossed out and
replaced above by§ here      ⁸| MS:Monsieur Antoine Mellerio's last  *CP4:*Monsieur
Alphonse §crossed out and replaced above by§ Léonce Miranda's last
⁹| MS:had wisely made §last two words crossed out and replaced above by three words§ been to
make      ¹⁰| MS:while slumbering and §last two words crossed out and replaced above by§
sleeping safe he §over comma§ lay,      ¹²| MS:apple stem, §over illegible word§
*CP2:*apple-stem,      ¹³| MS:Whence came §last two words crossed out and replaced above by
two words§ But watch the golden comfort §last two words crossed out and replaced above by two
words§ precious fruitage; somebody  *CP2:*fruitage. Somebody      ¹⁴| MS:Kept shop, in
short, §last four words altered and transposed to§ In short, kept shop, his §crossed out and
replaced above by§ played Paris substitute.  *CP2:*Kept shop, in short, played  *1889a:*played
Paris-substitute.      ¹⁶| MS:eye-glance, good §crossed out and replaced above by§ luck or ill,
§crossed out and replaced above by§ loss—      ¹⁷| MS:How commerce  *CP2:*Know
commerce      ¹⁹| MS:§line added between present ll. 18 and 20§
¹⁹⁻²⁰| MS:§no ¶§  *P2:*§¶§  *1889a:*§no ¶; emended to restore ¶; see Editorial Notes§

20   But one October morning, at first drop
     Of appled gold, first summons to be grave
     Because rough Autumn's play turns earnest now,
     Monsieur Léonce Miranda was required
     In Paris to take counsel, face to face,
25   With Madame-mother: and be rated, too,
     Roundly at certain items of expense
     Whereat the government provisional,
     The Paris substitute and shopkeeper,
     Shook head, and talked of funds inadequate:
30   Oh, in the long run,—not if remedy
     Occurred betimes! Else,—tap the generous bole
     Too near the quick,—it withers to the root—
     Leafy, prolific, golden apple-tree,
     "Miranda," sturdy in the Place Vendôme!

35   "What is this reckless life you lead?" began
     Her greeting she whom most he feared and loved,
     Madame Miranda. "Luxury, extravagance
     Sardanapalus' self might emulate,—
     Did your good father's money go for this?

---

²⁰| MS:first fall §crossed out§ drop        ²¹| MS:Of leafy §crossed out and replaced above by§
appled        ²²| MS:Because the other kind of turn §last four words crossed out and replaced
above by four words§ autumn is §crossed out and replaced above by§ came §crossed out§ in
§crossed out and replaced below by two words§ play turns earnest §inserted above§    *P2:*the
Autumn    *CP2:*the Autumn's play    *CP4:*Because rough Autumn's        ²³| MS: Monsieur
Antoine Mellorio was    *P2:* Monsieur Antoine Mellerio was    *CP4:*Monsieur Alphonse §crossed
out and replaced above by§ Léonce Miranda was        ²⁵| MS:With Madame-mother: who
§crossed out§ and        ²⁸| MS:§line added between present ll. 27 and 29§ Of §crossed out§
The §added in margin§ Paris        ²⁹| MS:inadequate    *P2:*inadequate—    *CP2:*inadequate:
³⁰| MS:—Oh, in <> run,—oh, no §last two words crossed out and replaced above by two
words§ not if    *P2:*Oh, in        ³¹| MS:Taken §crossed out and replaced above by§ Occurred
betimes!—might §crossed out and replaced above by§ But §crossed out and replaced above by§
Else,— tap the golden tree §last two words crossed out§ generous    *P2:*betimes! Else
³²| MS:quick,—and §crossed out and replaced above by§ it <> root,— §comma crossed out§
³³| MS:§line added between present ll. 32 and 34§        ³⁴| MS:"Mellerio," sturdy in the Street
of Peace!    *CP4:*"Miranda," sturdy in the Place Vendôme!        ³⁶⁻³⁷| MS:§line 36 added
between present ll. 35 and 37§ Madame Mellerio,—whom he <> loved,— / Her greeting:
wantonness §crossed out and replaced above by§ "Luxury    *P2:* /Her greeting. "Luxury
*CP4:*Madame Miranda,—whom    *C1873:* /Her greeting, she whom most he <> loved,— /
Madame Miranda, "Luxury    *1889a:*greeting she <> loved, / Madame Miranda. "Luxury

40  Where are the fruits of education, where
    The morals which at first distinguished you,
    The faith which promised to adorn your age?
    And why such wastefulness outbreaking now,
    When heretofore you loved economy?
45  Explain this pulling-down and building-up
    Poor Clairvaux, which your father bought because
    Clairvaux he found it, and so left to you,
    Not a gilt-gingerbread big baby-house!
    True, we could somehow shake head and shut eye
50  To what was past prevention on our part—
    This reprehensible illicit bond:
    We, in a manner, winking, watched consort
    Our modest well-conducted pious son
    With Dalilah: we thought the smoking flax
55  Would smoulder soon away and end in snuff.
    Is spark to strengthen, prove consuming fire?
    No lawful family calls Clairvaux 'home'—
    Why play that fool of Scripture whom the voice

---

41| MS:morals that §crossed out and replaced above by three words§ which at first <> you, in youth, §last two words crossed out§    42| MS:The firm §crossed out§ faith that §crossed out and replaced above by§ which <> age?    43| MS:why this §crossed out and replaced above by§ such    45| MS:Wherefo §crossed out and replaced above by§ Explain <> building up    *1889a:*building-up    46| MS:Of Tailleville that §inserted above and crossed out§ which §inserted above§    *P2:*Of Tailleville, which    *CP4:*Of Clairvaux, which    *1889a:*Poor Clairvaux
47| MS:Tailleville he <> left it you,    *CP2:*left to you,    *CP4:*Clairvaux he
48| MS:And §crossed out§ not §altered to§ Not a gilded modern §last two words crossed out and replaced above by three words§ gilt gingerbread gilt §crossed out§ big §inserted above§
51| MS:illicit tie, §crossed out and replaced above by§ bond—    *P2:*bond:
52| MS:§line added between present ll. 51 and 53§ manner, winked §altered to§ winking not §crossed out§ watched    54| MS:With Dalila    *P2:*With Dalilah    55| MS:Would wear its spark §last three words crossed out and replaced above by two words§ smoulder soon <> snuff;    *CP2:*snuff!    *1889a:*snuff.    56| MS:Is it §crossed out and replaced above by§ fire §crossed out and replaced below by§ spark to strengthen, and §crossed out and replaced above by§ prove consume §altered to§ consuming your life §last two words crossed out and replaced above by§ fire §crossed out§    *P2:*fire?    57| MS:calls Tailleville "home"—    *P2:*calls Tailleville 'home'—    *CP4:*calls Clairvaux 'home'—    58| MS:The very §last two words crossed out and replaced above by four words§ Why play that §crossed out§ the <> of scripture, whom §crossed out and replaced above by§ that §crossed out and restored§ the    *P2:*of Scripture that    *1889a:*play that fool of Scripture whom the

Admonished 'Whose to-night shall be those things
60    Provided for thy morning jollity?'
To take one specimen of pure caprice
Out of the heap conspicuous in the plan,—
Puzzle of change, I call it,—titled big
'Clairvaux Restored:' what means this Belvedere?
65    This Tower, stuck like a fool's-cap on the roof—
Do you intend to soar to heaven from thence?
Tower, truly! Better had you planted turf—
More fitly would you dig yourself a hole
Beneath it for the final journey's help!
70    O we poor parents—could we prophesy!"


Léonce was found affectionate enough
To man, to woman, child, bird, beast, alike;
But all affection, all one fire of heart
Flaming toward Madame-mother. Had she posed
75    The question plainly at the outset "Choose!
Cut clean in half your all-the-world of love,
The mother and the mistress: then resolve,

---

⁵⁹| MS:Admonished—"Whose shall <> things, to-night, §last word marked for transposition to
follow *Whose*; transposition cancelled§    *P2:*Admonished—'Whose <> things to-night,
*CP3:*Admonished 'Whose    *1889a:*Admonished 'Whose to-night shall <> things
⁶⁰| MS:for this §altered to§ thy morning's §altered to§ morning jollity?"    *P2:*jollity?'
⁶¹| MS:Of all the §last three words crossed out§ To      ⁶²| MS:in this plan,—    *1889a:*in the
plan,—      ⁶⁴| MS:"Tailleville Restored:" what means this §crossed out and restored§
*P2:*'Tailleville Restored:' what    *CP4:*'Clairvaux Restored:'      ⁶⁵| MS:§line added between
present ll. 64 and 66§ a fools' cap    *P2:*a fools'-cap    *1889a:*a fool's-cap
⁶⁶| MS:to soar to Heaven    *CP2:*heaven      ⁶⁷| MS:§line added between present ll. 66 and
68§ Towers, truly! Better if you    *P2:*Tower, truly    *CP2:*truly! Better had you
⁶⁸| MS:More fitly §altered to§ fitly    *CP2:*a hole §crossed out and replaced by§ grave §erased,
restoring *hole*§      ⁶⁹| MS:it, for <> journey's sake §crossed out and replaced above by§
help!    *1889a:*it for      ⁷⁰⁻⁷¹| MS:§¶§    *1889a:*§no ¶; emended to restore ¶; see Editorial
Notes§      ⁷¹| MS:Now, Antoine was affectionate enough,    *CP2:*Antoine was found
affectionate enough    *CP4:*Alphonse §crossed out and replaced above by§ Léonce was
⁷²| MS:man, and §crossed out and replaced above by§ to woman, child, §inserted above§ bird,
and §crossed out§ beast, alike:    *CP2:*alike;    *P3:*alike:    *CP3:*alike;
⁷⁴| MS:Flaming towards §altered to§ toward this §crossed out§ Madame- §inserted above§
mother      ⁷⁵| MS:outset—"Choose!    *CP3:*outset "Choose!    *P4:*outset. "Choose!
*CP4:*outset "Choose!      ⁷⁶| MS:all the world    *P2:*all-the-world      ⁷⁷| MS:§line added
between present ll. 76 and 78§ mistress—then resolve—    *CP3:*mistress: then resolve,

Take me or take her, throw away the one!"—
He might have made the choice and marred my tale.
80   But, much I apprehend, the problem put
Was "Keep both halves, yet do no detriment
To either! Prize each opposite in turn!"
Hence, while he prized at worth the Clairvaux-life
With all its tolerated naughtiness,
85   He, visiting in fancy Quai Rousseau,
Saw, cornered in the cosiest nook of all
That range of rooms through number Thirty-three,
The lady-mother bent o'er her *bézique*;
While Monsieur Curé This, and Sister That—
90   Superior of no matter what good House—
Did duty for Duke Hertford and Dumas,
Nay—at his mother's age—for Clara's self.
At Quai Rousseau, things comfortable thus,
Why should poor Clairvaux prove so troublesome?
95   She played at cards, he built a Belvedere.

---

[78] MS:Take me, §comma crossed out§ or §inserted above§ take her, but §crossed out§ throw
[79] MS:Well, he had made    *CP2:*He might have made       [81] MS:Was—"Keep both halves
yet    *P2:*halves, yet    *CP2:*Was "Keep        [82] MS:either!— §dash crossed out§ prize §altered
to§ Prize        [83] MS:the Tailleville-life,    *CP2:*the Tailleville-life    *1873:*the Clairvaux-life
[84] MS:§line added between present ll. 83 and 85§        [85] MS:He, saw §crossed out and
replaced above by§ visited §altered to§ visiting in fancy still the §last two words crossed out§
Quai Voltaire,    *CP4:*fancy Quai Rousseau        [86] MS:And §crossed out and replaced above
by§ Saw        [87] MS:That §over perhaps *The*§ range <> through §over illegible word§
Number Twenty five,    *P2:*through number Twenty-five,    *CP4:*number Thirty-three,
[88] MS:her *bezique* §altered to§ *Bezique,*    *P2:*her *Bézique,*    *CP2:*her *Bezique,*    *CP3:*her *Bézique,*
*1889a: bézique,*        [89] MS:With §crossed out and replaced above by§ While <> and Madame
§crossed out and replaced above by§ Sister That    *CP2:*and Sister That,—    *1889a:*and Sister
That—        [90] MS:what the §crossed out and replaced above by§ good        [91-92] MS:§lines
added in margin§        [92] MS:Nay,—at that §crossed out and replaced above by two words§
his mother's age, you know,— §last two words crossed out§ for Anna's self.    *P2:*age,—for,
Anna's    *CP3:*for Anna's    *CP4:*for Clara's self.    *1889a:*Nay—at <> age—for
[93] MS:§line added between present ll. 90 and 94§ Her Quai Voltaire made comfortable thus,
§line crossed out and replaced in margin by§ Things comfortable thus, at Quai Voltaire, §last six
words altered and transposed to§ At Quai Voltaire, things comfortable thus,    *CP4:*At Quai
Rousseau, things        [94-95] MS:And why §last two words crossed out§ Why §added in margin§
should poor §inserted above§ Tailleville §following word illegibly crossed out§ be so §last two
words crossed out and restored§ troublesome? / §line added between present ll. 94 and 95§
One builds a Belvedere with bricks §line crossed out§ / She plays §altered to§ played at cards,
he builds §altered to§ built §line crossed out and restored§ a not cards: §last two words crossed
out and replaced above by§ Belvedere!    *P2:*troublesome? / She <> Belvedere.
*CP4:*poor Clairvaux the <> / *1889a:*poor Clairvaux prove so <> /

But here's the difference: she had reached the Towers
And there took pastime: he was still on Turf—
Though fully minded that, when once he marched,
No sportive fancy should distract him more.

100   In brief, the man was angry with himself,
With her, with all the world and much beside:
And so the unseemly words were interchanged
Which crystallize what else evaporates,
And make mere misty petulance grow hard
105   And sharp inside each softness, heart and soul.
Monsieur Léonce Miranda flung at last
Out of doors, fever-flushed: and there the Seine
Rolled at his feet, obsequious remedy
For fever, in a cold Autumnal flow.
110   "Go and be rid of memory in a bath!"
Craftily whispered Who besets the ear
On such occasions.

                        Done as soon as dreamed.
Back shivers poor Léonce to bed—where else?
And there he lies a month 'twixt life and death,
115   Raving. "Remorse of conscience!" friends opine.
"Sirs, it may partly prove so," represents
Beaumont—(the family physician, he

---

96-99| MS:§lines added in margin§      103| MS:crystalize <> else evaporated §altered to§
evaporates  *P2:*evaporates,  *1889a:*crystallize      104| MS:make the §crossed out and
replaced above by§ mere      105| MS:inside the §crossed out and replaced above by§ each
<> and brain §crossed out and replaced above by§ soul.      106| MS:Monsieur Antoine
Mellerio, flung  *P2:*Monsieur Antoine Mellerio flung  *CP4:*Monsieur Alphonse §crossed out
and replaced above by§ Léonce Miranda flung      107| MS:fever-flushed—and
*P2:*fever-flushed: and      109| MS:in its §crossed out and replaced above by§ a <> flow:
*P2:*flow.      110| MS:and get §crossed out and replaced above by§ be <> bath,"  *P2:*bath!"
111| MS:Unwisely §inserted above§ Whispered  *P2:*whispered  *CP2:*Craftily whispered
112| MS:soon as said: §crossed out and replaced above by§ dreamed.
113| MS:poor Antoine to  *CP4:*Poor Alphonse §crossed out
and replaced above by§ Léonce to      115-16| MS:§¶§  *P4:*§no ¶§
116| MS:"Well—that §crossed out and replaced above by§ it  *P2:*"Well, it  *CP2:*"Sirs, it
117| MS:Pasquier—(the  *CP4:*Fouquier §crossed out and replaced by§ Beaumont—(the

Whom last year's Commune murdered, do you mind?)
Beaumont reports "There is some active cause,
120   More than mere pungency of quarrel past,—
Cause that keeps adding other food to fire.
I hear the words and know the signs, I say!
Dear Madame, you have read the Book of Saints,
How Antony was tempted? As for me,
125   Poor heathen, 'tis by pictures I am taught.
I say then, I see standing here,—between
Me and my patient, and that crucifix
You very properly would interpose,—
A certain woman-shape, one white appeal
130   'Will you leave me, then, me, me, me for her?'
Since cold Seine could not quench this flame, since flare
Of fever does not redden it away,—
Be rational, indulgent, mute—should chance
Come to the rescue—Providence, I mean—
135   The while I blister and phlebotomize!"


Well, somehow rescued by whatever power,
At month's end, back again conveyed himself
Monsieur Léonce Miranda, worn to rags,

---

118|   MS:The §crossed out§ Our §added in margin§ Commune murdered last year, do <>
mind?) §parenthesis over dash§   *CP3:*Whom last year's Commune murdered, do
119|   MS: Pasquier reports—"There   *P2:*reports: "There   *CP2:*reports "There   *CP4:*Fouquier
§crossed out and replaced above by§ Beaumont reports      120|   MS:mere memories §over
illegible word§ of the §crossed out and replaced above by§ a folly past,—   *CP2:*mere pungency
of quarrel past,—      121|   MS:That still §crossed out§ Cause §added in margin§ keeps
adding fuel to the fire.   *P2:*that   *CP2:*adding other food to fire.      122|   MS:signs: I say, . . .
.   *P2:*say, . .   *CP2:*signs, I say!      123|   MS:—Dear   *P2:*Dear      125|   MS:taught—
*P2:*taught.      126|   MS:standing full in face §last three words crossed out and replaced above
by two words§ here,—between      127|   MS:Of §crossed out§ Me      129|   MS:appeal:
*CP2:*appeal      130|   MS:"Will <> her?"   *P2:*'Will <> her?'      131|   MS:The §crossed out
and replaced above by§ Since <> flame, the §crossed out and replaced above by§ since
132|   MS:fever will not <> it to fade §last two words crossed out§ away,—   *CP4:*fever does not
133|   MS:rational, and acquiesce, §last two words crossed out and replaced above by two words§
indulgent, mute—should      134|   MS:Assist—or §last two words crossed out and replaced
above by four words§ Come to the rescue—providence <> mean to say— §last two words
crossed out§   *P2:*rescue—Providence      135|   MS:phlebotomize."   *CP2:* phlebotomize!"
*P3:*Tne   *CP3:*The      138|   MS:Monsieur Antoine Mellerio, worn   *CP4:*Monsieur Alphonse
§crossed out and replaced above by§ Léonce Miranda, worn

238

Nay, tinder: stuff irreparably spoiled,
140  Though kindly hand should stitch and patch its best.
Clairvaux in Autumn is restorative.
A friend stitched on, patched ever. All the same,
Clairvaux looked greyer than a month ago.
Unglossed was shrubbery, unglorified
145  Each copse, so wealthy once; the garden-plots,
The orchard-walks showed dearth and dreariness.
The sea lay out at distance crammed by cloud
Into a leaden wedge; and sorrowful
Sulked field and pasture with persistent rain.
150  Nobody came so far from Paris now:
Friends did their duty by an invalid
Whose convalescence claimed entire repose.
Only a single ministrant was staunch
At quiet reparation of the stuff—
155  Monsieur Léonce Miranda, worn to rags:

---

<sup>139</sup>| MS:And §crossed out and replaced above by§ Nay, tinder of irreparable trace,
*CP2:*tinder: stuff irreparable spoiled, *P3:*stiff *CP3:*stuff <sup>140-42</sup>| MS:Though friendly
§altered to§ kindly <> best. / §line added between present ll. 140 and 143§ Anna worked on,
worked ever: all the same, *P2:* / §¶§ Anna stitched on, patched ever *CP2:*best. / §no ¶§
Tailleville in Autumn is restorative / §¶§ Anna <> ever. All *P3:*best. / Tailleville <> /
*CP3:* / Tailleville <> restorative. / §no ¶§ Anna *CP4:*best. / Clairvaux in <> / Clara §crossed
out and replaced above by two words§ A friend stitched <sup>143</sup>| MS:Tailleville was §crossed
out and replaced above by§ looked <> ago, *P2:*ago. *CP4:*Clairvaux looked
<sup>144</sup>| MS:Unglossed the §crossed out and replaced above by§ was
<sup>145</sup>| MS:The woods §altered to§ wood §last two words crossed out and replaced above by two
words§ Each copse with §crossed out and replaced above by§ so wealthy of leaf: §last two words
crossed out and replaced above by§ how scant and dear. §last four words crossed out and
replaced above by two words§ the garden-plots *P2:*copse, so <> garden-plots, *CP2:*once; the
<sup>146</sup>| MS:§line added between present ll. 145 and 147§ The §added in margin; next word
illegibly crossed out§ orchard-walks, one dearth *CP2:*orchard-walks were dearth
*CP4:*orchard-walks showed dearth <sup>147</sup>| MS:distance pressed §crossed out and replaced
above by§ crammed <sup>148</sup>| MS:wedge, and *CP2:*wedge; and <sup>149</sup>| MS:§illegible
word, perhaps *Were,* crossed out and replaced above by§ Sulked <sup>150</sup>| MS:now—
*P2:*now: <sup>151</sup>| MS:They knew §last two words crossed out and replaced above by two
words§ Friends did <> duty to §crossed out and replaced above by§ by <sup>152</sup>| MS:Happily
§crossed out and replaced above by§ Whose convalescent, §altered to§ convalescence claiming
rest. peace. §last three words crossed out and replaced above by three words§ claimed such
quietude. §last two words crossed out§ entire repose. <sup>154</sup>| MS:At quiet §inserted above§
reparation <> the rags, §crossed out and replaced above by§ stuff—you see, §last two words
crossed out§ <sup>155</sup>| MS:§line added in margin§ Monsieur Antoine Mellerio, worn
*CP4:*Monsieur Alphonse §crossed out and replaced above by§ Léonce Miranda, worn

But she was Clara and the world beside.

Another month, the year packed up his plagues
And sullenly departed, pedlar-like,
As apprehensive old-world ware might show
160  To disadvantage when the new-comer,
Merchant of novelties, young 'Sixty-eight,
With brand-new bargains, whistled o'er the lea.
Things brightened somewhat o'er the Christmas hearth,
As Clara plied assiduously her task.

165  "Words are but words and wind. Why let the wind
Sing in your ear, bite, sounding, to your brain ?
Old folk and young folk, still at odds, of course!
Age quarrels because spring puts forth a leaf
While winter has a mind that boughs stay bare;
170  Or rather—worse than quarrel—age descries
Propriety in preaching life to death.
'Enjoy nor youth, nor Clairvaux, nor poor me?'

---

<sup>156</sup>|  MS:§line added between present ll. 154 and 157§ was Anna and   *CP4:*was Clara and
<sup>157</sup>|  MS:plagues,  *1873:*plagues      <sup>159</sup>|  MS:Who §crossed out and replaced above by§ As
apprehending §altered to§ apprehensive his §crossed out§ sorry ware will §crossed out and
replaced above by§ might   *CP4:*apprehensive old-world ware      <sup>160</sup>|  MS:disadvantage,
when §crossed out and replaced above by§ now §crossed out; original reading restored§
*CP3:*disadvantage when      <sup>161</sup>|  MS:§line added between present ll. 160 and 162§
*P2:*young, 'Sixty-eight,  *CP2:*young 'Sixty-eight,      <sup>162</sup>|  MS:bran-new <> whistled at
§crossed out and replaced above by§ o'er the gate §crossed out§ lea.  *1889a:*brand-new
<sup>163</sup>|  MS:hearth.  *P2:*hearth,      <sup>164</sup>|  MS:§line added between present ll. 163 and 165§ As
Anna kept §crossed out and replaced above by§ plied assiduously at work §last two words crossed
out§ her task.      <sup>164-65</sup>|  *CP2:*task. / "You look at me: why think and think of her? §entire
line crossed out§ / "Words      <sup>166</sup>|  MS:ear., §period crossed out§ go §crossed out and
replaced above by§ bite, sounding      <sup>167</sup>|  MS:young folk,—the old difference! §last three
words crossed out and replaced above by five words§ still at odds, of course!  *P2:*young folk,
still      <sup>168</sup>|  MS:They §crossed out and replaced above by§ Age quarrels that the §last two
words crossed out and replaced above by§ because Spring <> forth its §crossed out and
replaced above by§ a  *C1873:*spring      <sup>169</sup>|  MS:When §altered to§ While Winter <> mind
for §crossed out and replaced above by§ that boughs all §crossed out and replaced above by§
stay  *C1873:*winter      <sup>170</sup>|  MS:rather—not §crossed out and replaced above by§ worse the
§altered to§ than quarrel,—they supposed §last two words crossed out§ age  *CP2:*quarrel—age
<sup>171</sup>|  MS:Propriety of §crossed out and replaced above by§ in      <sup>172</sup>|  MS:"Do not §last two
words crossed out§ enjoy §altered to§ Enjoy nor §inserted above§ youth, nor §inserted above§
Tailleville, and your friend!" §last three words crossed out and replaced above by three words§
nor poor me?"  *P2:*'Enjoy <> me?'  *CP4:*youth, nor Clairvaux, nor

Dear Madame, you enjoy your age, 'tis thought!
Your number Thirty-three on Quai Rousseau
175    Cost fifty times the price of Clairvaux, tipped
Even with our prodigious Belvedere;
You entertain the Curé,—we, Dumas:
We play charades, while you prefer *bézique*:
Do lead your own life and let ours alone!
180    Cross Old Year shall have done his worst, my friend!
Here comes gay New Year with a gift, no doubt.
Look up and let in light that longs to shine—
One flash of light, and where will darkness hide?
Your cold makes me too cold, love! Keep me warm!"

185    Whereat Léonce Miranda raised his head
From his two white thin hands, and forced a smile,
And spoke: "I do look up, and see your light
Above me! Let New Year contribute warmth—
I shall refuse no fuel that may blaze."

---

173| MS:Dear lady §crossed out and replaced above by§ Madame <> age, I think §last two words crossed out§ 'tis    174| MS:And §crossed out and replaced above by§ Your number Twenty five on Quai Voltaire   *P2:*number Twenty-five   *CP4:*number Thirty three on Quai Rousseau *1873:*number Thirty-three   175| MS:Is §crossed out and replaced above by§ Cost <> the worth §crossed out and replaced above by§ price of Tailleville, here §crossed out§ tipped *CP4:*of Clairvaux   176| MS:§line added between present ll. 175 and 177§   our poor §crossed out§ prodigious §inserted above§ Belvedere.   *P3:*prodigious Belvedere;
177| MS:we, Dumas—   *P2:*we, Dumas:   *CP2:*we, Dumas;   *P3:*we, Dumas:
178| MS:He §crossed out and replaced above by§ We plays §altered to§ play <> *Bezique.* *P2:*prefer *Bézique.*   *CP2:* prefer *Bezique.*   *CP3:* prefer *Bézique.*   *1889a:* prefer *bézique.*
179| *P2:*Go lead   *CP2:*Do lead   180| MS:§line added between present ll. 179 and 181§ This old year shall <> done its worst   *CP2:*Cross Old Year shall have done §crossed out§ raged §crossed out; original reading restored§ his worst   181| MS:comes the New <> with its §crossed out and replaced below by§ a gifts §altered to§ gift, you know §last two words crossed out and replaced above by two words§ no doubt!   *P2:*comes gay New   *1889a:*doubt.
182| MS:let the §crossed out and replaced above by§ in   183| MS:hide?" §quotation mark crossed out§   184| MS:§line added between present ll. 183 and 185§
185| MS:Monsieur §crossed out and replaced below by§ Whereat Antoine Mellerio raised *CP4:*Whereat Alphonse §crossed out and replaced above by§ Léonce Miranda raised
186| MS:two poor thin   *CP4:*two white thin   187| MS:And said §crossed out and replaced above by§ spoke "I <> see your §crossed out and replaced above by§ some light *P2:*spoke: "I <> see your light   188| MS:contribute spark!" §crossed out and replaced above by§ warmth—   189| MS:§line added between present ll. 188 and 190§

190  Nor did he. Three days after, just a spark
     From Paris, answered by a snap at Caen
     Or whither reached the telegraphic wire:
     "Quickly to Paris! On arrival, learn
     Why you are wanted!" Curt and critical!

195  Off starts Léonce, one fear from head to foot;
     Caen, Rouen, Paris, as the railway helps;
     Then come the Quai and Number Thirty-three.
     "What is the matter, concierge ?"—a grimace!
     He mounts the staircase, makes for the main seat
200  Of dreadful mystery which draws him there—
     Bursts in upon a bedroom known too well—
     There lies all left now of the mother once.
     Tapers define the stretch of rigid white,
     Nor want there ghastly velvets of the grave.
205  A blackness sits on either side at watch,
     Sisters, good souls but frightful all the same,
     Silent: a priest is spokesman for his corpse.
     "Dead, through Léonce Miranda! stricken down
     Without a minute's warning, yesterday!
210  What did she say to you, and you to her,
     Two months ago? This is the consequence!
     The doctors have their name for the disease;
     I, you, and God say—heart-break, nothing more!"

---

189-90|  MS:§¶§  *P4*:§no ¶§       190|  MS:It §crossed out and replaced below by§ Nor did so
§crossed out and replaced below by§ he. three §altered to§ Three       191|  *CP4*:at Caen
§crossed out and restored§       192|  MS:Or §added in margin§ Whither goes §crossed out
and replaced above by§ reached  *P2*:whither       193|  MS:to Paris on §last three words
altered to§ to Paris! On       194|  MS:wanted . . . " curt §last two words altered to§ wanted!"
Curt       195|  MS:starts the man §last two words crossed out and replaced above by§ Antoine,
one  *1873*:starts Léonce, one       196|  *CP4*:Caen, Rouen §last two words crossed out and
restored§       197|  MS:Then comes §altered to§ come <> and Number Twenty-five.
*CP4*:and Number Thirty-three.       198|  MS:matter, Concierge?"—A  *P2*:a  *CP4*:concierge
200|  MS:mystery that §crossed out and replaced above by§ which
201|  MS:upon the §crossed out and replaced above by§ a bed-room  *P2*:bedroom
202|  MS:mother late. §crossed out and replaced above by§ once.       208|  MS:through
Antoine Mellerio, stricken  *P2*: through Antoine Mellerio! stricken  *CP4*:through Alphonse
§crossed out and replaced above by§ Léonce Miranda! stricken       213|  MS:God, I and you
§last four words transposed to§ I, you and God <> heart-break, all the same §last three words
crossed out and replaced above by two words§ nothing more!"  *P2*:I, you, and

242

Monsieur Léonce Miranda, like a stone
215   Fell at the bedfoot and found respite so,
While the priest went to tell the company.
What follows you are free to disbelieve.
It may be true or false that this good priest
Had taken his instructions,—who shall blame?—
220   From quite another quarter than, perchance,
Monsieur Léonce Miranda might suppose
Would offer solace in such pressing need.
All he remembered of his kith and kin
Was they were worthily his substitutes
225   In commerce, did their work and drew their pay.
But *they* remembered, in addition, this—
They fairly might expect inheritance,
As nearest kin, called Family by law
And gospel both. Now, since Miranda's life
230   Showed nothing like abatement of distaste
For conjugality, but preference
Continued and confirmed of that smooth chain
Which slips and leaves no knot behind, no heir—

---

²¹⁴|   MS:Monsieur Antoine Mellerio, like   *CP4:*Monsieur Alphonse §crossed out and replaced
above by§ Léonce Miranda, like        ²¹⁵|   MS:and had §crossed out and replaced above by§
found        ²¹⁶|   MS:§line added between present ll. 215 and 218§        ²¹⁶⁻¹⁸|   MS:company.
/ §¶§ Let me explain a little. This good priest   *CP4:*company. / §line added; no §¶§ What
follows you are free to disbelieve. / It may be true or false that this good priest
²¹⁹|   MS:instructions,—properly §crossed out§ who        ²²¹|   MS:Monsieur Antoine Mellerio,
had supposed   *CP4:*Monsieur Alphonse §crossed out and replaced above by§ Léonce Miranda
might suppose        ²²²|   MS:offer counsel §crossed out and replaced above by§ solace in
emer§crossed out and replaced above by§ such        ²²³|   MS:his cousinry §crossed out§ kith
and kin,   *CP3:*kin        ²²⁴|   MS:Was, they might worthily §inserted above§ be his §crossed
out§ substitutes   *CP4:*they were worthily his substitutes   *1889a:*Was they
²²⁵|   MS:commerce, do <> draw   *CP4:*commerce, did <> drew
²²⁶|   MS:What §crossed out and replaced above by§ But they remembered, was §crossed out and
replaced above by§ in additional: his §last two words altered to§ addition, this—
*CP2: they*        ²²⁷|   MS:That §crossed out§ they §altered to§ They were to §last two words
crossed out and replaced above by two words§ fairly might
²²⁸|   MS:As §added in margin§ Nearest of §crossed out§ kin, his §crossed out and replaced
above by§ called family §altered to§ Family   *P2:*nearest        ²²⁹|   MS:since the last eight years
*CP4:*since Miranda's life        ²³¹|   MS:conjugality, and §crossed out and replaced above by§
but        ²³²|   MS:§line added between present ll. 231 and 233§ continued <> smooth tie
*P2:*Continued   *CP4:*smooth chain        ²³³|   MS:Of tie §last two words crossed out§ which
§altered to§ Which slips, and §last two words inserted below§   *CP3:*slips and

Presumption was, the man, become mature,
235   Would at a calculable day discard
His old and outworn . . . what we blush to name,
And make society the just amends;
Scarce by a new attachment—Heaven forbid!
Still less by lawful marriage: that's reserved
240   For those who make a proper choice at first—
Not try both courses and would grasp in age
The very treasure youth preferred to spurn.
No! putting decently such thought aside,
The penitent must rather give his powers
245   To such a reparation of the past
As, edifying kindred, makes them rich.
Now, how would it enrich prospectively
The Cousins, if he lavished such expense
On Clairvaux?—pretty as a toy, but then
250   As toy, so much productive and no more!
If all the outcome of the goldsmith's shop
Went to gild Clairvaux, where remain the funds

---

235| MS:day, discard   *1889a:*day discard        236| MS:His §over perhaps *This*§ <> outworn . .
what   *1889a:*outworn . . . what        237| MS:amends:   *CP2:*amends;        238| MS:Not by
*CP4:*Scarce by        239| MS:marriage:, §colon crossed out§ that's   *P2:*marriage; that's
*CP2:*marriage: that's        240| MS:make the §crossed out and replaced above by§ a
241| MS:and unfit their age   *CP4:*and would grasp in age        242| MS:For grasping treasure,
youth   *CP2:*spurn!   *CP4:*The very treasure   *1889a:*treasure youth <> spurn.
243| MS:decently the past aside,   *CP4:*decently such thought aside,        244| MS:penitent
would straightway give his powers §crossed out and restored§   *CP4:*penitent must rather give
245| MS:§line added between present ll. 244 and 246§        246| MS:As, §added in margin§ To
§crossed out§ edify §altered to§ edifying his cousins—and §last three words crossed out and
replaced below by three words§ kindred, makes them enrich §altered to§ rich.
247| MS:how did §crossed out and replaced below by§ would this enrich   *CP4:*would it enrich
248| MS:The §crossed out and replaced above by§ A cousins §altered to§ cousin, that he
expence   *P2:*The Cousins, that <> expense   *CP4:*The Cousins, if he        249| MS:On
Tailleville? §question mark altered to comma and dash§ pretty <> toy, and as §last two words
crossed out and replaced above by two words§ but then   *P2:*On Tailleville?—pretty   *CP4:*On
Clairvaux?—pretty        250| MS:toy, productive, so much and   *CP4:*toy, so much productive,
and   *1889a:*productive and        251| MS:of the Street of Peace   *CP4:*of the Place Vendôme
§last two words crossed out and replaced above by two words§ goldsmith's shop
252| MS:Went §added in margin§ Was §crossed out and replaced above by§ Go §crossed out§ to
be §crossed out and replaced above by§ gild Tailleville, where would be §last two words crossed
out and replaced above by§ remained the   *CP4:*gild Clairvaux, where   *C1873:*remain

For Cousinry to spread out lap and take?
This must be thought of and provided for.
255   I give it you as mere conjecture, mind!
To help explain the wholesome unannounced
Intelligence, the shock that startled guilt,
The scenic show, much yellow, black and white
By taper-shine, the nuns—portentous pair,
260   And, more than all, the priest's admonishment—
"No flattery of self! You murdered her!
The grey lips, silent now, reprove by mine.
You wasted all your living, rioted
In harlotry—she warned and I repeat!
265   No warning had she, for she needed none:
If this should be the last yourself receive?"
Done for the best, no doubt, though clumsily,—
Such, and so startling, the reception here,
You hardly wonder if down fell at once
270   The tawdry tent, pictorial, musical,
Poetical, besprent with hearts and darts;
Its cobweb-work, betinseled stitchery,
Lay dust about our sleeper on the turf,
And showed the outer towers distinct and dread.

275   Senseless he fell, and long he lay, and much

---

253|  MS:For cousinry to spread the §crossed out and replaced above by§ out   *P2:*For Cousinry
254-56|  MS:for! / §¶§ Accordingly, the wholesome   *CP4:*for! / §no ¶§ I give it you as mere
conjecture, mind! / To help explain the wholesome   *1889a:*for. //      257|  MS:startled sin,
*CP4:*startled guilt,     258|  MS:white,  *P3:*white     262|  MS:lips, yonder §crossed out and
replaced above by§ silent now, make use of mine.   *CP2:*now, reprove through §crossed out and
replaced above by§ by mine.     264|  MS:harlotry] §punctuation altered to dash§ she
265|  MS:She had no warning §last four words altered and transposed to§ No warning had She
*P2:*she    266-68|  MS:receive?" / §¶§ Such   *CP4:*receive?" / Done for the best, no doubt,
though clumsily,— / §no ¶§ Such     269|  MS:You will not §last two words crossed out and
replaced above by§ hardly wonder that down   *CP2:*wonder if down     270|  MS:musical
*P2:*musical,     271|  MS:darts  *P2:*darts;     272|  MS:In betinseled stitchery, mere
§crossed out§ cobweb-work, §last five words transposed to§ In cobweb-work, betinseled stitchery,
*P2:*Its cobweb-work     273|  MS:To dust about the §crossed out and replaced above by§ our
*P2:*Lay dust     274|  MS:showed the §crossed out and replaced above by§ an outer wall
distinct <> dread,  *P2:*dread.   *C1873:*showed the outer towers distinct
275-77|  MS:§present ll. 276 and 277 reversed; l. 277 added between present ll. 275 and 276§
much— / To <> piece— / Seemed <> punishment   *CP3:*§ll. 277 and 276 transposed§

Seemed salutary in his punishment
To planners and performers of the piece.
When pain ends, pardon prompt may operate.
There was a good attendance close at hand,
280   Waiting the issue in the great saloon,
Cousins with consolation and advice.

All things thus happily performed to point,
No wonder at success commensurate.
Once swooning stopped, once anguish subsequent
285   Raved out,—a sudden resolution chilled
His blood and changed his swimming eyes to stone,
As the poor fellow raised himself upright,
Collected strength, looked, once for all, his look,
Then, turning, put officious help aside
290   And passed from out the chamber. "For affairs!"
So he announced himself to the saloon:
"We owe a duty to the living too!"—
Monsieur Léonce Miranda tried to smile.

How did the hearts of Cousinry rejoice
295   At their stray sheep returning thus to fold,
As, with a dignity, precision, sense,
All unsuspected in the man before,

---

much / Seemed <> punishment / To <> piece.  *P4:*much— / Seemed <> punishment— /
To  *CP4:*much / Seemed <> punishment / To        [278]|  MS:Never too §illegible words§
forgiveness §preceding words crossed out and replaced above by seven words§ When pains end,
may §crossed out§ pardon prompt may operate.  *CP2:*When pain ends        [278-79]|  MS:§¶
called for and cancelled§        [282]|  MS:All was §crossed out and replaced above by three
words§ things thus happily        [283]|  MS:Success, no wonder, was §crossed out and replaced
above by§ at §last four words altered and transposed to§ No wonder at Success commensurate.
*P2:*success        [284]|  MS:The §crossed out and replaced above by§ O swoon §altered to§
swooning at end §last two words crossed out and replaced above by§ stopped, the §crossed out
and replaced above by four words§ outburst §crossed out§ §word illegibly crossed out§ once
transport subsequent  *P2:*Once swooning <> once auguish subsequent  *CP2:*anguish
[286]|  MS:The §crossed out and replaced above by§ His <> changed the §crossed out and
replaced above by§ his        [287]|  MS:himself erect, §crossed out§ upright,
[289]|  MS:Then, turning, §inserted above§ put        [293]|  MS:Monsieur Antoine Mellerio tried
*CP4:*Monsieur Alphonse §crossed out and replaced above by§ Léonce Miranda tried
[293-94]|  MS:§¶§  *1889a:*§no ¶; emended to restore ¶; see Editorial Notes§        [294]|  MS:of
cousinry  *P2:*of Cousinry        [295]|  MS:returning safe §crossed out and replaced by§ thus

Monsieur Léonce Miranda made minute
Detail of his intended scheme of life
300 Thenceforward and for ever. "Vanity
Was ended: its redemption must begin—
And, certain, would continue; but since life
Was awfully uncertain—witness here!—
Behoved him lose no moment but discharge
305 Immediate burthen of the world's affairs
On backs that kindly volunteered to crouch.
Cousins, with easier conscience, blamelessly
Might carry on the goldsmith's trade, in brief,
Uninterfered with by its lord who late
310 Was used to supervise and take due tithe.
A stipend now sufficed his natural need:
Themselves should fix what sum allows man live.
But half a dozen words concisely plain
Might, first of all, make sure that, on demise,
315 Monsieur Léonce Miranda's property
Passed by bequeathment, every particle,
To the right heirs, the cousins of his heart.
As for that woman—they would understand!
This was a step must take her by surprise.

---

298| MS:Monsieur Antoine Mellerio made    CP4:Monsieur Alphonse §crossed out and replaced
above by§ Léonce Miranda made        299| MS:his determined §crossed out and replaced
above by§ intended        300| MS:Henceforward §altered to§ Thenceforward < > ever. Vanity
1873:ever. "Vanity        301| MS:Was over §crossed out and replaced above by§ ended
302| MS:And, certainly §altered to§ certain, would §inserted above§ continue: but how long?
§last two words crossed out and replaced above by two words§ since life    CP2:continue; but
303| MS:Was §over perhaps *Is*§        304| MS:moment, but    1889a:moment but
305| MS:The §crossed out§ immediate §altered to§ Immediate < > of this §crossed out and
replaced above by§ the        308| MS:in short,    CP2:in brief,        309| MS:by its §crossed
out and replaced above by§ who, lord so late,    CP2:by its, lord, who late    P3:its lord who late,
CP3:late        310| MS:§line added between present ll. 309 and 311§        311| MS:stipend
should §crossed out and replaced below by§ now sufficed the natural needs—    P2:natural
need:    CP2:sufficed his natural        312| MS:§line added between present ll. 311 and 313§
314| MS:Should, §crossed out and replaced above by§ May §crossed out; original reading
restored§ first < > that, at his death §last three words crossed out and replaced above by two
words§ on demise,    P2:Might, first        315| MS:Monsieur Antoine Mellerio's property
CP4:Monsieur Alphonse §crossed out and replaced above by§ Léonce Miranda's property
316| MS:Should, §crossed out and replaced above by§ Passed, §altered to§ Pass, §original
reading restored§ by    P2:Passed by        318| MS:for . . that    P2:for that

247

<sup>320</sup> It were too cruel did he snatch away
Decent subsistence. She was young, and fair,
And . . . and attractive! Means must be supplied
To save her from herself, and from the world,
And . . . from anxieties might haunt him else
<sup>325</sup> When he were fain have other thoughts in mind."

It was a sight to melt a stone, that thaw
Of rigid disapproval into dew
Of sympathy, as each extended palm
Of cousin hasted to enclose those five
<sup>330</sup> Cold fingers, tendered so mistrustfully,
Despairingly of condonation now!
You would have thought,—at every fervent shake,
In reassurance of those timid tips,—
The penitent had squeezed, considerate,
<sup>335</sup> By way of fee into physician's hand
For physicking his soul, some diamond knob.

And now let pass a week. Once more behold
The same assemblage in the same saloon,
Waiting the entry of protagonist
<sup>340</sup> Monsieur Léonce Miranda. "Just a week

---

<sup>319-20</sup>| MS:§lines added between present ll. 318 and 321§      <sup>319</sup>| MS:step would take < >
surprise!   *1889a:*step must take < > surprise.      <sup>320</sup>| MS:cruel should he take away
*P2:*cruel did he   *CP4:*he snatch away      <sup>322</sup>| MS:And . . and   *1889a:*And . . . and
<sup>324</sup>| MS:And . . from anxieties, might §crossed out and replaced above by§ would haunt < >
else! §exclamation mark crossed out§   *P2:*anxieties, might haunt   *1889a:*anxieties might
<sup>325</sup>| MS:§line added in margin§ he would have quite other thoughts   *P2:*When he were fain
have other thoughts in mind."      <sup>326</sup>| MS:to move a stone, the thaw   *P2:*to melt a stone,
that thaw      <sup>327</sup>| MS:disapproval, into dews   *P2:*disapproval into dew
<sup>330</sup>| MS:fingers tendered—so mistrustfully,— §dash crossed out§   *P2:*fingers, tendered so
<sup>331</sup>| MS:§line added between present ll. 330 and 332§      <sup>332</sup>| MS:One would < > every
fervent §crossed out and replaced above by§ timid §crossed out; original reading restored§
*C1873:*You would      <sup>333</sup>| MS:§line added between present ll. 332 and 334§
<sup>334</sup>| MS:penitent considerately §crossed out and replaced below by§ had, squeezed
*P2:*had squeezed      <sup>335</sup>| MS:into the §crossed out and replaced above by§ each §crossed
out§ physician's hand,   *CP2:*hand      <sup>338</sup>| MS:saloon—   *1889a:*saloon,
<sup>339</sup>| MS:All but §last two words crossed out and replaced above by§ Waiting
<sup>340</sup>| MS:Monsieur Antoine Mellerio! "Just   *P2:* Monsieur Antoine Mellerio. "Just
*CP4:*Monsieur Alphonse §crossed out and replaced above by§ Léonce Miranda. "Just

Since the death-day,—was ever man transformed
Like this man?" questioned cousin of his mate.
Last seal to the repentance had been set
Three days before, at Sceaux in neighbourhood
345 Of Paris, where they laid with funeral pomp
Mother by father. Let me spare the rest:
How the poor fellow, in his misery,
Buried hot face and bosom, where heaped snow
Offered assistance, at the grave's black edge,
350 And there lay, till uprooted by main force
From where he prayed to grow and ne'er again
Walk earth unworthily as heretofore.
It is not with impunity priests teach
The doctrine he was dosed with from his youth—
355 "Pain to the body—profit to the soul;
Corporeal pleasure—so much woe to pay
When disembodied spirit gives account."
However, woe had done its worst, this time.
Three days allow subsidence of much grief
360 Already, regular and equable,
Forward went purpose to effect. At once
The testament was written, signed and sealed.
Disposure of the commerce—that took time,

---

341| MS:death-day,—was §crossed out and replaced above by§ and §crossed out; original reading restored§ never §altered to§ ever        342| MS:man?" chatted §crossed out and replaced above by§ questioned cousin to §crossed out and replaced above by§ of
342-43| MS:§¶§  *P2:*§no ¶§        343| MS:the §over *his*§        344| MS:at Garges in *CP4:*at Sceaux in        346| MS:father: I shall §last two words crossed out and replaced above by two words§ let me <> rest—  *P2:*father. Let <> rest:  *P3:*Mot her y father  *CP3:*Mother by father        348| MS:bosom where the §crossed out and replaced above by§ heaped *CP2:*bosom, where        349| MS:Offered a shelter §last two words crossed out and replaced above by perhaps *hiding,* crossed out§ assistance §inserted above§ at  *CP2:*assistance, at
350| MS:And had to be §last three words crossed out and replaced above by three words§ there lay, §crossed out and replaced above by word illegibly crossed out; *lay* restored§ till
353| MS:impunity you §crossed out and replaced above by§ priests
354| MS:with, from  *P2:*with from        355| MS:soul:  *CP2:*soul;        356| MS:Corporeal comfort §crossed out and replaced above by§ pleasure <> much more §crossed out and replaced above by§ woe        357-58| MS:§¶§  *P2:*§no ¶§        358| MS:However, grief §crossed out and replaced above by§ woe        359| MS:§line added between present ll. 358 and 360§        363| MS:that takes §crossed out and replaced above by§ took

And would not suffer by a week's delay;
365   But the immediate, the imperious need,
The call demanding of the Cousinry
Co-operation, what convened them thus,
Was—how and when should deputation march
To Coliseum Street, the old abode
370   Of wickedness, and there acquaint—oh, shame!
Her, its old inmate, who had followed up
And lay in wait in the old haunt for prey—
That they had rescued, they possessed Léonce,
Whose loathing at recapture equalled theirs—
375   Upbraid that sinner with her sinfulness,
Impart the fellow-sinner's firm resolve
Never to set eyes on her face again:
Then, after stipulations strict but just,
Hand her the first instalment,—moderate

---

³⁶⁴| MS:That would <> by the due §last two words crossed out and replaced above by two words§ a week's delay: *CP2:*And would <> delay; ³⁶⁶| MS:That which §last two words crossed out and replaced above by two words§ The call demanded §altered to§ demanding <> cousinry *P2:*the Cousinry ³⁶⁷| MS:Utmost assistance, and §last three words crossed out and replaced above by two words§ Co-operation, what ³⁶⁸| MS:Was—that a §last two words crossed out and replaced above by four words§ how and when should deputation straight proceed §last two words crossed out§ march ³⁶⁹| MS:To Street Miromesnil §last two words transposed to§ Miromesnil Street *CP4:*To Coliseum Street ³⁷⁰| MS:shame!— *P2:*shame! ³⁷¹| MS:Her, §added in margin§ The §altered to§ the old *CP3:*Her, its old ³⁷²| MS:the old §inserted above§ haunt for him §crossed out§ prey— *CP2:*And §crossed out and replaced by illegible word, perhaps *who*§ lay <> wait for prey in <> haunt, *P4:*And lay <> wait in the old haunt for prey— ³⁷³| MS:§line added between present ll. 372 and 374§ Monsieur Antoine Mellerio, penitent, *CP2:*to catch §last two words crossed out and replaced above by two words§ For that §last two words crossed out and replaced below by six words§ That they had rescued, they possessed Antoine thus escaped §last two words added in margin§ §last two words crossed out and replaced below by§ now, §crossed out§ *CP3:*possessed Antoine. *CP4:*possessed Alphonse §crossed out and replaced above by§ Léonce, ³⁷⁴| MS:loathing for §crossed out and replaced above by§ at re-capture *1889a:*recapture ³⁷⁵| MS:Acquaint Debacker §crossed out and replaced above by two words§ that woman with her sin's result— §last word and dash crossed out§ award *CP2:*Upbraid that sinner with her sinfulness wished §added in margin and crossed out§ *P4:*sinfulness, ³⁷⁶| MS:Declare §crossed out and replaced above by two words§ And clinch the *CP2:*Impart the §crossed out and restored§ ³⁷⁷| MS:again:— §dash crossed out§ ³⁷⁸| MS:§line added between present ll. 377 and 379§ Then, §illegible word§ after *CP2:*Then, §altered to§ And then, with stipulations §original reading restored§ ³⁷⁹| MS:And §crossed out§ hand her §crossed out and restored§ the first §inserted below§ *P2:*Hand

<sup>380</sup> Enough, no question,—of her salary:
Admonish for the future, and so end.—
All which good purposes, decided on
Sufficiently, were waiting full effect
When presently the culprit should appear.

<sup>385</sup> Somehow appearance was delayed too long;
Chatting and chirping sunk inconsciously
To silence, nay, uneasiness, at length
Alarm, till—anything for certitude!—
A peeper was commissioned to explore,
<sup>390</sup> At keyhole, what the laggard's task might be—
What caused so palpable a disrespect!

Back came the tiptoe cousin from his quest.
"Monsieur Léonce was busy," he believed,
"Contemplating—those love-letters, perhaps,
<sup>395</sup> He always carried, as if precious stones,
About with him. He read, one after one,
Some sort of letters. But his back was turned.
The empty coffer open at his side,
He leant on elbow by the mantelpiece

---

<sup>380</sup>| MS:Enough, §added in margin§ No §altered to§ no <> salary: so end.— §last two words
and punctuation transposed to l. 381§        <sup>381</sup>|  MS:Admonish for the future, and §last five
words transposed to l. 380§ so end.—        <sup>382-83</sup>|  MS:§lines added between present ll. 380 and
384§        <sup>383</sup>|  MS:At intervals, §last two words crossed out and replaced above by§
Sufficiently, would have their §last three words crossed out and replaced above by two words§
only waited §last two words crossed out§ awaited §inserted above§ full    CP2:Sufficiently, but
waited full §crossed out and restored§    CP3:Sufficiently, were waiting full
<sup>384</sup>|  MS:Presently when the    P2:When presently the        <sup>385</sup>|  MS:appearance got delayed
<> long,    P2:appearance was delayed <> long;        <sup>386</sup>|  MS:And chat and    P2:Chatting and
<sup>387-88</sup>|  MS:silence. Nay, uneasiness, at length / Alarm, till,— §last six words and punctuation
inserted above§ Anything for certitude!—    P2:silence, nay <> / <> till—anything
<sup>390</sup>|  MS:be    CP2:be—        <sup>391</sup>|  MS:That §crossed out and replaced above by§ To caused
§altered to§ cause so <> disrespect.    P2:Which caused so    CP2:What caused <> disrespect!
<sup>392</sup>|  MS:the §over *one*§        <sup>393</sup>|  MS:"Monsieur Antoine was <> believed    P2:believed,
CP4:"Monsieur Alphonse §crossed out and replaced above by§ Léonce was
<sup>394</sup>|  MS:"Contemplating—perhaps, those love-letters, §transposed to§ "Contemplating—those
love-letters, perhaps,        <sup>396</sup>|  MS:him: he read one    P2:him. He read, one
<sup>397</sup>|  MS:§added in margin§ letters; but <> turned;    P2:letters. But    CP4:turned.
<sup>398</sup>|  MS:§line added between present ll. 396 and 399§ (The <> side,) §parentheses crossed
out§        <sup>399</sup>|  MS:He §added in margin§ Leaning §altered to§ Leant    P2:leant

251

⁴⁰⁰    Before the hearth-fire; big and blazing too."

    "Better he shovelled them all in at once,
    And burned the rubbish!" was a cousin's quip,
    Warming his own hands at the fire the while.
    I told you, snow had fallen outside, I think.

⁴⁰⁵    When suddenly a cry, a host of cries,
    Screams, hubbub and confusion thrilled the room.
    All by a common impulse rushed thence, reached
    The late death-chamber, tricked with trappings still,
    Skulls, cross-bones, and such moral broidery.
⁴¹⁰    Madame Muhlhausen might have played the witch,
    Dropped down the chimney and appalled Léonce
    By some proposal "Parting touch of hand!"
    If she but touched his foolish hand, you know!!

    Something had happened quite contrariwise.
⁴¹⁵    Monsieur Léonce Miranda, one by one,
    Had read the letters and the love they held,

---

⁴⁰⁰|  MS:the hearth- §inserted above§ fire; thats §crossed out§ big <> blazing there §crossed out and replaced above by§ too."     ⁴⁰²|  MS:the nonsense §crossed out and replaced above by§ rubbish" was   *P2:*rubbish!" was     ⁴⁰³|  MS:while:   *P2:*while.     ⁴⁰⁴|  MS:§line added between present ll. 403 and 405§ you, outside, snow <> fallen, I   *P2:*you, snow <> fallen outside, I     ⁴⁰⁵|  MS:cries—   *CP2:*cries,     ⁴⁰⁶|  MS:Screams—hubbub <> confusion— thrilled §over illegible word§ the room:   *P2:*room.   *CP2:*Screams, hubbub <> confusion thrilled     ⁴⁰⁷|  MS:by one §crossed out and replaced above by§ an §crossed out and replaced above by two words§ a common <> thence—reached as soon §last two words crossed out§   *P2:*thence, reached     ⁴⁰⁹|  MS:Skulls §altered to§ Skull §original reading restored§     ⁴¹⁰|  MS:Quoth cousin "Can §last three words crossed out§ Madame §inserted above§ Debacker might have §last two words inserted above§ play §altered to§ played   *CP4:*Madame Muhlhausen might     ⁴¹¹|  MS:Drop §altered to§ Dropped <> and appal §altered to§ appalled our friend §last two words crossed out§ Antoine,   *P2:*chimney, and <> Antoine   *CP2:*chimney and   *CP4:*appalled Alphonse §crossed out and replaced above by§ Léonce     ⁴¹²|  MS:By some §last two words added in margin§ Proposing §altered to§ Proposed a return to Tailleville?" §last four words crossed out and replaced above by five words§ —"One parting touch of hand! §¶; crossed out§ No, §crossed out§   *P2:*By some proposal—"Parting <> hand!"   *CP2:*proposal "Parting     ⁴¹³|  MS:§line added between present ll. 412 and 414§ touched that foolish <> know!—   *P2:*touched his foolish   *CP2:*know!   *P3:*know!!     ⁴¹⁴|  MS:This §crossed out§ thing §altered to§ Something     ⁴¹⁵|  MS:Monsieur Antoine Mellerio, one   *CP4:*Monsieur Alphonse §crossed out and replaced above by§ Léonce Miranda, one     ⁴¹⁶|  MS: love they held, §last two words over *there in*§

And, that task finished, had required his soul
To answer frankly what the prospect seemed
Of his own love's departure—pledged to part!
420 Then, answer being unmistakable,
He had replaced the letters quietly,
Shut coffer, and so, grasping either side
By its convenient handle, plunged the whole—
Letters and coffer and both hands to boot,
425 Into the burning grate and held them there.
"Burn, burn and purify my past!" said he,
Calmly, as if he felt no pain at all.

In vain they pulled him from the torture-place:
The strong man, with the soul of tenfold strength,
430 Broke from their clutch: and there again smiled he,
The miserable hands re-bathed in fire—
Constant to that ejaculation "Burn,
Burn, purify!" And when, combining force,
They fairly dragged the victim out of reach
435 Of further harm, he had no hands to hurt—
Two horrible remains of right and left,
"Whereof the bones, phalanges formerly,
Carbonized, were still crackling with the flame,"

---

417| MS:And that   *1889a:*And, that   418|   MS:prospect was §crossed out§ seemed
419|   MS:love's departing §altered to§ departure <> part,   *P2:*part.   *CP2:*departure— §altered
to§ departing— §crossed out; original reading restored§ pledged to part!   420|   MS:Then,
§added in margin§ And, §crossed out§ answer   422|   MS:and then §crossed out and
replaced above by§ so   424|   MS:hands besi §crossed out§ to   425|   MS:burning fire
§crossed out and replaced above by§ grate <> them fast §crossed out§ there.
426|   MS:"Burn, burn, and <> Past" cried he,   *P2:*Burn, burn and <> Past, cried   *CP2:*"Burn
<> my past!" said he,   427|   MS:all.   *P2:*all.   428|   MS:torture-place,   *P2:*torture-place:
429|   MS:with the soul of tenfold §last three words inserted above§   430|   MS:their arms
§crossed out and replaced above by§ clutch—and <> again was §crossed out and replaced
above by§ smiled   *P2:*clutch: and   432|   MS:ejaculation, "Burn,   *CP2:*ejaculation "Burn,
433|   MS:And §crossed out and replaced above by§ Burn, purify!" and §altered to§ And
435|   MS:harm, thus much was done—remained §last five words crossed out and replaced above
by six words§ he had no hand to hurt—   436|   MS:of left and right, §last three words
transposed to§ right and left,   437|   MS:the things §crossed out and replaced above by§ bones
438|   MS:Carbonised, still were §last two words transposed to§ were still   *1889a:*Carbonized

253

Said Beaumont. And he fought them all the while:
440　"Why am I hindered when I would be pure?
Why leave the sacrifice still incomplete?
She holds me, I must have more hands to burn!"
They were the stronger, though, and bound him fast.

Beaumont was in attendance presently.
445　"What did I tell you? Preachment to the deaf!
I wish he had been deafer when they preached,
Those priests! But wait till next Republic comes!"

As for Léonce, a single sentiment
Possessed his soul and occupied his tongue—
450　Absolute satisfaction at the deed.
Never he varied, 'tis observable,
Nor in the stage of agonies (which proved
Absent without leave,—science seemed to think)
Nor yet in those three months' febricity
455　Which followed,—never did he vary tale—
Remaining happy beyond utterance.
"Ineffable beatitude"—I quote
The words, I cannot give the smile—"such bliss
Abolished pain! Pain might or might not be:
460　He felt in heaven, where flesh desists to fret.
Purified now and henceforth, all the past

---

439| MS:Said Pasquier. and §altered to§ And <> while　P2:while:　CP4:Said Fouquier §crossed out and replaced above by§ Beaumont. And　440| MS:hindered, when　P2:hindered when　442| MS:§line added between present ll. 441 and 444§　443| MS:§line added in margin§　444| MS:Pasquier was　CP4:Fou §crossed out§ Beaumont was
445| MS:§line added between present ll. 444 and 448§　446-47| MS:§lines added in margin§
448| MS:for Antoine, a　CP4:for Alphonse §crossed out and replaced above by§ Léonce, a
452| MS:the earlier §crossed out and replaced above by two words§ stage of agonies that §crossed out and replaced above by§ which proved §over perhaps *were*§　P2:agonies (which
453| MS:think—　P2:think)　455| MS:That §crossed out and replaced above by§ Which
456| MS:"How he was §last three words crossed out and replaced above by§ Remaining <>
utterance—　P2:utterance.　458| MS:smile: "pure bliss　P2:smile—"pure
CP2:smile—"such bliss　459| MS:Abolished pain! pain <> be,　P2:be:　CP2:pain! Pain
<> be: §altered to *be,* and restored§　460| MS:He was §crossed out and replaced above by§
felt <> desists to §crossed out and replaced above by§ from fret.　P2:desists to fret.
461| MS:all that §crossed out and replaced above by§ the Past　CP2:past

Reduced to ashes with the flesh defiled!
Why all those anxious faces round his bed?
What was to pity in their patient, pray,
465  When doctor came and went, and Cousins watched?
—Kindness, but in pure waste!" he said and smiled.
And if a trouble would at times disturb
The ambrosial mood, it came from other source
Than the corporeal transitory pang.
470  "If sacrifice be incomplete!" cried he—
"If ashes have not sunk reduced to dust,
To nullity! If atoms coalesce
Till something grow, grow, get to be a shape
I hate, I hoped to burn away from me!
475  She is my body, she and I are one,
Yet, all the same, there, there at bed-foot stands
The woman wound about my flesh and blood,
There, the arms open, the more wonderful,
The whiter for the burning . . . Vanish thou!
480  Avaunt, fiend's self found in the form I wore!"

"Whereat," said Beaumont, "since his hands were gone,

---

462-64|  MS:defiled, §comma crossed out and restored§ / What moved such §last two words crossed out and replaced above by two words§ was to pity for §crossed out and replaced above by§ in <> patient, there? §crossed out§ pray?  CP2:defiled, / Why all those anxious faces round his bed? / What <> pray,  CP4:defiled! / /     465|  MS:§line added between present ll. 464 and 466§ The doctor <> went, the cousins watched:  P2:went: the Cousins  CP2:When doctors came <> went and Cousins watched?  P3:When doctor came <> went, and     466|  MS:Kindness, but thrown away!" §crossed out and replaced above by two words§ to waste §last two words crossed out; original reading restored§ he  P2:—Kindness  CP2:but in pure waste!" he     466-67|  MS:§¶§  P3:§no ¶§     469|  MS:corporeal transitory §inserted above§ pang. howe'er acute. §last two words crossed out§     471|  MS:not been §crossed out and replaced above by§ sunk <> dust §punctuation illegibly crossed out§  P2:dust,     472|  MS:And §added in margin§ Nothingness §crossed out and replaced above by§ nullity, if <> coälesce,— §comma crossed out§  P2:To nullity  CP2:To nullity! If <> coälesce  C1873:coalesce     473|  MS:And §crossed out§ Till §added in margin§ something <> get into §altered to§ to be §inserted above§     475|  MS:§line added between present ll. 474 and 476§     477-78|  MS:§line added between present ll. 476 and 479§     478|  MS:There the  P2:There, the     479|  MS:burning . . Vanish  1889a:burning . . . Vanish     480|  MS:Avaunt, thou §crossed out§ fiend's self found §inserted above§ in <> I knew §crossed out and replaced above by§ wore!"     481|  MS:said Pasquier, "since  CP4:said Fouquier §crossed out and replaced above by§ Beaumont, "since

255

The patient in a frenzy kicked and kicked
To keep off some imagined visitant.
So will it prove as long as priests may preach
485 Spiritual terrors!" groaned the evidence
Of Beaumont that his patient was stark mad—
Produced in time and place: of which anon.
"Mad, or why thus insensible to pain?
Body and soul are one thing, with two names
490 For more or less elaborated stuff."

Such is the new *Religio Medici.*
Though antiquated faith held otherwise,
Explained that body is not soul, but just
Soul's servant: that, if soul be satisfied,
495 Possess already joy or pain enough,
It uses to ignore, as master may,
What increase, joy or pain, its servant brings—
Superfluous contribution: soul, once served,
Has nought to do with body's service more.
500 Each, speculated on exclusively,
As if its office were the only one,

---

482| MS:frenzy used his §last two words crossed out and replaced above by two words§ kicked with feet  *CP2:*kicked and kicked  *1889a:*kicked and licked §emended to§ and kicked §see Editorial Notes§  483| MS:imagined enemy §crossed out§ visitant.

484| MS:§line added between present ll. 483 and 485§  485| MS:terrors,—" such §crossed out and replaced below by§ groaned  *P2:*terrors—" groaned  *CP2:*terrors!" groaned

486| MS:Of Pasquier that <> mad:  *CP2:*mad—  *CP4:*Of Fou §crossed out§ Beaumont that

488-90| MS:§line added between present ll. 487 and 491§  488| MS:Mad, or why thus §over illegible word§  *CP2:*"Mad  489| MS:soul—are <> names §punctuation illegibly crossed out§  *P2:*soul are  490| MS:stuff.  *P2:*stuff.  *CP2:*stuff."  490-91| MS:§¶§ *1889a:*§no ¶; emended to restore ¶; see Editorial Notes§  492| MS:The §crossed out and replaced above by§ But §crossed out§ Though §added in margin§

493| MS:but soul's §crossed out§ just  494| MS:servant: and when §last two words crossed out and replaced above by two words§ that, §over illegible word§ if <> be §over perhaps *is*§ *P2:*that if  *CP2:*that, if  495| MS:With its §last two words crossed out and replaced above by two words§ Possess already own §crossed out and replaced above by§ sufficient joy enough §crossed out§ or  497| MS:The minor §last two words crossed out and replaced above by two words§ What increase, joys §altered to§ joy or pains §altered to§ pain, its servant feels. §crossed out and replaced above by§ brings—  498| MS:§line added between present ll. 497 and 499§  499| MS:Served, what §last two words crossed out§ has §altered to§ Has soul §crossed out and replaced below by§ nought <> body's §inserted below§ service more? . §question mark crossed out§  501| MS:§line added in margin§

Body or soul, either shows service paid
In joy and pain, that's blind and objectless—
A servant's toiling for no master's good—
505    Or else shows good received and put to use,
As if within soul's self grew joy and pain,
Nor needed body for a ministrant.
I note these old unscientific ways:
Poor Beaumont cannot: for the Commune ruled
510    Next year, and ere they shot his priests, shot him.

Monsieur Léonce Miranda raved himself
To rest; lay three long months in bliss or bale,
Inactive, anyhow: more need that heirs,
His natural protectors, should assume
515    The management, bestir their cousinship,
And carry out that purpose of reform
Such tragic work now made imperative.
A deputation, with austerity,
Nay, sternness, bore her sentence to the fiend

---

502| MS:Shows, as the case may be, or §last seven words crossed out and replaced above by six words§ Body or soul, exhibits §crossed out§ shows—either, service paid §over illegible word§ *CP2:*shows either     *C1873:*soul, either shows service     503| MS:joy and §over illegible word§ pains §altered to§ pain, both §crossed out and replaced above by§ that's <> objectless, *CP2:*objectless—     504| MS:§line added between present ll. 503 and 505§ A servant toiling *C1873:*A servant's toiling     505| MS:Or pain and joy §last three words crossed out and replaced below by three words§ else shows good received, and   *P2:*received and 507| MS:As if no servants §last four words crossed out and replaced below by five words§ Nor needed body for a ministered §altered to§ ministrant, at all. §last two words crossed out§ 509-10| MS:§line added in margin§ Poor Pasquier could not: §last two words crossed out and replaced above by§ passive §crossed out and replaced above by§ silent §crossed out and replaced below by§ cannot, for <> ruled, / <> and when §crossed out and replaced below by§ ere <> his §over illegible word§   *P2:*Poor Pasquier cannot: for <> /     *CP4:*Poor Fou §crossed out§ Beaumont cannot <> /     *1873:*ruled /     511| MS:§line added between present ll. 508 and 512§ Monsieur Antoine Mellerio raved     *CP4:*Monsieur Alphonse §crossed out and replaced above by§ Léonce Miranda raved     512| MS:So he §last two words crossed out and replaced below by two words§ To rest; <> long month's §illegible word§ in   *P2:*months 514| MS:natural protection, §over perhaps *protectors*§ should   *CP2:*natural protectors, should 516-17| MS:§lines added between present ll. 515 and 518§     517| MS:Such tragedy §altered to§ tragic work §inserted above§     518| MS:austerity   *P2:*austerity, 519| MS:Redoubled, §crossed out and replaced above by two words§ Nay, sternness, <> the dame §crossed out§ fiend §crossed out and restored§

520   Aforesaid,—she at watch for turn of wheel
  And fortune's favour, Street—you know the name.
  A certain roughness seemed appropriate: "You—
  Steiner, Muhlhausen, whatsoe'er your name,
  Cause whole and sole of this catastrophe!"—
525   And so forth, introduced the embassage.

  "Monsieur Léonce Miranda was divorced
  Once and for ever from his—ugly word.
  Himself had gone for good to Portugal:
  They came empowered to act and stipulate.
530   Hold! no discussion! Terms were settled now:
  So much of present and prospective pay,
  But also—good engagement in plain terms
  She never seek renewal of the past! "

  This little harmless tale produced effect.
535   Madame Muhlhausen owned her sentence just,
  Its execution gentle. "Stern their phrase,
  These kinsfolk with a right she recognized—

---

520|   MS:You know of, still §last four words crossed out and replaced above by two words§ Aforesaid,—she   521|   MS:By §crossed out§ And §added in margin§ fortune's <> Street you   *CP2:*favour, Street—you   521-22|   MS:§¶§   *P2:*§no ¶§   522|   MS:roughness was §crossed out and replaced above by§ seemed   523|   MS:§line added between present ll. 522 and 524§ Trayer, Betrayer, whatsoe'er   *P2:*whatsoe'er   *CP4:*Steiner, Muhlhausen, whatsoe'er   524|   MS:catastrophe—"   *P2:*catastrophe!"—   525-26|   MS:§no ¶§   *P2:*§¶§   526|   MS:Monsieur Antoine Mellerio was   *CP2:*"Monsieur   *CP4:*Monsieur Alphonse §crossed out and replaced above by§ Léonce Miranda was   527|   MS:and forever with his partner late. §last two words crossed out and replaced above by two words§ —ugly word.   *P2:*for ever *P3:*word   *CP3:*word.   528|   MS:Himself had §over *was*§ gone <> to Italy: *CP4:*to Portugal:   529|   MS:They were §crossed out and replaced above by§ came   530|   MS:§line added between present ll. 529 and 531§ Pray, no <> were past dispute— §last two words and dash crossed out§ settled now—   *P2:*now:   *CP2:*Hold! no   532|   MS:also—such §crossed out and replaced above by§ good   533|   MS:Never to seek <> Past.   *P2:*the Past!   *CP2:*She never seek <> the tie §crossed out§ past!"   534|   MS:harmless lie had due §last two words crossed out and replaced above by§ produced   *CP2:*harmless lie §crossed out and replaced above by§ tale §crossed out§ produced *P3:*harmless lie produced   *CP4:*harmless tale produced   535|   MS:Madame Debacker owned the §crossed out and replaced above by§ her   *CP4:*Madame Muhlhausen owned   536|   MS:The §crossed out and replaced above by§ Its <> gentle—stern <> phrase— *P2:*gentle: stern   *CP2:*gentle. Stern <> phrase,   537|   MS:§line added between present ll. 536 and 538§ recognized,—   *P2:*recognised—   *1889a:*recognized—

But kind its import probably, which now
Her agitation, her bewilderment
540  Rendered too hard to understand, perhaps.
Let them accord the natural delay,
And she would ponder and decide. Meantime,
So far was she from wish to follow friend
Who fled her, that she would not budge from place—
545  Now that her friend was fled to Portugal,—
Never! *She* leave this Coliseum Street?
No, not a footstep!" she assured them.

                           So—

They saw they might have left that tale untold
When, after some weeks more were gone to waste,
550  Recovery seemed incontestable,
And the poor mutilated figure, once
The gay and glancing fortunate young spark,
Miranda, humble and obedient took
The doctor's counsel, issued sad and slow
555  From precincts of the sick-room, tottered down,
And out, and into carriage for fresh air,
And so drove straight to Coliseum Street,
And tottered upstairs, knocked, and in a trice

---

538| MS:kind the §crossed out and replaced below by§ its    539| MS:bewilderment,
*1889a:*bewilderment    540| MS:Rendered it §crossed out and replaced above by§ too
542| MS:meantime, §altered to§ decide. Meantime,    544| MS:she should §altered to§
would remove from place,  *P2:*place—  *CP2:*would not budge from    545-46| MS:§lines
added in margin§    545| MS:Seeing that §crossed out and replaced above by§ her < > to
Italy,  *P2:*to Italy,—  *CP2:*Now that her < > Italy,— §punctuation crossed out and restored§
*CP4:*to Portugal,—    546| MS:Never: she leave this Miromesnil Street?  *P2:*Never! *She*
*CP2:*Never! *She* leave §last three words altered to§ Nor ever leave §crossed out, restoring original
reading§ this < > Street,  *P3:*this < > Street?  *CP4:*this Coliseum Street?
547| MS:footstep,— §altered to§ footstep!—she  *CP2:*footstep!" she    548| MS:§line added
between present ll. 547 and 549§ saw that lie §last two words crossed out§ they should §crossed
out and replaced above by§ might < > that lie alone,  *CP4:*that tale untold    549| MS:more
had §crossed out and replaced below by§ were    551| MS:figure, first §crossed out§ once
552| MS:young spark, §over *man*§    553| MS:Mellerio, humbly §altered to§ humble in
§crossed out and replaced above by§ and obedience §altered to§ obedient  *CP4:*Miranda,
humble    557| MS:to Street Miromesnil, §last two words transposed to§ Miromesnil Street,
*P2:*to Coliseum Street,    558| MS:up stairs, knocked and  *P2:*upstairs, knocked, and

Was clasped in the embrace of whom you know—
560  With much asseveration, I omit,
Of constancy henceforth till life should end.
When all this happened,—"What reward," cried she,
"For judging her Miranda by herself!
For never having entertained a thought
565  Of breaking promise, leaving home forsooth,
To follow who was fled to Portugal!
As if she thought they spoke a word of truth!
She knew what love was, knew that he loved her;
The Cousinry knew nothing of the kind."

570  I will not scandalize you and recount
How matters made the morning pass away.
Not one reproach, not one acknowledgment,
One explanation: all was understood!
Matters at end, the home-uneasiness
575  Cousins were feeling at this jaunt prolonged
Was ended also by the entry of—
Not simply him whose exit had been made
By mild command of doctor "Out with you!
I warrant we receive another man!"

---

559| MS:Was locked §crossed out and replaced above by§ clasped        560| MS:Asse §crossed
out and replaced above by§ With        561| MS:end,—  P2:end.        562| MS:reward" was
here §last two words crossed out and replaced above by two words§ cried she  P2:reward," cried
she,        563| MS:§line added between present ll. 562 and 564§ her Mellerio by  P2:her
Mellerio herself  CP4:her Miranda by        565| MS:home at all, §last two words crossed out§
forsooth, §crossed out, restoring original reading§  1873:home forsooth,        566| MS:And
§crossed out and replaced above by§ To following §altered to§ follow who was §inserted above§
<> to Italy!  CP4:to Portugal!        567| MS:§line added between present ll. 566 and 568§
568| MS:was, and §crossed out and replaced above by§ knew <> her.  P2:her;
569| MS:cousinry  P2:The Cousinry        571| MS:What §crossed out and replaced above by§
How <> away—  CP2:away.        574| MS:Morning §crossed out and replaced above by§
Matters <> end—much home-uneasiness  CP2:end—the home-uneasiness  CP3:end, the
575| MS:At taste of air prolonged, six hours for one,  CP2:Cousins were feeling at this jaunt
prolonged  P3:prolonged,  CP3:prolonged        576| MS:ended also §inserted above§ by <>
of a pair— §last two words crossed out and replaced above by dash§  CP2:§following trial
revisions not adopted§ Was §crossed out and replaced above by two words§ So strangely,
§crossed out§ ended also §crossed out and replaced above by§ too by the §crossed out§
577| MS:him who made his exit moved  CP2:him whose exit had been made
579| MS:§line added between present ll. 579 and 581§

580    But—would that I could say, the married pair!
       And, quite another man assuredly,
       Monsieur Léonce Miranda took on him
       Forthwith to bid the trio, priest and nuns,
       Constant in their attendance all this while,
585    Take his thanks and their own departure too;
       Politely but emphatically. Next,
       The Cousins were dismissed: "No protest, pray!
       Whatever I engaged to do is done,
       Or shall be—I but follow your advice:
590    Love I abjure: the lady, you behold,
       Is changed as I myself; her sex is changed:
       This is my Brother—He will tend me now,
       Be all my world henceforth as brother should.
       Gentlemen, of a kinship I revere,
595    Your interest in trade is laudable;
       I purpose to indulge it: manage mine,
       My goldsmith-business in the Place Vendôme,
       Wholly—through purchase at the price adjudged
       By experts I shall have assistance from.
600    If, in conformity with sage advice,
       I leave a busy world of interests
       I own myself unfit for—yours the care
       That any world of other aims, wherein
       I hope to dwell, be easy of access
605    Through ministration of the moneys due,

580-81| MS:§¶§  P2:§no ¶§      582| MS:Monsieur Antoine Mellorio took  P2: Monsieur
Antoine Mellerio took  CP4:Monsieur Alphonse §crossed out and replaced above by§ Léonce
Miranda took     585| MS:To §crossed out§ take §altered to§ Take < > their prompt
§inserted above§ departure  P2:their own departure     586| MS:emphatically, next, §last
two words altered to§ emphatically. Next,     587| MS:cousins  P2:The Cousins
589| MS:advice;  P2:advice:    591| MS:myself: her  CP2:myself; her
592| MS:my Brother: he < > now  P2:now,  CP2:my Brother—he
593| MS:all the §crossed out and replaced above by§ my world      594| MS:kinship I esteem,
§crossed out§ revere,     597| MS:§line added in margin§ My Goldsmith-business < > the
Street of Peace,  P2:goldsmith-business  CP4:the Place Vendôme,     598| MS:Wholly—by
§crossed out and replaced above by§ through     599| MS:shall claim assistance of §altered
to§ from.  P2:shall have assistance     601| MS:leave that §crossed out and replaced above
by§ the busy  P2:leave a busy     602| MS:for,—yours  P2:for—yours
603| MS:To §crossed out§ that §altered to§ That new §crossed out and replaced above by§ any

As we determine, with all proper speed,
Since I leave Paris to repair my health.
Say farewell to our Cousins, Brother mine!"

And, all submissiveness, as brother might,
610　The lady curtseyed gracefully, and dropt
More than mere curtsey, a concluding phrase
So silver-soft, yet penetrative too,
That none of it escaped the favoured ears:
"Had I but credited one syllable,
615　I should to-day be lying stretched on straw,
The produce of your miserable *rente!*
Whereas, I hold him—do you comprehend?"
Cousin regarded cousin, turned up eye,
And took departure, as our Tuscans laugh,
620　Each with his added palm-breadth of long nose,—
Curtailed but imperceptibly, next week,
When transfer was accomplished, and the trade
In Paris did indeed become their own,
But bought by them and sold by him on terms
625　'Twixt man and man,—might serve 'twixt wolf and wolf,
Substitute "bit and clawed" for "signed and sealed"—
Our ordinary business-terms, in short.
Another week, and Clairvaux broke in bloom

---

608| MS:to my §crossed out and replaced above by§ our cousins, brother §altered to§ Brother  *P2*:our Cousins　　　610| MS:cutseyed  *P2*:curtseyed　　　611| MS:Beside the §last two words crossed out and replaced above by two words§ More than < > concluding word §crossed out§ phrase　　　612| MS:silver-soft, yet §over *so*§ penetrative still, §crossed out§ too  *P2*:too,
613| MS:ears,—  *P2*:ears:　　　614| MS:"Had I obeyed your §altered to§ you bidding, gentlemen, §last four words crossed out and replaced above by§ believed you §last two words crossed out§ but eyes §crossed out§ credited one §last two words inserted above§ syllable,
616| MS:miserable "rente"!  *P2*:miserable rente!  *CP2*:*rente!*  *P3*:*reute!*  *CP3*:*rente!*  *P4*:*retue!*
*CP4*:*rente!*　　　617| MS:But now §last two words crossed out and replaced above by§ Whereas
617-18| MS:§¶§  *CP4*:§no ¶§　　　619| MS:our Tuscans phrase, say, §crossed out and replaced above by§ laugh;　　　623-24| MS:§one line expanded into two§ In Peace-Street did indeed become their own, §last five words and comma inserted above§ But §inserted below§ bought by them §last two words inserted below§ and sould §altered to§ sold by him §last two words inserted below§ on those fair §last two words crossed out§ terms  *CP4*:In Paris did
625| MS:and man, which met §crossed out and replaced above by§ serve 'twixt  *CP2*:and wolf;
*CP4*:and man,—might serve < > and wolf,　　　626-28| MS:Read only §last two words crossed out and replaced above by§ Substitute < > sealed"! / §¶§ Another < > and Tailleville broke in

At end of April, to receive again
630    Monsieur Léonce Miranda, gentleman,
Ex-jeweller and goldsmith: never more,—
According to the purpose he professed,—
To quit this paradise, his property,
This Clara, his companion: so it proved.

635    The Cousins, each with elongated nose,
Discussed their bargain, reconciled them soon
To hard necessity, disbursed the cash,
And hastened to subjoin, wherever type
Proclaimed "Miranda" to the public, "Called
640    Now Firm-Miranda." There, a colony,
They flourish underneath the name that still
Maintains the old repute, I understand.
They built their Clairvaux, dream-Château, in Spain,
Perhaps—but Place Vendôme is waking worth:
645    Oh, they lost little!—only, man and man
Hardly conclude transactions of the kind

---

buds §crossed out§ bloom   *P2:*sealed"! / §no ¶§ Another   *CP4:*sealed"— / Our ordinary business-terms, in short. / Another <> and Clairvaux broke   <sup>630</sup>|   MS:Monsieur Antoine Mellerio, gentleman,   *CP4:*Monsieur Alphonse §crossed out and replaced above by§ Léonce Miranda, gentleman,   <sup>631</sup>|   MS:goldsmith, never   *CP2:*goldsmith: never
<sup>632</sup>|   MS:§line added between present ll. 631 and 633§ to the §over *his*§   <sup>634</sup>|   MS:And §crossed out and replaced above by§ This Anna, his <> so §over *as*§   *CP4:*This Clara, his
<sup>635</sup>|   MS:cousins each with §last two words inserted above§ unelongated §altered to§ elongated each §crossed out§ nose,   *P2:*The Cousins   <sup>636</sup>|   MS:reconciled themselves §altered to§ them   <sup>639</sup>|   MS:Proclaimed "Mellerio" to <> public late §crossed out§ "Called *CP4:*Proclaimed "Miranda" to   <sup>640</sup>|   MS:"Called §crossed out and replaced above by§ Now, Meller Brothers": there the colony,   *P2:*Now Meller, Brothers". There, a colony, *CP4:*Now Firm-Miranda". There   *1889a:*Now Firm-Miranda." There
<sup>641</sup>|   MS:§line added in margin§ Still flourish underneath that warrant, still   *P2:*They flourish underneath the name that still   <sup>642</sup>|   MS:Keep up §last two words crossed out and replaced above by§ Maintain the old §inserted above§ reputation §altered to§ repute rightly gained— §last two words and dash crossed out§ I understand.   *P2:*repute, I
<sup>643</sup>|   MS:§line added between present ll. 642 and 644§ They found their Tailleville, their Chateau in Spain:   *P2:*They built their <> Château   *CP4:*built their Clairvaux, dream-Château, in Spain,   <sup>644</sup>|   MS:"A branch §altered to§ Branch is at Madrid," goes on the gold. *CP4:*§line crossed out and replaced by§ Perhaps—but Place Vendôme is waking worth:
<sup>645</sup>|   MS:they §word crossed out§ lost nothing!—only, wolf and wolf   *CP4:*lost nothing!— §crossed out; correction missing§ only, man and man   *1873:*lost little!—only
<sup>646</sup>|   MS:Do not §last two words crossed out and replaced above by§ Hardly

As cousin should with cousin,—cousins think.
For the rest, all was honourably done,
So, ere buds break to blossom, let us breathe!
<sup>650</sup> Never suppose there was one particle
Of recrudescence—wound, half-healed before,
Set freshly running—sin, repressed as such,
New loosened as necessity of life!
In all this revocation and resolve,
<sup>655</sup> Far be sin's self-indulgence from your thought!
The man had simply made discovery,
By process I respect if not admire,
That what was, was:—that turf, his feet had touched,
Felt solid just as much as yonder towers
<sup>660</sup> He saw with eyes, but did not stand upon,
And could not, if he would, reach in a leap.
People had told him flowery turf was false
To footstep, tired the traveller soon, beside:
That was untrue. They told him "One fair stride
<sup>665</sup> Plants on safe platform and secures man rest."
That was untrue. Some varied the advice:
"Neither was solid, towers no more than turf."
Double assertion, therefore twice as false.
"I like these amateurs"—our friend had laughed,

---

<sup>647-49</sup>| MS:As Christian §crossed out and replaced above by§ cousin hop §crossed out§ should §over *would*§ with Christian §crossed out and replaced above by§ cousin,—Christians §crossed out and replaced above by§ cousins hoped §altered to§ hope §crossed out, restoring original reading§ think. / §¶§ Now, ere    *CP4:*think. / For the rest, all was honorably done, / §no¶§ So, ere    *1889a:*honourably          <sup>651</sup>| MS:wound half-healed before    *CP2:*wound, half-healed before,          <sup>652</sup>| MS:Freshly set §last two words altered and transposed to§ Set freshly <> sin, acknowledged so §last two words crossed out and replaced above by three words§ repressed as such,          <sup>653</sup>| MS:Loosened as now §over perhaps *new*§ necessity <> life— *P2:*Now loosened as necesity <> life!    *CP4:*New loosened          <sup>654</sup>| MS:revocation of §crossed out and replaced above by§ and          <sup>657</sup>| MS:With §crossed out and replaced above by§ By          <sup>658</sup>| MS:what was—was    *P2:*what was, was          <sup>659</sup>| MS:yonder wall *C1873:*yonder towers          <sup>660</sup>| MS:eyes but    *CP2:*eyes, but          <sup>661</sup>| MS:not—if <> would—reach    *P2:*not, if <> would reach    *CP2:*would, reach          <sup>664</sup>| MS:him—one *CP2:*him "One          <sup>665</sup>| MS:Plants sole §crossed out§ on safe §inserted above§ platform, and secures you §crossed out and replaced above by§ man rest:    *P2:*platform and    *CP2:*rest:" *P3:*rest."          <sup>666</sup>| MS:advice—    *CP4:*advice:          <sup>667</sup>| MS:Neither <> turf:    *CP2:*"Neither <> turf."    *P3:*turf"    *1889a:*turf."          <sup>669</sup>| MS:amateurs"—the man §last two words crossed out and replaced above by two words§ our friend <> laughed    *1889a:*laughed,

670 Could he turn what he felt to what he thought,
And, that again, to what he put in words:
"I like their pretty trial, proof of paste
Or precious stone, by delicate approach
Of eye askance, fine feel of finger-tip,
675 Or touch of tongue inquisitive for cold.
I tried my jewels in a crucible:
Fierce fire has felt them, licked them, left them sound.
Don't tell me that my earthly love is sham,
My heavenly fear a clever counterfeit!
680 Each may oppose each, yet be true alike!"

To build up, independent of the towers,
A durable pavilion o'er the turf,
Had issued in disaster. "What remained
Except, by tunnel, or else gallery,
685 To keep communication 'twixt the two,
Unite the opposites, both near and far,
And never try complete abandonment
Of one or other?" so he thought, not said.

And to such engineering feat, I say,
690 Monsieur Léonce Miranda saw the means

---

672| MS:like their §over perhaps *this*§ pretty trial what is §last two words crossed out and
replaced above by two words§ —proof of *P2:*trial, proof          673| MS:What §crossed out and
replaced above by§ Or          674| MS:eye aslant §crossed out and replaced above by§ askance
675| MS:Or touch §inserted above§ inquisition §altered to§ inquisitive of the §crossed out§
tongue §line transposed to§ Or touch of tongue inquisitive          676| MS:my gem §altered to§
jewels < > crucible, *P2:*crucible:          677| MS:§line added between present ll. 676 and 678§
680| MS:§line added in margin§          683| MS:That §crossed out and replaced above by§ Had
< > disaster: what resource §crossed out§ remained *P2:*disaster: "What *CP2:*disaster. "What
684| MS:tunnel or, else *P2:*tunnel, or else          685| MS:§line added between present ll. 684
and 686§ To §word crossed out§ keep          686| MS:the two erections §last two words crossed
out and replaced above by two words§ opposites, both < > far— *P2:*far,          687-88| MS:§one
line expanded into two§ try complete §inserted above§ abandonment / of §altered to§ Of one?
§question mark crossed out§ or other?" §next five words and punctuation inserted below§ —So
he thought—not said. *P2:*other?"—so < > thought, not *CP2:*other?" so          688-89| MS:§¶§
*1889a:*§no ¶; emended to restore ¶; see Editorial Notes§          689| MS:Now §crossed out and
replaced above by§ And, to *P2:*And to          690| MS:Monsieur Antoine Mellerio saw
*CP4:*Monsieur Alphonse §crossed out and replaced above by§ Léonce Miranda saw

Precisely in this revocation prompt
Of just those benefits of worldly wealth
Conferred upon his Cousinry—all but!

This Clairvaux—you would know, were you at top
695    Of yonder crowning grace, its Belvedere—
Is situate in one angle-niche of three
At equidistance from Saint-Rambert—there
Behind you, and The Ravissante, beside—
There: steeple, steeple, and this Clairvaux-top,
700    (A sort of steeple) constitute a trine,
With not a tenement to break each side,
Two miles or so in length, if eye can judge.

Now, this is native land of miracle.
O why, why, why, from all recorded time,
705    Was miracle not wrought once, only once,
To help whoever wanted help indeed?
If on the day when Spring's green girlishness
Grew nubile and she trembled into May,
And our Miranda climbed to clasp the Spring

---

692| MS:Of all §crossed out and replaced above by§ just     693| MS:cousinry—almost!
*P2:*his Cousinry—all but!     694| MS:This Tailleville—you would see, §crossed out and
replaced above by§ know, were   *CP4:*This Clairvaux—you     695| MS:its Belvedere,—§final
*e* crossed out and restored§   *P2:*its Belvedere—     696| MS:Is situate §crossed out and
restored§ in the §crossed out and replaced above by§ one angle-niche §inserted above§ out
§crossed out§ of three,   *1889a:*three     697| MS:from Saint Aubin—there—
*CP2:*from Saint-Aubin—there   *CP4:*from Saint-Rambert—there     698| MS:and The
Delivrande, beside—   *P2:*and The Délivrande   *CP2:*the   *CP4:*and The Ravissante, beside—
699| MS:There—steeple <> this Tainville-top,   *P2:*There: steeple <> Tailleville-top,
*CP4:*this Clairvaux-top,     700| MS:§line added between present ll. 699 and 701§ A <>
steeple constitute   *P2:*steeple, constitute   *CP2:* (A <> steeple) constitute
701| MS:break the §crossed out and replaced above by§ each sides §altered to§ side,
702| MS:so of §crossed out and replaced above by§ in     702-3| MS:§¶§   *1889a:*§no ¶;
emended to restore ¶; see Editorial Notes§     703| MS:Now, §inserted above§ This is the
§crossed out§ native   *P2:*this     705| MS:wrought, for §crossed out and replaced above by§
but only once,   *1889a:*wrought once, only once     707| MS:when April's §crossed out and
replaced above by two words§ Spring's green     708| MS:nubile and §crossed out and
replaced above by§ as §crossed out, restoring original reading§
709| MS:And §crossed out and replaced above by§ As §crossed out, restoring original reading§
poor Mellerio climbed to taste the   *CP3:*to clasp the   *CP4:*poor Miranda climbed

710    A-tiptoe o'er the sea, those wafts of warmth,
    Those cloudlets scudding under the bare blue,
    And all that new sun, that fresh hope about
    His airy place of observation,—friend,
    Feel with me that if just then, just for once,
715    Some angel,—such as the authentic pen
    Yonder records a daily visitant
    Of ploughman Claude, rheumatic in the joints,
    And spinster Jeanne, with megrim troubled sore,—
    If such an angel, with nought else to do,
720    Had taken station on the pinnacle
    And simply said "Léonce, look straight before!
    Neither to right hand nor to left: for why?
    Being a stupid soul, you want a guide
    To turn the goodness in you to account
725    And make stupidity submit itself.
    Go to Saint-Rambert! Straightway get such guide!
    There stands a man of men. You, jeweller,
    Must needs have heard how once the biggest block
    Of diamond now in Europe lay exposed
730    Mid specimens of stone and earth and ore,

---

710| MS:A-tiptoe on the sea, in §crossed out and replaced above by§ those   *P2:*A-tiptoe o'er the
711| MS:And §crossed out and replaced above by§ Those   712| MS:all that new §inserted
above§ sun, and §crossed out§ that fresh §inserted above, over illegible word§
714| MS:me, that §inserted above§ if < > then, and §crossed out§ just   715| MS:Some
§over illegible word§   716| MS:records the §crossed out and replaced above by§ for
§crossed out and replaced above by§ a   718| MS:And §crossed out and restored§ spinster
Jean §altered to§ Jeanne < > troubled much,—   *1889a:*troubled sore,—   719| MS:§line
added between present ll. 718 and 720§ angel with   *P2:*angel, with   720| MS:Had §over
illegible word§   721| MS:simply said §crossed out and replaced above by§ smiled §crossed
out, restoring original reading§ "Antoine, look   *P2:*said, "Antoine   *CP2:*said "Antoine
*CP4:*said Alphonse §crossed out and replaced above by§ Léonce, look   723| MS:a stupid
§crossed out and replaced above by§ foolish §crossed out, restoring original reading§ man
§crossed out and replaced above by§ soul, you need §crossed out and replaced above by§ want a
guide §punctuation illegibly crossed out§   726| MS:to Saint Aubin! and you §last two words
crossed out and replaced above by two words§ yonder §crossed out§ Straightway §punctuation
illegibly crossed out§ get your §crossed out and replaced above by§ such   *CP2:*to Saint-Aubin
*CP4:*to Saint-Rambert! Straightway   727| MS:There is §crossed out and replaced above by§
stands   728| MS:Must needs §last two words inserted above§ Have §altered to§ have heard
the story §last two words crossed out§ how once §inserted above§   730| MS:of §illegible
word crossed out and replaced above by two words§ metal, costly §last two words crossed out,
restoring illegible original§ earth < > ore   *P2:*of stone and earth < > ore,

On huckster's stall,—Navona names the Square,
And Rome the city for the incident,—
Labelled 'quartz-crystal, price one halfpenny.'
Haste and secure that ha'p'worth, on your life!
735    That man will read you rightly head to foot,
Mark the brown face of you, the bushy beard,
The breadth 'twixt shoulderblades, and through each black
Castilian orbit, see into your soul.
Talk to him for five minutes— nonsense, sense,
740    No matter what—describe your horse, your hound,—
Give your opinion of the policy
Of Monsieur Rouher,—will he succour Rome?
Your estimate of what may outcome be
From Œumenical Assemblage there!
745    After which samples of intelligence,
Rapidly run through those events you call
Your past life, tell what once you tried to do,
What you intend on doing this next May!
There he stands, reads an English newspaper,
750    Stock-still, and now, again upon the move,
Paces the beach to taste the Spring, like you,
Since both are human beings in God's eye.

---

731| MS:huckster's board §crossed out§ stall, St. Agnes §crossed out and replaced above by§ —
Navona     732|    MS:Rome was the    *P2:*And Rome the     733|    MS:Labelled "This
§crossed out and replaced above by§ Quartz-crystal <> halfpenny."    *P2:*Labelled 'quartz-crystal
<> halfpenny.'     736|    MS:Read §crossed out and replaced above by§ Mark
737|    MS:And §crossed out and replaced above by§ The breadth twixt    *1873:*breadth 'twixr
738|    MS:Italian eye will §last two words crossed out and replaced above by§ orbit, see
*CP4:*Castilian orbit     741|    MS:the ministry §crossed out and replaced above by§ policy
742|    MS:§line added between present ll. 741 and 743§     743|    MS:of what may §last two
words inserted above§ outcome probable §crossed out§ prove    *P2:*outcome be
744|    MS:there:—    *CP2:*there!     745|    MS:§line added in margin§ After the §last two words
crossed out§ After     746|    MS:through what §crossed out and replaced above by§ those
747|    MS:tell him §crossed out§ what once §inserted above§
748|    MS:doing, and then stop, §last three words crossed out and replaced above by§ presently.
§crossed out§ this <> May.    *P2:*next May!     749|    MS:stands, with §crossed out and
replaced above by§ reads     750|    MS:Reading, §crossed out and replaced
above by§ Stock-still, and, now again    *P2:*and now, again     751|    MS:Pacing §altered to§
Paces the Plage §crossed out and replaced above by§ beach    *P2:*Passes the
*CP3:*Paces the     752|    MS:§line added between present ll. 751 and 753§

He will have understood you, I engage.
Endeavour, for your part, to understand
755   He knows more, and loves better, than the world
That never heard his name, and never may.
He will have recognized, ere breath be spent
And speech at end, how much that's good in man,
And generous, and self-devoting, makes
760   Monsieur Léonce Miranda worth his help;
While sounding to the bottom ignorance
Historical and philosophical
And moral and religious, all one couch
Of crassitude, a portent of its kind.
765   Then, just as he would pityingly teach
Your body to repair maltreatment, give
Advice that you should make those stumps to stir
With artificial hands of caoutchouc,
So would he soon supply your crippled soul
770   With crutches, from his own intelligence,
Able to help you onward in the path
Of rectitude whereto your face is set,
And counsel justice—to yourself, the first,
To your associate, very like a wife
775   Or something better,—to the world at large,

---

753|   MS:understood what man §last two words crossed out§ you, are §crossed out§ I engage;
*P2:*engage.          755|   MS:more and <> better than      *P2:*more, and <> better, than
756|   MS:name,— §dash crossed out§ and never will §crossed out§ may.          757|   MS:recognized
how much of good, §last four words crossed out§ ere     *P2:*recognised    *1889a:*recognized
758|   MS:§line added between present ll. 757 and 759§          760|   MS:Monsieur Antoine
Mellerio worthy §altered to§ worth his §inserted above§ help:     *CP2:*help:—     *P3:*help;
*CP4:*Monsieur Alphonse §crossed out and replaced above by§ Léonce Miranda worth
761|   MS:And §crossed out and replaced above by§ While sounded §altered to§ sounding <>
bottom, ignorance     *CP2:*bottom ignorance          762|   MS:Historical, and philosophical,
*P2:*Historical and philosophical          763|   MS:moral, and     *P2:*moral and          765|   MS:And
§crossed out and replaced above by§ Then, §over illegible word§ just <> pityingly teach §over
illegible word§          766|   MS:maltreatment, try §crossed out§ give          767|   MS:§line added
between present ll. 766 and 768§          768|   MS:Two §crossed out§ With §added in margin§
769|   MS:would would §crossed out and replaced above by two words§ he soon supplement
§altered to§ supply          772|   MS:rectitude, whereto     *CP2:*rectitude whereto
773|   MS:With §crossed out§ And so do §last two words crossed out and replaced above by§
counsel          774-75|   MS:§one line revised into two lines§ associate, very like a wife §last four words
inserted above§ / Or something better, §last three words inserted below§ to     *P2:* / <> better,—to

269

Friends, strangers, horses, hounds and Cousinry—
All which amount of justice will include
Justice to God. Go and consult his voice!"
Since angel would not say this simple truth,
780    What hinders that my heart relieve itself,
Milsand, who makest warm my wintry world,
And wise my heaven, if there we consort too?
Monsieur Léonce Miranda turned, alas,
Or was turned, by no angel, t'other way,
785    And got him guidance of The Ravissante.

Now, into the originals of faith,
Yours, mine, Miranda's, no inquiry here!
Of faith, as apprehended by mankind,
The causes, were they caught and catalogued,
790    Would too distract, too desperately foil
Inquirer. How may analyst reduce
Quantities to exact their opposites,
Value to zero, then bring zero back
To value of supreme preponderance?
795    How substitute thing meant for thing expressed?
Detect the wire-thread through that fluffy silk

---

776| MS:cousinry— *P2:*and Cousinry— 778| MS:consult the §crossed out and replaced above by§ His voice!" §over *man*§ 779| MS:Since §over illegible word§ 780| MS:May not §last two words crossed out and replaced above by three words§ What hinders that < > itself, for once, §last two words crossed out§ 781| MS:O friend, my one friend that §last four words crossed out and replaced above by§ who < > warm the §crossed out and replaced above by two words§ my wintry world,? §question mark crossed out§ *C1873:*Milsand, who 782| MS:§line added between present ll. 781 and 783§ 782-83| MS:§¶§ *P2:*§no ¶§ 783| MS:Monsieur Antoine Mellorio turned *P2:* Monsieur Antoine Mellerio turned *CP4:*Léonce Miranda turned 784| MS:way. *P2:*way, 785| MS:of The Delivrande. *P2:*of The Délivrande. *CP4:*of The Ravissante. 787| MS:mine, Mellerio's, no enquiry *CP4:*mine, Miranda's, no *1889a:*inquiry 788| MS:For §crossed out and replaced above by§ Of 789| MS:causes, could I catch and §last two words inserted above§ §last four words altered to§ were they caught and 791| MS:Inquirer: how could §crossed out and replaced above by§ might §crossed out and replaced by§ may *P2:*Enquirer: how *CP2:*Enquirer. How *1889a:*Inquirer. How 792| MS:to the quantities §last two words crossed out and replaced above by§ exact 793| MS:Values §altered to§ Value to zero, then bring §last two words inserted above illegible word§ zero back again §crossed out§ 794| MS:preponderance? *1889a:*preponderance §emended to§ preponderance? §see Editorial Notes§ 796| MS:wire-thread, in §comma and *in* crossed out and replaced above by§ through

Men call their rope, their real compulsive power?
Suppose effected such anatomy,
And demonstration made of what belief
800    Has moved believer—were the consequence
Reward at all? would each man straight deduce,
From proved reality of cause, effect
Conformable—believe and unbelieve
According to your True thus disengaged
805    From all his heap of False called reason first?

No: hand once used to hold a soft thick twist,
Cannot now grope its way by wire alone:
Childhood may catch the knack, scarce Youth, not Age!
That's the reply rewards you. Just as well
810    Remonstrate to yon peasant in the blouse
That, had he justified the true intent
Of Nature who composed him thus and thus,
Weakly or strongly, here he would not stand

---

797|   MS:That's §crossed out and replaced above by§ Men called §altered to§ call <> rope, their
true §crossed out and replaced above by§ real     799|   MS:demonstration made of §last two
words inserted above§ what has moved §last two words crossed out§ belief     800|   MS:Made
to §last two words crossed out and replaced above by two words§ Has moved believer—would
§crossed out and replaced above by§ were     801|   MS:all? "You should §punctuation and last
two words crossed out and replaced above by§ Each §crossed out§ would each man straight §last
four words inserted above§ deduce, you see, §last two words crossed out and replaced above by§
perhaps §crossed out§     802|   MS:From this §crossed out and replaced above by§ proved
803|   MS:Conformable?—believe and disbelieve §altered to§ unbelieve   *P2:*Conformable?
believe   *C1873:*Conformable—believe     804|   MS:to this §crossed out and replaced above
by§ the §crossed out and replaced by§ your true I §crossed out and replaced above by§ thus
*CP2:*your True     805|   MS:all the §crossed out and replaced by§ his <> of falseness
§altered to§ false called reason here §crossed out and replaced above by§ first?" §quotation
mark crossed out§   *CP2:*of False     806|   MS:"My §quotation mark and last word crossed out
and replaced above by§ No: hand his §crossed out and replaced above by§ once <> thick rope,
*P2:*thick twist,     807|   MS:And §crossed out§ cannot §altered to§ Cannot now §inserted
above§ <> alone:   *1889a:*alone §punctuation decayed; emended to§ alone: §see Editorial
Notes§     808|   MS:Childhood perhaps §inserted above and crossed out§ might §crossed
out§ may §inserted above§ catch <> knack,—scarce Youth, §last two words inserted above
illegible words§ Age!" §quotation mark crossed out§   *P2:*knack, scarce     809|   MS:rewards
you. §crossed out and replaced by§ me §crossed out, restoring original reading§ Just
810|   MS:Demonstrate §altered to§ Remonstrate     811|   MS:That had   *CP2:*That, had
812|   MS:nature   *CP3:*Of Nature     813|   MS:Weakly and §crossed out and replaced above
by§ or <> here he §inserted above§ would not stand §over illegible word§

Struggling with uncongenial earth and sky,
815  But elsewhere tread the surface of the globe,
Since one meridian suits the faulty lungs,
Another bids the sluggish liver work.
"Here I was born, for better or for worse:
I did not choose a climate for myself;
820  Admit, my life were healthy, led elsewhere,"
(He answers) "how am I to migrate, pray?"

Therefore the course to take is—spare your pains,
And trouble uselessly with discontent
Nor soul nor body, by parading proof
825  That neither haply had known ailment, placed
Precisely where the circumstance forbade
Their lot should fall to either of the pair.
But try and, what you find wrong, remedy,
Accepting the conditions: never ask
830  "How came you to be born here with those lungs,
That liver?" But bid asthma smoke a pipe,
Stramonium, just as if no Tropics were,
And ply with calomel the sluggish duct,

---

<sup>814</sup>| MS:§line added between present ll. 813 and 815§ with uncongeniality §altered to§
uncongenial        <sup>815</sup>| MS:elsewhere on §crossed out and replaced below by§ tread
<sup>817</sup>| MS:Another makes §crossed out and replaced above by§ bids        <sup>818-20</sup>| MS:§three lines
added between present ll. 817 and 821§        <sup>818</sup>| MS:worse  *P2:*worse:        <sup>819</sup>| MS:—I
*P2:*I        <sup>820</sup>| MS:Suppose, by right, §last three words crossed out§ Admit, my healthy life
were §last three words transposed to§ life were healthy, led        <sup>821</sup>| MS:answers) "How am
§over illegible word§  *P2:*answers) "how        <sup>823</sup>| MS:And §over illegible word§ trouble
§inserted above§ uselessly attempt §crossed out§ with        <sup>824</sup>| MS:Or §altered to§ Nor soul
or §altered to§ nor        <sup>825</sup>| MS:That §added in margin§ Neither §altered to§ neither might
never §last two words crossed out and replaced above by§ haply have §altered to§ had
<sup>826-27</sup>| MS:§one line revised into two lines§ Precisely §added in margin§ where the §inserted
above§ circumstance forbade / their §altered to§ Their place to §last two words crossed out and
replaced above by two words§ lot should        <sup>828</sup>| MS:remedy  *P2:*remedy,
<sup>829-30</sup>| MS:§lines added between present ll. 828 and 831§        <sup>831</sup>| MS:As best you can. §last
four words and period crossed out and replaced below by three words§ That liver?" But < > pipe
*P2:*pipe,        <sup>832</sup>| MS:Stramonium just < > if no §inserted above§ Tropics were
not §crossed out§ §illegible word§  *P2:*Stramonium, just < > were,
<sup>833</sup>| MS:Slow biliary duct §last three words crossed out§ and ply §last two words inserted above§
with calomel, the < > duct  *P2:*And < > calomel the < > duct,

Nor taunt "The born Norwegian breeds no bile!"
835    And as with body, so proceed with soul:
Nor less discerningly, where faith you found,
However foolish and fantastic, grudge
To play the doctor and amend mistake,
Because a wisdom were conceivable
840    Whence faith had sprung robust above disease.
Far beyond human help, that source of things!
Since, in the first stage, so to speak,—first stare
Of apprehension at the invisible,—
Begins divergency of mind from mind,
845    Superior from inferior: leave this first!
Little you change there! What comes afterward—
From apprehended thing, each inference
With practicality concerning life,
This you may test and try, confirm the right
850    Or contravene the wrong which reasons there.

---

<sup>834</sup>|   MS:And never mind what of §inserted above and crossed out§ Iceland might have done—
§line crossed out and replaced above by new line§ Nor stop §crossed out and replaced above
by§ blame because cold Norway breeds no bile.    *CP2:*Nor taunt "a born Norwegian breeds no
bile!"    *P3:*taunt "The born Norwegian!"    *CP3:*born Norwegian breeds no bile!"
<sup>835-36</sup>|   MS:§one line revised into two lines§ And as with body §last four words inserted above§ So
deal §crossed out and replaced below by§ proceed <> soul: / nor §altered to§ Nor less
discerning §altered to§ discerningly grudge, §crossed out§ where faith is §crossed out and
replaced above by§ you          <sup>837</sup>|   MS:§line added between present ll. 836 and 838§
<sup>838</sup>|   MS:To somewhat §inserted below§ doctor malady §crossed out§ and    *P2:*To play the
doctor          <sup>839</sup>|   MS:Because of healthiness §last two words crossed out and replaced above by
three words§ a wisdom were          <sup>840</sup>|   MS:Whence it were to wander such a way. §last eight
words crossed out and replaced above by six words§ faith had sprung robust above disease.
<sup>841</sup>|   MS:Circumstance has ordained things otherwise: §line crossed out and replaced above by
new line§ Providence §crossed out§ Far above §crossed out and replaced above by§ beyond <>
things!          <sup>842</sup>|   MS:That §crossed out and replaced above by§ Since, in
<sup>843</sup>|   MS:at things seen by soul §last four words crossed out and replaced above by two words§
the invisible,    *1889a:*invisible,—          <sup>844</sup>|   MS:Immeasurably differs §last two words crossed
out and replaced above by three words§ Begins divergency §over illegible word§ of mind §over
*man*§ from mind, §over *man*§          <sup>845</sup>|   MS:Superior and §crossed out and replaced above by§
from inferior: from §crossed out and replaced above by§ leave <> first;    *P2:*first!
<sup>846</sup>|   MS:Let that alone: but §last four words crossed out and replaced above by four words§
Little to change there! what §altered to§ What    *CP2:*Little you change
<sup>848</sup>|   MS:With §illegible word inserted above§ practicality in common §last two words crossed out
and replaced above by§ concerning          <sup>849</sup>|   MS:That §altered to§ This
<sup>850</sup>|   MS:wrong which §over illegible word§ reasons you §crossed out§ there    *P2:*there.

The offspring of the sickly faith must prove
Sickly act also: stop a monster-birth!
When water's in the cup and not the cloud,
Then is the proper time for chemic test:
855   Belief permits your skill to operate
When, drop by drop condensed from misty heaven,
'Tis wrung out, lies a bowlful in the fleece.
How dew by spoonfuls came, let Gideon say:
What purpose water serves, your word or two
860   May teach him, should he fancy it lights fire.

Concerning, then, our vaporous Ravissante—
How fable first precipitated faith—
Silence you get upon such point from me.
But when I see come posting to the pair
865   At Clairvaux, for the cure of soul-disease,
This Father of the Mission, Parish-priest,
This Mother of the Convent, Nun I know—
They practise in that second stage of things;
They boast no fresh distillery of faith;
870   'Tis dogma in the bottle, bright and old,

---

851-52| MS:§lines added between present ll. 850 and 853§    853| MS:The §crossed out and replaced below by§ When    854| MS:Then is §last two words added in margin§ The §altered to§ the <> time is §crossed out§ for the §crossed out§ chemic
855| MS:Belief is brought to operate on earth §last six words crossed out and replaced above by five words§ permits your skill to operate    857| MS:bowl-full <> fleece; *P2:*fleece. *1889a:*bowlful    858| MS:dew came down, §comma crossed out§ to earth, §last two words inserted above§ let Gideon task his wit, §last three words crossed out and replaced above by word illegibly crossed out§ say: *1889a:*dew by spoonfuls came, let
859| MS:serves, a §crossed out and replaced above by§ your    861| MS:Accordingly, the vaporous Delivrande— *P2:*vaporous Délivrande— *CP2:*Concerning, then our vaporous *CP4:*vaporous Ravissante—    862| MS:How it precipitated faith at first, *CP2:*How fable first precipitated faith—    863| MS:points *CP2:*point
864| MS:But now §crossed out and replaced above by three words§ when I see came §altered to§ come <> the sickly §crossed out§ pair    865| MS:At Tailleville, for *CP4:*at Clairvaux, for
866| MS:the Mission, parish-priest, *P2:*the Mission, Parish-priest,
867| MS:That Mother <> Convent, nun I know, *P2:*the Convent, Nun I know—
*CP3:*This Mother    868| MS:§line added between present ll. 867 and 869§ practice <> things— *P2:*practise <> things: *CP2:*things;    869| MS:They make §crossed out and replaced below by§ boast <> faith, *CP2:*faith;    870| MS:But dogma *P2:*'Tis dogma

They bring; and I pretend to pharmacy.
They undertake the cure with all my heart!
He trusts them, and they surely trust themselves.
I ask no better. Never mind the cause,
875   *Fons et origo* of the malady:
Apply the drug with courage! Here's our case.
Monsieur Léonce Miranda asks of God,
—May a man, living in illicit tie,
Continue, by connivance of the Church,
880   No matter what amends he please to make
Short of forthwith relinquishing the sin?
Physicians, what do you propose for cure?

Father and Mother of the Ravissante,
Read your own records, and you find prescribed
885   As follows, when a couple out of sorts
Rather than gravely suffering, sought your skill
And thereby got their health again. Perpend!
Two and a half good centuries ago,
  Luc de la Maison Rouge, a nobleman

---

871| MS:and I §crossed out and replaced above by§ we pretend   *CP2:*and I pretend
872| MS:You §crossed out and replaced above by§ They <> the cure §over *case*§ then? Excellent!   *CP2:*cure with all my heart!   873| MS:trusts you §crossed out and replaced above by§ them, and you §crossed out and replaced above by§ they <> trust yourselves §altered to§ themselves   *P2:*themselves.   874| MS:We §over I§ ask <> better: never mind the rest §crossed out and replaced above by§ cause,   *CP2:*I ask <> better. Never
875| MS:§line added in margin§ malady,   *1889a:*malady:   876| MS:Apply your rules §last two words crossed out and replaced above by two words§ the drug <> Here's the §crossed out and replaced below by§ our   877| MS:Monsieur Antoine Mellerio asks §over illegible word§ of you §crossed out§ God,   *CP4:*Monsieur Alphonse §crossed out and replaced above by§ Léonce Miranda asks   878| MS:—Can §crossed out and replaced above by§ May <> in adultery, §last word and comma crossed out§ illicit ties, §over illegible word§   *CP2:*tie,
879| MS:Continue, thus §crossed out§ by licence §crossed out and replaced above by§ connivence   *P2:*connivance   880| MS:make,   *CP2:*make   881| MS:of forthwith §inserted above§ relinquishing the §over *that*§ sin at once?" §last two words crossed out§ *1873:*sin?   882| MS:what would §crossed out and replaced below by§ do <> cure! *CP2:*cure?   883| MS:the Delivrande,   *P2:*the Délivrande,   *CP4:*the Ravissante,
884| MS:records, where I §last two words crossed out and replaced above by§ and you
887-88| MS:§¶§   *P4:*§no ¶§   889| MS:Quoth §crossed out and replaced above by§ Jean de la Becquetière, nobleman of Vire,   *CP2:*la Becquetière, a nobleman of Vire, §last two words and comma transposed to l. 890§   *CP4:*Luc de la Maison Rouge, a

890　Of Claise, (the river gives this country name)
　　　And, just as noblewoman, Maude his wife,
　　　Having been married many happy years
　　　Spent in God's honour and man's service too,
　　　Conceived, while yet in flower of youth and hope,
895　The project of departing each from each
　　　Forever, and dissolving marriage-bonds
　　　That both might enter a religious life.
　　　Needing, before they came to such resolve,
　　　Divine illumination,—course was clear,—
900　They visited your church in pilgrimage,
　　　On Christmas morn: communicating straight,
　　　They heard three Masses proper for the day,
　　　"It is incredible with what effect"—
　　　Quoth the Cistercian monk I copy from—
905　And, next day, came, again communicants,
　　　Again heard Masses manifold, but now
　　　With added thanks to Christ for special grace
　　　And consolation granted: in the night,
　　　Had been divorce from marriage, manifest
910　By signs and tokens. So, they made great gifts,
　　　Left money for more Masses, and returned
　　　Homeward rejoicing—he, to take the rules,

---

890| MS:§line added in margin§ (The river §inserted above§ so-called gives　*CP2:*Of Vire, §last
two words and comma transposed from l. 889§ (The river gives　*CP3:*Of Vire, (the
*CP4:*Of Claise, (the　　　891| MS:noblewoman, Anne his　*CP4:*noblewoman, Maude his
892| MS:years,　*1873:*years　　　893| MS:Spent to §crossed out and replaced above by§ in < >
honor < > service both §crossed out and replaced above by§ too,　*1889a:*honour
895| MS:The purpose §crossed out and replaced above by§ project　　　896| MS:For ever and
*P2:*Forever, and　　　900| MS:visited this place §last two words crossed out and replaced above
by two words§ your church < > pilgrimage, §altered to§ pilgrimage.　*CP2:*visited your §altered
to§ our §erased, restoring original reading§　*1889a:*pilgrimage,　　　901| MS:On Christmas
Day §crossed out and replaced above by§ Morn, communicated §altered to§ communicating
*P2:*morn　*C1873:*morn: communicating　　　902| MS:They §added in margin§ Heard
§altered to§ heard the §crossed out§ three < > the time §crossed out and replaced above by§
day—　*P2:*day,　　　904| MS:the Cistertian Monk, I　*P2:*monk I　*CP2:*the Cistercian
905| MS:And, next §crossed out and restored§　　　906| MS:heard masses §altered to§ Masses
< > now—　*P2:*now　　　908| MS:the shape §crossed out§ night,
909| MS:Of that §last two words crossed out and replaced above by two words§ Had been
910| MS:tokens. So they　*P2:*tokens. So, they　　　912| MS:rejoicing—He　*P2:*he

As Brother Dionysius, Capucin;
She, to become first postulant, then nun
915 According to the rules of Benedict,
Sister Scolastica: so ended they,
And so do I—not end nor yet commence
One note or comment. What was done was done.
Now, Father of the Mission, here's your case!
920 And, Mother of the Convent, here's its cure!
If separation was permissible,
And that decree of Christ "What God hath joined
Let no man put asunder" nullified
Because a couple, blameless in the world,
925 Had the conceit that, still more blamelessly,
Out of the world, by breach of marriage-vow,
Their life was like to pass,—you oracles
Of God,—since holy Paul says such you are,—
Hesitate, not one moment, to pronounce
930 When questioned by the pair now needing help
"Each from the other go, you guilty ones,
Preliminary to your least approach
Nearer the Power that thus could strain a point
In favour of a pair of innocents
935 Who thought their wedded hands not clean enough
To touch and leave unsullied their souls' snow!

---

913| MS:As Brother Eliezer, Capuchin, *CP4:*As Brother Dionysius, Capucin, *1889a:*As Brother Dionysius, Capucin; 916| MS:Sister Elizabeth: so *CP4:*Sister Scolastica: so 917| MS:end, but not begin §comma and last three words crossed out and replaced above by three words§ nor yet commence 918| MS:One word of §last two words crossed out and replaced above by two words§ note or 918-19| MS:§¶§ *P4:*§no ¶§ 922| MS:And §crossed out and replaced above by§ If that *P2:*And that 923| MS:asunder" over-ruled §crossed out§ nullified 925| MS:that still *CP2:*that, still 926| MS:marriage vow, *P2:*marriage-vow, 927| MS:pass,—your §crossed out and replaced above by§ the oracles *P2:*pass,—you oracles 928| MS:§line added between present ll. 927 and 929§ are— *P2:*are,— 929| MS:Hesitates §altered to§ Hesitate, not §altered to§ no one, §crossed out and replaced above by§ a §crossed out, restoring original reading§ moment to *P2:*Hesitate, not one moment, to 930| MS:§line added between present ll. 929 and 931§ help— *CP2:*help 931| MS:Separ §crossed out and replaced above by§ "Each 934| MS:favor of this §crossed out and replaced above by§ a *P2:*favour 935| MS:Who feared §crossed out and replaced above by§ thought 936| MS:To touch and §last two words inserted above§ leave their souls' §inserted above§ snow unsullied §last four words transposed to§ leave unsullied their souls' snow! by their touch? §last three words and question mark crossed out§

Are not your hands found filthy by the world,
Mere human law and custom? Not a step
Nearer till hands be washed and purified!"

940   What they did say is immaterial, since
Certainly it was nothing of the kind.
There was no washing hands of him (alack,
You take me?—in the figurative sense!),
But, somehow, gloves were drawn o'er dirt and all,
945   And practice with the Church procured thereby.
Seeing that,—all remonstrance proved in vain,
Persuasives tried and terrors put to use,
I nowise question,—still the guilty pair
Only embraced the closelier, obstinate,—
950   Father and Mother went from Clairvaux back
Their weary way, with heaviness of heart,
I grant you, but each palm well crossed with coin,
And nothing like a smutch perceptible.
Monsieur Léonce Miranda might compound
955   For sin?—no, surely! but by gifts—prepare

---

937|  MS:Are not §last two words inserted above§ Your hands are §crossed out§ found   *P2:*your
938|  MS:By §crossed out and replaced above by§ Mere        939|  MS:till yours §crossed out and
replaced above by§ hands be §crossed out and replaced above by§ stand §crossed out, restoring
original reading§        941|  MS:kind;   *P2:*kind.        942|  MS:washing hands of §last two
words crossed out and restored§ him or her §last two words crossed out§ (Alack,   *P2:*him
(alack,       943|  MS:§line added between present ll. 942 and 944§ me? In < > sense!)
*P2:*me?—in   *1889a:*sense!),       946|  MS:remonstrance proving §altered to§ proved in
§inserted above§        947|  MS:Persuasion §altered to§ Persuasives tried, and threatening
§crossed out and replaced above by§ terrors put to use §last three words crossed out and
replaced above by two words§ brought to §last two words crossed out, restoring original
reading§ bear, §crossed out§   *P2:*tried and < > put in use,   *CP3:*put to use,   *P4:*put use,
*CP4:*put to use,        948|  MS:question,—when the   *C1873:*question,—still the
949|  MS:Only §added in margin§ Clasped hands §last two words crossed out and replaced above
by§ embraced the harder §crossed out and replaced above by§ closelier, and were §last two
words crossed out§ obstinate,—        950|  MS:and Mother went §crossed out and replaced
above by§ took §crossed out, restoring original reading§ from Tailleville back   *CP4:*from
Clairvaux back       951|  MS:To the Delivrande §last three words crossed out and replaced
above by four words§ Their way §crossed out§ weary way, with §over illegible word§ heaviness of
§last two words altered to§ heavy §crossed out, restoring original reading§ hearts, §altered to§
heart,       952|  MS:palm well §over *was*§        954|  MS:Monsieur Antoine Mellerio might
*CP4:*Monsieur Alphonse §crossed out and replaced above by§ Léonce Miranda might
955|  MS:but by §inserted above§ gifts—prepared §altered to§ prepare

His soul the better for contrition, say!
Gift followed upon gift, at all events.
Good counsel was rejected, on one part:
Hard money, on the other—may we hope
960 Was unreflectingly consigned to purse?

Two years did this experiment engage
Monsieur Léonce Miranda: how, by gifts
To God and to God's poor, a man might stay
In sin and yet stave off sin's punishment.
965 No salve could be conceived more nicely mixed
For this man's nature: generosity,—
Susceptibility to human ills,
Corporeal, mental,—self-devotedness
Made up Miranda—whether strong or weak
970 Elsewhere, may be inquired another time.
In mercy he was strong, at all events.
Enough! he could not see a beast in pain,
Much less a man, without the will to aid;
And where the will was, oft the means were too,
975 Since that good bargain with the Cousinry.

The news flew fast about the countryside
That, with the kind man, it was ask and have;
And ask and have they did. To instance you:—
A mob of beggars at The Ravissante
980 Clung to his skirts one day, and cried "We thirst!"

---

959| MS:other—might §crossed out and replaced above by§ may        962| MS:Monsieur
Antoine Mellerio, how by   *P2:*Monsieur Antoine Mellerio: how   *CP4:*Monsieur Alphonse
§crossed out and replaced above by§ Léonce Miranda: how   *1889a:*how, by
965| MS:Nothing §crossed out and replaced above by two words§ No ba §crossed out§ salve <>
more suitable §crossed out and replaced above by§ nicely        967| MS:ills,— §dash crossed
out§        969| MS:up Mellerio—whether   *CP4:*up Miranda—whether        970| MS:enquired
<> time:   *CP2:*time.   *1889a:*inquired        971| MS:§line added between present ll. 970 and
972§ mercy, he   *1889a:*mercy he        972| MS:Enough; he   *CP2:*Enough! he
973| MS:to help §crossed out and replaced above by§ aid;        974| MS:was, there the
*1889a:*was, oft the        975| MS:cousinry.   *P2:*the Cousinry.        977| MS:with these §altered
to§ the kind man §last two words inserted above§ folks there, §last two words crossed out§ it <>
have,   *P2:*have;        979| MS:the Delivrande   *P2:*at The Délivrande   *CP4:*at The Ravissante

Forthwith he bade a cask of wine be broached
To satisfy all comers, till, dead-drunk
So satisfied, they strewed the holy place.
For this was grown religious and a rite:
985    Such slips of judgment, gifts irregular,
Showed but as spillings of the golden grist
On either side the hopper, through blind zeal;
Steadily the main stream went pouring on
From mill to mouth of sack—held wide and close
990    By Father of the Mission, Parish-priest,
And Mother of the Convent, Nun I know,
With such effect that, in the sequel, proof
Was tendered to the Court at Vire, last month,
That in these same two years, expenditure
995    At quiet Clairvaux rose to the amount
Of Forty Thousand English Pounds: whereof
A trifle went, no inappropriate close
Of bounty, to supply the Virgin's crown
With that stupendous jewel from New-York,
1000    Now blazing as befits the Star of Sea.

Such signs of grace, outward and visible,
I rather give you, for your sake and mine,
Than put in evidence the inward strife,
Spiritual effort to compound for fault
1005    By payment of devotion—thank the phrase!
That payment was as punctual, do not doubt,
As its far easier fellow. Yesterday

---

983|   MS:And satisfied < > place—   *P2:*place.   *1889a:*So satisfied     984|   MS:For all §crossed out§ this was now §crossed out and replaced above by§ grown religion §altered to§ religious     986|   MS:Were §crossed out and replaced above by§ Showed < > the bounteous §crossed out and replaced above by§ golden     987|   MS:through hot §crossed out and replaced above by§ blind     993|   MS:at Caen, I find, §last two words and comma crossed out§ last   *CP4:*at Vire, last     995|   MS:At quiet §inserted above§ Tailleville rose   *CP4:*quiet Clairvaux rose     996|   MS:Of forty thousand §last two words altered to§ Forty Thousand < > pounds—whereof   *P2:*pounds: whereof     999|   MS:that enormous jewel from Madrid   *P2:*from Madrid,   *CP3:*that stupendous jewel   *CP4:*from New-York,     1001|   MS:This §crossed out and replaced above by§ Such sign §altered to§ signs     1003|   MS:inward thing §crossed out and replaced above by§ strife,

I trudged the distance from The Ravissante
To Clairvaux, with my two feet: but our friend,
1010 The more to edify the country-folk,
Was wont to make that journey on both knees.
"Maliciously perverted incident!"
Snarled the retort, when this was told at Vire:
"The man paid mere devotion as he passed,
1015 Knelt decently at just each wayside shrine!"
Alas, my lawyer, I trudged yesterday—
On my two feet, and with both eyes wide ope,—
The distance, and could find no shrine at all!
According to his lights, I praise the man.
1020 Enough! incessant was devotion, say—
With her, you know of, praying at his side.
Still, there be relaxations of the tense;
Or life indemnifies itself for strain,
Or finds its very strain grow feebleness.
1025 Monsieur Léonce Miranda's days were passed
Much as of old, in simple work and play.
His first endeavour, on recovery
From that sad ineffectual sacrifice,
Had been to set about repairing loss:
1030 Never admitting, loss was to repair.

---

1008| MS:from that §crossed out and replaced above by§ the Delivrande    P2:the Délivrande
CP4:from The Ravissante        1009| MS:To Tailleville with <> friend    P2:To Tailleville, with
<> friend,    CP4:To Clairvaux, with        1010| MS:§line added between present ll. 1009 and
1011§        1013| MS:Such §crossed out and replaced above by§ Snarled <> at Caen:
CP4:at Vire:        1015| MS:Bowed §crossed out and replaced above by§ Knelt
1016| MS:yesterday,—    CP2:yesterday—        1017| MS:§line added between present ll. 1016
and 1018§ eyes at watch,— §last two words and punctuation crossed out§ wide
1018-20| MS:all! / §¶§ Enough; incessant    CP2:all! / §¶§ Enough! incessant    P3:all! / §¶§
Enough incessant    CP3:all! / §¶§ Enough! incessant    CP4:§line added in ¶ space§ According
to his lights, I praise the man. / Enough        1021| MS:With one, you <> of, ever §crossed out
and replaced above by§ praying <> side.— §dash crossed out§    CP2:With her, you
1022| MS:tense:    1889a:tense;        1023| MS:Or §added in margin§ Life §altered to§ life must
§crossed out§ indemnify §altered to§ indemnifies        1024| MS:Or finds its very §last three
words inserted above§        1025| MS:Monsieur Antoine Mellerio's days were spent §crossed
out§ passed    CP4:Monsieur Alphonse §crossed out and replaced above by§ Léonce Miranda's
days        1026| MS:Just §crossed out and replaced above by§ Much <> old in    P2:old, in
1029| MS:repairing loss §crossed out§ harm. §crossed out and replaced above by§ things;
P2:things:    CP3:repairing loss:        1030| MS:§line added in margin§ repair    P2:repair.

No word at any time escaped his lips
—Betrayed a lurking presence, in his heart,
Of sorrow; no regret for mischief done—
Punishment suffered, he would rather say.
1035    Good-tempered schoolboy-fashion, he preferred
To laugh away his flogging, fair price paid
For pleasure out of bounds: if needs must be,
Get pleasure and get flogged a second time!
A sullen subject would have nursed the scars
1040    And made excuse, for throwing grammar by,
That bench was grown uneasy to the seat.
No: this poor fellow cheerfully got hands
Fit for his stumps, and what hands failed to do,
The other members did in their degree—
1045    Unwonted service. With his mouth alone
He wrote, nay, painted pictures—think of that!
He played on a piano pedal-keyed,
Kicked out—if it was Bach's—good music thence.
He rode, that's readily conceivable,
1050    But then he shot and never missed his bird,
With other feats as dexterous: I infer
He was not ignorant what hands are worth,
When he resolved on ruining his own.

So the two years passed somehow—who shall say
1055    Foolishly,—as one estimates mankind,
The work they do, the play they leave undone?—
Two whole years spent in that experiment

---

1031|   MS:escaped his §crossed out and replaced above by§ the lips   *CP2:*escaped his lips
1032|   MS:—Betrayed the §crossed out and replaced above by§ a < > in the heart,
*CP2:*in his heart,      1033|   MS:sorrow; least §crossed out and replaced above by§ no
1035|   MS:Good-tempered, school-boy-fashion   *CP2:*Good-tempered school-boy-fashion
*1889a:*schoolboy-fashion      1036|   MS:away the flogging, as fair price   *CP2:*away his flogging,
fair price paid      1039|   MS:scars,   *P2:*scars      1043|   MS:what they §crossed out and
replaced above by§ hands      1045|   MS:service; with   *P2:*service. With
1047|   MS:piano, pedal-keyed,   *CP2:*piano pedal-keyed,      1049|   MS:rode,—that's
*P2:*rode—that's   *CP2:*rode, that's      1053|   MS:his pair §crossed out§ own.
1056|   MS:And §crossed out and replaced above by§ The < > do, or §crossed out and replaced
above by§ the      1057-58|   MS:§lines added between present ll. 1056 and 1059§

I told you of, at Clairvaux all the time,
From April on to April: why that month
1060 More than another, notable in life?
Does the awakening of the year arouse
Man to new projects, nerve him for fresh feats
Of what proves, for the most part of mankind
Playing or working, novel folly too?
1065 At any rate, I see no slightest sign
Of folly (let me tell you in advance)
Nothing but wisdom meets me manifest
In the procedure of the Twentieth Day
Of April, 'Seventy, —folly's year in France.

1070 It was delightful Spring, and out of doors
Temptation to adventure. Walk or ride?
There was a wild young horse to exercise,
And teach the way to go and pace to keep:
Monsieur Léonce Miranda chose to ride.
1075 So, while they clapped soft saddle straight on back,
And bitted jaw to satisfaction,—since
The partner of his days must stay at home,
Teased by some trifling legacy of March
To throat or shoulder,—visit duly paid
1080 And "farewell" given and received again,—
As chamber-door considerately closed
Behind him, still five minutes were to spend.

---

1058| MS:at Tailleville all   CP4:at Clairvaux all         1060| MS:another luckless §crossed out§
notable   CP2:another, notable         1063| MS:proves—if you estimate §last three words
crossed out and replaced above by five words§ for the most part of   P2:proves, for
1064| MS:working—novel   P2:working, novel         1066| MS:folly, let <> advance,   CP2:folly
(let <> advance)         1067| MS:wisdom I see §last two words crossed out and replaced above
by two words§ meets me         1068| MS:of the thirteenth day §last two words altered to§
Thirteenth Day   CP4:of the Twentieth Day         1073| MS:And §added in margin§ Teach
§altered to§ teach him §crossed out§ the         1074| MS:Monsieur Antoine Mellerio chose the
ride.   P2:chose to ride.   CP4:Monsieur Alphonse §crossed out and replaced above by§ Léonce
Miranda chose         1075| MS:clapped the §crossed out and replaced above by§ soft saddle
straight §inserted above§ on his §crossed out§ back,         1076| MS:bitted him §crossed out and
replaced above by§ jaw         1078| MS:Teazed   1889a:Teased
1080| MS:again,— §dash crossed out§   P2:again,—         1081| MS:This §crossed out and
replaced above by§ As         1082| MS:him, still §over perhaps *some*§

How better, than by clearing, two and two,
The staircase-steps and coming out aloft
<sup>1085</sup> Upon the platform yonder (raise your eyes!)
And tasting, just as those two years before,
Spring's bright advance upon the tower a-top,
The feature of the front, the Belvedere?

Look at it for a moment while I breathe.

---

<sup>1085</sup>| MS:§line added between present ll. 1084 and 1086§ yonder—raise <> eyes—
*CP2*:yonder (raise <> eyes!)      <sup>1086</sup>| MS:years ago §crossed out and replaced above by§
before,      <sup>1087</sup>| MS:the Belveder §crossed out§ Tower §altered to§ tower
<sup>1088</sup>| MS:§line added between present ll. 1087 and 1089§ The Belvedere, §last two words crossed
out§ the §altered to§ The future <> front, the Belvidere? *P2*:front, the Belvedere?
<sup>1088-89</sup>| MS:§no ¶§ *P2*:§¶§      <sup>1089</sup>| MS:while I rest. §crossed out§ breathe.

IV

Ready to hear the rest? How good you are!

Now for this Twentieth splendid day of Spring,
All in a tale,—sun, wind, sky, earth and sea,—
To bid man "Up, be doing!" Mount the stair,
5    Monsieur Léonce Miranda mounts so brisk,
And look—ere his elastic foot arrive—
Your longest, far and wide, o'er fronting space.
Yon white streak—Havre lighthouse! Name and name,
How the mind runs from each to each relay,
10   Town after town, till Paris' self be touched,
Superlatively big with life and death
To all the world, that very day perhaps!
He who stepped out upon the platform here,
Pinnacled over the expanse, gave thought
15   Neither to Rouher nor Ollivier, Roon
Nor Bismarck, Emperor nor King, but just
To steeple, church, and shrine, The Ravissante!

He saw Her, whom myself saw, but when Spring
Was passing into Fall: not robed and crowned
20   As, thanks to him, and her you know about,

---

<sup>1-2</sup>| MS:§no ¶§  *P2:*§¶§       <sup>2</sup>| MS:thirteen  *P2:*this Thirteenth   *CP4:*this Twentieth
<sup>3</sup>| MS:Sun and air, §last two words inserted above§ earth and sky §last six words crossed out§
All in a tale,— §last four words inserted above§       <sup>4</sup>| MS:man, "Up  *1889a:*man "Up
<sup>5</sup>| MS:Monsieur Antoine Mellerio mounts  *CP4:*Monsieur Alphonse §crossed out and replaced
above by§ Léonce Miranda mounts       <sup>7</sup>| MS:Our longest far < > wide o'er fronting sea.
*P2:*Your longest  *CP2:*longest, far < > wide, o'er fronting space.       <sup>8</sup>| MS:Yon §added in
margin§ That §crossed out and replaced above by§ white streak is §crossed out and replaced
below by dash§ —Havre light-house; name  §altered to§ light-house! Name  *P2:*lighthouse
*CP4:*streak—Havre §crossed out and restored§       <sup>12</sup>| MS:That §crossed out and replaced
above by two words§ To all < > world that  *P2:*world, that       <sup>13</sup>| MS:But who stepped §over
perhaps *steps*§ out < > platform then, §over illegible word§  *P2:*platform here,  *C1873:*He who
<sup>17</sup>| MS:The §crossed out and replaced above by§ Yon §crossed out§ To §added in margin§
steeple < > shrine, the Delivrande.  *P2:*the Délivrande!  *CP4:*shrine, The Ravissante!
<sup>18</sup>| MS:saw her §altered to§ Her, as myself saw, but §inserted above§ when that §crossed out§
Spring  *CP2:*saw Her, whom myself       <sup>19</sup>| MS:into Fall,—not  *P2:*into Fall: not

She stands at present; but She smiled the same.
Thither he turned—to never turn away.

He thought . . .

        (Suppose I should prefer "He said?"
Along with every act—and speech is act—
25    There go, a multitude impalpable
To ordinary human faculty,
The thoughts which give the act significance.
Who is a poet needs must apprehend
Alike both speech and thoughts which prompt to speak.
30    Part these, and thought withdraws to poetry:
Speech is reported in the newspaper.)

He said, then, probably no word at all,
But thought as follows—in a minute's space—
One particle of ore beats out such leaf!

35    "This Spring-morn I am forty-three years old:
In prime of life, perfection of estate
Bodily, mental, nay, material too,—
My whole of worldly fortunes reach their height.
Body and soul alike on eminence:
40    It is not probable I ever raise
Soul above standard by increase of worth,

---

21|   MS:present,—but she  *P2:*present; but She     23|   MS:thought:— §¶§ (Suppose I were
to say §last three words crossed out and replaced above by two words§ should prefer, "He
*CP2:*thought . . §¶§ <> prefer "He    *1889a:*thought . . . §¶§      25|   MS:There §added in
margin§ Go §altered to§ go, in §crossed out§ a <> impalpable, §comma crossed out§
26|   MS:§line added between present ll. 25 and 27§     28|   MS:To be §last two words crossed
out and replaced above by two words§ Who is a poet is to §last two words crossed out and
replaced above by two words§ needs must     30|   MS:§line added between present ll. 29 and
31§     34|   MS:§line added between present ll. 33 and 35§
35|   MS:This Spring-morn, I <> forty three  *P2:*"This <> forty-three  *1889a:*"This Spring-
morn I    38|   MS:My very worldly fortunes at §crossed out and replaced above by§ reach
*1889a:*My whole of worldly    39|   MS:§line added between present ll. 38 and 40§
eminence,—  *CP2:*eminence:    41|   MS:Soul §added in margin§ Above this value, what I
now am §last six words crossed out and replaced above by four words§ standard,
by increase of worth,—  *P2:*Soul above standard by  *CP2:*worth,

Nor reasonably may expect to lift
Body beyond the present altitude.

"Behold me, Lady called The Ravissante!
45   Such as I am, I—gave myself to you
So long since, that I cannot say 'I give.'
All my belongings, what is summed in life,
I have submitted wholly—as man might,
At least, as *I* might, who am weak, not strong,—
50   Wholly, then, to your rule and governance,
So far as I had strength. My weakness was—
I felt a fascination, at each point
And pore of me, a Power as absolute
Claiming that soul should recognize her sway.
55   O you were no whit clearlier Queen, I see,
Throughout the life that rolls out ribbon-like
Its shot-silk length behind me, than the strange
Mystery—how shall I denominate
The unrobed One? Robed you go and crowned as well,
60   Named by the nations: she is hard to name,
Though you have spelt out certain characters

---

42|  MS:Just as I hardly §last four words crossed out and replaced above by two words§ Nor
reasonably <> to climb   *P2:*to lift     43|  MS:Body §added in margin§ Beyond §altered to§
beyond <> altitude. I reach. §last two words crossed out§     43-44|  MS:§no ¶§   *P2:*§¶§
44|  MS:Listen, §crossed out§ Therefore, §added in margin§ my Lady of the Delivrande!
*P2:* "Therefore <> Délivrande,   *CP2:* "Behold me, Lady <> Délivrande!   *P3:* "Behohld
*CP3:* "Behold   *CP4:*me, Lady called The Ravissante!     45|  MS:am, I gave <> you,
*P2:*am, I—gave   *CP2:*you     46|  MS:§line added between present ll. 45 and 47§ say "I give."
*P2:*say 'I give.'   *1889a:*give. §emended to§ give.' §see Editorial Notes§     47|  MS:life
*P2:*life,     48|  MS:submitted, wholly,—as   *P2:*submitted wholly—as     49|  MS:as I <>
weak not   *P2:*weak, not   *CP2:*as *I*     51|  MS:strength: the weakness   *P2:*strength: my
weakness   *CP2:*strength. My     52|  MS:felt the §crossed out and replaced above by§ a
fascination at   *P2:*fascination, at     53|  MS:me, of §crossed out and replaced above by§ a
power §altered to§ Power     54|  MS:To challenge life obedient to its §last five words crossed
out and replaced above by six words§ claim my §over illegible word§ soul should §over illegible
word§ recognize her   *P2:*Claim that my <> recognise   *CP2:*Claiming, my   *1889a:*Claiming
that soul <> recognize     57|  MS:Its startling §crossed out and replaced above by§ shot-silk
length before me   *CP2:*length behind me     58|  MS:Mystery,—how <> denominate?
§question mark crossed out§   *P2:*Mystery—how     59-61|  MS:§lines added between present
ll. 58 and 61§ unrobed one?—robed <> well. / Someone has spelt out thus the §last two words
crossed out and replaced below by§ certain characters   *P2:*unrobed One? Robed <> well, /
Named by the nations: she is hard to name, / Though you have spelt

287

Obscure upon what fillet binds her brow,
*Lust of the flesh, lust of the eye, life's pride.*
'So call her, and contemn the enchantress!'—'Crush
65    The despot, and recover liberty!'—
Cried despot and enchantress at each ear.
You were conspicuous and pre-eminent,
Authoritative and imperial,—you
Spoke first, claimed homage: did I hesitate?
70    Born for no mastery, but servitude,
Men cannot serve two masters, says the Book;
Master should measure strength with master, then,
Before on servant is imposed a task.
You spoke first, promised best, and threatened most;
75    The other never threatened, promised, spoke
A single word, but, when your part was done,
Lifted a finger, and I, prostrate, knew
Films were about me, though you stood aloof
Smiling or frowning 'Where is power like mine
80    To punish or reward thee? Rise, thou fool!
Will to be free, and, lo, I lift thee loose!'
Did I not will, and could I rise a whit?
Lay I, at any time, content to lie?
'To lie, at all events, brings pleasure: make
85    Amends by undemanded pain!' I said.
Did not you prompt me? 'Purchase now by pain

---

⁶²| MS:fillet serves for crown, §last three words crossed out§ binds          ⁶³| MS:"Lust <>
pride."  *P2: Lust <> pride.*          ⁶⁴| MS:"Call her so, and <> enchantress!"—"Crush
*P2:*'So call her, and <> enchantress!'—'Crush          ⁶⁵| MS:The potency §altered to§
potentate, §crossed out and replaced above by§ despot, why not as easily? §last four words
crossed out and replaced above by three words§ and recover freedom §crossed out§ liberty!"
*P2:*liberty!'  *C1873:*liberty!'—          ⁶⁶| MS:§line added between present ll. 65 and 67§ Cry
despot  *C1873:*Cried despot          ⁶⁹| MS:Spake §altered to§ Spoke          ⁷⁰| MS:I am §last
two words crossed out and replaced above by two words§ Born for          ⁷¹| MS:We §over
perhaps *One*§ cannot <> book;  *P2:*I cannot <> Book;  *1889a:*Men cannot
⁷³| MS:Before the servant be imposed  *C1873:*Before on servant is imposed          ⁷⁴| MS:best
and  *P2:*best, and          ⁷⁸| MS:me, while you  *CP2:*me, though you          ⁷⁹| MS:frowning
"Where  *P2:*frowning 'Where          ⁸¹| MS:loose!"  *P2:*loose!'          ⁸³| MS:Lay §over
illegible word§ I content, at any time, §last five words transposed to§ I, at any time, content
⁸⁴| MS:"To lie, is then forbidden §last three words crossed out and replaced above by four
words§ at all events brings  *P2:*'To <> events, brings          ⁸⁵| MS:pain!" you §crossed out
and replaced above by§ I  *P2:*pain!' I          ⁸⁶| MS:me? "Purchase  *P2:*Me? 'Purchase

Pleasure hereafter in the world to come!'
I could not pluck my heart out, as you bade:
Unbidden, I burned off my hands at least.
90 My soul retained its treasure; but my purse
Lightened itself with much alacrity.
Well, where is the reward? what promised fruit
Of sacrifice in peace, content? what sense
Of added strength to bear or to forbear?
95 What influx of new light assists me now
Even to guess you recognize a gain
In what was loss enough to mortal me?
But she, the less authoritative voice,
Oh, how distinct enunciating, how
100 Plain dealing! Gain she gave was gain indeed!
That, you deny: that, you contemptuous call
Acorns, swine's food not man's meat! 'Spurn the draff!'
Ay, but those life-tree apples I prefer,
Am I to die of hunger till they drop?
105 Husks keep flesh from starvation, anyhow.
Give those life-apples!—one, worth woods of oak,

---

87| MS:come!" *P2:*come!'    88| MS:bade:    *1889a:*bade §emended to§ bade: §see
Editorial Notes§    89| MS:least, *P2:*least.    92| MS:Yet §crossed out§ Well, §added in
margin§ <> reward, §comma altered to question mark§ the §crossed out and replaced above
by§ what    93| MS:content,—what *CP2:*content? what    94| MS:forbear,
*CP2:*forbear?    96| MS:to see §crossed out and replaced above by§ guess <> recognize
*P2:*recognise *1889a:*recognize    98-100| MS:§one line revised into three lines§ The other?
Less authoritative voice! §last three words and exclamation mark inserted above§ / But how
distinct enunciation—what §last five words inserted above§ / Plain-dealing! §inserted below§
Gain <> indeed. *P2:*voice, / But <> enunciating—how / Plain dealing! Gain <> indeed!
*CP2:*But she, the less <> voice, / Oh, how <> enunciating, how /    101| MS:deny—
contemptuous, that, you §last four words transposed to§ deny—that, you contemptuous call—
*P2:*deny: that <> call    102| MS:"Acorns, §quotation mark crossed out§ <> meat!"
§quotation mark crossed out§ Be it so §last three words crossed out§ Spurn <> draff?
*CP2:*meat! "Spurn <> draff!" *1873:* meat! 'Spurn <> draff!'    103| MS:Where are §last two
words crossed out and replaced above by two words§ Give me the golden §crossed out and
replaced above by§ life-tree <> I preferred §altered to§ prefer? §altered to§ prefer!
*CP2:*Ay, but those life-tree <> prefer,    104| MS:§line added in margin§
105| MS:Husks save §crossed out and replaced above by§ keep flesh §over illegible word§
106| MS:O that §altered to§ those gold §crossed out and replaced above by§ life-apples <>
oak,— *P2:*oak, *CP2:*Give those life-apples!—one §crossed out and replaced above by§ send
§crossed out, restoring original reading§

Worth acorns by the waggon-load,—one shoot
Through heart and brain, assurance bright and brief
That you, my Lady, my own Ravissante,
110  Feel, through my famine, served and satisfied,
Own me, your starveling, soldier of a sort!
Your soldier! do I read my title clear
Even to call myself your friend, not foe?
What is the pact between us but a truce?
115  At best I shall have staved off enmity,
Obtained a respite, ransomed me from wrath.
I pay, instalment by instalment, life,
Earth's tribute-money, pleasures great and small,
Whereof should at the last one penny piece
120  Fall short, the whole heap becomes forfeiture.
You find in me deficient soldiership:
Want the whole life or none. I grudge that whole,
Because I am not sure of recompense:

---

[107]  MS:And §crossed out and replaced above by§ With acorns   *P2:*Worth acorns
[108]  MS:brain,—assurance   *CP2:*brain, assurance        [109]  MS:§line added between present
ll. 108 and 110§ my Lady of the Délivrande,   *CP4:*my Lady, my own Ravissante,
[110]  MS:That §crossed out§ By famine, §last two words added in margin§ you at least §last two
words crossed out§ were served   *P2:*Were, though by famine, served   *CP2:*Feel, by my famine
*P3:*Feel my famine   *CP3:*Feel, through my        [111]  MS:You §crossed out and replaced above
by§ And reckoned me your §last three words crossed out and replaced above by four words§
owned the starved man soldier   *P2:*Would own your starved   *CP2:*Own me, your starveling,
soldier   *P3:*starving   *CP3:*starveling   *P4:*starveling   *CP4:*starveling        [112-13]  MS:§lines
added between present ll. 111 and 114§        [112]  MS:soldier—do   *P2:*soldier!—do
*CP2:*soldier! do        [114]  MS:is it §crossed out and replaced below by four words§ the pact
between us <> truce? between us two? §last three words and question mark crossed out§
[115]  MS:best I may §crossed out and replaced below by§ shall        [116]  MS:respite, paid your
§last two words crossed out and replaced above by three words§ ransomed me from wrath's
§altered to§ wrath delay §crossed out§   *P2:*wrath,   *CP4:*wrath.
[117]  MS:Paying, §added in margin§ Instalment by instalment, of my §last two words crossed out
and replaced above by§ paying §crossed out§ life,   *P2:*Have payed, instalment by   *CP2:*paid
*CP4:*I pay, instalment by        [118]  MS:§line added between present ll. 117 and 119§
[119]  MS:Whereof let §crossed out and replaced below by§ should <> penny-piece   *P4:*penny
piece        [120]  MS:short, and §crossed out and replaced above by§ straight all will §crossed
out§ be §altered to§ becomes a forfeiture.   *P2:*short, the whole heap becomes forfeiture.
[121]  MS:§line added between present ll. 120 and 122§ soldiership—   *P2:*soldiership:
[122]  MS:Want §added in margin§ The §altered to§ the whole of §crossed out§ life <> none. Why
not §last two words crossed out and replaced above by two words§ I grudge the whole?
*P2:*whole,   *CP2:*grudge that whole,        [123]  MS:§line added between present ll. 122 and 124§

Because I want faith. Whose the fault? I ask.
125 If insufficient faith have done thus much,
Contributed thus much of sacrifice,
More would move mountains, you are warrant. Well,
Grant, you, the grace, I give the gratitude!
And what were easier? 'Ask and have' folk call
130 Miranda's method: 'Have, nor need to ask!'
So do they formulate your quality
Superlative beyond my human grace.
The Ravissante, you ravish men away
From puny aches and petty pains, assuaged
135 By man's own art with small expenditure
Of pill or potion, unless, put to shame,
Nature is roused and sets things right herself.
Your miracles are grown our commonplace;
No day but pilgrim hobbles his last mile,
140 Kneels down and rises up, flings crutch away,
Or else appends it to the reverend heap
Beneath you, votive cripple-carpentry.
Some few meet failure—oh, they wanted faith,
And may betake themselves to La Salette,

---

124| MS:want the §crossed out§ faith. Whose the §inserted above§  *P2:*fault?—I  *CP2:*fault? I
125| MS:faith has done  *P2:*faith have done        126| MS:§line added between present ll. 125
and 127§        127| MS:you should surely see: §last three words crossed out and replaced above
by three words§ are warrant: well,  *P2:*warrant. Well,        128| MS:Be §crossed out and
replaced above by§ Give, yours §altered to§ you <> grace, and mine §last two words crossed out
and replaced above by two words§ I pay the  *P2:*Grant, you <> I give the        129| MS:easier?
"Seek §over perhaps *Ask*§ and have" say folk §last two words transposed to§ folk say,  *P2:*easier?
'Ask and have' folk call        130| MS:With me, the rule is: "Have <> to ask" §last word and
quotation mark crossed out§ seek!"  *P2:*Mellerio's method: 'Have <> to ask!'  *CP4:*Miranda's
method        132| MS:§line added in margin§        133-34| MS:You, the Délivrande, the
§crossed out and replaced above by§ who §crossed out§ you deliver man §altered to§ men /
From puny §inserted above§  *P2:*The Délivrande, you but deliver <> /  *CP4:*The Ravissante,
you ravish men away        135| MS:Elsewhere §crossed out§ by §altered to§ By vulgar §inserted
above§ Art  *P2:*By man's own art        137| MS:roused to set things  *P2:*roused and sets
things        138| MS:common-place;  *1889a:*commonplace;        140| MS:up, and §crossed
out§ flings        141| MS:That is, appends  *P2:*Or else appends        143| MS:failure—for
§crossed out and replaced above by§ oh, <> faith  *P2:*faith,        144| MS:to Lourdes or else
*P2:*to Lourdes, or seek  *CP2:*to La Salette, §last two words transposed from l. 145§ Lourdes,
§transposed to l. 145§ or seek §crossed out and transposed to l. 145§

145  Or seek Lourdes, so that hence the scandal limp!
     The many get their grace and go their way
     Rejoicing, with a tale to tell,—most like,
     A staff to borrow, since the crutch is gone,
     Should the first telling happen at my house,
150  And teller wet his whistle with my wine.
     *I* tell this to a doctor and he laughs:
     'Give me permission to cry—Out of bed,
     You loth rheumatic sluggard! Cheat yon chair
     Of laziness, its gouty occupant!—
155  You should see miracles performed. But now,
     I give advice, and take as fee ten francs,
     And do as much as does your Ravissainte.
     Send her that case of cancer to be cured
     I have refused to treat for any fee,
160  Bring back my would-be patient sound and whole,
     And see me laugh on t'other side my mouth!'
     Can he be right, and are you hampered thus?
     Such pettiness restricts a miracle
     Wrought by the Great Physician, who hears prayer,

---

145| MS:The §crossed out and replaced above by§ La Salette, so that §over illegible word§ hence they §crossed out and replaced above by two words§ the scandal limp! their best. §last two words crossed out§ *CP2:*Or seek Lourdes, §last three words transposed from l. 144§ so that §last two words crossed out and restored; other revisions illegibly crossed out§ 146| MS:grace, and let §crossed out§ go *CP2:*grace and 148| MS:borrow, now that crutch *P2:*borrow, since the crutch 149| MS:When the <> happens in my *P2:*Should the <> happen at my 150| MS:And with my wine the §crossed out§ teller his §inserted above§ whistle wets. §line transposed to§ And teller wets his whistle with my wine. *P2:*wet 151| MS:I tell this §over *a*§ Paris §crossed out and replaced above by two words§ to a *CP2:I* tell 152| MS:'Give <> cry" §quotation mark crossed out§ —Out 153| MS:You loth §inserted above§ rheumatic body! Cheat of §crossed out§ yon *CP2:*rheumatic sluggard! Cheat 155| MS:performed! For me, §last two words and comma crossed out§ But now *P2:*now, *1889a:*performed. But 156| MS:advice and *P2:*advice, and 157| MS:§line added between present ll. 156 and 158§ much then as the Delivrande. *P2:*much as does your Délivrande. *CP4:*your Ravissante. 158| MS:her plain §crossed out and replaced above by§ that <> cured, *1889a:*cured 159-60| MS:§lines added between present ll. 158 and 161§ 160| MS:And let my would-be patient lose the plague, *P2:*Bring back my <> patient sound and whole, 161-63| MS:And I shall laugh <> side of §crossed out§ my mouth!" / Such the §crossed out and replaced above by§ pettiness restriction §altered to§ restricts to §crossed out§ a miracle! *P2:*And see me laugh <> / Can he be right, and are you hampered thus? / Such <> miracle *CP2:*mouth!' // 164| MS:the Great Physician— who is there, §last two words and comma crossed out§ hears *P2:*the Great Physician, who

165 Visibly seated in your mother-lap!
He, out of nothing, made sky, earth, and sea,
And all that in them is—man, beast, bird, fish,
Down to this insect on my parapet.
Look how the marvel of a minim crawls!
170 Were I to kneel among the halt and maimed,
And pray 'Who mad'st the insect with ten legs,
Make me one finger grow where ten were once!'
The very priests would thrust me out of church.
'What folly does the madman dare expect?
175 No faith obtains—in this late age, at least—
Such cure as that! We ease rheumatics, though!'

"Ay, bring the early ages back again,
What prodigy were unattainable?
I read your annals. Here came Louis Onze,
180 Gave thrice the sum he ever gave before
At one time, some three hundred crowns, to wit—
On pilgrimage to pray for—health, he found?
Did he? I do not read it in Commines.
Here sent poor joyous Marie-Antoinette
185 To thank you that a Dauphin dignified

---

165| MS:mother-lap? *1889a:*mother-lap! 166-70| MS:sea, / Made §inserted above§ This §altered to§ this small insect on the §crossed out and replaced above by§ my parapet. / Should I go, kneel *P2:*sea, / And all that in them is, man, beast, bird, fish, / Down to this insect <> parapet. / Look how the marvel of a minim crawls! / Were I to kneel *1889a:*sea, / <> is— man, <> /// 171| MS:And say, who <> with eight legs *P2:*And pray, Who <> with ten legs, *CP2:*pray, 'Who 172| MS:where hands §crossed out and replaced above by§ ten <> once, *P2:*once!— *CP2:*once!' 173| MS:church, *CP2:*church. 174| MS:"What <> dare to ask §last two words crossed out and replaced above by§ expect?" *P2:*'What <> expect? 175| MS:faith gains that §last two words crossed out and replaced above by§ obtains <> least, *P2:*least— 176| MS:§line added between present ll. 175 and 177§ that! we <> though.' *P2:*though! *CP2:*that! We *P3:*though! *1873:*though!' 177| MS:Ay, were §crossed out and replaced above by§ bring <> again! *P2:*"Ay <> again, 178| MS:prodigy was §altered to§ were 179| MS:your records. §crossed out and replaced above by§ annals. Her <> Onze *P2:*came Louis Onze, 180-81| MS:§lines added between present ll. 179 and 182§ 183| MS:§line added between present ll. 182 and 184§ 184| MS:Here came §crossed out and replaced above by§ sent 185| MS:you, that §crossed out and replaced above by§ since a *CP2:*you that a

Her motherhood—called Duke of Normandy
And Martyr of the Temple, much the same
As if no robe of hers had dressed you rich;
No silver lamps, she gave, illume your shrine!
190 Here, following example, fifty years
Ago, in gratitude for birth again
Of yet another destined King of France,
Did not the Duchess fashion with her hands,
And frame in gold and crystal, and present
195 A bouquet made of artificial flowers?
And was he King of France, and is not he
Still Count of Chambord?

                "Such the days of faith,
And such their produce to encourage mine!
What now, if I too count without my host?
200 I too have given money, ornament,
And 'artificial flowers'—which, when I plucked,
Seemed rooting at my heart and real enough:
What if I gain thereby nor health of mind,
Nor youth renewed which perished in its prime,
205 Burnt to a cinder 'twixt the red-hot bars,
Nor gain to see my second baby-hope
Of managing to live on terms with both
Opposing potentates, the Power and you,

---

186| MS:motherhood—the Duke <> Normandy, *P2*:motherhood—since Duke *CP2*:of
Normandy *C1873*:motherhood—called Duke 188| MS:if that §crossed out and replaced
above by§ no <> rich, *1889a*:rich; 189| MS:No silver §inserted above§ lamp, she gave,
had lit your shrine. *P2*:lamps <> shrine! *CP4*:gave, illumed your *1889a*:illume
190| MS:Here, followed §altered to§ following the §crossed out§ example
193| MS:Did did §crossed out§ not 196| MS:of France and *P2*:of France, and
197| MS:Still §added in margin§ Count <> §¶§ Such were the §crossed out§ days *P2*:§¶§
"Such the 198| MS:their fruit §crossed out and replaced above by§ produce for my
§crossed out§ encouragement. *P2*:encouragement! *CP2*:produce to encourage mine!
199| MS:now if <> host?— *P2*:now, if <> host? 200| MS:I who have *P2*:I too have
201| MS:And "artificial flowers"—which when I plucked *P2*:And 'artificial flowers'—which,
when I plucked, 202| MS:Seemed clinging §altered to§ rooting <> enough—
*P2*:enough: 203| MS:gained *P2*:gain 204| MS:youth that §crossed out and
replaced above by§ which <> its infancy, *CP2*:youth renewed which <> its prime,
206| MS:Nor even §crossed out and replaced above by two words§ am to <> baby-hope—
*P2*:Nor gain to *1873*:baby-hope 207-8| MS:§lines added between present ll. 206 and 209§

Crowned with success? I dawdle out my days
210    In exile here at Clairvaux, with mock love,
That gives—while whispering 'Would I dared refuse!'—
What the loud voice declares my heart's free gift:
Mock worship, mock superiority
O'er those I style the world's benighted ones,
215    That irreligious sort I pity so,
Dumas and even Hertford who is Duke.


"Impiety? Not if I know myself!
Not if you know the heart and soul I bare,
I bid you cut, hack, slash, anatomize,
220    Till peccant part be found and flung away!
Demonstrate where I need more faith! Describe
What act shall evidence sufficiency
Of faith, your warrant for such exercise
Of power, in my behalf, as all the world
225    Except poor praying me declares profuse?
Poor me? It is that world, not me alone,
That world which prates of fixed laws and the like,
I fain would save, poor world so ignorant!
And your part were—what easy miracle?

---

208| MS:the world and   *CP2:*the power §altered to§ Power and    209| MS:success, but
dawdle   *C1873:*success? I dawdle    210| MS:at Tainville, with mock-love,   *P2:*at Tailleville
<> mock love,   *CP4:*at Clairvaux, with    211-12| MS:§lines added between present ll. 210
and 213§    211| MS:gives itself §crossed out§ with whisper— §inserted below§ "Would <>
refuse!'   *P2:*gives while whispering 'Would   *CP2:*gives—while <> refuse!'—   *P3:*gives, while
*1889a:*gives—while    212| MS:gift!   *C1873:*gift:    213| MS:Mock-worship, mock-
superiority   *P2:*Mock worship, mock superiority    214| MS:To those   *P2:*O'er those
215| MS:The irreligious   *P2:*That irreligious    216| MS:E'en Dumas, and §crossed out and
replaced above by§ nay, Lord Hertford <> Duke?   *P2:*E'en Dumas, e'en Lord Hertford, who
*CP2:*Dumas and even Hertford who   *C1873:*is Duke.    216-17| MS:§¶§   *1889a:*§no ¶;
emended to restore ¶; see Editorial Notes§    217| MS:Impiety   *P2:*"Impiety
218| MS:Not as §altered to§ if   *P2:*soul, I   *1889a:*soul I    221| MS:where I want the §last
two words crossed out and replaced above by two words§ need more faith! Declare §crossed out§
Describe    222| MS:sufficiency,   *P2:*sufficiency    223| MS:And be your
*P2:*Of faith, be warrant   *CP2:*faith, your warrant    224| MS:power in <> behalf as <>
world,   *CP2:*power, in <> behalf, as <> world    225| MS:Beside §crossed out and
replaced above by§ Except poor me, have testified profuse?   *CP2:*poor praying me declares
profuse?   *P3:*me, declare   *CP3:*declares   *1889a:*me declares    227| MS:§line added
between present ll. 226 and 228§ world which §over illegible word§    228| MS:I want to save
*CP2:*I fain would save    229| MS:miracle?"   *P2:*miracle?

<sup>230</sup>　Oh, Lady, could I make your want like mine!

Then his face grew one luminosity.

"Simple, sufficient! Happiness at height!
I solve the riddle, I persuade mankind.
I have been just the simpleton who stands—
<sup>235</sup>　Summoned to claim his patrimonial rights—
At shilly-shally, may he knock or no
At his own door in his own house and home
Whereof he holds the very title-deeds!
Here is my title to this property,
<sup>240</sup>　This power you hold for profit of myself
And all the world at need—which need is now!

"My title—let me hear who controverts!
Count Mailleville built yon church. Why did he so?
Because he found your image. How came that?
<sup>245</sup>　His shepherd told him that a certain sheep
Was wont to scratch with hoof and scrape with horn
At ground where once the Danes had razed a church.
Thither he went, and there he dug, and thence
He disinterred the image he conveyed
<sup>250</sup>　In pomp to Londres yonder, his domain.
You liked the old place better than the new.
The Count might surely have divined as much:

---

<sup>230</sup>| MS:§line added between present ll. 229 and 231§ your wish like mine! *P2:*mine!"
*CP2:*your want like      <sup>231-32</sup>| MS:§no ¶§ *P2:*§¶§      <sup>232</sup>| MS:sufficient! oh, my
happiness! *P2:*sufficient! Happiness at height!      <sup>233</sup>| MS:It solves the riddle, and converts
§last two words crossed out and replaced above by two words§ it persuades mankind. *P2:*I solve
the riddle, persuade mankind. *CP2:*riddle, I persuade      <sup>234</sup>| MS:stands,— *CP2:*stands—
<sup>235</sup>| MS:§line added between present ll. 234 and 236§ rights,— *1889a:*rights—
<sup>236</sup>| MS:shilly-shally, shall §crossed out and replaced below by§ may      <sup>237</sup>| MS:home,
*P2:*home      <sup>239</sup>| MS:is why §crossed out and replaced above by§ my      <sup>240</sup>| MS:power in
§crossed out§ you hold §inserted above§      <sup>241-43</sup>| MS:now! / §¶§ Count Baldwin built
*P2:*§¶§ My title—let me hear who controverts! / Count *CP4:* // Count Mailleville built
*1873:*now! / §¶§ "My < > /      <sup>248</sup>| MS:dug and *P2:*dug, and      <sup>249</sup>| MS:disinterred
your image he §crossed out and replaced above by§ and conveyed, *CP2:*disinterred the image
he conveyed, *CP3:*conveyed      <sup>250</sup>| MS:to Douvres yonder *P2:*pomp, to *CP3:*pomp to
*CP4:*to Londres yonder      <sup>251</sup>| MS:new: *CP2:*new.      <sup>252</sup>| MS:much, *CP2:*much:

He did not; someone might have spoke a word:
No one did. A mere dream had warned enough

<sub>255</sub> That back again in pomp you best were borne:
No dream warned, and no need of convoy was;
An angel caught you up and clapped you down—
No mighty task, you stand one *mètre* high,
And people carry you about at times.

<sub>260</sub> Why, then, did you despise the simple course?
Because you are the Queen of Angels: when
You front us in a picture, there flock they,
Angels around you, here and everywhere.

"Therefore, to prove indubitable faith,

<sub>265</sub> Those angels that acknowledge you their queen,
I summon them to bear me to your feet
From Clairvaux through the air, an easy trip!
Faith without flaw! I trust your potency,
Benevolence, your will to save the world—

<sub>270</sub> By such a simplest of procedures, too!
Not even by affording angel-help,
Unless it please you: there's a simpler mode:
Only suspend the law of gravity,

---

<sup>253|</sup> MS:not: someone <> word, *P2:*not; someone *CP2:*word: <sup>254|</sup> MS:did: then §crossed out§ a mere §inserted above§ dream <> enough, *P2:*did; a *CP2:*did. A *1889a:*enough <sup>255|</sup> MS:And §crossed out and replaced above by§ That <> pomp he bore §last two words inserted above and crossed out§ you straight be borne: *P2:*you best were borne: <sup>256|</sup> MS:dream was, and <> convoy; just *P2:*dream warned, and <> convoy was; <sup>257|</sup> MS:down,— *1873:*down— <sup>258|</sup> MS:No great task, since you are one metre *P2:*No mighty task, you are *CP2:*you stand one *1889a: mètre* <sup>260|</sup> MS:§line added between present ll. 259 and 261§ Why else did <> course, *P2:*Why, then, did <> course? <sup>261|</sup> MS:But you are §last two words crossed out and replaced below by two words§ that, the <> Angels, where are §crossed out§ you stand §inserted above§ *P2:*You are the <> Angels: where *CP2:*Because you are Angels: when <sup>262|</sup> MS:In story or in picture, there flock §over perhaps *are*§ *CP2:*You front us in a picture, there <sup>263-64|</sup> MS:§¶§ *1889a:*§no ¶§; emended to restore ¶; see Editorial Notes§ <sup>264-66|</sup> MS:Therefore to <> faith, / I *P2:*"Therefore, to <> faith, / Those angels that acknowledge you their queen, / I *CP2:* / <> you their §altered to§ as §original reading restored§ queen, / <sup>267|</sup> MS:From Tailleville through *CP4:*From Clairvaux through <sup>268|</sup> MS:flaw,: §colon crossed out§ I *P2:*flaw! I <sup>269-73|</sup> MS:world, / Not <> angel-help— / Do §crossed out§ For §added in margin§ but suspend *P2:*world / By simplest of procedures e'er conceived / Not <> angel-help, / Unless it please you: there's a simpler mode: / Only suspend *CP2:*world— / By such a simplest <> procedures, too! / Not <> / <> it please §altered to§ suit §original reading restored§ you <>

And, while at back, permitted to propel,
275   The air helps onward, let the air in front
Cease to oppose my passage through the midst!

"Thus I bestride the railing, leg o'er leg,
Thus, lo, I stand, a single inch away,
At dizzy edge of death,—no touch of fear,
280   As safe on tower above as turf below!
Your smile enswathes me in beatitude,
You lift along the votary—who vaults,
Who, in the twinkling of an eye, revives,
Dropt safely in the space before the church—
285   How crowded, since this morn is market-day!
I shall not need to speak. The news will run
Like wild-fire. 'Thousands saw Miranda's flight!'
'Tis telegraphed to Paris in a trice.
The Boulevard is one buzz 'Do you believe?
290   Well, this time, thousands saw Miranda's flight:
You know him, goldsmith in the Place Vendôme.'
In goes the Empress to the Emperor:
'Now—will you hesitate to make disgorge
Your wicked King of Italy his gains,
295   Give the Legations to the Pope once more?'

---

a simpler §last two words altered to§ an easier §original reading restored§ mode: /   *P3:* / < >
too? / Not < > //   *CP3:* / < > too! / Not < > //     274|   MS:while behind §crossed out and
replaced above by two words§ at back     277|   MS:Thus §crossed out and replaced above by§
As §crossed out, restoring original reading§ I < > railing, leg and leg,   *P2:*"Thus
*CP4:*railing, leg o'er leg,     278|   MS:And §crossed out and replaced above by§ Thus, lightly
§crossed out and replaced above by two words§ lo, I stand, thus §crossed out and replaced above
by§ a     279-81|   MS:At edge of dizziness and death,—so §crossed out and replaced by§
as sure / Your   *P2:*At dizzy edge of death,—no touch of fear, / As safe on tower above as turf
below! / Your     282|   MS:So lightly §last two words crossed out and replaced above by three
words§ And lifts along < > vaults—   *P2:*You lift   *CP2:*votary— §dash crossed out and restored§
who vaults,     284|   MS:Dropped safely   *CP2:*Dropt safely
287|   MS:saw Mellerio's flight!'   *CP4:*saw Miranda's flight!'   *1889a:*flight! §emended to§ flight!'
§see Editorial Notes§     289|   MS:buzz, 'Do   *CP2:*buzz 'Do     290|   MS:saw Mellerio's
flight,   *CP2:*flight:   *CP4:*saw Miranda's flight:     291|   MS:him, Paris knows the Jeweler.
§last four words crossed out and replaced above by six words§ goldsmith in the Street of Peace."
*P2:*of Peace.'   *CP4:*the Place Vendôme.'     292|   MS:to the Emperor—
*CP2:*to the Emperor   *1889a:*to the Emperor:     293|   MS:"Now   *P2:*'Now
294|   MS:This wicked   *P2:*Your wicked     295|   MS:more?"   *P2:*more?'

Which done,—why, grace goes back to operate,
They themselves set a good example first,
Resign the empire twenty years usurped,
And Henry, the Desired One, reigns o'er France!
<sup>300</sup> Regenerated France makes all things new!
My house no longer stands on Quai Rousseau
But Quai rechristened Alacoque: a quai
Where Renan burns his book, and Veuillot burns
Renan beside, since Veuillot rules the roast,
<sup>305</sup> Re-edits now indeed 'The Universe.'
O blessing, O superlatively big
With blessedness beyond all blessing dreamed
By man! for just that promise has effect,
'Old things shall pass away and all be new!'
<sup>310</sup> Then, for a culminating mercy-feat,
Wherefore should I dare dream impossible
That I too have my portion in the change?
My past with all its sorrow, sin and shame,
Becomes a blank, a nothing! There she stands,
<sup>315</sup> Clara de Millefleurs, all deodorized,
Twenty years' stain wiped off her innocence!

---

<sup>297|</sup> MS:And themselves *P2:*They themselves     <sup>298|</sup> MS:Resigning §altered to§ Resign the §inserted above§ empire wrongfully §crossed out and replaced above by two words§ twenty years usurped. *CP2:*usurped,     <sup>299|</sup> MS:And §crossed out§ 'Tis §added in margin§ Henry < > One, rule §crossed out and replaced above by§ reigns < > France— *P2:*And Henry < > France!     <sup>301|</sup> MS:on Quai Voltaire, *CP2:*on Quai Voltaire *CP4:*on Quai Rousseau     <sup>302|</sup> MS:But fraternizes with Quai §last three words crossed out and replaced above by four words§ Quai rechristened Quai Saint §last two words crossed out§ Alacoque: and there *P2:*rechristened Alacoque: a quai     <sup>303|</sup> MS:Renan shall §last two words altered and transposed to§ Shall Renan burn his < > Veuillot burn *P2:*Where Renan burns his < > Veuillot burns     <sup>304|</sup> MS:beside, the man's Prime Minister— §last four words crossed out and replaced above by five words§ since Veuillot rules the roast,— §dash crossed out§     <sup>305|</sup> MS:§line added between present ll. 304 and 310§     <sup>306-9|</sup> MS:§lines written on verso of previous leaf and marked for insertion between present lines 305 and 310§     <sup>307|</sup> MS:blessedness, beyond all blissing dreamed *P2:*blessedness beyond all blessing dreamed     <sup>308|</sup> MS:man, when just *CP2:*man! For just     <sup>310|</sup> MS:And §crossed out and replaced below by§ When, for last §crossed out§ a < > mercy-feat— *CP2:*Then, for < > mercy-feat,     <sup>311|</sup> MS:O what shall §last three words crossed out and replaced above by two words§ Wherefore should < > impossible §punctuation illegibly crossed out§     <sup>312|</sup> MS:§line added between present ll. 311 and 313§ That I, too, have *P2:*That I too have     <sup>313|</sup> MS:My §over illegible word§     <sup>314-16|</sup> MS:nothing,— there §altered to§ nothing?— There < > stands, / The §crossed out§ twenty §altered to§ Twenty §word inserted above and

There never was Muhlhausen, nor at all
Duke Hertford: nought that was, remains, except
The beauty,—yes, the beauty is unchanged!
320    Well, and the soul too, that must keep the same!
And so the trembling little virgin hand
Melts into mine, that's back again, of course!
—Think not I care about my poor old self!
I only want my hand for that one use,
325    To take her hand, and say 'I marry you—
Men, women, angels, you behold my wife!
There is no secret, nothing wicked here,
Nothing she does not wish the world to know!'
None of your married women have the right
330    To mutter 'Yes, indeed, she beats us all
In beauty,—but our lives are pure at least!'
Bear witness, for our marriage is no thing
Done in a corner! 'Tis The Ravissante
Repairs the wrong of Paris. See, She smiles,
335    She beckons, She bids 'Hither, both of you!'
And may we kneel? And will you bless us both?
And may I worship you, and yet love her?

---

illegibly crossed out§ years' stain §inserted above§ wiped <> innocence, §altered to§
innocence!   *P2:*nothing! There <> stands, / A Beaupré, all deodorized, / Twenty
*CP2:*stands, / Anna de Beaupré <> /   *CP4:*stands, / Clara de Millefleurs, all <> /
317|   MS:was Debacker—nor   *P2:*was Debacker, nor   *CP4:*was Muhlhausen, nor
318|   MS:Duke Hertford,—all is §last two words crossed out§ naught <> remains—except
*P2:*remains, except   *CP2:*Duke Hertford: nought        320|   MS:must §crossed out and
replaced above by word illegibly crossed out, restoring original reading§ keeps §altered to§ keep
<> same—   *P2:*same!        321|   MS:virgan   *P2:*virgin        322|   MS:mine,—'tis §crossed
out and replaced above by§ that's <> again, you know— §last two words crossed out and
replaced above by two words§ of course!        323-35|   MS:§lines written on verso of previous
leaf and marked for insertion between present lines 322 and 336§
323|   MS:Think <> self!—   *P2:*—Think <> self!        324|   MS:want. My   *P2:*want my
325|   MS:say—'I   *CP2:*say 'I <> you.   *P3:*say, 'I <> you—   *CP3:*say 'I
326|   MS:angels §over illegible word§ you <> wife,   *P2:*wife   *CP2:*wife!
328|   MS:know   *P2:*know!'        329|   MS:of you married <> have this §over perhaps *the*§ right
*P2:*have the right   *CP2:*of your married   *P3:*of you, married   *CP3:*of your married
*P4:*of you married   *CP4:*of your married        330|   MS:mutter—yes   *P2:*mutter 'Yes
333|   MS:corner! The §crossed out§ Tis the Délivrande   *CP4:*corner! 'Tis The Ravissante
334|   MS:of Paris. See, The §altered to§ She        335|   MS:beckons, she §altered to§ She

Then!"—

     A sublime spring from the balustrade
About the tower so often talked about,
340  A flash in middle air, and stone-dead lay
Monsieur Léonce Miranda on the turf.


A gardener who watched, at work the while
Dibbling a flower-bed for geranium-shoots,
Saw the catastrophe, and, straightening back,
345  Stood up and shook his brows. "Poor soul, poor soul!
Just what I prophesied the end would be!
Ugh—the Red Night-cap!" (as he raised the head)
"This must be what he meant by those strange words
While I was weeding larkspurs yesterday,
350  'Angels would take him!' Mad!"


               No! sane, I say.
Such being the conditions of his life,
Such end of life was not irrational.
Hold a belief, you only half-believe,
With all-momentous issues either way,—
355  And I advise you imitate this leap,
Put faith to proof, be cured or killed at once!

---

339|  MS:§line added between present ll. 338 and 340§     341|  MS:Monsieur Antoine
Mellerio on <> turf. beneath. §crossed out§   *CP4:*Monsieur Alphonse §crossed out and
replaced above by§ Léonce Miranda on    341-42|  MS:§no ¶§  *P2:*§¶§
344|  MS:straitening   *1889a:*straightening    345|  MS:his head §crossed out and replaced
above by§ brows "Poor  *P2:*brows—"Poor  *CP2:*brows "Poor  *CP3:*brows. "Poor  *1873:*soul
*C1873:*soul!    347|  MS:§line added between present ll. 346 and 348§ the Red night cap!'
(As  *P2:*the Red Night-cap!" (as    348|  MS:by muttering,  *P2:*by those strange words
349|  MS:was at the §last two words crossed out and replaced above by§ weeding larkspurs,
yesterday, §crossed out and replaced above by three words§ this day week, §last three words
crossed out, restoring original reading§  *1889a:*larkspurs yesterday,    350|  MS:'Angels
§over illegible word§ must §crossed out and replaced above by§ would <> him!' Mad!" §¶§ No;
sane, I  *P2:*§¶§ No; sane; I  *CP2:*§¶§ No! sane, I    351|  MS:of a life,  *P2:*of his life,
352|  MS:was §over perhaps *is*§ wholly §crossed out and replaced above by§ not rational §altered
to§ irrational.    353|  MS:Hold §over perhaps *have*§    355|  MS:§line added between
present ll. 354 and 356§ this man,  *P2:*this leap,    356|  MS:proof §over illegible word§

Call you men, killed through cutting cancer out,
The worse for such an act of bravery?
That's more than *I* know. In my estimate,
360   Better lie prostrate on his turf at peace,
Than, wistful, eye, from out the tent, the tower,
Racked with a doubt "Will going on bare knees
All the way to The Ravissante and back,
Saying my Ave Mary all the time, ·
365   Somewhat excuse if I postpone my march?
—Make due amends for that one kiss I gave
In gratitude to her who held me out
Superior Fricquot's sermon, hot from press,
A-spread with hands so sinful yet so smooth?"

370   And now, sincerely do I pray she stand,
Clara, with interposing sweep of robe,
Between us and this horror! Any screen
Turns white by contrast with the tragic pall;
And her dubiety distracts at least,

---

357| MS:Killed was the man, §last four words transposed to§ Was the man, killed by §crossed out and replaced above by§ through < > out,? §question mark crossed out§ *P2:*Call you man
*C1873:*men    358| MS:§line added between present ll. 357 and 359§    359| MS:than I
*CP2:*than *I*    360| MS:lie flat §crossed out and replaced above by§ prostrate upon §altered to§ on his face this way, §last three words crossed out and replaced above by three words§ turf at peace,    361| MS:Than sit indoors to read the Univers §last six words crossed out and replaced above by eight words§ wistful eye, from §over illegible word§ out the tent, the towers," *P2:*wistful, eye < > tent, the tower,    362| MS:with the §crossed out and replaced above by§ a doubt—would §crossed out and replaced above by§ will going on both knees *P2:*doubt—Will *CP2:*doubt "Will < > on bare knees    363| MS:Presently to the Délivrande and *P2:*All the way to *CP4:*to The Ravissante and    364| MS:the while, *CP2:*the time,
365| MS:§line added between present ll. 364 and 366§    366| MS:Make < > gave,
*P2:*—Make *CP2:*gave    367| MS:gratitude the hand that §last three words crossed out and replaced above by three words§ to her who held it me,— *P2:*held me out,— *CP2:*out
368| MS:§line added between present ll. 367 and 369§ Superior Picot's sermon < > press,—
*CP2:*press, *CP4:*Superior Fricquot's sermon    369| MS:yet so dear §crossed out and replaced above by§ smooth?" *P2:*smooth? *CP2:*smooth?" *P3:*smooth? *CP3:*smooth?"
370| MS:And now how gladly §last three words crossed out and replaced above by§ sincerely < > pray you §crossed out and replaced above by§ she *P2:*And now, sincerely
371| MS:§line added between present ll. 370 and 372§ Anna, with *CP4:*Clara, with
373| MS:pall: *P2:*pall;    374| MS:And your §crossed out and replaced above by§ her

<sup>375</sup> As well as snow, from such decided black.
With womanhood, at least, we have to do:
Ending with Clara—is the word too kind?

Let pass the shock! There's poignancy enough
When what one parted with, a minute since,
<sup>380</sup> Alive and happy, is returned a wreck—
All that was, all that seemed about to be,
Razed out and ruined now for evermore,
Because a straw descended on this scale
Rather than that, made death o'erbalance life.
<sup>385</sup> But think of cage-mates in captivity,
Inured to day-long, night-long vigilance
Each of the other's tread and angry turn
If behind prison-bars the jailer knocked:
These whom society shut out, and thus
<sup>390</sup> Penned in, to settle down and regulate
By the strange law, the solitary life—
When death divorces such a fellowship,
Theirs may pair off with that prodigious woe
Imagined of a ghastly brotherhood—
<sup>395</sup> One watcher left in lighthouse out at sea

---

<sup>375|</sup>  MS:well as snow-*skin* ermine §-*skin* and *ermine,* crossed out§ from such decided §inserted
above§ black!  *P2:*snow, from <> black.        <sup>376|</sup>  MS:With whitish §crossed out§
womanhood, at least, §last two words inserted above§        <sup>377|</sup>  MS:The §added in margin§
Ending §altered to§ ending with §crossed out§ Anna—is  *P2:*Ending with Anna  *CP4:*with
Clara—is        <sup>378|</sup>  MS:shock: there's  *P2:*shock! There's        <sup>379|</sup>  MS:what you §crossed
out and replaced above by§ one <> with a <> since  *P2:*with, a <> since,
<sup>380|</sup>  MS:happy is  *P2:*happy, is        <sup>382|</sup>  MS:for ever more  *P2:*for evermore,
<sup>384|</sup>  MS:o'er-balance  *1889a:*o'erbalance        <sup>385|</sup>  MS:But here, these cage-mates
*CP2:*But think of cage-mates        <sup>386|</sup>  MS:"Bound §crossed out§ Inured <> day-long night-
long  *P2:*day-long, night-long        <sup>388|</sup>  MS:When bolt came captive upon prison-bars:
*P2:*When, bolt captive came on prison-bars:  *CP2:*When, bolt on prison-bars, a captive came!
*1873:*came  *C1873:*If, behind prison-bars, the jailer knocked  *1889a:*If behind prison-bars the
<sup>389|</sup>  MS:These two, society <> out and  *P2:*out, and  *C1873:*These whom society
<sup>391-93|</sup>  MS:By the strange law, §last four words inserted above§ The §altered to§ the <> life— /
This may §inserted above§ pairs §altered to§ pair <> that old §crossed out§ prodious
*P2:*life— / When death divorces from such fellowship, / This <> prodigious  *CP2:* / <>
divorces such a fellowship, /  *C1873:* / <> fellowship, / Theirs may        <sup>394|</sup>  MS:of the
§crossed out and replaced above by§ a        <sup>395|</sup>  MS:The §altered to§ One watcher in the light-
house out  *P2:*lighthouse <> sea,  *CP2:*watcher left in lighthouse  *1889a:*sea

With leagues of surf between the land and him
Alive with his dead partner on the rock;
One galley-slave, whom curse and blow compel
To labour on, ply oar—beside his chain,
400      Encumbered with a corpse-companion now.
Such these: although, no prisoners, self-entrenched
They kept the world off from their barricade.


Memory, gratitude was poignant, sure,
Though pride brought consolation of a kind.
405      Twenty years long had Clara been—of whom
The rival, nay, the victor, past dispute?
What if in turn The Ravissante at length
Proved victor—which was doubtful—anyhow,
Here lay the inconstant with, conspicuous too,
410      The fruit of his good fortune!

---

³⁹⁶| MS:With miles of   *P2:*With leagues of < > him,   *1889a:*him
³⁹⁷| MS:rock:   *CP2:*rock;        ³⁹⁸| MS:Or galley-slave whom   *P2:*One galley-slave, whom
³⁹⁹| MS:labour at the oar—beside his §crossed out and replaced above by§ a chains §altered to§
chain,   *P2:*beside his chain,   *CP2:*labour on at oar   *C1873:*on, ply oar
⁴⁰⁰| MS:with his corpse-companion   *1889a:*with a corpse-companion
⁴⁰¹| MS:But you §crossed out and replaced above by§ these were brave,—no prisoners, you def
§last two words crossed out§ self-entrenched   *P2:*Such these: although, no < > self-entrenched,
*1889a:*self-entrenched        ⁴⁰²| MS:You §crossed out and replaced above by§ They < > from
your §crossed out and replaced above by§ their        ⁴⁰³| MS:Well, then §last two words
crossed out and replaced above by§ Beside,—the gratitude was hard to bear— §last three words
crossed out and replaced above by two words§ poignant, sure,   *CP2:*Memory, gratitude
*P3:*Memory, the gratitude   *CP3:*Memory, gratitude        ⁴⁰⁴| MS:§line added between
present ll. 403 and 405§        ⁴⁰⁵| MS:Near twenty years and you §last two words crossed out
and replaced below by two words§ since she had been   *P2:*Twenty years long, had Anna been   .
*1873:*had Clara been   *1889a:*long had        ⁴⁰⁶| MS:rival, if not §last two words crossed out
and replaced above by two words§ nay, the        ⁴⁰⁷| MS:Had She proved victor §last four
words crossed out and replaced above by§ Though in her turn the Délivrande §last two words
inserted above§ at length,—   *P2:*What if in turn   *CP2:*length   *CP4:*turn The Ravissante at
⁴⁰⁸| MS:Proved victor,—§last two words added in margin§ And even that §last three words
crossed out§ which §inserted above§ was doubtful,—any how,   *CP2:*victor—which < >
doubtful? any how,   *CP3:*doubtful—any   *1889a:*anyhow,        ⁴⁰⁹| MS:There §altered to§
Here < > the lover, and §last two words crossed out and replaced above by two words§
inconstant, with, conspicuously §altered to§ conspicuous   *P2:*inconstant, as conspicuous
*CP2:*inconstant with, conspicuous        ⁴¹⁰| MS:The fruits §altered to§ fruit < > fortune. §no
¶§ "Has   *P2:*fortune! §¶§ "Has   *1889a:* §no ¶; emended to restore ¶; see Editorial Notes§

"Has he gained
By leaving me?" she might soliloquize:
"All love could do, I did for him. I learned
By heart his nature, what he loved and loathed,
Leaned to with liking, turned from with distaste.
415    No matter what his least velleity,
I was determined he should want no wish,
And in conformity administered
To his requirement; most of joy I mixed
With least of sorrow in life's daily draught,
420    Twenty years long, life's proper average.
And when he got to quarrel with my cup,
Would needs outsweeten honey, and discard
That gall-drop we require lest nectar cloy,—
I did not call him fool, and vex my friend,
425    But quietly allowed experiment,
Encouraged him to spice his drink, and now
Grate *lignum vitæ*, now bruise so-called grains
Of Paradise, and pour now, for perfume,
Distilment rare, the rose of Jericho,
430    Holy-thorn, passion-flower, and what know I?

---

413| MS:what he §over illegible word§ liked §crossed out and replaced above by§ loved
414| MS:Made for §last two words crossed out and replaced above by two words§ Leaned to
§word inserted above and crossed out§ with §crossed out and restored§ liking, moved §crossed
out and replaced above by§ turned from with §§crossed out and replaced above by word
illegible crossed out, restoring original reading§ distaste;   *P2:*distaste.
416|   MS:wish—   *P2:*wish,            417|   MS:And thereupon §crossed out and replaced above by
two words§ in conformity administered the world §last two words crossed out§
418|   MS:For twenty years §last three words crossed out§ to §altered to§ To its §crossed out and
replaced above by§ his requirement: I mixed the §crossed out§ most of joy §last five words
transposed to§ most of joy I mixed   *CP2:*requirement; most            419|   MS:The §crossed out§
With §added in margin§ least < > draught   *P2:*draught,            420|   MS:For §crossed out§
Twenty years, §comma crossed out§ long, §inserted above§            422|   MS:out-sweeten honey
and   *CP2:*honey, and   *1889a:*outsweeten            423|   MS:That §over The§ gall-drop which
§crossed out§ we want §crossed out and replaced above by§ require            426|   MS:to dust his
< > and grate §crossed out§ now   *1889a:*to spice his            427|   MS:Now §crossed out and
replaced above by§ Grate < > *vitie*, < > bruise balsam seeds §last two words crossed out and
replaced above by§ so-called   *P2:vitae*            428-29|   MS:§one line revised into two lines§ Of
Paradise, pluck §crossed out and replaced above by eight words§ and now, for perfume, pour /
Distillment rare, the   *C1873:*and pour now, for perfume, /            430|   MS:Perfume with §last
two words crossed out and replaced above by§ Holy-thorn, < > I,   *P2:*know I?

Till beverage obtained the fancied smack.
'Twas wild-flower-wine that neither helped nor harmed
Who sipped and held it for restorative—
What harm? But here has he been through the hedge
435   Straying in search of simples, while my back
Was turned a minute, and he finds a prize,
Monkshood and belladonna! O my child,
My truant little boy, despite the beard,
The body two feet broad and six feet long,
440   And what the calendar counts middle age—
You wanted, did you, to enjoy a flight?
Why not have taken into confidence
Me, that was mother to you?—never mind
What mock disguise of mistress held you mine!
445   Had you come laughing, crying, with request,
'Make me fly, mother!' I had run upstairs
And held you tight the while I danced you high
In air from tower-top, singing 'Off we go
(On pilgrimage to Lourdes some day next month)
450   And swift we soar (to Rome with Peter-pence)
And low we light (at Paris where we pick
Another jewel from our store of stones
And send it for a present to the Pope)!'
So, dropt indeed you were, but on my knees,

---

431|  MS:Fill §crossed out§ Till §added in margin§ beverage till it §last two words crossed out§ gained §altered to§ obtained the rightful §crossed out and replaced above by§ fancied
432|  MS:§line added between present ll. 431 and 433§ wild-flower-wine, that did §crossed out§ helped   *CP2*:wild-flower-wine that     433|  MS:He §crossed out and replaced below by§ Who <> restorative;   *P2*:held such for restorative—   *CP2*:held it for     439|  MS:And §crossed out and replaced above by§ The     441|  MS:to take §crossed out and replaced above by two words§ enjoy a flight? from me? §last two words crossed out§     442|  MS:have §word illegibly crossed out§ taken     443|  MS:Me that   *CP2*:Me, that     445|  MS:crying, looked at me, §last three words crossed out and replaced above by two words§ with request,
446|  MS:"Make <> Mother!" I <> up-stairs   *P2*:'Make <> Mother!' I <> upstairs
448|  MS:from top of tower, sung "Off   *P2*:sung 'Off   *CP2*:from tower-top, singing 'Off
449|  MS:next year §crossed out and replaced above by§ month)     450|  MS:And on §crossed out and replaced above by§ swift we fly §crossed out and replaced above by§ soar *P2*:with Peter-pence),   *CP2*:with Peter-pence)     451|  MS:And down §crossed out and replaced above by§ low we drop §crossed out and replaced above by§ light     453|  MS:it for §inserted above§ a <> Pope)   *P2*:the Pope);   *CP2*:the Pope)!'     454|  MS:And §crossed out and replaced above by§ So, dropped <> knees   *P2*:knees,   *CP2*:dropt

<sup>455</sup> Rolling and crowing, not a whit the worse
For journey to your Ravissante and back.
Now, no more Clairvaux—which I made you build,
And think an inspiration of your own—
No more fine house, trim garden, pretty park,
<sup>460</sup> Nothing I used to busy you about,
And make believe you worked for my surprise!
What weariness to me will work become
Now that I need not seem surprised again!
This boudoir, for example, with the doves
<sup>465</sup> (My stupid maid has damaged, dusting one)
Embossed in stucco o'er the looking-glass
Beside the toilet-table! dear—dear me!"


Here she looked up from her absorbing grief,
And round her, crow-like grouped, the Cousinry,
<sup>470</sup> (She grew aware) sat witnesses at watch.
For, two days had elapsed since fate befell
The courser in the meadow, stretched so stark.
They did not cluster on the tree-tops, close
Their sooty ranks, caw and confabulate
<sup>475</sup> For nothing: but, like calm determined crows,

---

<sup>455|</sup> MS:a bit the    *1889a:*a whit the        <sup>456|</sup> MS:to the Délivrande and    *CP4:*to your
Ravissante and        <sup>457|</sup> MS:more Tailleville—that §crossed out and replaced above by§ which
*CP4:*more Clairvaux—which        <sup>459|</sup> MS:§line added between present ll. 458 and 460§ more
fine §inserted above§ house, trim §inserted above§ garden, pretty §inserted above§ park, §line
break called for§ and §crossed out§        <sup>460-61|</sup> MS:§one line revised into two lines§ All that I
made you do §last four words crossed out and replaced above by six words§ I used to busy you
about, / And made believe you did §last five words inserted below§ for    *P2:* / <> you worked
for    *CP2:*Nothing I <> /    *1873:* / <> surprise    *C1873:* / <> surprise!
<sup>462|</sup> MS:will things become    *CP2:*will work become
<sup>463|</sup> MS:not be §crossed out and replaced above by§ seem <> again—    *P2:*again!
<sup>465|</sup> MS:§line added between present ll. 464 and 466§        <sup>466|</sup> MS:stucco, and the looking-
glass,    *P2:*looking-glass    *CP2:*stucco o'er the        <sup>467|</sup> MS:§line added between present ll.
466 and 468§ toilet-table—dear    *P2:*toilet-table! dear        <sup>469|</sup> MS:crow-like were §crossed
out and replaced above by§ stood §crossed out and replaced by§ grouped, the cousinry,
*P2:*the Cousinry,        <sup>470|</sup> MS:§line added between present ll. 469 and 471§ She <> aware,
were witnesses <> watch;    *P2:*aware, sat witnesses    *CP2:*(She <> aware) sat <> watch.
<sup>473|</sup> MS:do    *CP2:*did        <sup>474|</sup> MS:confabulate,    *CP2:*confabulate        <sup>475|</sup> MS:nothing:
They were §last two words crossed out and replaced above by two words§ but, like

They came to take possession of their corpse.
And who shall blame them? Had not they the right?

One spoke. "They would be gentle, not austere.
They understood and were compassionate.
480  Madame Muhlhausen lay too abject now
For aught but the sincerest pity; still,
Since plain speech salves the wound it seems to make,
They must speak plainly—circumstances spoke!
Sin had conceived and brought forth death indeed.
485  As the commencement so the close of things:
Just what might be expected all along!
Monsieur Léonce Miranda launched his youth
Into a cesspool of debauchery,
And if he thence emerged all dripping slime,
490  Where was the change except from thin to thick,
One warm rich mud-bath, Madame?—you, in place
Of Paris-drainage and distilment, you
He never needed budge from, boiled to rags!
True, some good instinct left the natural man,
495  Some touch of that deep dye wherewith imbued

---

476-78|  MS:And §crossed out and replaced above by§ They <> of the corpse. / §¶§ One <>
gentle as in §last two words crossed out§ not    P2:of their corpse. / §¶§ <> gentle, not
CP4:corpse. / §no ¶§ And who shall blame them? Had not they the right? / §¶§ One
479|  MS:understood, and    1889a:understood and          480|  MS:Madame Debacker lay
CP4:Madame Muhlhausen lay        481|  MS:sincerest sympathy: §crossed out§ pity: still,
P2:pity; still   CP2:still,        482|  MS:Still §crossed out and replaced above by§ Since <>
speech may imply s §last two words and letter crossed out and replaced above by three words§
salves the wound      483|  MS:§line added between present ll. 482 and 484§ plainly.
Circumstances spoke—   P2:plainly—circumstances   CP2:spoke!
485|  MS:commencement, so <> things! §altered to§ things:    1889a:commencement so
487|  MS:Monsieur Antoine Mellerio early §crossed out§ launched   CP4:Monsieur Alphonse
§crossed out and replaced above by§ Léonce Miranda launched
488|  MS:Into extravagant §crossed out and replaced above by three words§ a cesspool of
489|  MS:if he §crossed out and replaced above by word illegibly crossed out, restoring original
reading§ <> emerged, all dripping wet, §crossed out§ slime,   P2:emerged all
CP2:And, if   1889a:And if          490|  MS:Why §altered to§ Where <> thick—   CP2:"Where
<> thick,   1873:—"Where   1889a:Where          494|  MS:True, the good instinct of the
P2:True, some good instinct left the          495|  MS:The tinge §last two words crossed out and
replaced above by two words§ Some touch of that §inserted above§          496|  MS:education in
his earlier §crossed out and replaced above by§ happier   P2:education, in

By education, in his happier day,
The hopeful offspring of high parentage
Was fleece-marked moral and religious sheep,—
Some ruddle, faint remainder, (we admit)
500  Stuck to Miranda, rubbed he ne'er so rude
Against the goatly coarseness: to the last,
Moral he styled himself, religious too!
Which means—what ineradicable good
You found, you never left till good's self proved
505  Perversion and distortion, nursed to growth
So monstrous, that the tree-stock, dead and dry,
Were seemlier far than such a heap grotesque
Of fungous flourishing excrescence. Here
Sap-like affection, meant for family,
510  Stole off to feed one sucker fat—yourself;
While branchage, trained religiously aloft
To rear its head in reverence to the sun,
Was pulled down earthward, pegged and picketed,
By topiary contrivance, till the tree
515  Became an arbour where, at vulgar ease,
Sat superstition grinning through the loops.
Still, nature is too strong or else too weak
For cockney treatment: either, tree springs back

---

497| MS:of such §crossed out and replaced above by§ high     499| MS:Some ruddle,
§inserted above§ faint remainder, we admit,   *P2*:remainder, (we admit)
500| MS:to Mellerio, rubbed   *CP4*:to Miranda, rubbed     502| MS:too—   *P2*:too!
503| MS:means—the ineradicable good,   *P2*:means—what ineradicable   *1889a*:good
504| MS:§line added between present ll. 503 and 505§     506| MS:monstrous that
the plant-stalk §crossed out and replaced above by§ tree-stock dead <> dry   *P2*:monstrous,
that <> tree-stock, dead <> dry,     507| MS:seemlier far §inserted above§ than such
flourishing §crossed out and replaced above by two words§ a heap grotesque—
*P2*:grotesque     508| MS:§line added in margin§ excrescence. Here,   *1889a*:excrescence.
Here     509| MS:Sap-like §inserted above§ Affectionateness §altered to§ Affection to the
family   *P2*:affection <> family,   *CP2*:affection, meant for family,     510| MS:off and fed
one   *CP2*:off to feed one     511| MS:branchage, meant religiously   *CP2*:branchage trained
religiously   *P2*:branchage, atried religiously   *CP3*:branchage, trained religiously
514| MS:§line added between present ll. 513 and 515§     515| MS:where at <> ease
*CP2*:where, at <> ease,     516| MS:Sat Superstition   *P2*:superstition
517| MS:But §crossed out and replaced above by§ Still,     518| MS:treatment—or the §last
two words crossed out and replaced above by§ either, tree   *P2*:treatment: either

To pristine shape, or else degraded droops,
520    And turns to touchwood at the heart. So here—
Body and mind, at last the man gave way.
His body—there it lies, what part was left
Unmutilated! for, the strife commenced
Two years ago, when both hands burnt to ash,
525    —A branch broke loose, by loss of what choice twigs!
As for his mind—behold our register
Of all its moods, from the incipient mad,
Nay, mere erratic, to the stark insane,
Absolute idiocy or what is worse!
530    All have we catalogued—extravagance
In worldly matters, luxury absurd,
And zeal as crazed in its expenditure
Of nonsense called devotion. Don't we know
—We Cousins, bound in duty to our kin,—
535    What mummeries were practised by you two
At Clairvaux? Not a servant got discharge
But came and told his grievance, testified
To acts which turn religion to a farce.
And as the private mock, so patent—see—
540    The public scandal! Ask the neighbourhood—
Or rather, since we asked them long ago,
Read what they answer, depositions down,
Signed, sealed and sworn to! Brief, the man was mad.
We are his heirs and claim our heritage.

---

519|   MS:or withers in despair— §last three words crossed out and replaced above by three
words§ else degraded droops,        520|   MS:§line added between present ll. 519 and 521§ to
powder §crossed out and replaced above by§ touchwood        522|   MS:His §over *The*§
523|   MS:Unmutilated, when §crossed out and replaced above by§ for the < > commenced—
§dash crossed out§   *P2:*Unmutilated! for, the        524|   MS:§line added between present ll.
523 and 525§ ago—when, both   *P2:*ago, when, both   *1889a:*when both
525|   MS:A < > loose, but lost what twigs thereby!   *CP2:*loose by loss of what choice twigs!
*P3:*loose, by loss what   *CP2:*loss of what   *C1873:*—A        526|   MS:for the mind
*CP2:*for his mind        527|   MS:moods from   *CP2:*moods, from        529|   MS:is worst!
*P2:*is worse!        531|   MS:matters of expen §last two words crossed out and replaced above by§
luxury        533|   MS:know,   *CP2:*know        534|   MS:—We cousins   *P2:*—We Cousins
536|   MS:At Tailleville? Not a servant, turned away, §last two words crossed out and replaced
above by two words§ got discharge   *CP4:*At Clairvaux? Not
539|   MS:so, patent   *P2:*so patent        542|   MS:answer—depositions   *P2:*answer, depositions
544|   MS:and take §crossed out and replaced above by§ claim

545 Madame Muhlhausen,—whom good taste forbids
We qualify as do these documents,—
Fear not lest justice stifle mercy's prayer!
True, had you lent a willing ear at first,
Had you obeyed our call two years ago,
550 Restrained a certain insolence of eye,
A volubility of tongue, that time,
Your prospects had been none the worse, perhaps.
Still, fear not but a decent competence
Shall smooth the way for your declining age!
555 What we propose, then . . . "

                            Clara dried her eyes,
Sat up, surveyed the consistory, spoke
After due pause, with something of a smile.

"Gentlemen, kinsfolk of my friend defunct,
In thus addressing me—of all the world!—
560 You much misapprehend what part I play.
I claim no property you speak about.
You might as well address the park-keeper,
Harangue him on some plan advisable
For covering the park with cottage-plots.
565 He is the servant, no proprietor,
His business is to see the sward kept trim,
Untrespassed over by the indiscreet:
Beyond that, he refers you to myself—
Another servant of another kind—
570 Who again—quite as limited in act—

---

545| MS:Madame Debacker,—whom  *CP4:*Madame Muhlhausen,—whom
547| MS:not our §crossed out and replaced above by§ that justice means no §last two words
crossed out and replaced above by§ stifles §word inserted above and illegibly crossed out§
mercy's here §crossed out§ prayer!  *P2:*not lest justice stifle mercy's   549| MS:obeyed the
call  *P2:*obeyed our call   550| MS:eye  *P2:*eye,   551| MS:And §crossed out and
replaced above by word illegibly crossed out, restoring original reading§ volubility
*P2:*A volubility   555| MS:then . . . " §¶§ Anna dried  *CP2:*then . . " §¶§ Anna  *CP4:*§¶§
Clara dried   *1889a:* then . . . " §¶§ Clara   556| MS:Sate <> consistory, said §crossed out§
spoke  *P2:*Sat <> spoke,   *1889a:*spoke   557| MS:pause with <> smile:
*P2:*pause, with   *CP2:*smile.   564| MS:Of covering <> with cottages:—  *P2:*For covering
<> with cottage-plots:—  *CP2:*cottage-plots.   567| MS:indiscreet,  *P2:*indiscreet:

Refer you, with your projects,—can I else?
To who in mastery is ultimate,
The Church. The Church is sole administrant,
Since sole possessor of what worldly wealth
575  Monsieur Léonce Miranda late possessed.
Often enough has he attempted, nay,
Forced me, well-nigh, to occupy the post
You seemingly suppose I fill,—receive
As gift the wealth entrusted me as grace.
580  This—for quite other reasons than appear
So cogent to your perspicacity—
This I refused; and, firm as you could wish,
Still was my answer 'We two understand
Each one the other. I am intimate
585  —As how can be mere fools and knaves—or, say,
Even your Cousins?—with your love to me,
Devotion to the Church. Would Providence
Appoint, and make me certain of the same,
That I survive you (which is little like,
590  Seeing you hardly overpass my age
And more than match me in abundant health)
In such case, certainly I would accept
Your bounty: better I than alien hearts
Should execute your planned benevolence
595  To man, your proposed largess to the Church.
But though I be survivor,—weakly frame,

---

<sup>572</sup>| MS:To what in   *P2:*To who in       <sup>573</sup>| MS:administrant   *P2:*The Church: the Church
*CP2:*The Church. The Church <> administrant,       <sup>575</sup>| MS:Monsieur Antoine Mellerio late
*CP4:*Monsieur Alphonse §crossed out and replaced above by§ Léonce Miranda late
<sup>579</sup>| MS:grace.   *CP2:*grace.       <sup>580</sup>| MS:This,—for   *P2:*This—for
<sup>581</sup>| MS:perspicacity,—   *1889a:*perspicacity—       <sup>582</sup>| MS:refused; and §over illegible
word§       <sup>583</sup>| MS:answer: 'We   *CP2:*answer 'We       <sup>585</sup>| MS:be the universe—or say,
*P2:*be the fools and knaves—or, say,   *CP4:*be mere fools       <sup>586</sup>| MS:Your cousins?—with
your utter love   *P2:*Your Cousins   *CP4:*Even your Cousins?—with your love
<sup>587</sup>| MS:Utter devotion to <> Church: §altered to§ Church. did §altered to§ Did fate
*CP4:*Devotion to the Church. Would Providence       <sup>588</sup>| MS:Decree, and   *CP4:*Appoint,
and       <sup>589</sup>| MS:you—which   *P2:*you (which       <sup>591</sup>| MS:health—   *P2:*health)
<sup>593</sup>| MS:bounty, better   *P2:*bounty: better       <sup>594</sup>| MS:Could §altered to§ Should
<sup>595</sup>| MS:the Church:   *P2:*the Church.       <sup>596</sup>| MS:frame   *P2:*frame,

With only woman's wit to make amends,—
When I shall die, or while I am alive,
Cannot you figure me an easy mark
600    For hypocritical rapacity,
Kith, kin and generation, couching low
Ever on the alert to pounce on prey?
Far be it I should say they profited
By that first frenzy-fit themselves induced,—
605    Cold-blooded scenical buffoons at sport
With horror and damnation o'er a grave:
That were too shocking—I absolve them there!
Nor did they seize the moment of your swoon
To rifle pocket, wring a paper thence,
610    Their Cousinly dictation, and enrich
Thereby each mother's son as heart could wish,
Had nobody supplied a codicil.
But when the pain, poor friend! had prostrated
Your body, though your soul was right once more,
615    I fear they turned your weakness to account!
Why else to me, who agonizing watched,
Sneak, cap in hand, now bribe me to forsake
My maimed Léonce, now bully, cap on head,
The impudent pretension to assuage

---

[597]| MS:And §crossed out and replaced above by§ With <> to counsel me,—
*P2:*to make amends,—    [599]| MS:easy prey  *CP4:*easy mark    [600]| MS:To those
rapacious cousin-hypocrites,  *CP2:*rapacious Cousin-hypocrites,  *CP4:*For hypocritical rapacity,
[601]| MS:low,  *1889a:*low    [602]| MS:On the <> on luckless me?  *P2:*Ever on the <> on
me?  *CP4:*pounce on prey?    [603]| MS:Do you forget how far they  *CP4:*Far be it I should
say they    [606-8]| MS:grave? / Did not they sieze  *P2:* / <> seize  *CP4:*grave: / That were
too shocking—I absolve them there! / Nor did they    [609]| MS:a Will from you,
*CP4:*a paper thence,    [610]| MS:Their rascally dictation, wh §crossed out§ and inrich
§altered to§ enrich  *CP4:*Their Cousinly dictation    [611]| MS:The knaves, each <> son of
them, enough  *P2:*The rogues, each  *CP4:*Thereby each <> son as heart could wish,
[612]| MS:codicil?  *CP4:*codicil.    [613]| MS:And when  *CP4:*But when
[614]| MS:The body though the soul <> right again,  *P2:*body, though  *CP4:*Your body, though
your soul  *1889a:*right once more,    [615]| MS:Did not they turn your <> account
*CP4:*I fear they turned your <> account!    [616]| MS:And come §crossed out and replaced
above by§ sneak to me, in §crossed out and replaced above by§ who <> watched,—
*CP4:*Why else to <> watched,    [617]| MS:And, §crossed out and replaced above by§ Not,
cap  *CP2:*And, cap  *CP4:*Sneak, cap    [618]| MS:maimed Antoine, now  *CP4:*maimed
Alphonse §crossed out and replaced above by§ Léonce, now    [619]| MS:impudent
pretender to  *CP2:*My impudent pretention to  *CP3:*pretension  *CP4:*The impudent

<sup></sup>620     Such sorrows as demanded Cousins' care?—
    *For you rejected, hated, fled me, far*
    *In foreign lands you laughed at me!*—they judged.
    And, think you, will the unkind ones hesitate
    To try conclusions with my helplessness,—
625     To pounce on and misuse your derelict,
    Helped by advantage that bereavement lends
    Folk, who, while yet you lived, played tricks like these?
    You only have to die, and they detect,
    In all you said and did, insanity!
630     Your faith was fetish-worship, your regard
    For Christ's prime precept which endows the poor
    And strips the rich, a craze from first to last!
    They so would limn your likeness, paint your life,
    That if it ended by some accident,—
635     For instance, if, attemptmg to arrange
    The plants below that dangerous Belvedere
    I cannot warn you from sufficiently,
    You lost your balance and fell headlong—fine
    Occasion, such, for crying *Suicide!*
640     *Non compos mentis*, naturally next,

---

620| MS:Those sorrows which demand a cousin's care?— P2:Such sorrows as demand
CP2:a Cousin's CP4:as demanded Cousin's 1889a:demanded Cousins'
621| MS:'For §crossed out and replaced above by§ 'Since you CP2:'For you 1873:For <> far
622| MS:me,'—they lied; §altered to§ lied. CP2:me!'—they CP4:they judged.
1873:In <> me!—they 623| MS:While you §last two words crossed out and replaced above
by three words§ And, think you <> the miscreants hesitate CP4:the unkind ones hesitate
625| MS:§line added between present ll. 624 and 626§ Pounce at §over on§ and plunder me, the
derelict, CP2:To pounce on, plunder CP4:on, misuse me your derelict
1873:me, your 1889a:on and misuse your 626| MS:At such §last two words crossed out
and replaced below by two words§ Helped by advantage that §over as§ bereavement lends,
P2:lends 627| MS:These §crossed out and replaced below by§ Rogues who
CP4:Folks, who 1889a:Folk 628| MS:detect CP2:detect,
629| MS:you said §over say§ and did, §over do§ insanity: P2:insanity!
631| MS:precept that endows P2:precept which endows 632| MS:craze: §colon crossed
out§ from 633| MS:So would they limn CP2:They so would limn
636| MS:dangerous balustrade §crossed out§ Belvedere 639| MS:Occasion, that, for crying
"Suicide"! P2:crying 'Suicide!' CP2:Occasion, such, for 1873:crying *Suicide!*
640| MS:"*Non <> mentis*," naturally P2:'*Non <> mentis*,' naturally 1873:*Non <> mentis*, naturally

Hands over Clairvaux to a Cousin-tribe
Who nor like me nor love The Ravissante:
Therefore be ruled by both! Life-interest
In Clairvaux,—conservation, guardianship
645 Of earthly good for heavenly purpose,—give
Such and no other proof of confidence!
Let Clara represent the Ravissante!'
—To whom accordingly, he then and there
Bequeathed each stick and stone, by testament
650 In holograph, mouth managing the quill:
Go, see the same in Londres, if you doubt!"

Then smile grew laugh, as sudden up she stood
And out she spoke: intemperate the speech!

"And now, sirs, for your special courtesy,
655 Your candle held up to the character
Of Lucie Steiner, whom you qualify
As coming short of perfect womanhood.

---

641-43| MS:Hands Tailleville over to your cousin-thieves! / Therefore <> by me! life-interest
*P2:*your Cousin-thieves! / <> Life-interest  *CP4:*Hands over Clairvaux to a Cousin-tribe! / Who
nor like me nor love The Ravissante, / <> by both! Life-interest  *1873:*a Cousin-tribe //
*1889a:* / <> love The Ravissante: /  644| MS:In Tailleville,—conservation  *CP4:*In
Clairvaux,—conservation  645| MS:purpose, give  *P2:*purpose,—give  646| MS:This
and <> confidence,  *P2:*confidence!  *CP4:*Such and  647| MS:Let Anna represent the
Délivrande!"—  *P2:*the Délivrande!"  *CP4:*Let Clara represent the Ravissante!"  *1873:*the
Ravissante!'  648| MS:To which §crossed out and replaced above by§ whom accordingly,
each stick and stone, §last four words and punctuation transposed to l. 649§ he then and there
§last four words and punctuation transposed from l. 649§  *P2:*—To <> there,  *CP4:*there
649| MS:He §altered to§ he then and there §last four words transposed to l. 648§ bequeathed
§altered to§ Bequeathed, §comma crossed out§ each stick and stone, §last four words and
punctuation transposed from l. 648§  650| MS:quill;  *P2:*quill:  651-54| MS:Go see
<> in Douvres, if <> doubt! / §¶§ "And <> special insolence,  *P2:*Go, see <> /
*CP2:*doubt!" / §¶§ Then smile grew laugh, as sudden up she stood. / §¶§ "And  *P3:* / §no ¶§
Then <> / §no ¶§ "And  *CP3:* / §¶§ Then <> / §¶§ "And  *P2:* / §¶§ Then <> / §no §¶§
"And  *CP4:*in Londres, if <> / <> stood. / And out she spoke: intemperate the speech! / §¶§
"And <> special courtesy,  *1873:* / <> stood / And <> /  *1889a:* /// §no ¶; emended to
restore ¶; see Editorial Notes§  655| MS:Kind critics of §last three words crossed out and
replaced above by three words§ Your candle held <> to my §crossed out and replaced above by§
the character! §altered to§ character.  *CP4:*character  656-57| MS:§lines added between
present ll. 655 and 658§  656| MS:Of Sophie Trayer, whom  *CP4:*Of Lucie Steiner, whom
657| MS:As coming §over illegible word§ far short of perfection. Well §crossed out and replaced
above by§ Why—  *P2:*perfection! Why—  *CP4:*coming short of perfect womanhood.

Yes, kindly critics, truth for once you tell!
True is it that through childhood, poverty,
660   Sloth, pressure of temptation, I succumbed,
And, ere I found what honour meant, lost mine.
So was the sheep lost, which the Shepherd found
And never lost again. My friend found me;
Or better say, the Shepherd found us both—
665   Since he, my friend, was much in the same mire
When first we made acquaintance. Each helped each,—
A two-fold extrication from the slough;
And, saving me, he saved himself. Since then,
Unsmirched we kept our cleanliness of coat.
670   It is his perfect constancy, you call
My friend's main fault—he never left his love!
While as for me, I dare your worst, impute
One breach of loving bond, these twenty years,
To me whom only cobwebs bound, you count!
675   'He was religiously disposed in youth!'
That may be, though we did not meet at church.
Under my teaching did he, like you scamps,
Become Voltairian—fools who mock his faith?
'Infirm of body!' I am silent there:
680   Even yourselves acknowledge service done,

---

658|   MS:critics, truth §last two words altered to§ critics! Truth   *P2:*critics, truth
659|   MS:that in childhood   *P2:*that through childhood   660|   MS:By §crossed out and replaced above by§ And pressure <> succumbed   *P2:*succumbed,   *CP2:*temptation I
*CP4:*Sloth, pressure <> temptation, I   661|   MS:And ere   *P2:*And, ere
*CP4:*honor   *1889a:*honour   662|   MS:lost which <> found,   *P2:*lost, which <> found
663|   MS:again: my <> me:   *P2:*again. My <> me;   665|   MS:For he   *P2:*Since he
666|   *CP2:*helped each,— §dash crossed out and restored§   667|   MS:And A §last two words
crossed out and replaced above by§ Wrought two-fold <> slough,   *CP2:*A two-fold <> slough;
668|   MS:then   *P2:*then,   674|   MS:me, whom   *CP4:*me whom
675|   MS:"He <> youth!"   *P2:*'He <> youth!'   676|   MS:church;   *CP2:*church.
677|   MS:Did he become Voltairian, like you all,   *CP2:*you scamps,   *CP4:*become Voltairian like
your scamps,   *C1873:*Under my teaching, §last three words and punctuation transposed from l.
678§ did he, become §altered to§ Become Voltairian §last two words transposed to l. 678§ like
*1889a:*teaching did <> like you scamps,   678|   MS:Under my teaching, you who
*CP4:*teaching, fools who   *C1873:*Become Voltairian— §last two words transposed from l. 677§
fools   679|   MS:"Infirm <> body!"—I   *CP2:*'Infirm <> body!' I

Whatever motive your own souls supply
As inspiration. Love made labour light."

Then laugh grew frown, and frown grew terrible.
Do recollect what sort of person shrieked—
685 "Such was I, saint or sinner, what you please:
And who is it casts stone at me but you?
By your own showing, sirs, you bought and sold,
Took what advantage bargain promised bag,
Abundantly did business, and with whom?
690 The man whom you pronounce imbecile, push
Indignantly aside if he presume
To settle his affairs like other folk!
How is it you have stepped into his shoes
And stand there, bold as brass, 'Miranda, late,
695 Now, Firm-Miranda'? Sane, he signed away
That little birthright, did he? Hence to trade!
I know and he knew who 'twas dipped and ducked,
Truckled and played the parasite in vain,
As now one, now the other, here you cringed,

---

681-82| MS:§¶§ *P2*:§no ¶§· 682-85| MS:made labour §inserted above§ light. / Such one
§crossed out§ was <> please, *P2*: / §¶§ "Such <> please: *CP2*:light. / §¶§ Then laugh grew
frown, and frown grew terrible. / "Such *P3*:light." / §no ¶§ Then <> / §no ¶§ "Such
*CP3*: / §¶§ Then <> / §¶§ "Such *CP4*: / <> terrible. / Do recollect what sort of person
shrieked— / §no ¶§ "Such 686| MS:you— *CP2*:you, *CP4*:you? 687| MS:The
§crossed out and replaced above by§ By <> showing, knaves—who bought *P2*:knaves? who
*CP2*:showing—knaves *CP4*:showing, sirs, you bought 689| MS:With whom abundantly
§inserted above§ did business but the madman here, §last three words crossed out§
*P2*:Abundantly did business, but with whom *CP2*:business, and with whom? *C1873*:whom?—
§dash crossed out§ 690| MS:Mellerio, you *P2*:Mellerio!—you *CP4*:Miranda!—you
*C1873*:The man whom you 693| MS:it that you stepped <> shoes, *CP4*:it you have
stepped *1889a*:shoes 694| MS:stand, as bold as brass, "Mellerio, late, *P2*:stand, there
bold <> late *CP2*:stand there, bold as brass, 'Mellerio, late, *P3*:late *CP2*:late, *P4*:late
*CP4*:brass, 'Miranda, late *C1873*:late, 695| MS:Now, Meller, Brothers? Sane §over
illegible word§ *P2*:Now, Meller, Brothers?" Sane *CP2*:Now, Meller, Brothers?' Sane
*CP4*:Now, Firm-Miranda?' Sane *1889a*:Now, Firm-Miranda'? Sane 696| MS:birthright,
did he? §last two words inserted above§ Out upon §last two words crossed out and replaced
above by two words§ Hence to trade! again! §crossed out§ 697| MS:know you, so did he?
§last three words crossed out and replaced above by three words§ and he knew! You dipped <>
ducked *CP2*:knew who dipped <> ducked, *C1873*:know and <> who 'twas dipped
699| MS:As now one, now the other, §last five words inserted above§ you sneaked here §last
three words transposed to§ here you sneaked, *P2*:sneaked *CP2*:sneaked, *CP4*:you cringed,

700      Were feasted, took our presents, you—those drops
Just for your wife's adornment! you—that spray
Exactly suiting, as most diamonds would,
Your daughter on her marriage! No word then
Of somebody the wanton! Hence, I say,
705      Subscribers to the *Siècle*, every snob—
For here the post brings me the *Univers*!
Home and make money in the Place Vendôme,
Sully yourselves no longer by my sight,
And, when next Schneider wants a new *parure*,
710      Be careful lest you stick there by mischance
That stone beyond compare entrusted you
To kindle faith with, when, Miranda's gift,
Crowning the very crown, the Ravissante
Shall claim it! As to Clairvaux—talk to Her!
715      She answers by the Chapter of Raimbaux!"
Vituperative, truly! All this wrath
Because the man's relations thought him mad!
Whereat, I hope you see the Cousinry
Turn each to other, blankly dolorous,
720      Consult a moment, more by shrug and shrug
Than mere man's language,—finally conclude

---

700| MS:drops,  *1873:*drops      701| MS:adornment, you  *P2:*adornment! you
702| MS:diamonds do,  *C1873:*diamonds would,      703| MS:her marriage-day §altered to§
marriage: no  *P2:*marriage! no  *CP2:*marriage! No      705| MS:the "Siècle," every soul—
*P2:*every snob—  *CP2:*the 'Siècle,' every  *C1873:*the '*Siècle*,' every  *1889a:* the *Siècle*, every
706| MS:me the "Univers!"  *P2:*me the "Univers"!  *CP2:*me the 'Univers'!  *C1873:*me the
'*Univers*'!  *1889a:*me the *Univers*!      707| MS:G §crossed out§ Home <> the Street of Peace,
*CP4:*the Place Vendôme,      709| MS:next Schneider §over illegible word§ wants <> *parure*
*P2:parure*,      710| MS:by mistake  *CP4:*by mischance      712| MS:faith from every §last
two words crossed out and replaced above by§ with, §crossed out§ when, §inserted above§ facet
§altered to§ faceted and §inserted above§ fixed,  *P2:*faith with, when, Mellerio's gift,
*CP4:*when, Miranda's gift,      713| MS:Crowning the §over *thy*§ very crown, the Delivrande!
§exclamation mark crossed out§  *P2:*crown, the Délivrande  *P2:*crown, the Ravissante
714| MS:Shall §added in margin§ Claims §altered to§ Claim it equally with §last two words
crossed out and replaced above by two words§ thanks to Tailleville—talk to her!—
*P2:*claim it: as to <> Her!  *CP2:*it! As  *CP4:*it! As to Clairvaux—talk
715-18| MS:of Bayeux!" / §¶§ Whereat I  *P2:* / §¶§ Whereat, I  *CP4:*of Raimbaux!" /
Vituperative, truly! All for what §last two words crossed out§ this wrath / Because the man's
relations thought him mad! / §no ¶§ Whereat      720| MS:moment, rather §crossed out and
replaced above by two words§ more by shrug with §crossed out and replaced above by§ and
shrug      721| MS:Than by §crossed out and replaced above by§ mere

To leave the reprobate untroubled now
In her unholy triumph, till the Law
Shall right the injured ones; for gentlemen
725   Allow the female sex, this sort at least,
Its privilege. So, simply "Cockatrice!"—
"Jezebel!"—"Queen of the Camellias!"—cried
Cousin to cousin, as yon hinge a-creak
Shut out the party, and the gate returned
730   To custody of Clairvaux. "Pretty place!
What say you, when it proves our property,
To trying a concurrence with La Roche,
And laying down a rival oyster-bed?
Where the park ends, the sea begins, you know."
735   So took they comfort till they came to Vire.

But I would linger, fain to snatch a look
At Clara as she stands in pride of place,
Somewhat more satisfying than my glance
So furtive, so near futile, yesterday,
740   Because one must be courteous. Of the masks
That figure in this little history,
She only has a claim to my respect,
And one-eyed, in her French phrase, rules the blind.

---

<sup>724-27</sup>|   MS:Should right <> one's; §¶§ so §altered to§ So, "Cockatrice"— / "Jezebel"—"Queen <> Camellias!" cried   *P2:*one's. §¶§ So, "Cockatrice!"— / "Jezebel!"—"Queen <> Camellia's!"—cried   *CP2:*Shall right <> /   *CP4:*one; for gentlemen / Can make §last two words crossed out§ Allow §illegible word§ the female sex, this sort at least, / Its privilege. So, simply "Cocaktrice!"— /   <sup>730</sup>|   MS:of Tailleville. "Pretty   *CP4:*of Clairvaux. "Pretty
<sup>731</sup>|   MS:What should you say, when once §crossed out and replaced above by§ proved our   *CP2:*What say you, when it proves our   <sup>732</sup>|   MS:with Courseuilles, §final *s* crossed out§   *CP2:*with Courseulle,   *P3:*with Courseuille,   *CP3:*with Courseulle,   *CP4:*with La Roche,
<sup>733</sup>|   MS:rival-oyster bed?—   *P2:*rival oyster-bed?—   *CP2:*oyster-bed?   <sup>735</sup>|   MS:to Caen,   *P2:*to Caen.   *CP4:*to Vire.   <sup>736</sup>|   MS:But I have lingered, fain   *CP2:*But I would linger, fain   <sup>737</sup>|   MS:§line added between present ll. 736 and 738§ At Anna as   *CP4:*At Clara as
<sup>739</sup>|   MS:futile yesterday,   *P2:*futile, yesterday,   <sup>740</sup>|   MS:the few §crossed out§ masks
<sup>742</sup>|   MS:You §crossed out and replaced above by§ She only have §altered to§ has
<sup>743</sup>|   MS:In your §crossed out and replaced above by§ her French phrase, you §crossed out and replaced above by§ the §crossed out and replaced by§ And one-eyed, §illegible word crossed out and replaced above by§ rules the blind. §line transposed to§ And one-eyed, in her French phrase, rules   *1889a:*blind §emended to§ blind. §see Editorial Notes§

Miranda hardly did his best with life:
745   He might have opened eye, exerted brain,
Attained conception as to right and law
In certain points respecting intercourse
Of man with woman—love, one likes to say;
Which knowledge had dealt rudely with the claim
750   Of Clara to play representative
And from perdition rescue soul, forsooth!
Also, the sense of him should have sufficed
For building up some better theory
Of how God operates in heaven and earth,
755   Than would establish Him participant
In doings yonder at the Ravissante.
The heart was wise according to its lights
And limits; but the head refused more sun,
And shrank into its mew and craved less space.
760   Clara, I hold the happier specimen,—
It may be, through that artist-preference
For work complete, inferiorly proposed,
To incompletion, though it aim aright.
Morally, no! Aspire, break bounds! I say,
765   Endeavour to be good, and better still,
And best! Success is nought, endeavour's all.
But intellect adjusts the means to ends,
Tries the low thing, and leaves it done, at least;
No prejudice to high thing, intellect

---

744|   MS:Mellerio hardly §inserted above§ did not do §last two words crossed out§ his
*P2:*Miranda hardly        745|   MS:exerted sense §crossed out and replaced above by§ brain,
748|   MS:say—   *P2:*say:   *CP2:*say;        750|   MS:Of Anna to   *CP4:*Of Clara to
751|   MS:And from perdition §last two words inserted above§ rescue soul forsooth!
*P2:*soul, forsooth!        752|   MS:sense in him   *P2:*sense of him
755|   MS:Than should §altered to§ would establish him participant   *P2:*establish God
participant   *CP2:*establish Him participant        756|   MS:the Délivrande.
*CP4:*the Ravissante.        757|   MS:heart of §crossed out§ was
758|   MS:limits—but   *P2:*limits: but   *CP2:*limits; but        759|   MS:mew nor wanted §last two
words crossed out and replaced above by three words§ and craved less
760|   MS:Anna, I < > specimen—   *P2:*specimen,—   *CP4:*Clara, I        763|   MS:incompletion,
though it §last two words inserted above§ aimed §altered to§ aim at sky and stars. §last four
words crossed out§ aright.        764|   MS:bounds!—we say:   *P2:*bounds! I say:   *CP2:*say,
765-66|   MS:§lines added between present ll. 764 and 767§        766|   MS:best: success is nought,
§last three words inserted above§   *P2:*best! Success        768|   MS:Does the   *P2:*Tries the

770   Would do and will do, only give the means.
      Miranda, in my picture-gallery,
      Presents a Blake; be Clara—Meissonier!
      Merely considered so by artist, mind!
      For, break through Art and rise to poetry,
775   Bring Art to tremble nearer, touch enough
      The verge of vastness to inform our soul
      What orb makes transit through the dark above,
      And there's the triumph!—there the incomplete,
      More than completion, matches the immense,—
780   Then, Michelagnolo against the world!
      With this proviso, let me study her
      Approvingly, the finished little piece!
      Born, bred, with just one instinct,—that of growth,—
      Her quality was, caterpillar-like,
785   To all-unerringly select a leaf
      And without intermission feed her fill,
      Become the Painted-peacock, or belike
      The Brimstone-wing, when time of year should suit;
      And 'tis a sign (say entomologists)
790   Of sickness, when the creature stops its meal
      One minute, either to look up at heaven,

---

771|  MS:Mellerio, in   *CP4:*Miranda, in      772|  MS:a Blake: but Anna—Gerard Dow!
*P2:*but Anna—Messionnier!   *CP2:*a Blake; be Anna—Meissonnier!   *CP4:*be Clara—
Meissonnier!   *1889a:*be Clara—Meissonier!    773-75|  MS:Only §crossed out and replaced
above by§ Merely considered as mere §last two words crossed out and replaced above by three
words§ so by artist, mind! / Bring art to   *P2:*so, by < > / Bring heart to
*CP2:*mind! / For break through Art and rise to poetry, / Bring Art to   *P3:* / < > through art
< > / Bring heart to   *CP3:* / < > through Art < > / Bring Art to   *C1873:*so by < > //
*1889a:* // Being Art §emended to§ Bring Art §see Editorial Notes§    780-81|  MS:§no ¶§
*P2:*§¶§   *1873:*§no ¶§   *CP2:*world! / —may I end discourse / —if you bear the ending . . / The
story's moral-obligatory / The winding up, / While we walk homeward?— §last five lines
cancelled§    782|  MS:Approvingly, this finished little §inserted above§ piece.
*P2:*Approvingly, the finished < > piece!    783|  MS:of life.   *P2:*of life:   *CP4:*of growth:
*C1873:*growth,—    784|  MS:Your §crossed out and replaced above by§ Her
785|  MS:select your §crossed out and replaced above by§ a    786|  MS:feed your §crossed
out and replaced above by§ here    787|  MS:the Painted Lady §crossed out and replaced
above by§ Peacock   *1889a:*the Painted-peacock    788|  MS:The Brimstone-winged, when
< > suit—   *P2:*The Brimstone-wing, when < > suit;    789|  MS:And §over illegible word§
'tis a sign—say entomologists—   *P2:*sign (say entomologists)
790|  MS:sickness when   *P2:*sickness, when    791|  MS:One moment, §crossed out and
replaced above by§ second §crossed out§ minute, §inserted above§ either

Or turn aside for change of aliment.
No doubt there was a certain ugliness
In the beginning, as the grub grew worm:
795 She could not find the proper plant at once,
But crawled and fumbled through a whole parterre.
Husband Muhlhausen served for stuff not long:
Then came confusion of the slimy track
From London, "where she gave the tone awhile,"
800 To Paris: let the stalks start up again,
Now she is off them, all the greener they!
But, settled on Miranda, how she sucked,
Assimilated juices, took the tint,
Mimicked the form and texture of her food!
805 Was he for pastime? Who so frolic-fond
As Clara? Had he a devotion-fit?
Clara grew serious with like qualm, be sure!
In health and strength he,—healthy too and strong,
She danced, rode, drove, took pistol-practice, fished,
810 Nay, "managed sea-skiff with consummate skill."
In pain and weakness he,—she patient watched
And wiled the slow drip-dropping hours away.
She bound again the broken self-respect,
She picked out the true meaning from mistake,

---

<sup>793</sup>| MS:No doubt, §last two words inserted above§ There §altered to§ there    *P2:*doubt there
<sup>794</sup>| MS:worm—    *P2:*worm:      <sup>795</sup>| MS:You §crossed out and replaced above by§ She
<sup>796</sup>| MS:parterre—    *P2:*parterre.      <sup>797</sup>| MS:Husband Debacker seemed fit stuff
*P2:*Husband Debacker served for stuff    *P2:*Husband Muhlhausen served
<sup>799</sup>| MS:Through §crossed out and replaced above by§ From <> "where you §crossed out and
replaced above by§ she <> awhile"    *P2:*From London, "when she <> awhile,"    *CP2:*From
London, "where she      <sup>801</sup>| MS:Now your are §last two words crossed out and replaced
above by two words§ she is      <sup>802</sup>| MS:on Mellerio, how you §crossed out and replaced
above by§ she    *P2:*on Miranda, how      <sup>804</sup>| MS:of your §crossed out and replaced above
by§ her      <sup>806</sup>| MS:As Anna? Had    *CP4:*As Clara? Had      <sup>807</sup>| MS:Anna grew serious
with §crossed out and replaced above by§ like such qualm    *P2:*serious with like qualm
*CP4:*Clara grew      <sup>808</sup>| MS:strength, why, healthy    *P2:*strength, he,—healthy
*CP2:*strength he      <sup>809</sup>| MS:fished    *P2:*fished,      <sup>810</sup>| MS:managed sea-skill
§*sea-* inserted above§ with §crossed out§ such consummate    *P2:*sea-skiff with consummate
<sup>811</sup>| MS:weakness—patiently she watched    *P2:*weakness, he,—she patient watched
*CP2:*weakness he    *P3:*weakness, he §emended to§ weakness he §see Editorial Notes§
<sup>812</sup>| MS:the miserable hours    *CP2:*the slow drip-dropping hours    *1873:*away    *C1873:*away.
<sup>814</sup>| MS:She recognized §crossed out and replaced above by two words§ picked out the full
§inserted above§ meaning from §crossed out and replaced above by§ from    *P2:*the true meaning

815     Praised effort in each stumble, laughed "Well-climbed!"
      When others groaned "None ever grovelled so!"
      "Rise, you have gained experience!" was her word:
      "Lie satisfied, the ground is just your place!"
      They thought appropriate counsel. "Live, not die,
820     And take my full life to eke out your own:
      That shall repay me and with interest!
      Write!—is your mouth not clever as my hand?
      Paint!—the last Exposition warrants me,
      Plenty of people must ply brush with toes.
825     And as for music—look, what folk nickname
      A lyre, those ancients played to ravishment,—
      Over the *pendule*, see, Apollo grasps
      A three-stringed gimcrack which no Liszt could coax
      Such music from as jew's-harp makes to-day!
830     Do your endeavour like a man, and leave
      The rest to 'fortune who assists the bold'—
      Learn, you, the Latin which you taught me first,
      You clever creature—clever, yes, I say!"

      If he smiled "Let us love, love's wrong comes right,

---

815| MS:Saw §added in margin§ The §crossed out§ effort in the §crossed out and replaced
above by§ each stumble, cried "Well climbed!"   *P2:*Praised effort <> "Well-climbed!"
*CP2:*stumble, laughed "Well-climbed!"     816| MS:others cried "None   *CP2:*others groaned
"None     817| MS:experience," was   *CP2:*experience!" was <> word;   *P3:*word:
818| MS:satisfied the <> place,"   *P2:*satisfied, the   *CP2:*place!"     819| MS:die!   *P2:*die,
820| MS:own!   *P2:*own   *CP2:*own,   *CP3:*own:     821| MS:What §crossed out and replaced
above by§ That <> interest.— §dash crossed out§   *P2:*interest!     822| MS:Write—is
*P2:*Write!—is     823| MS:Draw, §crossed out§ paint §altered to§ Paint!—the last §inserted
above§     824| MS:people must perform §last two words crossed out and replaced above by
four words§ must ply the §crossed out§ brush <> toes;   *P2:*toes.     825| MS:look at
§crossed out§ what they call §last two words crossed out and replaced above by two words§ folks
nickname   *P2:*look, what   *1889a:*folk     826| MS:lyre, the ancients <> ravishment!
*P2:*lyre, those ancients <> ravishment,—     827| MS:pendule <> Apollo holds §crossed
out§ grasps   *C1873:pendule*     828| MS:three-stringed nonsense §crossed out and replaced
above by§ gimcrack which no Litzt   *P2:*no Liszt     829| MS:jews-harp <> to-day.   *P2:*to-day!
*1889a:*jew's-harp     831| MS:to "fortune <> bold"—   *CP2:*to 'fortune <> bold'—
832| MS:Is not that §last three words crossed out and replaced above by two words§ Profit by Latin
<> me once,! §exclamation mark crossed out§   *P2:*Learn, you, the Latin <> me first,
833| MS:§line added between present ll. 832 and 834§   *P2:*Now clever creature—"Clever
*CP2:*You clever creature—clever     834| MS:When §crossed out§ If <> us love, it §crossed
out and replaced below by§ love must come right,   *P2:*us love, love's wrong comes right,

835   Shows reason last of all! Necessity
Must meanwhile serve for plea—so, mind not much
Old Fricquot's menace!"—back she smiled "Who minds?"
If he sighed "Ah, but She is strict, they say,
For all Her mercy at the Ravissante,
840   She scarce will be put off so!"—straight a sigh
Returned "My lace must go to trim Her gown!"
I nowise doubt she inwardly believed
Smiling and sighing had the same effect
Upon the venerated image. What
845   She did believe in, I as little doubt,
Was—Clara's self's own birthright to sustain
Existence, grow from grub to butterfly,
Upon unlimited Miranda-leaf;
In which prime article of faith confirmed,
850   According to capacity, she fed
On and on till the leaf was eaten up
That April morning. Even then, I praise
Her forethought which prevented leafless stalk
Bestowing any hoarded succulence
855   On earwig and blackbeetle squat beneath

---

835| MS:Show reason at the end §crossed out and replaced above by§ close: necessity
*P2:*Shows reason last of all! Necessity     836| MS:so, never mind   *P2:*so, mind not much
837| MS:What the priests menace!" back <> "Who does?"   *P2:*Old Picot's menace!"—back <>
"Who minds?"  *CP4:*Old Fricquot's menace     838| MS:When §crossed out and replaced
above by§ If  *P2:*side, "Ah  *CP2:*side "Ah     839| MS:§line added between present ll. 838
and 840§ all her smiling at the Délivrande,  *P2:*all Her mercy at  *CP4:*the Ravissante,
840| MS:And §crossed out and replaced above by§ She will not be  *P2:*She scarce will be
841-42| MS:gown!" §additional punctuation illegibly crossed out§ / Though lovelily it §last three
words crossed out§ I     843| MS:and f §*f* crossed out§
845| MS:in—I <> doubt at all— §last two words crossed out§  *P2:*in, I <> doubt,
846| MS:Was—Anna and her birthright:—to  *P2:*Was—Anna, and birthright to
*P2:*Was—Clara, and  *C1873:*Was—Clara's self's own birthright
848| MS:unlimited Mellerio-leaf.  *P2:*unlimited Mellerio-leaf;  *CP4:*unlimited Miranda-leaf;
849| MS:And, in that article <> confirmed  *P2:*In which prime article <> confirmed,
851| *CP2:*up,  *1889a:*up     852| MS:morning, even §last two words altered to§ morning.
Even then; I  *P2:*then, I     853| MS:The forethought which provided—stalk at least
*P2:*Her forethought which prevented leafless stalk     854| MS:Should not bestow its hoard
of succulence  *P2:*Bestowing any hoarded succulence     855| MS:blackbeetle down below
§altered to§ beneath:  *P2:*blackbeetle squat beneath;—  *C1873:*beneath

Clairvaux, that stalk whereto her hermitage
She tacked by golden throw of silk, so fine,
So anything but feeble, that her sleep
Inside it, through last winter, two years long,
860 Recked little of the storm and strife without.
"But—loved him?" Friend, I do not praise her love!
True love works never for the loved one so,
Nor spares skin-surface, smoothening truth away.
Love bids touch truth, endure truth, and embrace
865 Truth, though, embracing truth, love crush itself.
"Worship not me but God!" the angels urge:
That is love's grandeur: still, in pettier love
The nice eye can distinguish grade and grade.
Shall mine degrade the velvet green and puce
870 Of caterpillar, palmer-worm—or what—
Ball in and out of ball, each ball with brush
Of Venus' eye-fringe round the turquoise egg
That nestles soft,—compare such paragon
With any scarabæus of the brood

---

856| MS:Tailleville remained, and there §last two words crossed out and replaced above by§
whereto the hermitage    P2:Tailleville, that stalk whereto    CP2:whereto her hermitage
CP4:Clairvaux, that        857|    MS:Was tacked < > silks        P2:She tacked < > silk
858|    MS:Yet anything < > that who slept    P2:that her sleep    CP2:So anything
859|    MS:Inside through this last    P2:Inside it, through last
860|    MS:Was §crossed out and replaced above by§ Recked < > strife outside.    P2:strife without.
861|    MS:She loved him? Nay, §crossed out and replaced above by§ Friend, I should not < > her
so!    P2:"But loved him?"—Friend, I do not < > her love!    CP2:"But—loved him?" Friend
862|    MS:Since love worked never < > one thus,    P2:True love works never < > one so,
863|    MS:Nor §over illegible word§ spared skin-softness, smoothening < > away;
P2:Nor spares skin-surface, smoothening < > away.        864|    MS:But §crossed out§ Love
§added in margin§        865|    MS:love lose itself:    P2:love crush itself.
866|    MS:me, but God "all angels say:    P2:but God, "the angels urge:    CP2:but God! "the
1889a:me but        867|    MS:is the grandeur;—but in littleness    P2:is love's grandeur: still, in
pettier love        868|    MS:distinguish grade from §crossed out and replaced above by§ and
869|    MS:And §crossed out and replaced above by§ Shall I degrade this velvet < > puce,
P2:Nor mine degrades the velvet < > and pure    CP2:Shall I degrade the < > and puce
P3:Shall degrade    CP3:Shall mine degrade        870|    MS:This caterpillar, palmer-worm or
what?    P2:Of caterpillar < > what?—    CP2:palmer-worm—or what—
871|    MS:Ball, in < > of ball, with §crossed out§ each to §crossed out and replaced above by two
words§ ball with    P2:Ball in        872|    MS:Of Venus' eyelash §altered to§ eye-fringe < > the
ruby §crossed out and replaced above by§ turquiose        873|    MS:nestles there,—compare
P2:nestles soft,—compare        874|    MS:of them all    P2:of the brood

875 Which, born to fly, keeps wing in wing-case, walks
Persistently a-trundling dung on earth?
Egypt may venerate such hierophants,
Not I—the couple yonder, Father Priest
And Mother Nun, who came and went and came,
880 Beset this Clairvaux, trundled money-muck
To midden and the main heap oft enough,
But never bade unshut from sheath the gauze,
Nor showed that, who would fly, must let fall filth,
And warn "Your jewel, brother, is a blotch:
885 Sister, your lace trails ordure! Leave your sins,
And so best gift with Crown and grace with Robe!"

The superstition is extinct, you hope?
It were, with my good will! Suppose it so,
Bethink you likewise of the latest use
890 Whereto a Night-cap is convertible,
And draw your very thickest, thread and thrum,
O'er such a decomposing face of things,
Once so alive, it seemed immortal too!

This happened two years since. The Cousinry
895 Returned to Paris, called in help from Law,
And in due form proceeded to dispute

---

<sup>875|</sup> MS:That, born  *P2:*That born <> fly, keep wing <> wing-case, walk  *CP2:*That, born <>
fly, keeps wing <> walks  *C1873:*Which, born      <sup>878|</sup> MS:Not I, the  *P2:*Not I—the
<sup>879|</sup> MS:And Mother Nun who  *P2:*And Mother Nun, who      <sup>880|</sup> MS:this Tailleville,
trundled  *CP4:*This Clairvaux, trundled      <sup>882|</sup> MS:never once §crossed out and replaced
above by§ bade      <sup>883|</sup> MS:Showed that, to fly, you first should let  *P2:*Nor showed that,
who would fly, should  *C1873:*fly, must let      <sup>884|</sup> MS:Warned "Brother, your big jewel is a
blotch—  *P2:*Warning "Your jewel, brother, is a blotch:  *C1873:*And warn "Your
<sup>885|</sup> MS:ordure. Leave <> sins!  *P2:*sins,  *C1873:*ordure! Leave
<sup>886|</sup> MS:That shall best gift the crown §altered to§ Crown <> grace the robe §altered to§
Robe."  *P2:*And so best <> Robe!"  *C1873:*gift with Crown <> grace with Robe!"
<sup>886-87|</sup> MS:§no ¶§  *P2:*§¶§      <sup>887|</sup> MS:you smile §crossed out and replaced above by§ think
§crossed out and replaced above by§ hope      <sup>890|</sup> MS:a Nightcap  *P2:*a Night-cap
<sup>891|</sup> MS:draw the very thickest, threads §altered to§ thread and thrums §altered to§ thrum,
*CP2:*draw your very      <sup>892|</sup> MS:O'er the decomposing §inserted above§ face <> things,
§comma crossed out§  *P2:*O'er such a decomposing <> things,
<sup>893|</sup> MS:alive they seemed <> too.  *P2:*alive, they <> too!  *CP2:*alive, it seemed
<sup>895|</sup> MS:from law,  *P2:*from Law,      <sup>896|</sup> MS:to contest §crossed out§ dispute

Monsieur Léonce Miranda's competence,
Being insane, to make a valid Will.

Much testimony volunteered itself;
900　The issue hardly could be doubtful—but
For that sad 'Seventy which must intervene,
Provide poor France with other work to mind
Than settling lawsuits, even for the sake
Of such a party as the Ravissante.
905　It only was this Summer that the case
Could come and be disposed of, two weeks since,
At Vire—Tribunal Civil—Chamber First.

Here, issued with all regularity,
I hold the judgment—just, inevitable,
910　Nowise to be contested by what few
Can judge the judges; sum and substance, thus—

"Inasmuch as we find, the Cousinry,
During that very period when they take
Monsieur Léonce Miranda for stark mad,
915　Considered him to be quite sane enough
For doing much important business with—
Nor showed suspicion of his competence

---

897| MS:Monsieur Antoine Mellerio's competence, *CP4:*Monsieur Alphonse §crossed out and replaced above by§ Léonce Miranda's competence, 898| MS:a testamen §crossed out§ valid will. *P2:*valid Will. 898-99| MS:§no ¶§ *P2:*§¶§ 899| MS:itself, *P2:*itself; 901| MS:intervene *P2:*intervene, 902| MS:And give §last two words crossed out and replaced above by§ Provide <> France quite §crossed out and replaced above by§ with 903| MS:even such as this §last three words crossed out§ for 904| MS:the Délivrande. *CP4:*the Ravissante. 905| MS:summer *P2:*this Summer 907| MS:At Caen— Tribunal—Civil, Chamber *P2:*At Caen—Tribunal Civil—Chamber *P2:*At Vire—Tribunal 907-8| MS:§no ¶§ *P2:*§¶§ 908| MS:Here, §illegible word crossed out and replaced above by§ issued 910| MS:by ourselves *P2:*No wise *CP2:*Nowise *CP4:*by what few 911| MS:Who judge <> judges; in §crossed out§ sum <> thus. *CP2:*thus— *CP4:*Can judge 911-12| *P2:*§no ¶§ *CP3:*§¶§ 912| MS:Inasmuch as it appears §last two words crossed out and replaced above by two words§ we find the *P2:*"Inasmuch <> find, the 913| MS:period when §inserted above§ they declare say §last two words crossed out§ take 914| MS:Conspicuous for §last two words crossed out and replaced above by§ Monsieur Antoine Mellerio was §crossed out and replaced above by§ for *CP4:*Monsieur Alphonse §crossed out and replaced above by§ Léonce Miranda for 917| MS:thereby, *P2:*thereby,—

Until, by turning of the tables, loss
Instead of gain accrued to them thereby,—
920   Plea of incompetence we set aside.

—"The rather, that the dispositions, sought
To be impugned, are natural and right,
Nor jar with any reasonable claim
Of kindred, friendship or acquaintance here.
925   Nobody is despoiled, none overlooked;
Since the testator leaves his property
To just that person whom, of all the world,
He counted he was most indebted to.
In mere discharge, then, of conspicuous debt,
930   Madame Muhlhausen has priority,
Enjoys the usufruct of Clairvaux.

                     "Next,
Such debt discharged, such life determining,
Such earthly interest provided for,
Monsieur Léonce Miranda may bequeath,
935   In absence of more fit recipient, fund
And usufruct together to the Church
Whereof he was a special devotee.

"—Which disposition, being consonant
With a long series of such acts and deeds
940   Notorious in his life-time, needs must stand,
Unprejudiced by eccentricity

---

⁹²⁰|  MS:aside:  *P2:*aside.      ⁹²⁰⁻²¹|  MS:§no ¶§   *P2:*§¶§      ⁹²¹|  MS:—The §dash added
in margin§   *P2:*—"The      ⁹²²|  MS:right  *P2:*right,      ⁹²⁴|  MS:here:  *P2:*here.
⁹²⁵|  MS:despoiled nor overlooked   *P2:*despoiled, none overlooked,   *CP2:*overlooked;
⁹²⁶|  MS:When the   *P2:*Since the      ⁹²⁷|  MS:First to that <> whom of <> world
*P2:*To just that   *CP2:*whom, of <> world,      ⁹²⁹|  MS:discharge then of   *P2:*discharge,
then of      ⁹³⁰|  MS:Madame Debacker has priority   *P2:*priority,   *CP4:*Madame
Muhlhausen has      ⁹³¹|  MS:of Tailleville. §¶§ next §altered to§ Next,   *P2:*§¶§ "Next,
*P2:*of Clairvaux. ¶§¶      ⁹³³|  MS:Such earthly §crossed out and replaced above by§ human
§crossed out, restoring original reading§      ⁹³⁴|  MS:Fitting §crossed out and replaced above
by§ Monsieur Antoine Mellerio may   *CP4:*Monsieur Alphonse §crossed out and replaced above
by§ Léonce Miranda may      ⁹³⁷|  MS:devotee:  *P2:*devotee.      ⁹³⁷⁻³⁸|  MS:§no ¶§
*P2:*§¶§      ⁹³⁸|  MS:Which  *P2:*"—Which      ⁹³⁹|  MS:With §over illegible word§

Nowise amounting to distemper: since,
In every instance signalized as such,
We recognize no overleaping bounds,
945     No straying out of the permissible:
Duty to the Religion of the Land,—
Neither excessive nor inordinate.

"The minor accusations are dismissed;
They prove mere freak and fancy, boyish mood
950     In age mature of simple kindly man.
Exuberant in generosities
To all the world: no fact confirms the fear
He meditated mischief to himself
That morning when he met the accident
955     Which ended fatally. The case is closed."

How otherwise? So, when I grazed the skirts,
And had the glimpse of who made, yesterday,—
Woman and retinue of goats and sheep,—
The sombre path one whiteness, vision-like,
960     As out of gate, and in at gate again,
They wavered,—she was lady there for life:
And, after life—I hope, a white success
Of some sort, wheresoever life resume
School interrupted by vacation—death;

---

942|   MS:to unsoundness—since, §last two words crossed out and replaced above by two words§
distemper here:       944|   MS:There seems to be §last four words crossed out and replaced
above by two words§ We recognise   *P2:*over-leaping   *1889a:*recognize <> overleaping
945|   MS:Nor trespass out <> permissible   *P2:*No straying out <> permissible:
946|   MS:Allowed §crossed out and replaced above by§ Practiced by the religion <> land,—
*P2:*Duty to the Religion <> Land,—       947|   MS:Nothing excessive   *P2:*Neither excessive
948|   MS:The <> dismissed   *P2:*"The <> dismissed;       949|   MS:As proving freak
*P2:*They prove mere freak       951-53|   MS:generosities, / Nor §altered to§ Not meditating
mischief   *P2:*generosities / To all the world, no fact confirms the fear / He meditated mischief
*CP2:* / <> world: no <> /       954|   MS:The §over *That*§ morning <> met the §crossed out
and replaced above by§ an accident   *P2:*That morning <> met the accident
955|   MS:ended his career. The   *P2:*ended fatally. The       956|   MS:otherwise? So when <>
skirts   *P2:*otherwise? So, when <> skirts,       957|   MS:made yesterday,—
*P2:*made, yesterday,—       959|   MS:sombre way one   *P2:*sombre path one
960|   MS:of gate and in at §inserted above§   *CP2:*of gate, and       961|   MS:life;   *P2:*life:
962|   MS:And after   *P2:*And, after       964|   MS:death:   *P2:*death;

965     Seeing that home she goes with prize in hand,
     Confirmed the Châtelaine of Clairvaux.

                                True,
     Such prize fades soon to insignificance.
     Though she have eaten her Miranda up,
     And spun a cradle-cone through which she pricks
970     Her passage, and proves Peacock-butterfly
     This Autumn—wait a little week of cold!
     Peacock and death's-head-moth end much the same.
     And could she still continue spinning,—sure,
     Cradle would soon crave shroud for substitute,
975     And o'er this life of hers distaste would drop
     Red-cotton-Night-cap-wise.

                         How say you, friend?
     Have I redeemed my promise? Smile assent
     Through the dark Winter-gloom between us both!
     Already, months ago and miles away,

---

965|   MS:home you §crossed out and replaced above by§ she <> hand—    *P2:*hand,
966|   MS:the châtelaine §altered to§ Châtelaine of Tailleville. §¶§    *CP4:*of Clairvaux. §¶§
967|   MS:The §crossed out§ Such §added in margin§ prize <> insignificance—
*P2:*insignificance.       968|   MS:Just §crossed out§ Prize §added in margin§ to have <> her
Mellerio up,    *P2:*Though she have    *CP4:*her Miranda up,      969|   MS:a shroud of gold §last
three words crossed out and replaced above by§ cradle-cone from §crossed out and replaced
above by§ through which you §crossed out and replaced above by§ she pricked    *P2:*she pricks
970|   MS:Your §crossed out and replaced above by§ Her way and §last two words crossed out and
replaced above by two words§ passage, and proved a §crossed out§ peacock butterfly,
*P2:*proves peacock-butterfly,    *1889a:*proves Peacock-butterfly      971|   MS:In §crossed out§
This §added in margin§ Autumn. and §crossed out and replaced above by§ Wait <> week or
§altered to§ of two §crossed out§ cold,    *P2:*This autumn—wait <> cold!    *CP2:*This Autumn
972|   MS:That §crossed out§ Peacock §added in margin§ and a §crossed out§ death's-head-moth
are much    *CP2:*death's-head-moth end much      973|   MS:could you §crossed out and
replaced above by§ she <> sure   *P2:*sure,      974|   MS:The cradle would have shroud
*P2:*Cradle would soon crave shroud      975|   MS:life of hers §last two words inserted above§
distaste, §comma crossed out§ oblivion §crossed out and replaced above by§ would
*P2:*her's    *1889a:*hers      976-77|   MS:Red-cotton-Night-cap-wise. §¶§ How <> /
*CP2:*Red-cotton-Night-cap-wise. / But §over perhaps *Well*§ / Story's done; / And pardon granted
for its length and breadth? / Tell me as homeward we retrace our steps! / §date added in
margin§ August, 1872 §rule added§ / Once more, and yet once more, we meet, §last two words
crossed out§ fair friend! / Have §all inserted lines cancelled§    *CP3:*§rule called for§
*CP4:*§rule called for§      978|   MS:dark winter-gloom    *CP2:*dark Winter-gloom

<sup>980</sup> I just as good as told you, in a flash,
The while we paced the sands before my house,
All this poor story—truth and nothing else.
Accept that moment's flashing, amplified,
Impalpability reduced to speech,
<sup>985</sup> Conception proved by birth,—no other change!
Can what Saint-Rambert flashed me in a thought,
Good gloomy London make a poem of?
Such ought to be whatever dares precede,
Play ruddy herald-star to your white blaze
<sup>990</sup> About to bring us day. How fail imbibe
Some foretaste of effulgence? Sun shall wax,
And star shall wane: what matter, so star tell
The drowsy world to start awake, rub eyes,
And stand all ready for morn's joy a-blush?

---

<sup>982</sup>| MS:this long story   *P2:*this poor story        <sup>983</sup>| MS:Here is that <> flashing amplified
*P2:*Accept that <> flashing, amplified,        <sup>985</sup>| MS:Conception brought to §last two words
crossed out and replaced above by two words§ proved by birth, no <> change;   *CP2:*birth,—no
<> change!        <sup>986</sup>| MS:And what Saint Aubin gave §crossed out and replaced above by§
flashed <> a flash, §crossed out§ thought,   *P2:*Can what Saint Aubin   *CP2:*what Saint-Aubin
*1873:*what Saint-Rambert flashed        <sup>987</sup>| MS:of—   *P2:*of?        <sup>988</sup>| MS:Such I maintain
it! Could §crossed out and replaced above by§ if §crossed out and replaced below by§ can I
come §crossed out§ so close §crossed out§ precede,   *P2:*Such ought to bc whatever dares
precede,   *CP2:*be        <sup>989</sup>| MS:Play herald ruddy §last two words transposed to§ ruddy herald
star to <> white orb §crossed out§ blaze   *P2:*herald-star        <sup>990</sup>| MS:bring the day; §altered
to§ day, and not §last two words crossed out and replaced above by two words§ I must §crossed
out, restoring original reading§ imbibe   *P2:*bring us day. How fail imbibe
<sup>992</sup>| MS:matter so it §crossed out§ I tell   *P2:*so star tell   *CP2:*matter, so
<sup>993</sup>| MS:start wide §inserted above§ awake   *P2:*start awake
<sup>994</sup>| MS:stand, up §crossed out and replaced above by§ all <> for the §crossed out and
replaced above by§ your joy a-blush?   *P2:*stand all <> for morn's joy        §MS ends with
date§ (Finished, Jan. 23. '73. L. D. I. E. R. B.)   *P2:*§no date§   *CP2:*January 23, 1873.

## FIFINE AT THE FAIR

*Emendations to the Text*

The following emendations have been made to the 1889a copy-text:

l. 5: The stanza number (II) just above l. 5, present in both the MS and the 1872 edition, is missing from the 1889a edition. It has been inserted.
l. 6: The end punctuation of the line in both MS and 1872 is a comma, but it has been changed in 1889a to a question mark; this incorrectly separates the sentence's subject in l. 6 from its modifiers in l. 7 and from its predicate in l. 8. The comma has been restored.
l. 1421: The end of this line is the conclusion of the quoted words of "mind" (l. 1414), which began at l. 1418. B, however, did not provide closing quotation marks in any text, in this line or any other in the vicinity. The reversion to Elvire as the subject of the next line shows that Don Juan is speaking in his own voice again; on the basis of this rhetorical shift, we have inserted double closing quotation marks at the end of line 1421.

"Epilogue: the Householder," l. 16: The copy-text prints a single opening quotation mark at the beginning of the line, where a double quotation mark is required; the correct MS-1872 reading is restored.

*Composition*

In his amazingly productive decade of the 1870s, B published ten volumes of poetry. *Fifine at the Fair* was the third volume, following *Balaustion's Adventure* (August 1871) and *Prince Hohenstiel-Schwangau* (December 1871). In December, the month in which the latter work appeared, he began writing *Fifine*. At the end of the manuscript he notes that he had begun the poem in December and finished it on 11 May 1872, just four days after his sixtieth birthday.

He must have begun this poem of almost 2500 lines early in December since at the beginning of January he reports to Edith Story that "this thing I am now engaged upon" was "half-done" (Hood,153). At the end of March he tells Isa Blagden that he is nearly finished: "I have been hard at work, the poem *growing* under me, and seeming worth attending to: it is *almost* done: but I am very tired & bilious" (McAleer, 376). Ten days later he was done. Alfred Domett, just returned from New Zealand, called on the poet on 9 April and recorded in his diary that "Browning tells me he has just finished a poem" (Domett, 52). If B told Domett on 9 April that he had finished *Fifine*, why did he date the completion of his manuscript over a month later, on 11 May? Horsman, Domett's editor, reasonably speculates that B revised the poem during that month and did not consider it really done until the changes and additions were made. It may also be that on 9 April he had not yet written the prologue and epilogue. The manuscripts of both of these poems, "Amphibian" and "The Householder," are fair copies with no corrections, unlike the manuscript of *Fifine* itself, which is heavily marked. The pagination of the prologue manuscript is by letter rather than number, suggesting that it was written after the main poem. It is clear that B sent the epilogue to Smith, Elder after he had received proof sheets for the rest of the poem. Alongside the title of the epilogue B instructed the printer in parentheses, "Print this to correspond exactly with Prologue—p. vii." The Roman numeral page number is the one where the prologue appears in the first edition and, one would assume, in the lost page proofs.

*Sources*

The source for the setting of the poem is Pornic, a Breton town just S of the mouth of the Loire, where B spent his August-September holidays in 1862, 1863, and 1865. In the intervening year of 1864 he was at the Basque town of Cambo, not far from Biarritz, and in 1866 he went to Le Croisic, some forty miles N of Pornic. Accompanied on these holidays by his father, Sarianna, Pen, and the Brackens—Mary Bracken and her son, Willy—B actually stayed not at Pornic but at Ste. Marie, or as it is sometimes styled, Ste. Marie-sur-Mer, then two miles S of Pornic. There they resided in the house of the mayor, who tragically lost his wife and the mother of his four children during their first visit in 1862. On this visit B described the countryside to his friends the Storys as "solitary and bare enough, but the sea is everywhere and the land harmonizes entirely with it. I like the rocky walks by the sea [such the one taken by Don Juan and

Elvire in the poem] and complete loneliness. At Pornic, gaiety enough, but it does not reach us" (Hood, 70). During his last visit, in 1865, B described the place to Isa Blagden in these terms:

> Nothing is changed—Pornic itself, two miles off, is full of company, but our little village is its dirty, unimproved self—a trifle wilder than before, if possible. The weather is not good: rain every day, with intervals of sun, but a contrast to the wonderful Biarritz and Cambo blaze of last year: at the same time, it suits me, and I think the others, better by far: the sea is the great resource. I used not to care about it inordinately till of late years—now, it seems to be the *obbligato* accompaniment to my last home but one. I bathe daily— and feel much the better for it.
>
> (Hood, 89)

The prologue to *Fifine*, "Amphibian," draws directly from B's delight in swimming off the Breton coast, as does a parallel passage in the poem itself when Don Juan tells Elvire of his swim that morning (stanza LXIV). These visits to the environs of Pornic furnished B not only with his setting, but also with his title character, the starting and ending point of his speaker's monologue. During one of his three holidays there—most critics assume, but without evidence, the last in 1865—B attended the festival of St. Giles (*fête de la Saint-Gilles*) at Pornic, where, as he said, there was "gaiety enough," and at this fair he saw a gipsy who became the model for Fifine. The source of this information is Sarianna, who told Alfred Domett in August of 1872, two months after *Fifine's* publication, that "the original 'Fifine' was a fine fierce gipsey [sic] woman they had seen at the fair at Pornic where they had been staying" (Domett, 54-55). The festival of St. Giles is celebrated on 1 September.

The title character is therefore of Pornic; on the other hand, the speaker and his auditor are from Molière's *Don Juan*, a passage from which serves as the poem's epigraph. Readers have objected that B's speaker has little in common with Molière's character or indeed with the Don Juan of legend. Stopford Brooke, for instance, observes that "the name of Don Juan is a mistake. Every one knows Don Juan, and to imagine him arguing in the fashion of this poem is absurd" (*The Poetry of Robert Browning* [London, 1902], 425). Similarly, Edward Dowden complained that "No more unhappy misnomer than this 'Don Juan' could have been devised for the curious, ingenious, learned experimenter in life, no man of pleasure, in the vulgar sense of the word, but a deliberate explorer of thoughts and things, who argues out his case with so much fine casuistry and often with justest conceptions of human character and conduct" (*The Life of Robert Browning* [New York, 1915], 303). Byron had carefully distinguished his Don Juan from all others by that name, but B had not. Yet he did tell Dr. Furnivall that his purpose "was to show merely how a Don Juan might justify himself, partly by truth, somewhat by sophistry" ( *Browning Society Papers* 2.242, quoted in Dowden, op. cit., 303). His use of the indefinite article is telling. His character is not *the* Don Juan of Molière or of legend but instead *a* Don Juan. Barbara Melchiori is exactly right in saying that the poet's purpose was to create "a Victorian Don Juan. How would Don Juan behave in the mid-nineteenth century? . . . What, too, would Elvire, his Victorian wife, be like?" (*Browning's Poetry of Reticence* [New York, 1968], 160).

As for the particular passage from Molière's play quoted by B, it clearly serves as a cue for the speaker's long monologue. In the passage Donna Elvira challenges Don Juan to defend his inconstancy, and, accepting the challenge, B's Don Juan proceeds to do precisely that.

A much less obvious source than either the fair at Pornic or Molière's *Don Juan* is B's proposal to Louisa, Lady Ashburton in September 1869. For one discussion of the influence of this biographical episode on the poem, see William O. Raymond's "Browning's Dark Mood: A Study of *Fifine at the Fair*" (*Studies in Philology* 31 [1934], 578-99; rpt. as Ch. 7 in his *The Infinite Moment and Other Essays in Robert Browning*, 2nd ed. [Toronto, 1965]). Briefly put, Raymond begins with Mrs. Sutherland Orr's comment that "Some leaven of bitterness must, nevertheless, have been working within him" in the writing of *Fifine* (Orr, *Life*, 294) and then argues that the bitterness derived from his regret at having been inconstant to the memory of Elizabeth by proposing to another woman. The facts of the matter remain somewhat unclear, but it seems that in September 1869 B proposed to Lady Ashburton and was refused, or perhaps had couched the proposal in such terms that she had no other option. Whatever the case may be, the relationship between the two continued till a final meeting in October 1871, just two months before B began writing *Fifine*. Raymond explicitly rejects identifying B with Don Juan, Elvire with Elizabeth, and Fifine with Lady Ashburton, but he does argue that the autobiographical element influenced the choice and development of the subject. In *Browning's Later Poetry: 1871-1889* (Ithaca, NY, 1975) Clyde de L. Ryals has added two further examples of inconstancy that may also have been on B's mind: that of his own father, who proposed to another woman little more than a year after becoming a widower, and that of Shelley, who, as B discovered in 1851, had abandoned his wife and child (60-61).

Yet another influence, at once both biographical and literary, was Dante Gabriel Rossetti, who read *Fifine* shortly after publication and went into a rage, believing that the poem was an attack upon himself and his poem "Jenny." Rossetti, who had greatly admired B as a poet and who had cherished a long friendship with him, never spoke to B again. At the time William Michael Rossetti accounted for his brother's behavior as the result of an unstable mental and emotional state, but William Clyde DeVane has argued that Rossetti had reason to be offended and that B did in fact have "Jenny" in mind when he wrote *Fifine* ("The Harlot and the Thoughtful Young Man," *Studies in Philology* 29 [July 1932], 463-84).

In April 1870 Rossetti published "Jenny" in his *Poems*. In October 1871 Robert Buchanan anonymously attacked the volume in an article titled "The Fleshly School of Poetry—Mr. D. G. Rossetti." Rossetti defended himself in "The Stealthy School of Criticism" in December 1871 and was then attacked once more by Buchanan in May 1872 by an enlarged version of the earlier essay, now published in pamphlet form as *The Fleshly School of Poetry and other Phenomena of the Day*. Rossetti was distraught, and B, who followed the controversy along with everyone else in the London literary world, sympathized with Buchanan. His response was *Fifine*, composed during the height of the controversy, and designed to parallel the situation in "Jenny," one of the poems singled out by Buchanan. Both poems, as DeVane's title indicates, involve harlots and thoughtful young men, but B's young man acts very differently at the end of the poem that does Rossetti's, who compassionately leaves the sleeping Jenny with unearned gold coins. By leaving to meet Fifine, Don Juan represents for B a more truthful version of what would have happened, but Rossetti, who identified himself with his own young man and thus, by extension, with B's, took personal offence.

The criticism of Byron in stanza LXVII is much more overt and is one of numerous examples of B's expressing his distaste for that poet in his own poems. These examples appear as early as *Sordello*, but they increase in frequency in the 1870s, starting with ll. 517-55 of *Prince Hohenstiel-Schwangau* (this edition, 10.141ff.), then to this stanza in *Fifine*, and then to stanzas XX-XXIII of the Epilogue to *Pacchiarotto and How He Worked in Distemper: with Other Poems* (this edition, 13.269ff.). In all three of these poems B ridicules the apostrophe to the ocean at the end of Canto IV of *Childe Harold's Pilgrimage* and especially Byron's preference of the sea to his fellow man. In the last two poems B draws attention to Byron's ungrammatical use of the word *lay*. Quite possibly the reason for the increased frequency of these criticisms in the 1870s was the publication in 1870 of Alfred Austin's *The Poetry of the Period*, a book in which the author disputed Tennyson's reputation as a first-rank poet, denied that B was even a third-rank poet, and placed Byron on a level unapproachable by any contemporary poet. When asked by Alfred Domett who Austin was, B replied "A scurvy little fellow who always abuses me" (Domett, 67). B struck back at Austin in "Of Pacchiarotto," whose editorial notes by Ashby Bland Crowder in Volume 13 of the present edition give a full account of the dispute between B and Austin. Although as a young man B had admired Byron's poems, he later came to dislike the elder poet, and even more so once Austin championed him at B's expense.

A final word about the sources should be given to the *Prometheus Bound* of Aeschylus. When the chorus first appears to Prometheus, the Titan, uncertain of who its members are, asks if they are "God, man, or both together mixed." B quotes the Greek in ll. 905 and 2210 of *Fifine* and the English translation in ll. 907, 2188, and 2216. This source would not warrant a place with the more important ones previously mentioned were it not for its direct bearing on *Fifine's* themes of true and false, soul and sense, and of how these opposites are mixed in the world and in humans. The poem's prologue, "Amphibian," strikes the keynote to these dualities, and Don Juan plays variations on it throughout the piece.

### Text and Publication

Three texts of *Fifine at the Fair* have been collated for this edition; the significance of each is discussed below, in the order in which they appear in the variant list.

*The Balliol Manuscript* The manuscript of *Fifine at the Fair*, in the Balliol College Library, is bound with the manuscripts of *Balaustion's Adventure* and *Prince Hohenstiel-Schwangau* in Volume III. For a description of this volume see the editorial notes on these poems in Volume 10 of the present edition. *Fifine* comprises the last eighty-nine pages of the Balliol volume. B numbered every other page. Someone else, probably a compositor, numbered the intervening pages by adding the letter *a*, so that, for example, the unnumbered page following the first page became *1a*. For some reason no one added numbers between page 24 and page 39, resulting in fifteen unnumbered alternate pages. B apparently numbered the 132 stanzas after he completed the poem because there are no changes in these numbers despite the addition of some one hundred paragraph/stanza divisions made in revisions.

That the MS was the printer's copy is evident from the addition of page numbers, from the signing of compositors' names throughout, and from B's instructions regarding the type size for the epigraph, prologue, and epilogue. The extensive revisions B made on the MS indicate that it was the compositional copy as well. The prologue and epilogue, as noted above in *Composition*, are fair copies. The most heavily revised sections are stanzas in the range of XL-LV and of LXXI-LXXXI. See the textual notes for a description of these.

There are two unrhymed lines of the 2355 lines of alexandrine couplets: ll. 622 and 1488. Both seem to be deliberate in that neither is the result of a revision or addition. On the other hand, ll. 53-55 are a triplet, created by the later insertion of l. 55. This triplet and others further on account for there being an odd number of lines (2355) in a poem of couplets.

On the title page of the MS B wrote diagonally in large Greek letters l. 488 of Aristophanes's *Acharnians*, which may be translated as "Take courage! Forward! March! O well done, heart!" And in the lower right corner, in smaller Greek letters, he quoted ll. 11-13 of Pindar's *Olympian* 13, which translates as "Fair is the tale I have to tell, and courage that maketh straight for the mark prompteth my tongue to speak; it is a hard struggle to quell one's inborn nature."

On the last page of the MS and within parentheses, B again quoted in Greek, this time from Aeschylus's *Choephorae*. The English for these lines (816-18) is "And reading this doubtful word he has dark night before his eyes, and he is nothing clearer by day." Within the parenthesis marks B added "—if any of my critics had Greek enough in him to make the application!" Beneath this is yet another Greek passage, dated 5 November 1872, from Aristophanes's *Thesmophoriazusae*. "To what words are you turned, for a barbarian nature would not receive them. For bearing new words to the Scaeans you would spend them in vain" (1128-31).

At the end of *Fifine* B wrote the letters "L. D. I. E." followed by the beginning and ending dates of December and May. At the end of the epilogue, "The Householder," he repeated the letters, this time adding his initials. These letters appear on most of the Balliol manuscripts and stand for *Laus Deo in excelsis*, "Praise God in the highest," B's thanksgiving for the completion of his work.

*The First English Edition (1872)*    *Fifine at the Fair* was published by Smith, Elder probably on 3 June 1872, the earliest date of B's presentation copies (*Reconstruction*, C330-44), and sold for five shillings. As mentioned above, the Balliol MS was the copy text for this edition. B made over a thousand changes, most of them involving punctuation, before the poem was printed, but the page proofs on which he made these changes are now lost. A set of uncorrected proofs for the first edition went through the 1913 Sotheby sale, but its present location is unknown

(*Reconstruction*, A424). The volume has 171 pages in addition to twelve preliminary pages for the title, epigraph, and prologue. There was no second edition.

*Collected Edition (1889a)* *Fifine at the Fair* was published in Volume 11 of the 1888-89 *Poetical Works* along with *Balaustion's Adventure* and *Prince Hohenstiel-Schwangau*. B made over a hundred changes, most of them again to punctuation, in preparing the poem for this edition.

*Reception*

When B described *Fifine* to Alfred Domett as "the most metaphysical and boldest he had written since *Sordello*" and then added that he "was very doubtful as to its reception by the public (Domett, 52-53), he foresaw clearly how his critics would react. They objected not so much to its being bold, if by that B meant the subject of a man arranging a meeting with a prostitute while in the company of his wife, nor even to its being metaphysical, but rather to its metaphysics being presented in a style so difficult and obscure as to be unintelligible. One of the earliest reviews, appearing 15 June in the *Examiner*, had more favorable things to say about the poem than later reviews. Describing B as "our great poet and our wonderful character-painter," the reviewer concluded that *Fifine*, though perplexing and hard to understand, "is a poem worth puzzling over. It is rich in gems of thought that sparkle through their rugged setting" (601). What was so frustrating and maddening about B for his critics was that the obscurity seemed deliberate. For this reviewer, "Mr. Browning's willful incoherencies are inartistic, and he is artist enough to avoid, if he chooses, being incoherent by accident" (601). The reviewer for the *Illustrated London News*, also published on 15 June, put it more strongly: "The wayward genius of Mr. Robert Browning has perpetrated another monstrosity of deliberate clumsiness and affected incoherence" (35).

Subsequent reviews in the *Spectator* (6 July 1872, 853-55), the *Fortnightly Review* (July 1872, 118-20), and the *Guardian* (25 September 1872, 1215-16) all complained of the poem's obscurity. The *Westminster Review* did approve the poem's subject and found reason to praise B for having "put more substance into 'Fifine at the Fair' than into any other poem." On the other hand, "for the ordinary reader it might just as well have been written in Sanscrit" (1 October 1872, 545). One of the last of the British reviews, appearing in the *Times* for 2 January 1873, chided B for his criticism of Byron and defended the passage from *Childe Harold's*

*Pilgrimage* as one "which, for all its bad grammar, teaches us that in every word and in it sublimest flights the English tongue may be so written that it can be read and understood, not merely by students and experts, but by ordinary Englishmen" (5).

In the United States *Fifine* was published in the summer of 1872 by James Osgood of Boston as *Fifine at the Fair, and Other Poems,* the others being *Prince Hohenstiel-Schwangau* and "Hervé Riel." Reviews in the *Galaxy* (August 1872, 277-78), San Francisco's the *Overland Monthly* (October 1872, 385-87), and *Scribner's Monthly* (October 1872, 775-76) generally followed the British reviews in finding some parts praiseworthy but the whole incoherent and obscure. A notable exception to the unfavorable reviews was one written by C. C. Everett for the Boston journal *Old and New* in November 1872. Everett, unlike the other reviewers, took the trouble to read the poem carefully, and while he acknowledged that there is "the occasional harshness of diction," he dismissed this as "a fault which the habitual reader of Browning has learned to expect in his poems, and, we may add also, has learned to pardon, it is so associated with his rugged strength" (613). He argued that readers are wrong to demand that poetry should be clear at first reading and to fail to recognize that it should be studied before being comprehended (615).

In the years following publication readers did not warm to the poem. Even so ardent a champion as Mrs. Sutherland Orr called it "that piece of perplexing cynicism" and a "perverse poem" (Orr, *Life,* 294, 297). Eleven years later, in 1902, Stopford Brooke complained that *Fifine* was "pitilessly long" and that Don Juan "had much better have stayed with Elvire, who endured him with weary patience. I have no doubt that he bored Fifine to extinction" (*The Poetry of Robert Browning* [London, 1902], 422, 425).

In addition to the modern discussions of the poem by DeVane, Raymond, and Melchiori previously mentioned above in *Sources,* there are good ones by Roma A. King, Jr. in *The Focusing Artifice: The Poetry of Robert Browning* (Athens, OH, 1968), Philip Drew in *The Poetry of Browning: A Critical Introduction* (London, 1970), and in Irvine and Honan, where *Fifine* is praised for being "as fine a work as he wrote in his later years" (463). *Fifine* is also the subject of an entire book, Samuel B. Southwell's *Quest for Eros: Browning and Fifine* (Lexington, KY, 1980).

*Epigraph*

7]   *chap-fallen*   Crest-fallen, dejected.
11]   *erst*   Formerly (archaic).

*PROLOGUE: AMPHIBIAN*

11-16]   *butterfly . . . soul*   The butterfly is a common symbol of the soul.
58]   *disport*   Relaxation, amusement.


*FIFINE AT THE FAIR*

9]   *Autumn*   Specifically 1 September, the feast of St. Giles.
10]   *Pornic*   The town in Brittany close to Ste. Marie, where B spent holidays in 1862, 1863, and 1865. See *Sources* above.

   *Saint Gille*   Usually spelled Gilles in French, Giles in English. He was a seventh-century saint whose festival, as noted above, is celebrated on 1 September. According to legend he was a hermit whose only companion was a hind, ordinarily portrayed with him in iconography. In Pornic the Église St. Gilles was founded by Guy de Laval in the late fourteenth century, and when the saint answered Guy's prayers for a child, the father named him Gilles in gratitude. This child grew up to be the notorious Gilles de Retz (or Rais) (1404-40), the murderous pedophile upon whom Perrault based Bluebeard. The present church of St. Giles was built in 1864-75.

   *boon*   Gift, something to be thankful for.
11]   *parterre*   A garden with ornamental flower beds.
12]   *Bateleurs*   Mountebanks, jugglers, tumblers.

   *baladines*   Theatrical dancers, mountebanks, buffoons, from the French word *baladin*.
14]   *O pleasant land of France*   Possibly from l. 4 of Macaulay's poem "Ivry" (celebrating Henry of Navarre's victory in 1590): "Through the corn fields green, and sunny vines, O pleasant land of France." Mark Twain quoted the line in Ch. 12 of *Innocents Abroad*. Cf. also the first line of Pierre Jean de Béranger's "Les adieux de Marie Stuart": "Adieux, charmant pays de France."
24]   *Tricot*   A woolen knitted fabric (*OED* cites this line).
27]   *Perpend*   An archaic word meaning to consider, ponder, reflect on.
28]   *Gawain . . . Grail*   Sir Gawain quested for the Holy Grail, but lacking the purity of Percival, he was not vouchsafed the vision of it.
47]   *losels*   Scoundrels, good-for-nothings, rascals.
82]   *hunger . . . wood*   "Hunger drives the wolf out of the wood," a fourteenth-century French proverb.
90]   *thistle-fluffs*   The thistle-down, which carries the seeds in the wind.

   *bearded windlestraws*   Dry, thin stalks of grass (*OED* cites this line).

92] *blow-bell-down* The *OED* does not list "blow-bell-down," but its definition of "blow-ball" is appropriate: "the globular seeding head of the dandelion and allied plants."

101] *Bateleurs, baladines* See l.12.

102] *pique* Take pride in.

111] *Graces* A sarcastic reference to the three Graces, Greek goddesses of beauty and charm: Aglaia, Thalia, and Euphrosyne.

121] *five sous* A very small sum, there being one hundred sous to the franc.

125] *Nondescript* Earlier in the nineteenth century the English explorer and naturalist Charles Waterton (1782-1865) had perpetrated a hoax by returning from Guiana with a human-like specimen he called the Nondescript, a picture of which appeared as the frontispiece to his *Wanderings in South America* (1825). The creature, apparently fashioned from a red howler monkey, bore a striking resemblance to J. R. Lushington, the Secretary of the Treasury, who had imposed a duty tax on the specimens Waterton brought home with him.

129] *Knight . . . Fleece* The Order of the Golden Fleece was founded in 1430 by Philip the Good, Duke of Burgundy.

150] *pourtray* A variant of *portray.*

151] *swarth* Dusky complexion (rare; *OED* cites this line).

154] *velvet of the mole* Fifine's eyebrows, likened to the velvety fur of the mole.

159] *bistre* Brown, in keeping with "swarth" in l. 151 and "shade" in l.160.

163] *almandines* Violet-red garnets, but instead of true gemstones, these are glass, just as the turquoise is mock (*OED* cites this line).

169] *quarte and tierce* The fourth and third positions in fencing from which to parry or thrust (*OED* cites this line).

190] *flavourous* Full of flavor, pleasing to the taste and smell.

    *venomed bell* Perhaps belladonna, or deadly nightshade.

    *wot* Know (archaic).

202-5] *Louis . . . Onze* Louis XI (1423-83), King of France from 1461, was infirm during the last two or three years of his life, which he lived in seclusion at Plessis-les-Tours. B's source for the pageant mentioned in l. 201 is unknown. Neither the memoirs of Philippe de Comines (which B knew and referred to in *Red Cotton Night-Cap Country*) nor the *Biographie universelle* says anything about this.

210-11] *Helen . . . hand* Helen guided by Venus in accordance with the goddess's promise to Paris.

216] *Beldame* An old woman.

218]   *Cleopatra*   The other famous beauty of antiquity, referred to again in l. 362.

225]   *haught*   Haughty (archaic)

230]   *Pornic Church*   The church which had provided the setting for "Gold Hair" (*Dramatis Personae* [1864]; this edition, 6.193). In 1865 B wrote to Isa Blagden that the church was being pulled down: "since our arrival a fortnight ago, they have pulled—or are busy pulling down Pornic Church, mentioned in a poem of mine ["Gold Hair"]: on arriving, I went inside and found all as I had left it—last evening I looked through great gaps in the walls and saw the inside a mere shell: it was very old, and built on a natural pedestal of living rock—and there's the whole bare country round about to build on" (McAleer, 219).

234]   *pent-house*   Canopy, roof.

239]   *Besprent*   Strewed.

246]   *enough's a feast*   "Enough is as good as a feast," a proverb included in Charles Lamb's *Popular Fallacies* (1836) and described there as "a vile cold-scrag-of mutton sophism."

259]   *paragon*   Match (*OED* cites this line).

262]   *braving*   Facing danger with bravery, defying.

263]   *blinking*   Evading, shirking.
   *Troy-town* A frequent compound form in Homer and the title of one of Rossetti's poems.

264]   *purple prows*   The prows of Greek ships were painted red or purple. See the description of the twelve ships led by Odysseus to Troy in the catalogue of captains and ships in Homer, *The Iliad*, Book 2.

265]   *seigneur-like*   Like a nobleman, in this case by giving money.

267]   *franc*   In the latter part of the nineteenth century a common laborer would earn three to four francs per day.

273]   *becks*   Mute gestures.

275]   *nice*   Delicate or refined.

291]   *quintal*   Either a hundred pounds or a hundred kilograms (220 pounds), more likely the former if the Strong Man also has a cart wheel between his teeth.

304-24]   *Helen . . . time*   In *Helen* Euripides combined the version of Stesichorus (7th-6th centuries B.C.) that only the phantom of Helen went with Paris to Troy with Herodotus's account that Helen was in Egypt throughout the Trojan War.

334]   *extern*   A rare or poetical form of *external.*

336]   *outward . . . grace*   In the Catechism of *The Book of Common Prayer,* a sacrament is defined as "an outward and visible sign of an inward and spiritual grace."

348]  *facette*  Variant spelling of *facet,* one of the sides of a gem or other object with numerous faces.

360]  *blind beaks*  Rams attached to the bows of ships below the prows. Those beneath the waterline are blind in the sense of being hidden or out of sight.

361]  *equal-sided ships*  Greek ships had square ("equal-sided") sails.

362]  *Ptolemaic witch*  Cleopatra (69-30 B.C.) was the last ruler of the Ptolemaic dynasty. The notion of her as bewitching is continued in the passage beginning at l. 436.

371]  *lozenged blue*  The lozenge-shaped pane of the stained glass oriel window in l. 366.

  *benefic*  Beneficient.

374]  *sherd*  Shard, a fragment.

  *sun-smit*  Sun-smitten.

375]  *mope*  One who mopes.

377]  *Gloze*  Explain or comment (*OED* cites this line).

378]  *premiss*  Variant spelling of *premise.*

381]  *Pariah*  Originally, a member of one of the lower castes in India.

  *Nautch*  A kind of ballet dance performed by East Indian women, but used by B here and in "Natural Magic" to refer to the dancer (*OED* cites this line).

439]  *three-times-three*  A magical number in casting spells.

445]  *boots*  Avails.

469]  *graved*  Engraved.

473]  *dew-prime*  A nonce word, *prime* being the first canonical hour of the day, six o'clock or sunrise, when dew is plentiful.

482]  *white-night's*  Translation of the French "nuit blanche," a sleepless night.

483]  *Solon's self*  Athenian lawgiver (c. 639-559 B.C.), famous for his wisdom and known as one of the seven wise men of Greece.

486]  *acquist*  Acquisition.

501]  *fen-fire*  A will of the wisp, "ignus fatuus."

504]  *cribs*  Steals (informal).

505]  *tallow-rush*  A rush dipped in tallow and used as a candle, a rush-light or rush-candle.

  *squibs*  Firecrackers.

507]  *fizgig*  A firework, a squib (l. 505); also, a light, frivolous woman.

514-15]  *third . . . Manner*  The works of Raphael are divided into three periods: the first, the most religious, influenced by Pietro Perugino; the second, or Florentine, from 1504-1508; and the third, the Roman and most classical. Most connoisseurs prefer the third.

518] *Rafael* In B's time Raphael (1483-1520) was the most highly regarded of the Italian Renaissance painters. See B's "Andrea del Sarto."

524-25] *sell . . . pottage* Esau sold Jacob his birthright for a pottage of lentils (Gen. 25:29-34).

551] *Doré's last picture book* Gustave Doré, 1832 (not 1833, as it is sometimes given)-83, was a popular and prolific French illustrator.

565] *glad* Make glad (archaic).

566] *pochade* A rough sketch (*OED* cites only this line).

638] *Bazzi's lost profile* Giovanni Antonio Bazzi, known as Il Sodoma, (1477-1549) was a minor Sienese painter. For an explanation of why B refers to him as Razzi in the manuscript, see Ashby Bland Crowder's note to ll. 17-19 of "Of Pacchiarotto, and How He Worked in Distemper," this edition, 13.335.

639-40] *pillared cloud . . . fire by night* "And the Lord went before them by day in a pillar of a cloud, to lead them the way; and by night in a pillar of fire, to give them light; to go by day and night" (Exod. 13:21).

641] *modulating* Modulation is the change from one key to another within a musical composition.

*enharmonic change* "The respelling of a note in accordance with its changing function" (*Grove Dictionary*). The note remains the same, but the spelling changes, e.g. from C-sharp to D-flat.

642] *augmented sixth resolved* "An augmented 6th chord characteristically resolves to the chord of the dominant" (*Grove Dictionary*). The augmented sixth is an interval that is enharmonically equivalent to a minor seventh. However, the notes resolve in different directions depending on how they are spelled. If a dominant seventh chord in the key of D-sharp minor were to be respelled as an augmented sixth chord, this would facilitate modulation from D-sharp minor to D major. Normally these keys are considered to be rather distantly related, but the use of an augmented sixth chord makes it easy to modulate from the first key to the second. Resolution is the movement from a dissonant sound to a consonant sound.

644] *D major natural* A natural note is one that is neither sharpened nor flattened.

672] *deform* Deformed, ugly (archaic, *OED* cites this line).

684] *Plato* The Greek Philosopher (c. 428-347 B.C.) whose *Symposium* deals with the nature of love.

692] *superflux* Superfluity, surplus (*OED* cites this line).

693] *fiat lux* "Let there be light" (Gen. 1:3 in the Vulgate).

706] *Gérôme's* Jean-Leon Gérôme (1824-1904), popular French painter and sculptor of classical and oriental subjects.

710] *haled* Pulled, hauled.

720] *monadic* Single, indivisible, although the context suggests a reference to Leibnitz (1646-1716) and his belief that the soul is the dominant monad.

724-27] *Reynolds . . . Melpomene* A reference to Sir Joshua Reynolds's *Garrick Between Tragedy and Comedy* (ca. 1761, private collection), a painting of David Garrick (1717-79), in which the great actor is pulled with both hands by Thalia, muse of comedy, as he smiles at Melpomene, muse of tragedy, who holds him by the wrist with her right hand and raises her left above her head in a declamatory manner. Melpomene is "stiff-stoled" in that she wears a green stole about her head in the manner of a Roman matron.

755] *Michelagnolo* The unfinished sculpture by Michelangelo (1475-1564) described in the following lines is imaginary, but B may have had in mind the unfinished sculptures of the captives series in Florence.

759] *Master's* Michelangelo's.

778] *old man o' the sea* The sea god Proteus, subordinate to Poseidon.

779] *Eidotheé* In Book 4 of *The Odyssey*, Menelaus tells Telemachus of how Eidotheé, daughter of Proteus, assisted him on his return from Troy. Becalmed on the island of Pharos at the mouth of the Nile, Menelaus encounters Eidotheé, who explains how Menelaus and three of his men might disguise themselves as seals in order to seize Proteus when he counted his flock and so learn from him how to escape from the island.

781] *Mab* In *Romeo and Juliet* Mercutio describes Queen Mab as the fairy who brings dreams (1.4.53-95).

*Hero* Menelaus.

782] *isle* Pharos.

785] *told their tale* Counted the seals.

786] *fine . . . breath* Quoting from Homer, *Odyssey*, 4.451. The stench of the seals was so rank that Eidotheé put ambrosia under the men's nostrils as a sort of nosegay.

793] *Emprise* Enterprise.

796] *tool of triple tooth* The tooth chisel is used by the sculptor to refine forms and to remove the peaks and valleys left by the point chisel, which is used to rough out the shape. The flat and rondel chisels are used to smooth the texture left by the tooth chisel.

798] *dollars* Presumably Spanish dollars, or pieces of eight, each worth eight reales.

799] *five pauls* The paul, or *pado*, was an Italian silver coin of little value. A century earlier, Sterne mentioned in *Tristram Shandy* that five pauls purchased two hard boiled eggs.

816]  *Conquering and to conquer*  "And I saw and behold a white horse: and he that sat on him had a bow; and a crown was given unto him: and he went forth conquering, and to conquer" (Rev. 6:2).

861]  *triple-tine's*  The triple tooth chisel mentioned in l. 796.

903]  *Glumdalclich*  Gulliver's "little nurse," as he translates her name, during his voyage to Brobdingnag in Swift's *Gulliver's Travels*. The nine-year-old farmer's daughter was "not above forty foot high, being little for her age."

905]  *Theosutos e broteios eper kekramene*  Aeschylus, *Prometheus Bound*, 116, translated by B in l. 907. Spoken by Prometheus at the first approach of the chorus. Later references occur in ll. 2188, 2210, and 2216.

931]  *bombed*  Rounded, convex (rare; *OED* cites only this line.)

  *chrysopras*  The golden-green color of the gem by this name, a variety of the beryl.

935]  *gastroknemian*  The chief muscle of the calf of the leg (*OED* cites this line).

948]  *thrid*  Archaic form of *thread*.

949]  *Electrically*  With the suddenness, rapidity, or force of electricity.

951]  *transpierce*  Pierce from side to side.

952]  *tricksily*  In a playful, sportive manner.

957]  *suspirative*  Sighing.

975]  *Sainte Marie*  The  village two miles distant from Pornic, where B holidayed in 1862, 1863, and 1865.

980]  *rope-wreath . . . bead-blooms*  A wreath of artificial flowers made by stringing beads on wire. The craft dates back to the sixteenth century and was especially popular in France. These flowers were used as bouquets, altar decorations, and, as here, memorial wreaths.

983]  *camomile*  An aromatic creeping herb with white and yellow blooms.

986]  *bay*  The Bay of Bourgneuf, famous for its oysters and production of sea-salt. Pornic is on the NE coast of the bay.

987]  *Île Noirmoutier*  An island lying SW across the bay from Pornic. Now connected to the mainland by causeway and bridge, it was accessible in B's time only by boat.

1009-10]  *bathed . . . morning*  This stanza recalls the Prologue.

1046]  *illude*  Trick, deceive.

1049]  *sowse*  With a sudden or deep plunge, a variant spelling of *souse* (*OED* cites this line).

1050]  *dowse*  To plunge into water, a variant spelling of *douse* (*OED* cites this line).

1106-7]  *Man . . . gods*  From Byron's apostrophe to the ocean at the end of *Childe Harold's Pilgrimage*: "send'st him, shivering in thy playful spray / And howling, to his Gods" (Canto IV, CLXXX).

1107] *Childishest childe* Punning on Byron's title, as below in l. 1115.

1108] *flat-fish* In a letter to Annie Egerton Smith (16 August 1873) B denied calling Byron a flatfish but did admit to saying that Byron should associate with sea creatures if he meant what he said and did in fact prefer the sea to human society (Hood, 159). For a similar passage on Byron see ll. 566-70 of "La Saisiaz." An excerpt from the letter to Miss Smith is quoted in the note on these lines in this edition, 14.406.

1122] *'Who . . . hand'* "Who hath measured the waters in the hollow of his hand" (Isa. 40:12).

1126] *there . . . lay* Quoting from the last line of stanza CLXXX, *Childe Harold's Pilgrimage*, Canto IV.

1132] *beryl* A precious stone of pale green, or the pale sea-green color of the beryl.

1147] *Thalassia* Personification of the sea, which is the meaning of the Greek word.

1148-49] *Triton . . . conch* Triton, son of Poseidon and Amphitrite, used a conch shell as a trumpet.

1157] *Descents to Hell* Among the possibilities are those of Orpheus, Odysseus, Aeneas, and Dante.

1164-65] *life's . . . phrase* The phrase "Life's little hour" appears in l. 7 of Susan Evance's poem, "To Miss [Maria] Barton. This poem was published in Evance's *Poems* (1808).

1171] *pelf* Stolen property, booty.

1188] *bubble-fish* A jellyfish, B's coinage.

1191] *globose* Globe-shaped, spherical.

   *opaline* Having the color and iridescence of an opal.

1192] *amethysts* Precious stones of a purple or bluish violet color, as in the colors mentioned in the next two lines.

1193] *sea-flower* A sea-anemone, that is, the jellyfish.

1195] *head* The jellyfish has no head, only a mouth.

1198] *nine-tenths* The jellyfish is ninety-five percent water.

1208-9] *fisher-bird* The kingfisher.

1232] *Immurement* Confinement.

1235] *snuff* Examine by smelling.

1243] *Indian* The preceding lines describe how American Indians hunted by camouflaging themselves in animal skins.

1245] *belled* Bellowed, roared (*OED* cites this line).

1257] *loathlier* The standard comparative form in Anglo-Saxon but unusual in modern English.

1280] *swell . . . ox-size* In Aesop's fable "The Frog and the Ox," the father frog bursts in attempting to blow himself up to the size of an ox. The fable illustrates the danger of self-conceit.

1284] *brag* Loud noise.

1285] *ramp* Act of ramping (*OED* cites this line).

1291] *fable* The fable B recounts in this stanza comes from the first book of Herodotus's *History*.

1294] *Arion* Arion, the greatest musician of his time, enjoyed the patronage of King Periander of Corinth. During Arion's return voyage from a tour of Italy, he was robbed by the sailors and forced overboard. A dolphin rescued him by carrying him on its back to his home in Greece.

1299] *Methymnaean hand* Arion was originally from the city of Methymna on the island of Lesbos.

1300] *Phoebus'* Phoebus Apollo, the god of lyric poetry.

1303] *shattering dithyramb* Arion invented the dithyramb, dance music associated with the cult of Dionysus.

1309] *Orthian lay* Herodotus writes that just before hurling himself overboard, Arion sang the Orthian lay. *Orthia* is a word of unknown meaning associated with the worship of Artemis at Sparta. It now refers to singing in a high pitch (*OED* cites this line).

1315] *Stem* Make headway against.

1316] *grim* Grimness (obsolete as a noun).

*gulph* Obsolete spelling of *gulf.*

1318] *stems on* Keeps on course.

*saves* Makes a dangerous voyage safely.

1319] *Taenarus* The dolphin brought Arion to Taenarus, in Laconia, at the S tip of the Peloponnesian peninsula.

1322] *crab* The wild apple tree, or the sour fruit of it.

*love-apple* The tomato.

1323] *toil and moil* Rhyming synonyms, frequently paired, both meaning labor, drudgery.

1330] *god o' the grape* Bacchus, or Dionysus, god of wine.

1333-34] *indignant . . . press* "And the angel thrust in his sickle into the earth, and gathered the vine of the earth, and cast it into the great winepress of the wrath of God" (Rev. 14:19).

1335] *amimalcule* A small animal.

1336] *blotch* A shapeless object (*OED* cites this line).

1340] *thought, or word, or deed* The phrase appears as "thought, word, and deed" in the general confession of the Holy Communion service in *The Book of Common Prayer.*

1347] *furify* To render furious (rare; *OED* cites only this line).

1348] *pismire* Ant.

1349] *black bottle* Possibly the black bottle fly.

1351] *cuckoo-spits* A frothy secretion used by some insects to envelope their larvae on plants.

1394] *cockle-shell* A small boat.

1395] *crank* A nautical word meaning easily capsized.

1400] *firmland* Terra firma.

1431-37] *breast . . . deep* These lines paraphrase ll. 9-24 of Horace's *Odes* 1.3 ("On Virgil's Journey to Greece").

1438-41] *Horace . . . ode* Horace wrote the ode on the occasion in 19 B.C. when Virgil took his fatal trip to Greece.

1441] *comfortable* In the obsolete sense of encouraging, inspiriting, reassuring, cheering, perhaps intended to be ironic since the ode is not in fact very comforting.

1446] *Attica* The area around ancient Athens.

*thrid* Thread, see l. 948.

1454] *Long Walls* The walls built to protect the road from Athens to its seaport, Piraeus. The walls were destroyed by the Spartans in 404 B.C. but rebuilt in the next century. Sections remained until the nineteenth century.

1461] *Iostephanos* "The violet-crowned," Pindar's description of Athens: "O glittering violet-crowned, chanted in song, / Bulwark of Hellas, renowned Athens, / Citadel of the gods" (*Dithyrambs*, trans. C. M. Bowra).

1465] *plash* The sound of water splashing.

*plaint* Audible expression of sorrow (poetic).

1473] *express* Clearly (obsolete).

1484] *stoled* Wearing a stole.

1485] *cobbler in the king* The lowest in the highest, as exemplified in the eastern folk tale, "The Happy Cobbler."

1507] *excepted* The context indicates *exceptional*, but the *OED* gives no example of the word in this sense.

1511] *parti-coloured* Varied, diversified.

1516] *threescore years and ten* "The days of our years are threescore years and ten" (Ps. 90:10).

1527] *mind, sound in body sane* "*Mens sana in corpore sano*" (Juvenal, *Satires* 10.356).

1560] *four-cornered world* "And after these things I saw four angels standing on the four corners of the earth, holding the four winds of the earth" (Rev. 7:1).

1588] *Schumann's 'Carnival!'* Robert Schumann (1810-56) was inspired to write *Carnaval: scenes mignonnes sur quatre notes* during the Leipzig carnival in 1835. Published in 1837, it is a set of twenty-one scenes for solo piano, each of which depicts a character, scenario, or idea. The four notes referred to in the subtitle are based on the letters A, S, C, and H. These letters spell out the town of Asch, home of

Schumann's sweetheart at the time, Ernestine von Fricken, and are also present in his own last name. The notes are A, C, E flat (represented in German by S), and B flat (represented in German by H). In 1873 B heard Clara Schumann play this piano piece in London (Domett, 77).

1593] *spice-nut* Gingerbread nut.

1598] *crack of doom* "What, will the line stretch out to th' crack of doom?" (*Macbeth* 4.1.117).

1599] *merceries* Wares sold by a mercer, a dealer in textiles. According to the *OED*, the word usually occurs in the collective singular, only rarely in the plural.

1618] *bespread* Spread over, covered.

1619] *trow* Believe, suppose (archaic).

1622] *board-head* Head of the table.

1624] *way* Away, which is what B first wrote in the manuscript before striking through the first letter of the word.

1635] *obtuse* Dull, not acutely sensitive.

   *gust* Pleasing taste of food.

   *smack* Pleasant or agreeable to taste.

1644] *amber's* Ambergris, an ingredient in perfume, was formerly used in cooking.

1660] *canting* Whining, begging.

1662] *Columbine, Pantaloon* Characters from the commedia dell'arte and popular carnival costumes. They are the subject of scene fifteen in Schumann's *Carnaval*.

1663] *staccato,—legato* Antonyms, the first meaning notes separated by a pause, the second meaning notes connected smoothly.

1664] *Fi la folle* Fie the madwoman (French).

1666] *Harlequin* Another character from the commedia dell'arte that was popular for carnival. He is the subject of Schumann's third scene.

1680] *abductor* A muscle that draws any part of the body from its normal position.

1681] *tenths' and twelfths' unconscionable stretch* Notes ten or twelve diatonic degrees above or below a given note, requiring a stretch of the hand in this piano piece. Both tenths and twelfths are wide intervals. The tenth is an octave plus a third. The twelfth is an octave plus a fifth. The stretch of a tenth is awkward for many players and impossible for some. An unbroken twelfth is even more difficult.

1684-85] *Venice . . . proper* Famous for its carnivals, Venice had celebrated with masks and costumes as early as the thirteenth century.

1686] *Mark's Church* The eleventh century Byzantine Basilica of St. Mark.

1687] *Mark's Square* Named for the church but also enclosed by the doge's palace.

1688] *Procuratié-sides* So called because they housed the offices of the nine procurators, Venice's most important citizens after the doge.

1691] *casqued* Wearing a helmet.

1695] *frontispiece* Face (jocular; *OED* cites this line).

1696] *vizard* Mask.

1701] *chap* Jaw.

1736] *simulacra* Things existing in appearance only, not in substance.

1737] *plumb* Either immediately or straight down.

1738] *groundling* One of humble rank, low breeding or taste (obsolete and rare).

1743] *lightlier* An example of B's fondness for idiosyncratic comparative (as here) and superlative forms.

1744] *nearlier* Another idiosyncratic comparative.

1754] *checked* Curbed, repressed.

1790] *pelf* See l. 1171.

1794] *orbs ... temple* On 5 August 1846 B wrote to Elizabeth that "Our Druids used to make balls for divining out of such *all-but*-solid gems with the central weakness—I have had them in my hand" (*Correspondence*, 13.226).

1810] *elate* Exultant, flushed with success.

1822] *Timbuctoo* The ancient African city in present-day Mali. Tennyson had written a prize-winning poem on the subject while at Cambridge.

1835] *momently* Every moment.

1844] *meseemed* It seemed to me (archaic).

1869] *baluster-rope* Rope supported by balusters, or posts, along the side of a staircase.

1888] *cirque* Circle (poetic).

1912] *Commercing with the skies* "And looks commercing [communing] with the skies" (Milton's "Il Penseroso," 39).

1918] *chimeric* Imaginary, fanciful (*OED* cites this line).
    *supermundane* Belonging to a region above the world.

1922] *threescore years and ten* See l. 1516.

1926] *days are long i' the land* "Honor thy father and thy mother: that thy days may be long upon the land which the Lord thy God giveth thee" (Exod. 20:12).

1927] *chop and change* A change, alteration.

1942] *coign of vantage* Cornerstone affording a position of observation. "No jutty, frieze, / Buttress, nor coign of vantage, but this bird [martlet] / Hath made his pendent bed and procreant cradle" (*Macbeth* 1.6.6-8).

1943] *house not made with hands* "For we know that if our earthly house of this tabernacle were dissolved, we have a building of God, an house not made with hands, eternal in the heavens" (2 Cor. 5:1).

1955] *fullness of the days* "the fulness of times" (Eph. 1:10).

1986] *raree-show* A show or spectacle of any kind.

1996] *Behindhand* Too late or out of date.

2000] *fine gold grew dim* "How is the gold become dim! how is the most fine gold changed! the stones of the sanctuary are poured out in the top of every street" (Lam. 4:1).

2000-1] *brass . . . was* Solomon engaged Hiram of Tyre to make two pillars of brass for his palace (I Kings 7:13-15).

2003] *Harlequinade* Buffoonery, referring back to ll. 1662 and 1666.

2007] *evanishment* Disappearance.

2008] *marmoreal* Marble

2045] *Druid monument* On the outskirts of Pornic, the Tumulus des Mousseaux is a megalithic funeral chamber, dating from about 3500 B.C. Built with seventy blocks of stone, it has two transept galleries and several small secondary rooms. See Figure 1. There are a number of Druidic monuments in Brittany, the most spectacular of which is at Carnac.

FIGURE 1. Tumulus des Mousseaux

2056] *Bar-sinister* In heraldry an emblem of illegitimacy, but the context suggests a pun meaning evil barrier.

2062-63] *Just . . . land* Archaeologists believe that the stones, some weighing ten tons, were rolled on logs.

2100] *run their rigs* Played pranks, frolicked.

2103] *Curé* Curate, parish priest.

2109-24] *rungs . . . Heaven* Jacob "took of the stones of that place, and put them for his pillows, and lay down in that place to sleep. And he dreamed, and behold a ladder set upon the earth, and the top of it reached to heaven; and behold the angels of God ascending and descending it . . . . And Jacob awaked out of his sleep . . . . And he was afraid, and said How dreadful is this place! this is none other but the house of God, and this is the gate of heaven. And Jacob rose early in the morning, and took the stone that he had put for his pillows, and set it up for a pillar, and poured oil upon the top of it" (Gen. 28:11-18). The comparison to Jacob's stone had been made by J. M. Jephson in his *Narrative of a Walking Tour in Brittany* (London, 1859), 199.

2130] *arch-word* Original or initial word, although the context also allows for *arch* in the sense of most important.

2131] *charactery* Letters of the alphabet, writing (*OED* cites this line).

2138-51] *stone . . . again* In stanzas XII-XVI of "The Two Poets of Croisic" (this edition, 14.134ff.) B had described a similar repression of the Druids' fertility rites by local religious authorities, and in a letter to the Baron Seymour Kirkup he mentioned how at Le Croisic "women used to dance round a phallic stone" (Hood, 106). There is, however, no such stone at Pornic.

2142] *bleedings* Sap from a wound.

2152] *pert* The context suggests the meaning of "forward in speech and behavior, unbecomingly ready to express an opinion."

2156] *Saint Gille* Saint Giles, whose feast day is the occasion for the fair; see note to l. 10.

2162] *founderingly* In a falling down way. The *OED* does not list this adverb form of the present participle.

2165] *Protoplast* The first creator (*OED* cites this line).

2178] *triad* A chord of three notes, consisting of a given note with the third and fifth above it.

2188] *God . . . mixed* See l. 905.

2197] *excepted* See l. 1507.

2210] *Theosuton e broteion eper kekramenon* See l. 905.

2213] *poet . . . bird-phrase* Aeschylus, and *bird-phrase* perhaps because the chorus wears wings and so appears birdlike. The quoted lines in 2217-23 are from the chorus's first song in *Prometheus Bound*.

2215]   *Titan*   Prometheus

2216]   *God . . . mixture*   See l. 905.

*nymph*   The chorus in *Prometheus Bound* is composed of the daughters of Oceanos.

2225]   *poet's Titan*   Aeschylus's Prometheus

2225-26]   *Three-formed Fate, / Moirai Trimorphoi*   Aeschylus, *Prometheus Bound*, 516. The English phrase translates the Greek. In the play the chorus asks Prometheus who steers necessity, and he answers "triple formed Fate and remembering Furies."

2240]   *league*   About three miles.

2241-42]   *circuit . . . began*   "Thy firmness draws my circle just [perfect], / And makes me end where I begun" (John Donne, "A Valediction Forbidding Mourning," 35-36).

2256]   *plumes up his will*   "To plume up my will" (*Othello* 1.3.399).

2302]   *bell on bell*   The foam-bells, or bubbles, referring back to "foam-flake" in l. 2299 and to "Foam-flutter" in this line.

2321]   *stickle*   Strive or contend for.

2330]   *freak*   Vagary, sudden change.

*fret*   Disturbance, agitation.

2347]   *inconsciously*   Unconsciously (rare).

2351]   *silver whites*   Silver coins, perhaps referring to the franc in l. 2346, a silver coin worth less than a shilling in B's time.

*yellow double yolk*   Either two gold coins (Napoleons) or a double Napoleon, worth forty francs.

## EPILOGUE: THE HOUSEHOLDER

30]   *Affliction sore . . . bore*   The phrase is common in English epitaphs of the 18ᵗʰ and 19ᵗʰ centuries; it has this literary analogue: "Instruction sore long time I bore, / And cramming was in vain; / Till heaven did please my woes to ease / With water on the brain" (Mrs. Bedonebyasyoudid's epitaph for the turnip in Ch. 8 of Charles Kingsley's *The Water-Babies* (1863).

*RED COTTON NIGHT-CAP COUNTRY*

*Emendations to the Text*

The following emendations have been made to the 1889a text:

1.193:  The copy-text prints a single closing quotation mark at the end of this line, where a double mark is required. The MS-1875 reading is restored.

1.220:  The 1889a edition omits the required punctuation at the end of the line. The MS-1873 comma is restored.

1.434:  The 1889a edition omits the required punctuation at the end of the line. The MS-1873 exclamation mark is restored.

1.912:  In the copy-text, the last two letters of *succeeds* are missing; the correct MS-1873 reading is restored. This correction was made in later impressions of 1888-89, though at whose direction is unknown.

2.1050:  The 1889a edition omits the required punctuation at the end of the line. The P2-1873 comma is restored.

3.482:  The copy-text reading *licked* is not inherently erroneous, but the earlier reading *kicked* is rhetorically preferable and continues the sense of the MS-P2 reading *kicked with feet*. The CP2-1873 reading is restored.

3.794:  The 1889a edition omits the required punctuation at the end of the line. The MS-1873 question mark is restored.

3.807:  In all copies of 1888-89 collated, the punctuation at the end of this line is decayed to a single elevated point. The MS-1873 reading *alone:* is restored.

4.46:  The 1889a edition omits the required punctuation at the end of the line. The quotation mark in P2-1873 is restored.

4.88:  The 1889a edition omits the punctuation at the end of the line, running together two independent clauses. The colon in MS-1873 is restored.

4.287:  The 1889a edition omits the required punctuation at the end of the line. The quotation mark in MS-1873 is restored.

4.743:  The omission of the punctuation at the end of the line in 1889a runs together two independent sentences. The period in MS-1873 is restored.

4.775:  The 1889a reading *Being Art* is emended to *Bring Art* in accordance with 1873 and earlier texts. The 1889a text damages the sense by destroying the syntactic and semantic parallels with 4.774.

4.811:  The CP2 reading *weakness he* is restored. In CP2, B deleted the comma before the pronoun *he* in this line and in the parallel construction of line 808. The compositor made the change to line 808 but failed to make it here.

In addition, the compositors of 1888-89 frequently used B's paragraph breaks to divide one page from another. As a consequence, certain interruptions and shifts in the discourse disappeared in the copy-text. We have restored paragraph breaks lost in this way in *Red Cotton Night-Cap Country* at ll. 1.98-99, 1.138-39, 1.528-29, 1.1017-18, 2.190-91, 2.337-38, 2.586-87, 2.1060-61, 2.1085-86, 3.19-20, 3.70-71, 3.293-94, 3.490-91, 3.688-89, 3.702-3, 4.216-17, 4.263-64, 4.410, 4.653-54.

*Composition and Date*

In early October 1872, B wrote to Isa Blagden from Fontainbleau, "I bring back with me, for winter-work in London, a capital brand-new subject for my next poem" (McAleer, 385). Before arriving at Fontainbleau, B had been at St. Aubin-sur-Mer on the Norman coast, where he had found the subject for *Red Cotton Night-Cap Country*. He may have heard the story of Antonio Mellerio during his previous sojourn at St. Aubin in 1870, but the full details did not emerge until the trial contesting his will occurred in June and July of 1872. On 24 November 1872, B again referred to the poem in a letter, hoping to see Miss Thackeray "when my piece of work is done" (DeVane and Knickerbocker, 210). This reference implies that he had already begun to write the work, but he noted on the manuscript itself that he had begun on 1 December 1872, and finished on 23 January 1873.

When the poem was first set in proof in February, B's publisher, George Smith of Smith and Elder, became concerned about the possibility of a libel suit from some of the living individuals named in the work. The poet's first reaction was to write the following disclaimer— labeled an "Advertisement" and apparently intended as a preface— which he sent to George Smith on 26 March 1873:

> I premise, and wish to have distinctly borne in mind by any reader of this poem, that it is no more nor less than a mere account treated poetically, of certain problematic facts taken just as I find them given, by parties to a dispute, in the published pleadings of their respective legal advocates and the formal decision of a Court of Law. Each and every such statement, therefore, affecting the conduct of either party, must be considered as depending absolutely upon public authority and pretending to no sort of

guarantee for its truth obtainable from private sources of information—into none of which have I the will or power to enquire. My business confines itself to working a sum from arbitrary or imaginary figures: if these be correct, the result should follow as I give it—not otherwise. Nor would I attempt the working at all, had not the parties themselves begun by proposing the figures for examination. No fact has been purposely changed, although conversations, declared and described, could only be re-produced by a guess at something equivalent. Either party may—and one must have—exaggerated or extenuated or invented: my concern is exclusively with these presumable exaggerations and extenuations and inventions as they were presented to and decided upon by the Court of the Country, as they exist in print, and as they may be procured by anybody.

(DeVane and Knickerbocker, 211-12; See *Reconstruction*, E400)

However, Smith and B must have decided that it was not enough to declare that the poem was a factual account of public records and that the names would have to be changed. The poet also sought the advice of his friend John Duke Coleridge, the Attorney-General, as well as that of Robert Cumming Schenk, a lawyer and the American ambassador to Great Britain. Both men assured him that with the change of names he would be safe from legal action in Britain and the United States, and so he proceeded to make these changes in revising the final proof sheets of 15 March 1872.

Shortly before his death B answered an inquiry by T. J. Nettleship about *Red Cotton Night-Cap Country*: "the facts are so exactly put down, that, in order to avoid the possibility of prosecution for Libel—that is, telling the exact truth—I changed all the names of persons and places, as they stood in the original 'Proofs,' and gave them as they are to be found in Mrs. Orr's Hand-book" (Hood, 309). In the following list from the *Handbook* (Orr, *Hbk.*,261-62), the substituted names are to the left, followed by the original ones. [Mrs. Orr's page numbers have been replaced by the line numbers of the present edition, and misspellings are followed by the correct form in brackets.] These and all other such changes are indicated in the notes for those lines where they appear.

1.11 The Firm Miranda—Mellerio, Brothers
1.41 St Rambert—St. Aubin
1.42 Joyeux, Joyous-Gard—Lion, Lionesse
1.82 Vire-Caen
1.362 St. Rambertese—St. Aubinese

1.422 Londres—Douvres
1.424 London—Dover
1.427 La Roche—Courcelle [Courseulles]
1.428 Monlieu—Bernières
1.430 Villeneuve—Langrune
1.430 Pons—Luc
1.432 La Ravissante—La Délivrande
1.495 Raimbaux—Bayeux
1.499 Morillon—Hugonin.
1.506 Mirecourt—Bonnechose
1.513 Miranda—Mellerio
1.522 New York—Madrid
1.614 Clairvaux—Tailleville
1.638 Gonthier—Bény
1.643 Rousseau—Voltaire
1.645 Léonce—Antoine [Antonio]
1.785 Of "Firm Miranda, London and New York"—"Mellerio Brothers"—
Meller, people say
2.158 Rare Vissante—Dell Yvrande
2.160 Aldabert—Regnobert
2.164 Eldebert [Eldobert]—Ragnebert
2.174 Mailleville—Beaudoin
2.184 Chaumont—Quelen
2.186 Vertgalant—Talleyrand
2.304 Ravissantish—Delivrandish
2.483 Clara de Millefleurs—Anna de Beaupré
2.489 Coliseum Street—Miromesnil Street
2.629 Steiner—Mayer [Trayer]
2.630 Commercy—Larocy [Lalory]
2.630 Sierck—Metz
2.637 Muhlhausen—Debacker
2.661 Carlino Centofanti—Miranda di Mongino
2.800 Portugal—Italy
2.1017 Vaillant-Mériel
3.87 Thirty-three—Twenty-five
3.117 Beaumont—Pasquier
3.344 Sceaux—Garges
3.889 Luc de la Maison Rouge—Jean de la Becquetière
3.890 Claise—Vire
3.891 Maude—Anne
3.913 Dionysius—Eliezer
3.916 Scolastica—Elizabeth

3.1068 Twentieth—Thirteenth
4.368 Fricquot—Picot

*Sources*

*Red Cotton Night-Cap Country* is based on a story B heard while vacationing at St. Aubin-sur-Mer, Normandy. He had gone there initially to be near his close friend, Joseph Milsand, in August of 1870, but had left earlier than planned, returning to England by boat from Honfleur at the urging of Milsand, who feared for his safety during the Franco-Prussian War. After a holiday in Scotland in 1871, the poet and his sister returned to St. Aubin in 1872 and yet again in 1873, the year of the poem's publication.

The story is that of Antonio (sometimes Antoine) Mellerio (1827-70), who lived at Tailleville, only a short distance from St. Aubin. On 13 April 1870, a few months before the poet's first visit there, Mellerio, wealthy heir to the Paris jewelry firm, "Mellerio Brothers," leaped or fell to his death from the tower of his chateau at Tailleville, where he had lived in retirement with his mistress Madame Debacker, the wife of a Paris tailor. Mellerio willed his entire estate to his mistress, giving her a life interest in the Tailleville property with instructions that after her death it be given to the nearby Convent de la Délivrande for use as a hospital for the maimed.

In 1872 Mellerio's relatives contested the legitimacy of this will, arguing not only that he was mentally incompetent but that both his mistress and the representatives of the Convent de la Délivrande had cowed him into submission. The public hearings and the newspaper accounts revealed the details of his troubled life, which included a youthful period of dissipation followed by retirement to Tailleville with the mistress, moments of self-reproach accompanied by impulsive self-destructive acts, as when he deliberately burned both his hands to charred stumps, and occasions of excessive religious zeal.

It is likely B heard of Mellerio's violent death during his first visit to St. Aubin in August 1870, but he did not gather materials for his poem until his second visit in 1872, shortly after the court had passed judgment on the cousins' law suit. The Franco-Prussian war, which had cut short his 1870 visit to St. Aubin, had also delayed the Mellerio relatives' legal action for two years. The suit was heard in the court at Caen from 17 June through 8 July 1872, and the arguments were reported in detail in the newspaper *L'Ordre et la Liberté* from 19 June to 10 July, and perhaps in other newspapers. B vacationed in St. Aubin from mid-August to 14

September 1872, when the scandal was still fresh. He recalled the experience years later in a letter to J. T. Nettleship:

> I heard, first of all, the merest sketch of the story on the spot. Milsand told me that the owner of the house had destroyed himself from remorse at having behaved unfilially to his mother. In a subsequent visit (I paid one every year while Milsand lived there) he told me some other particulars, and they at once struck me as likely to have been occasioned by religious considerations as well as passionate woman-love,—and I concluded that there was no intention of committing suicide; and I said at once that I would myself treat the subject *just so.*
>
> Afterward he procured me the legal documents. I collected the accounts current among the people of the neighbourhood, inspected the house and grounds, and convinced myself that I had guessed rightly enough in every respect.
>
> (Hood, 309)

Although B acquired his information from a combination of sources—local informants, newspaper accounts of the trial, legal documents, as well as his own observations—there is no telling exactly which documents or newspapers he saw. Mellerio's wills and some of the depositions in the legal suit were filed with the *notaire* at Douvre la Délivrande, where they remain to this day. Other documents survive in archives at Caen. In his useful study, *Rough in Brutal Print: The Legal Sources of Browning's Red Cotton Night-Cap Country* (Columbus, 1981), Mark Siegchrist provides a translation of the newspaper articles on the trial from *L'Ordre et la Liberté* and of the handwritten court documents. B may have read the account of the trial in *L'Ordre et la Liberté,* which ran the story from 19 June through 10 July 1872, or he may have followed the trial in the *Journal de Caen,* but this paper's archives go back no further than 1877. The Armstrong Browning Library at Baylor University has copies of the *Journal de Caen*'s coverage of the cousins' appeal in July of 1873, copies on which B wrote "affaire Mellerio" and signed and which he probably had collected when he returned to St. Aubin in 1873, but these are not among the sources since they appeared two months after the poem's publication (*Reconstruction,* A1327-35).

The Huntington Library has a working paper of B's—partly in French, partly in English—that reveals some of the data he collected (see Figure 1). He records the names, the places and dates of birth and death, and the addresses of his principals, their relationships to one another, their movements about the country, and the locations and dates of key events in their lives. He lists chronologically Mellerio's wills, noting with each one the amount left to Madame Debacker, and he copies in full the last will of 21 October 1869.

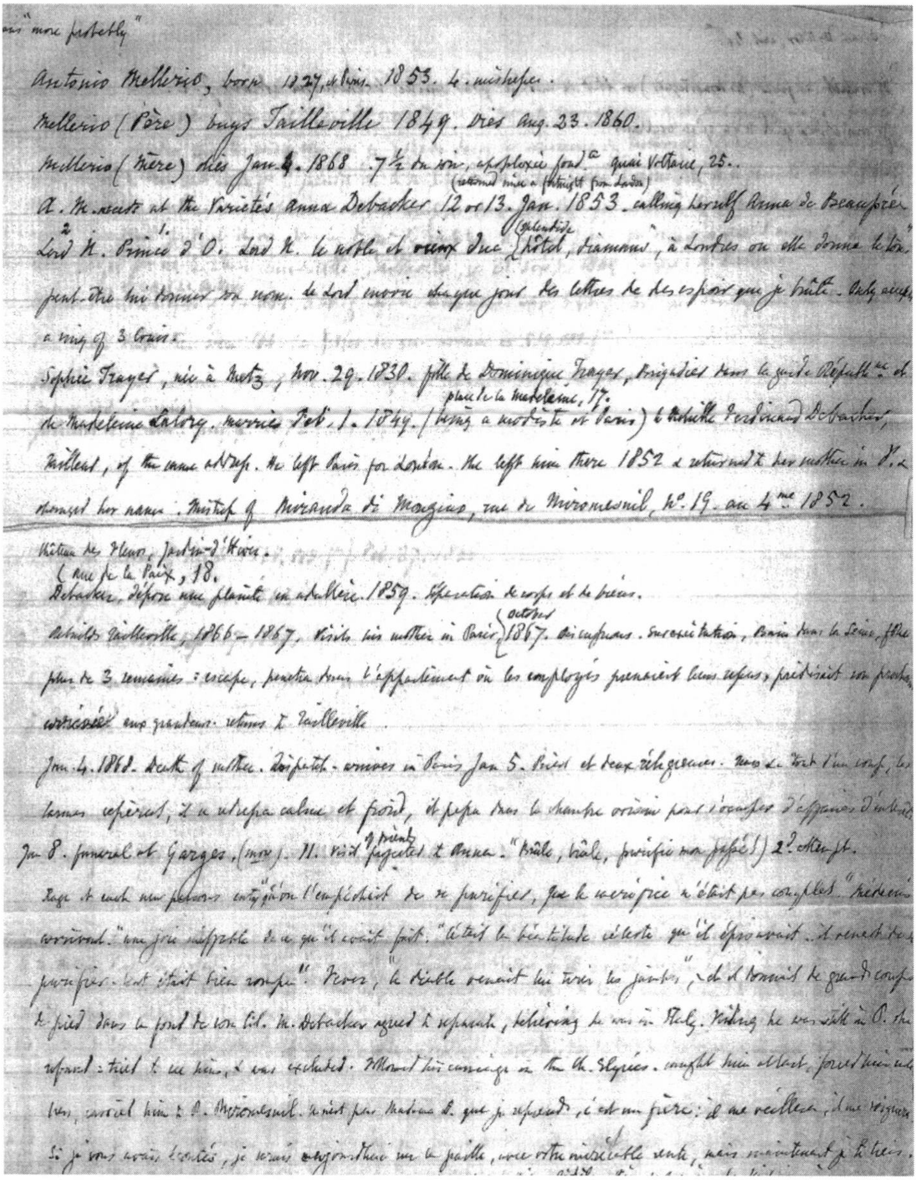
Mellerio (Père) buys Tailleville 1849. Dies Aug. 23. 1860.
A. M. meets at the Variétés Anna Debacker 12 or 13. Jan. 1853. calling herself Anna de Beaupré
rue de la Paix, 18.

FIGURE 1. First Page of Browning's Notes

*Text and Publication*

Because of B's extensive alterations in numerous sets of proofs, evidence survives from more than a dozen stages in the composition and revision of *Red Cotton Night-Cap Country*. The collated texts represented in our variant lists are discussed below.

*The Balliol Manuscript* (MS)   The manuscript of *Red Cotton Night-Cap Country* is in the Balliol College Library, Oxford, bound together with that of *The Inn Album* in a single volume. The text is written exclusively on the recto except for three instances when B used the verso for additional lines to be inserted into the text on the facing page. B inscribed a motto from Pindar, in Greek, on the title page, and lines from Euripides' "Rhesus," also in Greek, as a marginal comment on the tribute to Joseph Milsand in Part III. Neither of the Greek passages is in any edition B saw through the press. That this MS was the compositional one is shown by the dates in B's hand mentioned above. Its use as printers' copy is evidenced by the pencilling of compositors' names and take-marks throughout the MS in another hand. (*Reconstruction*, E399).

*Proofs of the First Edition*   Perhaps because of his rapid composition, B made extensive revisions to the text in the proof sheets. Since the earliest surviving proof sheets differ substantially from the MS, one can assume there was an initial set of proof sheets, produced in early February 1873 and now missing. B made additional changes to the text of the poem in later proof-stages, when fears of a libel suit led to a delay in publication. He substituted fictitious names for actual ones and sometimes softened his derisive language, but he also made revisions that had nothing to do with the legal threat. Thus even the last extant proofs, dated 15 March, include extensive revisions that are incorporated into the first edition. The surviving phases of proofing and correction include the following:

*P2*   Proof sheets for the first edition. Printers' labels identify this as "Author's Proof 2," dated 22-26 February, 1873. These proofs, in the Berg Collection of the N.Y. Public Library (*Reconstruction*, E402), contain corrections and additions in B's hand. Since the printed text of this proof differs substantially from the MS, it is reasonable to assume there was an intervening set of proof sheets, [*P1*], now missing. Nothing is known of [*P1*] or its date. Printed readings from these proofs are entered in the variants as *P2*; corrections are entered as *CP2*.

*P2a*   A duplicate of *P2* except for signature K$^8$ which derives from a set of *P3*. Labelled "Author's Proof 2," dated 22-26 February, 1873. *P2a* contains a few corrections and additions in B's hand, but these proof sheets seem not to have been used by the printers. Since they record a small part of the poet's creative process, the alterations are included in our variant list. *P2a* is housed in the Humanities Research Center of the University of Texas, Austin (*Reconstruction*, E403). Printed readings from these proofs are entered as *P2a*; corrections are entered as *CP2a*.

*P3* Later proofs for the first edition. Labelled by the printers "Author's Proof 3," dated 6-10 March, 1873. Some signatures are labeled "Author's Proof 2," but the dates on these labels and internal evidence suggest this number is incorrect. These proof sheets, in the Armstrong Browning Library at Baylor University (*Reconstruction*, E404), contain corrections and additions in B's hand. B's revisions include the substitution of some fictitious names for real ones for the first 614 lines of the poem, but in most cases B uses different fictitious names in both the subsequent *P4* and the first edition. This set of proof sheets contains some printed changes not found in *P3a*. Printed readings from these proofs are entered as *P3*; corrections are entered as *CP3*.

*P3a* A duplicate of *P3* except for signature K$^8$, which derives from a set of *P2*. These proof sheets contain corrections and additions by B and in another hand. B's revisions include the substitution of the fictitious names found in *P3*, this time up to 2.907 of Part 2, i.e., through signature I$^8$. A portion of signature K$^8$ heavily revised by B helps establish the sequence of authorial revisions. This signature predates and takes precedence over K$^8$ in *P2*. A printers' label affixed to signature P$^8$ is dated 10 March, 1873. These proof sheets, in the Armstrong Browning Library at Baylor University, are not listed in *Reconstruction*. Printed readings from these proofs are entered as *P3a*; corrections are entered as *CP3a*.

*P4* Proof sheets for the first edition with corrections and additions in B's hand. Although printers' labels continue to call this "Author's Proof 3," they are dated 15 March, 1873, later than both *P3* and *P3a*. Furthermore, some corrections to *P3* are incorporated into the printed text of these proof sheets, providing additional evidence that they are revises of *P3*. They are thus identified as *P4* in our variants. In revising these proofs for the first edition, B adopted the set of fictitious names of persons and places that he uses throughout the poem. *P4* is in the Berg Collection of the N.Y. Public Library (*Reconstruction*, E405). Corrections to these proofs are entered as *CP4*.

*The First Edition (1873)* *Red Cotton Night-Cap Country*, published by Smith, Elder, & Co. during the first week of May, 1873, in a green octavo volume of 282 pages. The earliest date on B's presentation copies is "May 3. '73" (*Reconstruction*, C509).

*Corrected Copy of the First Edition* (*C1873*)   A copy of the first edition of "Red Cotton Night-Cap Country," with corrections and additions in B's hand, prepared by the poet as copy for the 1888-89a edition. It is in the Berg Collection of the N.Y. Public Library (*Reconstruction*, E406).

*Collected Edition* (*1889a*)   In the *Poetical Works* of 1888-89, *Red Cotton Night-Cap Country* appears in Volume 12, pages 3-177. The copy-text for this edition is the first impression, 1888-89a (see above, *Preface*, sections II and III).

### Reception

The British reviews of *Red Cotton Night-Cap Country* appeared in May, June, and July of 1873, shortly after the volume's publication in early May. Though not enthusiastic in their praise of the poem, most of the reviewers were favorably inclined towards it, and those who were not at least found something good to say about parts of it.

Highest praise came from the reviewer in the *Examiner*, who particularly liked the moral lesson of the poem. Because of "the force of its teachings, and . . . the moral that Mr. Browning deduces from his very searching study of a very matter-of-fact present-day romance . . . it will deserve to be ranked among the most useful and memorable of all the good poems that he has written" (10 May 1873, 482). The review concludes with equal warmth: "With all our heart we thank Mr. Browning for his brave and eloquent unfolding of some of the chief social abuses of the present day" (484).

The review in the *Graphic* praised generally "the power and excellence of this fine work" and particularly the characters of the lovers, depicted by Browning with "wonderful power, insight, and subtlety" (31 May 1873, 515). As to be expected of a close friend, Alexandra Orr wrote a very favorable (and long) review, describing the poem as "surpassing as a work of art anything he has yet done" (*Contemporary Review*, June 1873, 87).

More critical reviews, on the other hand, found fault with the awkward title, the unpleasant subject, and the discordant mixture of the playfulness in the beginning of the poem and the tragic events that constitute its main subject. For the most part, though, these reviews repeated the two old complaints against Browning's poetry: it was unpoetical and obscure. The reviewer in the *Illustrated London News* criticized the poem on both counts, saying that "little of the poetical faculty is discernable in the unmusical poem under consideration" and that "Language so far as the use of it is to conceal thought, has been most skilfully and ingeniously employed in *Red Cotton Night-Cap Country* . . . . the poem . . . will be found a hard nut to crack" (21 June 1873, 590).

Few of his fellow reviewers disagreed about the poem's being unpoetical, but many considered it to be far less obscure than B's previous poems. For example, the reviewer in the *Spectator* concluded his article by remarking "that there is far less of obscurity . . . than usual with Mr. Browning. There is the same faulty, short-hand, article-eliminating hurry of style, as if the poet had to get his story told within a certain number of minutes, and every superfluous word, and many words by no means superfluous, must therefore be left to the reader to guess at. But there are a very few passages the meaning of which is not quite clear at the second reading" (10 May 1873, 607). The reviewer in the *Examiner* concurred, both about the compression and the clarity: "But while its thought is as compressed as usual, the thought is, for the most part, unusually clear and intelligible" (484). It was Mrs. Orr who paid the most attention to this aspect of the poem: "The 'new poem' possesses one quality at least which no one will dispute. It is easy to understand. . . . We are heartily glad that he has this time avoided his old ground of offence, and none the less so for believing that he has been more sinned against than sinning in the profound irritation which his so-called obscurities have created" (*Contemporary Review*, 105-6). She went on to explain that the fault was with readers who misunderstood the nature of Browning's poetry: "Many of his readers to whom it is irksome to substitute an active effort of attention for that state of receptive dreaminess which poetry is expected to encourage, resent his frequent ruggedness of form as if it were a real obstacle to comprehension and cannot be convinced that a style of expression which was more caressing to the ear would not find its way more easily to the understanding. There could be no greater mistake" (106).

On the other hand, even those reviewers who made this mistake in criticizing the poem for being obscure and ruggedly unpoetical acknowldeged the excellence of what one called B's "peculiar power; the ability to follow up the windings of involved and doubtful motives" (*British Quarterly Review*, 1 July 1873, 241). Even the reviewer for the *Illustrated London News*, so censorious of all other aspects of the poem, conceded that the characters of the two lovers "are analysed with much subtlety, shrewdness, quaintness and force" (590).

The American reviewers found no such redeeming value in what they considered the poem's obscurity, and, in addition, were offended by the subject, not, as with their British counterparts because it was unfit for poetry, but because it was immoral. The reviewer for the *Atlantic Monthly* described the story as "horrible and revolting . . . . the uncleanly history of M. Miranda's intrigue and lunacy. The poem—if it is a poem—is as unhandsome as it is unwholesome" (July 1873, 115). The reviewer for *Harper's New Monthly Magazine* admitted that he had not read through all of this "intolerably wearisome book," explaining, "We have read enough to know both the story and the manner in which it is told, and to enter our strong protest against the endeavor to glorify an illicit love with one who had been in succession a profligate woman and an unfaithful wife. The very abstruse and scarcely comprehensible moral which is tacked on at the close does not save the story from its essential spirit of immorality" (August 1873, 461).

From the very beginning readers objected to the poem's subject, not necessarily on moral grounds. Carlyle, in his typically blunt way, told William Allingham that "nobody out of Bedlam ever thought of choosing such a theme" (*A Diary*, ed. H. Allingham and D. Radford [London, 1907], 225). Ernest Dowden wrote that the subject was suitable enough for a realistic short story but "an unfortunate subject for a long poem" (*Robert Browning* [London, 1904], 308). Stopford Brooke described the poem as "the story of the man and woman in all its sordid and insane detail" (*The Poetry of Robert Browning* [New York, 1902], 419).

Later readers would not object so to the subject matter, but the poem was neither well liked nor widely read. In 1934 Saxe Commins edited *The Poems and Plays of Robert Browning* for the Modern Library Giant series, and despite the volume's 1223 pages, he had to exclude a few works: *Sordello* ("wholly unintelligible"), *Strafford* ("presupposes a considerable knowledge of the period"), *King Victor and King Charles* ("told in such a faltering manner"), and finally "the vague and perplexing *Red Cotton Night-Cap Country*" (xvii).

There are a few modern scholarly discussions of the poem, the most illuminating of which so far is Mark Siegchrist's *Rough in Brutal Print: The Legal Sources of Browning's Red Cotton Night-Cap Country* (see *Sources*). As the subtitle indicates, this study is more about the legal proceedings than about the poem itself.

*Title*

The poet offers one explanation for the title in the first section of the poem. His auditor, Anne Thackeray (see *Dedication* n.), referring to the innocent, peaceful, and somnolent appearance of the neighborhood, proposes "White Cotton Night-Cap Country" as an appropriate title for a book about the region. White cotton caps are indeed the traditional head-gear worn by Norman women (see Figures 2 and 3). But

FIGURE 2.  Norman Cap          FIGURE 3.  Norman Caps

appearances are deceiving, as the speaker insists: he will prove red the more appropriate color, since the region borders on a larger world, and its people are not insulated from the stormy passions of human experience represented by the red night-cap. The specific tale of Léonce Miranda's turbulent life and violent death will illustrate just that point.

Further, the speaker associates the red night-cap with the *bonnet rouge* worn by the *sans-culottes* of the French Revolution and displayed again as a symbol of revolutionary independence by supporters of the Paris Commune of 1871. Such political events and the convictions that motivated the opposing parties form the backdrop to the narrative. Indeed, the poem's title seems prefigured in a letter F. T. Palgrave wrote to B on 25 May 1871. Distraught over the burning of Paris and the horrors of "la semaine sanglante" then in progress, Palgrave suggests: "At the Herbert Cowper breakfast might not your toast be, 'May she make the bonnet rouge & convert it into a nightcap'" (A.J. Armstrong, ed. "Intimate Glimpses from Browning's Letter File," *Baylor Browning Interests Series Eight,* Waco:1934, 52). Ten years after the poem's publication, in 1882, the title was to figure humorously in its author's life when an Oxford undergraduate lowered from the gallery a red cotton night-cap upon the occasion of B's receiving the D.C.L. from the university.

An explanation of the subtitle, "Turf and Towers," emerges in the second section of the poem. "Turf" refers to the immediate pleasures of this world, particularly pleasures of the flesh, the amusements of "the Boulevard" (2.268); whereas "towers" pertain to religious faith, the Christian life of the spirit calling for self-denial and devotion to the Church. Léonce Miranda's efforts to reconcile his worldly desires with his religious belief reflect, in little, the controversies in the larger world over secular and religious authority, the powers of the state and the limits of individual freedom, the secular and religious grounds for judging moral conduct, and the association between reason and faith.

Title and subtitle join in the climactic episode, where they refer quite literally to Miranda's leaping from the tower and falling to the turf:

> A sublime spring from the balustrade
> About the tower so often talked about,
> A flash in middle air, and stone dead lay
> Monsieur Léonce Miranda on the turf.
>
> (4.338-41)

Miranda's bloody head stains his cap, "the Red Night-cap" (4.347), as the gardener says in lifting the head. In this episode literal blends with figurative as title combines with subtitle.

*Dedication*]   *To Miss Thackeray*   Anne Isabella Thackeray (1837-1919), the eldest daughter of the English novelist William Makepeace Thackeray. In 1877, she married a cousin, Richmond T. W. Ritchie, becoming Lady Ritchie when he was knighted in 1907. A popular prose writer in her time, Miss Thackeray was the author of novels, sketches, essays, and memoirs, as well as the entry for EBB in the *Dictionary of National Biography*.

Shortly after the Bs arrived in Rome in December, 1853, William Makepeace Thackeray called on them, accompanied by his daughters Anne, then age 15, and Harriet, age 13. B thought them "very genial and kind" (letter to Sarianna Browning, 19 December 1853, DeVane and Knickerbocker, 68). Anne visited the Brownings at other times in Rome, Paris, and Florence; and she maintained the connection throughout B's lifetime. She describes their friendship in her book *Records of Tennyson, Ruskin, and Browning* (London: 1892).

In 1872 Miss Thackeray chanced to be vacationing in Normandy at Lion-sur-Mer when B was gathering material for *Red Cotton Night-Cap Country* in the neighboring town of St. Aubin. Although a rift had developed between them (see 1.12-15n. below), their mutual friend Joseph

Milsand (see 3.726-82n.) brought about a reconciliation at this time, entertaining both B and Miss Thackeray at his house in Luc-sur-mer. On the return journey to Lion-sur-Mer, Miss Thackeray's party visited B's cottage. Afterwards, in a cordial letter to Miss Thackeray's sister-in-law, B expressed his pleasure at the unexpected company: "it makes the sky bluer and the sea brinier and the little house bigger in my memory," he wrote, and he advised her of the role Miss Thackeray would have in his forthcoming publication: "how I keep her in mind, she is going to see, if I may be so honored when my piece of work is done" (DeVane and Knickerbocker, 210). B not only dedicated the work to Miss Thackeray, he also included her in the poem, dramatized as the narrator's auditor.

1.1] *here . . . friend*  The setting is St. Aubin-sur-Mer, Calvados, in Lower Normandy (Basse- Normandie), which Browning fictionalized as St. Rambert (see 1.41n.). The friend, though not identified by name in the poem, is Anne Isabella Thackeray, and the speaker is B's dramatization of himself. See *Sources* and *Dedication* nn.

1.3-6] *Rome . . . sleep*  William Makepeace Thackeray and his daughters were among B's acquaintances in Rome in the winter of 1853 and the spring of 1854 (see *Dedication* n.). The Bs often picnicked with their friends in the Campagna, the plains of Rome with their ancient ruins. The setting inspired B's similar description in "Two in the Campagna," probably written in May of 1854. Cf. stanza V (this edition, 6.127):

> The champaign with its endless fleece
> Of feathery grasses everywhere!
> Silence and passion, joy and peace,
> An everlasting wash of air–
> Rome's ghost since her decease.

1.7] *Paris Boulevard*  The Bs stayed in Paris from 24 June to 11 July 1855 and again from 17 October 1855 to 29 June 1856. During both occasions they entertained the Thackeray girls.

1.9] *Place Vendôme*  B's substitute name for the Rue de la Paix, where the Mellerio jewelry firm is located at number 9. The Rue de la Paix extends from the Place Vendôme to the Place de l'Opéra.

1.10] *Golconda*  A ruined city and fort, just W of Hyderabad in India, famous for its trade in the diamonds mined nearby. The Koh-i-noor and Hope diamonds probably came from here.

1.11] *"The Firm-Miranda"*  B's fictitious name for Mellerio dits Meller (Mellerio known as Meller). The phrase "dits Meller" was added at the time of the French Revolution to give the firm a more French sounding name. The firm was *blazed about the world* as one patronized by the French royal family and, after establishing a shop in Madrid in 1850, by the Spanish royal family as well. Today the Paris store remains in its location at 9 Rue de la Paix, next to Cartier. See Figure 4.

FIGURE 4. Mellerio dits Meller, 9 Rue de la Paix

1.12-15]   *London . . . rib*   Perhaps an allusion to the misunderstanding between B and Miss Thackeray. Believing Miss Thackeray had spread rumors about his remarrying, B in London had been cool to her, "apparently going so far at a soirée as to dig her with his elbow" (Irvine and Honan, 471). Although aware that something was wrong between her and B, Anne Thackeray told Joseph Milsand that she did not know what it was. Milsand spoke to B, who visited Miss Thackeray at Lion to make amends (*Records of Tennyson, Ruskin, and Browning* [London: 1892], 174-75). The square may be one of London's residential garden squares, sometimes used for parties by those living in the surrounding terraces.

1.18]   *little village*   St. Aubin.

1.20]   *un-Murrayed*   Not included in Murray's popular travel guide.

1.22]   *mine . . . house*   B wrote to Isa Blagden on 27 August 1872, "our house here consists of five rooms: a parlour, kitchen, & room for the 'bonne' [maid] down*stairs* I was going to say—whereas there are no *stairs* at all, one goes outside and mounts by stone steps to Sarianna's bedroom & my own. In front is a little field, and then comes the sea— very wide, warm and enjoyable, as I walk into it straight from the 'parlour' aforesaid" (McAleer, 383). Anne Thackeray (later Lady Ritchie) visited the Bs and gave this description: "We entered the Brownings' house. The sitting-room door opened to the garden and the sea beyond–a fresh-swept bare floor, a table, three straw chairs, one book upon the table. Mr. Browning told us it was the only book he had with him. The bedrooms were as bare as the sitting-room, but I remember a little dumb piano standing in a corner, on which he used to practice in the early morning. I heard Mr. Browning declaring they were perfectly satisfied with their little house. That his brains, squeezed as dry as a sponge, were only ready for fresh air" (*Records of Tennyson, Ruskin, and Browning* [London: 1892], 177).

1.25]   *luzern*   Obsolete spelling of lucerne or lucern, a plant resembling clover, with blue or purple flowers and used as fodder (*OED* cites this line).

1.33]   *pipy . . . worm*   Probably the lugworm or sandworm, which can be as large as nine inches long on the coasts of Europe and which burrows in the sand, raising coiled castings in little mounds.

1.36]   *varech*   Seaweed. Baedeker's *Northern France* notes that along this coast seaweed is "cast up in large quantities by the sea" and is "used as manure by the peasants" (Karl Baedeker, *Northern France, from Belgium and the English Channel to the Loire, excluding Paris and its environs; handbook for travellers* [London, 1899], 177). Gustave Courbet included the seaweed in his painting, *The Beach at Saint Aubin-sur-Mer* (1867).

1.37-38] *Burnt . . . size* Brown seaweed, actually an algae, has air-filled, berry-like polyps to aid in flotation and turns black when exposed to the sun.

1.39-40] *And . . . vain* In 1.26-40 B describes his walk from his house to the beach, where he regularly went swimming, a great pleasure for him on his holidays in Brittany and Normandy. He wrote to Isa Blagden in September of 1870, "I have had–or shall have had today, my three dozenth good swim in the sea. The water washes away the cobwebs from my brain" (McAleer, 346).

1.41] *Saint-Rambert* B's alternative place name for St. Aubin. Saint Aubin-sur-Mer is on the Côte de Nacre, which is between Ouistreham and Courseulles. On D-Day it was on Sword Beach and liberated by Canadians. There are several Saint-Ramberts in France, none close to St. Aubin. Perhaps B chose the name because Rambert is a spelling variation of Ragnebert, B's substitution for Eldobert (see 2.165 n.). As for its being wilder than Joyeux, B described St. Aubin to Isa Blagden as "this little wild place" (McAleer, 342). In a letter to Annie Egerton Smith dated 4 August 1870, B wrote that "The wildness, savageness of the place, its quiet and remoteness, suit me exactly" (Hood, 140).

1.42] *Joyeux . . . Joyous-Gard* B's substitute place name for Lion-sur-Mer, where Anne Thackeray was staying. Joyeux is a small village in the Rhône-Alpes, not far from Lyons and the various Saint-Ramberts. Joyous Gard is Lancelot's castle in the Arthurian legends. Perhaps the similarity of Lion to Lyonesse suggested the Arthurian Joyous Gard.

1.43] *five miles* Actually closer to four, along the coast and to the east.

1.45-47] *Only . . . time* The speaker's first reference to the legend and miraculous events associated with the statue of Notre Dame de la Délivrande, referred to in the poem as la Ravissante (see 1.432n.).

1.49] *prig* The *OED* cites this as a figurative use of the word.

1.49-50] *Joyeux . . . masterpiece* The church at Lion (Joyeux), Saint-Pierre de Lion, has a Romanesque choir and a bell tower dating from the eleventh century. The *masterpiece*, on the other hand, is the basilica of Notre-Dame de la Délivrande, begun in 1854 and consecrated in 1895. See Figure 5.

1.72] *Rome's Corso* The Via del Corso is a principal thoroughfare in Rome, linking the Piazza del Popolo and the Piazza Venezia.

1.74] *Next . . . Saint* Internal evidence (see 1.444n.) fixes the date of the speaker's address as 29 August 1872. *Saint* probably refers to the Virgin Mary, Notre Dame de la Délivrande. The celebration of the Nativity of the Blessed Virgin Mary is 8 September, which would be *next Sunday* after Thursday, 29 August.

FIGURE 5. Church of Notre Dame de la Délivrande

1.78]   *Assembly from Versailles*   After the fall of Napoleon III's Second Empire with its defeat in the Franco-Prussian War, the new French government, including the National Assembly, moved to Versailles in March of 1871. It would not be until November 1879 that the Assembly returned to Paris.

1.82]   *Vire*   B's substitute place name for Caen. Caen is the chief city of Calvados, Normandy, and is twelve miles S of St. Aubin. Vire is also in Calvados, Normandy, forty miles SW of Caen.

1.83 *I fear me*   Archaic form of "I fear" or "I am afraid."

1.104]   *walk*   The distance from Lion to St. Aubin is only $3\frac{1}{2}$ miles.

1.120]   *lace*   "In Caen . . . we saw continually women seated at the house-doors, as one sees them in Belgium, engaged either in lace-making or much more frequently in embroidering tulle" (Katherine S. Macquoid, *Through Normandy* [London, 1874], 309).

1.132]   *immobilities*   Immovables (nonce word; *OED* cites only this line).

1.134-36]   *placards . . . populace*   The Emperor, Napoleon III of France (1808-73), declared war on Prussia in mid-July 1870, but his military resources were not equal to those of the Prussians. In early September the French suffered a disastrous military defeat at Sedan, where the Emperor, fighting with his army, surrendered to the Germans and was made prisoner. When the news reached Paris, he was summarily deposed and the Third Republic proclaimed. The poem echoes B's letter to Isa Blagden, written from St. Aubin on 19-22 August 1870: "I don't think he [Napoleon III] has a chance of re-entering Paris as Emperor. . . . oh, the caricatures which filled the shops at Rouen, of a Zouave kicking Bismark, King, Prussia & all, leagues away over the Rhine,—the soldier who, turning a mitrailleuse [machine-gun] too quickly, cleared the field before any sport could be had,–& so on,—surely all this 'brag,' and immorality too,—wanted the treatment it is getting only too energetically" (McAleer, 343-44).

1.139]   *drowsihead*   An archaic form of drowsiness (*OED* cites this line).

1.146]   *"White Cotton Night-cap Country?"*   See *Title* n.

1.147-49]   *For . . . repose*   Katherine Macquoid described the cap as "the snowy *bonnet de coton*, with its tassel a little on one side" (*Through Normandy*, 106).

1.160]   *idlesse*   An archaic and romantic form of idleness (*OED* cites this line).

1.165]   *Composite . . . too*   A combination pencil and dip pen.

1.250-54]   *This . . . forefinger-plucked*   B is referring to the special exhibition of ancient musical instruments at the South Kensington Museum (later the Victoria and Albert) in 1872. There is a catalogue, written by Carl Engel. B writes of *your* Kensington because this was the area of London where the Thackerays lived and the subject of Anne Thackeray's novel, *Old Kensington,* to be published in the next year (1873).

1.257] *Guarnerius, Straduarius* The Guernari family and Antonio Stradivari (1644-1737), renowned Italian violin makers of Cremona, crafted their finest instruments in the latter half of the seventeenth century and the early eighteenth century. See 1.270n.

1.264-65] *woods . . . gum* All of these features influence the tone and quality of the instrument. At one time the superb acoustics of the Stradivarius violin were attributed primarily to its varnish, which has never been duplicated.

1.267] *Corelli* Arcangelo Corelli (1653-1713), Italian violinist, conductor, composer, and teacher.

1.268] *cushat-dove* The European wood-pigeon or ring-dove (Scottish and northern dialect).

1.269] *Giga . . . Saraband* The giga and the saraband are two of several dance forms that became popular as movements in instrumental music in the seventeenth and eighteenth centuries. Corelli uses both forms.

1.270] *Paganini* The Italian virtuoso violinist, Niccolò Paganini (1782-1840). Paganini's favorite violin was a Guarneri (see 1.257n.) of 1742, made by the most accomplished violin maker of the family, Giuseppi Guarneri (1687-1745), called "del Gesù" because he used the letters IHS as his mark.

1.271] *tenuity* Thinness of voice.

1.282-83] *Pope's . . . frame* Throughout his life, the English poet Alexander Pope (1688-1744) suffered from severe headaches. His frame was stunted and misshapen as a consequence of childhood illness. Pope was embroiled in complicated and bitter literary quarrels that provoked some of his best satires. Dr. Johnson writes that as Pope grew older, "His hair had fallen almost all away; and he used to dine sometimes with Lord Oxford, privately, in a velvet cap (*Life of Pope,* ed. Peter Peterson [London, 1899], 75).

1.287] *Voltaire's* François Marie Arouet de Voltaire (1694-1778), the French author. The Italian writer Saverio Bettinelli described Voltaire as wearing "a cap of black velvet, which came down to his eyes" (Quoted by James Parton in his *Life of Voltaire* [Boston, 1882], 2.261).

1.287-90] *Hogarth . . . blood* William Hogarth (1697-1764), the English painter and engraver whose work is distinguished by realistic detail and sharp characterization. Thus B describes Hogarth eyeing and later painting *with true flesh and blood . . . some alley-phyz,* the face or physiognomy of a street person. B's Fra Lippo Lippi, another painter of flesh and blood, also uses the word *phiz* and also in an alley ("Fra Lippo Lippi," 327, this edition, 5.193). In both *The Painter and his Pug* (1749) and his self-portrait of 1757, Hogarth depicts himself wearing a soft cloth cap.

1.291]   *Poor . . . sarsnet-stripe*   The English poet William Cowper (1731-1800) suffered from recurrent bouts of insanity characterized by religious delusions, severe mental depression, and repeated attempts at suicide. George Romney, among other portraitists, painted Cowper in a large, white, soft cap. *Sarsnet* is a fine, soft, silk material.

1.296]   *hangman's toilet*   The hood traditionally worn by the hangman.

1.302]   *story-books*   Possibly Thomas Carlyle's *The French Revolution*, according to Charlotte Crawford Watkins in "Browning's 'Red Cotton Night-Cap Country' and Carlyle," *Victorian Studies*, 7 (1964), 363.

1.300-330]   *Well . . . place*   The incident described in these lines occurred on 20 June 1792, when a Parisian mob stormed Louis XVI's Tuileries palace and humiliated him by placing the red cap of revolution on his head. On this occasion he escaped unharmed. However, two months later, on 10 August 1792, the mob again stormed the palace, this time massacring the nine-hundred-man Swiss Guard and taking the king prisoner. The next month, September, the monarchy was abolished and a republic proclaimed. Bonaparte, the *Corsican lieutenant* of 1.324, did indeed witness the invasion of the palace on 20 June. While out walking with his friend and, later, private secretary, Bourrienne, he followed the mob to the Tuileries palace and the two of them, according to Bourrienne, watched from "the banks of the river. It was there that he [Napoleon] witnessed the scandalous scenes which took place; and it would be difficult to describe the surprise and indignation which they excited in him. When the King showed himself at the windows overlooking the garden, with the red cap, which one of the mob had put on his head, he could no longer repress his indignation. '*Che coglione,*' he loudly exclaimed. 'Why have they let in all that rabble! They should sweep off four or five hundred of them with the cannon; the rest would then set off fast enough'" (Louis Antoine Fauvelet de Bourrienne, *Memoirs of Napoleon Bonaparte*, ed. R. W. Phipps [NY, 1895], 1.18).

1.304]   *Commune*   The revolutionary government of Paris from 1789-95.

1.313-14]   *Phrygian . . . Freedom*   Phrygia, an ancient country in Asia Minor, was a principal source of slaves for classical Greece. Greek art depicts a soft conical cap as part of Phrygian dress. In ancient Rome such caps were presented to slaves when they were granted their freedom.

The cap thus became a symbol of liberty, especially in the eighteenth century when the red cap of freedom, the *bonnet rouge*, was adopted by the people during the French Revolution.

1.321] *did him stead* Did him service (archaic; *OED* cites this line).

1.324] *The Corsican lieutenant* At this time, in 1792, Napoleon Bonaparte (1769-1821) was a first lieutenant in the artillery, only one rank above that which he received upon his graduation from the École Militaire in 1785. In 1794, however, because of his conduct in the victorious siege of Toulon the previous year, he was promoted to brigadier general. Just two years later he was commander-in-chief of the Army of Italy.

1.327] *street-flags* Flagstones.

*canaille* Rabble, mob.

1.328] *droll* Buffoon (*OED* cites this line).

1.337] *Quod . . . ubique* The Latin translates "what was and is always and everywhere." The cleric is probably St. Vincent of Lerins, who wrote in his *Commonitorium* (434 A.D.) that "Quod ubique, quod semper, quod ab omnibus creditum est" ("What all men have at all times and everywhere believed must be regarded as true").

1.356] *Rahab-thread* The harlot Rahab protected the two spies Joshua sent to Jericho. In return, they told her to hang a scarlet cord from the window of her house as a sign that all therein were to be spared from the destruction of the city (Josh. 2 and 6:17-25).

1.361] *ruddy . . . blank* Red on the white (obsolete sense of *blank*).

1.364] *Octroi* The name given to a local tax on commodities brought into the city and to the tax collectors.

1.393] *strain point* Exceed one's obligation (*OED* cites this line).

1.402] *musicalest* One of B's idiosyncratic superlatives.

1.404] *Though . . . wool* "though your sins be as scarlet, they shall be as white as snow; though they be red like crimson, they shall be as wool" (Isa. 1:18).

1.406] *Liebig* The German scientist Baron Justus von Liebig (1803-73) was considered the ultimate authority in matters of chemistry. He made major contributions to the study of organic and inorganic chemistry and was among the first to systematize the teaching of laboratory methods of chemical research.

1.422] *Londres* B's substitute place name for Douvres, or Douvres-la-Délivrande, just three miles inland from St. Aubin. It is the site of the church of Notre-Dame de la Délivrande. There is no such place as Londres in France, but it is the French spelling of London.

1.422-24] *mother-mouse . . . birth* "Parturient montes, nascetur ridiculus mus" ("The mountains labor, a ridiculous mouse is brought forth," Horace, *Ars Poetica*, 139).

1.425] *the Conqueror's country* William the Conqueror (c.1028-87), Duke of Normandy, became William I, King of England, with the defeat of Harold at the battle of Hastings in 1066. William was born in Normandy at Falaise and buried in Normandy at Caen.

1.427] *La Roche* B's substitute place name for Courseulles-sur-Mer. There are some ten towns in France named La Roche, none close to the actual site of the poem. Courseulles-sur-Mer, not quite four miles W of St. Aubin, is well known for its oysters.

1.428] *Monlieu* B's substitute place name for Bernières-sur-Mer, halfway between Courseulles-sur-Mer and St. Aubin. There is no town by the name of Monlieu in France.

1.430] *Villeneuve* B's substitute place name for Langrune-sur-Mer, just over a mile E of St. Aubin. There are some ten Villeneuves in France, none of them in Normandy.

*Pons* A substitute for Luc-sur-Mer, E of Langrune-sur-Mer, a mile and half from St. Aubin. There are four French towns named Pons, none in Normandy.

1.432] *La Ravissante* "The Ravishing One," B's substitute name for La Délivrande.

1.435] *three . . . France* Pilgrimage shrines of France, dedicated to the Virgin Mary and noted for producing miraculous cures are at Douvres, Lourdes, and La Salette. After the virgin Mary appeared to two children at La Salette in 1846, and to Bernadette Soubirous at Lourdes in 1858, shrines were erected at the two sites. The tradition of pilgrimage associated with Notre Dame de la Délivrande is much older. Gustave Flaubert, who visited the area in 1877 in preparation for writing *Bouvard et Pécuchet*, has the two title characters make a pilgrimage there, and in chapter nine names these pilgrims: "Louis XI, Louis XIII, deux filles de Gaston d'Orleans, le cardinal Wiseman, Samirrhi, patriarche d'Antioche; Mgr Véroles, vicaire apostolique de la Manctrourie; et l'archevêque de Quélen vint lui rendre grâce pour la conversion du prince de Talleyrand" (*Bouvard et Pécuchet* [Paris, 1881], 310). ("Louis XI, Louis XIII, two daughters of Gaston d'Orleans, Cardinal Wiseman, Samirrhi, Patriarch of Antioch; Monseigneur Véroles, Vicar Apostolic of Manchuria; and Archbishop Quélen came to give thanks for the conversion of Prince Talleyrand.") The two daughters of Gaston d'Orleans, nieces of Louis XIII, were the Grand Duchess of Florence and the Duchess d'Alençon. Their pilgrimage occurred in 1678. Cardinal Wiseman, first Archbishop of Westminster, came in July 1851. Ignatius Anthony Samhiri (or Samhery) was Patriarch of Antioch for the Syrian Catholic Church from 1853 to 1864 and probably visited Douvres in 1855. Monseigneur Véroles came in September of 1845. See 4.179n. for the pilgrimage of Louis XI and 2.184-86n. for that of Archbishop Quélen. By the middle of the nineteenth century, some 150,000 pilgrims visited the shrine at Douvres each year. In *Bouvard et Pécuchet*, Flaubert also names several miracles: "Ses miracles sont innombrables. Un marchand de Bayeux, captif chez les Sarrasons, l'invoqua: ses fers tombent et il s'échappe. Un avare découvre dans son grenier un troupeau de rats, l'appelle à son secours et les rats s'éloignent. Le contact d'une médaille ayant effleuré son effigie fit se repentir au lit de mort un vieux matérialiste de Versailles. Elle rendit la parole au sieur Adeline, qui l'avait perdue pour blasphéme; et, par sa protection, M. et Mme. De Becqueville eurent assez de force pour vivre chastement en état de mariage" (310). ("Her [the Virgin's] miracles are countless. A merchant from Bayeux, held captive by the Saracens, appeals to her; his shackles fall off and he escapes. A miser discovers in his granary a pack of rats; he calls upon her help and the rats leave. The touch of a medal that had been brushed against her statue causes an old materialist of Versailles to repent on his death bed. She restores the ability to speak to Lord Adeline, who had lost it because of blasphemy; and by her influence Monsieur and Madame De Becqueville had enough strength to live a chaste life in a state of marriage.") Chains, reputed to be those of the merchant of Bayeux, presently hang in the chapel of St. Anne as a votive offering.

1.438]    *Lourdes and La Salette*   See 1.435n.

1.443-44]    *This . . . observed*   The coronation of Notre Dame de la Délivrande, B's La Ravissante, took place during his stay at St. Aubin on 22 August 1872, one week before the time of the poem's monologue, 29 August (see 1.503n.). Each year the event is celebrated on the first Thursday following 15 August. Strictly speaking, the midsummer month is June, the time of the summer solstice. The coronation at Lourdes was not until 1876.

1.460]    *Pope's . . . crowns*   B accurately amends this statement in 1.466-69. As a rule, the crowns for such ceremonies were provided by the Pope, but in January 1870 Pius IX gave approval to the coronation of La Délivrande with the proviso that the faithful of the diocese supply the crowns. Shortly before the coronation ceremony, Father Picot (see 4.368n.) took the completed crowns to Rome to be blessed by the Pope. There were two crowns, one for the Virgin and one for the infant Jesus, whom she holds.

1.463-65]    *fund . . . year*   In 1631 Count Alexander Sforza-Pallavicini of Piacenza (not to be confused with a better known fifteenth-century Count Sforza) paid the expenses for crowning a painting, *Santa Maria della febbre*, in one of the sacristies of St. Peter's in Rome. The count left considerable property in his will of 1636 to the Chapter of St. Peter to pay for the crowning of pictures and statues of the Virgin. The rite of coronation is a symbolic honoring of the sacred image. A pamphlet published for the coronation ceremony, a copy of which is in ABL, signed and dated by B ("Robert Browning, St. Aubin, Sept. 14. '72."), states that "Le comte Alexandre Sforza, pour continuer, méme après sa mort, les actes de sa piété envers Marie, fit au vénérable Chapitre de Saint-Pierre un legs important, à la charge d'offrir chaque année une couronne d'or aux madones les plus célèbres de l'univers catholique"(*Fête du Couronnement de Notre-Dame de la Délivrande* [Caen, 1872], 5; *Reconstruction*, A946). ("Count Alexander Sforza, in order to continue even after his death acts of piety for Mary, left a considerable bequest to the venerable Chapter of Saint Peter on the condition that it offer each year a golden crown to the most celebrated madonnas in the Catholic world.")

1.466] *prison-house* When Victor Emmanuel II seized Rome in 1870 and made it the capital of Italy in 1871, Pope Pius IX refused to recognize his authority and considered himself a prisoner in the Vatican.

1.469] *the faithful . . . sum* See 1.460n.

1.477] *fifty-franc* The modern value is about one hundred euros.

1.488-94] *but . . . bare* In 1850 the rector of Notre Dame de la Délivrande in Douvres, Msgr. Etienne Jean François Le Herpeur, was appointed first bishop of Martinique, where he founded at the town of Morne-Rouge a church named after the one he left in Normandy. In 1853 the church commissioned an artist in Normandy to make a statue of the Virgin, and this statue was crowned 8 December 1868, four years before the coronation at Douvres. On the matter of the church in Martinique being honored before the one at Douvres, the *Fête du Couronnement de Notre-Dame de la Délivrande* (see 1.463-65n.) states that "Cet étonnement s'accrut encore, dans le diocèse de Bayeux, lorsqu'un pèlerinage issu du nôtre, mais sur une terre lointaine, Notre-Dame de la Délivrande à la Martinique, reçut cet honneur bien mérité, mais qui, disait-on naïvement, mettait *la Fille avant la Mère*" (6). ("This astonishment [that the church had not yet been honored with a coronation] grew even greater in the diocese of Bayeux when a shrine having come from us but in a faraway land, Notre Dame de la Délivrande in Martinique, received this well deserved honor, but which, as it was said naively, put *the Daughter before the Mother*.")

1.495-503] *Bishop . . . since* At the first Vatican Council, the Bishop of Bayeux, Msgr. Hugonin (1823-98), with the support of many other church officials from Normandy, successfully petitioned for papal approval of a crown for Notre Dame de la Délivrande. B substitutes the names *Raimbaux* for *Bayeux* and *Morillon* for *Hugonin*. The coronation ceremony took place on 22 August 1872, seven days before 29 August, the date of the poem's monologue (see 1.443-44n.). The pope was Pius IX (1792-1878), pontiff from 1846-78.

1.506]   *Cardinal Mirecourt*   B's substitute name for the Archbishop of Rouen, Cardinal Bonnechose (1800-1883), who presided at the ceremony.

1.508]   *August-strippage*   Branches stripped from trees. (Rare; *OED* cites only this example.)

1.513-20]   *Miranda . . . Stone*   Miranda is B's substitute name for Mellerio. The pamphlet titled *Fête du Couronnement de Notre-Dame de la Délivrande* (see 1.463-65n.) states that "un des jouaillers les plus célèbres de Paris, M. Mellerio, se chargea de confectionner les couronnes, auxquelles il voulut contribuer lui-même par le don d'une pierre de grand prix" (8). ("one of the most famous jewellers of Paris, Mr. Mellerio, was commissioned to make the crowns, to which he wanted to contribute himself with the gift of a stone of great value.") B marked this passage in the margin. See Figure 6.

FIGURE 6. Crown made by Mellerio for the Coronation of the Virgin

1.522] *New-York* Substituted for Madrid. The Mellerios had established a shop in Madrid in 1850, Mellerio-Hermanos (Mellerio-Brothers).

1.525-28] *since . . . brocade* The reference is to Mme. Muhlhausen, Miranda's mistress rather than his wife. The program for the ceremony (*Fête du Couronnement*, see 1.463-65n.) states that the robe of the Virgin's statue was made by the Parisian house of Poussielgue and that "une main accoutumé à parer Notre-Dame de la Délivrande ajoutait au voile d'or, une riche parure de dentelles." (9) ("a hand accustomed to dressing Notre Dame de la Délivrande added a golden veil, richly ornamented with lace.") B also marked this passage in the margin. The statue of the Virgin is dressed in a robe, changed several times a year from among a wardrobe of some twenty-four. See Figure 7.

1.532] *devotions at high tide* Most likely swimming.

FIGURE 7. Statue of the Virgin and Child wearing crowns made by Mellerio

1.542-43]   *liquid . . . Miranda*   The original name, Mellerio, is more
aptly described as *liquid* than the substitute Miranda.

1.545]   *Abaris*   A servant of Apollo who rode through the air on a
golden arrow, the symbol for the god of archery.

1.556-57]   *Heaven . . . man*   Possibly a reference to Luke 17:21: "for,
behold, the kingdom of God is within you."

1.595]   *diamond-necklace-dealing*   A reference to a scandal in the French
court in the 1780s, the subject of Thomas Carlyle's *The Diamond Necklace*
(1837) and Alexander Dumas's *The Queen's Necklace* (1848). The scandal
added to the public's disapproval of the monarchy and especially of
Marie Antoinette, though she was probably blameless.

1.610]   *lucarnes*   Dormer windows.

1.614-15]   *Clairvaux . . . Priory*   Clairvaux is the substitute name for
Tailleville. B's note reads, "Tailleville was originally a Priory belonging
to the Abbaye aux Hommes at Caen: became a Bien-National [a national
or state-owned property], was several times sold, till bought by M. [Mel-
lerio]." See Figure 8.

FIGURE 8.  Mellerio chateau at Tailleville

1.616-19]    *Abbey-for-the-Males . . . retain*    William, Duke of Normandy (later, the Conqueror) founded the Abbaye-aux-Hommes in Caen in 1063, three years after his duchess, Matilda, founded the Abbaye-aux-Dames. They built these abbeys to receive pardon from Pope Leo IX for their consanguineous marriage. Upon his death in 1087, William was buried, according to his wish, in the choir of the abbey. In 1562 Huguenots desecrated the tomb, an act repeated by the Revolutionaries in 1793.

1.622-24]    *And . . . Domain*    With the French Revolution (*Red Cap*) the ownership of all church property was transferred to the state.

1.627]    *three-and-twenty years ago*    1849, twenty-three years before 1872, the time of the poem's monologue.

1.630-31]    *French . . . Miranda*    That is, Miranda père (*Father Miranda*).

1.632]    *Madrilene*    A resident of Madrid. B substitutes Madrid for Turin.

1.636]    *Place Vêndome*    Actually 9 Rue de la Paix.

1.638]    *Gonthier . . . Villeneuve*    Gonthier is a fictitious name for Bény-sur-Mer, four miles S of St. Aubin. For Monlieu and Villeneuve, see 1.428n. and 1.430n. Mellerio mentioned his property in Bernières, Langrune, and Bény in his last will (see 1.749n.).

1.639-40]    *twelve . . . demise*    The father died 23 August 1860. He was born Jean-Antoine (in Italian, Giovanni Antonio) Mellerio in 1798.

1.643]    *Quai Rousseau*    B's substitute name for Quai Voltaire. The exact address is 25 Quai Voltaire. See Figure 9.

1.652]    *branchage-roof*    A roof of branches in the mass    (*OED* cites only this line and one other, from *The Ring and the Book*, 10.274).

1.653]    *affronts*    An archaic sense of the word, meaning to front or face in position (*OED* cites this line).

1.655]    *Hey, presto, pass*    A phrase said by a magician or conjurer when performing a trick.

1.656-57]    *park . . . l'Anglaise*    A park in the English style is based on Romantic aesthetics, that is, irregular, picturesque, and *natural*, as opposed to the formal, neo-classical gardens and parks that had been fashionable previously. The English style grew in popularity, in Europe as well as Britain, from the mid-eighteenth century onward.

1.659]    *bosses*    Raised or protuberant designs.

   *embosomings*    Shelters or enclosures.

1.666]    *coquetry*    Prettiness (*OED* cites this line).

1.670]    *lightsome*    Light-hearted, cheerful, merry.

1.671]    *late*    Recently (poetical; see 1.610 and    1.613).

1.672]    *mansarde-roof*    The mansard roof has two slopes on each of four sides, the lower steeper than the upper. It takes its name from the

FIGURE 9. Mellerio family residence at 25 Quai Voltaire

French architect François Mansard (1598-1666), who revived and popularized this style.

1.704] *Parc Anglais* English park (see 1.657n.).

1.705] *shrub-embossment* See 1.659n.

1.706-9] *bauble . . . ball-convexity* B here describes the effects of an ornamental reflecting globe, variously called a garden ball, gazing globe, or garden globe, invented in thirteenth-century Venice.

1.714] *Elysées . . . Boulogne* The Champs [*Fields*] Elysées and the Bois [*wood*] de Boulogne, famous avenue and park in Paris.

1.719] *six . . . elapsed* Six years since he inherited Clairvaux (Tailleville) upon the death of his father in 1860.

1.720] *made . . . smile* "The wilderness and the solitary place shall be glad for them: and the desert shall rejoice, and blossom as the rose" (Isa. 35:1). See also Alexander Pope's "Eloisa to Abelard": "You rais'd these hallow'd walls; the desert smil'd, / And Paradise was open'd in the wild" (133-34). Thomas Moore as well uses the figure of speech in the second stanza of his "One Bumper at Parting" from *Irish Melodies*: "These few sunny spots, like the present / That 'mid the dull wilderness smile!"

1.744]   *regalized*   To make regal or royal (rare; *OED* cites only this example).

1.749]   *last bequeathment*   Antonio Mellerio's last will, dated 21 October 1869, bequeathed to the Convent of la Charité des Orphelines de la Délivrande (La Ravissante) his estate at Tailleville (Clairvaux); properties at Berniéres, Langrune, and Bény; and 200,000 francs. However, the will stipulated that the convent was not to take possession of this legacy until after the death of Mme. Debacker (Mme. Muhlhausen), who was to have use of it during her lifetime and to receive as his beneficiary the remainder of the estate. B copied out this will in his notes and also wrote down the dates of the previous four wills: 27 February 1865, 4 June 1868, 17 September 1868, and 27 June 1869.

1.755]   *as I told you*   See 1.520 and   1.544-45.

1.760]   *prophet*   In Num. 22-23, King Balak of Moab orders the prophet Balaam to curse the Israelites, but Balaam obeys God and blesses them instead.

1.764]   *Bride*   The statue of Notre Dame de la Délivrande.

1.772]   *Cousinry*   A group of cousins. Ten of Antonio Mellerio's first cousins unsuccessfully contested his will, first in 1872, and then through appeals in 1873 and 1874. Seven of these cousins were the children of Mellerio's father's sister and three were the children of his mother's sister. Mark Siegchrist's *Rough in Brutal Print* (see *Sources*) gives a full account of the legal proceedings.

1.777-85]   *Heirs . . . New-York*   Antonio Mellerio sold the jewelry business to his cousins for 180,000 francs in 1869. The descendant of one of the cousins, Jean François Mellerio, operates the business today at the same address, 9 Rue de la Paix.

1.804]   *sidelingly*   Side by side. Not recorded in the *OED* but used by Melville in *Moby Dick*. As both an adjective and an adverb, *sideling* does not require the *-ly* suffix.

1.815-19]   *That . . . Ravissante*   Mellerio's fourth will (27 June 1869) added to the previous one of 17 September 1868 that after the death of Mme. Debacker, Tailleville should be made into a hospital for crippled paupers to be called St. Joseph's Asylum. The building was never used for this purpose. Instead, the convent rented it out. During World War II it was a German radar station. Undamaged by the Normandy invasion, it now belongs to the Chiffoniers d'Emmaüs, a charitable organization.

1.834]   *darlinglike*   Labeled a nonce-word by the *OED*, which cites this line.

1.840]   *forty*   Mme. Debacker was born 29 November 1830 and would have been almost forty-two at the time of the poem's dialogue in August of 1872.

1.853] *impressment* Exertion of pressure.

1.885] *suits* Matches in color (obsolete or archaic).

1.888] *Châtelaine* Lady of the manor.

1.898] *Isleted* Like an islet (*OED* cites this line).

1.950] *benefic* Benign, beneficent (*OED* cites this line).

1.951-52] *She . . . first* In Matt. 20:1-16 Jesus tells the parable of the landowner who hires laborers for his vineyard at different times of the day and yet pays them all, the last hired as well as the first, the same: one penny.

1.971] *Peter-pence* Peter's Pence was originally a donation to the pope of a penny per household in eighth-century England. The practice continues in modern times throughout the Catholic world with donations, no longer limited to a penny, collected the Sunday closest to 29 June, the Solemnity of Saints Peter and Paul.

1.973] *imprisoned* See 1.466n.

*Lord, how long* See Rev. 6:10 and the last line of B's "Filippo Baldunucci on the Privilege of Burial" (this edition, 13.387-88 and nn.).

1.983] *baignoire* A theater box.

1.986] *parure* Matched set of jewelry.

1.1021] *laurustines* An Anglicized form of laurustinus (*Viburnum Tinus*), a flowering evergreen shrub.

1.1025] *sinistrous* Ill-omened, baleful (*OED* cites this line).

*Section 2*

2.5] *fane* Temple.

*cirque* A hollow space, usually in the mountains, surrounded by cliffs.

2.10] *Time's tooth* Cf. "the tooth of time" (*Measure for Measure*, 5.1.12), and the fourth line of Thomas Hood's sonnet, "To an Enthusiast": "Spite of the world's cold practice and Time's tooth . . . ." B had previously used the phrase in *The Ring and the Book*: "Granite, time's tooth should grate against, not graze" (1.660).

2.12] *Gallic Tuileries* This French royal palace built in Paris during the sixteenth century was rarely used until the French Revolution, when Louis XVI was forced to move there from Versailles in 1789. It became the chief residence of Napoleon I and subsequent rulers, including Napoleon III. In the Paris rebellion of 1871, the palace was burned down by the Communards on 23 May, as they retreated from the Versailles troops during *La Semaine Sanglante*, "the bloody week" of fighting that ended the rebellion. The ruins were not demolished until 1883 and thus were still standing when B wrote this line.

2.67-68]   *Father Secchi . . . transit*   Pietro Angelo Secchi (1818-78), a Jesuit priest and astronomer known as the "father of astrophysics," was director of the Vatican observatory. He placed the observatory on the roof of St. Ignatius Church in Rome. Venus passed directly between the sun and earth in December 1874; B's reference anticipates the event by two years. The transit had last been observed by Captain Cook on his first voyage to the South Sea in 1769.

2.83-88]   *statue . . . still*   The statue or *Idalian shape* is Aphrodite, Greek goddess of love and beauty. A temple in the ancient town of Idalium in Cyprus was dedicated to her. One of the epithets ascribed to Venus was *Victrix*, Venus the Victorius.

2.91   *Exalt*   Shortened form of "exalted" (*OED* cites only this line and *Prince Hohenstiel-Schwangau*, 1832; this edition, 10.197).

2.122-24]   *Castilian . . . cold*   Instead of *Castilian* B had originally written *Italian*, which was in fact the heritage of the Mellerios. Mellerio's mother was Swiss rather than French.

2.122]   *blind*   Reckless.

2.152]   *Ravissante*   B's substitute name for *Délivrande*. Although the French *Délivrande* may be taken as equivalent to *Libératrice*, the Virgin as deliverer, rescuer, or liberator (see 2.155), the name actually is derived from the fusion of two ancient words, the Saxon *Delle* and the Celtic *Yvrande*, that describe the Norman topography—a valley (*delle*) where a stream forms the border between two peoples (*yvrande*). When B substituted *La Ravissante* (she who ravishes, charms, or delights) for *La Délivrande*, he invented the etymology given in these lines.

2.160]   *Saint Aldabert*   Aldabert is the substitute name for St. Regnobert, an evangelist from Bessin and early bishop of Bayeux. He is credited with making the transition from pagan to Christian worship, probably in the early part of the seventh century. By tradition he founded the church at Douvres. B may have been following a local legend that dated the event much earlier.

2.163]   *Raimbaux*   The substitute name for Bayeux.

2.164]   *Eldobert*   B's substitute name for St. Ragnebert, bishop of Bayeux in the seventh century. His responsibility for bringing the Virgin's statue to the church is undocumented.

2.171-80]   *Northmen's . . . again*   The best known account of the Virgin's statue is that of a Franciscan friar, F. G. Fossard, in *L'ancienne fondation de la chapelle de Notre-Dame De La Délivrande* (Caen, 1642):

> Mais durant le règne de Louis, Roi de France, premier de ce nom, les Normands, hommes barbares et idolâtres, sortirent de Norvège accompagnés des Danois, et descendirent des gaules l'an huit cent

trente, depuis encore, ils firent plusieurs courses, où ils pillèrent et
ravagèrent toute la Neustrie dont une partie s'appelle la Nor-
mandie, du nom de ces infidèles. Ils profanèrent et brûlèrent
toutes les églises qui tombèrent en leur puissance; jusqu'aux
faubourgs de Paris. Ce fut en ce temps déplorable, tout au com-
mencement de ces embrasements et ravages universels, que ladite
chapelle de la Délivrande fut brûlée et ruinée de fond en comble
par Haistinc, le premier conducteur de ces infidèles, qui brûlèrent
et pillèrent l'église cathédrale de Bayeux. Ces cruautés, plus que
brutales, donnèrent sujet d'insérer aux Litanies "*a furore Normano-
rum.*" (quoted in *Le pèlerinage et la basilique de Notre Dame de la
Délivrande, Art de Basse-Normandie,* 119 [1999], 12).

(But during the reign of Louis, king of France [814-840], first of
that name, the Normans, barbaric and idolatrous men, left Norway
accompanied by Danes and descended on the Gauls in the year
eight hundred thirty, then made several raids, in which they pil-
laged and ravaged all of Neustrie [a Merovingian kingdom in the
northwest of France] of which a part is called Normandy, from the
name of these infidels. They profaned and burned all the churches
which they captured; even to the outskirts of Paris. It was in this de-
plorable time, just at the beginning of this widespread burning and
devastation, that the aforesaid chapel of la Délivrande was burned
and destroyed from top to bottom by Hastinc, the main leader of
these infidels who burned and pillaged the cathedral church at
Bayeux. These acts of cruelty, beyond mere savagery, were the rea-
son for inserting in the Litanies, "from the fury of the Normans.")

Fossard reports that the statue of the virgin in the chapel was buried
beneath the ruins for two hundred years, that is to say, until 1030, when
it was miraculously discovered. He is about a hundred years short in this
estimate, for Beaudouin de Reviers, one of the principals in the discov-
ery, was born in the last quarter of the eleventh century and died in
1140. Fossard continues with the story of finding the statue:

En ce tempe-ci vivait un seigneur, nommé Beaudoin, comte du
Bessin, qui se tenait en sa baronnie de Douvre, de l'évêché de
Bayeux, le berger duquel seigneur aperçoit que l'un de ses mou-
tons par plusieurs fois, se retirait du troupeau et courait en un lieu
auprès de la pâture, là de pied et de cornes, frappait et fouillait la
terre, puis étant las il se couchait à la place même où de présent est
la niche de l'image de la Vierge, en la chapelle de la Délivrande. Ce

mouton ne prenait aucune nourriture et était néanmoins le plus gras de la bergerie; le comte croyant que celui-ci était un avertissement envoyé du ciel, se transporta sur le lieu, accompagné de la noblesse et d'un saint ermite, avec le peuple qui y courut des lieux circonvoisins! Il commanda de parachever la fosse que le mouton avait commencée, on y trouve l'image de Notre-Dame, il y a à présent plus de 800 ans. Cette image fut portée en procession solennelle, avec une commune allégresse de tout le peuple dans l'élise de Douvres: mais tôt après elle fut rapportée par le ministère d'un ange, au lieu même où elle fut trouvée. Dieu montra, par ce transport et invention miraculeuse, qu'il l'avait choise plus particulièrement pour son service, et pour celui de la glorieuse Vierge Marie, sa Mère. Alors le comte connaissant la volonté divine, it fit édifier et fonder la chapelle qui est encore à présent, et la donna à messieurs du chapitre de Bayeux (p. 12).

(At this time [c. 1130] lived a lord named Beaudoin, count of Bessin, who dwelled in his barony of Douvres, in the diocese of Bayeux, the shepherd of this lord noticed that one of his sheep would a number of times leave the flock and run to a place near the pasture, there, with hoof and horns, it struck and dug the earth, then being tired it lay down on the same place where at present is the niche of the image of the Virgin, in the chapel of la Délivrande. This sheep took no nourishment, and was nevertheless the plumpest one in the sheep-fold; the count believing that this was a message sent from heaven, visited the scene of this occurrence, accompanied by his court and a saintly hermit, along with the people who hurried there from the neighborhood! He commanded that they finish digging the hole that the sheep had begun. They found there the image of Notre Dame, now more than 800 years ago. This image was carried in a solemn procession, with a joyfulness shared by all the people in the church of Douvres: but soon after it was carried back through the ministry of an angel, to the same place where it was found. God showed, by this conveyance and miraculous method, that He had chosen it very particularly for His service, and for that of the glorious Virgin Mary, His Mother. When the count knew the divine will, he had built and established the chapel that is still here, and gave it to the gentlemen of the chapter of Bayeux.)

This chapel, built in the twelfth century, was pulled down in 1872 to make way for the construction of the new church. Two of its arches were preserved and incorporated into the new building. The statue of the Virgin was destroyed by Protestants in May of 1561 during the wars of religion. It was replaced by the present statue, probably carved by a local artist, in 1580. When the church was closed during the French Revolution, the statue was placed in the Museum of Caen, and during the German occupation, it was replaced by a replica and hidden at the Convent de la Vierge Fidéle. The statue is a *Vierge Noir* (Black Virgin), possibly influenced by an Isis-like goddess in the original Gallo-Roman temple built by legionnaires from Africa.

2.174]   *Mailleville*   B's substitute name for Beaudoin de Reviers, Count of Bessin and Viscount of Douvres, son of Richard de Reviers, a knight who fought with William the Conqueror at Hastings. He inherited from his father numerous possessions and titles, among them Count of Bessin, Viscount of Douvres, Count of Exeter, and Lord of the Isle of Wight. Upon his death in 1140, he was buried in the abbey of Quarr on the Isle of Wight.

2.176]   *carved . . . plain*   In the tympanum above the central door of the church is a carving of the statue being dug up by the sheep. See Figure 10.

2.184-86]   *Archbishop . . . Vertgalant*   Prince Vertgalant is B's fictitious name for Charles-Maurice, Prince de Talleyrand (1754-1838). Although unsuited for the priesthood, Talleyrand was ordained and then, through the influence of his father, elevated to the bishopric of Autun. He found his way to his true vocation of politics during the French Revolution and later became, during the reign of Napoleon and then the restoration of the monarchy, the greatest French diplomat of his time. Both his public

FIGURE 10. Carving of sheep and statue

and private lives separated him from the Church, to which he was reconciled with a death-bed confession. Hyacinthe-Louis de Quélen (Archbishop Chaumont) was instrumental in bringing about the so-called conversion of Talleyrand. Archbishop of Paris, Msgr.de Quélen (1778-1839) had not only made the practical arrangements for the conversion but also had been praying for Talleyrand to the Virgin himself as well as soliciting prayers from the sisters of the convent of Notre-Dame de Fidélité in Douvres. When their prayers were answered, Bishop de Quélen presented a bronze statue of the Virgin to the convent, where it still remains.

2.193]    *Voltaire*    See 4.678 for another reference to Voltaire as an opponent of religion.

2.194]    *Alp, Apennine*    Mountain ranges of southern Europe and the Italian peninsula.

2.204]    *Rabelais*    François Rabelais (c.1490-1553), French physician, humorist, and satirist, known for his coarsely ribald tales about the giant Gargantua and his son Pantagruel.

2.215]    *acromia*    The extreme points of the shoulder blades.

2.216]    *Black . . . head*    One of his nephews described Mellerio as being blond. It is not known where B got this information to the contrary.

2.224]    *Saint Eldobert*    See 2.165n.

2.226-30]    *Prince . . . bee*    A reference to Talleyrand's reconciliation with the Church shortly before his death. See 2.184-86n.

2.228]    *octogenary joints*    Talleyrand was eighty-four when he died.

2.231]    *Sganarelle*    A character in some seven of Moliere's plays and the title character in one of them. The description and the context in B's poem seem to fit the Sganarelle in *Don Juan* best. In this play Sganarelle is the sanctimonious valet of Don Juan, constantly criticizing his master for his immorality and unsuccessfully trying to reform him. B had drawn upon the same play for *Fifine at the Fair*.

2.266]    *First Communion*    Roman Catholic children receive their first communion at the age of discretion, usually seven or eight years old. In preparation, children will make their first confession and say prayers in penance and thus, as B puts it in the preceding line, *emerge soul-cleansed*.

2.279]    *Saint-Sauveur . . . Saint-Jean*    All churches in Caen: Saint-Sauveur (12th-16th centuries), Notre-Dame de la Gloriette (1684-87), Saint-Pierre (13th-16th centuries), and Saint-Jean (14th-15th centuries).

2.289]    *Inveni ovem quæ perierat*    Quoted from the Latin Vulgate and translated in the King James Version as "I have found my sheep which was lost" (Luke 15:6).

2.305-10]    *Voltaire . . . significant*    Antonio Mellerio's parents lived at 25 Quai Voltaire, which B changed to 33 Quai Rousseau when he altered the actual names in the poem. Alfred de Musset had lived at this address between 1839 and 1849. Next door, at number 27, Voltaire died in the house of the Marquis Charles de Villette on 30 May 1778. The name of the street was changed from Quai des Théantins to Quai Voltaire in 1791, after the Revolution. That he died *mad and raving* was a canard spread by his enemies and exposed long before B wrote this line. B had read all of Voltaire's works in his father's library but later ridiculed him, as here and in *The Two Poets of Croisic* (this edition, 14.125). Other references to Voltaire are in 1.287, 2.193, and 4.678. The fireworks (*squibs and crackers*) may refer to the celebration outside the house following the production of *Irène* two months before his death.

2.316-30] *deposed . . . Law* B here resorts to the depositions, the courtroom evidence, and the lawyers' arguments in the cousins' suit challenging Mellerio's will. These documents were at Caen (Vire), where the trial was held.

2.317] *confirmed . . . words* Antonio Mellerio described his conquests in letters to his younger brother, Victor. Excerpts from these letters were read in court by both the defense and the prosecution.

2.350] *rampired* Fixed firmly (obsolete and rare; *OED* cites this line).

2.363] *transitive* Transient or transitory, passing away.

2.374-75] *Bat-fowling . . . hedge* Bat-fowling is the method of catching birds at night by rousing them from their roosts in hedges and then, attracting them with the light of a lantern, either clubbing them with bats or snaring them with nets. The clap-net, designed for such a purpose, can be closed quickly with a drawstring.

2.391] *Gay . . . lives* B's translation of the refrain from "Le Grenier" ("The Garret"), a song by Pierre-Jean de Béranger (1780-1857): "Dans un grenier qu'on est bien à vingt ans!" ("In a garret how happy you are at twenty years!")

2.394] *Winter-garden and Mabille* Both the Jardin d'Hiver and the Jardin Mabille were pleasure gardens where young people could meet. The Jardin d'Hiver was a glass hall built on the Champs Elysées in 1848. The Jardin Mabille was in the Avenue Montaigne, near the Champs Elysées. It was described by Mark Twain in *Innocents Abroad* (1869) and by G. A. Sala in *Paris Herself Again in 1878-1879* (1880).

2.396] *read . . . Court* See 2.317n.

2.406] *New Year* B's notes indicate that Mellerio met Anna Debacker on 12 or 13 January 1853.

2.407] *favoured five* Perhaps the top five theatres in Paris as listed by Baedecker's *Paris* (1878): Opéra, Comédie Français, Théâtre Italien, Opéra Comique, and Odéon.

2.408-9] *Varieties . . . named* In his worksheet for this poem, B writes: "A. M. [Antonio Mellerio] meets at the Varietés [sic] Anna Debacker 12 or 13. Jan. 1853. calling herself Anna de Beaupré." The Théâtre des Variétés is still at 7 Boulevard Montmartre. Perhaps it is a *Playhouse appropriately named* because it offered a variety of entertainment: vaudeville, operettas, and farces.

2:460]  *falsish*  Somewhat false (*OED* cites only this line).

2:477]  *ruddle*  Red ocher used for dyeing and marking sheep (*OED* cites this line).

2.478]  *devils'-dung*  Another name for the plant asafetida, so called because of its odor.

2.480]  *ruby and topaz*  The same colors as the violins in 1.265.

2.483]  *Clara de Millefleurs*  Literally "Clara of a thousand flowers," B's substitute name for Anna de Beaupré.

2.487]  *Miss Pages*  Adèle Page (1822-82), a popular French actress, known as much for her beauty as for her talent. She was born Adèle Chateaufort and took the stage name of Page.

2.488]  *Noble . . . denotes*  A reference to the nobiliary particle *de* in the name "de Millefleurs."

2.489]  *Coliseum Street*  B's substitute for Rue de Miromesnil. The Rue du Colisée is an actual street in the 4th arrondissement, where B had rented an apartment in 1855-56. Anna's residence was 19 Rue de Miromesnil, a street that runs between the Elysée palace and the Boulevard Haussman, intersecting the Rue du Colisée. See Figure 11.

2.548]  *Court Guide*  Probably *Robson's Royal Court Guide and Peerage,* published in London by William Robson and Company.

2.549-50]  *Lord . . . Duke*  A translation of B's notes, "Lord N. Le noble et vieux duc" and not further identified.

2.552]  *Prince of O*  Identified only as "Prince d'O." in B's notes.

2.554]  *Giving . . . Thames*  This line comes directly from B's notes: "á Londres ou elle donne le ton."

2:564]  *darlingly*  A nonce word (*OED* cites only this line).

2.571]  *Louis'-worth*  A louis is a French gold coin, worth twenty francs.

2.588]  *brother*  See 2.796n.

2.596]  *Set . . . Breeze*  *Set Fair* is the position on barometers between Very Dry and Fair, meaning the fair weather will last some time. *Favonian* is the adjective form of Favonius, the Roman counterpart of the Greek Zephyros and god of the west wind. Unlike Shelley's, this is a gentle, favorable wind.

2.597]  *warrants*  Guarantees immunity (rare; *OED* cites this line).

   *Auster's*  Auster was the brother of Favonius and god of the south wind.

2.601]  *Commissary*  A police official, just below the rank of chief.

2.609]  *pip*  A disease of birds.

FIGURE 11.  19 rue de Miromesnil

2.613] *haschisch-man*  A nineteenth century spelling for hashish, an intoxicating and euphoric drug derived from the hemp plant.

2.629-30] *Lucie . . . Sierck*  With the exception of *Dominique*, B substitutes fictitious names here, Lucie Steiner for Sophie Trayer, Magdalen Commercy for Madeleine Lalory, and Sierck for Metz. The family history is recorded briefly in B's working notes: "Sophie Trayer, née à Metz, Nov. 29. 1830. fille de Dominique Trayer, Brigadier dans la garde République et de Madeleine Lalory. marries Feb. 1. 1849. place de la Madeleine, 17. being a modiste at Paris to Achille Ferdinand Debacker, Tailleur, of the same address."

2.631] *Social Couch*  A Gallicism from the French phrase "couches sociales," meaning social strata, classes of society. In this phrase *couche* is to be translated not as "couch" but as "layer" or "stratum."

2.634] *professed*  Made a business of.

   *mode-merchandize*  B has Anglicized the French phrase for milliner, "marchande de modes."

2.635] *roughlier*  One of B's idiosyncratic comparatives.

2.637] *Monsieur Ulysse Muhlhausen*  B's substitute name for Achille Ferdinand Debacker.

2.640] *marriage*  B's notes give the date as 1 February 1849.

2.641] *quicklier*  An obsolete form of the comparative.

2.652] *escape to Paris*  In 1852.

2.661] *Carlino Centofanti*  A fictitious name. B's notes record that at this time Mme. Debacker became the mistress of Miranda di Mongino, but in court her legal representatives denied the charge. This name, however, may very well be the source of Miranda, B's substitute name for Mellerio.

2.662-63] *Found . . . one*  A playful reference to Heb. 13:2: "Be not forgetful to entertain strangers: for thereby some have entertained angels unawares." This verse is a reference to Abraham and Sarah entertaining angels (Gen. 18).

2.680] *yesterday*  See 1.821ff.

2.684] *chignon*  This women's hair style, a large knot or coil of hair worn at the back of the neck, was fashionable in 1870. See also  1.900-904.

2.692] *dreadful cannonry*  The Franco-Prussian War. The trial had been interrupted by the war two years previously, in 1870.

2.711] *Twenty years*  A few months less than twenty years, between their meeting in January1853 and the poem's dramatic time of August 1872.

2.725] *first stone*  Of the woman taken in adultery, Jesus says, "He that is without sin among you, let him first cast a stone at her" (John 8:7).

2.736]   *aurorally*   From Aurora, the goddess of the dawn, and thus like Homer's "rosy-fingered dawn" (*OED* cites this line).

2.737]   *women-wreaths*   Garlands; crowns; or here specifically, nightcaps.

2.740]   *clout*   A piece of cloth (archaic).

2.742-43]   *God's . . . fire*   A reference to Pentecost: "And there appeared unto them cloven tongues like as of fire" (Acts 2:3).

2.747]   *cupping-cloth*   Presumably a cloth bloodied from "cupping," the process of drawing blood to remove poisons and cure disease.

2.796]   *brother died*   Antonio Mellerio's younger brother, Victor, born in 1830, died in 1857.

2.800]   *Portugal*   Originally Italy, where in fact Victor died.

2.811]   *Next . . . cave*   B's working notes read: "Mellerio (Père) buys Tailleville 1849. Dies Aug. 23. 1860." B refers to the familiar tale of Aladdin in *The Thousand and One Nights*. From a subterranean cavern, Aladdin takes the magic lamp whose power brings him wealth and enables him to build a marvelous castle for the Sultan's daughter, whom he marries.

2:847]   *perdue*   Hidden.

2.849]   *Deity-like . . . fog*   The theatrical convention of *deus ex machina*, god appearing from the machine, in this case, a fog machine rather than the crane of ancient drama.

2.851]   *rubies*   "Who can find a virtuous woman? for her price is far above rubies" (Prov. 31:10)

2.857-59]   *Gustave . . . ruby-mine*   Gustave is the substituted name for Alfred, the professional name of Debacker, who set up shop at 18 Rue de la Paix, just across the street from Mellerio's jewelry store at 9 Rue de la Paix.

2.868]   *griffin*   This dragon-like, mythical animal with the head, wings, and talons of an eagle and the body of a lion, often is depicted as the guardian of a treasure but also is associated with Nemesis, hence revenge or retribution.

2.883]   *Deposing . . . wrong*   A translation of B's note, "Debacker, dépose une plainte en adultère. 1859."

2:884]   *divorce*   Although M. Debacker filed charges of adultery, a settlement was reached short of a legal dissolution of the marriage. M. Debacker retained a husband's legal authority in his wife's financial affairs, while Mme. Debacker renounced her claim to his property.

2.890]   *Body . . . separate*   A translation of B's note, "Séparation de corps et de biens."

2.917]   *Sganarelle*   See 2.231n.

2.920]   *Magdalens*   Sinners or prostitutes. Mary Magdalene, the woman whose evil spirits Jesus cast out, is traditionally associated with the repentant sinner who anointed his feet. See Luke 7:37-50 and 8:2.

2.949]   *Clairvaux-Priory*   See 1.614-15n.

2.1005-6]   *They . . . Paris*   They turned their back on Paris, from the Italian expression *dare un calcio a* ("to give a kick to").

2.1017-18]   *Vaillant . . . civilities*   Vaillant is the substitute name for the original Mériel. The lines are based on B's notes: "M. Mériel, ami, marchant de musique, Caen, 'prie M. Mellerio d'être son interprète auprès de madame pour lui présenter ses civilités'" ("M. Mériel, friend, music seller, Caen, 'asks M. Mellerio to convey to Madame his kind regards'"). Possibly this man was Albert Mériel, born in 1840, who served as mayor of Caen from 1882 to 1892.

2.1019-20]   *Next . . . you*   The French writer Alexandre Dumas (1802-70), referred to as Dumas père, is best known as the author of the popular romances *The Three Musketeers* (1844) and *The Count of Monte Cristo* (1844-46). B's note: "'mes complements à Madame et à vous'" ("'my compliments to Madame and to you'").

2.1021-27]   *And . . . Affectionate*   Richard Seymour-Conway (1800-70), 4th Marquess of Hertford and owner of the Chateâu of Bagatelle; MP, 1819-26; a member of the Light Dragoons and for a time attached to the British Embassy in Constantinople. From 1830 until his death, he lived primarily in Paris as an eccentric recluse and avid art collector. His father, the 3rd Marquess of Hertford (1777-1842), was the model for Thackeray's Lord Steyne in *Vanity Fair* (1848) and Disraeli's Lord Monmouth in *Coningsby* (1844). The quotation in 2.1023-27 is a translation from the French in B's notes. "Un riche propriétaire de Paris, M. Hertford, auquel appartenait la belle propriétaire de Bagatelle; près de Bois de Boulogne, et qui assure Mad^e. D. de ses hommages et de ses compliments affectueux" ("A rich property owner of Paris, M. Hertford, to whom belonged the beautiful property, Bagatelle; close to the Bois de Boulogne, and who assures Madame D [Debacker] of his esteem and his affectionate compliments"). The Bois de Boulogne is the celebrated park in Paris.

2.1037]   *Elysian Fields*   The Champs Élysées of Paris with perhaps a hint of the Elysian Fields of Greek mythology.

2.1070]   *seigneur-like*   In a lordly style.

2.1090]   *L'Ingegno*   The Genius, nickname of Andrea Luigi of Assisi (1470-1556), who, Vasari tells us in *The Lives of the Artists*, vied with Raphael in his youth, but who was afflicted with cataracts and became blind.

2.1093]   *Who . . . deaf*   The mention of deafness indicates that B is referring to Beethoven's *Missa Solemnis*, which premiered 7 April 1824 in St. Petersburg.

2.1099-1103] *Sieur . . . sustenance* Nicolas Boileau-Despréaux (1636-1711), French literary critic and poet; Louis XIV (1638-1715), King of France from 1643-1715, called the Sun King for the brilliance of his court; Pierre Corneille (1606-84), French dramatist, master of neo-classicism. After early successes Corneille became less popular, eclipsed by Racine, and lapsed into penury. Boileau successfully petitioned the King on Corneille's behalf, but by then it was too late: Corneille was seriously ill and died in 1684.

2.1106-7] *Dumas, Hertford* See 2.1019-20n. and 2.1021-27n.

2.1114-15] *So . . . gay* B's working notes read simply, "Rebuilds Tailleville, 1866-1867."

2.1118] *Park . . . preference* See 1.656-57n.

2.1119] *desert smile* See 1.720n.


*Section 3*


3.11-13] *Somebody . . . fruitage* The golden apples in the Garden of the Hesperides were guarded by a never-sleeping dragon.

3.20] *October* B's working notes read, "Visits his mother in Paris, October 1867."

3.38] *Sardanapalus' self* A legendary Assyrian monarch, famous for his wealth, Sardanapalus destroyed his court and himself by fire after being besieged in Nineveh for two years by the Medes. Reputed to be voluptuous, effeminate, and extravagant, he was the subject of a play by Byron and a painting by Delacroix.

3.45] *pulling-down . . . building-up* See 2.1114-15n.

3.54] *Dalilah* Delilah, the woman paid by the Philistines to discover the secret of Samson's strength (Judg. 16).

3.54-55] *smoking . . . snuff* A reference to Isa. 42:3: "A bruised reed shall he not break and the smoking flax shall he not quench"; see also Matt. 12:20, where Jesus refers to this verse.

3.58-60] *Why . . . jollity* In a parable a rich man accumulates great wealth and plans on living a life of ease and pleasure. God rebukes him, saying, "Thou fool, this night thy soul shall be required of thee: then whose shall those things be, which thou hast provided?" (Luke 12:20).

3.85] *Quai Rousseau . . . Thirty-three* Actually 25 Quai Voltaire. See 2.307n.

3.88] *bézique* A popular card game introduced in the mid-nineteenth century.

3.91] *Hertford . . . Dumas* See 2.1021-27n. and 2.1019-20n.

3.107]     *Seine*   His mother's house on Quai Voltaire was directly on the left bank of the river. None of the court testimony says that Mellerio jumped into the Seine, only that he took a cold bath. However, in his notes B writes that following discussions with his mother, there was a "bain dans la Seine."

3.114-15]     *And . . . Raving*   B's note says that following the plunge into the Seine, he was in a state of "folie plus de 3 semaines" ("madness for more than three weeks").

3.117-18]     *Beaumont . . . murdered*   Beaumont is the substitute name for Dr. Pasquier, the Mellerio family physician, who wrote one of the two principal documents the cousins used as evidence to support their argument that Antonio Mellerio was not of sound mind when he wrote his wills. As B records here, Pasquier achieved celebrity through his death at the hands of the Paris Communards. When French troops from Versailles marched on Paris, in 1871, Pasquier was with them as Surgeon Major of the Gendarmerie. They entered Paris by a strategic bridge at Neuilly. Pasquier, carrying a white flag, was sent forward to negotiate, but the Communards, apparently misunderstanding his intentions, shot him. The Versailles government exploited the event to inflame public animosity. Pasquier's affidavit of 23 August 1870, claiming Mellerio's insanity, was effectively discredited in court since Pasquier had had no personal meeting with Antonio Mellerio after 1867 and was merely conjecturing about events he had not witnessed.

3.123-24]     *Book . . . tempted*   St. Anthony of Egypt (251?-356?), the founder of Christian monasticism. As a young man he went into seclusion, where he experienced and successfully resisted every temptation the devil could devise.

3.135]     *blister and phlebotomize*   Raising blisters and bloodletting were standard medical procedures in the nineteenth century.

3.161]     *'Sixty-eight*   The year 1868.

3:165]     *Words . . . wind*   "Words are but wind," a proverb, used memorably by B in *The Ring and the Book* 12.836 (this edition, 9.283).

3.177]     *Dumas*   See 2.1019-20n.

3.178]     *bézique*   See 3.88n.

3.191]     *Caen*   Here and in 3.196 B keeps the actual name and does not substitute Vire.

3.196]     *Caen, Rouen*   The principal cities on the train route to Paris.

3:271]     *besprent*   Dotted about (*OED* cites this line).

3:282]     *to point*   To the smallest detail, completely (archaic; *OED* cites this line).

3.294-95] *rejoice . . . fold* The parable of the lost sheep: "Rejoice with me; for I have found my sheep which was lost" (Luke 15:6). Matthew also records the parable, 18:12-13).

3.344] *Sceaux* B's working notes read, "Jan 8. funeral at Garges, (snow)." Garges is a suburb on the N side of Paris, next to the present-day airport Le Bourget. Sceaux, the substituted name, is a suburb to the S of the city.

3.362-63] *testament . . . commerce* B's working notes read, "Sale of commerce to his cousins, Apr. 24. 1868." Mellerio wrote several testaments. B lists five of these in his working notes and copies the last testament of 21 October 1869, in full. See 1.749n.

3.369] *Coliseum Street* Actually Miromesnil Street; see 2.489n. B's working note reads, "[Jan] 11. Visit of friends projected to Anna."

3:386] *inconsciously* Unconsciously (rare; *OED* cites only this line and *Sordello*, 6.148 [this edition, 2.308]).

3.426] *Burn . . . past* A translation of B's note: "'Brûle, brûle, purifie mon passé!'"

3.439] *Said Beaumont* Dr. Pasquier (see 3.117-18n.), who described the injuries in his affidavit of 23 August 1870.

3.439-41] *And . . . incomplete* These lines come from the notes: "Rages at each new person's entry 'qu'on l'empéchait de se purifier, que le sacrifice n'était pas complet'" ("that they kept him from purifying himself, that the sacrifice wasn't complete").

3.447] *next Republic* Mellerio's self-mutilation occurred in 1868, during the Second Empire of Napoleon III. The next Republic was proclaimed in 1870, after Napoleon's defeat at Sedan in the early stages of the Franco-Prussian War. Dr. Pasquier himself was killed (see 3. 117-18n.) in the fighting to establish the authority of the Versailles government.

3:454] *febricity* Feverishness (*OED* cites only this line).

3.457] *Ineffable beatitude* From B's notes: "une joie ineffable . . . la beatitude céleste" ("an ineffable joy . . . the celestial bliss").

3.491] *Religio Medici* I. e., *Religion of a Doctor*, first published in 1642. This book by Sir Thomas Browne (1605-82), author and physician, is noted for its expression of Christian faith tempered by reasoned skepticism.

3.503] *blind* Purposeless (*OED* cites this line).

3.509-10] *Commune . . . him* Dr. Pasquier's death at the hands of the Communards (see 3.117n.) was used by the Versailles government to justify the killing of hostages, escalating the brutality on both sides. On 24 May 1871, the Communards executed Mgr. Darboy, the Archbishop of

Paris, along with five priests. This event was followed by the group exe-
cution of other captive priests.

3.512]   *bliss or bale*   Cf. Coleridge's "Christabel": "Her face resigned to
bliss or bale" (288).

3.528]   *Portugal*   Actually Italy, and again in 3.545 and 3.566. B's work-
ing notes read, "M. Debacker agreed to separate, believing he [Mellerio]
was in Italy. Finding he was still in P. [Paris] she refused: tried to see him,
& was excluded."

3.592]   *This . . . now*   B's notes quote Mellerio as saying, "Ce n'est pas
Madame D que je reprend, c'est un frère: il me veillera, il me soignera"
("It is not Madame D. [Debacker] that I take back, it is a brother: he will
look after me, he will take care of me").

3.614-17]   *Had . . . comprehend*   These lines translate B's notes: "Si je
vous avais ecoutés [sic], je serais aujourd'hui sur la paille, avec votre mis-
érable rente, mais maintenant je le tiens" ("If I had listened to you,
today I would be on straw, with your miserable allowance, but now I have
him").

3.629]   *April*   B's working notes read, "in April (68) return to
Tailleville."

3.643]   *Spain*   Clairvaux is their "castle in Spain."

3.703]   *Now . . . miracle*   A reference to the legend of how the statue of
the Virgin was found and to the cures it effected. See 1.435n. and
2.171-80n.

3:722]   *Neither . . . left*   "Turn not to the right hand nor to the left"
(Prov. 4:27).

3.726-82]   *Go . . . too*   These lines contain B's tribute to his close friend
the French essayist and literary critic Joseph Milsand (1817-86). In Au-
gust 1851, the *Revue des deux Mondes* published Milsand's enthusiastic
essay on Browning's poetry, and shortly thereafter the two men met in
Paris to form a lasting friendship. B had profound respect for Milsand's
character and intellect. The revised *Sordello* of 1863 and this passage in
*Red Cotton Night-Cap Country* were dedicated to the living Milsand, while
*Parleyings with Certain People of Importance in Their Day* (1887) was dedi-
cated to his memory. It was Milsand's presence that drew B to St. Aubin
in the summers of 1870, 1872, and 1873, and of course Milsand helped
B acquire the documents he needed for the composition of *Red Cotton
Night-Cap Country*.

3.727-33]   *You . . . halfpenny*   B is probably referring to the Florentine
diamond, of Indian origin and weighing over 137 carats. The story goes
that a Jesuit priest bought the diamond for a pittance in the Piazza
Navona, Rome, where it was sold as a piece of crystal. The priest, in turn,

sold it to the Grand Duke Peter Leopold of Tuscany (hence the name Florentine) for an enormous profit. The diamond has been missing since the First World War.

3.734] *ha'p'worth* Contraction for *halfpennyworth*, a very small amount (*OED* cites this line).

3.738] *Castilian* See 2.122-24n.

*orbit* Eye (*OED* cites this line).

3.742] *Monsieur Rouher* Eugène Rouher (1814-84), a French politician who wielded such influence and power in Napoleon III's government that he was called the Vice-Emperor.

3.744] *Œcumenical Assemblage* The twentieth ecumenical council of the Catholic Church was summoned by Pope Pius IX, opened in 1869, and suspended in 1870 because of the Franco-Prussian War. Its main topic was the doctrine of papal infallibility.

3:764] *crassitude* Gross ignorance or stupidity.

3.781] *Milsand* See 3.726-82n.

3.832] *Stramonium* A narcotic drug made from the thorn apple or jimson weed and used as an anodyne and antispasmodic.

3.833] *calomel . . . duct* Calomel, also called mercurous chloride, is a purgative.

3.855-58] *Belief . . . say* Gideon, instructed by the angel of the Lord to lead the Israelites against the Midianites, wanted assurance that God would give him the needed power. On two successive nights Gideon spread a fleece on the threshing floor. The first night he asked that dew fall only on the fleece and not on the surrounding ground. This happened, and Gideon wrung out the fleece, filling a bowl with water. The second night, he asked that dew fall only on the ground and not the fleece. When this also happened, he knew he was in the presence of the Lord (Judg. 6:36-40).

3.875] *Fons et origo* Latin for "source and origin."

3.887] *Perpend* Archaic for "consider."

3.889-90] *Luc . . . Claise* These are the substituted names, Luc de la Maison Rouge being fictitious and Claise being an actual town, named for a river, and located E of Poitiers, near Châteauroux. The original was Jean de la Becquetière of Vire (1593-1626), an actual person from a town in Calvados, Normandy. His full name was Jean Halbout de la Becquetière before becoming a Capuchin monk, whereupon he took the name of Brother Eliezer (Fr. *Elzear*). He founded the Convent of Capuchins at Vire and died caring for those stricken by the plague.

3.891] *Maude* The substitute name for Anne, the wife of Jean Halbout de la Becquetière. She was born Anne Le Fevre de la Boderie at

Vire on 25 July 1593. She changed her name to Elizabeth when she joined the Cistercian order of nuns at the abbey of Villers-Canivet, S of Caen, on 30 July 1633.

3.904]    *Cistercian monk*    Joseph le Chevalier, a monk at the Cistercian abbey of Aulnay. He is the author of *La Vie de Fr. Elzear de Vire, clerc capucin, fondateur du Convent des Capucins de la ville de Vire, et de la Mère Elisabeth de Ste. Anne, son épouse, et depuis religieuse de l'Ordre de Citeaux au monastère de Villers Canivet* (*The Life of Brother Eliezer of Vire, capuchin monk, founder of the Convent of Capuchins in the city of Vire, and of Mother Elisabeth of St. Anne, his spouse, and afterwards nun of the Cistercian Order at the monastery of Villers Canivet* (Caen, 1696).

3.913]    *Dionysius*    B's substitute name of Eliezer (see 3.889-90n.).

3.915]    *rules of Benedict*    The Cistercians follow the rules of St. Benedict, even more strictly than do the Benedictines.

3.916]    *Scolastica*    B's substitute name for Elizabeth (see 3.891n.)

3.922-23]    *What . . . asunder*    See Matt. 19:6, Mark 10:9, and the marriage service in the *Book of Common Prayer*.

3.927-28]    *oracles . . . Paul*    Rom. 3:2.

3.949]    *closelier*    One of B's idiosyncratic comparatives.

3.1000]    *Star of the Sea*    The Virgin Mary, English equivalent of the Latin *Stella Maris*, which, in turn, is an etymological rendering of the name Mary.

3.1047]    *pedal-keyed*    Possibly a piano pédalier, which has thirty-two pedals, ranging from bottom A through D above middle C. The piano has a standard keyboard in addition to the pedals, but Miranda could have played it with only the pedals. Indeed, the French composer Charles-Valentin Alkan (1813-88) wrote some pieces for feet alone. Such a piano was built by the Parisian firm of Érard and shown at the 1855 Paris Exhibition.

3.1048]    *Bach's*    The celebrated German composer Johann Sebastian Bach (1685-1750). B admired Bach's music. Though worried about his son's narrow education, B confessed to Isa Blagden, "how can I regret that he plays Bach & Beethoven understandingly?—as he certainly does" (McAleer, 202).

3.1068]    *Twentieth*    Altered from the thirteenth, the actual date of Mellerio's death, along with the other changes made to avoid libel.

3.1069]    *Of . . . France*    1870 was *folly's year* in France because that was when the French foolishly declared war on Prussia. B wrote Isa Blagden from St. Aubin on 19 August 1870 that "the French have been wrong as well as foolish, and wanted the lesson they have so effectually got" (McAleer, 342).

*Section 4*

4.2]   *Twentieth*   Actually 13 April; see 3.1068n.

4.8]   *Havre lighthouse*   The lighthouse visible from B's cottage at St. Aubin conjured up memories of his life with EBB. He describes the experience to Isa Blagden in a letter from St. Aubin, 19 August 1870: "Exactly opposite this house,—just over the way of the water,—shines every night the lighthouse of *Havre*—a place I know well & love very moderately: but, it always gives me a thrill as I see, afar, *exactly* a particular spot which I was at, along with her. At this moment, I see the white streak of the phare [lighthouse] in the sun from the window where I write and I *think*" (McAleer, 343).

4.13]   *platform*   The belvedere that had been added with the rebuilding of the house and from which Mellerio fell. See Figure 12.

4.15]   *Rouher*   Eugène Rouher; see 3.742n.

   *Ollivier*   Émile Ollivier (1825-1913) in this year of 1870 was Prime Minister of France and in favor of war with Prussia. After the catastrophe of the war, he never regained political power.

   *Roon*   General Albrecht Graf von Roon (1803-79) was the Prussian Minister of War during the Franco-Prussian War.

FIGURE 12.  The platform from which Mellerio fell at the house at Tailleville

4.16] *Bismarck* Otto von Bismarck (1815-98), the great statesman and unifier of Germany, was Prime Minister of Prussia during the war and immediately afterward; in 1871 he became the first Chancellor of Germany.

*Emperor* The Emperor Louis Napoleon of France (see 1.134-36n.).

*King* Kaiser Wilhelm I (1797-1888) became King of Prussia in 1861 and Emperor of Germany in 1871.

4.18-21] *Her . . . present* The statue of the Virgin Mary. The coronation of Notre Dame de la Délivrande took place in August 1872, two years after Antonio Mellerio's death (see 1.443-44n.).

4.57] *shot-silk* Silk made by a special weaving process in which threads of alternating colors are used to give an iridescent effect.

4.63] *Lust . . . pride* "For all that is in the world, the lust of the flesh, and the lust of the eyes, and the pride of life, is not of the Father, but is of the world" (1 John 2:16).

4.71] *Men . . . masters* "No man can serve two masters: for either he will hate the one, and love the other; or else he will hold to the one, and despise the other. Ye cannot serve God and mammon" (Matt. 6:24).

4.127] *More . . . mountains* "And though I have the gift of prophecy, and understand all mysteries, and all knowledge; and though I have all faith, so that I could remove mountains, and have not charity, I am nothing" (1 Cor. 13:2).

4.144-45] *La Salette . . . Lourdes* Shrines (see 1.435n.).

4.146-47] *go their way / Rejoicing* Echoing Acts 8:39.

4.164] *Great Physician* Certain Biblical passages (e.g. Mark 2:17 and Luke 4:23) indirectly describe Jesus as a physician, but apparently the phrase itself was coined by the Church Fathers.

4.166-67] *He . . . is* "For in six days the Lord made heaven and earth, the sea, and all that in them is" (Exod. 20:11).

4:169] *minim* Smallest or least important creature (*OED* cites this line).

4.179-81] *Louis . . . crowns* Louis XI (1423-83), King of France from 1461-83, made pilgrimages to La Délivrande from 7 September to 10 September 1470 and again from 14 August to 19 August 1473. It was on the second of these pilgrimages that the king, not known for his generosity, gave 303 crowns, each crown having the value of three francs.

4.183] *Commines* Philippe de Commines (c.1445-c.1511), a French historian and diplomat who served in the courts of Louis XI and his successor Charles VIII and who recorded his experiences there in his *Mémoires sur les règnes de Louis XI et de Charles VIII*. His name is also spelled Comines and Commynes.

4.184-89] *Marie-Antoinette . . . shrine* Marie Antoinette (1755-93) was the queen consort of King Louis XVI from 1774 to 1793, when they both were guillotined. Her first son died in 1789. Her second son, Louis

Charles (1785-95), Duke of Normandy, was imprisoned with his parents in the Temple in 1792, where he remained until his death, thus his sobriquet, "Martyr of the Temple." When he was born in 1785, Marie Antoinette gave thanks to Notre Dame de la Délivrande with gifts of a silver lamp and a gown brocaded in gold.

4.190-97]   *Here . . . Chambord*   The Duchess was Caroline Ferdinande Louise, Duchess de Berry (1798-1870), wife of Charles Ferdinand, Duke de Berry (1778-1820). The Duke was the son of King Charles X of France. The Duchess's son was Henri, Count of Chambord, whose birth in 1820 was *fifty years* previous to the present year of 1870. His father having died in the year of his birth, Henri stood next in line to his grandfather as king, which he briefly became upon his grandfather's abdication as a consequence of the 1830 July Revolution. He reigned as Henri V for only one week, at which time the National Assembly proclaimed his cousin, the Duke d'Orleans, king as Louis Philippe. Henri resumed his title of Count of Chambord and lived until 1883. There is a record of a visit by the Duchess to Notre Dame of Liesse on 24 May 1821 to give thanks for the birth of a son, but none to Délivrande.

4.216]   *Dumas . . . Hertford*   See 2.1019n. and 2.1021n.

4.220]   *peccant part*   Perhaps alluding to Pope's use of the expression: "Imagination plies her dangerous art, / And pours it all upon the peccant part" ("An Essay on Man," 2.143-44).

4.243-57]   *Count . . . down*   Count Mailleville is the substitute name for the Count of Bessin (see 2.174n.). The story of the statue in the following lines repeats the first account of it in 2.171-80.

4.258]   *you . . . high*   The statue is precisely 123 centimeters high.

4.259]   *And . . . times*   During a cholera epidemic in 1832 the statue was carried through the streets of Douvres, and the Virgin was credited with ending the pestilence.

4.283]   *in the twinkling of an eye*   Echoing the language of religious transformation in 1 Cor. 15:52.

4.292-302]   *Empress . . . Alacoque*   Miranda imagines that the miracle of his flight will resurrect the past by restoring the temporal authority of the Pope, re-establishing the Bourbon monarchs, and reviving the Catholic faith. In his fantasy, Napoleon III, persuaded by the *Empress* Eugenie, will compel the King of Italy, Victor Emmanuel II, to return the Papal States to the Pope. The Emperor and Empress, having reigned since 1852 (eighteen rather than twenty years), will resign in favor of the Bourbon pretender, Henry, Count of Chambord (see 4.190-97n.). And the streets of Paris named for secular rationalists will be re-christened for champions of Catholicism. *Quai Rousseau* is the substitute name for Quai Voltaire. There is in Paris a Rue Jean-Jacques Rousseau, named for the writer (1712-78). Margaret Mary *Alacoque* (1647-90) was a French nun who initiated the cult of devotion to the Sacred Heart of Jesus. Jesus appeared to her in numerous visions. She was canonized as Saint Margaret Mary in 1920.

4.303]  *Renan*  Ernest Renan (1823-92), French historian and critic whose best known book is *La Vie de Jésus* (1863), a life of Christ presented from an historical rather than theological perspective.

4.303-5]  *Veuillot . . . 'The Universe'*  Louis Veuillot (1813-83) became editor of the Catholic paper *l'Univers* in 1848. By *Re-edits* B may mean that the paper was revived in 1867 after its supression in 1860 for its extreme Ultramontanism.

4.309]  *Old . . . new*  "Therefore if any man be in Christ, he is a new creature: old things are passed away; behold, all things are become new" (2 Cor. 5:17).

4.342]  *gardener*  A gardener named Richer was present at the scene of Mellerio's death, but he saw the body only just as it reached the ground.

4.362-64]  *Will . . . time*  Mellerio's cousins charged him with numerous acts of religious mania, including crawling from Tailleville to la Délivrande on his knees while reciting prayers.

4.368]  *Superior Fricquot*  The substitute name for the Reverend Father Picot, Superior of the Missionaries of Notre Dame de la Délivrande. In 1872 he preached the sermon at the ceremony of the coronation of the Virgin (see 1.443-44n.).

4.405]  *Twenty years*  Actually a little over seventeen years since they first met in January 1853.

4.427-30]  *lignum vitae . . . passion-flower*  Clara suggests spices or medicinal plants whose names have religious connotations. *Lignum vitae* (wood of life) is a tropical hardwood whose resin has various medicinal uses; *grains of paradise* (cardamom) is of the ginger family; the *rose of Jericho*, of the mustard family, is also called the resurrection plant because of the way the dried up plant revives with moisture; *holy-thorn* (hawthorn) purportedly planted by Joseph of Glastonbury, blooms twice a year; the *passion-flower* gets its name from parts of its flower being imaginatively associated with elements of Christ's passion—crown of thorns, nails, wounds.

4.437]  *Monkshood . . . belladonna*  Although these plants are the source of beneficial drugs, they also are deadly poisons.

4.449]  *Lourdes*  See 1.435n.

4.450]  *Peter-pence*  See 1.971n.

4.484]  *sin . . . death*  "Then when lust hath sin, when it is finished, bringeth forth death (James 1.15). See also Book 2 of *Paradise Lost*, where Milton portrays sin as the mother of death.

4.499] *ruddle* See 2.477n.

4:501] *goatly* Goatlike (a nonce word; *OED* cites only a line by EBB).

4.511] *branchage* See 1.652n.

4.518] *cockney* An archaic sense of the word, meaning an over-coddled or squeamish person (*OED*, s.v.2).

4.526-30] *register . . . catalogued* For the 1872 trial, the cousins listed sixty-three alleged "statements of fact" as evidence of Mellerio's mental instability. In their appeal of 1873, the list was enlarged to 109.

4.542] *depositions* Although the cousins made numerous allegations regarding dismissed servants, their case depended principally on two unreliable documents, the affidavit of Dr. Pasquier (see 3.117-18n.) and a letter written by a wandering musician to whom Mellerio had briefly granted hospitality.

4.553] *competence* The cousins did propose an out-of-court settlement with Mme. Debacker, but their efforts were frustrated by her increasing demands and by the interference of M. Debacker, her estranged husband.

4.605] *scenical* Theatrical.

4:631-32] *Christ's . . . rich* "If thou wilt be perfect, go and sell that thou hast, and give to the poor, and thou shalt have treasure in heaven" (Matt. 19:21).

4.640] *Non compos mentis* Latin, "not of sound mind."

4.651] *Londres* Mellerio's holograph wills are on file with the *notaire* at Douvres-de-la-Délivrande; see 1.422n.

4.662-63] *sheep . . . again* The parable of the lost sheep, previously referred to in 2.294-95.

4.678] *Voltairian* An opponent of organized religion, Voltaire's most famous statement on the subject is "Écrasez l'infâme" (crush the infamy).

4.686] *casts stone* A second allusion to the woman caught in adultery (see 2.725n.).

4.700] *drops* Earrings.

4.701] *spray* Brooch.

4.705] *Siècle* *Le Siècle* (1836-1932) was a popular and influential newspaper. Its subtitle was *Journal politique, littéraire et d'économie sociale.*

4.706] *Univers* See 4.305n.

4.709] *Schneider* Hortense Catherine Schneider (1833-1920) was an acclaimed soprano who starred in Offenbach's operettas.

4.726] *Cockatrice* A mythical serpent-like monster whose look or breath was fatal.

4.727] *Jezebel* The wicked wife of King Ahab of Israel (1 Kings 21:5-23 and 2 Kings 9:7-10).

*Queen of the Camellias* The courtesan heroine of *La Dame aux*

*Camélias* (1848), the popular novel by Alexandre Dumas fils. Verdi's opera *La Traviata* (1853) is based on the novel.

4:732]     *concurrence*   Rivalry (a Gallicism; *OED* cites this line).

4.743]     *And . . . blind*   "In the land of the blind, the one-eyed man is king" ("In regione caecorum rex est luscus"), from Erasmus's *Adagia*, 3.4.96.

4.772]     *Blake . . . Meissonier*   William Blake (1757-1827), English poet and artist whose visionary works qualify him as an example of the artist who aspires to *break through.* Jean Louis Ernest Meissonier (1815-91), French artist, noted for his military paintings, especially of the Napoleonic wars, and for his small, meticulously detailed genre paintings in the manner of the Dutch school, is thus an example of the artist who *Tries the low thing, and leaves it done* (4.768). Coincidentally, the 4th Marquess of Hertford, whom B names as an admirer of Clara (see 2.1019n.), also collected Meissonier's paintings.

4.780]     *Michelagnolo . . . world*   B substitutes Michelangelo (1475-1564) for Athanasius, Bishop of Alexandria, in Richard Hooker's phrase "Athanasius contra mundum" (see *La Saisiaz*, 546n., this edition, 14.405).

4.787-88]     *Painted-peacock . . . Brimstone wing*   Types of butterflies.

4.799]     *From . . . awhile*   See 2.554n.

4.812]     *drip-dropping hours*   Hours measured by sand dropping in an hourglass.

4.827]     *pendule*   Clock.

      *Apollo*   The Greek god of music, especially associated with the lyre.

4.828]     *Liszt*   The Hungarian composer Franz Liszt (1811-86), the foremost virtuoso pianist of the time.

4.831]     *fortune . . . bold*   From Virgil's *Aeneid*: "audaces fortuna juvat" (10.284).

4.837]     *Fricquot's*   Picot's (see 4.368n.).

4:857]     *throw*   A twist of a fiber (rare; *OED* cites this line).

4.860]     *storm . . . strife*   The Franco-Prussian war.

4.870]     *palmer-worm*   The term applies to a variety of caterpillars who wander like a palmer, or pilgrim.

4.872]     *Venus' eye-fringe*   Possibly the eyelash-like edge of the trap bar of the Venus flytrap plant.

4.874-77]     *scarabæus . . . hierophants*   Some varieties of the dung beetle form balls of dung that they roll along with their hind legs as they move about. The beetles bury these balls and lay their eggs in them. The ancient Egyptians venerated the black dung beetle that breeds in the mud of the Nile, the *Scarabaeus sacer*, which they associated with ideas of resurrection and immortality.

4.901]    *'Seventy*    1870, the year of the Franco-Prussian War.

4.905-7]    *It . . . First*    The Civil Court of Caen made its judgment on 9 July 1872, closer to seven weeks before the date of the monologue (29 August) than two weeks.

4.956]    *How otherwise*    This is the same question that B's Ivàn Ivànovich asks upon learning the verdict ("Ivàn Ivànovich," 424; this edition, 14.248).

4.969]    *cradle-cone*    Cocoon.

4.976-94]    *How . . . a-blush*    In this epilogue to the poem, the time and place of the poem have moved from August in St. Aubin to January in London.